W9-CCI-477

PILGRIMS TO THE NORTHLAND

PILGRIMS

to the Northland

The Archdiocese of St. Paul,
1840 – 1962

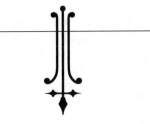

MARVIN R. O'CONNELL

UNIVERSITY OF NOTRE DAME PRESS
Notre Dame, Indiana

The author and publisher are grateful for permission to reproduce images
from the Archdiocesan Archives, Archdiocese of St. Paul and Minneapolis,
and from the Archives of the University of Notre Dame
(for James Shields and Ignatius A. O'Shaughnessy).

Designed by Wendy McMillen
Set in 10.8/13.2 Stempel Garamond by EM Studio
Printed in the U.S.A. by Thomson-Shore, Inc.

Manufactured in the United States of America

Library of Congress Cataloging-in-Publication Data

O'Connell, Marvin Richard.
Pilgrims to the northland : the Archdiocese of St. Paul, 1840–1962 /
by Marvin R. O'Connell.
p.   cm.
Includes bibliographical references and index.
ISBN-13: 978-0-268-03729-1 (cloth : alk. paper)
ISBN-10: 0-268-03729-9 (cloth : alk. paper)
1. Catholic Church. Archdiocese of St. Paul (Minn.)—History—19th century.
2. St. Paul Region (Minn.)—Church history—19th century.
3. Catholic Church. Archdiocese of St. Paul (Minn.)—History—20th century.
4. St. Paul Region (Minn.)—Church history—20th century.   I. Title.
BX1417.S3O36   2009
282'.776—dc22
2008050096

In Memoriam

To the O'Connells and the Sheas
who came as pilgrims from the west of Ireland

to forge for themselves a new and better life
in St. Thomas the Apostle Parish,

Derrynane Township, Le Sueur County,
Minnesota Territory

CONTENTS

MY REVERED MENTOR, THE EMINENT ENGLISH HISTORIAN, Monsignor Philip Hughes—dead now these forty years—had little patience for colleagues in the profession who purported to discern in historical data large themes of cosmic significance. He had in mind savants like Oswald Spengler, who promoted a deterministic theory of the cyclical rise and decline of civilizations; and Arnold Toynbee, whose twelve-volume *A Study of History* (1934–1961) put forward the argument that the bringing to light, as he aimed to do, of certain "universal rhythms" within the human experience amounted to what he chose to call "metahistory." It is hard now to overstate how fashionable such approaches were during the middle third of the last century. Such was the case as well with R. G. Collingwood, whose *The Idea of History* (published posthumously in 1946) was for many years required reading in graduate courses in historiography. When I mentioned to Father Hughes how perplexing I found working my way through Collingwood's dense prose, he replied, with his inimitable chuckle: "I knew old Collingwood [they were indeed contemporaries]. He was mad at the end, you know. And the trouble with *The Idea* is that nobody can make out which parts he wrote when he was mad and which parts when he was sui compos."

That Spengler and Toynbee each brought to his sweeping synthesis a preconceived leftist secular agenda was enough to arouse Hughes's suspicions. But he differed also from those historians with whom he shared a basic confessional and cultural sympathy if, in his judgment, they strayed too far into philosophical ruminations. The comprehensive and discernible designs the convert Christopher Dawson, for instance—"that immensely learned amateur," as one critic described him—claimed to uncover within the history of Catholicism seemed extravagant to a journeyman historian, as Hughes considered himself to be. (In fairness it should be added that Philip Hughes, a born Catholic, always maintained a certain reserve with regard to his fellow countrymen, like Dawson, whose conversions to Catholicism attracted more attention than they deserved and whose Oxbridge accents, he thought, unjustifiably overawed American audiences. Nevertheless, his own English accent lent him a platform presence he used to his advantage.)

I too am a journeyman, and so I subscribe cheerfully to my master's definition of this discipline I have engaged in for more than half a century: History is the reconstruction of the past by the mind from sources. An abstract noun qualified by three prepositional phrases. For practical purposes this means past human experience inquired into by limited human intelligence based upon fallible human witnesses. Not therefore an intellectual enterprise that can allege the kind of certitude achieved by a syllogism or a mathematical formula or a chemical exposition. Nor one, or so it seems to me, capable of producing a Spenglerian worldview. History at any rate is the humblest of the sciences, and besides, since it is a construct of him who practices it, it is to a degree no less an art. Never can he who does the constructing completely escape his own predispositions and personal circumstances.

For this very reason the employment, evaluation, and identification of sources remains always the crucial ingredient in the historian's endeavors; otherwise the artist in him may be carried away and deliver an unsubstantiated opinion or, at worst, a fictional fantasy. To be sure the source material is always less than apodictic, because the witness contained in it is often fragmentary, sometimes mendacious or self-serving, never complete—which fact serves to make obvious the deficiency of the historian as scientist. But even taking into account such limitations, a more or less accurate picture of the past can be drawn so long as the available evidence is carefully enough sifted and analyzed and its credibility authenticated.

That evidence, at least since the time of the Renaissance, has consisted largely of written documentation—letters, diaries, official pronouncements, minutes of meetings, press reports, and the like, all of which in one way or another provide contemporary witness to past events. And, of course, which have been preserved. If the French missionary had not recorded the transaction in his memoirs, no one could know that in the early months of 1850 Father Augustin Ravoux purchased for $900 twenty-two lots in what was to become the heart of the business district of the city of St. Paul, and in doing so provided the infant Catholic community not only with needed space but also, over the long term, with a real estate investment of inestimable value.

Needless to say, this written documentation needs to be made available to the researcher. And in an institutional history of the sort attempted in this book, that means the institution itself must be prepared to open its books, so to speak, so that the pertinent sources—its own record of its past—can be thoroughly examined. Other external witness there may be, useful and valuable, but none so essential as the institution's own collective memory. In this account of the past of the archdiocese of St. Paul till 1962—the courteous addition of Minneapolis, St. Paul's twin, to the canonical title did not occur until 1966—I was given nothing but the fullest access to relevant materials, thanks to the professionalism of the archdiocesan archivist. But the archbishop, now deceased, who originally asked me to take on this project, was anxious that I should carry the story forward into the 1990s. His intentions were perfectly honorable and appropriate; important "initiatives"—his word—were launched, he argued, during his administration and during that of his immediate predecessor, initiatives that took into account the radical challenges faced by the Church in Minnesota and, indeed, across the United States in the wake of the Second Council of the Vatican (1962–1965).

One could not quarrel with the late archbishop's overall if somewhat superficial assessment; much indeed, especially in the development of an overarching ecclesiastical bureaucracy, had been established to meet the realities of the post-conciliar era, clearly a time that manifested a culture very different from what had prevailed before. Still, my instincts as a journeyman historian were troubled. The more recent the events under inspection, the more suspect the historical analysis. This is because the sources are in a state of flux, still expanding and not seldom contradicting one another, leaving little time or opportunity to assess their credibility. Many of those who have been witnesses are still among the living; they have the desire—indeed, the obligation—to argue their own point of view about what has happened or not happened. Recent episodes quite rightly receive the attention of serious investigative reporting which, needless to say, puts to shame anything like tabloid exploitation; but what the French call *haut journalisme* is journalism nonetheless. Clio, the muse of history, requires of her votaries a greater reflective distance than that possible in a busy newsroom.

The proposal to chronicle the positive accomplishments in the archdiocese of St. Paul (and Minneapolis) since Vatican II—the "initiatives" the late archbishop spoke about—had a certain congruity, since these activities were without doubt worthy of genuine commendation. This was particularly the case with regard to the social apostolate, in areas like race relations, housing, ministry to the divorced and separated, care for the homeless and for the immigrant and for those afflicted with HIV/AIDS. Despite the pressures of the secular culture, the defense of life, from conception to natural death, never faltered. Considerable strides were made in ecumenical dialogue. Catholic higher education for laymen and women within the archdiocese achieved a remarkable expansion. Deliberative bodies developed within parishes, thus giving lay opinion significant weight really for the first time. If the impetus for liturgical reform sometimes seemed to stumble due to the eccentricity of this or that individual priest, by and large across the archdiocese the *novus ordo* was exercised with a dignity and reverence which won the acceptance and participation of the people.

But there was a complication. If a great deal had gone right within the archdiocese after 1962, a great deal had also gone wrong. Or at least progress was countered by unprecedented deterioration, if the matter were to be judged by the criteria in place since Father Galtier arrived at Fort Snelling in 1840. Of course such a mix of good and ill was by no means restricted to one locality; how could it have been when the whole country—though none of us recognized it at the time—was experiencing a cultural revolution? Still, I had been asked to tell the local story, and that meant, out of professional integrity, I had to deal with its dark side as well as its bright. To do so I had to have access to all pertinent documentation, including that which was official and, in many instances, sensitive. When I made this point, I received authoritative assurance that such would be the case. In the end, however, various important sources remained unavailable.

And so this book ends in 1962, a few months after the death of Archbishop William O. Brady and a few months before the first session of Vatican II. This is a circumstance with which I, as an historian, am perfectly at ease. The succeeding tumultuous decades have yet to be played out, and in due time the sources that illuminate those years will become grist for a later historian's mill. Perhaps then—who knows?—the events will be evaluated by standards other than those that apply to the archdiocese of St. Paul between 1840 and 1962. In any case, the story as it stands seems to me worth telling, even if it fails to exhibit the philosophical significance required by a Toynbee or a Dawson.

AMONG THOSE WHO HELPED ME IN THE PREPARATION OF THIS book I am bound to mention first Steven T. Granger, archivist of the Archdiocese of St. Paul and Minneapolis, who cheerfully accommodated me in every possible way; I am grateful as well to Mr. Granger's associate, Patrick Anzelc. Professors Scott Wright and Anne Klejment of the Department of History, the University of St. Thomas, read large portions of the manuscript and favored me with their wise and encouraging comments; Professor

Klejment moreover kindly shared with me unpublished material drawn from her research into the history of the *Catholic Digest*. My thanks to the editor and staff of the *Catholic Spirit,* the archdiocesan weekly, who allowed me access to the files of the *Spirit's* predecessor, the *Catholic Bulletin,* so often cited in the pages that follow. I was able to augment work in this source due to the helpful people in the Document Center, Hesburgh Library, the University of Notre Dame. As he always has in the past, W. Kevin Cawley of the Notre Dame Archives answered any stray question I may have had that required prompt and professional attention. For references to correspondence in the *Archivio Segreto Vaticano* I owe thanks to my old Roman friend, Monsignor Charles Burns. Mary Martin, former director of the Ireland Memorial Library, the St. Paul Seminary School of Divinity, provided me with admittance to a large cache of specialized and unpublished material under her care. Ann Regan, acting director and editor in chief of the Minnesota Historical Society Press, lent me much bibliographical help, but also—and more importantly—gave me her encouragement and friendship. As did my esteemed colleague of nearly forty years, the dean of American Catholic historians, Philip Gleason.

And last, but certainly not least, my warm thanks to Barbara Hanrahan, director of the University of Notre Dame Press, and to her colleagues Rebecca DeBoer, Margaret Gloster, Wendy McMillen, and, particularly, Margaret Heyr—a formidable regiment of women who made this book much better than it might otherwise have been.

Among those to whom this book is dedicated *in memoriam,* I have no difficulty in summoning to my mind's eye with special reverence the figures of my paternal grandparents, William O'Connell and Hannah Shea O'Connell.

Marvin R. O'Connell
25 April 2008

CHAPTER 1

Sky-Tinted Waters

"CONTINUING TO ASCEND THIS RIVER TEN OR TWELVE LEAGUES more, the navigation is interrupted by a cataract which I called the Falls of St. Anthony of Padua, in gratitude for the favors done me by the Almighty through the intercession of that great saint, whom we had chosen patron and protector of all our enterprises. This cataract is forty or fifty feet high, divided in the middle of its fall by a rocky island of pyramidal form."[1] The Belgian priest who wrote these lines some years after the event had been at the time a prisoner of a band of Dakota Indians. His captors viewed the Falls in a different supernatural light than did he. One of them "climbed an oak opposite . . . with a well-dressed beaver robe, whitened inside and trimmed with porcupine quills" which, in a manner "admirable and frightful," he offered "in sacrifice to the Falls," all the while "shedding copious tears" as he intoned the ritual chant: "'Thou who art a spirit, grant that the men of our nation may pass here quietly without accident, that we may kill buffalo in abundance [and] conquer our enemies.'"[2]

---

1. For the extensive iconography prompted by Hennepin's sight of the Falls, see Patricia Condon Johnston, "Portrayals of Hennepin, 'Discoverer' of the Falls of St. Anthony, 1680," *Minnesota History* 47 (Summer 1980): 57–62.

2. Louis Hennepin, *A Description of Louisiana*, ed. and trans. John Gilmary Shea (New York, 1880), 199–200, 242–243. *Description de Louisiane* was first published in Paris in 1683. It was succeeded by *Nouveau Voyage* (1696) and *Nouvelle Découverte* (1697). Hennepin has often been suspected of excess elaboration—the Falls of St. Anthony were not nearly so high as he asserted—and perhaps of sheer invention. It is possible also that his manuscripts were amended by other writers. The value of Shea's critical edition of *Description* lies partly in the recognition of these faults and in its appendices, where he adds information from the memoirs of Duluth and La Salle, and from Hennepin's own later writings.

This small confrontation of cultures at the headwaters of the Mississippi, chronicled by the forty-year-old Louis Hennepin, occurred in the spring of 1680. Born in Flanders, Hennepin had in his youth joined the Recollect Friars, a recently founded group of Franciscans who had adopted the relatively more rigorous and explicitly fervent lifestyle characteristic of religious orders during the era of the Catholic Counter-Reformation. After ordination he had served in various ministries, including a stint as an army chaplain during the seemingly interminable wars in the Low Countries. Along with the personal austerity and zeal to make converts to the true faith appropriate to his station, Hennepin added a zest for travel and a desire to expand his horizons as broadly as could be. He does not appear to have found his situation as a Recollect friar a hindrance to such aspirations. Indeed, long before the age of passports and border controls, his restless temper had led him to undertake missions in Germany, Italy, and France. In the early 1670s his superiors granted him permission to settle in the Pas de Calais, "to act," as he put it, "the part of the mendicant there in the time of herring-salting." In that port city on the English channel he was fascinated by the adventurous tales he heard told by the sailors and shipmasters, even though the taverns where he encountered them were choked by tobacco smoke, which was "offensive to me and created pain in my stomach"—a reaction he would have occasion to recall when offered a calumet pipe by Native Americans a few years later.

In the summer of 1675 the several ambitions of Louis Hennepin—the religious zeal, the insatiable curiosity, the wanderlust—came together, and he took ship at La Rochelle for the voyage to the New World of America. Once landed in Quebec, he attached himself, appropriately, to the house of Recollect Franciscans already established there for some years. His first duties were the conventional ones of preaching and ministering to the handful of French settlers who had migrated to la Nouvelle-France since that sailor's son, Samuel de Champlain, had first fixed the fleur-de-lys banner on the banks of the St. Lawrence sixty years before. But Hennepin at the same time busied himself learning as best he could the languages and customs of the Indian tribes in the immediate neighborhood of Quebec, the Huron and the Algonquin, with the hope that he might win converts to the Christian Catholic faith. Tedious journeys to their camps by foot and by sled in the winter brought him few consolations in this regard, a result shared by all his fellow missioners, whose dedication nevertheless won a real if somewhat self-serving respect from the often puzzled tribesmen.

Father Hennepin was not unique among the denizens of Quebec in combining a genuine desire to spread the faith with a romantic urge to seek out faraway lands and exotic peoples. Nor was such a twofold aspiration inconsistent with the euphonic axiom enthusiastically endorsed by all French élites during an epoch of heightened national feeling. *Une loi, une foi, un roi*—one law, one faith, one king—included in its writ the contention that the expansion of New France would result in the establishment of a superior civilization, the promotion of true religion, and the enhancement of French political power. If the process should also bring about monetary gain, so much the better. Indeed, in accord with human nature, this latter consideration was never really absent.

But the religious motivation of these Catholic explorers remained always a prominent feature of their endeavors. Thus, in 1673, two years before Hennepin's arrival in Quebec, Louis Jolliet and Jacques Marquette, commissioned by the governor of New France, headed a small company in two canoes up the St. Lawrence and across the lakes to Green Bay, on Lake Michigan's western shore, and from there up the swift-running Fox River to a portage to the Wisconsin, which carried them finally to the upper Mississippi. Then they turned their canoes southward and rode the current of "the great river of the West," about which their Indian contacts had so often spoken, to the mouth of the Arkansas, at a point not far from where De Soto and his Spaniards, the first Europeans to do so, had reached the Mississippi 130 years earlier. The Spanish were there still, to the south, and so the Frenchmen prudently decided to head for home. During their spectacular journey Marquette mapped—crudely, to be sure—the country through which the expedition had passed, and noted down a detailed description of its flora and fauna, of the scattered villages of its native inhabitants, and, perhaps most important, of its complex river system. It is not without significance that Jacques Marquette was a Jesuit priest and that Louis Jolliet had spent his youth as a Jesuit seminarian.

Marquette never returned to Quebec: he died in an Indian village on the eastern shore of Lake Michigan in the spring of 1675, aged thirty-nine. Jolliet, however, though he lost some important maps and papers when his canoe capsized, brought back sufficient information to whet the political appetite of his patron the governor, the able if imperious and quarrelsome Louis de Baude, comte de Frontenac. The governor, loyal servant of Louis XIV, promoted the view that the discovery of a river by a subject of the Sun King brought with it the right to royal sovereignty over all the territory drained by it and its tributaries. Marquette and Jolliet had theoretically implemented this policy, the success of which would at a stroke confine the Spanish to the area south of the Arkansas and the English to their string of colonies east of the Alleghenies. But what of the unknown lands north of the Wisconsin River? About fifteen years before a couple of intrepid but unlicensed French traders—*coureurs de bois*—had indeed paddled to the western edge of Lake

Superior, the first white men to set foot in what is now Minnesota; lacking government sanction, however, they were arrested when they tried to sell their furs in Montreal.[3]

But that had happened before Frontenac had assumed the direction of New France. In 1678 the governor heartily endorsed the project of forty-two-year-old Daniel Greysolon—who bore the gentry-title sieur du Luth—a seasoned veteran of Louis XIV's European wars, to pursue again the route to the west by way of Lake Superior. This expedition had the twofold purpose of revivifying the fur trade and of ascertaining whether there existed an access by water across the continent to the Pacific—the oft-rumored but elusive Northwest Passage. By the following spring Duluth—to use the more familiar anglicized spelling—had with a few companions traversed Superior and had penetrated into the interior. The immediate problem he encountered, both as an explorer and an entrepreneur, was the hostility between the Dakota Indians among whom he now found himself and their inveterate enemies to the east, the Ojibwe. Duluth accordingly summoned and presided over a council of the chieftains of the two tribes, at which he proclaimed—with a hubris characteristic of the hardy if arrogant explorer—that both nations should henceforward live in harmony, since they were all subjects of the great King Louis across the sea. The Frenchmen then proceeded southward to the shores of a vast lake where various Dakota subclans maintained villages. Duluth promptly dubbed the lake *le lac du Baude,* in honor of the comte de Frontenac's family name, and nailed a royal emblem to a tree. "On the second of July, 1679," he reported, "I had the honor to plant his majesty's arms . . . where never had a Frenchman been [before]."[4] No doubt this ceremony had no meaning whatever to the natives who observed it, save for the axes, steel knives, needles, and other less useful "presents" they received at the end of it.

Frontenac meanwhile, in pursuit of his overall policy, had found another kindred spirit in René-Robert Cavelier, sieur de La Salle, resident in Quebec since 1666. La Salle too, like so many of his explorer-colleagues, was a deeply committed Catholic. Born in Rouen in 1643, he like Jolliet had seriously pondered a calling to the religious life, but had ultimately given up the idea, not

---

3. The two interlopers were Pierre Radisson and his brother-in-law Médart Chouart, sieur des Groseilliers, who, out of disgust at their treatment, allied themselves with the English Hudson's Bay Company. See William E. Lass, *Minnesota: A History* (New York, 1998), 56–57.

4. See Duluth to Seignelay, 1685, printed as an appendix in Hennepin, *Description,* 374–375.

however without absorbing some of the puritanical earnestness associated with the Jansenist movement so influential in France during his formative years. Once settled in Canada La Salle studied unobtrusively but minutely the topography along the lakes, listened carefully to the accounts of the local Indians about the mysterious regions to the west, and explored the waterways linked to the St. Lawrence—including the majestic falls of the Niagara—which he came to believe, with Frontenac, were the highways of empire. To install a series of military posts and missions along the western rivers would secure a vast region for *le roi* and *la foi,* and, not coincidentally, provide an unprecedented opportunity for expanded trade and, perhaps someday, for colonies. But none of this grandiose enterprise could come to pass without following up Jolliet's and Marquette's penetration of the Mississippi valley.

In the high summer of 1679 La Salle, with Frontenac's license in his pocket and with credit reluctantly accorded him by merchants in Quebec and Montreal, completed organizing his expedition at the western extremity of Lake Ontario. Included on the roster were Louis Hennepin and two other Recollect Franciscans who, though not Jansenists, nevertheless enjoyed a reputation for austerity that appealed to La Salle's strict moral and ascetic code. (Frontenac, too, though generally suspicious of clerical pretensions, maintained a friendly relationship with the Recollects.) The company departed the Niagara aboard a forty-five-ton brigantine, the *Griffon,* which carried them across the lakes to the little French trading post at Green Bay. There the *Griffon* was loaded with furs and sent back to Canada in hopes of assuaging La Salle's creditors; she was never seen or heard of again, presumably the casualty of a storm.[5] Meanwhile the expedition proceeded by canoe to the southeastern shore of Lake Michigan, to the mouth of a river called, by the pious explorers, the St. Joseph. There, after erecting a little stockade, La Salle and his companions paddled southward up the St. Joseph to the point where the river bent to the north.[6] A difficult portage brought them to the Kankakee and then to what Hennepin called "the River of the Illinois," on the banks of which, on January 1, 1680, Mass was celebrated and new year's wishes extended to the sieur de La Salle. Here, near what would one day be the city of Peoria, a fort was built, called Crève-coeur, because, said Hennepin, "the desertion of our men and the other difficulties we labored under had almost broken our hearts." At this moment, for reasons unclear, La Salle determined that he had to return to

---

5. See Theodore C. Blegen, *Minnesota: A History of the State* (Minneapolis, 1963), 49.

6. The site today of South Bend, Indiana.

Quebec—perhaps to settle his parlous financial circumstances. In any case he left in charge at Crève-coeur his lieutenant, a tough Neapolitan named Enrico di Tonti. For Louis Hennepin he reserved a crucial assignment.

> He begged me to consent to take the pains to explore in advance the route which he would have to take to the River Colbert[7] on his return from Canada, but as I had an abscess in the mouth, which suppurated continually, and which had continued for a year and a half, I manifested to him my repugnance, and told him I needed to return to Canada to have it treated. He replied that if I refused this voyage he would write to my superiors, that I would be the cause of the want of success of our new missions.[8]

The threat of delation served its purpose. On February 29, 1680, sore-mouthed Father Hennepin, with two companions, both French-born—Antoine Augelle and Michel Accault—departed Crève-coeur and canoed their way down the Illinois "as deep and broad," Hennepin remembered, "as the Seine at Paris" and "skirted by hills whose sides are covered with fine large trees," behind which stretched out "fields of black earth, the end of which you cannot see, all ready for cultivation, which would be very advantageous for a colony."

Late in March they reached the Mississippi—the "Colbert"—and began the laborious task of paddling upstream. "This great river is almost everywhere a short league in width, and in some place[s], two leagues; it is divided by a number of islands covered with trees, interlaced with so many vines as to be almost impassable." But on April 11, 1680, these prosaic observations all at once gave way to an alarming spectacle.

> At two o'clock in the afternoon we suddenly perceived thirty-three bark canoes, manned by a hundred and twenty Indians, coming down with extraordinary speed to make war on the Miamis [and the] Illinois. These Indians surrounded us, and, while at a distance, discharged some arrows at us; but as they approached our canoe the old men, seeing us with the calumet of peace in our hands, prevented the young men from killing us. These brutal men leaping from their canoes, some on land, others in the

---

7. The name tentatively given to the Mississippi in honor of Louis XIV's chief minister, Jean-Baptiste Colbert (1619–1683).

8. Hennepin, *Description*, 188–189.

water, with frightful cries and yells, approached us, and as we made no resistance, being three against so great a number, one of them wrenched our calumet from our hands, while our canoe and theirs were made fast to the shore. We first presented to them a piece of . . . French tobacco, better for smoking than theirs.[9]

Tobacco fumes, which had made Hennepin ill all those years ago in Calais, now saved his life.

From the beginning their captors adopted an ambivalent attitude toward Hennepin and his companions. Some were clearly quite ready to slay these intruders, who had to endure many a fearful display of Dakota hostility. The prevailing view, however, appears to have been that the white men might be of some long-term material use, or at least so opined Hennepin afterward. Thus, once the Europeans' large canoe had been forced to the shoreline and a score of tomahawks had been raised menacingly, Hennepin felt "compelled . . . to go to the war chiefs . . . and throw into their midst six axes, fifteen knives, and six fathom of our black tobacco." Then, "bowing down my head I showed them with an axe, that they might tomahawk us if they thought proper. This present appeased several individuals among them who gave us some beaver to eat." The Indians could surely have seized axes and knives and any goods they wanted, but Hennepin's act of bravado—if indeed it happened—seems to have given them pause. They turned round in any case and, with their prisoners in tow, paddled northward.

The water journey took nineteen days "of very painful navigation. . . . These Indians paddle with great force, from early in the morning till evening, scarcely stopping to eat during the day." Father Hennepin was intent on remaining faithful to his religious obligations, whatever the obstacle or hazard. "The greatest difficulty I had was say[ing] my office before these savages," who became immediately suspicious of the priest's moving lips. Accault "told me that if I continued to say my breviary we should all three be killed." But Hennepin persisted, though more discreetly, until it became clear that "these savages [assumed] that the book I was reading was a spirit" toward which "they . . . showed a kind of aversion. . . . To accustom them to it, I chanted the Litany of the Blessed Virgin in the canoe with my book open." This maneuver apparently appeased the warriors, "for these people are naturally fond of singing." But not all of them were so soothed by the chanting, or at least not all the time. When the convoy of canoes reached a northward point where the

---

9. Hennepin, *Description*, 204–206.

Mississippi, between a set of lowering bluffs, swelled into an expanse several miles long and unusually wide—Lake Pepin—Hennepin called it "the Lake of Tears," because "the Indians who had taken us, wishing to kill us, some of them wept the whole night to induce the others to consent to our death."[10]

When they reached the Falls of St. Anthony, the Dakota pulled their canoes ashore and hid them. After some lively deliberation, they decided not to kill their captives. But "they seized all our property and broke our canoe into pieces . . . and compelled us to go sixty leagues by land, forcing us to march from daybreak to two hours after nightfall and to swim over many rivers. . . . Our legs were all bloody from the ice which we broke as we advanced [across the streams] which we forded." On the sixth day they reached the collection of Dakota camps along the shores of the complex of waters called by Duluth the summer before *le lac de Baude* but which, once the maps had assumed definitive form and the aggressive governor of *Nouvelle France* was no more than a hazy memory, assumed the designation it has borne ever since, still French, Mille Lacs. By then Hennepin's captors had appropriated "our brocade chasuble and all the articles of our portable chapel, except the chalice, which they durst not touch; for seeing that silver gilt, they closed their eyes saying that it was a spirit that would kill them." In one sense the seizure of the priestly vestments meant little; Hennepin could not have said Mass anyway, because his supply of wine had long since been exhausted.[11]

Hennepin, Accault, and Augelle were kept at the camp at Mille Lacs for three months, during which time they endured as much indignity as uncertainty. The priest, however, managed to learn a smattering of the Dakota language and to ingratiate himself to a degree among his captors by tending their sick, a development that aroused some jealousy in his two companions. Hennepin did not sympathize: "If they were well received in this country, it was only in consequence of my bleeding some asthmatic Indians and giving some orvietan and other remedies which I kept in my sleeve."[12] "Well received"

---

10. Hennepin, *Description*, 198, 207–215. Hennepin's assertion here may be an instance of a tendency to embellish or even fabricate in order to heighten the drama of his account. Another explanation for the sobriquet "Lake of Tears" rests upon the tale of a chief who wept along its shores mourning the death of his son in battle. Still another story associated with Lake Pepin is that of Winona, an Indian princess who, rather than marry a man she did not love, killed herself by jumping from Maiden Rock into the lake.

11. Hennepin, *Description*, 219–223, 259.

12. Hennepin, *Description*, 240. Orvietan was a folk remedy allegedly useful to combat the effects of snakebite.

surely overstated their circumstances, but at least they were still alive. Then, at the end of July, came a dramatic intervention. Duluth had mounted a second expedition from French Canada into the territory west of Lake Superior. This time he portaged his way to the Saint-Croix and followed that stream south through an indescribably gorgeous countryside of hills and inlets till he and his small company reached the Mississippi. There he learned that three white men were prisoners of the Dakota with whom he had reached agreement the previous summer. "This intelligence surprised me so much," Duluth recalled, that he hastened to Mille Lacs and "caused a council to be summoned, exposing the ill-treatment [the Indians] had been guilty of, both to the . . . Reverend Father and to the other two Frenchmen, . . . having robbed them and carried them off as slaves, and [having] even taken the priestly vestments of the said Reverend Father." He scorned, he said, to smoke a calumet of peace with such ungrateful and wicked subjects of King Louis. This tongue-lashing by the soldier of fortune—who had only a half dozen men at his back—had its effect upon the assembled chiefs. "Each one in the council endeavored to throw the blame from himself." Their "excuses" notwithstanding, as Duluth explained to an uneasy Hennepin, "it would be to strike a blow at the French nation in [this] new discovery [if we were] to suffer an insult of this nature without manifesting resentment." The tactic worked and the captives were released: "I put them into my canoes and brought them back to Mackinac," at the head of Lake Michigan, and from there they returned to Quebec the following spring.[13]

When he came to record his recollections of his adventures on the upper Mississippi, Louis Hennepin proved reluctant to give much credit to Duluth for the rescue. "On the 25th of July, 1680," he wrote laconically, "we met the Sieur du Luth who came . . . with five French soldiers." And he quoted with relish a Dakota chieftain who had told Duluth, "'Père Louis is a greater captain than you, for his robe (meaning our brocade chasuble) . . . is more beautiful than that which you wear,'" and observed as well, reproachfully, that Duluth and his men "had not approached the sacraments for two years."[14] But Hennepin's memories, as they appeared in the books he published after he went back to Europe for good in 1682, were not always to be trusted—he claimed, for example, to have explored the Mississippi valley *south* of the Illinois during the summer of his captivity, a manifest impossibility. Duluth for his part returned to the upper valley twice more during his distinguished

---

13. Duluth to Seignelay, 1685, in Hennepin, *Description*, 375–377.
14. Hennepin, *Description*, 254–256.

career as explorer, soldier, and administrator. Thanks largely to his efforts the fur trade matured into New France's most flourishing enterprise, but his hopes to find a Northwest Passage never advanced beyond the tantalizing story the Indians told him of a great body of saltwater twenty days march to the west from Mille Lacs.

THE EIGHT DECADES FOLLOWING FATHER HENNEPIN'S FIRST SIGHT of St. Anthony Falls were, in what would one day be the state of Minnesota, the years of the French. Men with names like Le Sueur and Varennes, Charlevoix and Pénicaut, paddled up and down the waterways and crisscrossed the woods and grasslands, drawing maps on which rivers were named for Catholic saints, and setting up little forts and missions and, above all, trading posts, most of which flourished for a few years and then gave way to others in other places. But it would be wrong, of course, to suppose that they were the first inhabitants of this immense expanse of land, with its thousands of lakes, with its evergreen forests in the northeast and the hardwood forests of oak, maple, and basswood in the center and southeast, with its fertile and treeless prairie stretching in an enormous L-shaped arc from the northwest to the southeast. Indeed, except for a tiny fraction, the French and their Quebecois descendants could scarcely be called inhabitants at all. The blackrobes came to convert the Indians to *la foi,* as Marquette and Hennepin had hoped to do; their success was minimal. The *voyageurs* came in the early summer, to be sure, plying their huge canoes and sporting their colorful garb and singing their lusty songs—the stuff of legend now—but they went away too, every autumn, with a rhythm of their own dictated by the all-embracing fur trade. The farmers did not come, nor the lumbermen, not yet. Then, in 1759, on the Plains of Abraham above Quebec City, the imperial dreams of Frontenac and La Salle dissolved in the smoke of battle, and, as Wolfe and Montcalm both lay dying, Nouvelle-France passed away.

The Frenchmen's interlude in Minnesota was as but a moment when compared with the aeons it had taken to form the land as they found it. Measured in terms of a billion years or more—hardly comprehensible in any case—the succession of physical upheavals, of volcanoes spewing lava, of seas rising and disappearing, of species of plant and animal flourishing and then lurching into extinction, bore its cosmic effects deep into the earth, not least in the northeast where it left a rich residue of iron ore. The most immediate of these colossal episodes, covering a period of perhaps two million years and lasting until ten or twelve thousand years before Christ, had been the series of glaciers that pushed relentlessly down from the north and northwest, leveling mountains, crunching boulders, scooping out hollows, and, in short, reshaping the landscape in accord with the ineluctable power of their icy tendrils, often as much as a mile thick. Over several millennia the climate slowly warmed and the last of the glaciers melted, leaving in its wake an inland sea greater in size than all the Great Lakes combined, until it too ultimately disappeared and left as a memorial the lakes, great and small, the river valleys, the fertile soil that could nourish trees and grassland and, in time, crops planted by *homo sapiens*. It left as well a triangle of watersheds: along the western border the Red River flowed north through its lush valley into Lake Winnipeg and so joined the system that ended finally on the chilly shores of Hudson Bay; in the northeast the St. Louis and its tributaries emptied into Lake Superior and so were linked ultimately with the Atlantic Ocean; and the Mississippi made its majestic way south to the Gulf of Mexico. (When Ronald Knox, in 1950, offered to the public his translation of the Old Testament, his rendering of the opening verses of Genesis seemed to reflect a theist's reaction to such events: "God, at the beginning of time, created heaven and earth. Earth was still an empty waste, and darkness hung over the deep; but already, over its waters, brooded the Spirit of God.")

Sometime after the last Ice Age, Asiatics crossed over a land bridge, long since gone, between what are now Siberia and Alaska, in one of those migrations of prehistoric peoples as common as they were mysterious. Archeological and fossil remains suggest that the descendants of these first arrivals in North America had settled in Minnesota as early as six or seven thousand years before Christ. A few bones, some sherds of pottery, and a few bits of tools can shed little light on what these people may have been like, but thousands of burial mounds argue for their presence and their permanence.[15] The discovery of conch shells also provides evidence that there was a continuous, if slow, movement of these Native Americans—as they can be rightly designated—in various directions, including into Minnesota from as far south as the Gulf of Mexico. When the French first arrived in the upper Mississippi valley, the dominant tribe there was the Dakota. How long they—a hunting and gathering people—had prevailed in the area cannot be established with certainty, but it must have been for several centuries. Nor should the word "tribe" be understood as presuming a centralized or bureaucratic structure. Besides their seven subclans or "council fires" the Dakota—or Sioux as the

---

15. See Lloyd A. Wolford, "The Prehistoric Indians of Minnesota," *Minnesota History* 31 (September and December, 1951): 163–171, 231–237.

French came to call them from the name of one of the clans—were related ethnically and linguistically to other groups settled nearby, like the Winnebago, the sad remnant of whom had been gradually driven out of what is now southern Wisconsin. The Dakota demonstrated on every recorded occasion a fierce individualism—which appears to have saved Father Hennepin's life—so much so that each teepee had to be considered a political entity in itself.[16] These were the people whom a company of Vikings would have encountered had it wandered into the area during the fourteenth century—a highly unlikely occurrence.[17]

When Duluth in 1678 beached his canoes at the western extremity of Lake Superior, the Dakota were already being pressed from the east by the Ojibwe or Chippewa. They in turn were moving westward because of the aggression of the Iroquois confederation, which, since Champlain's day, had been hostile to any tribe allied to the French. The British, understandably, had taken as much advantage as they could of such belligerent feelings, for they too entertained dreams of imperial sway in North America. At the great council of 1678, Duluth demanded that the Ojibwe and the Dakota smoke the pipe of peace. They did so, but without for a moment understanding that

---

16. For an eloquent evocation of the decentralized character of the Dakota polity, see Larry McMurtry, *Crazy Horse* (New York, 1999). McMurtry deals specifically with the nineteenth century, but the evidence clearly indicates his conclusions apply validly to the earlier period as well.

17. In 1897, near Kensington in west-central Minnesota, a large stone was unearthed by a local farmer of Norwegian extraction, which appeared to bear a message chiseled in runes proper to medieval Scandinavia. The inscription described how "eight Goths and twenty-two Norwegians" had come under attack from some unidentified hostile force. It was dated 1362. Heated and sophisticated debate over the authenticity of the Kensington Runestone has raged from the day of its discovery to the present and has produced a considerable literature. The circumstantial evidence accepted today generally, though by no means universally, strongly suggests that the Runestone is a brilliant and elaborate hoax. For a recent analysis see David A. Sprunger, "Mystery & Obsession: J. A. Holvik and the Kensington Runestone," *Minnesota History* 57 (Fall 2000): 141–154, and the authorities cited there. Ethnic pride was involved in the debate, since, were the Runestone authentic, Minnesota's large Scandinavian population could claim their forebears had "discovered" America 130 years before Columbus. But Catholics too had a stake in the argument, because fourteenth-century "Goths and Norwegians" would have been Catholic; indeed, the Runestone appeared to have on it an invocation of the Virgin Mary. Thus the first chapter of James M. Reardon, *The Catholic Church in the Diocese of St. Paul* (St. Paul, 1952), 3–11, argues for authenticity.

such an act committed them to an agreement such as what might have been reached by diplomats meeting, over champagne and canapés, in Paris or London. War between American tribes was a harsh game, in which individuals set out their emblem of virility, but in essence they amounted to occasional raids for food or ponies, and fatal casualties were few. The notion that such confrontations possessed some geopolitical political significance was unknown. Even so, the Ojibwe possessed an advantage, since they had firearms, supplied by the French, lacking to the Dakota.[18]

But the French were gone now, at least politically and administratively, for, as they had lost to the British by the misfortunes of war Canada and indeed all the territory east of the Mississippi they had heretofore claimed, they had also ceded to Spain by secret treaty the vast area to the west of the river, what they called, after the long dead Sun King, *Louisiane*. Thus did the monarchies of Europe draw and redraw the maps of a continent far away, maps which were anyway rudimentary at best. The practical effect in the Minnesota region was simply the continuation and expansion of what had gone on before. The myth of an El Dorado, a city of gold, in the New World had long since been exploded, but the voracious appetite for furs among the luxury markets of the Old World was a persistent reality. The trade in furs—otter, marten, mink, and above all prime beaver pelts—drove the new political masters no less than the old. The British entrepreneurs, organized into joint stock companies like the Hudson's Bay and the North West, opened dozens of new trading posts or expanded existing ones. Most famous among the latter was Grand Portage, on the northern shore of Lake Superior, which linked the rivers and lakes westward into the interior with the St. Lawrence system and which during the summers for thirty years and more was a hubbub of noisy commerce, swarming with white and mixed-blood traders and Indians. Anglos to be sure assumed new prominence, some British-born, others Yankees like the soldier and surveyor Jonathan Carver from Massachusetts colony, and Peter Pond, an outstanding cartographer from Connecticut. But the French flavor did not entirely dissipate, for, though Montreal and Quebec were British entrepots now, the *voyageurs* still carried the commodities back and forth in their long canoes and still sang their songs in their own language. Nor did the search for a Northwest Passage to the Pacific flag under British administration. Major Robert Rogers, headquartered at Mackinac, assigned Carver among others to pursue this objective, the fruit of which effort

---

18. Blegen, *Minnesota*, 21–23.

produced not knowledge of a waterway to the riches of Cathay but a literary gem, Carver's *Travels through the Interior Parts of North America.*[19] The Spanish, putative rulers of the western lands between the Mississippi and the Rockies, were notable only by their absence and indifference.

And so, after their successful revolution, were the Americans. By the Treaty of Paris of 1783, Great Britain ceded to the newly independent United States the territory east of the Mississippi and south of British Canada. Over the next two decades and more, however, this agreement made little practical difference in the Minnesota region. British chartered companies continued to control the fur trade, and Grand Portage, if anything, increased its standing as a uniquely great emporium.[20] Indeed, the negotiators at Paris had only the haziest notion of where the northern boundary of American jurisdiction should lie, this because, despite a century of exploration and map making, nobody knew precisely where the source of the Mississippi River was located. Only desultory attempts were made to solve the problem, mostly because the Americans had so far demonstrated little interest in their northernmost acquisition.

Even so, in 1787 the Northwest Territory was formally organized, out of which six states of the Union ultimately evolved.[21] Then, in 1803, came the dramatic purchase by President Jefferson of "Louisiane" from Napoleon Bonaparte, which the hapless Spaniards had ceded back to France three years earlier. Thus at the stroke of a pen (and at a remarkably modest payment of $15,000,000, or three cents an acre) the sovereignty of the United States suddenly stretched from the Atlantic to the Rocky Mountains, and what was to be the state of Minnesota was no longer bounded by the Mississippi. There followed one of the great adventures of all time, the expedition to explore the

---

19. Blegen, *Minnesota*, 65–81, and Lass, *Minnesota*, 67–75. Carver's *Travels* was published in 1778. For a helpful analysis, see Russell W. Fridley, "The Writings of Jonathan Carver," *Minnesota History* 34 (Winter 1954): 154–159. The swashbuckling Rogers is most familiarly evoked in Kenneth Roberts's novel *Northwest Passage* (1937), a minor classic of historical fiction.

20. Nancy L. Woolworth, "Grand Portage in the Revolutionary War," *Minnesota History* 44 (Summer 1975): 199–208.

21. Ohio (1803), Indiana (1816), Illinois (1818), Michigan (1837), Wisconsin (1848), Minnesota east of the source of the Mississippi and south to there from Lake of the Woods (1858).

Louisiana Purchase commissioned by Jefferson and led by William Clark and Meriwether Lewis, which trekked up the Missouri River from St. Louis and across the prairies and the mountains to the Columbia River and the western ocean.

About the time, in the late summer of 1805, when Captain Lewis first caught sight of the Pacific, another expedition, much less pretentious in size and significance, was laboring its way up the Mississippi, also out of St. Louis. Twenty-six-year-old Lieutenant Zebulon Montgomery Pike—his name immortalized by a spectacular mountain in Colorado he traveled to a year later—led a contingent of twenty soldiers with instructions to investigate the native peoples in the upper valley, to ascertain the extent of the British presence there, and to look into the feasibility of establishing American military installations and trading posts in the region. By September 21 the little company had reached the junction of the Mississippi and the river flowing into it from the west, which the French had called the Saint-Pierre. There he held a council with the local Dakota, during which he urged the assembled chiefs to convert their allegiance from the British king to the Great White Father in Washington. He promised that a new system would be inaugurated whereby the trade in furs would be more justly administered than before. Most significantly, Pike negotiated with the Dakota the cession of two tracts of land: one at the mouth of the St. Croix and the other along the Mississippi, from below the mouth of the St. Peter River—the Dakota called it the Minnesota, "sky-tinted water"—to above St. Anthony Falls, nine miles on each side. In return Pike offered a variety of "presents," including a consignment of liquor and other merchandise to the value of $2,000. There were no immediate consequences of this agreement, but in the long term it proved of seminal importance.

Pike, in accord with his orders, continued upriver, and, as autumn turned into a bitterly cold winter—he and his troopers camped on a snowy Christmas day near the site of the present town of Brainerd—arrived early in the new year at the large British trading post at Leech Lake. They were cordially received, but, though grateful for the hospitality, Pike immediately ordered that the Union Jack be taken down and the American flag hoisted in its place. He further insisted that from then on the proprietors recognize United States sovereignty by paying duties on all goods imported for use in trade with the Indians. The Scotsman in charge of the post raised no objection and cheerfully pledged to fulfill all legal obligations, mindful, of course, that there was not a single American customs officer anywhere in the territory, and confident as well that this young subaltern and his handful of soldiers would soon go away. As indeed they did, but not before Pike held council with the Ojibwe and also satisfied himself that Leech Lake was the source of the Mississippi. In this judgment he proved mistaken; the true source of the great river remained as elusive as the Northwest Passage itself.[22]

WHEN ZEBULON PIKE RETURNED TO ST. LOUIS ON APRIL 30, 1806, his superiors read with interest the notes and diary he had kept on the journey. They did not, however, take any follow-up action, and it appeared that the expedition, by raising the Stars and Stripes for the first time along the upper Mississippi, had had merely a symbolic significance. Nevertheless, circumstances in the region were inexorably if slowly changing. After a hundred years of exploitation, the center of the fur trade was moving north and west, into what would one day be the Canadian province of Manitoba. Even Grand Portage, for thirty years the hub of a frenzied commerce, witnessed the sharp diminution of trading activity, until the British decided to move the operation up the shore of Lake Superior to Fort William, unarguably within their own jurisdiction. In 1808, a wealthy German-born New York merchant named John Jacob Astor organized the American Fur Company, just as the growing scarcity of pelts was leading the established British companies into an ever-fiercer competition.[23] During the War of 1812—one fatality was Brigadier General Zebulon Pike—the British at first had the best of the fighting along the Great Lakes and in the Ohio River basin, and, allied with the Dakota and the Ojibwe, they maintained without challenge their control of the upper Mississippi. But at war's weary end, with Napoleon still finally to be dealt with, they agreed to withdraw from their Midwestern outposts and to negotiate a northern frontier which, they believed, would still leave the bulk of the fur trade in their hands.[24]

The prosecution of the war, and particularly the defeats endured by American forces in the Northwest Territory, had a sobering effect on the

---

22. Blegen, *Minnesota*, 87–90.

23. K. G. Davies, "From Competition to Union," *Minnesota History* 40 (Winter 1966): 166–177. Hudson's Bay and North West merged in 1821.

24. William E. Lass, "How the Forty-ninth Parallel Became the International Boundary," *Minnesota History* 44 (Summer 1975): 209–219.

government in Washington. In response to the movement of population westward—Indiana became a state in 1816 and Illinois two years later—an explicit policy was adopted to fortify the region as well as to promote settlement there. The war department established or, in some instances, enhanced a line of military installations from Detroit through Chicago to St. Louis, and northwestward from there into the Missouri country.[25] Included in the overall plan was a determination to locate a fort in the upper Mississippi valley—a project heavily lobbied for by Astor and his American Fur Company. In 1817 an exploratory commission reported that the best site for such a post lay at the congruence of the Minnesota and Mississippi rivers, putting to use the land acquired by Pike from the Dakota twelve years before. Accordingly a detachment two hundred strong, dispatched from Detroit, set up camp there in the summer of 1819 to survey first of all what precise piece of ground would be best suited for the construction of Fort St. Anthony. Their efforts were severely hampered by the harsh winter that followed and by an epidemic of scurvy that caused an alarming number of fatalities among the troops. Their morale was at low ebb when, the next year, a new commandant arrived.

Colonel Josiah Snelling, thirty-eight-year-old Boston-born veteran of the War of 1812, was a man of extraordinary vigor and decisiveness. He immediately selected the site for the fort, on a bluff at the exact angle where the two rivers met, on the west bank of the Mississippi and the north of the Minnesota. He then put his men to work building the installation. Waterpower available at the Falls eight miles upriver prompted him to set up a sawmill there to supply the needed timber, and local limestone quarries provided the wherewithal for the enclosing walls ten feet high, punctuated by loopholes for musket-fire and adorned with handsome round towers and a platform for cannon. Inside the compound, after four years of strenuous labor, were barracks, a commissary, a hospital, even a little school. Outside, two hundred acres were utilized for the cultivation of corn and fruits and vegetables, so that scurvy would never again menace the soldiers and their dependents. So impressed was the war department by this remarkable achievement on the edge of the wilderness that in 1824 it decreed that the post should be renamed for its commandant, whose productive assignment there continued

---

25. John S. Galbraith, "British-American Competition in the Border Fur Trade of the 1820s," *Minnesota History* 36 (September 1959): 241–249.

for another three years.[26] For the most part his successors proved themselves similarly competent executives, as did the agents assigned to deal directly with the Indians. In 1836 the fort witnessed an event, hardly noticed at the time, that was to have immense symbolic importance. The medical doctor appointed to serve there brought with him a Negro slave who, when taken south again later, claimed that his residence in a free territory furnished rationale for his own emancipation. The slave's name was Dred Scott.[27]

Fort Snelling, though it never came under hostile attack, remained for the next several generations the symbol and reality of United States authority in the Minnesota region. Here was the center of a revivified fur trade,[28] here was a presence which encouraged whites to immigrate little by little, and here or in the environs were negotiated—dishonorably for the most part—the covenants through which those immigrants, bolstered by the power the fort represented, cheated the Native Americans of their hunting grounds. And here, in 1832, passed the last of the explorers, Henry Rowe Schoolcraft, who finally found the true source of the Mississippi. He called the small body of water Lake Itasca, an awkward fusion of two Latin nouns, *veritas* (truth) and *caput* (head).[29] There is something poignant in that Itasca sounds as though it might have been the name of an Indian princess—and for a long time it was assumed to be so—when in fact it was taken from a European language, and a dead language at that. The maturation of Fort Snelling was an even more potent sign that one civilization was giving way to another, a reality embossed on the official seal a little later when Minnesota was admitted to the Union: a white farmer plowing his field, and a mounted Native American galloping away, all under the inscription *L'Etoile du Nord*—Star of the North.

---

26. Blegen, *Minnesota*, 99–104. The next year, 1828, Zachary Taylor—later hero of the Mexican War and twelfth president of the United States—assumed command at the fort. His tenure was brief and unpleasant. "We are here entirely out of the world, & very seldom hear from the civilized part of our country." He had arrived at the end of May and found it so cold "that I could not divest myself of the opinion that it was the commencement of winter instead of summer." Taylor to Lawson, August 28, 1828, in *Minnesota History* 28 (Spring 1947): 15–19. Snelling died in Washington D.C. in 1829.

27. Blegen, *Minnesota*, 102.

28. See David Lavender, "Some American Characteristics of the American Fur Company, 1808–1834," *Minnesota History* 40 (Winter 1966): 178–187.

29. Philip P. Mason, ed., *Schoolcraft's Expedition to Lake Itasca* (East Lansing, Mich., 1958), 350–352.

What had happened before in the states and territories to the east was about to happen along the upper Mississippi. Good intentions and official federal policy to treat the Indians fairly collapsed beneath the rapid and chaotic onrush westward of white settlers lusting after cheap land.[30] Once the farmers came, and then the lumberjacks and the miners, in ever increasing numbers, the relative handful of natives—six or seven thousand Dakota, perhaps five thousand Ojibwe[31]—had no chance to preserve their culture and their way of life. One need not succumb to the myth of the "noble savage" to regret that that culture was destroyed by trinkets, whiskey, small pox, and a series of disgraceful "treaties"—the most celebrated of which was that of Traverse des Sioux in 1851 when the Dakota ceded no less than twenty-four million acres west of the Mississippi[32]—which the Indians could not possibly have understood. But the hard fact was that two such different societies could not coexist in the land of sky-tinted waters, and in the unequal struggle that ensued victory went, as it always does, to the big battalions. One frontiersman, given to versifying, put the reality bluntly if quaintly:

Give way, give way, young warrior,
Thou and thy steed give way—
Rest not though lingers on the hills
The red sun's parting ray.
The rocky bluff and prairie land
The white man claims them now.
The symbols of his course are here,
The rifle, axe and plow.[33]

One hundred sixty years after Louis Hennepin traveled up the great river and first saw the Falls of St. Anthony, another French-speaking priest embarked on the same journey, though by a conveyance more modern and more comfortable than a long canoe. He boarded "on the 26th day of April, 1840, in the

---

30. See the perceptive remarks of Gordon S. Wood, "The Greatest Generation," *The New York Review of Books* 48 (March 29, 2001): 21.

31. See the detailed population figures in Mitchell E. Rubenstein and Alan R. Woolworth, "The Dakota and Ojibway," in June Drenning Holmquist, ed., *They Chose Minnesota: A Survey of the State's Ethnic Groups* (St. Paul, 1981), 19–23.

32. See the retrospective account in the *St. Paul Pioneer Press*, June 24, 1903.

33. Quoted in Blegen, *Minnesota*, 170.

afternoon, a St. Louis steamboat, the first of the season, . . . bound for St. Peter and Fort Snelling."[34] Two or three days later he reached his destination not as a captive or an explorer or even an itinerant missionary, but as a parish priest—which meant that the Catholic presence in the upper Mississippi, ephemeral until now, would assume a conventional permanence. A new adventure had begun.

---

34. Galtier to Grace, January 14, 1864, Archives of the Archdiocese of St. Paul and Minneapolis (AASPM), Grace Papers. This letter is printed in *Acta et Dicta* (*A&D*) 1 (July 1908): 184–190, and quoted extensively in M. M. Hoffman, *The Church Founders of the Northwest* (Milwaukee, 1937), 156–159 (with the original spelling corrected), as well as in Richard P. Moudry, "The Chapel of Saint Paul: The Beginnings of Catholicity in Saint Paul, Minnesota, 1840–1851" (Master's thesis, St. Paul Seminary, 1950), a model of its kind.

CHAPTER 2

From Pig's Eye
to Saint Paul

LUCIEN GALTIER, A SLENDER, DARK-EYED MAN OF TWENTY-NINE, had been ordained priest only a few months before his arrival at Fort Snelling at the end of April 1840. Recruited as a subdeacon in France by the newly appointed bishop of Dubuque, Mathias Loras, Galtier had spent his first year in the United States at a seminary in Maryland, completing his theological studies and learning a rudimentary English. In temperament he was reserved and introspective, and his foray into the wilderness of the upper Mississippi filled him with both awe and foreboding.

> The boat landed at the foot of Fort Snelling [he recalled], then garrisoned by a few companies of Regular soldiers. . . . The sight of the Fort, commanding from the elevated promontory the two rivers, the Mississippi and the St. Peter, pleased me; but the discovery, which I soon made, that there were only a few houses on the St. Peter side, and but two on the side of the Fort, surrounded by a complete wilderness, and without any sign of fields under tillage, gave me to understand that my mission and life must henceforth be a career of privation, hard trials, and suffering, and required of me patience, labor, and resignation.[1]

Galtier still used the old French names for the river and for the little settlement on its south bank, which had already become anachronistic in favor of Minnesota and Mendota respectively; but the linkage, natural to his ecclesiastical mind, between "St. Peter" and St. Paul was to have its consequences in due course.

---

1. Galtier to Grace, January 14, 1864, AASPM, Grace Papers.

Zeal is one Christian virtue that seems to require redefinition from one generation to the next. The sentiments that prompted Ignatius of Antioch to confront joyfully the wild beasts in the Roman coliseum appear far removed from those that inspired Archbishop Cranmer to submit to the fires of Smithfield and Oxford or Isaac Jogues to the tortures of the Mohawks so many centuries later. And yet there exists a discernible continuity among such persons of different times and cultures. They shared an unalterable conviction that they professed the ultimate truths, that God had chosen them for a special mission, that it was their solemn duty, whatever the hardships, to share the graces divinely afforded them, even to the point of taking literally Jesus' injunction in the parable about the man who gave a great banquet: "Go to the open roads and the hedgerows and force people to come in to make sure my house is full."[2] Such was the spirit that spurred on the zealous Lucien Galtier and his fellow missionaries in middle America during the middle years of the nineteenth century—Protestant circuit riders no less than a variety of Catholic blackrobes—even if their endeavors, unlike those of some of their spiritual forebears, were not crowned with martyrdom. At the beginning of the twenty-first century, when certainty among Christians about the tenets of their faith and about the matchless value of their moral code has so often dwindled into equivocation, such heroic self-denial and uncompromising dedication perhaps engender as much puzzlement as they do admiration.

Among Catholics, at any rate, the cutting edge of the missionary project had to be entrusted to priests like Father Galtier, because of the unique status Catholicism bestows upon the ordained minister, who alone enjoys the capacity to confect the sacraments of grace, particularly the Eucharist. And so it was that across the Upper Midwest, names like Samuel Mazzuchelli the Italian (d. 1864), Pierre De Smet the Belgian (d. 1873), and Francis Pierz the German-speaking Slovenian (d. aged ninety-five 1880) earned a place on the sacerdotal roll of honor. "Mazzuchelli," wrote John Ireland, "was the missionary. With him zeal for the welfare of the Church, for the salvation of souls, was a burning passion. It had sent him in his youth to the wilderness, away from so much that was naturally dear, so much that was legitimately alluring. It remained forceful into the days of old age."[3] These and other sturdy evange-

---

2. Luke 14:15–24.
3. Samuel Mazzuchelli, *Memoirs Historical and Edifying of a Missionary Apostolic* (Chicago, 1915). The quotation is from Ireland's "Introduction," xiii.

lists came to Mid-America from every corner of Catholic Europe, but in the Minnesota region, and elsewhere as well, the predominant nationality among the missioners was French. "No matter where the traveler rests his feet"— Ireland again—"in whatever part of the globe tribes and peoples are awaiting the announcement of the Gospel of Christ the French missionary greets him. . . . Heaven-lit pages in the history of France, which no shortcomings along other lines of action, however grievous now and then these may seem to be, can ever throw into obscurity . . . those that tell us of its contributions to the Catholic missions in foreign lands."[4]

This French connection is not without its enigmas as far as the American missions were concerned. From the time of the great Revolution of 1789, and indeed in anticipation of it, France, the eldest daughter of the Church, endured a kind of ideological schizophrenia. In some areas—particularly in the west and in the southeast—there occurred a remarkable religious revival during the early nineteenth century, a response no doubt to the perceived excesses of the Enlightenment and the Revolution, while in other parts of the country a culture of indifference and anticlerical hostility continued to prevail and even to intensify.[5] Thus the western provinces of Brittany and Maine, where partisans had taken up arms against the revolutionary state, sent squads of men and women to the missions,[6] as did the region around Lyons, in the valley of the Rhone. Galtier hailed from the mountainous area south of Lyons, the *département* of Ardéche; here too resistance to the ideals embodied in the *tricoleur* was common. In another sense, however, Galtier and his colleagues were typical of their time and place; the romantic reaction to the cerebral certitudes of the Enlightenment was in full swing among Frenchmen of all religious persuasions and of none. That deep sense of hopefulness, that rush of enthusiasm, that restless hankering after adventure—those qualities encompassed in the untranslatable word *élan*—could inspire some to mount the barricades to attain an elusive political objective and others to build cathedrals in the wilderness.

---

4. John Ireland, "Life of Bishop Cretin," *A&D* 5 (July 1917): 58–59.

5. See the very important study of Ralph Gibson, *A Social History of French Catholicism, 1789–1914* (London, 1989).

6. See, for example, Charles Lemarié, *Les missionaires bretons de l'Indiana aux xix siècle*, 3 vols. (n.d., n.p. [Montsurs, 1973]).

MATHIAS LORAS CAME FROM AN OLD AND HIGHLY RESPECTED bourgeois family in Lyons.[7] In 1793, when he was a toddler scarcely a year old, his father and two of his father's brothers were beheaded by the guillotine. Shortly afterward, at the height of the Reign of Terror, two of his mother's sisters suffered the same grisly fate. All property held in the name of those executed was confiscated by the regime, and Madame Loras, mother of eleven, found herself destitute. But she was a woman of remarkable vigor and courage and shrewdness, and by the time Napoleon had put an end to the persecution, she had managed to restore a good portion of the family's fortune. She brought the same intensity to the practice of her religion, and she did not allow her children to forget what loyalty to the Catholic faith had cost her and them. Two of her daughters entered the convent, and Mathias was ordained priest for the archdiocese of Lyons in 1815.[8]

The shortage of clergy was acute in a Church first racked by persecution and schism during the revolutionary era and then hobbled in its activities during the Napoleonic. This circumstance, together with his family's social standing—further adorned by its martyrs—and his own considerable gifts, led many to predict for young Loras swift promotion to honors and high office as he pursued his ecclesiastical career. And indeed he did assume notably responsible posts at a relatively tender age. Between 1817 and 1824 he was superior of the archdiocesan *petit séminaire* at Meximieux. When that institution was incorporated into the refounded diocese of Belley,[9] Loras was assigned to direct the larger and more prestigious preparatory seminary in l'Argentière. In both places he oversaw significant expansion and substantial building projects. But, as he complained to his mother in 1820, "I am perpetually assailed by a thousand little affairs, one more vexing than another. All my free moments find themselves absorbed in such a manner." Administrative tasks, many of them trivial, distracted him from "prayer and study, the principal occupations of a minister of Jesus Christ." Such concerns were perhaps to be expected from one who had been a schoolfellow of Jean-Marie Vianney,

---

7. See Louis de Cailly, *Memoirs of Bishop Loras* (New York, 1897), 6–8, 40–42, 52–56. Cailly was Loras' nephew.

8. John Ireland, "Mathias Loras, the First Bishop of Dubuque" (St. Paul, n.d. [1898]), 4–7. The material in this pamphlet was first published in two issues of the *Catholic World* 67 (September 1897): 721–731, and 68 (October 1897): 1–12.

9. The diocese of Belley traced its origins back to the fifth or sixth century. It was suppressed by the Revolution and restored in 1822. See Louis and Gabrielle Trenard, *Le diocèse de Belley* (Paris, 1978), 154–155.

the saintly and soon to be celebrated curé of Ars: "If I do not make some spiritual provisions, how would I be able to nourish [my students] on the bread of Life, how instruct them in the truths of salvation, if I myself am not spiritually prepared?"

Sentiments such as these led Loras to resign his position at l'Argentière after only three years and to join the so-called mission band newly established in the archdiocese of Lyons. Assignment to this group of priests, who preached retreats and days of recollection in parishes in the city and across the countryside, relieved him of the niggling preoccupations involved in institutional direction. But it did not relieve his restlessness, nor his sense that as the child of a martyr some great labor for the faith had been reserved for him. Late in 1828 there arrived in Lyons a native son who as a seminarian had departed his homeland to serve in the missions in America. Michel Portier had been ordained in New Orleans, and, after ministering in various capacities there, had been appointed by Rome Vicar Apostolic of Alabama and western Florida.[10] He had returned home now to solicit funds[11] and to secure recruits for his new jurisdiction where, aside from himself, not a single priest was at hand. Loras met with him and was beguiled by his account of a vast territory where the Catholic faith had scarcely been heard of. He, Father Loras, was aware of the prospectus recently circulated in France which portrayed the mission in America in the direst terms:

> We offer you no salary, no recompense, no holidays, no pension. But we offer you much hard work, a poor dwelling, few consolations, many disappointments, frequent sickness, a violent and lonely death. An unknown grave.

These admonitions, however exaggerated, were calculated to appeal to a romantic generation, and so they did in Loras' case. In October 1829, he joined

---

10. A vicar apostolic was a prelate, ordained a bishop, whose jurisdiction extended over a wide area where no definite center had yet been established. By 1829 the situation had been regularized canonically, and Portier was designated first bishop of Mobile.

11. The Society for the Propagation of the Faith (SPF, not to be confused with the Propagation of the Faith or *Propaganda Fide,* the department of the Roman curia in charge of activities in mission regions) provided significant sums of money to support mission activities around the world. There were headquarters of the Society both in Paris and in Lyons.

the bishop, in the company of another French priest and five subdeacons, aboard the ship bound for New Orleans. As he watched the harbor and the shoreline recede, he fingered the medallion given him by his formidable mother. It bore an emblem of the Sacred Heart entwined with flowers. The inscription read: "Dans ce divin Coeur, O mon fils! Pensez à moi; c'est là que tu me trouveras toujours. La Veuve Loras à son fils le missionaire, Obre 1829."[12]

Mathias Loras spent more than seven years amid the hardwood forests and cotton fields of Alabama. No missionary labor did he fail to experience, from canoeing to back country settlements to sharing in the foundation of a *collège* at Spring Hill in Mobile—which flourishes to this day. There were inevitably many frustrations to be endured but there were some triumphs as well. "Ma chère Mère," he wrote in 1832, "I have the pleasure of announcing to you that I have lately achieved the greatest consolation which the good God has been able to procure for me, that is, to have preached in English for the first time. . . . I had never believed that God would bless my efforts as he has deigned to do." Even in this, to him, primitive environment, Loras remained, as John Ireland put it, "a gentleman of the old French school."

He was most polite in manner, without giving room to the smallest suspicion of affectation or studied formalism, scrupulously exact in his attire, which often betrayed poverty but never meanness or untidiness, always dignified in bearing, even when stooping to apparently menial tasks that circumstances of the time commended to his spirit of zeal and humility. His word always revealed the honesty of his soul. . . . He was of gentle temper, too gentle almost for the hard, rough humanity amid which his lot was cast. . . . He was most kind and affable to the lowliest as to the highest, seeking to serve and please others and, in order to do so, forgetful and even harsh toward self. His conversation was always charitable and genial, at times witty; his purpose was never to offend but to do good, to diffuse around him innocent joy.[13]

Loras' growing reputation as a more than effective missioner—not least his ability to hold his own in an overwhelmingly and sometimes hostile Protestant environment—soon caught the attention of the American ecclesiastical

---

12. "In this divine Heart, O my son, remember me; it is there will you find me always. The widow Loras to her missionary son, October 1829."
13. Ireland, "Loras," 11.

powers that were, and his name began to appear on the *ternae* sent to Rome.[14] When the third provincial council of Baltimore met in the spring of 1837, the assembled bishops recommended that new dioceses be established at Natchez for the state of Mississippi, Nashville for Tennessee, and Dubuque for the immense territory that stretched from the Missouri border to the north and west. For this last post, the fathers of the council endorsed the candidacy of Mathias Loras.[15]

The new bishop-elect, however, did not go immediately to his see city, the little town in Iowa Territory, perched on the western bank of the Mississippi. Following Bishop Portier's example of eight years earlier, he went home instead, to Lyons and its environs, in search of money and recruits. In both these endeavors he was moderately successful. The Society for the Propagation of the Faith pledged 50,000 francs ($10,000) to the support of the diocese of Dubuque for the year 1839; the generosity of this remarkable organization continued unabated over the next quarter of a century.[16] As for securing priestly personnel, a tour of nearby seminaries produced four volunteers, all of them already in subdeacon's orders, along with a thirty-two-year-old priest from the diocese of Rodez, Jean-Antoine Perlamorgues. Among the subdeacons were Lucien Galtier and another named Augustin Ravoux. These young men were strangers to Loras; not so the sixth recruit.

AN OLDER, RIPER MAN WAS JOSEPH CRETIN. BORN IN 1799, SON and namesake of a prosperous baker and innkeeper in the small town of Montluel, fifteen miles or so east of Lyons, he had been a student in the *petit*

---

14. A *terna* was (and is) a submittal to the Roman curia of the names of three candidates locally deemed worthy of promotion to episcopal rank.

15. Hoffmann, *Church Founders*, 26–36.

16. Between 1839 and 1864 Dubuque received more than half a million francs in donations from the SPF. From 1850, when the territory now comprising Minnesota and the Dakotas east of the Missouri River was detached from Dubuque to form the new diocese of St. Paul, the contributions were, so to speak, divided. In all, the two Catholic dioceses during these years received from Lyons and Paris contributions totaling 910,916 francs (nearly $200,000). For a summary, see Hoffmann, *Church Founders*, 370–373. For an account of the beginnings of the SPF in 1822, see Edward J. Flahavan, "A Quarter Century of Alms: The Aid Given to the Diocese of St. Paul by the Society for the Propagation of the Faith" (Master's thesis, St. Paul Seminary, 1956), 6–14.

séminaire at Meximieux when Loras had been superior there. Like the Loras, though not so spectacularly, the Cretin family too had provided witnesses to the faith during the Reign of Terror: Joseph's great-uncle had gone under the guillotine, and his mother had spent some time in prison. An altar at which fugitive priests had secretly said Mass remained a treasured heirloom and relic within the household. The family was close-knit, fiercely religious, and included, besides Joseph, his sister Clemence and his brother Jean; a second girl had died in infancy.

Joseph Cretin completed his theological studies at the celebrated *grand séminaire* of Saint-Sulpice in Paris, an indication of the high regard in which his teachers at the preparatory level held him. He distinguished himself there more for his piety, regularity, and scrupulous attention to duty than for his intellect; he was no deep thinker, then or ever. But seminaries—even the premier Catholic seminary in France and, for that matter, in the world at the time—were schools of virtue, not universities or research centers. They were institutions designed to prepare a young man for a particular profession in which he would be expected to offer Mass for his parishioners, preach the traditional gospel, hear the confessions of simple peasants, artisans, and shopkeepers, and catechize their children, all the while living a sober, prayerful, and celibate life. The strict regimen at Saint-Sulpice, with its careful and elaborate schedules, its exclusiveness, its often petty preoccupation with detail, suited Cretin perfectly. "I am entirely at home," he wrote his family. "It seems to me that all I see, all I hear of the clerical spirit, of the ecclesiastical life, is of my very nature."[17]

But that "clerical spirit," as molded in the Catholicism of post-Napoleonic France, could manifest some distinctly unattractive features, among them a certain priggishness of which Joseph Cretin gave evidence even as a seminarian.

I pray the Lord [he wrote Clemence] that he may grant you his peace and his holy grace! This is how the first Christians greeted one another, and they believed no better greeting could be found. There is indeed no better greeting, for only inner peace can make us happy. Neither material things, nor wealth, nor honors and power, for which men are so greedy, fill the heart, but rather the sole joy of a pure and tranquil soul. Other people wish one another happiness, but of what does their kind of happi-

---

17. Cretin to his parents, July 6, 1821, AASPM, Cretin Papers.

ness consist? Of fragile and short-lived comforts which cause them anguish instead. Yes, only the peace of the Lord can cause the soul's
happiness, if there is to be happiness here on earth. May my prayers be
granted! What more can I add to that? Except to say that may you be renewed in righteousness and fervor.

Then he invoked an imagery unknown in the long tradition of Christian iconography, from the mosaics in Ravenna to the depictions of Christ's nativity
and infancy as rendered by the likes of Fra Angelico, Raphael, and Leonardo.

Let us imitate the suffering and humbled God. Let us, time and again,
travel in spirit back to the manger in Bethlehem, to the sight of the suffering and crying Christ child. O, how he must have loved us, to put himself in the body of a weak and suffering infant. Ah! If little sister were still
alive, you would have a perfect opportunity to be reminded of the presence of God. For in holding her in your arms, you would be able to imagine yourself holding the little Christ child, and would you not have found
yourself always drawn to this thought?

And finally he concluded on a curiously condescending note.

Farewell! I won't be able to write you as often as you [sic] would like, but
you can write me at any time. They don't scrutinize what comes through
the mail.[18]

Such were the thoughts, preachy at best, with which the eighteen-year-old
Levite addressed the person dearest to him in all the world.

Yet it would be wrong not to look just as carefully at the other side of the
coin. Joseph Cretin, even as he imagined a weeping baby Jesus, set out for
himself the agenda of a spiritual hero. He wrote down in a little notebook a
list of personal rules.

To remember that God is my beginning and my last end. . . . To ask often
of myself, when I pass from one exercise to another, what ought I do?
What am I doing? Why and to what intention? . . . To perform the
present act as if it were the last of my life. To act as if there were on earth

---

18. Cretin to Clemence Cretin, December 10, 1817, AASPM, Cretin Papers.

only God and myself. . . . To examine myself carefully after each act, . . . and should I be obliged to acknowledge guilt, to humble myself before God, crave pardon from him, and impose upon myself some act of self-denial. To beg from God that he make me more humble, more void of myself[,] that he extirpate within me all love of myself.[19]

These spiritual principles, however strange and perhaps distasteful they may sound to modern ears—too introspective, it might be argued, too individual-istic and self-centered, too little scriptural or sacramental, tinged more than a little by Jansenistic pessimism—guided Joseph Cretin all his life. They in-spired and sustained him through many trials, physical and emotional, and, to his mind at least, explained why he, a man of modest natural gifts, achieved what he did. The notebook, well-thumbed, lay at his bedside when he died thirty-five years later in a rude village on the American frontier, a world away from Paris.

Ordained in 1823 by Alexandre Devie, bishop of Belley, Cretin was as-signed as curate and then as pastor of the parish in Ferney, virtually a suburb of Calvinist Geneva and once the home of Voltaire. These geographic and historic connections were reflected in the town where Protestants and lapsed Catholics abounded. If this state of affairs occasioned difficulties for the young priest, it did not inhibit him. His work in Ferney over a fifteen-year tenure covered the full spectrum of pastoral activities. He built a new church and raised the money to pay for it. He established a convent of cloistered Carmel-ites in the town, and brought there as well an order of teaching nuns, who opened a school for girls. He also founded a boarding school for boys—the Pensionnat of Ferney—which he supervised and in which he regularly taught. Always punctilious about ceremonial—a source of edification, he argued, for true believers living in the midst of heretics and the godless—liturgical cele-brations were carried out with considerable pomp, and the more or less mori-bund parish displayed a new liveliness in the gusto of its congregational singing, both in French and in Latin, often accompanied by the curé on the organ or the flute. If his parishioners found Abbé Cretin somewhat reserved and even rigid, they also admired his urbanity of manner—attributable, they no doubt thought, to his Parisian education. His concern for the material al-leviation of the poor became legendary, as did his personal austerity. And many remembered that during the Revolution of 1830 their curé, with only a

---

19. Ireland, "Life of Cretin," *A&D* 4 (July 1916): 187–218.

few boys at his back, confronted an anticlerical mob at the doors of the Pen-sionnat "and in strong words bade them dare come no further." They did not.[20]

Yet, through the faithful performance of his parochial duties, there tugged at Joseph Cretin's heart a different ambition, his own version of *élan*. He wanted to be a missionary; he wanted specifically to preach the Christian gospel among the pagans of China. When he requested a release from the di-ocese for this purpose, the bishop refused and gently reminded him that there were plenty of nonbelievers to convert at home. Some years later, however, the intervention of Cretin's former teacher, Mathias Loras—scion of one of the first Catholic families of Lyons—produced a different result. The bishop of Belley, albeit reluctantly, granted the curé of Ferney a temporary leave of absence for service in the diocese of Dubuque. This proviso was to play its part later when Cretin was pondering the most crucial decision of his life.[21]

But long before that a small family tragedy had to be played out. Cretin took care to stay in touch with his parents and siblings, and he habitually ad-dressed them in the pietistic and somewhat saccharine tones considered ap-propriate within the culture they shared. His New Year's greeting in 1837 was typical: "May God bless you a thousand times over," he wrote his father. "May he keep you by your children for a long time to come. . . . May your old age be like the evening of a pure and serene summer's day. May the love and bond among your children . . . be like the freshness and sweetness of flowers."[22] A year later Madame Cretin died, and Joseph, some weeks after he presided at her funeral, sent further condolences to Montluel: "Give all my love to father," he told Clemence. "Let him not despair like those who have no hope. Take good care of him; he will love you all the more. . . . I can see him steeped in sorrow and mournful silence, tears rolling down his face. . . . Be a comfort to him."[23] Then, shortly afterward, he composed a poem in honor of his own and his father's nameday, the feast of St. Joseph, the last stanza of which read:

Keep sadness far away
From his whitened hair;
Lengthen his advanced age
By adding to his years.

20. Ireland, "Life of Cretin," *A&D* 5 (July 1917): 19–41.
21. See chapter 3, below.
22. Cretin to his parents, January 1, 1837, AASPM, Cretin Papers.
23. Cretin to Clemence Cretin, January 30, 1838, AASPM, Cretin Papers.

O Spouse of Mary,
Joseph, her protector,
Watch over his life
And over our happiness.[24]

Despite such invocations the elder Cretin's health rapidly deteriorated after his wife's passing, so that by the summer he stood himself at death's doorstep. What followed was by no means his son's finest hour. Joseph had securely in hand the bishop of Belley's license to go to America, but he had told no one of his designs. After the customary observance at Ferney of the feast of the Virgin's Assumption, August 15, 1838—solemn high Mass in the morning, fireworks in the evening—in the early light of the next morning he crept stealthily out of the presbytery and made his way to Geneva, where he boarded the stage bound for Paris to join Loras and the other five men the latter had also recruited for the mission in Iowa. Why he indulged in this seemingly pathological secrecy—especially in the light of the fact that he knew his father was dying—remains puzzling, at least at first blush. He let the burden at any rate fall upon Clemence.

I beseech you in the name of the faith in your heart, do not blame me for what I have done; do not sorrow too much over my departure. Console my father, or rather refrain from telling him of my absence. . . . For a long time I have been preparing myself for this great sacrifice, foreseeing and weighing all circumstances, and striving to overcome all obstacles nature was putting in my way. . . . I am quite tranquil, because my conscience is my witness that I followed upon the ways of God. . . . Yes, I am to be a missionary in a country where there is a large number of savages to be converted. . . . Rejoice that your brother is perfectly resigned to the sacrifices, however heavy, that God may require of him. . . . At the break of day I escaped [from Ferney] as a fugitive. I had not the strength to make resistance to the manifestations of sorrow and sadness; the sorrow and sadness should have weighed even more heavily upon myself. That is why I did not make known my intentions to you or go to see you. Your letters, your tears, would have been desolation of soul.[25]

---

24. "*Ecarté la tristesse/ Loin de ces cheveux blancs;/ Prolongé sa vieilesse/ Aux dépens de ses ans./ O Epoux de Marie,/ Joseph son protecteur,/ O veillez sur la vie/ Et sur notre bonheur.*" Cretin to his father, March 19, 1838, AASPM, Cretin Papers.

25. Cretin to Clemence Cretin, August 25, 1838, AASPM, Cretin Papers.

One could hardly find more striking testimony to the vein of self-indulgence that ran through nineteenth-century French spirituality, this despite all its other grandeurs; at least Cretin showed a measure of good taste in not citing to his sister the ninth chapter of the Gospel of St. Luke.[26] In any event, delayed some weeks by inclement weather, Loras and his party boarded the American-licensed brig *Lion,* which set sail from Le Havre on September 17, 1838. They landed in New York on October 10. Even then Cretin could not shake free of his pietistic mode of expression. "Is my father still living?" he asked Clemence. "This was the first question Joseph addressed to his brothers when he met them again.[27] It is also the one I am addressing to you with the most intense solicitude. Answer me as soon as possible. I do not know why I have not as yet received any news from you," he added testily.[28]

After depositing the young subdeacons at Mount St. Mary's in Emmitsburg, Maryland, where, under the auspices of the archbishop of Baltimore, they could finish their theological studies and learn some English, Loras and Cretin proceeded westward overland by rail and stagecoach, and then by riverboat, till at the end of November they reached St. Louis, where Perlamorgues joined them early in the new year. Not till April did the Mississippi open for steamer traffic northward, and on the eighteenth of that month, as Cretin described it in a letter to Clemence: "We arrived at last at Dubuque, . . . at six o'clock in the evening, and there, . . . although it was already late, many people were on the bank. We were soon recognized, and the good Catholics rejoiced at our arrival. We were directed to a little hotel at eleven o'clock, where we took our repose."[29]

THE REPOSE DID NOT LAST LONG, NEITHER FOR THE BISHOP NOR for his newly appointed vicar general, Father Cretin. This ordinarily prestigious title meant little on the American frontier. Loras, counting the recruits he brought with him from France, had at his disposal only two or three priests

---

26. Luke 9:59–60: "Jesus said to another, Follow me. And he said, Lord, suffer me first to go and bury my father. And Jesus said to him, Let the dead bury their dead, but go thou and preach the kingdom of God."

27. The reference was to the patriarch Joseph, whose father, Jacob, was still alive. Genesis 45:3.

28. Cretin to Clemence Cretin, October 16, 1838, AASPM, Cretin Papers.

29. Cretin to Clemence Cretin, April 20, 1839, AASPM, Cretin Papers.

to serve the enormous territory assigned to him, and one of them, the peripatetic Dominican Samuel Mazzuchelli, soon departed and went back to the scenes of his earlier labors in central Wisconsin. Cretin, as vicar general, had few bureaucratic responsibilities outside the ministries he performed up and down both sides of the Mississippi. He was like all frontier clergymen, of whatever denomination, essentially a circuit rider. Sixty or seventy miles a day astride his little black pony was not unusual,[30] and in the evening—after hearing a confession or two, witnessing a marriage, baptizing a mixed-blood baby—a bed of skins spread out on the dirt floor of a fur trader's shack. Each season presented its own perils. Winters harsh beyond the imagining of a man brought up in the valley of the Rhone chilled blood and bones, and made travel by horseback difficult and dangerous, if not impossible. In the summers, he told his sister, "the two greatest inconveniences are rattlesnakes and gnats. One cannot walk with security in the woods and meadows, particularly near the rivers, where, at every step, one hears rattle the tail of this frightful reptile. . . . The gnats are still more annoying; I am devoured by them. . . . I wear silk gloves, I put on my boots, I cover my face with gauze to avoid the sting of this troublesome insect. But during Mass it settles on my [bald] crown which is then defenseless; and my head swells immediately half an inch for half the day."[31]

Cretin, technically headquartered at Dubuque, expended much of his time and energy in the little river towns of Prairie du Chien and Galena. His service to the parishes there, both east of the Mississippi as was the large Winnebago encampment at Fort Atkinson, illustrated how flexible was the writ with which the bishop of Dubuque governed his newly created jurisdiction. By church law Loras was responsible for that territory north of the Missouri state line and west of the Mississippi, stretching to the Canadian border and to the Missouri and White Earth rivers in Dakota. This immeasurable area had been designated successively Michigan, Iowa, and Wisconsin Territory. Then, as increase in population gradually warranted it, new states were admitted to the union—Michigan (1837), Iowa (1846), Wisconsin (1848)—and the former territorial polity accordingly contracted.

---

30. As recalled by his admiring colleague, Augustin Ravoux, "The Labors of Mgr. A. Ravoux among the Sioux or Dakota Indians" (St. Paul, n.d. [1897]), 8. The material in this pamphlet appeared first in the *St. Paul Pioneer Press*, March 7, 1897.

31. Cretin to Clemence Cretin, June 22, 1845, AASPM, Cretin Papers. Printed in *A&D* 1 (July 1907): 38.

Organization of the Catholic hierarchy kept pace as best it could with the development of territory and statehood, but the niceties of the canon law could not be strictly adhered to on the frontier. Thus, for example, when Loras began to exercise his authority out of Dubuque, all Wisconsin and what would be the eastern section of Minnesota were canonically subject to the ailing bishop of Detroit,[32] hundreds of miles away, until 1843, when a bishop assumed office in Milwaukee. But this prelate had no more resources or personnel than did his colleague in Detroit to serve a place as far away as Prairie du Chien, and so the burden willy-nilly fell upon Dubuque and its handful of priests. "When . . . I took possession of my new diocese," Loras recalled ruefully, "I found only one priest, Samuel Mazzuchelli, and even he was obliged to devote one half of his time to the town of Galena. . . . When I was first installed in Dubuque [in 1839] there was but one church in the whole diocese, and even that was scarcely covered in."[33]

The bishop himself, however, soon after his arrival, began a series of pastoral visitations within the diocese that was canonically his own.

I left Dubuque on the 23rd of June [1839], on board a large and magnificent steam vessel, and was accompanied by the Abbé Perlamorgues. . . . After a successful voyage of some days along the superb Mississippi and the beautiful Lake Pepin we reached St. Peter's. Our arrival was a cause of great joy to the Catholics, who had never before seen a priest or a bishop in these remote regions; they manifested a great desire to assist at divine worship and to approach the sacraments of the Church.

He remained about two weeks at Mendota, where he found 185 Catholics, "fifty-six of whom we baptized, administered confirmation to eight, communion to thirty-five adults, and gave the nuptial benediction to four couples."[34] The names of these people, which he carefully registered when he returned to Dubuque, gave off a predictably Gallic sound: Latourelle, Brunelle, Morin, Leclaire. Most of them were associated in one way or another with the headquarters of the American Fur Company, and many of them were colonists who had originally arrived at the headwaters of the Mississippi with loads of

---

32. For Bishop Resé and his problems, see Leslie Tentler, *Seasons of Grace: A History of the Archdiocese of Detroit* (Detroit, 1990), 13–17.

33. Extract of a letter of Loras, January 26, 1854, AASPM, Kempker Papers.

34. Loras to his sister, July 26, 1839, *Annales de la Propagation de la Foi*, 110 vols. (Lyons, 1825 ff.), 3:339.

furs gathered from as far away as the Red River valley in the northwest—the last, so to speak, of the *voyageurs*, driving creaking oxcarts made of skins and wood instead of paddling canoes. There were as well a few Celtic names, like Graham and Quinn, for the bishop to write down in his sacramental register.[35] During their stay, for example, he and Father Perlamorgues lodged with one Scott Campbell, who served as an interpreter for the officers and Indian agents at Fort Snelling. Campbell was not untypical of the overall population in that he was of mixed blood, Scottish and Dakota, and his wife was pure Dakota; she and her seven children were among those baptized during this visitation.

Bishop Loras took pains as well to pay his respects to the commandant of the fort, anxious as he was to accommodate to the spiritual needs of any Catholics among the garrison. In satisfying this concern he encountered no difficulty, but the moment of contact between Church and state was tense for another reason. After twenty years of relative tolerance, a new and stricter policy was evolving with regard to those civilians, most of them at least nominally Catholics, who had settled in Snelling's shadow and so adjacent to the great trading center in Mendota. Indeed, as the government in Washington annexed more and more land by treaty with the Indians, those whites or métis already residing thereon were technically "squatters"; their right of possession remained dubious at best until the newly acquired tracts were formally put up for sale. By the time of Loras' sojourn, the officers at the fort had determined that the squatters on the military reservation secured by Lieutenant Pike from the Dakota in 1805[36] had become a nuisance and, in many instances—some selling whiskey to the Indians, others stripping away the all-important timber supply—a danger. The next year the new policy was implemented, and the soldiers expelled the squatters from their holdings and destroyed their cabins. Most of them moved upriver a few miles, where they settled just at the edge of the military reservation, on the east bank of the Mississippi. Prominent among them was a peculiarly ugly mixed-blood whiskey trader named Pierre Parrant, whose sobriquet came to be attached to the new little riverside settlement: Pig's Eye Landing.[37]

---

35. For the names of the newly baptized—forty-one by Loras and eleven by Perlamorgues—see the list in AASPM, Kempker Papers.

36. See chapter 1, above.

37. According to Reardon, *Diocese of St. Paul,* 63 (without attribution), this "name of the locality [Pig's Eye] . . . never became current among the French colonists."

Included in Bishop Loras' prior schedule during his stay at St. Peter's were visits to the several Dakota villages located in the immediate vicinity of Mendota. This intention was frustrated, however, when a Dakota hunter encountered several Ojibwe and was casually murdered by them; the chronic hostility between the two tribes then flared up into violence once more. In Campbell's house on the fourth of July, Loras recorded, "I was at the altar offering my prayers to heaven in favor of my adopted country, when a confused noise suddenly burst upon my ears." He looked out the window and saw "a band of savages, all covered with blood, executing a barbarous dance and singing one of their death songs. At the top of long poles [they] brandished fifty bloody scalps, to which a part of the skulls was still attached." The local tribesmen were whipping themselves into a fury in preparation for taking the warpath against their ancient enemies. "I finished the holy sacrifice as well as I could, and recommended to the prayers of the audience those unfortunate beings." Loras heard later that on their vengeful campaign the Dakota killed more than a hundred Ojibwe. Still, he remained optimistic and nurtured the illusions so common among Christian missionaries. "We baptize a great number of children, and find the women favorably disposed toward religion," he wrote wistfully. "May the sentiments of hatred which this frightful war has awakened present no insurmountable obstacle to the progress of our missionaries amongst those poor people. Instead of discouraging me, these events have only inflamed my desire to labor in the civilization of those unfortunate beings by imparting to them the blessing of the Christian faith."[38]

It was not easy for "a French gentleman of the old school" to grasp that the Native Americans did not so much resist "the Christian faith" as the "civilization" in which that faith was encapsulated; their own civilization, their own immemorial way of life, bound up with a timeless nature religion, stood on the brink of dissolution, and resistance, scarcely articulated and fruitless as it may have proved, appeared to be the only intelligible course open to them. Even so, Loras' concern for them was deeply and genuinely felt. In mid-July 1839, as he departed St. Peter's for the south in a dug-out canoe instead of waiting for the next available steamer, he promised to send soon one priest to care for the congregation at St. Peter's and another to serve exclusively the Indian population.

---

38. Loras to the Propagation of the Faith, Lyons, July 1839, in *Annales* 3:342.

LUCIEN GALTIER, ORDAINED TO THE PRIESTHOOD IN DUBUQUE IN January 1840, was the first fruit of that pledge. He took up residence at the end of April in Scott Campbell's stone house just outside the walls of Fort Snelling. "For about a month I was there as one of the family," he recalled many years later. "But though kindly treated by all the members of the house, I could not feel sufficiently free to discharge my pastoral duties." So a separate room was set aside for him, "and henceforth I made of it a kitchen, a parlor, and a chapel. With a few boards I made a little altar, open in time of the h[oly] service and neatly closed the balance of the day by a little white canopy and drapery." During his first weeks he acquainted himself with his little flock: a few Catholic soldiers in the Snelling garrison, five families besides the Campbells living near the fort, and, across the Minnesota River in Mendota, five more families, along with some unmarried employees of the American Fur Company. On May 3 he baptized a baby girl, and on June 17 he buried an old lady. By that time he had already presided at a funeral "at St. Croix," as he laconically entered the fact in his register, which meant that Galtier, like Joseph Cretin in Prairie du Chien, had exercised his ministry to the pockets of Catholics living as far east of the Mississippi as the valley of the St. Croix, who strictly speaking were not his responsibility.[39] Nor did such ministrations cease, one of them with unhappy results: "In the month of August I returned sick from a visit I made to some few families settled in the vicinity of St. Croix Lake. Prostrated by bilious fever and the ague at the military hospital, I could not have recovered had it not being [sic] for the skill of Doctor Turner and the continued and kind attentions of his good lady. . . . If my body was truly prostrated, my spirit was still more depressed. I was panting after a priest, but none was around me, the nearest being three hundred miles distant."[40] "Fever and ague" were commonplaces among the pioneers during an era of primitive medicine; loneliness with its usual companion, boredom, was the peculiarly heavy cross borne by the solitary and celibate missionary, who could not even enjoy the sacramental solace he offered to others.[41]

---

39. The register is housed in AASPM. See also Moudry, "Chapel of St. Paul," 31–33.

40. Galtier to Grace, January 14, 1864, AASPM, Grace Papers.

41. This was the common lot of the missionaries. Stephen Badin, the first Catholic priest ordained in the United States and a veteran of fifty years of missionary activity, often complained at not being able to make his sacramental confession. See J. Herman Schauinger, *Stephen Badin: Priest in the Wilderness* (Milwaukee, 1956), 107.

Once released from the Snelling infirmary and the tender care of Dr. and Mrs. Turner, Galtier found his attention drawn more and more to the area east of the Mississippi, not so much to the St. Croix valley now but upstream six miles or so from the fort, where the bulk of the squatters expelled from the military reservation had relocated. Eighteen families had settled here in the vicinity of Pig's Eye Parrant's tavern, thirteen of them Catholic and virtually all of them French-speaking. Father Galtier began to offer Mass for these people with some regularity, though none of the shanties available was large enough to accommodate everybody. In the mid-autumn of 1840, a meeting was convened to discuss what might be done to alleviate the situation. "It was suggested that a shelter, that is, a cover supported by posts, be erected," one who had been present remembered long afterward. This idea attracted little support, and "so it was decided to erect a log chapel sixteen by twenty-four feet. . . . Nothing further was done until late the next summer."[42] During that interval Lucien Galtier, upon whom the inhabitants conferred the right to make the final decision, pondered as to what would be the best location for the structure. All the sites under consideration, it must be observed, were on land literally owned by the federal government; the squatters had indeed staked their claims, as they had earlier done on the military reservation, but the ultimate determination of ownership depended on the moment when Washington would put the tracts up formally up for sale. "Three different points were offered," Galtier remembered.

One [was] called *la pointe basse* or Pointe Leclair, . . . but I objected, because that part was the very extreme of the new settlement and, in high water, the greatest part of the low ground was exposed to inundation; in a word, the idea of having the church carried down the stream to St. Louis did not smile at me, [and so] I refused. Two and a half miles or so [away from there] . . . a Catholic . . . made to me the offered [sic] an acre of his ground.[43] But this place did not suit my purpose. I was truly looking ahead and for the future, as well as for the present time. Steamboats could not stop there[;] the bank was too steep and the room [i.e., the area] above too narrow. . . . I gave it up after mature reflection. Several

---

42. See Moudry, "Chapel of St. Paul," 35–38. The testimony was that of Isaac Labisonnière, originally published in *The Northwestern Chronicle* (Milwaukee), June 1, 1907. "Labisonnière's memory was very retentive," says Moudry.

43. "This site," says Moudry, "was located at the southern point of what is now known as Dayton's Bluff." "Chapel of St. Paul," 36.

persons had asked me to put up the church at the nearest possible point [where it would be] more convenient there for me to cross there the river from St. Peter [Mendota] and the nearest point to the head of navigation out of the [military] reservation line.

The best site appeared to Galtier to be situated between the squatter claims of Benjamin Gervais and Vital Guerin, "two good and peaceable farmers. . . . They both consented to give me the ground necessary for a church and a garden together with a small graveyard." So the building was to stand on a bluff overlooking the Mississippi, two hundred feet back from the river's bank, at a point easily accessible to boat traffic. Once the village was platted, the chapel would be located between Cedar and Minnesota streets and between Bench and Third streets.[44]

Construction under the direction of Joseph Labisonnière began in late October 1841. Long afterward Labisonnière's son Isaac, one of the workers, recalled the experience.

Eight of us at first volunteered for the work; others offered themselves later. The ground selected for the site of the church was thinly covered with groves of red oak and white oak. . . . The logs for the chapel were cut on the spot, and the tamarack swamp in the rear was made to contribute rafters and roof pieces. We had poor building tools in those days, and our work was not beautifully finished. The logs, rough and undressed, prepared merely by the ax, were made secure by wooden pins. The roof was made of steeply slanted bark-covered slabs . . . [which] were likewise put to good use in the construction of the floor and of the benches. The chapel, as I remember it, was about twenty-five feet long, eighteen feet wide, and ten feet high. It had a single window on each side, and it faced the river. It was completed in a few days, and could not have represented an expenditure in labor value of more than $65.[45]

On November 1, 1841, the feast of All Saints, the rude little chapel was crowded with the devout and the curious, as Father Lucien Galtier offered

---

44. Use of these street names cannot determine the precise location of the chapel. It faced Bench Street which, however, has long since disappeared. Third Street is now Kellogg Boulevard.

45. Quoted in A. McNulty, "The Chapel of St. Paul, the Cradle of the Catholic Church in Minnesota," in *A&D* 1 (July 1907): 66.

Mass there for the first time. He also dedicated the building to a special saintly patron and thus gave it its name. "Already I was residing at St. Peter [Mendota]," he explained,

> and as the name of *Paul* is generally connected with that of *Peter*, [and with] the gentiles here being well represented in the persons of the Indians, I called it St. Paul. Henceforth we could call him our protector, and for apostolic life could I desire for a better pattern? Thus with the great apostle could I say: *Cum infirmior tunc potens sum!*[46] A good motto, I am sure. . . . St. Paul, as applied to a town or city, was well appropriated. This monosyllable is short, sounds good, [and] it is understood by all Christian denominations. Hence when an attempt was made to change it, I opposed the vain project. The church remained thus dedicated to St. Paul, and I expressed the wish to call the place by no other name. I succeeded.

Galtier's name for the place did indeed endure, to the discomfiture perhaps of Monsieur Parrant. For the Chapel of St. Paul, aside from its religious significance, provided as well a sense of cohesion and community where none had existed before. When people build houses of worship, they signal their intention to put down roots in that locale, to raise their children and earn their living there. "Pig's Eye," appropriate enough for a bit of land occupied by a collection of drifters, would never do for a real town. Galtier witnessed signs of a new permanence almost immediately: "An American named Jackson put up a new store, and a grocery was opened at the foot of Gervais's claim, so this soon caused steamboats to land there, henceforth to be known as St. Paul's Landing."[47]

By the time of the construction of the chapel in St. Paul, Galtier had vacated Scott Campbell's house near Fort Snelling and moved to Mendota. He lodged and said Mass there in the residence of the prominent fur trader, Jean-Baptiste Faribault, until mid-1842, when he directed the building of another church which also provided him accommodation; this edifice he dedicated, it need hardly be said, to St. Peter. He continued to minister to both congregations and on occasion to Catholics living as far east as St. Croix Falls and as far south as Lake Pepin. But physical strain, the climate, and the loneliness little by little exacted their toll. For a man of some cultivation, as Galtier was, the lack of refined company and conversation was a severe trial. There was

---

46. "When I am weak, then I am strong." 2 Corinthians 12:10.
47. Galtier to Grace, January 14, 1864, AASPM, Grace Papers.

less subtle hardship to contend with, too. "God is my witness of what I had to suffer there," he wrote after his departure. And not God only: "All St. Peter and St. Paul and the Fort can serve as my witnesses in proof of my sufferings." Three times he was almost killed, "once [when] I was thrown into a slough with my horse which had dragged me along in its fall. For all that I was cheerful. The rain, the storms, the snow, and the ice also gave me much occasion to suffer. Meanwhile two churches were built. They are neither costly nor masterpieces of architecture; but they attest [to] the sentiments of a poor priest." His relations with Loras grew increasingly tense, particularly after the bishop heard that Galtier had "found advantages that very few other priests of the diocese have, . . . [being] able to make some savings and purchases each year."[48] In the spring of 1844 Loras removed him and assigned him to another mission in the extreme southeast corner of Iowa Territory. Galtier's bitterness spilled over.

> The time of departure arrived. . . . Soon I was aboard the steamboat, tears in my eyes. I loved the place that had cost me toil and sweat, despite the fact that it was unpolished, not very docile, effusive at times, yet hardly grateful. This was the place where my desire for the spiritual did not find enough of an outlet. O missions of Iowa, how difficult and sterile you are! O generous priests of Iowa, how much you have to suffer![49]

Within a year he returned to France, intending to remain there. But the lure of the missions coursed through Lucien Galtier's veins and would not be denied. In 1847 he came back to the American Midwest, though not to Dubuque. Incardinated into the new diocese of Milwaukee, he served honorably as pastor, ironically enough, at Prairie du Chien till he died in 1866. Before that he paid two cordial visits to his old haunts in St. Paul and Mendota and was able to recall much less harshly his original departure: "At last, on the 25th of May, 1844, I was leaving to better hands the yet barren field of my first mission, neither without regret nor without friends."[50]

---

48. Cretin to Loras, May 8, 1844, AASPM (translated copy), Cretin Papers.

49. Galtier to Loras, November 8, 1844, quoted in Moudry, "Chapel of St. Paul," 61–62.

50. Galtier to Grace, January 14, 1864, AASPM, Grace Papers.

THE "BETTER HANDS," OR AT LEAST THE STRONGER ONES, BELONGED
to Augustin Ravoux. Born in the Auvergne in 1815, he, like Galtier, had been
in subdeacon's orders when he answered Loras' appeal to serve in the missions in Iowa Territory.[51] After his ordination in January 1840, he was assigned
to the parish in Prairie du Chien. He remained there until September of the
following year, at which time the bishop decided he could now honor the second of the promises he had made at St. Peter's in 1839. Father Ravoux, whose
long-held ambition had been to serve as missionary to the Native Americans,
was appointed to minister exclusively to the Dakota, a charge he accepted
with alacrity. Without delay he made his way upriver and, after a few days
spent with Galtier at Mendota, he proceeded to the great Dakota encampment along the Minnesota River, which Ravoux still called by its old French
name, Traverse des Sioux. There followed three years of unremitting toil for
the young priest at Traverse and at Little Rock, and eastward to Little Prairie
and northwestward to Lac qui Parle, and indeed at any point in between
where the tribesmen, always on the move, might have been found.[52] He recognized immediately that the largest problem he confronted—not counting
the Indians' own cultural reluctance to listen to him and the hostility of Protestant missioners already active in the area—was the linguistic one. Preaching and instruction delivered through interpreters was a temporary expedient at best. He set himself therefore to learn the extremely difficult Dakota
language—totally unrelated as it was to any Indo-European tongue—and not
only to learn it but to put it into written form. During these hectic years he
produced a prayer book and a wide-ranging manual-catechism, entitled *Wakantanka Ti ke Tanku* or *The Path to the House of God*.[53] These writings he
caused to have printed on the press maintained then in Prairie du Chien—the
Wisconsin rivertown haunts the accounts of these early days—by the pastor
there, Joseph Cretin.[54]

---

51. Ravoux attended the seminary at Puy-Guillaume, near Lyons, and received
minor orders and the subdiaconate from the bishop of Annecy. For documents so
attesting and other administrative documents, see AASPM, Ravoux Papers.

52. Traverse des Sioux was located near the present town of St. Peter (not to be
confused with the former St. Peter, Mendota); Little Rock between New Ulm and
Redwood Falls; Lac qui Parle just west of Willmar; and Little Prairie near what is
now Chaska.

53. Ravoux, "Labors of Ravoux," 4–5.

54. For printed excerpts, accompanying holograph notes, and related documents, see AASPM, Ravoux Papers.

But for all Ravoux's efforts and good will—"It would not be easy to describe the virtues of this Missionary," observed an admiring Samuel Mazzuchelli[55]—the results were meager. "The progress of religion among the Indians is not very consoling," he confessed to Loras at the beginning of 1844. "Conversions are rare." Scarcely a handful of the Dakota were then under instruction, and over the course of the previous month he had baptized only six persons and witnessed two marriages; the long-term effect of such sacramental ministrations remained problematical at best. "I know enough of the Sioux tongue to explain the truths of Christianity to the savages and to hear confessions," but even so, it was a hard struggle to unravel forms of expression representing a culture so remote from his own, while at the same time trying to master the intricacies of English. He lived in unheated houses—the wine in the chalice sometimes froze when he said Mass during the winter—and, since in his poverty he had to do all the menial tasks himself, he thereby earned the contempt of the Indian men he wanted to convert. Nor was Ravoux's burden lightened when the bishop sent him an assistant in the person of French-born Antoine Godfert, ordained at Dubuque in 1842. From the beginning of their association the two did not get along, partly due to Ravoux's rather imperious temperament and even more so to Godfert's obstinacy and self-serving imprudence.[56] Loras soon had to recall the younger man, but not before Galtier visited them while they were in residence at Little Prairie. "Their furniture is pitiable," he reported to the bishop. "They have only one chair, broken, which fell to them by charity; a single table knife, one coffee cup, two spoons, two napkins, the rest in proportion to their poverty. In spite of these discomforts and because of his sufferings, Father Ravoux had all the merit that a holy priest can desire in his ministry." He added no such encomium for Godfert.[57]

When in the spring of 1844 Lucien Galtier left Mendota and St. Paul for good, the bishop dispatched Augustin Ravoux as a replacement, with the assurance that the assignment was temporary and that he could soon return to his beloved Indians; as things turned out, he stayed for more than sixty years. This change in ministry was momentous for Ravoux personally, and, at the same time, it represented a fateful shift of emphasis in the whole missionary

---

55. Mazzuchelli, *Memoirs*, 296.

56. See Eugene J. Roden, "Augustin Ravoux, Pioneer Priest" (Master's thesis, St. Paul Seminary, 1954), 57–61.

57. See Reardon, *Diocese of St. Paul*, 53–55, and Hoffmann, *Church Founders*, 162–164, and especially 167–169. Godfert shortly afterward left the diocese of Dubuque.

enterprise.[58] Men like Joseph Cretin and Ravoux had come from across the sea imbued with a romantic yet imprecise conviction that their task was to convert and "civilize" the Indians—"these poor savages," as Cretin invariably called them. But the resistance of the natives to their message as well as demographic reality imposed upon them a different set of priorities. The ever more numerous white Catholic immigrants also needed and deserved ministry from the handful of priests available. And this pressing obligation meant that more and more they turned to duplicating the parochial and institutional structures with which they had grown up. So they bought property, and built churches, and opened rude little schools, and exhorted monks and nuns to found establishments as part of a conventional European diocese. Bishop Loras indeed launched an advertising campaign in eastern newspapers urging Catholics to come and settle in the salubrious confines of Iowa Territory. Augustin Ravoux, for his part, never lost his zealous interest in the Dakota whom he had tried with so little success to transform; he still visited their villages whenever he could and even forayed once or twice to encampments as far west as the Missouri.[59] But in fact the Dakota hunters were galloping, galloping away toward the sunset, and the white plowmen were taking their place.

Over the next six years Ravoux proved himself a zealous steward. He carried on Galtier's ministry in Mendota, St. Paul, and the outlying districts without displaying the kind of thin skin that had hampered his predecessor's endeavors. By 1850 he could report that the Catholics under his charge numbered about 1,000, by far the largest concentration of them in St. Paul. Many of them were rough and crude, some of them drank too much—"I had some whose conduct was far from edifying for their neighbors." He felt himself obliged not only to insist on the moral improvement of his flock but also to protect it from dire outside influences: "Bigoted ministers, Infidels, and even Atheists were around, and now and then vomited forth their pestiferous poison."[60] Such challenges merely sharpened Ravoux's naturally combative temper, and, since like all zealots he suffered from no internal doubts, he was

---

58. Similarly, French-born Father Edward Sorin, founder of the University of Notre Dame, expressed a desire shortly after his arrival in Indiana to work exclusively with the local Indians. This aspiration vanished almost as soon as it had been given voice. See Sorin to Moreau, December 5, 1842, Archives of the Generalate of the Congregation of Holy Cross (Rome), Sorin Papers.

59. See Roden, "Ravoux," 93–113.

60. Augustin Ravoux, *Reminiscences, Memoirs, and Lectures* (St. Paul, 1890), 52.

more than a match for his environment. Still in his early thirties, this short, spare man, his severe demeanor emphasized by the wide, thin-lipped mouth, his full head of dark hair puffed out from beneath the biretta, speaking a patois of French, English, and Dakota and gesturing with the thick-fingered hands of a laborer, had already achieved a singular status among his fellow pioneers.

In 1849 a young French Canadian priest named Albert Lacombe arrived in St. Paul on his way to the mission in the Red River valley. "I came all the way by boat and stage," he remembered long afterward. "The city then consisted of only a few little log cabins and shacks. Father Ravoux . . . held service in a little log church, and had quite a large congregation. He met me when I arrived on the steamboat and entertained me like a brother during the [two months] I spent in St. Paul organizing my expedition into the Northwest."[61] By then, however, "little" as it remained in absolute terms, Ravoux, at a cost of $400, had had an addition built to Galtier's chapel that doubled its capacity, as well as, next to it, a modest belfry which housed a steamboat bell donated by a prominent Protestant business man.[62] And though Lacombe saw only "log cabins and shacks," Ravoux had seen the steady growth of his flock and so had kept a sharp eye on the opportunity for real estate expansion. Squatters' rights, established simply by erecting a building, however primitive, on the property, would be transformed into owners' rights when federal lands were put on the market. By the first public sale, in 1848, he had secured title to the four acres upon which stood the chapel and its out-buildings, including a shanty where he lodged himself when not in Mendota.[63] But he realized that much more property would shortly be needed.

Especially was this the case in the light of rumors that St. Paul would soon be detached from Dubuque and preside over a diocese of its own. Meanwhile, Ravoux did not refrain from pointing out what he discerned as the shortcomings of his ecclesiastical superiors. He was vexed specifically at the bishops of Dubuque and Milwaukee for failing to send more missionaries to serve the rapidly expanding population along the upper Mississippi. Bishop Martin Henni of Milwaukee, he complained to Loras,

is not sending anyone to St. Paul. I am very far from judging him guilty before God, yet if your Grace would like to inform him that his children

---

61. Reminiscences printed in the *St. Paul Globe,* January 15, 1904.
62. See chapter 3, below.
63. Roden, "Ravoux," 90–91, 117.

in Jesus Christ in St. Paul and the neighborhood, to the number of eleven or twelve hundred, have been begging for several years that he deign to help them immediately, you would be performing a great act of charity.[64]

Several times he appealed directly to Henni, "describing to him the great wants of the Catholic population in this part of his diocese, and spoke to him on the necessity of sending a priest to reside in St. Paul." On the last day of January 1850, Milwaukee responded good naturedly: "I heartily forgive you for the kind lecture you read to a bishop; you are perfectly right, but you ought to be aware of the trouble, nay, the impossibilities, on the other side." Henni also, however, added a broad and consoling hint that the canonically anomalous situation would soon be resolved.[65]

In 1848 Wisconsin was admitted to the Union as the thirtieth state. A year later Minnesota Territory was formally organized. A dispute arose as to the proper boundary between these two entities, but in the end the emerging political class centered in St. Paul—including prominently Galtier's patron, Vital Guerin—managed to fend off the Wisconsinites' proposal to fix the border along the entire length of the Mississippi. Instead a line was drawn from the mouth of the St. Louis River (what became the city of Duluth) to the St. Croix, which then meandered its way to its juncture with the Mississippi, some thirty miles south of Fort Snelling. Westward the new Territory, like those that had preceded it, stretched to the Missouri River in Dakota.[66] In accord with these adjustments the American Catholic bishops, meeting in Baltimore in the late spring of 1849—Mathias Loras among them—petitioned Pope Pius IX to set up "a new episcopal See in the town of St. Paul, in the Territory of Minnesota, to be co-terminous with that Territory in jurisdiction."[67] There followed a delay; the pope and his curia had been driven from Rome by the Revolution of 1848, and did not return there till April 1850. The following July 19 a papal brief officially established the diocese of St. Paul, and four days later Joseph Cretin was named its first bishop.

---

64. Ravoux to Loras, December 19, 1849, quoted in Moudry, "Chapel of St. Paul," 124.

65. Ravoux, *Reminiscences*, 60.

66. See William W. Folwell, *A History of Minnesota*, 4 vols. (St. Paul, 1921–1930), 1:489–495; and Blegen, *Minnesota*, 160–165.

67. *Concilia Provincialia, Baltimori Habita ab anno 1829 usque ad annum 1849* (Baltimore, 1851), 273.

Ravoux on his own ground moved swiftly. "I bought of Mr. Vital Guerin twenty-one lots for $800, and for $100 the lot on which now [1890] stands the cathedral. . . . I considered the purchase . . . a very good bargain for the church, as also a good one for Mr. Vital Guerin, because it was understood that the [proximity of the] cathedral and other buildings . . . would increase the value of Mr. Vital Guerin's property." In both assumptions Ravoux proved correct. Over the years Guerin enjoyed handsome income from his adjoining property. As for the Catholic community, ownership of these lots in the heart of what would become St. Paul's business district was of incalculable consequence.[68] In the midst of their negotiations Guerin asked the priest: "Why do you buy so many lots, Father?" "I wish to buy a block for a cathedral and another for school purposes," came the reply.[69] And indeed in due course these intentions were fulfilled; but besides such explicitly parochial uses the property produced revenue that sustained the diocese of St. Paul during its infancy and far beyond.

Perhaps the most remarkable feature of this transaction was that Ravoux did not have $900 or any amount close to that figure. He simply gave assurances that the new bishop, when he arrived, would pay in full, and Guerin, benefactor as well as business man, accepted his bond. Little wonder that when he was a very old man Augustin Ravoux could look back with proud complacency on his bold initiative. "In favor of historical facts, of truth and justice," he observed in the third person,

> Mgr. A Ravoux . . . [states] that he sincerely believed . . . that the Catholic Church of the Diocese or Archdiocese of St. Paul has contracted towards him a debt of gratitude of about one million dollars, including the produce [sic] or income of blocks and lots in St. Paul proper, even before the arrival of the Rt. Rev. Bishop Cretin in our city.[70]

Indeed, his estimate of the debt of gratitude was doubtless much too low.

---

68. Employing the modern street names, the first twelve lots were bounded by St. Peter Street on the west, Seventh Street on the north, Wabasha Street on the east, and Sixth Street on the south, a full block comprising 300 square feet. The other ten lots, not quite a full block between Eighth and Exchange Streets, boasted a frontage of 300 feet on St. Peter Street. See Moudry, "Chapel of St. Paul," 127–129.

69. See the appreciation by Marjorie Knowles, *St. Paul Pioneer Press*, June 22, 1941.

70. Augustin Ravoux, "Tempus Tacendi et Tempus Loquendi [A Time for Silence and a Time to Speak]" (St. Paul, 1901), 2.

CHAPTER 3

"An Exile in Frozen Lands"

"ON THE DAY OF THE FEAST OF THE VISITATION OF THE BLESSED Virgin Mary, July 2, 1851, I had the long expected and desired visit of the Right Reverend Bishop, who arrived at St. Paul, accompanied by two priests and three seminarians. To describe the pleasure I felt at their arrival would be a difficult task. I had been for seven years without any brother priest, if I except a few weeks, during which another clergyman resided with me in St. Paul." Thus did Augustin Ravoux recall, long afterward, that moment of exaltation when Joseph Cretin arrived aboard the steamboat *Nominee* to assume his duties in his new diocese. Eleven years and three months had passed since Lucien Galtier had made the same journey. Ravoux chose to describe the event in ironic terms for a later and more opulent and jaded generation, which he thought appreciated too little the labors of the pioneers.

> My first interview with the . . . Bishop and his companions was on the boat where I went to meet them. I had the honor of accompanying them from the boat to the episcopal palace. It did not take his lordship much time to visit all the apartments of the palace and the cathedral. The episcopal palace was a building one story and a half high, about seventeen or eighteen feet square. And the cathedral . . . was a log building about forty-five feet long and eighteen wide. Near the palace stood another remarkable monument from ten to twelve feet square, which was used as a kitchen; a little farther was the stable. . . . The Right Reverend Bishop was not much surprised at the poverty of the Catholic Church in St. Paul, for he had been informed of everything. From the first, he saw hard labor before him, and, full of confidence, was not discouraged.[1]

---

1. Ravoux, *Reminiscences*, 62–63.

Ravoux was no doubt correct in concluding that the new bishop was "not much surprised" at what he found at the northern navigational terminus of the Mississippi. After all, he had already labored in the Midwestern missions for thirteen years and, as vicar general of Dubuque, had officially visited Mendota and St. Paul on occasion. Even so, Cretin had not accepted the new mandate without much searching of soul, due partly to religious scruple and, perhaps more so, to the restlessness that had characterized him since his days at Ferney. Thus early in 1849 he had petitioned Bishop Loras for permission to accompany the Iowans headed for the gold fields in California, so that he could minister to the Catholics among them. The bishop had refused this rather bizarre proposition.[2]

Nor had Cretin entirely ruled out the prospect of returning to France. After all, his leave of absence from the diocese of Belley had been granted only on a temporary basis, and presumably he could take up his priestly duties there again.[3] He still owned property in Montluel, inherited at the time of his parents' death,[4] and he remained keenly interested in local affairs. And through the years he had kept in close touch with his siblings. He rejoiced in his brother Jean's success in business: "I blessed the Lord for having granted you favors that he has withheld from others. You have succeeded in most of your endeavors while so many others have seen their hopes and plans overturned." This good fortune of the younger son gave rise to some nostalgia in the elder, whose hopes and plans in the New World had not matured as he had expected. Sure enough, he explained to Jean, the soil in the Mississippi valley was rich and bountiful, and "a very good cow" could be purchased for as little as fifty francs. But, he added quickly,

> do not think that I am trying to tempt you to come to this country. No, do not leave your homeland. Please remain a good Christian and a good citizen of France. Those who come here from Europe, despite the earthly advantages they find here, almost all experience the sorrow of seeing their children reject their faith and their ancestral home. Yes, it is all too true, especially of the French, that they degenerate rapidly when abroad.[5]

---

2. Cretin to Clemence Cretin, April 12, 1849, AASPM, Cretin Papers.

3. See chapter 2, above.

4. In his last will Cretin took care to distinguish between the property and chattels he owned in America, which he left to the diocese of St. Paul, and his holdings in France, which he did not. See Reardon, *Diocese of St. Paul*, 108–109.

5. Cretin to Jean Cretin, January 1 and 12, 1846, AASPM, Cretin Papers.

In the spring of 1847 Father Cretin combined a trip to France in search of priestly recruits for the diocese of Dubuque with a pilgrimage to Rome. While in Montluel he discussed the possibility of returning permanently to his native land with his closest confidante, his unmarried sister, Clemence. Her devotion to him was total, and he recognized that delicate health and loneliness were heavy burdens for her to carry. Though the manner he adopted toward her was often peremptory and sometimes condescending, his affection for her was deep and genuine. Nothing was settled in the course of their conversations, and before a decision could be reached the outside world intervened.

The Revolution of 1848 that ushered in the Second French Republic did not, in the end, manifest the anticlerical and antireligious characteristics of its predecessors in 1789 and 1830, though no one could have been certain of that when the barricades went up in Paris in June of that year. Back in Iowa at any rate the uncertain political climate in France gave Joseph Cretin pause. The acute shortage of priests here was such, he told Clemence, that "I do not think I can in good conscience leave the country, not this year at any rate. I will see how things turn out in France. . . . Remember that it is folly to ponder dreams. . . . I will not make a decision about my return until next spring."[6] By the spring of 1849 his indecision had, if anything, increased; the aborted plan to exchange Iowa for California was followed by an abrupt reversal of view about the expediency of his brother emigrating to America. "If your father were able to sell a part or half of his property at a profit," he wrote Jean's daughters, "I would urge him to come here. There is no doubt he could do very well here and could double his revenue in a few years without much trouble, and just by tilling the land." But this recommendation did not extend to the girls' Aunt Clemence, whatever her aspirations: "She would be homesick for her native land after a mere three days at sea."[7]

Cretin's ambivalence continued into the next year, heightened by a falling-out with Jean over money matters, by the still unpredictable ecclesiastical policies of the Second French Republic, by a hankering to abide once again in the land of his birth, and, perhaps most of all, by Clemence's increasingly poignant yearning to be with her brother and mentor, whether in France or America.[8] Then, in mid-July, came the news of the establishment of the diocese of St. Paul and Joseph Cretin's appointment as its first bishop. The

---

6. Cretin to Clemence Cretin, September 8, 1848, AASPM, Cretin Papers.

7. Cretin to Marie and Géneviève Cretin, June 20, 1849, AASPM, Cretin Papers.

8. Cretin to Clemence Cretin, June 15, 1850, AASPM, Cretin Papers.

formal documents, however, did not reach Dubuque till the end of September, and they put their recipient into an emotional quandary. There followed upward of three months of hesitancy, a kind of midlife crisis for a man, now fifty-one years old, firmly committed to his vocation as a missionary and yet distracted by family concerns and apprehensive at the sheer difficulty of the task he was being asked to assume. He applied to Augustin Ravoux for counsel, and that formidable individual, who seldom entertained doubts of any sort, showed none on this occasion.

> In his letter he told me he was about to start for Europe, and that no determination would be taken by him for some time. He asked me to give him my advice on the acceptation or refusal of the new bishopric. Such a question surprised me very much. In my answer I pressed him to accept, showing him, by many reasons, how very necessary it was for the Catholics of this territory. . . . I did all in my power to encourage him to accept the bishopric offered to him. I went so far as to tell him in my letter that things were in such a condition in this new territory that, according to my opinion, he was obliged *sub gravi* to give his consent to bear the load imposed upon him by Divine Providence.[9]

But Cretin departed for Europe without offering Ravoux any reassurances, and indeed still unsure himself. Whatever lingering nostalgia he entertained about returning to France permanently, the basic sticking point was the utter lack of resources he could count on were he to take up the charge in Minnesota Territory. He determined therefore to rest his decision upon securing prior pledges of financial support. Early in December he submitted to the Society for the Propagation of the Faith an appeal for funds needed to meet even the minimum requirements of an assignment to St. Paul, and then added a kind of challenge: "I could not bring myself to accept this important position without assuring beforehand whether I could rely upon indispensable help for a diocese where everything is to be established. . . . I shall decide according to your decision."[10]

If the gentlemen of the Society in Paris and Lyons judged that this statement amounted to a solicitation of a kind of religious bribe, they declined to pay it. All available funds at any rate had already been committed, they said.

---

9. Ravoux, *Reminiscences,* 60–61. *Sub gravi:* under the penalty of mortal sin.
10. Cretin to the Society for the Propagation of the Faith (SPF), AASPM, SPF Papers.

As the new year of 1851 began, Cretin felt a certain sense of relief, until old Bishop Devie intervened—the same Devie who had ordained him twenty-eight years earlier and who, ironically, had allowed him to leave for America only temporarily.

> Far from being grieved at [the Society's] answer, I was pleased with it. At last, I thought, I have found the excuse I was looking for to free myself [from acceptance]. I told this to Monseigneur Devie. "Not at all, my dear Abbé," he said. "The apostles began the conquest of the world with nothing, and the first bishops of America did not have the help of the Propagation of the Faith. Therefore, prepare yourself immediately for your consecration, and do not lose any more time in deliberation and hesitation."[11]

Accordingly, on the morning of January 26, 1851, Joseph Cretin lay prostrate on the floor of the bishop of Belley's private chapel and then was anointed with oils of episcopal consecration. A few days later he confided his feelings with admirable candor to a friend back in Iowa.

> I have to give you the great news. I am affixed to the cross of St. Paul since last Sunday. After three months of anxiety, of consultations, of prayers, I was induced to yield to the advice of the able men I have consulted. But it is not without some fears that I have made up my mind to say a perpetual farewell to my country and friends and to consent to so distant an exile in frozen lands. The labors more than the honors attached to that dignity were making me shrink from it.[12]

Once Cretin's decision had been reached and had been sacramentally sanctioned, the doubts and vacillations of the years immediately preceding his consecration seemed to fall from him. Consistent with the biblical imagery, he put his hand to the plow and did not look back. Whatever his shortcomings, from then on, irresolution was not one of them. As for his siblings,

---

11. Cretin to Bernard, January 11, 1851, quoted in Flahavan, "A Quarter Century of Alms," 21. Abbé Bernard was a priest of the diocese of Avignon from whom Cretin hoped to secure financial help.

12. Cretin to Donaghoe, January 30, 1851, quoted in Hoffmann, *Church Founders*, 289.

he was quickly reconciled to his brother, and if he imposed upon his beloved sister a painful and permanent separation, it proved, as things turned out, the proper course to have adopted.

> I will repeat in earnest what I have told you before. You must not think of following me, no matter who were to accompany you. Not one more word about this to anyone. I understand what a help you could be [to me], but I also know well the toll it would take on you. I love you too much to expose you to all the inconveniences which beset one when starting over in a new country. . . . So let us talk of this no further. Think rather of helping me by your prayers and by the other little things you can do in France.[13]

During the months immediately following the assumption of his new dignity, Bishop Cretin, adhering to the pattern set by so many French missionary prelates, scoured his homeland for recruits and for money. In the latter regard, the results were disappointingly modest, a total of about $800. Before he sailed for America, however, the Society for the Propagation of the Faith relented, allotting him $4,000 and pledging another $2,500 to be paid later in the year. These sums, together with $2,400 of his own money, meant that he boarded ship with a little over $7,000 in hand—not an opulent amount, to be sure, but sufficient for a rough beginning.[14] Then came that memorable July day, 1851, when his friend and comrade Augustin Ravoux boarded the *Nominee*, embraced him, and welcomed him to his see city, the little village of St. Paul. The group of Catholic notables who waited on the landing to greet him saw step ashore a man of medium height, somewhat corpulent—"I am really ashamed at being so stout," he had confessed ruefully to Clemence a couple of years earlier[15]—balding, his round face most remarkable for the piercing blue eyes behind the spectacles.[16] "In the evening," recorded a local newspaper, "large numbers assembled at the log chapel on the bluff to see him and to hear his voice. The Te Deum and Magnificat were chanted, and the Bishop addressed the congregation both in English and

---

13. Cretin to Clemence Cretin, April 4, 1851, AASPM, Cretin Papers.

14. I have rounded off the figures as calculated in Flahavan, "A Quarter Century of Alms," 27–28.

15. Cretin to Clemence Cretin, January 6, 1848, printed in *A&D* 3 (July 1911): 17.

16. See the description on Cretin's French passport, dated 1851, AASPM, Cretin Papers.

French. He said that the purpose of his mission and residence among them was their religious and temporal welfare."[17]

During the days that followed, the new bishop took stock of his environment, and all in all he was favorably impressed. "We have found the countryside charming," he reported back to France,

and the town is growing rapidly. Already one can discern the wealth (*luxe*) and bustle of large cities. Butchers, bakers, vegetable merchants, milkmen come every morning in their carts to sell at one's door their indispensable products. Three or four times a day I see splendid carriages, drawn by four horses, coming and going in all directions.[18]

And Joseph Cretin's very presence in the town—starkly treeless, in contrast to leafy Ferney, because of the acute need for building materials and fuel—had converted the log chapel on the bluff into a cathedral.

THE SEVENTH PROVINCIAL COUNCIL OF BALTIMORE HAD DECREED— and the Roman curia had confirmed—that the diocese of St. Paul should be coterminous with the polity formally created by Congress in 1849 and called Minnesota Territory. Territory and diocese were geographically defined on the east, south, and north by the boundaries of the future and present state of that name and on the west by the Missouri and White Earth rivers in what would become eventually the states of North and South Dakota.[19] Across this area encompassing 166,000 square miles there dwelt, according to the census of 1850, about 6,000 persons, not, of course, counting the Native Americans. A year later Joseph Cretin in a report to a funding source in France reduced that number by a third and stated it laconically in confessional terms: "3,000 Catholiques, 1,000 hérétiques, 27,000 infidèles." Whatever the accuracy of his estimate, he at least showed himself more humane than the census takers by including in it the nature-worshiping Indians.[20]

In any case the growth of the white population during the nine years of the territorial experience (1849–1858) was prodigious. Between 1850 and 1852

---

17. *Minnesota Pioneer*, July 10, 1851.

18. Cretin to Géneviève Cretin, August 21, 1851, AASPM, Cretin Papers.

19. For much of what follows see Blegen, *Minnesota*, 159–230; Lass, *Minnesota*, 97–135; and Folwell, *Minnesota*, 1:365–421.

20. Quoted in Hoffmann, *Church Founders*, 291–291.

its number tripled. By 1857, the year Bishop Cretin died, the total had risen to 150,000, virtually all of them migrants and representing an overall increase of 2,500 percent. Seven of ten of them had been born in states to the east, notably in New England, New York, and other mid-Atlantic states where the Yankee mystique was the strongest. Indeed, a cultural élite soon emerged, unabashedly committed to reestablishing in the bracing climate of the Territory a society based upon the values and aspirations first enshrined, as they thought, at Plymouth Rock. Thirty percent of those who came to Minnesota Territory during these years were foreign-born, just less than 60,000 altogether. The Germans, at 18,000, were the most numerous, and the Irish, at 12,000, were second. But perhaps most significant in the long term were the 8,000 Norwegians, precursors as it were to the vast influx of Scandinavians who in due course would provide Minnesota its dominant ethnic character.

What is striking about these summary figures is the virtual nonappearance of persons of French origin. Switzerland (1,085) and even tiny Wales (422) contributed more immigrants to swell the Caucasian population in the Territory than did France and French Canada combined. This was a momentous demographic fact as far as the Catholic Church was concerned. Names of explorers akin to Hennepin and Duluth, and more recently to successful traders like Faribault and Le Sueur, or to priests like Galtier and Ravoux, became increasingly submerged in a flood of Smiths and Joneses, of Schneiders and O'Briens. Smith and Jones aside—Presbyterian, Episcopal, Congregationalist—many of the German immigrants, and virtually all the Irish, were nominally Catholic. Although for a time the ox carts from the Red River, driven by the colorful *coureurs de bois,* continued to roll into St. Paul, the long era of French and métis ascendancy along the upper Mississippi vanished during the rambunctious 1850s, a circumstance which, to his lasting credit, Joseph Cretin was not slow to appreciate.

The boisterous energy of the Territory's expanding population was characteristic of the wider American phenomenon that would come to be called Manifest Destiny. The farmers and the lumber men hardly waited for the treaties with the Indians to be ratified before they rushed into the vacated lands with plow and ax. Townsites were platted at a furious pace, no less than 400 of them, though many—most notably "Niniger City," near Hastings, creation of the flamboyant young Ignatius Donnelly, later the stormy petrel of Minnesota politics[21]—existed only on paper or on shady land-speculation schemes. But

---

21. Martin Ridge, *Ignatius Donnelly: The Portrait of a Politician* (Chicago, 1962), 14–27.

river settlements did flourish, St. Paul first—its population soared to more than 10,000 by the end of the decade—as did its neighbors', St. Anthony and Minneapolis, while down the Mississippi Winona counted 2,500 inhabitants. Similar growth gave rise to new towns along the Minnesota River, like New Ulm and Mankato, and along the St. Croix, like Stillwater. Stillwater indeed became the center of a lumber industry destined to monumental increase, as Minneapolis, with its waterpower, would eventually emerge as the milling capital of the world. But it was predictably agriculture that provided the Territory's economic underpinning: by 1859 Minnesota farmers produced annually between two and three million bushels of corn, wheat, and oats, to say nothing of an abundance of potatoes, cabbages, turnips and other vegetables, as well as a variety of fruits. Cretin brought with him from France apple seed which in time brought forth trees the whole community admired. "We were presented . . . yesterday with a specimen of apples grown in the garden of the Cathedral from a tree brought from France by . . . Bishop Cretin. They are a splendidly flavored fruit, and the perfection to which they have been brought proves conclusively that with proper care as fine an apple can be raised in this state as in any other in the union."[22]

Such rather defensive assertions reflected the sensitivity of local worthies to the negative reputation of Minnesota's long and harsh winters. And certainly the bounty of the Territory's farms and orchards belied the claims that the Star of the North was too cold to bring forth abundant harvests and, consequently, a viable economy. Nonetheless, the winters were long and harsh, and until a grid of passable roads was laid out and before the railways came in the 1860s, the residents had to depend on the rivers for movement and markets, especially on the Minnesota and the Mississippi, frozen and scarcely navigable over five months of the year. Yet when the ice broke on Lake Pepin every April the steamboats, laden with freight and new settlers, pushed their way north to the St. Paul Landing, and left again with a cargo comprised of grain and timber and other primary commodities. In 1855 more than a hundred boats made the journey upstream, carrying amid a jumble of furniture and farm machinery no fewer than 30,000 immigrants. Two years later the dockings reached nearly three hundred, and in 1858 more than a thousand. Before that, in mid-May 1852, when the rate of immigration was still relatively moderate, the *Nominee*—the same vessel that had transported Cretin northward ten months earlier—put ashore "two respectable and intelligent Irish

---

22. *St. Paul Pioneer,* October 10, 1863.

families," as a local newspaper put it, headed by Richard Ireland and John O'Gorman.[23]

Some immigrants were indeed respectable, and some were not. Some who came to the Territory because they had failed somewhere else inevitably failed again, but most learned to cope with the rough and raw conditions, learned to deal with the loneliness of a remote homestead or with the sheer newness and unfamiliarity of everything around them. Most of them proved hardy and determined enough to do the grinding work necessary to make their lives better than they had been before. Such stamina, to be sure, carried in its train a certain coarseness, exhibited perhaps most prominently in occasional violence and in the high incidence of drunkenness. Whiskey, at twenty-five cents a quart, plagued the whole frontier, and not just the Native Americans, despite a proliferation of temperance societies and the routine passage of blue laws. Yet the overall atmosphere was one of hope and opportunity, with the unavoidable defects and discomforts smoothed out by a robust egalitarianism.

To earn a decent living remained the top priority for the immigrants, whatever their ethnic background, but not all was getting and spending on this new frontier. For example, the pioneers, especially those with roots in New England, were strong advocates of education. Space and funds were quickly set aside to support it: by the end of the territorial period seventy-two school districts had been created, and three years later 466 schools were functioning. The academic year, with its no-nonsense curriculum stressing basic verbal and numerical skills, usually lasted only between autumn harvest and spring planting, and teachers—paid $13 a month for women and $21 for men—mostly took to the classroom only when their ordinary jobs were in abeyance. Nevertheless, even if as yet there were no high schools, the basic structure of a system of free common education "to all persons between the ages of four and twenty-one," as one of the first laws passed by the territorial legislature expressed it, had been established. So too were the beginnings of a land-grant university when Congress, in 1851, awarded the Territory 46,000 acres of the public domain to charter and endow such an institution. It took time for a great university to develop; meanwhile, the legislators authorized

---

23. See Ann Regan, "The Irish," in Holmquist, *They Chose Minnesota,* 140. The two families were not named in the *Minnesota Democrat* of July 19, but Reardon, *Diocese of St. Paul,* 214, and Helen Angela Hurley, *On Good Ground: The Story of the Sisters of St. Joseph in St. Paul* (Minneapolis, 1951), 88, appear likely correct in assuming so. (Two of Richard Ireland's daughters became Sisters of St. Joseph.)

the founding of three normal schools to train teachers, while in Red Wing—another river town—a genuine four-year coeducational college, named after Methodist Bishop Leonidas Hamline, opened its doors in 1854.[24]

This concern for information and self-betterment revealed itself in another way: an astonishing number of newspapers, eighty-nine in all, catered to readers during the territorial era. The most memorable of them was the *Minnesota Pioneer,* inaugurated in St. Paul in 1849 by James Madison Goodhue, a New Englander blessed with a gift for the piquant phrase—bad government, he used to say, was "infamy on stilts"—and with a zealous conviction that Minnesota—its "lands as fertile as the banks of the Nile," its cornfields "jungles of rustling maize," its cold winters merely indicative of a "fresh, bracing climate"—was indeed the new promised land. Such boosterism was a commonplace among the local papers, and Goodhue and his fellow publishers saw to it that copies of their publications that recorded such enthusiasms were dispatched widely east and south. There is no reason to suppose that Minnesotans at large disagreed with printed promotion of this sort, but, even so, they manifested as well broader and more cosmopolitan interests: the subscription list of the *New York Tribune* was longer than that of any organ published in the Territory.

During these hectic and seminal years politics, as usual, preoccupied the attention of the press, both local and national. For residents of the Territory the overriding issue was preparation for statehood. Growth in population and economic progress guaranteed that admission to the Union would eventuate in due course, but to the minds of politically engaged Minnesotans, the sooner this result the better. Meantime the federal Congress approved a territorial constitution, which provided for a judiciary and a bicameral legislature chosen by manhood suffrage. Democrats dominated the elections, but to the governorship, an appointive office in the territories, President Zachary Taylor—years earlier the reluctant commandant at Fort Snelling[25]—named his fellow Whig, Alexander Ramsey, a thirty-four-year-old former congressman from Pennsylvania.[26] Partisan differences notwithstanding, when Ramsey arrived to take up his duties, he was welcomed by Henry Hastings Sibley,

---

24. The institution in Red Wing closed in 1869, only to be reconstituted in St. Paul in 1880 as Hamline University.

25. See chapter 1, above.

26. See Holman Hamilton, "Zachary Taylor and Minnesota," *Minnesota History* 30 (June 1949): 104–110.

sometime head of the American Fur Company, and was housed in Sibley's handsome stone mansion in Mendota.[27]

Sibley was the leading Democrat in the Territory, rivaled within the party only by Henry Mower Rice, another baron of the fur trade. Both immigrants themselves (Sibley born in Michigan, Rice in Vermont), they had both extended their business interests, especially in St. Paul (it was Rice who had given Father Ravoux the bell for the log chapel[28]), and they had both been instrumental in securing territorial status from Washington. Nor did they hold fundamental disagreement with the Whig governor as to ultimate objectives: the expulsion of the Indians from their hunting grounds, the encouragement of white immigration, and the consequent achievement of statehood for Minnesota. Indeed, this trio of politicians was to dominate civic affairs for years to come, even after Ramsey's Whig Party had collapsed and disappeared.

That collapse was fueled by the growing national crisis over slavery. A generation of provisional compromises—in 1820, 1850, 1854, all purporting to deal with controlling the spread of chattel slavery into new territories and states—had resulted only in exacerbating mutual hostility on the matter in both North and South. The attempt to apply the principle of popular sovereignty in Kansas Territory led to a scramble by slaveholders and abolitionists alike to gain a majority there and ended, in the late 1850s, with an outbreak of particularly ugly violence. Minnesota's drive for admission to the Union as a free state was therefore played out against the background of "Bleeding Kansas," and further complicated by the dismay provoked across the North by the Dred Scott decision. Both major parties were deeply divided along sectional lines over the issue, but the Whigs fared worse, and with the emergence of the explicitly antislavery Republican Party, they were swept from the board. Ramsey had no difficulty in accommodating himself to this latest political reality, and toward the end of 1857, after a convention had drawn up a new state constitution, he contested the governor's office, running as a Republican against Sibley, the Democrat. Sibley won by a handful of votes. Early in the new year, Henry Rice in Washington formally submitted to President Buchanan the text of the constitution and other relevant documents, including the results of the recent elections, and, despite heated opposition raised by southern senators and representatives, on May 11, 1858, Minnesota was admitted to the

---

27. See Frances Vreviga, ed., "With Governor Ramsey to Minnesota in 1849," *Minnesota History* 35 (December 1957): 352–357. These reminiscences of Ramsey appeared first in the *St. Paul Pioneer Press*, November 9, 1899.

28. See chapter 2, above.

Union as the thirty-second state. "She extends a friendly hand to all her sisters, north and south," proclaimed Governor Sibley, "and gives them assurance that she joins their ranks, not to provoke sectional discord or to engender strife, not to enlist in a crusade against such of them as differ with her in the character of their domestic institutions, but to promote harmony and good will, and to lend her aid, on all occasions, in maintaining the integrity of the Union." Brave words, but overly sanguine: only weeks later a somber Abraham Lincoln reminded the nation that "a house divided against itself cannot stand."[29]

INTO THIS EXPANDING, BOOMING, SOMETIMES BRAWLING community came the former parish priest of an ancient town located on the edge of Lake Geneva. Yet Joseph Cretin was no stranger to the American frontier experience. Steeled by a long experience as a missionary along the Mississippi, he brought few illusions with him to St. Paul in the summer of 1851. If unlike his famous French contemporary—Alexis de Tocqueville was six years his junior[30]—Cretin took no interest in analyzing the society in which Providence, as he believed, had situated him, he did not fail to adjust to its realities. He did not need to study Tocqueville's brilliant exposition of Jacksonian democracy to appreciate both the achievements and the limitations of this great American experiment. He lived daily within the scope of its noble political and social aspirations, its optimism and generosity and devotion to hard work; but he remained cognizant also—consistent with Tocqueville's prescient warnings—of the spiritual dangers of its raw and protocapitalist individualism, its get-up-and-go materialism, its tendency to identify the Declaration's assertion of the right to pursue happiness with the drive to make money.[31]

Nationhood, defined within these aggressive parameters, had abruptly deprived Joseph Cretin of his original missionary *raison d'être*, though he never completely recognized this reality. The romantic purpose that had attracted him first to China and then to the New World, the conversion of pagans to Christianity, had had to give way to a different perspective. He had

---

29. Lincoln thus invoked the Gospel of Mark 3:25 in a speech to the Illinois Republican Convention, held in Springfield, June 16, 1858.

30. The first volume of *Democracy in America* appeared in 1835, the second in 1840.

31. See the perceptive remarks of Gordon S. Wood, "Tocqueville's Lesson," *The New York Review of Books* 48 (May 17, 2001): 46–49.

witnessed already the beginnings of the massive influx of white settlers into the Midwest—indeed, along with Bishop Loras had encouraged it—and had had as a result to accommodate himself to new preoccupations and challenges. Not that Cretin or Augustin Ravoux or others of their priestly colleagues ever explicitly repudiated their ambition to bring to the Native Americans what they considered the inestimable solace of their religion and their civilization, nor did they cease to try to do so. But—one might say with the wisdom of hindsight—the contending cultures remained so fundamentally opposed that never the twain could have met. Nominal converts there may have been, but—not unlike the "rice Christians" who crowded the missions in China during the late nineteenth and early twentieth centuries—some of the local Dakota and Ojibwe, ruthlessly deprived of their livelihood, might have been persuaded to listen to spiritual admonition in exchange for food and shelter. Sheer numbers swiftly decided the issue.

And the numbers of Catholics coming into Minnesota Territory expanded during the 1850s at roughly the same geometric rate as did those of persons of other faiths. The thousand *catholiques* over whom Bishop Cretin claimed jurisdiction upon his arrival increased perhaps fortyfold by the time he died in 1857, and the growth continued apace over the next two years before his successor was appointed. Such statistics are not verifiable in detail, but there is no doubt of their overall accuracy. Nor is there any doubt about the radically different status Cretin assumed once the pope had named him a bishop. In Catholic doctrine a bishop, as the anointed successor of the apostles, is in his time and place the unique witness to the faith. His writ goes back to the shores of the Sea of Galilee, when Jesus imposed upon St. Peter the obligation to nourish the faithful lambs and sheep. Over the eighteen centuries that followed, many such shepherds had been martyrs, many others had been great scholars and administrators, still others, to their shame, had been timeservers and political hacks. But the tradition had continued uninterrupted and, in July 1851, it had manifested itself once again only a short distance from Pig's Eye Landing.

Galtier's log chapel had been automatically converted "by the grace of God and the favor of the Apostolic See"—to invoke the official language—into a cathedral, because within its humble confines stood a *cathedra,* a simple chair which was the new bishop's throne and from which he formally exercised his authority as chief priest, teacher, and ruler of the faithful of his diocese. For Joseph Cretin personally the change was profound: no longer the peripatetic missioner riding from one settlement or camp to another astride his black pony, but now a leader responsible for a determined area—vast as it was—and fixed at a headquarters in a specific locale. This new commission did not mean that he ceased to travel extensively in the service of his scattered flock; it meant that he did so with a mandate in accord with the traditional practice of the Roman Church: St. Anselm, after all, had made his authority felt across the whole province of Canterbury, as had St. Boniface over the ecclesiastical jurisdictions of southern Germany. On the American frontier in the 1850s Bishop Cretin demanded no less sanction, and he harbored no doubts about the efficacy of his teaching or about his personal status. To one of the young seminarians accompanying him on a pastoral visitation to an outlying district of the diocese, he said: "When you preach, always bear in mind that you represent the Bishop, and speak as you would think he would speak."[32]

But a dilapidated log shack would not do as a cathedral even in a frontier village, especially when it could accommodate only a fraction of a growing congregation. Thanks to Father Ravoux's shrewd negotiation of a year earlier,[33] a handsome site was available for a new building, and, even before Cretin arrived and paid the $900 to close the purchase of the property, Ravoux had initiated discussions of plans and construction strategies with local contractors. "The Catholic Church," reported one newspaper, "owns two blocks of lots on Wabasha Street. Upon one is to be erected a Cathedral, and upon the other a College."[34] This projection was only partially accurate; what Cretin first intended was to provide a church and a residence, but limited funds obliged him to modify that modest objective and to have built instead a single multi-purpose facility. No time was wasted: as early as July 14, 1851, a group of volunteers, mostly Irish immigrants, set to work clearing the site, and soon the foundation and lower walls of local limestone were going up. By the end of September the upper brick walls were in place and the fastening of the roof had begun. Meanwhile Bishop Cretin fretted over the unexpectedly high cost of labor and matériel, which amounted in the end to about $7,000. Local contributions in cash were minimal, and, since the total expenditure pretty much exhausted the funds he had brought with him from France, Cretin found it

---

32. Anatole Oster, "Personal Reminiscences of Bishop Cretin," *A&D* 1 (July 1907): 61. Cretin ordained Oster priest on December 14, 1856. Oster lived till 1910 and filled many responsible posts within the diocese, as will be seen in the pages below. See Thomas Monahan, "The Life of Anatole Oster, a Pioneer Priest" (Master's thesis, St. Paul Seminary, 1958).

33. See chapter 2, above.

34. *Minnesota Democrat*, April 8, 1851.

necessary to borrow some money and to donate some more of his own. Even so, the interior of the building remained unplastered and unadorned for some time into the future.

On November 3 the bishop went into residence on the third story, accompanied by the priests and seminarians who had come with him from France. Directly beneath the rooms, dormitories, and study areas they occupied, was the church proper which, at a pinch, could seat as many as five hundred worshipers. A corridor ran the full length of the ground floor, opening on one side into a kitchen, a parlor, and a schoolroom of considerable size, and, on the other, into a dining area, a little library, a storeroom, and small quarters for a housekeeper. The building thus proved genuinely functional, but neither Cretin nor, it would seem, the local population ever considered it a proper cathedral or even a proper church: "I cannot apply that name to the large room where we say Mass," the bishop observed.[35] Nevertheless, the people of St. Paul, Catholic and Protestant alike, took some pride in an edifice that was quite splendid when compared with most of the architecture in the village. Soon gardens planted to the north and east of the building, tended by the seminarians when not occupied by their theology books, enhanced the site even further with vegetables, bright flowers, and Cretin's sprouting apple trees.[36]

THE CLERICS WHO TOOK UP RESIDENCE ON THE THIRD FLOOR OF the new Catholic Building (as the local newspapers dubbed it), though it was still unfinished, included Bishop Cretin himself and those he had recruited in France: the two priests, Denis Ledon and Francesco di Vivaldi, the three subdeacons, Jean Fayolle, Edouard Legendre, and Maurice Rochette, and a seminarian in minor orders, Marcellin Peyragrosse.[37] An Irish priest named

---

35. Cretin to SPF, June 5, 1852, AASPM, SPF Papers. For a description of the building by one who knew it well, see Anatole Oster, "Personal Reminiscences of Bishop Cretin," *A&D* 1 (July 1907): 74–76.

36. Robert Christian Nygaard, "The Second Cathedral of St. Paul . . . 1851–1857" (Master's thesis, St. Paul Seminary, 1964), 8–18.

37. See the brief notice in Cretin's "Memorialis Tabella" (appointment diary), May 29, 1851, AASPM, Cretin Papers and printed in *A&D* 1 (July 1907): 41.

Prior to the changes introduced during the 1970s, an aspirant for ordination to the Catholic priesthood proceeded through several rubrical steps: the ceremony of tonsure inducted him into the clerical state, and this was followed by the several "minor orders" (porter, lector, exorcist, acolyte). "Major orders" began with the sub-

Moran drifted into the community for a brief period and then drifted away—
an occurrence experienced by no means rarely within the frontier Church.
Augustin Ravoux, now vicar general of the new diocese, continued as pastor
of St. Peter's in Mendota. Ledon was soon dispatched to found a new parish in
St. Anthony, while the enigmatic Vivaldi went off to Long Prairie, a hundred
miles north of St. Paul, to serve the Winnebago Indians, driven first from
Wisconsin and then into Iowa—where Father Cretin had tried to minister to
them[38]—and finally into a reservation awkwardly carved out between the already sullen Ojibwe and Dakota.[39] By the end of 1852 Cretin had ordained
Legendre, Fayolle, and Peyragrosse to the priesthood; Rochette unaccount-
ably had simply disappeared. It was not, however, the removal of the men
from the episcopal "palace"—the shanty Ravoux had put up in 1848—that
renders November 3, 1851, a hallmark in the history of Catholicism in the
upper Midwest; it was rather the arrival of the four women who replaced
them there.

Their names, given their accomplishments and those of their successors,
must adorn perpetually any roll of honor drawn up within that history: Julie
Alexise Fournier, born in France thirty-seven years before; Anne Marie
Vilaine, aged forty, also of French birth; Celestine Vasques, twenty-two, of
Creole ancestry and a native of St. Louis, Missouri; and Eliza Ellen Ivory,
twenty-seven, the daughter of Irish immigrants who had settled in eastern
Pennsylvania. In religion they were called, respectively, Mother St. John, the
superior, and Sisters Philomene, Scholastica, and Francis Joseph.[40] They belonged to a religious congregation founded in the seventeenth century in Le
Puy, not far from Lyons, which in itself was a talisman not without significance for the infant diocese of St. Paul. Cretin himself hailed from that southeastern part of France, as had Galtier, and Augustin Ravoux had been a
seminarian at Le Puy when Bishop Loras had recruited him for the missions.

---

diaconate, which imposed the obligations of celibacy and recitation of the breviary,
and the (temporary) diaconate, which granted the candidate permission to exercise
certain sacramental functions. These incremental steps were designed as a means of
discernment as to the aspirant's fitness and worthiness. Of them only the sacramental diaconate is preserved today.

38. See chapter 2, above.

39. For Vivaldi's strange apostolate, see chapter 4, below.

40. For biographical details, see Ann Thomasine Sampson, *Seeds on Good
Ground* (St. Paul, 2000), 1–61. Sister Ann Thomasine has made admirable use of a
variety of material she has found—letters, diaries, personal reminiscences—in several archival collections.

The Sisters of St. Joseph, as they were called, had served with distinction as teachers and nurses and custodians of orphans in that region of the country until the Revolution of 1789 had rendered their status, like those of all the religious orders, untenable. Suppression was the ordinary coin of the 1790s, but martyrdom at the guillotine was not unheard of. Survival of the community during these parlous years depended upon the skills and dedication of its young superior general, Mother St. John Fontbonne, who, after the persecution had abated in the wake of the concordat agreed to between Napoleon Bonaparte and the Holy See in 1801, had sought and secured the patronage of the archbishop of Lyons. That eminent churchman, Cardinal Fesch, was Bonaparte's uncle, and though he lost his office when his imperial nephew was finally defeated at Waterloo in 1815, by that time the revival of the Sisters of St. Joseph had been safely launched: they stood ready to contribute to the renaissance in the religious life that so marked French Catholicism during the nineteenth century.[41]

An essential characteristic of that renaissance was the same missionary spirit that motivated secular priests like Loras, Cretin, and Ravoux. Nor was it restricted by gender: French women religious had, if anything, more long-term impact upon the development of Catholicism in Mid-America than did their male counterparts. In the case of the Josephites, the commitment to the New World assumed permanent form on March 25, 1836, when six sisters, one of them Anne Marie Vilaine—all prudently in lay garb lest they provoke bigoted gibes from the rough river men—disembarked from the *George Collier* at St. Louis after a four-day voyage up the Mississippi from New Orleans. They settled in a village just south of the city called Carondelet. This apostolic initiative had been undertaken with the blessing of Mother St. John Fontbonne—who continued to guide the congregation until her death in 1843—and at the explicit urging of a pious French noblewoman named Félicité de Duras, who had succeeded Cardinal Fesch as the order's benefactor. Long a supporter of the Propagation of the Faith in Lyons, the *comtesse* met there by chance a priest from St. Louis, who told her of the desperate needs of that fledgling diocese. She promptly got into contact with the bishop, Joseph Rosati, and offered to pay the travel expenses of a company of sisters if he would receive them.

> It seems to me [she wrote], that if I succeed in establishing the Sisters of St. Joseph in your America, near the savages and near so many heretics in

---

41. Hurley, *On Good Ground*, 5–7.

your diocese, I shall have done during my life something pleasing to God to win his mercy for my sins. I know what I have given is not enough, but I will give more. I will help; only say, my Lord, what you think is necessary for the beginning. . . . I am confident that [the sisters will] bring to America the true and admirable spirit of their congregation, and that the grain of mustard seed which is to be sown in St. Louis will become a large tree. My hope is that, with time, the fruits of the establishment of these good sisters in America will be immense and that they will comprise all works which charity may suggest. . . . I shall aid them to the best of my ability whenever it will be necessary.[42]

Rosati gladly accepted this generous offer, though he asked in addition for a further benefaction: would it be possible, he wondered, if one or two nuns specially trained in care of the deaf might also be sent to Missouri? This request too was granted; the next year, 1837, two young sisters, who had spent the previous twelve months in intensive study of sign language and related disciplines, arrived in St. Louis. One of them was the novice Julie Fournier.

Countess Félicité had shrewdly assured Bishop Rosati that the Sisters of St. Joseph would be of particular value on the frontier precisely because they were not specialists. Along with swearing the conventional vows and following the venerable Rule of St. Augustine, she explained,

they promise, without exception, to perform *all* works of charity. . . . Hence piety, recollection, abnegation, humility flourish on the one hand; and, on the other, free schools or pay boarding institutions, large hospitals, hospices for the aged or foundling asylums—prisons, relief of the poor, of the sick in their homes, care of the scurfy, of the mangy, it matters not—the care of dispensaries. . . . Ah, my Lord, if you had only seen, as I have, the spirit of poverty, that evangelical *littleness*! I speak truly: I have known them for thirty years. . . . My little sisters work . . . according to reason and suitableness of the place.[43]

This paean did not in the long run prove extravagant. Whatever nonsacramental tasks the mission called for the sisters did, as catechists, nurses, sacristans, teachers, caregivers to orphans and to the sick and poor. And there

---

42. Quoted in Sampson, *Seeds*, 28–29.
43. Quoted in Hurley, *On Good Ground*, 8–9.

were plenty of poor to care for in Carondelet and its environs and equally so in Cahokia, just across the Mississippi in Illinois, at that time the bishop of St. Louis's canonical responsibility, where the nuns shortly opened a house. One touch of specialization, Julie Fournier's service in a local asylum for the deaf, could not have displeased Félicité de Duras, since she had paid for the novice's prior training in this therapy. The sisters' own poverty at any rate went far beyond "the spirit" the *comtesse* spoke of. Thus there was nothing genteel about their first convent in Carondelet: a two-room log cabin with an attic that could be reached only by an outside ladder, where the sisters slept on straw-stuffed mattresses. Almost immediately this shack became a free day school and a little orphanage as well. The sisters in their habits of black serge, with long skirt and sleeves, a headdress also black with a touch of white linen, a cross with a brass figure of Christ crucified on it hanging from a cord around the neck, and a rosary suspended from the cincture at the waist, soon were familiar sights around Carondelet and Cahokia. To most they seemed angels of light, but to others, to deeply primitive Protestants, their garb made them objects of derision. And they had to cope with an even more atavistic display of bigotry. By virtue of the celebrated Compromise of 1820 Missouri had been admitted to the Union as a slave state. "In 1843 or 1844," recalled Julie Fournier, by then Sister St. John,

> the first mission was opened in St. Louis as a school for free Negroes. . . . We also prepared slaves for the reception of the sacraments, which vexed many of the whites. After a time they threatened to drive us away by main force. Threats came every day. Finally one morning a number of people . . . told me that the next night they would come and drive us from the house. . . . At eleven o'clock we heard a great noise which aroused the sisters with a start. A crowd of people in the street were shouting and blaspheming. We recited together the *Memorare* and other prayers. All at once a patrol of armed police dispersed the demons who were trying to force the door. They came back three times that same night, but our good [Blessed] Mother protected us, and they were not able either to open the door or to break through from the outside.[44]

As though the ordinary cultural difficulties they confronted daily were not severe enough, the sisters also had to contend with the internal disagreements

---

44. Quoted in Hurley, *On Good Ground*, 102.

and tensions inevitable within so closed and highly charged a company, as well as, initially, with an unsympathetic and alcoholic parish priest in Carondelet.[45]

Despite these threats and alarums, the community continued its dedicated labor and showed a modest amount of growth. In 1847 the bishop of Philadelphia, Francis Patrick Kenrick, at the recommendation of his brother, Peter Richard Kenrick, now bishop of St. Louis, invited the Sisters of St. Joseph to open a house in his see-city. To this mission, composed of four nuns, Sister St. John Fournier was assigned, not least because of her expertise in the ministry to the deaf. She was given besides the responsibility of overall supervision of the local convent, and so merited the title Mother St. John. She opened in due course a school, an orphanage, and a hospital in the City of Brotherly Love, but the rigors and burdens of the apostolate there undermined her always delicate health. Meanwhile, the inspiration of the presence of the hardworking sisters in Philadelphia inspired Pennsylvania-born Eliza Ellen Ivory to join the community as Sister Francis Joseph, and back in St. Louis Celestine Vasques, as Sister Scholastica, did the same.

By the early months of 1851, Mother St. John Fournier was back at Carondelet, enjoying a well-earned period of rest from her exertions in Philadelphia, when she was shown an impassioned plea from the recently consecrated bishop of St. Paul. Monseigneur Cretin, whom the sisters remembered from a retreat he had preached to them a decade earlier, described himself as in desperate need of personnel-support in his vast new diocese. The nuns in Carondelet did not need to know that Cretin had already petitioned other religious orders only to be refused for a variety of reasons, so he did not tell them so. After due consideration by the sisters' ruling council, the bishop's request was agreed to, and in the fading days of October 1851 Mother St. John, joined by Sisters Philomene, Scholastica, and Francis Joseph, boarded the steamboat for the journey northward. During a brief stop at Prairie du Chien they were greeted by the local parish priest and heard from him some details about what they might expect in St. Paul; and who better to provide them than Lucien Galtier? Finally, after skirting the ice already forming on Lake Pepin, the captain deposited his passengers on the wharf at the end of Jackson Street on the night of Sunday, November 2. Next day, Sister Francis Joseph

---

45. See Sampson, *Seeds*, 5, 30. The alcoholic priest was probably French-born Augustin Saunier, who had been dismissed from the Congregation of Holy Cross in Kentucky and had relocated in Missouri. See Marvin R. O'Connell, *Edward Sorin* (Notre Dame, Ind., 2001), 230–231.

remembered long afterward, "we were shown our future home, a low frame shanty on a bluff over the Mississippi. . . . The furniture was a few old mattresses on which we took our brief rest. These were located in the upper story. . . . We had a small stove on the first floor, the pipe of which was set upright through the roof. Around this opening we could count the stars."[46]

---

46. Quoted in Sampson, *Seeds,* 49.

CHAPTER 4

New Horizons

SISTER FRANCIS JOSEPH AND HER COMPANIONS SPENT LITTLE time stargazing through the hole in the roof of their wretched abode. Within days of their arrival in St. Paul they had opened a little school for girls in the vestry of Galtier's log chapel. A week later they welcomed the first boarding pupil in what would become the celebrated St. Joseph's Academy. Martha Ellen Rice was her name, daughter of the prominent businessman and leading Democrat, Henry Mower Rice.[1] "We fixed up an old shed back of the shanty. Mr. Rice furnished her room, a good bed, etc., and very comfortable. The next month we received a second boarder, . . . Miss Mary Fridley, daughter of [Indian Agent Abram] Fridley. . . . The young ladies seemed happy." That the nuns were perceived to fill a civic need beyond confessional allegiances was testified to by the fact that neither Rice nor Fridley was a Catholic—indeed, the latter proved hostile later to proposals to provide Catholic schools for the Native Americans under his charge. "We had a well-attended school, as it was the only one," Sister Francis Joseph explained sensibly. "In the spring [of 1852] we moved the school into the [Galtier's] old church. We had the building filled. . . . We had happy times, yet some days we did not taste food until night."[2]

The recollection that the sisters' primitive school was "well-attended" because it was "the only one" missed the mark. The "academy," destined to flourish for more than a century, was, to be sure, unique in attracting both female boarders and day pupils, and unique also perhaps in the promise it seemed to offer the daughters of the pioneers of something of the ambience of a French

1. See chapter 2, above.
2. Hurley, *On Good Ground*, 24–25, 36–37.

finishing-school education. Indeed, Bishop Cretin grasped early on how important an overall influence such an institution might have within the community at large. The sisters had hardly disembarked before he was already planning a new venue for them. By the autumn of 1852, thanks to monies received from the Propagation of the Faith in Lyons, a one-story building had been constructed on the "Catholic block" to house the nuns and their pupils. "We had," recalled Mother St. John, "nearly seventy day-scholars and seventeen boarders." Such success was consolation, at least to a degree, for the hazards of religious life on the American frontier: "Every morning that winter until the snow came, we made a number of genuflections on the way to [Mass in the cathedral], and to conclude we kissed the ground. When the snow came, we sank into it two or three feet or we walked on it, as if on ice. It was on one of those mornings that a starved wolf had a mind to take a bite . . . of my person! The next day and all the rest of the winter Monseigneur [Cretin] came to say Mass [for us] in his old [Ravoux's] palace."[3]

The territorial government, meanwhile, in accord with its Yankee predispositions,[4] proved anxious to set up within Minnesota a program of universal, secular, and free education. But "secular" in the context of the time meant a system that took due account of the predominant Protestant culture which prevailed in the Territory and indeed across the nation. Thus Governor Ramsey appointed a Presbyterian minister to be superintendent of the common schools. This gentleman, eschewing for public consumption any sectarian bias—and he did so with an admirable abundance of good will—nevertheless could not abate the suspicion among Catholics that he, or those allied with him, would in the end undermine the faith of Catholic youth. These were highly unecumenical times.

Parallel to the sisters' foundation for girls Bishop Cretin had established a boys' school in the ground floor of the "Catholic Building." The first instructors were the newly ordained Fathers Peyragrosse and Legendre, whose rudimentary English proved a challenge both to themselves and their pupils. Early in 1852 they were joined by a young man fluent enough in the Territory's official language but heavily burdened with mixed emotions about the task he found himself confronted with. Daniel Fisher was a seminarian attending St. John's, the Jesuit college in New York,[5] when recruited by Cretin for service

---

3. Hurley, *On Good Ground*, 30–32, 27.

4. See chapter 3, above.

5. Founded in 1841, St. John's evolved into the present-day Fordham University.

in the fledgling diocese on the frontier. "What am I doing, do you think?" Fisher asked a friend at St. John's rhetorically and sardonically.

I am teaching the Catholic School—my mission is among the dirty little ragged Canadian and Irish boys. Every day, morning and afternoon, I practice patience with these wild little fellows, try to teach them who God is, and then to instruct them in the mysteries of A. B. C. I left N. Y. to go among the Indians, and I was hoping for strength to undergo the hardships of a savage life, or to meet a martyr's death. I felt the difficulty of the sacrifice more than anybody thought, but the greatest trial was one I never dreamed of: to take charge of these impudent and insulting children of unthankful parents was the greatest mortification I ever underwent.

This mordant testimony to the evangelical realities might have been mitigated somewhat had the young and bumptious Fisher realized that his bishop had also come to the American Midwest with similarly romantic aspirations. Joseph Cretin, curé of Fermey, had likewise dreamed of "the hardships of a savage life" and of the conversion of a host of pagans, only to find himself obliged to devote his energies to the humdrum duties of the ministry. Hardships there were aplenty, but the drums of glory remained muted.

Daniel Fisher at any rate possessed an acute and critical eye as well as a quixotic ardor.

The Catholics [are] very poor here, and, what is worse, very irreligious and indifferent. They are half-breeds, Canadian, and Irish. There are three [news]papers published weekly here. There are six churches and any number of doctors, lawyers, and parsons. But there is no money, as all the wealth is controlled by a [i.e., the American] Fur Company, who [sic] own nearly all the shops and employ a great number of workmen and never circulate any money—they loan at 60 percent! . . . It is well for those who thought of coming here that they did not come. I think they would have been disappointed in everything. The only thing that can sustain a New Yorker in this wild country is the hope of a speedy release.

But Fisher did not include himself among such slackers.

I would not lead the inactive life of a priest in New York for a great deal of wealth and comfort. Talking of comfort, if you take it in its worldly sense, there is none here. I have not had a moment of it. But as for peace of mind, I never enjoyed it until now. I am perfectly in love with the hard lot of a Minnesota missionary. . . . I am entirely weaned from New York.[6]

He wrote in the same vein to a priest he had known in New Jersey who had sensed that the young man had not found what he had hoped for in his foray into the West: "I hope you will believe me, Father Mac, when I say that I do not seek a comfortable life in the ministry—for that reason the offer of a reception from a Bishop in the east has not even a momentary charm to tempt me." Nevertheless, being consigned to teaching "the dirty little ragged Irish boys" (among them John Ireland and Thomas O'Gorman) had taken its toll on Fisher's considerable self-esteem, as did the delay in the date of his ordination.

My expectation was to be ordained soon and sent on the mission immediately; if I have been presumptuous in expecting this, I was led to it by what Bishop Cretin said to me several times before leaving New York. . . . I knew that whether I remained at Fordham or came to Minnesota I should, before the year expired, be a priest, because I was of the required age and finishing my seminary studies. Well, I have been nearly ten months in Minnesota and not yet ordained, first disappointment.

But sacramental ordination, which Cretin conferred upon him in 1853,[7] proved insufficient to preserve Fisher's "love of the missionary's hard lot." He grew ever more homesick and frustrated as he judged adversely—with all the cocksureness of youth and inexperience—the ecclesiastical scene at hand. "There is not half the need of priests here as in New York city. In St. Paul, the largest town in the Territory, there is no need of more than one priest. The Bishop has the charge of the Church there, and the priest who is assisting him has nothing to do—second disappointment."[8] Shortly afterward Father Fisher

---

6. Fisher to Donnelly, n.d. [Autumn 1852], AASPM, Catholic Historical Society Papers.

7. "Next Saturday . . . I shall ordain an American priest who will do well, I think. I am confident that he will not cause any trouble; he is modest and he has good sense." Cretin to Loras, March 10, 1853, AASPM, Cretin Papers (copy).

8. Fisher to McQuaid, February 19, 1853, AASPM, Catholic Historical Society Records. Bernard McQuaid (1823–1909), at this date a pastor in northern New Jer-

returned to the East, and, after a respectable life in the ministry, died in the salubrious confines of Hoboken, New Jersey.

But not before he performed an important if futile service to the infant diocese. "At the request of the Bishop," Fisher recorded, "I drew up a petition, asking for an amendment of the School law, and for a share of the School fund to Catholic Schools. It was referred to a committee of the Lower house [of the Territorial Legislature], and after a first and second reading was laid on the table to be printed." The petition, however, was denied a third reading in committee by a vote of twelve to five. So, in Minnesota in 1853, the argument that Catholics who contributed their proportionate share to the public treasury should receive support from that treasury for confessional schools within an overweening Protestant culture fell upon deaf ears, as it continued to do across the United States over the next century and more. Meanwhile Bishop Cretin hoped to solve his immediate educational problem by turning over the school for boys to a group of religious brothers, drawn from his native diocese of Belley; but these Frenchmen foundered in their new and unfamiliar environment and soon dispersed, in marked contrast to the hardihood exhibited by the Sisters of St. Joseph.[9]

CRETIN'S BRIEF ENCOUNTER WITH DANIEL FISHER UNDERSCORES the difficulty frontier bishops experienced in recruiting American-born priests. Indeed, not till well past the turn of the century—sixty years after Cretin's death—did the number of native-born ordinands outpace that of immigrants. Between 1901 and 1910, for example, sixty-seven percent of the priests ordained for service in the archdiocese of St. Paul were foreign-born.[10] And this at a time when the total Catholic population of the jurisdiction was approaching 175,000. In one sense such statistics are not at all surprising. The Catholic community during these years was overwhelmingly immigrant, and many of its subgroups—Bohemian, Polish, German, Italian, to say nothing of

---

sey, still part of the archdiocese of New York, became first bishop of Rochester in 1868. A bitter antagonist of Archbishop Ireland of St. Paul during the so-called Americanist Controversy of the 1890s, McQuaid, once tempers had cooled, sent Fisher's letters to Ireland to be deposited with the Catholic Historical Society. See *A&D* 1 (July 1907): 42–51.

9. Reardon, *Diocese of St. Paul*, 78–79.

10. See the statistics in the admirable study by Daniel Patrick O'Neill, "St. Paul Priests, 1851–1930: Recruitment, Formation and Mobility" (Ph.D. dissertation, University of Minnesota, 1979), 13–15.

the English-speaking Irish—clung inflexibly to the linguistic and devotional habits they had brought with them from their mother countries. Such people predictably preferred to be served by priests of their own nationality.

The fact remained, however, that for Joseph Cretin, and indeed for any Catholic missionary, a primary charge was to promote the creation of a native clergy. With this obligation in mind, early in April 1853 the bishop singled out two boys from Daniel Fisher's schoolroom—John Ireland, aged fourteen, and Thomas O'Gorman, barely eleven. As O'Gorman reconstructed the scene a half century later, Cretin led the two lads into the church, placed their hands on the altar, and said: "I put you under the protection of God and his Blessed Mother; you are the beginning of my diocesan seminary, the first seminarians of St. Paul."[11] Four months later John and Thomas were sent off to France, to the preparatory seminary at Meximieux, where Joseph Cretin had once been a student and Mathias Loras a professor,[12] and where, thanks to the largesse of the bishop of Belley, these "first seminarians of St. Paul" would receive their training gratis. But this initiative on Cretin's part—momentous as it proved ultimately to be for the history of Catholicism in the upper Midwest—did not satisfy the bishop's immediate need for priestly personnel. Father Augustin Ravoux, who had conducted young Ireland and O'Gorman to Europe—and had been victim of their boyish pranks[13]—returned to Minnesota in the spring of 1854 with seven recruited seminarians in tow. One of them, who was to be an especial familiar of the bishop—Anatole Oster, destined for a long and dis-tinguished priestly career[14]—recalled that when they disembarked the river steamer and made their way to the church, they found Cretin conducting a catechism class.[15]

It was true enough—as Daniel Fisher, to his chagrin, had observed—that Cretin, in these early days of his episcopate, acted in effect as though he were curé of the village in which Providence, as he believed, had situated him. He was seen early and late plying the muddy streets of St. Paul on one pastoral mission or another, not disdaining, despite his inbred distaste for heresy, an

---

11. See M. Seraphica Marx, "The Life of Thomas O'Gorman, Bishop of Sioux Falls" (Master's thesis, University of South Dakota, 1959), 9–10, and the authorities cited there.

12. See chapter 2, above.

13. See Marvin R. O'Connell, *John Ireland and the American Catholic Church* (St. Paul, 1988), 42–43.

14. See Thomas Monahan, "The Life of Anatole Oster" (Master's thesis, St. Paul Seminary, 1958).

15. Oster, "Bishop Cretin," 73.

occasional foray into a Protestant home that he had learned stood in some spiritual or temporal need. He remained as punctilious about ceremonial as he had been in Fermey, and, primitive as present circumstances may have been, he insisted that the full circle of liturgical fast and feast be carried out with as much pomp as possible, from elaborate Corpus Christi processions to the long and scarcely comprehensible rituals of Holy Week. Certainly one lasting memorial to Cretin's ministry was the continuing devotion to music and singing among the people he had served. Some years after the bishop's death, a young priest, "lost on crosspaths and trails" to the west of Minneapolis, "began to feel rather perplexed and stood still in the midst of a cool, shady wood. Wiping his brow and trying to find his bearings, he thought he heard the tune of a church song, . . . real French psalmody, well known to him from his years of study in France." He followed "the angelic sounds" through the woods and thickets until he came to a newly erected frame building. "There was a Catholic congregation gathered together without a priest praying and singing psalms."[16] Singing perhaps Joseph Cretin's favorite hymns, among them "Jerusalem, My Happy Home" and, in his beloved native tongue, "En ce jour, O bonne Madonne" ("On this day, O beautiful Mother").[17]

Cretin lived with the utmost simplicity, cleaning his little room himself and chopping the wood for the stove that heated it during the harsh winters. When in residence in St. Paul—which was the case most of the time—Cretin invariably celebrated Mass at 5:00 a.m. on weekdays and 7:00 a.m. on Sundays. Anatole Oster, who as a seminarian lived with him on the third story of the "Catholic Building," remembered long afterward how the bishop would knock on his door shortly before Mass time, invoke the conventional Sulpician invocation on awaking (*Benedicamus Domino,* "Let us bless the Lord") and, fully vested for the liturgy, would await the younger man in the sacristy on the floor below. "After Mass, at half past five, priests, students, brothers, and all the members of the household would attend morning prayer and meditation." Here at work in the wilds of middle America were the spiritual principles imbibed so long ago at Saint-Sulpice-de-Paris. Following a Spartan breakfast the bishop often repaired to a confessional, the one nearest the side altar dedicated to the Virgin Mary. On at least one occasion, the Sisters of St. Joseph, who came weekly to the cathedral to be shriven, discovered that

---

16. Mathias Savs, "The Catholic Church in Wright County, Minn.," *A&D* 4 (July 1916): 222. The young priest was John Ireland.

17. Oster, "Bishop Cretin," 73.

their spiritual shepherd had fallen asleep, perhaps not unexpectedly, within the warm and drowsy confines of the confessional box.[18]

Once the snow had melted and travel became feasible, the bishop, accompanied by Oster, paid pastoral visits to the settlements scattered across the southern part of the Territory. Nor did he leave his principles behind him. On one occasion, for example, "[we were] directed to a house on Main Street. It proved to be a saloon kept by a Catholic. On inquiry the bishop was informed that Mass was said in the room occupied by the saloon, the bar serving as an altar." Cretin, a teetotaler himself and a strong advocate of temperance—he knew full well the ravages effected on the frontier by strong drink, among whites and Indians alike—"without a word . . . crossed the street to a large house and asked the owner, a Protestant lady, whether she would allow him to use her large sitting room . . . to say Mass in. She consented; an altar was erected, confessions heard, and Mass said. After the services she gave us breakfast."

Aside from a natural compatibility there was another reason why Cretin chose young Oster as his companion on these missionary expeditions. The bishop spoke no German, and the Catholics in many settlements spoke nothing else. This linguistic barrier proved particularly awkward in dispensing the sacrament of penance. "My knowledge of the German language," the Alsatian-born Oster recalled, "though imperfect, enabled me to act as interpreter whenever [Cretin] was called upon to hear confessions in that language."

On such occasions I wore a surplice and, when I was a deacon, a stole, said the Veni Sancte Spiritus, and sat near him. The first time I acted in this capacity was at a place called Mary's Town, near Shakopee. It was a new thing to the people, and for a while they were uncertain what to do. At length, one man came forward and made his confession, and the others followed his example. When the confessions were heard I had to say the Rosary by way of thanksgiving.[19]

The number of German immigrants swelled in the territorial capital as well as in the countryside, so much so that in 1855 Bishop Cretin organized a parish in St. Paul for their exclusive use; the Church of the Assumption of Mary opened its doors a year later.

---

18. Oster, "Bishop Cretin," 77.
19. Oster, "Bishop Cretin," 78–79.

THE FOUNDING OF THE ASSUMPTION WAS ITSELF REFUTATION
of the brash Daniel Fisher's claim that a single priest could readily serve the
needs of the burgeoning Catholic population of St. Paul. And the early career
of that parish's first pastor testifies further to Cretin's desperate need for ever
more personnel. The German-speaking George Keller, ordained in 1855, did
indeed oversee the Assumption through its first year or two, but before that
he was instrumental in establishing congregations and supervising the construction of humble log churches in the outlying communities at Centerville
and Mary's Town—in the latter place, presumably, he did not need an interpreter when hearing confessions. In neither of these locations, however,
nor in the dozen or so other rural settlements across the southeast of the
Territory—among them Le Sueur, Hastings, Shieldsville—where formal
Catholic parishes were set up could the bishop afford to assign resident pastors. Mass in such locales was offered and the sacraments administered only
occasionally. But after he left the Assumption in St. Paul (and after Cretin
died), Father Keller arrived in the lively town of Faribault—named for the
prominent French-Canadian fur-trading family which had befriended Lucien
Galtier[20]—and there he remained for a dozen years, erecting in the course of
his pastorate a handsome stone church and inducing Dominican Sisters to
come and open a school.[21] Here was an intimation, obvious enough though
perhaps never minutely calculated, of future missionary strategy: assignment
of permanent clergy, and all that that suggested, would depend on the demographic realities.

One settlement that clearly required a resident pastor was Galtier's original mission, St. Peter's in Mendota. The fur trade, though gradually lan-
guishing, still attracted enough commerce to the environs of Fort Snelling to
support a considerable population. Once Cretin had taken up the reins in
St. Paul, Augustin Ravoux was left free to assume a full-time status at St. Peter's. In 1853, to replace Galtier's log chapel, he supervised construction of
a stone church—the first such in the diocese—on a bluff overlooking the
confluence of the Mississippi and Minnesota rivers. It cost $4,500—paid off
within three years—and continues in use a century and a half later.[22] This

---

20. See chapter 2, above.
21. Reardon, *Diocese of St. Paul,* 607.
22. A personal note. In 1959 I served for some months as a part-time assistant at
St. Peter's and performed my duties in what is now called the "historic" church.
Since then a new and much more capacious church has been built (1991) nearby, but
Ravoux's building—with a spire added after his time—is still in use. See Scott

larger edifice testified to the steady influx of Catholics into the area, as did Ravoux's meticulously kept registers: during his five and a half years as pastor in Mendota he recorded nearly five hundred baptisms, a hundred weddings, and sixty-five funerals.[23] Unsurprisingly, the bishop also appointed this old and trusted friend his vicar general. A small room was reserved for him in the Catholic Building in St. Paul, and—it was said—whenever Cretin wanted to consult Ravoux, whose experience in the Territory made him uniquely useful, a banner was hung outside the bishop's window, a signal which, on a clear day and with no tall structures intervening, could be seen from Mendota and which would assure the vicar's prompt presence.[24]

Also close to St. Paul, to locales that would ultimately become suburbs of a vast metropolitan complex—Osseo, Edina, Oakdale among others— permanent pastors could be assigned by the bishop only when the numbers of Catholics justified such an expenditure of clerical personnel. In most instances this sign of normal parochial development did not occur during Cretin's time. Thanks to recruits from Europe, he had available to him eleven priests in the mid-1850s, but this number could hardly keep pace with the demands that an increasing wave of immigration confronted him with. There were places, however, like Mendota, that could not be neglected. Upriver from St. Paul, for instance, north and east of the Falls Father Hennepin had named for St. Anthony of Padua, a village numbering several hundred people, a large proportion of them French and Irish, had grown up by the time of Cretin's arrival. And even before that, Augustin Ravoux, shrewd as ever, had secured property and had presided over the building of a chapel there; he realized that the entrepreneurial and industrial possibilities afforded by waterpower guaranteed the area a bright and populous future.[25]

Ravoux's original plan had called for a stone structure, but funds were insufficient and a more modest frame church, after several delays, was put up instead; even so, it stood upon completion as the most impressive edifice under Catholic auspices in the Territory.[26] The parish enjoyed the honor of

Wright, *Gather Us In: A History of the Parishes of the Archdiocese of St. Paul and Minneapolis* (St. Paul, 2000), 1.

23. See the registers in AASPM, Ravoux Papers. Till the end of 1852 the entries are in French, after that in English.

24. *St. Paul Pioneer Press,* January 30, 1906.

25. Roden, "Ravoux," 136–137.

26. See Frederic Fleming, "A History of the Parish of Saint Anthony of Padua, Minneapolis, Minnesota, to 1866" (Master's thesis, St. Paul Seminary, 1955), 7–14.

receiving Bishop Cretin's first diocesan visitation, at the end of July 1851, on which occasion he announced that he was assigning Denis Ledon to be the first pastor of what would be the mother church of the city of Minneapolis. The twenty-seven-year-old Ledon, ordained for the diocese of Belley in 1848 and long acquainted with the Cretin family, had enthusiastically answered the new bishop's appeal for missionary volunteers. He was to remain Joseph Cretin's confidant throughout the brief years of that prelate's episcopate: "I esteem him and am very attached to him," the bishop told his sister.[27] The work at St. Anthony was arduous, as the population of the village doubled and then doubled again, and yet it proved fruitful for him and for his parishioners, thanks in large part to the Sisters of St. Joseph who, despite a grinding poverty, opened a flourishing convent school. (Board, tuition, and washing cost $35.00 per quarter of twelve weeks duration; day pupils paid $3.00.) The good first impression the pastor made—"He is very content, and they are quite content with him"[28]—lasted throughout his four years at St. Anthony. But Father Ledon's health, never sturdy, was undermined by the unfamiliarly harsh climate and by the exertion involved as the flood of immigrants rolled in unabated, in visiting, not infrequently on foot, mission stations as far from St. Anthony as what is now Dayton and Medicine Lake. Cretin hoped to relieve something of his burden by transferring him in 1856 to the cathedral, and, though somewhat paradoxically Ledon sorely missed the enervating labors of his first assignment,[29] his presence in St. Paul afforded him the opportunity to administer the last rites when his friend the bishop died the following year. After that, and after several bouts of illness,[30] Denis Ledon returned to France in the summer of 1859 and served in the parochial ministry in the diocese of Belley till his death twenty-two years later.

The community at Little Canada provides another example of Cretin's need to husband his human resources carefully, and an example too of the difficulties that might arise in the attempt to establish a viable parish. Jean Fayolle, whom the bishop had recruited in France and whom he had ordained a few months after his arrival in 1851, discovered that the rough French Canadians who peopled this village harbored some harsh animosities toward one another, a situation that augured ill for any cooperative efforts. The priest managed, however, to soothe his new parishioners and persuade them to set

27. Cretin to Clemence Cretin, April 20, 1853, AASPM, Cretin Papers.
28. Cretin to Clemence Cretin, August 21, 1851, AASPM, Cretin Papers.
29. Cretin to Clemence Cretin, October 14, 1856, AASPM, Cretin Papers.
30. Ledon to Clemence Cretin, November 5, 1858, AASPM, Cretin Papers.

aside their mutual resentments. "A gentle peace has succeeded to our late deplorable divisions," Fayolle reported. "All appear now to have learned how to bridle their tongues, as becomes good neighbors, and to abstain from those imprudent and bitter expressions which formerly lighted the fires of discord."[31] The immediate result of this harmony was a successful construction project which included the completion of a church building dedicated to St. John the Evangelist and the beginning of a presbytery.

AFTER A COUPLE OF YEARS, HOWEVER, BISHOP CRETIN REQUIRED Jean Fayolle to exchange the tranquility he had achieved in Little Canada for a much more problematic scene. Far away to the northwest—nearly six hundred miles away, in fact, from the Catholic enclaves springing up in the southern regions of Minnesota Territory—along the Red River of the North a mission in precarious circumstances had struggled for survival over decades before the diocese of St. Paul had been instituted. Cretin's responsibility for this distant place arose out of a history not only of the canonical uncertainties so common on the American frontier—and with which, from his experience in Dubuque, he was fully familiar[32]—but also of how a long-standing disagreement about national boundaries had been finally settled.

At the beginning of the century, when the Hudson's Bay Company was pushing its operations west and south, efforts were made by the British to introduce colonists—Scotch-Irish, Irish, and Germans primarily—into what is now southern Manitoba Province. The object of this policy was at once philanthropic and imperialist: hardworking but impoverished farm families brought from over the sea could find, it was argued, a new chance to prosper and fulfill themselves; and, at the same time, they could by their very presence fix the Union Jack firmly into what had been a largely empty land and thereby thwart any American hankering after continental hegemony. The lot of these immigrants did not, however, prove a happy one. Beset by drought and regular infestations of locusts, they watched their crops, season after season, wither in the fields. They had to grapple moreover with the fierce competition between Hudson's Bay and the North West Company over the still

---

31. Jean Fayolle to Joseph Fayolle, October 10, 1852, AASPM, Catholic Historical Society Records.

32. Cretin had served routinely outside the canonical confines of the diocese of Dubuque. Indeed, Galtier's mission in St. Paul was, strictly speaking, uncanonical. See chapter 2, above.

lucrative fur trade, which led to sporadic bouts of violence. Eventually a goodly number of them moved sixty miles or so southward, up the valley of the Red—which, it will be recalled, flows northward—and across the ill-defined frontier between British Canada and the United States, to a trading post called Pembina.[33] Here and nearby a remnant of the old *coureurs des bois* still perdured, a community perhaps three hundred strong characterized by almost universal intermarriage between the French Canadians and the local Native American women. As to the pilgrims from the north, fortune showed herself fickle as she often does, and not a few of them, after subsisting for some years on buffalo meat and wild rice, returned to the original colony around Lake Winnipeg. Those who remained in Pembina and its vicinity naturally adapted to the way of life they found in possession there.

In 1818 the long-debated question between Washington and London about where precisely the line lay between British and American jurisdictions was at last resolved. West of Lake of the Woods, and indeed all the way to the Rockies, the 49th parallel of latitude determined the line between the two entities.[34] By virtue of this agreement Pembina now became definitively part of the United States. But this bureaucratic resolution made little practical difference to the people who actually lived in the region concerned; a line drawn on a map did not discernibly alter their situation, material or spiritual. From the beginning the number of Catholics among the colonists in Manitoba had been statistically significant: indeed, they had been originally accompanied by an Irish priest who, however, did not remain with them long. "Our spiritual wants increase with our numbers," wrote the governor of the settlement, himself a Catholic. "We have many Catholics from Scotland and Ireland, . . . besides those Canadians already with us. . . . A vast religious harvest might also be made among the natives around us."[35] This appeal for missionaries was sent to the far-off bishop of Quebec who responded in 1818—the year of the boundary settlement—by dispatching one Joseph Provencher to establish a permanent mission near Lake Winnipeg. This station, dedicated to St. Boniface, became headquarters during all of Provencher's long and productive life,

---

33. For the disputed boundary line and the competition between Hudson's Bay and North West, see chapter 1, above. The name Pembina may have been derived from two Ojibwe words signifying a meeting place for buffalo-hunting bands. The present town is located in what is now the extreme northeast corner of North Dakota. See the excellent study by James M. Reardon, *George Anthony Belcourt: Pioneer Missionary of the Northwest, 1803–1874* (St. Paul, 1955), 8–11, 100–101.

34. See Blegen, *Minnesota*, 94.

35. Macdonnell to Plessis, April 4, 1816, quoted in Reardon, *Belcourt*, 12.

ultimately a bishopric (1847) and then an archbishopric (1871). Long before that, however, in 1822, Provencher himself was raised to episcopal rank as vicar apostolic of Hudson Bay, and thus became Roman Catholic bishop of all of western Canada—his writ indeed stretched, theoretically, to the North Pole—an area in square miles larger than continental Europe.

But at little Pembina the French trappers and their Ojibwe wives and the remainder of the immigrants from Manitoba, most of them at least nominally Catholics, found themselves, after 1818, in ecclesiastical limbo. An eccentric Canadian Jesuit dwelt among them for a few years, but after that they were left mostly to their own devices. Though Provencher had no canonical responsibility for these new American citizens—and the nearest American bishop was in St. Louis—he sent them a priest whenever he could for a week or a month to say Mass, baptize, hear confessions, regularize sexual liaisons, and otherwise shore up this fragile community of faith. But given the vicar's huge obligations and the paucity of his resources, such occasions were rare. Desperate for money and personnel as were all churchmen in his circumstances, French-born Provencher traveled several times to his native land in search of aid and was moderately successful in doing so. He also heard about a zealous young Canadian priest named Georges Antoine Belcourt.

Son of a Quebecois farmer, representative of a family that had settled in Canada seven generations before, in the mid-seventeenth century, Belcourt had been ordained, aged twenty-four, in 1827. In accord with conventional practice he had during the early years of his ministry assisted as curate in several parishes. In 1830 he was named curé of a congregation near Montreal. From his childhood, however—not unlike Joseph Cretin and the callow Daniel Fisher—he had entertained a romantic ambition to work wondrous deeds of conversion among the aborigines. Bishop Provencher's appeal for priestly aid in the Red River Valley was music to his ears. At first Belcourt's superiors in Quebec forbade his transfer westward, but in the end his own predilections prevailed. In the autumn of 1831 he accompanied Provencher to St. Boniface and began sixteen years of strenuous ministry all across the region. Among the strengths he brought to the mission was his innate linguistic ability: he already spoke English fluently—a rarity among the Quebecois clergy of his time—and he soon showed that the very differently-rooted Native American tongues posed no insuperable obstacles for him. Indeed, as Ravoux was to do later among the Dakota,[36] Belcourt fashioned an Ojibwe grammar and dictionary.

---

36. See chapter 2, above.

This remarkable gift for languages served Belcourt well. So did his immense vitality and his collateral skills. He demonstrated early on the ability of a carpenter and an iron worker and indeed a whole plethora of proficiencies in the material arts that forwarded an apostolate needing above all to demonstrate its permanence. Little churches were built under Belcourt's charge, and schools, most of the skilled labor done by the priest himself. He identified completely with the colonists and the métis he served, even to the extremity of publicly championing their cause when they attempted to challenge the monopoly over the fur trade of the all-powerful Hudson's Bay Company. Besides this bonding with the whites and mixed-bloods, Belcourt's sure and ready ability to communicate with them quickly won him the regard of the Indians, as did his manifest sympathy toward many aspects of their way of life. His toughness and unabashed masculinity appealed to them, and so, when they invited him to join in their great buffalo hunts, he accepted with gusto.

And yet an element of the haphazard clung to Belcourt and his frenetic energy. Projects were taken up with enthusiasm, only to be put aside in favor of something else. He displayed as well authoritarian inclinations which did not sit well with a similarly authoritarian superior. At first Bishop Provencher rejoiced in the dynamism and seemingly tireless dedication of his young recruit. But as the years passed the vicar gradually grew disenchanted. His directives no less than his suggestions seemed to leave little impression upon Belcourt, who went his own restless way and who, the bishop thought, expended too much time and effort on the material demands of his ministry at a cost to the spiritual. When scrutinized carefully, Belcourt's various initiatives and proposals appeared to have produced only meager results. To claim that hunting buffalo with the Indians was a means of converting them smacked, to the bishop, of frivolity. Moreover, always desperately short of money, Provencher, perhaps understandably, exhibited many of the characteristics of a skinflint, and he resented deeply what he considered Belcourt's wasteful ways. His bill of indictment found partial expression in a private letter of the summer of 1841, commenting on Belcourt's latest plans for one of his mission stations.

If I did as I wish at [Baie] St. Paul, I would not undertake to repair, much less complete, the chapel. I'd let it be as it is till it falls down, which won't be long. . . . [Belcourt] intends to finish the basement for an industrial school to make linen from nettles and cloth out of buffalo hair, without reflecting that he has not the essentials of success—teachers and pupils. He is worse off this year. . . . This project will go up in smoke. . . .

He is about to build a house at Baie St. Paul, and for that money will be required.

At issue, aside from differing views of the missionary endeavor and its priorities, was the clash of two rugged individualists—hardly surprising in a milieu in which only the strong could survive. But for Provencher, Father Belcourt's espousal of the campaign against Hudson's Bay—an unwarranted meddling in politics as he saw it—was the last straw. When the regional governor demanded that the archbishop of Quebec recall Belcourt, Provencher could offer only this laconic observation: "If I were in his place, I'd be happy to quit a country where I am not welcome."[37] In the autumn of 1847 George Belcourt duly departed the upper Red River Valley and returned to Montreal. But, neither bowed nor in the least content that his endeavors as a missionary were over, he did not stay there very long.

When in 1837 Mathias Loras was named first bishop of Dubuque, his immense diocese extended northward—it may be recalled—to the Canadian frontier. His immediate concerns, to be sure, centered on service to the little settlements along both banks of the Mississippi, including the one in the shadow of Fort Snelling and the Falls of St. Anthony. But in fact Pembina, located just a few miles south of the 49th parallel, was an American community and therefore also his canonical responsibility. Loras had only the haziest notion of this utterly remote mission, and, even had he had intimate knowledge of it, he could have done nothing to succor it, given the pitiful resources at his disposal. But late in 1847 he received an appeal from George Anthony Belcourt asking for assignment to Pembina and offering as credentials a record of sixteen productive years as a missionary operating out of St. Boniface, Manitoba. For Bishop Loras this proposition was a godsend, almost literally so. Belcourt may have annoyed his Canadian superiors—why and to what degree Loras hardly had the luxury to inquire—but he remained a priest in good standing and one whose experience of the region and its people was unique. Departing Montreal at the beginning of the following year, in a procession of wagons that crossed the plains from Detroit to Milwaukee to St. Paul, Belcourt, endowed with full faculties of the diocese of Dubuque, reached Pembina at the beginning of June 1848.

He stayed there for eleven years and displayed during that span the same qualities, positive and negative, that had marked his earlier career. The verve

---

37. Provencher to Signay (archbishop of Quebec), July 23, 1841, and same to same, June 11, 1847, quoted in Reardon, *Belcourt*, 57, 84.

and inventiveness and the willingness to work with his hands soon made him the leading personality in a community that now approached in numbers a thousand souls up and down the Red River Valley. He refurbished the pathetic little mission buildings that went back in their foundation to the 1820s and added several more. He opened a school which soon attracted upwards of two hundred pupils drawn from among the métis population. He even founded an "order" of nuns, the Sisters of the Propagation of the Faith, seven young mixed-blood women to teach in the school, to offer special instruction to the Ojibwe squaws in the locality, and to bring solace and nursing to the sick. Two or three of these "religious" he sent to a convent in Montreal for a brief indoctrination, while the others—to Belcourt's ultimate undoing[38]— remained at home in Pembina and attached to their families and their former way of life. Meanwhile, he even carried on his earlier feud with the Hudson's Bay Company, drawing up in 1849 a petition signed by a hundred local traders. It protested to the new territorial governor, Alexander Ramsey, the incursion of the Company's agents across the international boundary in a bid both to corner the fur market and, he intimated darkly, to promote British interests in the area. But at the same time the politically astute Father Belcourt kept in touch as carefully with the leader of the Democratic Party, Henry Sibley, as he did with the Whig Ramsey.[39] Indeed, even as he made his way across the trackless prairies on his way to Pembina, he sent a note to Sibley informing him of his ultimate destination and mission.[40]

As for the Indians in the vicinity of Pembina, Belcourt wrote a long report to Loras, in which he maintained—Bishop Provencher would have shaken his head in skepticism—that joining the natives in their pursuit of the buffalo was the best way to bring these primitive sons of the land into conformity with the Christian message. The burden of his argument reflected a charming naïveté: "Unquestionably a priest would, by accompanying the hunters do much good, not only as regards their temporal welfare, but in a moral and religious point of view. His presence would prevent much disorderly conduct. He could catechize the children who are roving from tent to tent."[41] Yet in a later moment of candor Belcourt admitted what, in the end, all the missionaries had to admit: "I am in ignorance as yet [after twenty-one years experience] to the best means of effecting [the Native Americans']

---

38. See chapter 5, below.
39. See chapter 3, above.
40. See Reardon, *Belcourt*, 99, 108–109.
41. Belcourt to Loras, February 16, 1850, printed in *APF* 12 (July 1851): 232–241.

conversion; but I presume it will be necessary for several years to travel about as they do, under the tent, that we may always have them under our eyes."[42]

Still, "unquestionably" was the kind of word that characterized Belcourt's ordinary *modus operandi,* and it also indicated that he would brook no opposition to, or competition with, his settled views. So it was that though he constantly pleaded—to his friends in eastern Canada, to Loras in Dubuque, and, after 1851, to Cretin in St. Paul—for priests to be sent to the Red River region to help him, once they did, disillusion set in all too quickly. Thus the idealistic young Father Albert Lacombe, who had visited with Augustin Ravoux at Mendota on his way to Pembina in 1849,[43] lasted in the latter place only two years. Overcome by what Belcourt portrayed contemptuously as moodiness and depression, Lacombe returned to Montreal, where, while declining to criticize Belcourt explicitly, he stated clearly that he could not possibly serve with him again.[44] Three years later—by which time Belcourt had shifted the headquarters of the mission to St. Joseph, later renamed Walhalla, thirty miles to the west—Bishop Cretin dispatched Jean Fayolle from relatively peaceful Little Canada to Red River. The young man's stay there was mercifully brief, and he was only too happy to retrace his steps southward again and to assume the pastorate at St. Anthony in the place of the ailing Denis Ledon.[45]

Angular and difficult though George Belcourt may have been in his professional relationships, neither his zeal nor his willingness to work was ever in question. Always desperately in need for money, he did not disdain, in the spirit of St. Paul the tent maker, to accept income from his skills as a carpenter and a cabinet maker. He oversaw construction of a saw mill and a flour mill, as well as the installation of a wind-driven threshing machine. But poverty, his own and that of his scattered, motley parishioners, remained the overwhelming fact of life in Pembina. Belcourt's appeals for funds to the Society for the Propagation of the Faith in France went unheeded, due in part, perhaps, to his penchant for strong language and exaggeration.[46] Bishop Loras, from his virtually depleted treasury, advanced Pembina one hundred dollars in 1850, a sum which, in retrospect, may appear a trivial amount but which at that moment may well have spelled the difference between the extinction and the survival of the mission. Joseph Cretin, once Pembina became his respon-

---

42. Belcourt to Cretin, September 13, 1852, AASPM, Cretin Papers.

43. See chapter 2, above.

44. Reardon, *Belcourt,* 116–119.

45. Jean Fayolle to Joseph Fayolle, September 20, 1854, AASPM, Catholic Historical Society Records.

46. See Flahavan, "A Quarter Century of Alms," 26, 68.

sibility after 1851, sought financial support for it from Washington. "Certain sums are commonly granted," he wrote to a friendly United States senator, "to those who cultivate the lands among the Indians." A mere four or five hundred dollars could see the mission through the year. Since the government's Indian policy was so muddled, inequitable, and badly administered, the bishop can be forgiven for stretching the truth a little in presenting his petition.

> One of our missionaries, Mr. Belcourt, a very talented and industrious man, is these twenty-four years among the Chippewa [Ojibwe]. He is the founder of Pembina. The Hudson's Bay Company of the Red River having opposed him, he crossed the English line and came on the land of the United States accompanied by more than eight hundred half-breeds, who left [Manitoba] . . . to become citizens of the United States. His influence is great over all the Indians around. He is a precious man for that colony and for the Government. . . . Could not the Government allow him some pecuniary help?[47]

No federal money was forthcoming, but the mission at Pembina survived, and, for some years yet, so did its tempestuous leader.

JUST AS REMARKABLE IN HIS OWN WAY AS GEORGE BELCOURT, and perhaps even more so, was another priest whose success in converting Native Americans to Christianity—though finally as ephemeral as that of his missionary colleagues, Catholic and Protestant alike—nevertheless earned him at the time special notoriety. Francis Xavier Pierz[48] was fifty years old and twenty-two years ordained when, in 1835, he left his native Slovenia to serve the missions in Michigan Territory. He had been persuaded to exchange a settled and successful parochial ministry at home for an unpredictable future in a strange land largely through the influence of his countryman, Frederic Baraga.[49] The ardent Baraga—later vicar apostolic and first bishop of

---

47. Cretin to Jones, January 18, 1853, AASPM, Cretin Papers. Cretin had come to know Senator George W. Jones of Iowa during his days in Dubuque.

48. See Grace McDonald, "Father Francis Pierz, Missionary," *Minnesota History* 10 (June 1929): 107–125.

49. See Bernard J. Lambert, *Shepherd of the Wilderness: A Biography of Bishop Frederic Baraga* (Sidney, Australia, 1968).

Marquette—had arrived in America five years before, and, thanks to financial support from the Leopoldine Society[50]—the Austrian equivalent of France's Society for the Propagation of the Faith—he succeeded in establishing a string of mission stations in the north of the Territory. He also wielded an eloquent pen, and the pamphlets and little descriptive tracts he sent back to his homeland made a deep impression upon Pierz. When he announced his determination to join Baraga, many associates, including his bishop, tried to dissuade him, arguing that his advanced age and ingrained habits left him ill-prepared to start life anew among a host of savages. But Pierz persisted and ultimately won canonical permission to join the American missions; and, incidentally, he outlived all those who had doubted his capacity. Baraga and the bishop of the two-year-old diocese of Detroit welcomed him with open arms.

Pierz labored in the missions of Michigan for nearly seventeen years, about the same span, that is, as Belcourt, much the younger man, did in Manitoba. Though not as proficient linguistically as the Canadian, Pierz eventually mastered the language of the Ottawas, among whom he primarily worked. And since their tongue was related to that of the Ojibwe, he was able to communicate with the members of this tribe also, when he made several temporary forays along the north shore of Lake Superior, experiences he had found particularly rewarding. Pierz's tale is the typical one of the foreign missionary in Mid-America at this time, one of privation and great courage, of genuine zeal and untroubled faith, of restless energy and stubbornness and a tendency toward impatience whenever contradicted, and an assumption that converting the Indians to Christianity involved "civilizing" them along European lines. For Father Pierz this latter factor had very specific implications. Sprung himself from sturdy peasant stock, he had served in Slovenia in exclusively rural parishes, and he had taken a lively interest in the development of scientific agricultural methods. He took it for granted that the Indians' salvation, and even their physical survival, depended upon making them good Catholic farmers. And indeed at Arbre Croche, his principal mission, he succeeded for a while in creating a serene Ottawa community of blossoming fields and cottage industry. Still, thanks to the white man's greed and the red man's incomprehension, Arbre Croche proved in the end to be a Potemkin village, not because of conscious deceit but because of the incompatibility of two radically diverse cultures. Meanwhile, Pierz himself cheerfully testified to the

---

50. *Die Leopoldinen-Stiftung,* founded specifically to support missions in North America, was set up in 1829, seven years after its French counterpart.

same unambiguous convictions that had sustained the likes of Mazzuchelli, Cretin, Ravoux, Belcourt, and all the others.

> A missioner in America is like a plaything in the hand of God. Sufferings and joys alternate constantly. No conquest for the Kingdom of God can be achieved here without exertion and the sweat of one's brow. . . . I am perfectly content, in the most joyous sense of the word, in my present and very arduous but also consoling field of labor. And I thank the Father of all for having led me with his protecting hand into this great continent, where so much good can be done for the salvation of the souls of others and one's own soul.[51]

Pierz predictably got along well with Frederic Baraga, though he thought his Slovenian mentor less than astute when it came to practical matters. Not that such naiveté was in the eternal scheme of things reprehensible. His "boundless generosity," Pierz confided to Baraga's sister, "will always preserve him in apostolic poverty."[52] The bishops of Detroit, to whom Pierz was canonically responsible, were a different matter. These prelates—Frederic Resé, a north German native and, after 1841, Pierre-Paul Lefèvre, a Belgian, both of them veteran missionaries—never quite measured up to Pierz's episcopal ideal. The altercations between him and them appear trivial taken individually, but in accumulation they amounted to a growing mutual disenchantment. When it became clear to Father Pierz that he had done as much as he could have for the indigenous Ottawa, he began to hanker after the possibility of moving farther west and ministering to the Ojibwe whom he had encountered on earlier occasions during his brief incursions into Grand Portage and its environs. The bishop of Detroit, quite understandably, since he was so desperately short of priests, did not agree. What could Pierz require, so the bishop contended, more than had already been granted him from the bishop's extremely limited resources? Here was one of those classical disputes, not between right and wrong but between right and right. Or, as the overall record of Catholic missionary activity in the American Midwest affirms, an argument between conventional authority, without which Catholicism as a system could not exist, and individual endeavor, without which the gospel could not in fact be preached or the sacraments administered. If in a particular instance

---

51. See William P. Furlan, *In Charity Unfeigned: The Life of Father Francis Xavier Pierz* (St. Cloud, Minn., 1952). The quotation, 84, is from a letter dated May 1, 1836.

52. Quoted in Furlan, *Charity Unfeigned*, 120.

the twain could not meet, then the parties had to accept the inevitable. The bishop of Detroit finally granted Francis Xavier Pierz his formal release.

Joseph Cretin received Pierz, now sixty-eight years old, into his infant diocese in 1852, and in the same spirit and for the same reasons that Loras had originally welcomed George Belcourt. West and north of St. Paul were concentrations of Ojibwe whom Father Pierz was anxious to evangelize— recalling as he did the happy times he had enjoyed among elements of that tribe at Grand Portage and along Pigeon Creek years before. From one Indian encampment to another the Slovenian brought his Mass kit, his Bible, and the other accouterments of his profession, and, as usual, he achieved a certain measure of success. But Pierz was also a realist, in that he recognized that white immigration into Minnesota Territory—as had already occurred in Michigan—would in the end determine the character of society there. In the wake of the scandalous treaties of the early 1850s, the Indians gradually withdrew westward, while white settlers rushed in to assume "squatters' rights" on the hunting grounds thus vacated, especially after 1854, when the Chicago and Rock Island Railroad stretched its line to the east bank of the Mississippi.

As a Slovenian nationalist, young Pierz had resented the Austrian sovereignty over his homeland; but because the Habsburg overlords in Vienna had mandated the curriculum, the schools he attended had endowed him with fluency in spoken and written German. Now, with Cretin's endorsement, he shrewdly put this skill to use in a small propaganda campaign that featured a series of pamphlets and letters published in German newspapers as well as in German American periodicals in such places as Cincinnati and New York, advertising the wondrous benefits to be derived by immigrating to Minnesota Territory. Thanks largely to these efforts the clusters of German Catholics already in and around St. Paul and St. Anthony expanded rapidly and began to spread westward along the Minnesota River—the townsite of New Ulm was laid out in 1855[53]—and northward eighty or a hundred miles toward the fertile land of the Sauk River valley, the very region in which Pierz had been striving to evangelize the Ojibwe.

Nor was the old Slovenian loath to take the credit. "More than fifty German families have already responded to my invitation," he boasted in 1855, "and have settled on government land on both sides of the Sauk River, where

---

53. Germain Kunz, "Diocese of New Ulm," in Patrick H. Ahern, ed., *Catholic Heritage in Minnesota, North Dakota, South Dakota* (St. Paul, 1964), 125.

they have the finest claims with every advantage. Most of them have already put up their houses and fences and are preparing to farm with the blessing of God and with bright prospects for the future." And to what siren song had they responded? "Our splendid prairie and meadowlands," rhapsodized the peasant boy turned veteran missioner, "which can hardly be equaled any-where in the world, produce an immense amount of hay, . . . enough to feed many million head of cattle." Hogs flourished too, and sheep—"Sheep too might be raised here with profit. . . . [They] will grow better wool in a temper-ate than in a torrid zone." As for the produce of the land itself:

> In the past year I saw very fine oats cut at Belle Prairie on the first of Au-gust, and it had been sown at the end of May. We have cucumbers an ell [forty-five inches] in length, melons weighing twenty-eight pounds, cabbages of twenty-four pounds, and eighteen pound rutabagas. Winter wheat yields forty-two bushels to the acre, and one can infer that the rest of the crops are equally good.

But the farmer's craft by no means exhausts the natural bounty. Wild rice abounds, as do cranberries—"A single person can pick from three to five tubs a day"—as well as plums, cherries, gooseberries, currants, blackberries, rasp-berries. The streams are alive with sturgeon, trout, and pike, while "on the prairies the pheasants jump about like grasshoppers. In the woods . . . [are] such game as deer, elk, moose, and bear." And the notoriously cold weather? Here Father Pierz indulged in some equivocation. "Our winter, indeed, is somewhat longer but not more severe than in the southern states." During his three years' residence in Minnesota Territory, he maintained, he experienced only fifteen or twenty cold days and saw no more "than one foot of snow" on the ground. "During the past winter I have seen German settlers at work in their shirt-sleeves, cutting their wood for building and fencing." And so, on the basis of this firsthand evidence, he issued his appeal:

> Several hundred families can still find good claims along the Sauk River, and in the surrounding country no doubt several thousand families can find favorable places for settlement. I do wish, however, that the choicest pieces of land in this delightful Territory would become the property of thrifty Catholics who would make an earthly paradise of this Minnesota which heaven has so richly blessed, and who would bear out the opinion that Germans prove to be the best farmers and the best Christians in America. I am sure that you will likewise do credit to your faith here in

Minnesota; but to prove yourselves good Catholics, do not bring with you any freethinkers, red republicans, atheists, or agitators.[54]

No evidence survives to determine whether or not such undesirables crept into Minnesota Territory under the cover of Father Pierz's invitation. That indomitable missioner himself at any rate, once satisfied that the German Catholic immigration he had sponsored had in fact taken root, returned to the apostolate that had brought him from across the sea in the first place. Until 1873, when he had reached his eighty-eighth year, he continued to serve as best he could the Ojibwe missions he had established along the shore of Mille Lacs at Crow Wing—for which a modern county is named—and, much to the north, those at Red Lake. His constant appeal for priestly help in these endeavors went pretty much unheeded, but the golden jubilee of his ordination to the priesthood was observed in St. Paul in 1865—two years after the fact—with appropriate pomp. Even so, Pierz's incredible stamina took him back to his original commitment and into the primitive confines that had intrigued him all those years ago as a callow youth in the Slovenian seminary of Ljubljana. Little by little, however, his physical powers failed—"During the past year [1872] my eyesight has failed me so that I am not able to read newspapers any longer"—and a year later the remarkable career came to an end. He returned to his Slovenian home, and, in 1880, in his ninety-sixth year, he died. Toward the end he experienced some confusion of mind: he was known on occasion, for example, to hail a taxi on the streets of his native Kamnik "and request the driver to take him to Wabasha or some Indian mission he attended in America." Perhaps such senile preoccupation was itself tribute to what he had accomplished.[55]

FRANCIS XAVIER PIERZ'S ACCOMPLISHMENTS, HOWEVER, NEED TO be viewed with a measure of discrimination. By the nature of the role he played, the endeavors of the lone missionary in Mid-America, particularly one who labored exclusively among those whose culture was fast disappearing, necessarily betray a transient character. Augustin Ravoux provides a case in point. His ambition—certainly a noble one as he judged it—was to serve

---

54. Quotations are taken from a lengthy appendix Pierz added to his *Die Indianer in Nord-Amerika* (St. Louis, 1855). For a translation see Furlan, *Charity Unfeigned,* 245–256.

55. See Furlan, *Charity Unfeigned,* 226–240.

and convert the Indians to Christianity; but the long-term significance of his apostolate rests upon a shrewd real estate transaction he negotiated in a town where the Indians were not welcome[56]—and, needless to say, upon all sorts of priestly ministrations he performed over the half century that followed. Pierz for his part, that sturdy and single-minded individualist, never slackened in his zealous striving to effect the conversion of his beloved Ojibwe, even when he was very old and practically blind. But the Native Americans, misunderstood, disdained, and cruelly displaced, went away, and, toward the very end of his life, so did Pierz, a kind of charming and romantic will o' the wisp. Nevertheless, because he added to his work among the Indians a program to promote German Catholic immigration into Minnesota Territory, his ministry did bequeath a lasting testament: the settlers from Bavaria and the Rhineland had remained, as had Augustin Ravoux. The difference was monumental. In the real world Catholicism depends for its very existence upon a coherent institutional permanence. And this is why Bishop Cretin's invitation to German-speaking Benedictines to come to Minnesota Territory, eventually to establish a monastery, and so to carry on Pierz's apostolate, was matched in historical import only by his similarly successful entreaty to the Sisters of St. Joseph from Carondelet.

Catholic Slovenia, during Francis Pierz's youth, had felt the almost cosmic tremors set in motion by Napoleon Bonaparte's military and political successes. And so had Catholic Bavaria.[57] French ascendancy meant the imposition of the liberal principles of the Revolution of 1789, so long as those principles did not interfere with Napoleon's personal ambitions. One result was the widespread suppression of the religious orders and the confiscation of their property and endowments. No congregation suffered more in this regard than did the most ancient and venerable, the Benedictines. When the ruthless policy of secularization was finished, barely thirty abbeys remained of the hundreds upon hundreds that had flourished in western Europe for more than a thousand years. Among the Bavarian houses shut down was that of Metten, founded on the banks of the Danube in 792, during the reign of Charlemagne. Of Metten's twenty-three monks thus expelled, some simply disappeared, while others, if they had been ordained, found what employment they could as parish priests.

---

56. See chapter 2, above.

57. For what follows see Colman J. Barry, *Worship and Work* (Collegeville, Minn., 1956), 5–17.

But as tyrants often do, Napoleon overreached himself, and defeats at Moscow, Leipzig, and Waterloo wrote finis to his grand strategy of conquest and domination. There followed a reaction which assumed many forms, not least among them a religious revival that affected all the Christian denominations.[58] In Bavaria a king came to the throne unfettered as his predecessor had been by connections to the revolutionary contempt for religion or to the Napoleonic obsession to keep religion firmly under the state's thumb. Ludwig I, a cultivated as well as a pious man, held special regard for the Benedictine tradition, and in 1830, under his patronage, Metten reopened. Two of the original monks, now old men, took up residence there again, and two years later they were joined by five novices.

Among these latter was a young secular priest from Ratisbon named Sebastian Wimmer. For a decade he played a not insignificant part in the restoration of Benedictinism in the German-speaking lands of Europe. But little by little, particularly as he studied the reports of missionaries in the New World, he came to believe that that restoration should not be confined to the Old. Though he received scant encouragement at first, once again the king of Bavaria intervened decisively. The establishment in 1838 of the Ludwig Missionsverein, the Bavarian counterpart to the mission societies already active in France and Austria,[59] meant the availability of funds and of continuing support for the venture Wimmer had in mind. Mixed in with his conventional zeal was a conviction, not out of harmony with nineteenth-century nationalism, that German Catholic immigrants in the United States were being routinely neglected by their largely French and Irish bishops. Whatever the justice of this contention, the widespread perception of it guaranteed Wimmer—who, significantly, chose Boniface for his name in religion, in memory of the eighth-century monk honored as "the Apostle of Germany"— a sympathetic hearing in his homeland. A monastery with a school attached, and with personnel able to provide parochial ministry, could offer the religious permanence and stability German American communities were in need of. If Benedictine monks traditionally stood for anything, they stood for permanence and stability. In the summer of 1846, Father Boniface, accompanied by four aspirants to the priesthood and fourteen to the brotherhood, landed in New York.

---

58. For the contemporaneous revival in the west of France, see O'Connell, *Sorin*, 6–16.

59. See note 50, above.

After a false start or two, they settled on a property ceded to them by the bishop of the newly instituted diocese of Pittsburgh—Mount St. Vincent, it was called. They endured all the usual vicissitudes that other European missionaries encountered: the homesickness, the inability to speak English, the backbreaking work of clearing fields and nurturing orchards, the utter poverty which left them vulnerable to the harshest whims of nature: "We froze even under the woolen coverlings" on mattresses stuffed with straw and strung out under the leaky roof of a log shack. There was trouble too with the Irish bishop of Pittsburgh, who characteristically resisted the independence of exempt religious within his jurisdiction[60] and who, as a teetotaler, was scandalized by Wimmer's insistence that the German monks, especially the elderly, needed to have beer accessible to their diet and indeed to maintain a brewery under their direction. But, inspired by Wimmer's relentless and sometimes ruthless leadership, these obstacles did not prevent St. Vincent's from flourishing. By the early winter of 1856 Abbot Boniface—Pope Pius IX

---

60. Specialized personnel within the Roman Catholic Church have been traditionally divided into two broad groups. The "secular" or "diocesan" clergy were ordained priests directly subject to the jurisdiction of a diocesan bishop; they were attached to the diocese itself and served only within its geographical limits. Their normal function was to staff the parishes within the diocese, though they were not infrequently assigned some different work like teaching or diocesan administration. They took no vows, but upon ordination they solemnly promised to obey their bishop and to remain unmarried, thus theoretically retaining scope and freedom to perform their parochial duties in the fullest possible way. There were no restrictions upon them as to the ownership of property.

"Religious" belonged to a larger category, which included ordained priests as well as nuns and brothers who had not received the sacrament of order. All religious, ordained or not, took the classic vows of poverty, chastity, and obedience. Benedictines from time immemorial added to these obligations the vow of stability, whereby they agreed to abide in the community in which they had been professed. All religious theoretically found in the fulfillment of these commitments their ordinary means of sanctification. They were also called "regulars," from the Latin *regula* or "rule" fashioned by a founder, who imposed requirements and recommendations concerning priorities and lifestyle, by virtue of which each group of religious was distinguished from another—Dominicans, Franciscans, Jesuits, Redemptorists, and the rest. The long-established religious orders—among them the Benedictines, the most venerable of them all—were international corporations and maintained a headquarters in Rome, where they dealt directly with Vatican officials. They enjoyed what the Church's canon law labeled an "exempt" status in the dioceses in which they served. The result was an inevitable tension between them and the diocesan bishops, though differences were for the most part eventually worked out.

the year before declared St. Vincent's a full-fledged monastery, the first in the United States—could number the professed members in his community at nearly a hundred, and could consider the petitions for Benedictine foundations from various bishops in the Midwest a heartening sanction of his original ambition. From among those solicitations Wimmer and his confreres, with admirable courage, chose to establish a priory[61] in the most remote and difficult of the missions open to them.

Late in the evening of May 2, 1856, five monks disembarked from the steamer *Minnesota Belle* onto the levee in St. Paul.[62] The voyage upriver from St. Louis had taken a hard eleven days over a Mississippi swollen by tempestuous rains and cluttered with floating debris. Two of the party, Bruno Riess and Cornelius Wittman, were clerics shortly to be ordained priests, and two were brothers, Benno Muckenthaler and Patrick Greil; all four were natives of Bavaria. Their superior, the prior, was one of the more exotic figures to grace the early Minnesota scene. Father Demetrius di Marogna, a muscular and comely man of fifty-three, carried himself with all the aplomb of his patrician background. Born into the Veronese aristocracy, Carlo Giuseppe di Marogna as a young boy had served as a page at the court of the Grand Duke of Tuscany in Florence. In 1809 the family removed from Italy to Germany—another indication of the unstable social circumstances unleashed, even for the prominent and well-fixed, by Napoleon—and settled near Frankfurt-am-Main. When he was twenty-three Carlo was ordained for the diocese of Augsburg, and for the next two decades he ministered to various parishes there and elsewhere in Germany. But he too, like Pierz and Wimmer, was a restless man, and he too had been enthralled by the accounts he read of the missionaries in America. Again like Wimmer, he also accepted as true the allegation that the spiritual needs of German Catholic immigrants were not adequately attended to by the American hierarchy. In 1847 he gained release from his bishop, crossed the sea, and ultimately went to work in the diocese of Chicago. The service Marogna provided them won him warm plaudits from the German Catholics in various communities across Illinois, but he often found himself at odds with the local clergy, especially the Irish, over jurisdictional matters. By 1852 he had decided that the itinerant individual missionary, without insti-

---

61. Traditionally a "prior" was the officer in a monastery second in rank to the abbot. Later Benedictine usage extended the meaning to a monk who headed a house—a "priory"—founded by and dependent on an older monastic institution.

62. For a brief but informative overview, see Vincent Tegeder, "The Benedictines in Frontier Minnesota," *Minnesota History* 32 (Spring 1951): 34–43.

tutional support, could not do an effective job, that "the secular priest seems like a skiff coursing upon high sea and in constant danger of being wrecked on some hidden rock."[63] He therefore applied for entry into St. Vincent's, where Boniface Wimmer gave him warm welcome. So, once the preliminaries of postulancy and novitiate were satisfied—much foreshortened in this instance—Carlo was exchanged for Demetrius, and Marogna, with his severe features, deep-set eyes, and luxuriant gray beard contrasting with the flowing black habit he now wore, appeared the very model of a Benedictine monk.

From the beginning of their association Wimmer placed Marogna in positions of authority and trust—understandable enough, given the latter's age and experience, as well, perhaps, as his social standing. This did not always sit well with other members of the abbey, some of whom resented their new confrere's sometimes peremptory style. Nevertheless, when the decision was reached to accept Bishop Cretin's invitation, Father Demetrius was the logical—indeed, the only—choice to head the enterprise. Nor did he fail to make a positive impression once he and his companions had arrived in St. Paul: his patriarchal appearance, his elegant manners, his knowledge of languages—on his first Sunday in the town he preached in English at the cathedral and in German at the Assumption—his obvious zeal for the task ahead, all these combined to gain him approval all round during his brief stopover.

The stay in St. Paul was rather stressful, however, for the two clerics, Riess and Wittman. Cretin had agreed to ordain them to the priesthood, with Wimmer's assurance that they had completed their seminary course at St. Vincent's. But this frontier bishop, a product of Saint-Sulpice in Paris, was a stickler when it came to judging the theological training of candidates for ordination—as Daniel Fisher had learned to his annoyance. Cretin conducted Riess's and Wittman's examination himself, and he was not pleased. "The results were mediocre," Marogna admitted, "and their clumsy manners were still more disturbing. The bishop was so disturbed that he perspired." Upon Marogna's promise that he "would continue their instruction," Cretin consented to give the young men a second hearing. Apparently he was not the only one who perspired. "First there was a question of Moral theology," Riess remembered, "then in Church History, Dogma, Canon Law, Holy Scripture of the New and Old Testament, and especially Liturgy. He demands quick answers. . . . If the first word of the answer doesn't hit the last word of the question, then he answers himself. He is quite a strict moralist and especially strict

---

63. Quoted in Barry, *Worship,* 26.

in liturgy."[64] The results of this examination were more satisfactory, and on Trinity Sunday, May 18, 1856, Bruno Riess and Cornelius Wittman were ordained priests. During the modest banquet that followed the ceremony, Bishop Cretin observed wistfully that if he could ordain five Benedictines a year for five years his diocese would achieve a solid footing.

Had he had his way, he would have kept the five Benedictines at hand in St. Paul—indeed, he offered them thirty acres of land within the precincts of the town—or, if not that, then he urged them to turn their eyes toward the growing settlements in the Minnesota River valley. But, as Father Demetrius gently pointed out, monks are farmers, not city dwellers. As for the other suggested sites, like Shakopee or Stillwater, these were set aside in favor of the region first recommended by Francis Pierz. Accordingly, the morning after the ordination, May 19, the five set out northward on the eighty-mile trek that would take them to the confluence of the Mississippi and Sauk rivers. Bishop Cretin, not at all distressed by their choice, accompanied them; here was at least one French-born prelate of whom the Germans could not complain. Their final destination encompassed two hamlets, Sauk Rapids on the east bank of the river juncture, and St. Cloud on the west. In Sauk Rapids they found the log chapel built by Father Pierz, who had left there a written list of its accouterments, including "my personal property as a present to Fr. Prior: 1 altar picture of the Assumption, 1 altar cloth, 2 altar hangings, 2 candle sticks, 1 altar bell, 1 Mass vestment, alb with amice and cincture, 2 Mass cruets," all from "your friend, F. Pierz."

With few exceptions the German Catholics who had heeded Pierz's counsel and settled in the area in increasing numbers welcomed the Benedictines warmly. Most notable among them were two bachelor brothers named Rothkopp who had immigrated from the Rhineland in 1854 and who had "squatted" on 320 acres of formerly Winnebago land on the west bank of the Mississippi, just south of St. Cloud. They were intensely religious men, though eccentric and stubbornly resistant to adapting to American ways. They had been offered $3,000 for their claims by a St. Cloud business man, but, after a visit with Father Bruno Riess, they expressed their intention to donate their holdings to the monastic community, in return for board, room, and other necessities during their lifetime. Marogna accepted their proposal, and the deeds were duly registered by the clerk of court of the recently formed

---

64. Quoted in Barry, *Worship*, 30. In fairness it should be noted that the first examination was conducted in English and the second in Latin, neither of them the native language of the candidates.

Stearns County, with the pledge that the Benedictines would pay $400 for the holding—the usual $1.25 an acre for federal land—once the government in Washington put these properties up for formal sale. By the beginning of June 1856, the five monks had moved in with the Rothkopps in the two primitive cabins already erected on the claim and had begun work to link them across a front seventy-two feet in length that would include a chapel and a kitchen. Here was the priory, placed under the patronage of St. John the Baptist, as St. Benedict's Monte Cassino had been. Much of the labor on this project was done by Brothers Benno and Patrick, and help was furnished by Catholic volunteers from St. Cloud and Sauk Rapids.

But money was also spent, exorbitantly, Demetrius's young colleagues thought, in hiring more skilled workers from the surrounding communities. The monks had brought with them from Pennsylvania necessary pieces of furniture and trunks of books and liturgical paraphernalia valued at perhaps $1,500, and the prior had had at his discretion $540 in cash from Abbot Boniface for traveling expenses. This latter sum was almost gone, but not his associates' suspicion that he had expended their resources too freely. Combined with this skepticism was the uneasy feeling that Marogna's noble antecedents had left him less than able to deal with the essentially democratic Benedictine ethos, which, it might have been argued, bore at least some resemblance to the spirit prevailing on the American frontier. After all, though he was a man in late middle age, the prior had been a monk for only a couple of years, hardly longer than Riess or Wittman. Marogna's lack of business acumen resulted in unacceptable debts, and his disdainful failure to honor the legal niceties of his adopted country would cause a worse predicament shortly afterward. But it was his reluctance to consult with his brethren that occasioned the most resentment.

Such in-house tensions were complicated by a larger structural problem directly associated with the missionary enterprise. At the heart of traditional Benedictinism, enshrined in the founder's *Holy Rule,* lay a profound sense of community, of familial interdependence. Like-minded men came together in a particular place to pray and to work together; indeed, the motto attributed to St. Benedict, *laborare est orare,* to work is to pray, suggested that the two activities melded into one. This was not to deny, however, the centrality of formal prayer: the *Rule* decreed that the monk's primary obligation was the daily recitation in choir of the psalms, hymns, and lessons of the eight "hours"[65] of the Divine Office. But this *opus Dei,* this work of God, was a

---

65. Matins, lauds, prime, terce, sext, none, vespers, and compline.

communal exercise, not a private or individualistic one, and, as it assumed a measure of cloister, it also imposed a certain removal from the kind of ministry routinely carried on by the secular clergy. Yet Bishop Cretin, with Abbot Wimmer's agreement, had assigned to the monks responsibility for six mission stations set up by Francis Pierz and scattered over an area of six hundred square miles. And every day, it seemed, another group of German Catholic families arrived to stake their claims in the Sauk River valley. The remarkable achievement of the founding monks of St. John's and their immediate successors was to adjust the Benedictine ideal to the realities of the fluid American frontier without sacrificing the essence of that ideal. Parishes were established in Sauk Rapids, St. Joseph, and St. Cloud—there were already two hundred Catholics in St. Cloud—and outlying stations were attended to regularly, increasingly so as personnel expanded. Schools were opened, necessarily small and crude at first, but, even so, in accord with an ancient Benedictine tradition.[66] Though it took a fierce partisan struggle and tireless lobbying by Demetrius Marogna—who managed to persuade a few Republicans to join the sympathetic Democrats—a charter for a seminary was obtained from the territorial legislature, and so St. John's became the first Catholic institution of higher learning in Minnesota. But in the midst of these hectic comings and goings the *opus Dei* was not neglected, far from it. "Although we were but three priests," Bruno Riess recalled in his old age,

> [and] worked hard throughout the day and had poor fare, choir was never intermitted, even if only two priests were at home [at the priory]. And this exertion, I must confess, did not shorten the life of any of us. Two of us are still alive [in 1889], and Father Demetrius, in spite of the effort choir attendance cost him, reached a venerable age. Let the rising generation remember that the service of God does not shorten life.[67]

Father Bruno, young, strong, perhaps even headstrong, gave definition to these early monks of St. John's in a way the austere and rather remote Father

---

66. See John Henry Newman, "The Mission of St. Benedict" (1858) and "Benedictine Schools" (1859). These much-neglected articles are now available under the title *Rise and Progress of Universities and Benedictine Essays* (Notre Dame, Ind., 2001), 365–487. See especially the introduction by Mary Katherine Tillman, xii–lxxvi.

67. Quoted in Barry, *Worship*, 43. The three priests as "choir monks" recited the Office in chapel, while the two brothers—were they literate?—prayed the rosary in the kitchen or elsewhere.

Demetrius could not. And he was shrewd, too. Indeed, by scoring a coup reminiscent of Augustin Ravoux's acquisition of the twenty-one lots in downtown St. Paul,[68] it might be said that he was the savior of what was to become in time the largest Benedictine foundation in the world. To the west of St. Cloud lay a parcel of land dubbed Indianbush, because the local Ojibwe, now gone, had often hunted there. Riess realized immediately that its upwards of 2,000 lush acres of meadow, timber, and water were an ideal setting for a monastic community, particularly one which aimed to support someday a seminary and perhaps a university. He prudently saw to it that little shacks were thrown up all over the property, thus signaling the claim of squatters' rights to what was still technically federal land. This initiative proved crucial when, a few years later, a sharp real estate speculator in St. Cloud filed a complaint in the courts that the Rothkopp brothers' transfer of their claim to the Benedictines had been legally flawed, that in fact the Rothkopps themselves, notoriously suspicious of and resistant to an unfamiliar judicial system, had never secured legitimate title to the river front property. Nor had Marogna been alert enough to foresee the crisis their recalcitrance would bring about. The litigation dragged on from magistrate to judge to commissioner well into the next decade, until the Secretary of the Interior in Washington finally ruled against the Benedictine claim.[69]

It was a severe blow, but in the long run a blessing in disguise. For nearby lay the splendor of Indianbush.

IF THE REFINED DEMETRIUS MAROGNA REPRESENTED THE EXOTIC on the Minnesota frontier, Francesco di Vivaldi represented the bizarre. Born in 1824 like Marogna into the lesser Italian nobility, Vivaldi had been ordained in his early twenties and, through his family's social connections, had been appointed canon of the cathedral in Ventimiglia on the coast of Savoy, near Monaco. He edited a local journal for awhile, but during the revolutionary turmoil of 1848 he fell afoul of one faction or another—which cannot be determined precisely; specifics were always hard to come by in Vivaldi's case— and he was expelled from the principality. He traveled into southeastern France and came to rest, again mysteriously, in the vicinity of Montluel, Joseph Cretin's birthplace. There this tall and strikingly handsome man, so imbued with charming *savoir faire*, cultivated Cretin's sister, Clemence, and his

---

68. See chapter 2, above.
69. Barry, *Worship*, 50–51, 77.

niece, Marie. (Indeed, the time would come when the bishop would advise his female relations to curtail their communications with Vivaldi.[70]) Once Cretin had overcome his hesitations and accepted the call to Minnesota Territory,[71] he spent some months after his consecration scouring his home region for funds and clerical recruits. Among the latter was an enthusiastic Vivaldi. The new bishop could not but rejoice at having enlisted for his demanding apostolate a priest with such blue blood and such a plethora of apparent talents. So it was that when Ravoux welcomed Cretin and his entourage to St. Paul on July 2, 1851, the sometime canon of Ventimiglia was among the party.

Toward the end of the year Cretin, never forgetful of his responsibility to convert and civilize "these poor savages," assigned Vivaldi to the Winnebago reservation at Long Prairie, some 120 miles north of St. Paul. To this relatively small tribe, cruelly displaced by the federal government from Wisconsin to Iowa and now located in mid-Minnesota as a buffer, so to speak, between the dominant and mutually hostile Dakota and Ojibwe, the bishop felt particularly accountable, since his earlier attempts to minister to them in Iowa had been largely rebuffed. Vivaldi was accompanied by Sister Scholastica Vasques, who was to open a school for Winnebago children; she was joined on the mission the following summer by a second nun, a young recruit from Carondelet. Meanwhile Bishop Cretin tried to come to terms with the largest obstacle to success, the chronic shortage of funds. The federal government budgeted $12,000 for the education of the Indians still living in Minnesota Territory, and the bishop determined to secure some share of it. In the spring of 1852, he traveled to Baltimore to attend the first plenary council of the American hierarchy. He then made the short trip to Washington, having first asked his friend, Senator Jones of Iowa, to pave the way for him. "Your influence may be very useful to the object of my visit. I entertain no doubt that you [can] help me to obtain from the Department of Indian Affairs for our Missionaries the same privileges that are granted to those of other denominations. The Government cannot be ignorant that these Indians . . . and their half-breeds have repeatedly asked for Catholic missionaries."[72] Jones succeeded at least to the extent that President Millard Fillmore granted the bishop of St. Paul an interview. But the same privilege had been offered the Protestants, who, Cre-

---

70. Cretin to Clemence Cretin, June 23, 1852, and Cretin to Marie Cretin, January 19, 1855, AASPM, Cretin Papers.

71. See chapter 3, above.

72. Cretin to Jones, May 16, 1852, AASPM, Cretin Papers.

tin reported to the Society for the Propagation of the Faith in Paris, "have presented themselves for three days to the President to the number of 150 and they have reminded him that this country is *Protestant*. I have seen the President, and I am convinced that he would like to oblige the Catholics, but he does not wish to displease the Protestants. So far he has given me only promises." Then the usually apolitical Cretin added an afterthought: "We can intimidate the President by giving publicity to the denial of justice to the savages. The Catholic vote is beginning to hold the balance in elections. They do not dare to disregard it."[73]

Whether or not such electoral considerations played a role in the decision, the bishop won his point. In the summer of 1852 the government awarded him a five-year contract for support of a school for the Winnebagoes at Long Prairie. The terms called for a seventy-five dollar annual subsidy for each enrolled child between the ages of five and eighteen. "According to their Treaty," remembered one sister who taught in the school for a time, "each pupil received a certain amount of flour, pork, blankets, and everything needed for food and raiment. Each of us received $40 per month, the Superintendent $60 per month. . . . All of which came out of school funds."[74] Cretin was duly grateful to "President Fillemore [sic]" and to Senator Jones, to whom he wrote:

I have appointed for Superintendent of this school an excellent clergyman, the Rev. M. de [sic] Vivaldi, an accomplished scholar and gentleman, who has a great influence over the Half-Breeds and the Indians. He had a high position in Piedmont, even in civil matters, being the head of a Newspaper. I have sent two Sisters of St. Joseph who do a great deal of good among these Indians. They are very much respected.[75]

Though at first the arrangement at Long Prairie appeared to promise well, trouble soon arose in the person of Abram Fridley, the agent on scene of the Bureau of Indian Affairs. Fridley's complaint, directed to Governor Ramsey, was basically ideological, although his personal dislike of Vivaldi was hardly obscured. Education for the Indians, the agent argued, should be based on practicality. "Manual labor becomes the principal object of instruction and secondary to this is a reasonable devotion to litterary [sic] pursuits with a

73. Cretin to SPF, AASPM, SPF Papers.
74. Sister Ursula Murphy, quoted in Hurley, *On Good Ground*, 50.
75. Cretin to Jones, January 18, 1853, AASPM, Cretin Papers.

view to learning the scholars the English language, with moral and religious teachings as an auxiliary. . . . It is futile to begin civilization among Indians by attempting to force on there benighted understanding mysterios truths which no previos habits of there minds or bodies has prepared them to receive or comprehend aright." Not too sure-footed in a "litterary" way himself, Fridley nevertheless made the valid point that one hundred and fifty years of Catholic proselytizing among native Americans, and fifty years of Protestant, had left "no monument of piety or civilization or belief to their descendants."[76] Long Prairie thus became a house divided, and Fridley and Vivaldi exchanged barbs in correspondence with the governor, in the public press, and in person.

The canon won this first skirmish: Fridley was dismissed in the summer of 1853. "So you see," Cretin told Vivaldi, "God does not treat with impunity those trustees of public authority who do not act in good faith. Learn to have greater trust in God. All will go better than you think."[77] All, however, did not go well. Fridley's replacement proved similarly hostile. Moreover, bureaucratic sluggishness resulted in late government payment, so that the bishop had to dip into his scanty resources to keep the Winnebago project afloat. But worse was the increasingly erratic behavior of Vivaldi. By that same summer Cretin had begun to suspect that the canon might be playing fast and loose with the mission's finances. Of the required financial reports, Cretin complained, "I have received nothing, notwithstanding my repeated requests. You need not be surprised at my astonishment; I remained here all during the month of July [1853] to dispose of the financial matter and to bring you the balance which is due to you. Is it possible that you do not feel responsible in this matter? I am equally surprised that the Sisters have not written me a single word, notwithstanding my well-known wishes and my repeated requests."[78] In fact Father di Vivaldi was running up a score of debts which ultimately amounted to $4,000, an immense sum given the diocese's empty coffers. Still the bishop continued to hope for the best and to do his part: "I am sending you one quarter's worth of first-rate pork," the bishop announced in the summer of 1853, "plus three crates addressed to you and one barrel of nails. I wanted to send you flour and some hens which arrived for you from Galena [Illinois], but the driver didn't want to take on those extra items; he

---

76. Quoted in Hurley, *On Good Ground*, 42–43.
77. Cretin to Vivaldi, July 15, 1853, AASPM, Cretin Papers.
78. Cretin to Vivaldi, July 30, 1853, AASPM, Cretin Papers.

was overloaded as it was. Please write! Are you not speaking with St. Paul? I hope you are not setting out to prove the proverb *qui multum peregrinatus* [he who wanders much]."[79] But nothing came from Long Prairie but resounding silence.

In November the bishop made a visitation to the Winnebago reservation and had an awkward and embarrassing interview with the Indian agent. "Not having received your reports is a nuisance," he scolded Vivaldi a month later. "Please be accurate in your accounting; do not repeat what you did in your reports [last month] which left me looking very confused in front of the agent after I had assured him that everything was correct. He found references to items which were identified as donated but which had never been donated." And what did the canon know, Cretin wondered, about accusations registered at the Propagation's headquarters in Paris "regarding how our allocated funds have been spent. I do not know where the complaints came from. What I do know is that the originator of the complaints is doing a bad turn to the mission. This will have the effect of reducing by much on which we could have depended otherwise."[80] Perhaps the bishop suspected even then that Vivaldi was the "originator," as indeed he was.

But much worse than sloppy bookkeeping or ill-intentioned gossip spread abroad was about to be revealed. In the spring of 1855, the Winnebagoes were removed from Long Prairie—a wretched, swampy place, infested by mosquitoes and vermin—to a reservation near Blue Earth, in the Minnesota River valley. In the course of this proceeding it gradually came to light that Vivaldi, to line his own pockets, had systematically withheld food and other necessities from the Indian children that Cretin's contract with the government had called for. Needless to say, the contract was *ipso facto* negated. Vivaldi tried for a while to brazen his way out of the scandal: at Blue Earth he would set up a Native American utopia—to be called "Piopolis" in honor of the pope—where his auxiliaries would be the "Sisters of the Love of God," a group of mixed-blood women he had gathered round him, ten times more spiritual and unselfish, he said, than the Sisters of St. Joseph. This charade, however, quickly melted away, and by the end of the year Vivaldi was on the run. He hoodwinked the bishop of Milwaukee for a brief period into assigning him to a pastorate, until that prelate received a stern warning lest the scapegrace "might not involve you and others in so many difficulties as he has our good bishop and others in the diocese of Minnesota. Reverend canon de

---

79. Cretin to Vivaldi, n.d. [Summer 1853], AASPM, Cretin Papers.
80. Cretin to Vivaldi, December 18, 1853, AASPM, Cretin Papers.

[sic] Vivaldi," Augustin Ravoux continued, writing in his capacity as vicar general, "with his good, sweet, and polite manner has been very imprudent, and by his imprudence he has been the cause of many evils." Debts, theft, ill-treatment of the Sisters of St. Joseph who labored under his supervision—ultimately "they were forbidden by their Superior of [sic] St. Louis to go to any mission under his direction. More than once he caused disturbance in the house of our good bishop. . . . He desired too much his own elevation!"[81]

L'affaire Vivaldi was the bitterest disappointment Cretin endured during his years in Minnesota, not least because it underscored the ruin of the dream that had brought him to America in the first place. "It is true," he told Bishop Loras just before Vivaldi absconded from Blue Earth, "that he has many savage children at his school. But it is the hunger that attracts them and the provisions which they receive. He does not occupy himself with their Christian instruction."[82] Shortly afterward he learned that Vivaldi had also stolen the provisions. By the late spring of 1856 Joseph Cretin's disillusionment was complete. "I do not know where this priest is," he explained to the gentlemen of the Propagation in Lyons.

> I believe he has fled. Should his debts not be paid for, horrible imprecations will be vomited against our holy religion by poor families he has ruined and by his Indians. I cannot consent to keep up that mission of the Winnebagoes, as then I should be obliged to pay all the [additional] debts contracted, which is quite impossible for me to do. May your society have pity on me in such a sad circumstance.[83]

As for the balance of the career of the erstwhile canon of Ventimiglia, it was not without its piquancy. In 1858 he married a wealthy widow, then went off to Kansas and purchased a small-town newspaper. During the campaign 1860 his editorials strongly supported Mr. Lincoln and other Republican candidates, the reward for which was appointment the next year as United States consul in an obscure port in southern Brazil. By 1870 he had settled in Rio de Janeiro, and the consulate, of such little significance, had been closed down. In 1882 he left his wife and daughter in Rio to take, he said, a sentimental journey to his old haunts in the south of the country; they never heard from

---

81. Ravoux to Henni, June 5, 1856, AASPM, Ravoux Papers.
82. Cretin to Loras, Christmas, 1855, quoted in Hoffmann, *Church Founders*, 340.
83. Cretin to SPF, June 1, 1856, AASPM, SPF Papers.

him again. In 1883 Vivaldi, now in his sixtieth year, turned up on the doorstep of the archbishop of Buenos Aires and applied for readmittance to the priesthood. The charm had apparently not vanished with age, and before long he had secured reinstatement and indeed prominence as a missionary among the Indians of southern Argentina. The illusions of grandeur had not vanished either, nor the taste for intrigue. In 1892 Father di Vivaldi (as canonically he was again entitled to designate himself) was in Rome lobbying the papal curia for an Argentine bishopric. He did not succeed in that venture, but he did by chance—small world—meet the archbishop of St. Paul, who was also in Rome seeking the pope's approval of his Faribault school plan.[84] John Ireland, always interested in lore from the pioneer days of the diocese he now headed—he was planning to write a biography of Joseph Cretin—found the white-haired old scalawag and his stories fascinating, especially when Vivaldi revealed that he possessed a cache of Cretin's letters which he would cheerfully hand over to Cretin's successor. In the course of their conversations the archbishop mentioned the imminence of a litigation pending in St. Cloud concerning a parcel of land in which in the old days at Long Prairie Vivaldi had acquired some interest. He immediately set off for Minnesota and, to the kindly amusement of the people of St. Cloud, zestfully filed his suit. "The Patagonian Prelate," as one newspaper dubbed him, predictably lost the case. He disappeared from view after that, until 1911, when Ireland heard that he was living in a hostel for the poor in Paris conducted by the Sisters of Charity. The archbishop promptly sent the dying old man a bank draft—a characteristic *beau geste* that seemed to close a tortuous and mysterious circle.[85]

---

84. See chapter 13, below.

85. Compare the account of Vivaldi's latter years in Hoffmann, *Church Founders*, 340–342, with the fuller, less romanticized, and more credible account in Hurley, *On Good Ground*, 60–63.

CHAPTER 5

The Passing
of the Torch

BISHOP CRETIN DESCRIBED HIM AS "ONE OF OUR MOST RESPECTED
citizens and an edifying member of our Catholic congregation," and Auguste
Larpenteur no doubt deserved such accolades. But he represented as well a
melding together within the Catholic community in St. Paul of the old French
Canadian strain, the recent Irish and German immigrants, and a newer, more
native element. For, though his surname and paternal ancestry were French,
Larpenteur was born in America of a woman herself American-born, and he
married an American wife. Not that the process of amalgamation was all that
abrupt: as a young man Auguste had been a fur trader, and when he settled in
Minnesota in the mid-1840s he could speak the language of his neighbors
Benjamin Gervais and Vital Guerin. Nevertheless, he was perfectly comfortable within the larger society, and notably among the commercial élite of the
town, largely Anglo and Protestant.

Larpenteur was not without romantic antecedents. His paternal grandparents operated an inn at Thomery, a village forty-five miles from Paris and
near the royal palace of Fontainebleau. While in residence there, Napoleon
Bonaparte had occasion to sample Madame Larpenteur's cooking, of which
he grew exceedingly fond. One day, while munching *foie gras truffé* and *boeuf
bourguignon* in the inn's public room, he encountered the glamorous and fascinating Josephine Beauharnais, a recent refugee from the slave uprising in
Santo Domingo. For the rest of his life Monsieur Larpenteur boasted that, in
the best tradition of *l'amour à la français,* he had conducted to the table of the
world's greatest general his beautiful future consort. The marriage of course
did not last, nor, after awhile, did Napoleonic grandeur, and after Waterloo
Auguste's grandfather, his loyalty to the fallen emperor undiminished, decided it prudent to emigrate. He came first to New York and then to Balti-

more, where his wife and children joined him. The eldest son among these married a local girl, and from this union Auguste was born.

His parents died young, and the boy was raised by the somewhat rascally old Monsieur Larpenteur, who told him endless stories about his beloved Napoleon. In 1840, when he was eighteen, Auguste struck out for St. Louis, where two of his father's brothers operated a fur-trading post. The business, however, did not fare well, and Auguste fell in with two Anglo entrepreneurs, William Hartshorn and Henry Jackson. These men scented opportunity in the upper Mississippi valley, and they recruited young Larpenteur to join them, mostly because of his fluency in French. The party reached St. Paul (or Pig's Eye Landing) in mid-September 1843. From the beginning Auguste felt at home, and the Jacksons were particularly kind to him—Mrs. Jackson, he said, became the mother he did not remember. "The white population at that date," he recalled, "in the territory out of which [emerged the states] of Minnesota and the two Dakotas, . . . did not exceed three hundred." He got along very well with the Dakota with whom Hartshorn and Jackson were eager to trade, learned their language, and earned for the firm not a few advantageous bargains. Henry Sibley's American Fur Company was fiercely competitive, particularly as the availability of profitable furs dwindled, and, as a result of more than one tumult, Hartshorn decided to withdraw from the enterprise. But Jackson remained in St. Paul, and, as the frontier milieu receded and more conventional business practice came to the fore, established himself as the foremost merchant in the Territory. Meanwhile, his young colleague, Larpenteur, played as zestfully as he worked. "The country abounded in game, and soon I became expert in the chase." He remembered fondly one outing with "old Scott Campbell," who had befriended Loras and Galtier[1] and who was a man "very fond of his nips." On one occasion, when on a trading expedition with Larpenteur, Campbell, hopelessly drunk, had fallen into a snow bank where, had he not been swiftly extricated, he might well have smothered to death. In 1845 Larpenteur wooed and won a girl he had met in St. Louis. The wedding had to be held in St. Paul, because the groom had not enough money to take him down river to the bride's parish church. Ten years later, however, thanks to his Jackson connections, Auguste Larpenteur had prospered and could justifiably be called, as Joseph Cretin did, "one of our most respected citizens."[2]

---

1. See chapter 2, above.
2. Auguste Larpenteur, "Recollections" and "Reminiscences," AASPM, Larpenteur Papers.

The occasion for the bishop's tribute was Larpenteur's willingness to head a fund drive for a new cathedral. Cretin had never been satisfied with the "Catholic Building," as the local newspapers called it. To him its second floor remained "the large room where we say Mass."[3] As the immigrants over a few years swelled the number of Catholics in the Territory to 30,000 and then to 50,000, the bishop argued that a more spacious and embellished building was a necessity. Blueprints were accordingly drawn up as early as 1853 that called for a structure 175 feet by 75, surmounted by a steeple 250 feet high, located at what would become the corner of St. Peter and Sixth Streets, well within the bounds of the property Augustin Ravoux had shrewdly acquired in 1850. The steeple never eventuated, but the third cathedral of St. Paul did become a reality and served the diocese for sixty-five years. Not, unhappily, in Joseph Cretin's time. By the beginning of September 1855, the committee headed by Auguste Larpenteur had managed to raise locally $1,350, only a fraction of the overall cost, to be sure, but not paltry when the resources of the Catholic community are taken into account. The next year construction went forward, and by the autumn the walls had risen to twelve feet. "We are making progress on the Church despite the scarcity of workers and their high wages of fifteen francs [$3.00] a day." But even the ever-generous Propagation of the Faith could not cover the growing deficit, and a month later construction had to be suspended.[4]

The bishop fared better financially in the pastoral care of the dead. The original Catholic cemetery near Galtier's chapel was soon inadequate, and after a few temporary expedients proved likewise,[5] Cretin bought sixty acres some three miles away, at the outskirts of the town. "I blessed the new [Calvary] cemetery last Friday," he told his sister. "It cost me 25,000 francs, [but] it's happily paid off. . . . We are selling a good number of plots in this cemetery for 100 francs per plot."[6] More pressing still, however, was the ministry to the living, especially to the sick and deprived. Cretin had listed high among the desiderata for the new diocese the erection of a combination hospital-orphanage, and once the Sisters of St. Joseph had arrived he wasted no time in drawing up plans for it. The cornerstone was laid in the summer of 1853, and by late October, he reported, just as "the cold weather is setting in, they started

---

3. See chapter 3, above.
4. Cretin to Clemence Cretin, October 14 and November 23, 1856, AASPM, Cretin Papers.
5. Cretin to Jean Cretin, April 15, 1853, AASPM, Cretin Papers.
6. Cretin to Clemence Cretin, November 23, 1856, AASPM, Cretin Papers.

the roof on the hospital today. . . . This building is by far the largest of its kind in St. Paul."[7] But even before the facility could be put into full use, the sisters proved their worth as nurses. In June 1854, the first cases of the dreaded cholera appeared in St. Paul. During the epidemic that followed, the nuns converted Galtier's log chapel into a makeshift infirmary, where they heroically cared for the stricken. St. Joseph's Hospital, a handsome four-story stone edifice located at the platted corner of Ninth and Exchange Streets—property donated by the civic leader, Henry M. Rice, always friendly toward Catholic good causes[8]—opened its doors the following September 24.

A frontier "hospital" might have appeared an anomaly to later generations blessed by more sophisticated medical techniques. It was in reality a kind of hostel which aimed to provide as clean, healthful, and comfortable an environment as possible for the sick poor who had nowhere else to go. The sisters charged eight dollars a week for a private room, but they seldom realized even a fraction of that sum. Their training as nurses may have been minimal, but their dedication was not, a circumstance testified to by the journalists who toured the new facility and in the pages of their newspapers lavishly praised these "truly Christian and self-sacrificing ladies for [their] humanity and Christian benevolence." Such encomiums, offered by solidly Protestant commentators, had social and political implications. The mid-1850s witnessed the brief but sorry eruption of the Nativist Movement, the so-called Know-Nothing Party, with its bigoted attacks upon immigrants in general and Catholics in particular. St. Paul had its share of public men—and not all of them Protestant preachers—who inveighed regularly against the guile of popery and priestcraft and warned good Americans that, did they not look sharp, the Inquisition would be imposed on them. But invoking the shade of the legendary Maria Monk could not obscure the contribution to the community at large of the Sisters of St. Joseph, who had risked their lives during the cholera epidemic and who now proposed to care for sick people and orphans—thirty of the latter from the start—regardless of creed.[9] Nor, in connection with the building of the hospital-orphanage, could Joseph Cretin's own good citizenship have been challenged: once the land was secured by virtue of Rice's generosity, the bishop paid for most of the construction out of his

---

7. Cretin to Clemence Cretin, October 29, 1853, AASPM, Cretin Papers.

8. Helen Angela Hurley, "The Sisters of St. Joseph and the Minnesota Frontier," *Minnesota History* 3 (June 1949): 6–8.

9. Hurley, *On Good Ground,* 74–84.

own pocket, with money received from property sold in France.[10] Not a penny of public funds was expended.

Not that Cretin endorsed all American habits and mores. He found the ethos of frontier egalitarianism especially irksome.[11] Perhaps that was why he did not apply "to become a citizen of the United States and to renounce forever all [other] allegiance and fidelity" until 1854.[12] He by no means severed his French connections, though his one intention, declared in the autumn of 1855—to visit Ireland and France in search of the ten priests he needed "and the money to bring them here as well as to support them," not to mention the hundred thousand francs he required to complete his cathedral—was, for some reason, thwarted.[13] By then his health had begun to fail, a process hastened by the almost daily increase of the pastoral demands on him, to say nothing of the anxiety about the questionable goings-on of mavericks like Belcourt and Vivaldi. He stayed in touch by letter, even so, with his brother, his nieces, and particularly his sister. On rare occasions he was testy with her, as he had been in earlier years. "I saw with sadness in your last letter," he wrote her in the spring of 1853, "that you threatened to withdraw your support of my work. And for what? Because I thought it necessary to carry out my brotherly duty to correct you with a friendly observation about your expenses."[14]

But later that year a new bond drew the siblings closer together: "I understand you saw Monsieur Ravoux and the two young missionaries from St. Paul."[15] Joseph had entrusted to Clemence the care of John Ireland and Thomas O'Gorman, who had been virtually left on her doorstep by Augustin Ravoux.[16] The boys were enrolled in the *petit séminaire* at Meximieux, but Mademoiselle Cretin, throughout their matriculation, kept a close, stern, and, it must be said, loving eye on them. "Guard your vocation well," she instructed them early on. "Be faithful to your sublime vocation, and my brother will be happy to have made sacrifices for your happiness in procuring an excellent

---

10. Ravoux, *Reminiscences*, 63.

11. See Cretin to Jean Cretin, April 23, 1853, AASPM, Cretin Papers.

12. See the official document of Minnesota Territory and Ramsey County, signed by Cretin and notarized, dated June 27, 1854, AASPM, Cretin Papers.

13. Cretin to Clemence Cretin, October 23, 1855, AASPM, Cretin Papers.

14. Cretin to Clemence Cretin, March 20, 1853, AASPM, Cretin Papers.

15. Cretin to Clemence Cretin, October 29, 1853, AASPM, Cretin Papers.

16. See chapter 4, above.

education for you."[17] She lived nearby, in the family home in Montluel, from where she saw to mundane matters, too: "You will keep on your knitted jackets during the night." "You are to try on the new shirt and tell me if it fits well and you like it." "You have received your clothes. They cost a good deal. Take care of them. Do not soil them or wrinkle them." "I am sending you the box of pens you asked for. . . . Take care of them. They are very expensive."[18] No doubt exercise of maternal prerogatives could, on occasion, seem somewhat oppressive to a sixteen-year-old far from his own home. "I have told you," she wrote John Ireland, "that I wished to replace your mother, who, perhaps, cannot now render you the services of which you have need. If it gives you pleasure that I have for you the feelings and the care of a mother, prove it to me by the conduct of a good son."[19]

For his part the bishop kept track of "the first two seminarians of St. Paul" largely through his sister but now and then directly. He was pleased with their communications to him: "Dear Boys," he wrote early in 1854, "your French is pretty correct." Toward the end of that year he demonstrated that his English was "pretty correct," though still a mite stilted after nearly twenty years in America: "Dear Children. You may have been surprised because I have delayed so long to answer your letters. Please to believe that it has been out of my power to write sooner. My occupations are increasing with our population, and I have not been able to write to my sister these three months."[20] Punctilious as always about money matters, he wanted strict records maintained. "John Ireland's father," he told Clemence the next summer, "has just given me fifty francs [$10.00] destined for his son; please give that sum to John for me. You were to have given him," he reminded her, "a watch from me for his New Year's gift. Give twenty-five francs to Thomas Gorman [sic]. I will keep account of all this . . . and any other expenses you deem necessary for the children. I don't want them to be your responsibility during their vacation."[21] In due time both Ireland and O'Gorman would achieve heroic status within their Church and country; how much they owed to the Cretins, brother and sister, remains incalculable.

17. Clemence Cretin to Ireland and O'Gorman, February 11 and April 1, 1854, AASPM, Ireland Papers.

18. Clemence Cretin to Ireland and O'Gorman, January 1, 1854, and February 5 and November 1, 1856, AASPM, Ireland Papers.

19. Clemence Cretin to Ireland, October 19, 1854, AASPM, Ireland Papers.

20. Cretin to Ireland and O'Gorman, February 24 and November 8, 1854, AASPM, Cretin Papers.

21. Cretin to Clemence Cretin, July 12, 1855, AASPM, Cretin Papers.

Toward the end of 1856 Joseph Cretin felt all too palpably the intimations of mortality. "I have a fairly heavy cold," he told Clemence in mid-October.[22] But this discomfort was merely symptomatic of a far more severe malady. He was suffering from dropsy, accompanied by a chronic and cruel insomnia. "Pastoral care has chased the sleep from my eyes," he wrote his sister just after Christmas, "eyes which have furthermore not been shut for over three weeks. I don't know how this will all end. My legs are very swollen; every step feels like I am walking on thorns. I've seen two doctors, but they give me no relief." With the new year he grew progressively weaker, and he celebrated Mass for the last time, within the Spartan confines of his little room in the Catholic Building, on January 26, 1857. Ten days later he sent what amounted to a farewell to his beloved siblings: "I have been seriously ill for three months now. I've not been able to get four hours of sleep in this long span of time. Ah! But in the midst of the sadness and excruciating pain, I was never in want of God's patience." He fretted even then, on the edge of the grave, over the kind of financial concerns that had necessarily absorbed him all his active life: why, he asked rhetorically, should the New York Customs Authority charge 400 francs duty on imported ecclesiastical "adornments, though most [of them] were old." But in his last agony he remembered too the future of the diocese he had founded in the wilderness: "Please pray for me. My affectionate greetings to those two good little Missionaries [Ireland and O'Gorman]."[23]

Joseph Cretin, in the fifty-eighth year of his age, died on the morning of Sunday, February 22, 1857. In attendance at the deathbed were his young friend from Belley, Denis Ledon,[24] and the austere Benedictine monk from St. John's, Prior di Marogna, who had heard the dying man's general confession. The young levite, Anatole Oster, the man perhaps closest to the bishop in his latter years—the similarly young Father Peyragrosse who might otherwise have been Cretin's confidant had died in the spring of 1855[25]—had been sent the day before on mission to Mendota. Before he left Oster knelt for a final blessing. "It is the last time," Cretin had said, "but we must meet in heaven." Hurry back, the bishop had added in closing, but for Oster his return was hours too late. Cretin's obsequies were the most spectacular in the brief history of Minnesota Territory. Local Protestant clergymen had petitioned

---

22. Cretin to Clemence Cretin, October 14, 1856, AASPM, Cretin Papers.

23. Cretin to Jean and Clemence Cretin, February 6, 1857, AASPM, Cretin Papers.

24. For a description of Cretin's last illness, see Ledon to Clemence Cretin, February 3, 1857, AASPM, Cretin Papers.

25. See chapter 4, above.

permission to attend the requiem Mass, and in the procession to the new Calvary cemetery afterward, Catholics walked the three miles while the *crème de la crème* of St. Paul's Yankee ascendancy followed in their carriages. All this signaled how profound had been the effect of the small, plump sometime curé of Ferney on this frontier community, the doleful influence of the fading Know-Nothings notwithstanding. But what Oster remembered best were the penultimate words from the dying bishop, as he fingered the book of devotions he had composed during his student days at Saint-Sulpice: "In my life I have asked neither for health nor for sickness, for riches nor poverty, for success nor failure; but only that the will of God be done. In the long nights when I cannot sleep, I always pray for you."[26]

STATISTICALLY, BISHOP CRETIN LEFT BEHIND IN HIS HUGE AND fledgling diocese thirty-one churches built, seventeen under construction, and as many as ninety other stations ministered to on an occasional basis. A Catholic population of about 50,000 was served by twenty-seven priests, including the monks of St. John's Priory, and by the Sisters of St. Joseph, as well as by a recently arrived group of Benedictine nuns.[27] This remarkable growth, however, did not lead to a rush of candidates to don the miter in St. Paul. In the summer of 1858, the see still vacant more than a year after Cretin's death, this situation drew comment from a distinguished Eastern source. "We learn," observed the editors of the *Boston Pilot*,

> that the Very Rev. A. Perlamorgues of Iowa has succeeded in obtaining his request to be excused from accepting the Bishopric of St. Paul, Minnesota. The Pope urged him to accept, but the firmness of Father Perlamorgues in refusing the office and dignity carried the day. The Catholics of Iowa feel themselves the gainers by the result. The important and promising Diocese of St. Paul is meanwhile vacant. The piety and zeal of the administrator, Very Rev. A. Ravoux, leaves nothing to complain of; but St. Paul, so young, so growing, calls earnestly for one clothed with the permanent authority and responsibility of the Episcopate.[28]

---

26. Oster, "Bishop Cretin," 80–81.

27. See Ravoux to Grace, November 13, 1858, AASPM, Grace Papers. In his *Reminiscences*, 69–71, written of course much later, Ravoux claimed that at Cretin's death only seventeen priests were serving in the diocese and that that number increased by ten over the subsequent eighteen months—a most unlikely occurrence.

28. *Boston Pilot*, August 21, 1858.

Augustin Ravoux had indeed been appointed interim administrator of the diocese—the obvious and really the only possible choice. "The afflicting, but not unexpected, news of the death of your late saintly and devoted Bishop," the archbishop of St. Louis wrote him a month after Cretin's death, "has been received here with profound regret by all his friends, and none more so than by myself." In the same letter the archbishop formally conferred upon Ravoux all the faculties necessary to act authoritatively *sede vacante,* as was his prerogative as metropolitan.[29] His decision was ratified by Rome the following summer.

The course adopted by Jean-Antoine Perlamorgues was, as the *Pilot* indicated, more circuitous—and indeed more mysterious. Perlamorgues had been among the recruits—along with Cretin, Galtier, and Ravoux—whom Mathias Loras had brought with him from France to the new diocese of Dubuque in 1839.[30] At the time of Cretin's death he was the pastor in Davenport. At the end of March 1858, he received word that Pius IX had appointed him bishop of St. Paul. Once his designation was officially confirmed, two months later, he sent Father Ravoux a most peculiar directive.

> I appoint you my Vicar General, and I send you all the faculties I have received from Rome. You can then act as Vicar general of St. Paul till my resignation is accepted; and if not accepted I hope you will be to me a counselor during the rest of my days. You will be the only priest having the powers of Vicar General in the diocese of St. Paul. I have far more confidence in your wisdom than in mine.[31]

Perlamorgues claimed that the curious canonical arrangement he suggested— a bishop-elect granting full powers to a particular individual, even though said bishop-elect was intent upon quashing his own appointment—enjoyed

---

29. See Kenrick to Ravoux, March 8, 1857, AASPM, Ravoux Papers. Peter Richard Kenrick (1806–1895) had been bishop of St. Louis since 1840. In 1847, in a sweeping reorganization of the American hierarchy, St. Louis was raised to an archdiocese and given, in the technical terminology, "metropolitan" status. Among St. Louis's "suffragan sees" were Milwaukee, Dubuque, and after 1850, St. Paul. As archbishop, Kenrick exercised ordinary jurisdiction only within his own immediate geographical area. As "metropolitan" he enjoyed some vaguely defined appellate powers among his suffragans, as well as the right to grant the kind of authority, with the death of a suffragan, that he gave to Ravoux.

30. See chapter 2, above.

31. Perlamorgues to Ravoux, May 22, 1858, AASPM, Ravoux Papers.

the sanction of the archbishop of St. Louis. However that may have been, Perlamorgues, who hastened off to Rome, succeeded in persuading the mandarins of the curial bureaucracy that he should be absolved from the obligation of succeeding Joseph Cretin as bishop of St. Paul. His reasons remained obscure; no evidence exists, for example, that he suffered from unusually bad health. Of course, Augustin Ravoux already executed full authority within the diocese thanks to Archbishop Kenrick's mandate.

One intriguing question remains. Surely Ravoux himself, given his broad and deep experience of the apostolate at the upper reaches of the Mississippi valley, should have been considered at the highest authoritative levels as the appropriate successor to Joseph Cretin. Yet such a judgment apparently never figured in the counsels in St. Louis or in Rome. And the predilections of Ravoux himself may well have played a part. Unlike a sizable proportion of Catholic clerics, the prospect of a miter gave off little glitter for him. A decade after these events, he was nominated to be vicar apostolic of Montana, an honor he declined because he maintained that given his thirteen discernible ailments, among them "palpitation of the heart, poor digestion, and overall weakness in my members," if he were to be transferred to the west he stood in danger of "disease, sadness, and continual pain."[32] This catalogue of physical woe served its turn, and the man who composed it died in St. Paul a few days after his ninety-first birthday.

In the wake of the uncertainty caused by Perlamorgues' *gran rifuto,* Augustin Ravoux soldiered on. His first concern was to complete the third cathedral on St. Peter Street, to the degree at least that the swelling number of Catholics in the town could have a building to serve their basic liturgical and devotional needs. The early pangs of the sharp economic downturn known as the Panic of 1857 had forced Cretin to suspend construction, and Ravoux, if anything, faced even more severe financial constraints. Still, he managed to scrape together enough money to proceed, and Mass was celebrated in the edifice for the first time in June 1858; collections at the various services that day amounted to $428. Hardly a thing of beauty, the interior remained unadorned and unplastered, but the work continued, and by Christmas, 2,000 worshipers were more or less comfortably accommodated at midnight Mass.

---

32. Ravoux to Barnabò, July 15, 1868 (copy), AASPM, Ravoux Papers. Archbishop Alessandro Barnabò was secretary of the Propaganda Fide, that department of the curia responsible for activities in mission countries, which included the United States until 1908.

Father Ravoux kept meticulous accounts: total expenditure came to just over $33,000 but left an indebtedness of only $4,500, thanks to the munificence of the French Propagation of the Faith and to the endeavors of the local committee chaired by Auguste Larpenteur, which, despite a shaky beginning, raised a respectable $10,000.[33]

Another initiative undertaken by Administrator Ravoux also affected the parochial life in St. Paul. The Assumption, founded to minister to German-speaking Catholics, grew at such a pace as to put one more intense strain on the resources of the diocesan clergy. Accordingly, at the end of 1857, Ravoux offered the parish to the Benedictines of St. John's, specifically to the prior, Demetrius di Marogna. This arrangement served a double purpose: it freed the peripatetic and apparently tireless George Keller to be assigned elsewhere, and it relieved a tension within the community of monks at St. John's occasioned by the prior's sometimes headstrong behavior. Di Marogna had never been entirely at ease within the monastic setting; he had acted too long as a relatively independent parish priest, unhampered by the demands of communal living, and the pastorate of the German Assumption suited him much better.[34] The transfer, however, might have foundered because of di Marogna's rather too artful encouragement of a group of Benedictine Sisters intent on bringing their apostolate to Minnesota Territory. This venture was sternly judged premature at best by Abbot Wimmer, the prior's superior back in Pennsylvania. Ravoux was similarly annoyed when the seven nuns, for whom he had neither specific work nor sources of support, appeared unexpectedly in St. Paul in the summer of 1857. But in the end both abbot and administrator sensibly relented, recognizing what a boon these women represented, and the sisters went off to St. Cloud to begin a ministry that flourishes to this day.[35] As for the Assumption, the parish was staffed by the Benedictines continuously till 1912.

A less pleasant event for Ravoux to preside over was the abrupt conclusion of George Anthony Belcourt's career at Pembina and St. Joseph.[36] The causes of his departure remain shrouded in mystery. The most likely explanation is that he physically—but not sexually—abused some of the young women who made up the "religious order" he had founded. These girls had

---

33. Ravoux, *Reminiscences,* 67–68.
34. See chapter 4, above.
35. See Barry, *Worship,* 53–55.
36. See chapter 4, above.

all been recruited from the locality, and when they showed their bruises, so it was said, to relatives and friends, loud complaints were sent to St. Boniface and St. Paul. After an investigation conducted by the bishop of St. Boniface, the upshot was that, though contradictory testimony left much in doubt, it was no longer possible for Belcourt to remain in the mission. Ravoux, always a stickler for proper priestly discipline and decorum, endorsed this conclusion. Belcourt accordingly returned to Quebec, and spent the remaining fifteen years of his life working honorably in several parishes in eastern Canada. That he did not have his faculties removed, at least in Canada—a rumor persisted that Ravoux had "interdicted" him—suggests that his misdeeds, however gross, did not merit what for a priest is the ultimate penalty. Nevertheless, enough smoke continued to rise that a fire cannot be ruled out. In 1860, when Father Belcourt petitioned the new bishop of St. Paul to be restored to his beloved Indians and métis, the negative decision was unequivocal.

But there occurred a dramatic footnote to the saga of George Belcourt's zealous labors in Minnesota Territory, marred though they may have been by his own idiosyncrasy and imprudence. Pembina and St. Joseph still needed a resident missionary to replace Belcourt. Ravoux had at hand a thirty-five-year-old Frenchman who had arrived in Minnesota in 1857 and who, incidentally, was an alumnus of the seminary at Meximieux—the alma mater of Cretin and, eventually, of Ireland and O'Gorman—where, Joseph Goiffon admitted, he had survived academically "not without difficulty." His career at Pembina was brief but memorable; indeed, his hair-raising experience, albeit unique, nevertheless can stand as emblematic of the courage and endurance of the early missioners. Returning north to his station by horseback from a visit in St. Paul, Goiffon was caught in a freakish mid-autumn blizzard. He was only a few miles from his destination, but his horse bolted into a swamp and died. Goiffon scooped out some snow and placed the saddle beneath and a buffalo robe over himself. The storm raged for three days, and once his small store of berries was gone, he had nothing to eat but the frozen flesh of the dead horse. By the end of the third day, when he was finally rescued, he knew his feet were frozen. Taken first to Pembina and then to St. Boniface, in excruciating pain, his gangrenous right leg was amputated below the knee. After eight days of convalescence in the bishop's house he began to hemorrhage, and there seemed little doubt that he would bleed to death. Just then a fire broke out in the rectory, which destroyed the house and the nearby cathedral but which, ironically, saved Goiffon's life: having been necessarily laid in a snowbank by the harried firefighters, the cold stopped the hemorrhaging.

The sick man was then carried to a little hospital staffed by the Grey Nuns,[37] where his left foot was amputated. Despite such horrendous sufferings, Father Goiffon survived and even returned for a brief spell to the mission in Pembina. Later he served with admirable effect in several parishes in the diocese of St. Paul located in a relatively more gentle climate—Little Canada, Centerville, White Bear, Moundsville. He made himself a wooden leg and foot which he refused to exchange for more professionally crafted prostheses. If any man deserved to indulge his eccentricities in dress and demeanor, it was Joseph Goiffon. So said his parishioners when they met him on a winter day, garbed in an old fur cap and an odd assortment of cast-off clothing. He was eighty-six years old when he died in 1910. Endurance indeed.[38]

THE BISHOP OF ST. PAUL WHO PUT THE FINAL QUIETUS TO GEORGE Belcourt's ambition to resume his apostolate in the Red River valley was named Thomas Langdon Grace, of the Order of Preachers.[39] "Monsieur Belcourt will, I trust," he wrote Bishop Taché of St. Boniface, "give no further trouble, as I have removed from him every vestige of hope of ever being permitted to return to his former mission in St. Joseph [and Pembina]." Still, the needs of the missions there required attention, and Grace hoped that spiritual sustenance might be provided for them from Manitoba, so much closer physically to the scene than southeastern Minnesota. "I have made application through the Representative of this district to the general government in Washington for an appropriation in favor of the Indians and half-breeds of St. Joseph and Pembina. Monsieur Belcourt drew an annual allowance in their favor for several years."[40] As a short-term solution to the geographical conundrum, Grace, in accord with canon law—so he assured the archbishop of St. Louis, his metropolitan—persuaded Taché "to accept the appointment

---

37. A congregation of religious women founded in Montreal in 1738, so called by reason of the color of the habit they wore.

38. See Agnes Keenan, "Joseph Goiffon (1824–1910)," typescript, AASPM, Catholic Historical Society Records.

39. One of the great medieval mendicant orders, the Friars Preachers were founded by St. Dominic Guzman and so are more popularly known as the Dominicans.

40. Grace to Taché, October 6, 1860, AASPM, Grace Papers. In 1853 Alexandre-Antoine Taché (1823–1894) succeeded Joseph Provencher (see chapter 4, above) as bishop of St. Boniface.

as our vicar general . . . in the heart of Minnesota and Dakota territory . . . and [to enjoy] full authority to grant or refuse faculties to any clergyman either residing or transient in said district."[41] International boundaries should not interfere with the cure of souls, or so the bishop appeared to be saying. Nor did he intend by this arrangement to renounce his ultimate title to jurisdiction along the Red River of the North.[42]

The sure-handed and decisive manner in which Thomas Grace handled this early quandary in his administration was reminiscent of the conduct of his predecessor. Joseph Cretin had shrunk from assuming the responsibilities of a frontier American diocese, but, once he did, he confronted them dutifully and without reservation. Similarly, Grace had no desire to don a miter in the northern wilderness, a headgear, as one sympathetic observer put it, that was hardly more comfortable than "a crown of thorns."[43] Grace knew full well that Jean-Antoine Perlamorgues had managed to persuade the curial officials in Rome to reverse their first decision,[44] and so, when the news came that the Vatican had designated him to head the derelict diocese at the headwaters of the Mississippi, he determined to adopt the same stance. Indeed, he sent the bulls[45] of appointment back to the curia, along with a Latin statement replete with conventional platitudes and pieties: "I have tried in vain," he wrote in his crabbed hand, "to bend my will, after much prayerful consideration, to accept so great an apostolate." However, his own "incapacities, which are enormous," as well as work still undone in his present position, led him "to implore humbly" that due consideration be taken of his "unworthiness" and that he be allowed to decline the honor.[46] But the Vatican was not to be thwarted a second

---

41. Grace to Kenrick, July 5, 1861, AASPM, Grace Papers.

42. For Grace's personal concerns about the Red River settlement, see chapter 6, below.

43. *Freeman's Journal* (New York), July 9, 1859, commenting on Grace's reluctant acceptance. The *Journal*'s editor was the brilliant but volatile James McMasters, a convert to Catholicism. He was an admirer of Grace, with whom he carried on a serious if fitful correspondence (see chapter 6, below).

44. Poignantly in his personal papers, AASPM, Grace kept a clipping of the article in the *Boston Pilot* (see note 28, above) in which it was announced that Perlamorgues had successfully refused to accept the miter of St. Paul.

45. A *Bulla*, or seal, refers to the formal nature of a papal document, properly "sealed" by apostolic authority and thus expressive of that authority.

46. Grace to Barnabò, March 26, 1859, Rome, Archives of the Sacred Congregation of Propaganda Fide.

time, and the bulls were promptly returned to him. "Roma locuta est," Grace's Dominican superior observed with a shrug. "Causa finita."[47]

At the time of his appointment to St. Paul, Grace, aged forty-four, had been the parish priest down the Mississippi at Memphis for more than twelve years. He had been born in Charleston, South Carolina, in 1814, four years after his newly wedded parents, both surnamed Grace, had immigrated from Ireland. Both hailed from County Kilkenny, Margaret from Newchurch and Pierce from Kilkenny City. Thomas Grace's mother's forebears were solidly middle class, as stable and well-off as any Catholic family could have hoped to be during those unhappy penal times. They included a soldier who had fought under Wolfe at Quebec, as well as a civil servant attached to the Dublin Parliament[48] and, more recently, another employee of the state who worked for nearly half a century as a supervisor in the British prison system. Even so, large numbers of offspring and restricted vocational opportunities for them meant that, even for the relatively substantial Graces of Newchurch, the option of emigration was routinely discussed around the fireside. Some of the family in due course settled in Tasmania and others in Canada, just as Pierce and Margaret came to South Carolina. On such distant shores their religion, discriminated against at home, continued to provide a social no less than a spiritual cohesion to their lives. One of Margaret's brothers joined the Trappists at their celebrated monastery at Mount Melleray, County Waterford, and later was among the monks who founded New Melleray in Iowa, where he died in 1884; meanwhile a cousin of Margaret's, Catherine Grace, ultimately became superior of a convent of nuns in Harrisburg, Pennsylvania.[49] Less is known of the bishop's paternal connections, though a family tradition had it that Pierce Grace had served his adopted country with distinction during the War of 1812 and that he was a man of no little intellectual cultivation. For reasons unknown—though most likely for economic ones—he moved his young family out of the deep south first to Pennsylvania and then to Ohio.

---

47. O'Daniel to Ireland, August 24, 1917, AASPM, Ireland Papers. Victor F. O'Daniel was a Dominican historian who wrote about the beginnings of Catholicism in Tennessee. John Ireland (d. 1918), Grace's successor, was toward the end of his life gathering material for a biographical sketch of Grace.

48. The parliament was suppressed in 1800 with the creation of a unitary state embracing both islands, the United Kingdom of Great Britain and Ireland.

49. See "Memorandum" of William Grace, December 3, 1887, AASPM, Grace Papers. William, the bishop's third cousin on his mother's side, was an amateur genealogist. He had left Ireland about 1850 and settled in Ontario.

It was in Cincinnati that teenaged Thomas Grace first encountered the Order of Preachers. A generation earlier a well-fixed Maryland native named Edward Fenwick, along with three companions, had established near Springfield, Kentucky, the first Dominican priory in the United States. Placed under the patronage of St. Rose of Lima, the first person born in the Americas to be canonized (and herself a Dominican), this institution soon became a hub of missionary activity. Consistent with the Dominican intellectual tradition, St. Rose's Priory almost immediately founded two schools, in one of which Jefferson Davis, the eight-year-old scion of a prominent plantation family from Mississippi, matriculated in 1816. Nor was the presence of this little Protestant—and future rebel chieftain—in a Catholic school an anomaly: given the demographic realities, in their early days such missionary schools predictably attracted a clientele predominantly non-Catholic; Davis, for his part, in later life recalled his days at St. Rose's with gratitude and affection.

But these frontier Dominicans also deemed it their responsibility to administer the sacraments and preach the gospel to the pockets of Catholic settlers scattered across a vast virgin territory. This was particularly true of Fenwick, who, though his modest fortune had paid for the construction of St. Rose's, soon grew restless within the groves of academe, however unsophisticated. Always more the itinerant missionary than the studious friar, in 1817 he brought his personal apostolate north across the Ohio river into the state of that name, where, he said, a half million people lived and not a single Catholic priest. He founded a second Dominican priory at Zanesville, and when, five years later, a new diocese was set up in Cincinnati, he was named its first bishop.[50]

Thus emanating out of St. Rose's Priory, the Dominicans made their presence felt all the way from mid-Ohio south across Kentucky into Tennessee. If he thought he heard a call to the priesthood, young Thomas Grace would quite naturally have answered it by donning their white habit, which he did in June 1830. As a lad barely into his seventeenth year, he was assigned for preparatory studies to St. Rose's. There he distinguished himself so remarkably that in 1838 his superiors sent him to Rome to complete his theological training and to earn an advanced degree. The quality of clerical education available in Italy during the 1830s and 1840s may not have been particularly good, but it compared favorably enough with what a young friar might have received

---

50. See Thomas Stritch, *The Catholic Church in Tennessee* (Nashville, 1987), 43–50.

amidst his poverty-stricken brethren in Ohio and Kentucky. But perhaps the exposure to a cosmopolitan Catholic culture meant more in the long run to young Grace's development than did lectures in a classroom. He attended such lectures first in the college attached to Santa Maria Sopra Minerva, the six-century-old mother church of the Dominican order, the magnificent gothic pile built in the center of Rome on the ruins of an ancient temple dedicated to the Roman goddess Minerva, and hard by the Pantheon. Here reside the bones of heroic Dominicans like St. Catherine of Siena, who died in a shabby street nearby, and of Fra Angelico and a host of other ecclesial celebrities of earlier centuries. And here, in these gorgeous and edifying confines, Grace was ordained priest in the Order of Preachers on December 21, 1839.[51]

Altogether Grace spent seven years in Italy, not returning to the United States until 1845. This span of time, unusual in its length, suggests that his training may have been interrupted by some unspecified illness. So does the fact that before long he was removed from the Minerva, and so from the notoriously unhealthy climate in *la Città,* and sent up the Tiber to Perugia, where, amid the serene purple hills of Umbria, he completed his studies. But since Grace seldom wrote or spoke about himself, the record in this regard remains incomplete. Consistent with that same reticence, he did not often refer to his European experience, which, however, had left its clear mark upon him. A certain sophistication, a gravity of manner, a verbal dexterity and even, on occasion, elegance—all of which qualities he manifested without the slightest trace of pretentiousness—lent him a demeanor that stood out among the citizenry of raw river towns like Memphis and St. Paul. Not that he hankered after Old World styles or social and political arrangements, as perhaps Joseph Cretin had; in Grace the American ethos ran deep, and he embraced it with all its brashness.

It would be presumptuous to claim that all the products of Roman seminaries during the 1840s took away with them studious habits, but Thomas

---

51. Reardon, *Diocese of St.Paul,* 138–139, observes that exactly twenty-two years later, in 1861, Grace ordained as priest his successor in St. Paul, John Ireland, and that on that same date fourteen years afterward he consecrated Ireland a bishop. Added to this alleged symmetry is the fact that Joseph Cretin was ordained priest December 21, 1823. But there remains some uncertainty about the exact date of Ireland's ordination to the priesthood, which may have taken place a day later. See O'Connell, *Ireland,* 530–531. For those who discern mystical significance in the conjuncture of numbers, the fact remains that Joseph Cretin died on February 22, 1857, and his successor, Thomas Grace, died on February 22, 1897.

Langdon Grace certainly did.[52] While at the Minerva he copied out long Latin extracts from the *Summa Theologica* of St. Thomas Aquinas, the great Dominican thinker of the thirteenth century, and similarly lengthy passages, in Italian, from standard authors in philosophy, theology, and canon law. But his interests went beyond the conventional: demonstrating that liberal bent that he would display all his life, he delved in detail into the highly controversial works of Antonio Rosmini.[53] Once back in America, Grace incorporated into these scholarly texts longhand additions and cuttings drawn from a wide range of contemporary journals, mostly, though not exclusively, Catholic. Thus he regularly read, among others, *The Rambler, Freeman's Journal, Brownson's Quarterly,* and the *North British Review.* He subscribed as well at one time or another to several newspapers, including the *Louisville Courier,* the *Brooklyn Eagle,* and the *Catholic Telegraph* of Cincinnati. What caught his attention ranged across a spectrum from the recondite to the winsome. Thus in 1850 he extracted from *The Rambler* a long, two-part review of Newman's *Discourses Addressed to Mixed Congregations.* But ten years later he also cut out of the *Boston Transcript* an article arguing that the literary achievement of Washington Irving, whose only true love had died just before the scheduled wedding, had been enhanced by his celibacy, in that it gave him a breadth of affectionate associations and "a heroic self-denial." In neither of these instances nor in the compilation as a whole is there a trace of the slipshod or the casual. When, for example, he cited a comment of Macaulay on the constitution of the Church of England, Grace carefully noted the precise source, much as he had done when quoting the Italian theologians during his schooldays.

Much of Grace's collection had to do with apologetics, intended no doubt to furnish him with material to use in sermons and lectures. Such subjects as religious freedom, the evils of sectarianism, the apostolic succession, the place of the Bible in the Christian life, and the validity of Anglican Orders figured prominently. As for moral standards, he kept open a keen apologetic eye for any excerpt affirming that Catholic behavior was superior to Protestant. For

---

52. What follows is based upon a very large scrapbook, kept by Grace till 1860, AASPM, Grace Papers.

53. Antonio Rosmini-Serbati (1797–1855), founder of the Institute of Charity (the so-called Rosminians), was a philosopher whose works aroused much displeasure in some ecclesiastical circles, as did his call for internal reform of the Church. He was formally silenced in 1849, and forty propositions drawn from his writings were condemned by Pope Leo XIII thirty years after his death. Pope John Paul II, however, has restored to a degree Rosmini's reputation as an orthodox thinker. See *Fides et Ratio,* n. 74.

example, he clipped a piece indicating that statistically the crime rate was much lower in Ireland than in England, where, it was asserted, even infanticide was practiced. In the spring of 1850, to rebut the frequent indictment of the countries of the Mediterranean basin for their alleged social miseries, he cut out a long article from the *Freeman's Journal* which described the horrors prevailing in the crowded and fetid tenements of New York City, again with statistics. That was the year John C. Calhoun died, and, though Charleston-born Grace seldom adverted to politics in his self-composed manual, it must have been with some poignancy that he pasted into it an article analyzing the prophetic speech delivered on the senate floor by his fiery fellow South Carolinian shortly before his death. Neither the great Protestant religions nor the great political parties, Calhoun declared, had been able to unite the country when faced with the slavery question: "To this extent the Union has already been destroyed by agitation in the only way it can be, by snapping asunder and weakening the cords which bind it together."

Upon his return home early in 1845, Father Grace was appointed to the teaching staff at St. Rose's, from which missionary center, in accord with the priory's routine practice, he also ministered to the nascent parishes in the district. Like Fenwick before him, however, he was not destined to remain long in a classroom. The following year Grace was sent to assist temporarily at St. Peter's parish in Memphis; he remained there for thirteen years. A bishopric had been established in Nashville in 1837 by virtue of the same papal decree that had set up the diocese of Dubuque and had brought Mathias Loras out of Alabama to Iowa Territory.[54] Geography, not an abundance of resources, had induced the American hierarchy in council to petition Rome to found these new jurisdictions. The designated bishop of Nashville, a Dominican product of St. Rose's named Richard Miles, found even fewer assets at hand than did Loras in Iowa: one small chapel and not a single priest besides himself. Since his diocese embraced the whole state of Tennessee, Memphis far to the west was his responsibility.

By the time Grace arrived there nine years later it was a bustling town of 8,000 and growing. Unskilled and semi-skilled laborers were much in demand at the Navy Yard and on the river front generally, as well as in the manual trades and construction. Irish Catholic hod carriers and bricklayers, soon joined by Germans, some of whom could boast of clerical proficiencies, naturally aspired to a religious presence akin to what they had known in the old country. Indeed, before long there were more Catholics in Memphis than in

---

54. See chapter 2, above.

Nashville itself. St. Peter's had been organized by an Irish missionary in 1841. Bishop Miles then mournfully watched a succession of secular priests depart St. Peter's for greener pastures,[55] until he finally turned to his religious brethren in hopes of bringing some stability to the parish. But the Dominican pastors came and went at a similar pace. The first of them was very soon promoted to a bishopric in California,[56] and two of his successors died during cholera and yellow fever epidemics of the kind that so often in these times blighted life in the Delta.[57]

So, in the wake of all these mishaps, the mantle of Catholic leadership in Memphis fell willy-nilly upon the shoulders of the scholarly young Father Grace. His temporary assignment to St. Peter's became a permanent one. It was remarkably successful. Under his direction a fine new stone church was built, the most splendid gothic edifice, so the Catholic press boasted, west of the Alleghenies.[58] He opened a parochial school, and then an orphanage, both under the supervision of a half dozen Dominican nuns recruited from their Kentucky convent. Such administrative achievements appear prosaic enough, but they must be seen as merely a part of the ordinary burden of the missionary pastor. Grace presided over a congregation mostly, though not exclusively, Irish, and mostly poor. It took a good deal of financial prudence and acuity to keep the enterprise afloat. It took as well a supple and zealous temper of mind for the Roman-educated young priest to preach with appropriate eloquence to his proletariat parishioners, to listen with due sympathy to their sacramental confessions, to catechize with proper playfulness their children. All these challenges Grace met with aplomb, so much so that after only a few years in Memphis Bishop Miles named him vicar general for western Tennessee. This honorific title meant little in practice, but even more significant was the inclusion of Grace's name—when he was thirty-nine years old—on a *terna* sent to Rome by the archbishop of St. Louis to head the proposed diocese of

55. No less than three pastors of St. Peter's, Memphis, during the 1840s were incardinated into the Diocese of New York.

56. Joseph Alemany (1814–1888), born in Spain, was named bishop of Monterey, California, in 1850, and first archbishop of San Francisco in 1853.

57. See Raymond A. Lucker, "Some Aspects of the Life of Thomas Langdon Grace, Second Bishop of St. Paul" (Master's thesis, St. Paul Seminary, 1952), 9, 14.

58. See Victor O'Daniel, *Fathers of the Church in Tennessee* (Washington, D.C., 1926), 506–507. For a physical description of the church—"romantic, lush, ardent, heavily decorated, bursting inside with arches and statues," its "exterior bold and fascinating"—see Stritch, *Church in Tennessee*, 94.

Quincy, Illinois.[59] As it turned out, various bureaucratic complications nullified the erection of a see at Quincy; even so, the existence of the pastor of St. Peter's, Memphis, became formally recognized within the labyrinth that was (and is) the Roman curia.

Not least among the qualifications noted about Grace was his ability to relate positively to the different constituents of the typical American community, not all of them natively friendly, in which he labored: "He is described as a courteous, temperate, and pious man," registered a functionary in Propaganda, "eloquent and worthy. . . . He is known to have gained the good opinion of all."[60] Nor was this characterization an exercise in hyperbole. Grace's cultivated manner, no less than his zeal in service of his own people, had won him the high regard of virtually every element of Memphis society. Thus, for example, the ground upon which he built the beautiful St. Peter's had been donated by a non-Catholic fellow townsman. His communal merit, however, came to be recognized fully only after it was clear that, despite his own inclinations, he was to be removed from the seat of his longtime apostolate and dispatched northward. A purse was presented to him on the eve of his departure, along with a testimony of high regard from the Catholics of Memphis:

> Your zeal, your example, and your eloquence have done much to awaken and preserve the faith of those entrusted to your pastoral care, and to command the respect of our fellow citizens who are not of our communion. . . . We are aware that you go now not of your own accord but in obedience to a mandate that you are not permitted to disregard; and it is no small satisfaction for us to know that not even the honor of a miter—an honor to which we feel you are entitled—could induce you to leave us.

That this tribute represented a public esteem wider than merely confessional was confirmed by an editorial in the *Memphis Bulletin,* a newspaper known at times to have shown sympathy for the Know-Nothing party.

---

59. See Reardon, *Diocese of St. Paul,* 140. Candidates on *ternae* were routinely ranked from first to third—"most worthy" (*dignissimus*), "more worthy" (*dignior*) and "worthy" (*dignus*). On the list for Quincy, Grace was placed second, *dignior*.

60. See the Archives of the Propaganda de Fide, A222 (1858): 595: 606–607: "E depinto come un uomo cortese, morigerato, e pio, eloquente e benemerito. . . . Ha saputo conciliarsi e la benevolenza di tutti."

Our readers will learn with poignant regret that the application of this excellent Christian pastor for the privilege to decline the appointment of [sic] Bishop of St. Paul, Minn., has been refused; and that it is now a fixed fact that he will ere long remove to his wider and more responsible field of labor. The regret will be shared by Protestants and Catholics alike; for during his residence amongst us, so blameless and exemplary has been his conduct as a minister of religion—so enlightened and useful has been his way of life as a citizen; so irreproachable his entire bearing as preeminently a gentleman—that it may truly be said that the range of those who esteem and love him is limited only by the circle of those who know him. . . . His departure will leave many hearts full of tears.[61]

The language may have been somewhat stilted, at least when judged by later rhetorical standards, but for a Catholic priest to have won at that date such plaudits in a southern city, was no mean accomplishment.

The reluctant Thomas Grace was consecrated in the Cathedral of St. Louis on Sunday, July 24, 1859. In attendance at the ceremony was a small delegation from St. Paul, headed by Augustin Ravoux. A day or two later the new bishop and the Minnesotans boarded the *Northern Belle* for the journey up the Mississippi. They reached their destination on Friday, July 29, and were greeted on the levee by a large crowd. In the evening Grace took the episcopal chair within the bare walls of the cathedral, now, despite his reluctance, formally his own. After his clergy had come forward to pledge their loyalty, he presided at a Eucharistic Benediction. The next day he received callers at his residence, "Protestant and Catholic," as one admirer put it, "men of rank and position, influential and otherwise, . . . to bid him welcome to Minnesota. . . . As people met on the streets afterwards, the talk was of the new Bishop, such a noble personage, so elegant in his manner, so charming in his conversation." On Sunday morning a crowd of as many as five thousand thronged the cathedral and spilled out along the streets outside to witness Grace celebrate pontifical Mass. Reverence no doubt mingled with curiosity as they watched him mount the pulpit to preach from the text, "Beware of False Prophets"—an intriguing choice. One who listened to it found the sermon "so clear, lucid, and expressive—nothing vague or indefinite—but the most profound knowledge of the system of Church government and the economy of God's providence to fallen man, wrought out so naturally, logically, and consistently."

---

61. Quoted in William Busch, "The Coming of Bishop Grace," *A&D* 7 (1936): 179–181.

This same enthusiast thought these early manifestations indicated that "the good Bishop, under God, to be a great agent to work a future for Minnesota. From this time will commence a new era." Yet one could not fail to recognize that "there is much work to be done, and the laborers are few." Admittedly "'tis a great task, but with God's divine help he will succeed. We feel that he is the right man in the right place, at a fit and proper time, too."[62]

Indeed, time, the remorseless arbiter of human affairs, would tell.

*

---

62. Lawrence Cotter to the *Boston Pilot,* August 1, 1859, quoted in Busch, "Coming of Grace," 183–185. Cotter was a sometime St. Paul City Clerk. Thirty years later his son, Joseph, would become first bishop of Winona.

CHAPTER 6

The Heart of
the Matter

THOMAS LANGDON GRACE SERVED AS BISHOP OF ST. PAUL FOR A quarter of a century. When he arrived in 1859 the diocese comprised the same awesome dimensions as before: Minnesota—a state now—and the Dakota Territory west to the Missouri River, 166,000 square miles in all. He had at his disposal twenty-seven priests, nine of them Benedictines who owed first allegiance to their priory at St. John's in Stearns County, and two small groups of religious women. To minister to a Catholic population of roughly 50,000, thirty-one churches, mostly rude log shanties, had been built. There were, to be sure, also ninety-seven "mission-stations" technically on the books, but these out-of-the-way settlements, in a land with few decent roads and, as yet, no railways, were visited only spasmodically and rarely. In St. Paul itself a nascent hospital-orphanage and a girls' academy pointed more to a promising future than to a vibrant present.

By the time he retired in 1884, Grace's jurisdiction had been limited by erection of vicariates to the north and west to the southern third of Minnesota, and so reduced in size by five-sixths. In this relatively small area lived 130,000 Catholics, served by 147 priests, fourteen orders of religious women and six of men. One hundred ninety-five churches were in full operation including the maintenance, by many of them, of a parochial school, while the fifty-one stations, now that they could be reached more readily, expected and received regular and predictable ministrations. Instead of the lonely duo of young Ireland and O'Gorman,[1] twenty-nine young men were preparing for the diocesan priesthood in American and European seminaries. Seventeen parishes flourished in the Twin Cities—as St. Paul and Minneapolis could by

---

1. See chapter 4, above.

then at least informally be called—where only four struggling ones had existed in 1859.[2] In 1884 ten boarding schools for girls were functioning, as well as five orphanages and two fully equipped and staffed hospitals.[3] And, the year before his retirement, the bishop blessed the plans of the Franciscan nuns located in Rochester, who, in the wake of a tornado that had devastated southern Minnesota, determined to found a hospital there, so long as they could secure the cooperation of the young Doctors Mayo, William and Charles; the destiny and the international fame of St. Mary's Hospital and the Mayo Clinic have been linked ever since.[4]

Statistics by definition are cold and abstract. Nonetheless, they tell a tale that sheds light upon larger and more humane data. During the twenty-five years of Thomas Grace's episcopate in St. Paul the floods of European immigrants, dwarfing what had happened before, brought profound changes to America. These refugees from the Old World unavoidably carried cultural baggage with them. In Minnesota, a plurality of them were Scandinavian Lutherans—Swedes, Norwegians, Danes, and in the northeast, Finns—who more than any other immigrant group endowed the state with its characteristic entrepreneurial and hardy individualistic spirit. But others too came to the upper waters of the Mississippi seeking economic and political solace, first Catholic Irish and Germans, later Poles, Slovenians, and Bohemians, and still later Italians. Some who greeted Bishop Grace in 1859 exhibited an aggressively chauvinistic demeanor—"It is peculiarly pleasing to the Irish portion of the congregation (for they are, as usual, the vast majority) that now, at last, they can be understood and appreciated as they deserve, and that their offering will be accepted with a spirit that will do justice to the Irish heart."[5] The implied slur upon the likes of Galtier, Ravoux, and Cretin would hardly have won the approval of a sophisticated churchman like Thomas Grace, his Irish roots notwithstanding. For if the French and French Canadian tradition were now indeed receding proportionately, he recognized that these pioneers had laid the foundations upon which to build—and not these clerics only, but also faithful laymen like Vital Guerin, Benjamin Gervais, Jean-Baptiste Faribault, and Auguste Larpenteur. And the future would depend on believers of similar spirit and dedication, whatever their nationality.

---

2. In St. Paul, the Cathedral of St. Paul (1841) and the Assumption of the Virgin (1856); in St. Anthony, St. Anthony of Padua (1851); in Minneapolis, St. Boniface (1858).

3. See Reardon, *Diocese of St. Paul,* 198–199.

4. See Helen Clapesattle, *The Doctors Mayo* (Minneapolis, 1941), 247–253.

5. Cotter, quoted in Busch, "Coming of Grace," 184.

As a veteran and very successful pastor, Grace knew full well that the one indispensable unit within the institutional Church was, and had been since time immemorial, the parish. Various overarching bureaucratic structures within a diocese were, to be sure, necessary and useful, in order to preserve good order and administrative consistency. But the point at which the institution and the people met and melded was the parish. Here was the heart of the matter. Little wonder, then, that hardly more than a month after his arrival in St. Paul, Grace set out to visit the communities of believers now under his charge. Accompanied by Augustin Ravoux—vicar general once again—he traveled north first, to the Benedictine foundations around St. Cloud and Sauk Rapids. "It had been raining all day, and the stage, true to its nature, broke down while crossing the prairie. . . . In St. Cloud the bishop confirmed fifty-nine persons and preached in English. Father Demetrius [di Marogna] preached in German." The following week, late September, the small episcopal party arrived in Faribault, "a beautiful and flourishing village" of 1,500, forty miles or so south of St. Paul, where twenty persons, one of them a convert, were confirmed. Grace went next to New Trier, "a town whose name is not yet on the maps of the state"; here the bishop confirmed twenty-five and, again, preached in English. The indefatigable Father George Keller did the same in German. In early October Grace was in Winona where this same procedure was repeated: the administration of the sacrament of confirmation (seventy recipients) and a learned preachment in English. Wabasha was next, on October 12, where the predominantly French congregation heard a sermon from Ravoux, and then Stillwater in the Saint Croix valley, and here "a large and very attentive audience" listened respectfully to the oration of their new bishop.[6]

In 1859 the demographic realities, except in the mid-north around St. John's Priory, determined that the booming river towns—Stillwater, New Ulm, Mankato, Winona, and, of course, St. Paul and Minneapolis—would receive the bishop's primary attention. In allocating scanty personnel, it only made sense for him to assign resident pastors to parishes with relatively large numbers of communicants. But reality also obliged each resident to be circuit rider to neighboring settlements, some of them at a considerable distance from his base. Thus the energetic pastor in Mankato usually said Mass in his home parish only one Sunday in four; his counterpart in Winona had to

---

6. An anonymous letter in the *Western Banner* (St. Louis), November 26, 1859, quoted in Busch, "Coming of Grace," 190–191.

assume responsibility for sacramental ministration throughout the eponymous county and across three adjoining counties besides.

The origin and development of these parochial communities inevitably shared certain characteristics. They were all, needless to say, the result of immigration, and almost all of them depended on the initiative of local laymen. Yet each of them manifested its unique individuality and spirit. A necessarily foreshortened and random catalogue clearly demonstrates both points.

BY 1853, A GROUP OF MOSTLY IRISH IMMIGRANTS HAD SETTLED the fertile lands around Inver Grove, south of St. Paul. Augustin Ravoux celebrated the first Mass there, at the home of one John McGrath; twelve persons were present. In 1856 John Egan ceded ten acres to Bishop Cretin "for the benefit of the Catholic Church." At the same time Charles McGroarty—who had been instrumental in the naming of the village after his home town in Ireland—donated five acres for a cemetery. Logs for the first church were cut in neighboring woods, hauled to the site, their ends beveled, then augured through and held together with stout wooden pegs. The only cash expended paid for hinges and a door lock, window frames and glass, and a large heating stove. This structure remained in use till 1867 when it was replaced by a frame building at a cost of $6,000. Despite such physical progress, Inver Grove did not have a resident pastor until 1880.[7]

Nor did St. Anne's parish in Le Sueur, though by 1860 at least twenty-five Catholic families were living in the area. That year the priest from Mankato conducted the first Catholic marriage there in the home of Henry Cantwell. During the Civil War plans were set out for a stone church, which, though duly completed in 1864, could not be used in wintertime till four years later, when a heating apparatus was installed. The total cost was about $4,000, a sum that did not include the twelve stained glass windows donated by individual parishioners. Once the church was built, a good-natured dispute arose as to whose saintly patronage it should be under: the Irish predictably opted for St. Patrick, while other nationals nominated St. John. When a vote taken at a parish fair and bazaar ended in a virtual tie, a visitor from St. Paul, young Father John Ireland, suggested St. Anne as a compromise.[8]

---

7. Anon., "Blessing of St. Patrick's Church, June 3, 1962, Inver Grove, Minnesota" (n.p., n.d. [1962]), 11–12.

8. Anon., "Centenary of the Completion of the First St. Anne's Church, 1864–1964" (n.p., n.d. [1964]), 4–6. Ireland may have been moved to make his sug-

The beginnings of Holy Trinity parish in New Ulm—destined ultimately to have its own bishop—was more problematic. In Chicago in 1853, a group of German immigrants, mostly socialists and freethinkers, proposed to establish a western colony which would advocate equal rights and equal shares in the earth's bounty to every member "except lawyers and clergymen." Soon the society had attracted eight hundred applicants. A scouting party twenty-six strong was commissioned to find a suitable locale. After many vicissitudes and false starts they came upon the site in Minnesota Territory where the Cottonwood River flowed into the Minnesota. By 1855 New Ulm—most of the settlers hailed from the Kingdom of Württemberg—boasted a population of 1,600, so large so suddenly that a barrel of flour cost $20.00 and a bushel of potatoes $3.00.

The next year an itinerant Jesuit named Franz X. Weninger, famous among German Catholics for his eloquence, preached a mission on the farm of one Anton Kraus, located on the north edge of the town. This religious exercise brought together enough Catholics to bespeak the need and feasibility of setting up a parish. A series of planning meetings followed, but progress was slow, due perhaps as much to a lack of resources as to the hostility of the town's anticlerical élite. Although construction of a church began, only the outer walls stood when the Dakota War broke out in 1862, and they were demolished for fear the hostile Indians might fortify them as a barricade or a forward position. Meantime Catholics in the New Ulm area were served occasionally by Valentine Sommerreisen from Mankato. This sturdy missionary—a native of Alsace, recruited by Ravoux in 1853, ordained by Cretin in 1856—took care over the years of thirty-six missions scattered across fourteen counties.

In 1865 the congregation of New Ulm determined to try again. With $325 from the federal government in compensation for the destruction of their unfinished church, $500 from the Ludwig Missionsverein,[9] and $500 from the estate of a German noblewoman donated to Bishop Grace for the purpose, enough money was at hand to launch another building project. Michael

---

gestion out of chivalry as well as diplomacy, since the Christian name of the wives of both the leading opponents was Anne. See Ann Regan, "The Irish," in Holmquist, *They Chose Minnesota*, 136. A personal note: My parents, Richard O'Connell and Anna Mae Kelly, were married in the present St. Anne's in 1929. Their remains lie now in the lovely little cemetery some blocks away.

9. See chapter 4, above.

Lauterbach gave the diocese two lots for a church, and on April 10, 1866, he hauled the first load of bricks to the site. Other parishioners—with names like Rauch, Stocher, Schmitz—pitched in, and the cornerstone was laid on September 1, at which ceremony a collection netted $35.95. Gradually more money was raised, but as before the enterprise proceeded at a snail's pace, so that when the first resident pastor arrived in January 1869, he entered a partially completed Church of the Holy Trinity and assumed responsibility for a debt of $462.48.

Handsome, wavy-haired Alexander Berghold was thirty-one when he came to New Ulm. Born in Austria of artisan stock, and educated in gymnasium and university there, a strong admiration for the achievements of Father Pierz brought him to Minnesota at the beginning of 1864. After six months intensive study of English, he was ordained by Grace, who immediately assigned him as missioner to Belle Plaine, Jordan, and St. Patrick in Scott County and St. John in Carver County. He proved to be a veritable dynamo, organizing viable parishes and getting churches built in all these places. In New Ulm he displayed the same high level of energy as the first resident priest in Brown County, who also served settlements as far away as Lamberton, Springfield, and Birch Coolie, as well as closer locations like West Newton. Articulate and cultivated, dogged, tireless, a genuine leader, Berghold—rivaled perhaps only by Sommerreisen and George Keller—stands as *le beau idéal* of the second generation of European-born priests who conducted the Catholic Church in Minnesota out of its infancy. As time went on, and that process matured, Father Berghold tended to concentrate most of his remarkable enterprise on the congregation in New Ulm itself. The church was finished, a school built, and an assortment of pious societies set up—the Confraternity of Christian Mothers, the St. Joseph Benevolent Society, Young Men's and Young Ladies' Sodalities—all designed to give permanence and coherence to what would soon be reckoned one of the great parishes in the diocese, whatever the disgruntlement of New Ulm's original agnostic founders.[10] Indeed, it may have been some satisfaction to Berghold and his people that they had done battle with the kind of German immigrants Franz Pierz had warned them about.[11]

Not far to the east from New Ulm lay another settlement with high secular aspirations. St. Peter was the brainchild of Captain William Bigelow Dodd

---

10. Anon., "The Church of the Holy Trinity of New Ulm, Minn." (n.p., 1944), 11–26.

11. See chapter 4, above.

of Montclair, New Jersey, who, with like-minded promoters, formed the St. Peter Company, just one more organization lured westward by the prospect of cheap and available land. The town was duly platted in 1857, and it was widely noted that it boasted an unusually wide central thoroughfare. This physical largesse was apparently related to a dispute that had for some time raged in the territorial legislature, as to where the capital of Minnesota—on the very cusp of statehood, which came in 1858—ought to be located. The conventional position was that St. Paul should continue after admission to the Union to enjoy that honor, while others urged that a more central site, one that emphasized the inevitable expansion of the new state westward, would be more appropriate. The St. Peter Company underwrote this latter claim not only with its broad main street but also by offering to furnish gratis the ground upon which a suitable capital could be constructed and pledging a substantial amount of money to defray the costs of the building. The territorial legislature indeed approved this proposal, but before it could be finalized by the governor's signature, a maverick legislator—from Pembina, of all places—absconded with the unsigned bill and hid out until time ran out for its implementation. Dodd and his colleagues went ahead with construction anyway, but they had to be content that the edifice once built would serve only as the seat of Nicollet County. How consoled they may have been that the state established its first lunatic asylum in St. Peter (1866) has not been recorded.[12]

The first Mass in St. Peter was celebrated in 1855 in "the Ewing house" by Canon Vivaldi. Shortly afterwards a church was built: "It was unplastered and unfurnished inside. The pews for many years were rough planks placed on kegs. Many times there were broken windows, for the boys were as mischievous then as they are now. It had no belfry, nor bell, and was little more than four square walls." The parish, such as it was, was served from Henderson by the indefatigable Sommerreisen and, intermittently, from St. Paul. John Ireland was among those priests who came and went. Resident pastors, named, significantly, Zuzek and Tori, brought with them a measure of stability. Father John Zuzek refurbished and enlarged the primitive church and opened a school—he bought an abandoned public school for $562.50, with sufficient lots for a cemetery thrown in by the official sellers.[13]

In 1856 Patrick Maher preempted eighty acres of land along what was then called the Dubuque Road, about eleven miles southeast of St. Peter. Soon

---

12. For details see Blegen, *Minnesota*, 218–220.

13. David McGuire, "The Catholic Community of St. Peter, Minnesota, the First 140 Years" (n.p., n.d. [1993]), 10–14.

two of his brothers, a brother-in-law, and their families joined him. Born in County Cork, Maher had been working in a textile mill in New Hampshire. He was typical not only among his relatives but of the Irish and Germans generally who settled after him here in the vicinity of Lake Washington and Lake Ballantyne—typical in that all of these men, when first in America, had been employed in the eastern states and now came west looking for land of their own. Maher proposed to his neighbors the organization of a parish and, to press his point, he donated two acres for a church and five for a cemetery. The log church—forty feet by twenty, with a low roof, four windows on each side, an oak floor, and a plastered ceiling—accordingly went up late in 1857. Beyond that, he also had the southern end of his farm platted into streets and blocks, and called the place Marysburg.

In the early years life was hard, and Marysburg remained for many years a rustic village, hemmed in by towering forest. Many of the men had to supplement their income by hiring out their labor in nearby and thriving St. Peter. The most remarkable building in the settlement was Maher's large cabin, dubbed "Paddy's Castle." Here Father Sommerreisen probably said the first Mass in the parish of the Immaculate Conception even before the church was finished, and he continued to include Marysburg among his stations till 1867. That year the parish was assigned its first resident pastor, a forty-one-year-old Bohemian immigrant named Peter Maly, but when he departed after a year due to chronic ill health, Sommerreisen resumed responsibility from Mankato. Under his direction a frame church was built, exactly twice as large as the original and boasting an eighty-foot spire. Pews were added in 1871 and the interior plastered three years later.[14]

Before his short tenure among the Irish in Marysburg, the delicate Father Maly had served for awhile among his own compatriots who had settled about thirty-five miles to the northeast. In the spring of 1856 a small group of men with names like Hanzel, Stehlik, Stepka, and Bruzek, all hailing from the Vlatava River valley in Bohemia, turned up in the village of Shakopee. A later local tradition, perhaps apocryphal, suggested that they had intended to locate in the St. Cloud area, but, once they had traveled north by steamer from Dubuque, at the crucial junction they mistook the Minnesota River for the Mississippi. However that may have been, they heard in Shakopee of a settlement just beginning on a claim twenty miles away staked by a Bavarian named Anton Philipp. Loading their spare belongings on their backs, they walked

---

14. Anon. [Frank Sullivan], "Church of the Immaculate Conception, Marysburg, Minnesota, 1857–1957" (n.p., n.d. [1957]), 10–16.

through the woods till they arrived on the banks of Sand Creek. Herr Philipp emerged from his half cabin, half dugout, by no means thrilled to see them, until, when he reluctantly shared a meal with them, he discovered they were Catholics—they made the sign of the cross before they ate. He welcomed them then, as he did other Bohemians as they came to the site over the next few years in increasing numbers. Cabins were thrown up, swamps drained, and—the usual pattern—a log church erected in 1859, dedicated to St. Wenceslaus. Not surprisingly the village that subsequently grew up was soon called not New Munich but New Prague.

Anton Philipp apparently took in stride this non-Bavarian ascendancy. The first primitive school in the area was conducted in his cabin by a Bohemian-born laywoman. Moreover, he, along with Albert Vitis, J. Bernas, and Frank Bruzek, contributed for the support of the church forty contiguous acres. Philipp may, however, have indulged in a certain wry amusement that the first priests to serve the settlement, even before the church was built, were Benedictines from St. John's, who, for a brief span, had charge of the mission in Shakopee, and who were all German-speaking. This circumstance led to the same sort of conundrum that had confronted the French Joseph Cretin when he heard confessions in a German congregation.[15] The procedure adopted at St. Wenceslaus manifested rather more sophistication. The priest faced the penitent, and both of them were separated from the interpreter by a thin wall. The priest enunciated in turn the Ten Commandments in German, which the interpreter translated loudly into Bohemian. The penitent either nodded—meaning he had transgressed in that regard—or shook his head in denial. Thus secrecy was observed and embarrassment avoided, and sacramental absolution could be duly administered.

When the Bohemian Peter Maly arrived in New Prague in 1861, this elaborate procedure could be set aside. But Maly was not a lucky man: two years later the original church burned down, and many of his parishioners, more for economic than for religious reasons, talked about returning to the old country. They were for the most part dissuaded, and under a new pastor, Alois Plut—destined for a long and distinguished priestly career—a new church was constructed and, more importantly, a new optimism about the future inculcated. Nevertheless, the Czech tradition since the Hussite days of the fifteenth century has exhibited a stubborn streak of independence from ecclesiastical authority. In 1877, a dispute arose in New Prague between the clerical estate and the lay trustees over control of church property. Bishop

---

15. See chapter 4, above.

Grace interdicted St. Wenceslaus for some months, until Father Plut, by then pastor in Shakopee, managed to mediate the altercation. Even so, a significant fraction of St. Wenceslaus's congregation seceded from the mother church.[16]

Not far from New Prague, maybe fifteen or eighteen miles to the south, lay the most memorable of the early Catholic colonies in Minnesota, not, to be sure, by reason of its intrinsic importance but because of the romantic associations connected with its founder. James Shields (1810–1879), born in County Tyrone, emigrated from Ireland to Illinois at the age of sixteen. Industrious and boundlessly ambitious, he made of himself a lawyer—not too difficult a feat in those far-off days—and without much ado flung himself into the political arena. He attained local office first, then secured a seat on the state's supreme court, and from that position of judicial eminence was appointed governor of Oregon Territory. In the early 1850s he won election to the United States Senate from Illinois. None of these triumphs, however, could satisfy him, any more than did the reputation and medals he had earned for gallantry during the Mexican War (1846–1848), when, twice wounded, he was awarded brevet rank of major general. Always restless, he came to Minnesota Territory in the mid-1850s, intent upon carving out even more fame and fortune.

Shields settled first in Faribault in Rice County, but he soon fell out with local residents. With every intention of founding a town of his own, he bought a large tract ten miles away from a mixed-blood squatter and proceeded to plat the area and lay out streets and avenues. He sold shares to several budding entrepreneurs, and in St. Paul he persuaded others, mostly Irish immigrants, to join the widening venture. He placed advertisements in eastern newspapers prophesying the brilliant future of Shieldsville, and soon the village and the surrounding countryside were swarming with settlers. With statehood in 1858 Shields was elected to the United States Senate; he won this surprising victory less because of his own admittedly immense charm than

---

16. Robert Dobihal, "History of St. Wenceslaus Parish, New Prague, Minnesota" (n.p., 1957). This pamphlet has no pagination, but see its first sixteen leaves. "Interdict" is an ecclesiastical penalty that deprives a person or a place of sacramental ministration. "Trusteeism," an administrative phenomenon that troubled the Catholic Church in the United States during its early years, turned upon a tension between laity and clergy as to control over the material fabric of a parish. The problem in New Prague arose at a time when by and large the clergy, led by the local bishop, had successfully asserted its ultimate jurisdiction. John Hus (c. 1369–1415) was a Czech priest and theologian of heterodox views, whose condemnation and execution at the Council of Constance sparked a full-scale revolt across Bohemia.

because other prominent and ambitious Democrats quarreled among themselves.[17] His short term expired in 1860, and then, for reasons unknown—aside from his own wild Celtic restlessness—he moved to California. When the Civil War broke out, he hastened back East, was commissioned a brigadier general, and, along with several other Union commanders, fell victim to Stonewall Jackson in the latter's brilliant Shenandoah Valley campaign of 1862. Shortly after that humiliation, Shields resigned his commission and returned to California. By the mid-1870s he had relocated once again, now to Missouri, and when he died he once again held a seat in the Senate, for the third time and for the third state.

So General Shields, ever on the move, was hardly more than a remote, if benign and celebrated, onlooker of the little town he had established. Most of the inhabitants of Shieldsville and the vicinity were Catholics, and in the fall of 1856 Augustin Ravoux offered Mass there in the home of Patrick Hanlon. After the service he took several of the men in attendance with him out behind the house. They sat down on a pile of logs, and during their conversation Ravoux told them that Bishop Cretin wanted them to form a proper parish. The $25.00 donated to him for his services, he said, would be returned to them as the first contribution to the building of their church. Construction began promptly, not with logs but with finished lumber, to the cost of $800. A crisis loomed, however, when, with funds pretty well exhausted, the unpaid carpenters locked the building's door and refused anyone entry. Two farmers accordingly rode over to Faribault and, by mortgaging their property, secured enough money to pay the workmen. Such efforts notwithstanding, no resident priest was available for St. Patrick's of Shieldsville until 1867. He was an abrasive Irishman named McCullough who soon departed, leaving behind a reputation for incessant quarreling. By contrast his successor, the gentle, French-born Father Robert, was beloved by all his parishioners, including now, besides the predominant Irish, a goodly number of Belgians and Canadians. By the time he left in 1880, he had accumulated much of the stone and other material for a new and more spacious church.[18]

---

17. See Blegen, *Minnesota*, 227–228. Henry M. Rice, another Democrat, was the other senator elected in 1858. At this date, as was the case until the early twentieth century, U.S. senators were chosen by state legislatures rather than by popular vote. The most powerful Democrat in Minnesota, Henry H. Sibley, could surely have taken the Senate seat awarded to Shields had he not just been elected first governor of the state. See chapter 3, above.

18. Mary Hagerty, *Meet Shieldsville: The Story of St. Patrick's Parish, Shieldsville, Minnesota* (n.p., n.d. [1940]), 19–22.

Till the unpleasant Father McCullough came there in 1867, Shieldsville
was ministered to by the dogged George Keller, resident in Faribault but responsible during the early years for a broad swath of nascent parishes from
Rosemount in the north to Blooming Prairie in the south, from Kilkenny in
the west to Pine Island in the east. By wagon or buggy or, sometimes, simply
on horseback, Keller brought the gospel and the sacraments to these widely
scattered settlements as best he could, without neglecting his home base.
That base had a history and a peculiar importance of its own. In 1826, Alexandre Faribault—son of the venerable Jean-Baptiste, one of Lucien Galtier's
patrons[19]—was persuaded by the local Indians to open a trading post at a location more convenient for them, somewhere south of Mendota. Much time
and energy were expended in seeking a suitable site, and temporary stations
were set up in the vicinity of what are now the towns of Northfield and War-
saw. Ultimately Faribault, beguiled by the physical beauty of the place, asked
the approval of the Dakota—this occurred many years before the formal Indian treaties of the 1850s—to set up his business at the juncture of the Straight
and Cannon rivers. Here, on the west bank of the Straight, he built a log
house, fifteen by twenty-five feet, and by 1847 he had expanded his fur-trading
enterprise into conventional farming and livestock husbandry. That year, or
perhaps the next, Ravoux said Mass in the Faribault manse, attended by Alexandre, his métis wife, and the handful of French Canadians and Indians in his
employ. Over the following years an influx of Catholic immigrants into the
area, with names as diverse as LeMay, Fitzsimons, Armstrong, and Payant, all
clamored for the establishment of a parish. But others with very different confessional priorities also settled in the area. In 1856 a Congregationalist minister claimed about forty communicants and was anxious to put up a church for
them. "The followers of His Holiness the Pope," he wrote to a funding source
in New England, "ever ready to seize upon the best points, have contracted to
have a church built here early in the summer. Oh! Shall that be the first
church-edifice in this lovely region? God and the faithful forbid!"

But indeed the church for the local Roman Catholics, under the patronage of St. Anne—a gesture to the large number of French Canadians in the
area—was built on a hilly, attractive site, whatever the fulminations of the
local Protestant clergy. A year later, however, that primitive structure burned
down. Then, in 1858, upon the scene strode the sturdy figure of Father Keller,
impressive in his virile demeanor, symbolized best perhaps by his thick black
beard. Under his direction a new church went up, one hundred feet by fifty-

---

19. See chapter 2, above.

two, built of stone from local quarries, its inner walls tinctured by lime from local kilns. He dedicated the new edifice to Our Lady immaculately conceived.[20] A couple of years later he opened a two-room school in the basement of the church; this was pretty much a crude and hit-and-miss affair until the arrival in 1865 of five Dominican sisters—four of them, significantly, with Irish surnames—who then initiated their long and fruitful educational apostolate.[21]

Unsurprisingly, given his far-flung activities, it was George Keller who, on January 1, 1856, offered the first Mass in what would become the thriving town of Shakopee. Shortly afterward the Benedictines from Stearns County, with the approval of Administrator Ravoux, opened a permanent mission there, under the patronage of St. Mark. Their original plan to found a college in Shakopee did not materialize—happily, as the later history of St. John's University was to show.[22] But for some years their services filled a ministerial vacuum spreading out from the Minnesota River valley across Scott and Carver counties and the northern edge of Le Sueur, an area rapidly filling up with Catholic immigrants, many of them Germans. One such settlement, near Sand Creek, was called Holmes Mill, because the abundant water supply had induced one William Holmes to build a flour mill there. As early as 1854 Bishop Cretin had visited the handful of Catholics who lived in the huts thrown up in the shadow of the mill. Four years later Benedictine Cornelius Wittman oversaw the construction of a small church, dedicated to St. John the Baptist, and seven years after that, the Benedictines having departed and the settlement now called Jordan, the energetic Alexander Berghold replaced it with a more spacious edifice.[23]

But before he left the area Wittman persuaded another group of largely German settlers to establish a parish of their own some five miles south of

---

20. In 1854 Pope Pius IX proclaimed that traditional Christian doctrine revealed that Mary, the Mother of Jesus, had been conceived without the stain of original sin.

21. Johanna O'Leary, *Historical Sketch of the Parish of the Immaculate Conception, Faribault, Minnesota* (Faribault, 1938), 6–17. A personal note. From 1936 till 1939—that is, from grades one through four—I was a pupil in the Immaculate Conception school in Faribault and thus a debtor, among countless others, to the Dominican Sisters of Sinsinawa, Wisconsin, whom I remember with nothing but affection.

22. See Barry, *Worship*, 61, 66–67.

23. Germain Kunz, "History of St. John the Baptist Parish, Jordan, Minnesota, 1855–1900" (Master's thesis, St. Paul Seminary, 1957), 4–8, 20–22.

Jordan. The project enjoyed its initiation when, in the early autumn of 1859, he said Mass there in the home of John Berndgen, just as a twelve-acre parcel was formally donated to the diocese jointly by Berndgen and his wife Eva and by Christ and Margaret Busch. This tract, however, proved too hilly to sustain extensive construction; nevertheless, it furnished an endowment for the parish, while the first church was built a mile away on an acre bestowed by another resident, Nicholas Lennerths. From the beginning a certain Teutonic thoroughness prevailed in parochial arrangements. For example, the bylaws decreed that every family had to contribute $4.00 a year to support church and pastor, and a recording fee of $2.00 was required of every new member. Father Wittman was especially pleased that the settlement as well as the parish bore the name of St. Benedict.[24]

"In 1856," reads an old Scott County chronicle, "a Catholic church of logs was built on the southeast corner of section 35, and was named St. Mary's Church. This formed a nucleus about which a settlement was begun. The first dwelling-house was built by John H. and Peter Theis. The place was named Marystown, after the church." The account went on to describe how the local men, when they had dragged the logs to the site they had chosen, realized that it was the feast of lights, the Purification of the Virgin, February 2, Maria Lichtmesse. Characteristic of German Catholic immigrants, they soon set up a parochial school as well as an organization to maintain it, a Schule-Bau-Verein. The first schoolmaster was John Theis, who in after hours operated a saloon. As numbers increased the school was moved into one of the two rooms in the priest's Spartan residence. That accommodation shortly proved inadequate, and so the priest moved into the sacristy of the church. By the mid-1860s a two-story frame building housed the classrooms and the Sisters of St. Joseph who now staffed the institution.[25]

Not far away from Marystown another collection of German Catholic farmers had put down roots in a corner of Scott County called Union Hill. They had come there recently from temporary colonies in Wisconsin, though originally they had emigrated to the United States from the Rhineland, from the vicinity of Cologne and Trier. Old timers remembered many years later that, upon their arrival, they had been most fearful of the wolves roaming the

---

24. Anon., "Diamond Jubilee, St. Benedict's Church, Scott County, Minn." (n.p., n.d. [1935]), 7–13.

25. James Klein, "History of St. Mary's Parish of the Purification, Marystown, Scott County, Minnesota" (n.p., n.d. [1930]), 25–38.

vicinity freely and most puzzled about the peculiarly acrid smoke arising for a nearby swamp. The crude houses they put up were all of log, usually of a story and a half in height. The religious ministrations they received from the Benedictines at Shakopee were irregular at best; even so, by 1860 they had constructed a primitive church building. "With all our prayers and home devotions," a chronicler explained, "we nevertheless felt like pagans having no church to which we could go to adore God." By then Wittman and Bruno Riess[26] as well were riding the circuit across these counties. Whenever either of them approached the vicinity of Union Hill, he would ring a handbell, the word would spread that the missionary was nigh, and the congregation would gather. There emerged, however, a difficulty with Bishop Grace, who had laid down the rule that rural parishes needed to be at least six miles apart, so that each could count upon adequate financial support. Accordingly, since the Church of St. John the Evangelist of Union Hill was too close to Wittman's St. Benedict's, a new site was found some four miles away. This location too, where Mass was celebrated once a month from New Prague, came under challenge, until the ubiquitous and forceful Father Berghold, then centered in Belle Plaine, directed in 1867 the building of a third church which cost the by then bemused parishioners about $1,000.[27]

The Benedictine apostolate out of Shakopee in these years just before the Civil War extended also into the northern reaches of Le Sueur County, where German and Irish immigration was later augmented by Bohemians and Poles. At first, however, Ireland predominated, at least to the extent that the township where they all lived was named Derrynane, after Daniel O'Connell's country estate in County Kerry. In April 1857, Benedictine Father Benedict Heindl celebrated Mass in the home of John Carey, and the priest also on that occasion baptized thirteen-month-old Anne Connolly, the first in the area to pass through traditional Christian initiation. At the end of that year, a series of meetings was held, which resulted in the contribution of fifteen contiguous acres, half from Patrick and Catherine Ronan and the rest from Patrick and Elizabeth Cassin. In 1858, with Ravoux's endorsement, a log church was put up, 30 feet by 60, with shingled roof and roughboard floor, a crude altar against the east wall, no pews or sanctuary rail, and, more

---

26. See chapter 4, above.

27. Hilarion Duerk, "St. John's Parish of Union Hill, Minnesota" (n.p., n.d. [1940]), 19–32.

importantly, no stoves, so that in winter Mass could be celebrated only in private houses. No resident pastor was assigned to this parish of St. Thomas the Apostle till 1881.[28]

To the north and west of Scott lay Carver County, named for Jonathan Carver, the celebrated eighteenth century travel writer. When the first white settlers came there—2,000 of them by 1855—the area was heavily forested, what the Indians referred to as "the Big Woods." Ravoux had said Mass within its confines as early as 1842, at the Dakota camp called Little Prairie, where old J. B. Faribault maintained a trading post. With the Indians removed, Little Prairie became the village of Chaska, and in 1859 the Benedictines from Shakopee presided over the formation of Guardian Angels parish there. In nearby Cologne both Bruno Riess and Cornelius Wittman were instrumental in organizing St. Bernard's parish, the former overseeing in 1860 construction of a little frame church that cost $500. Catholic immigrants had settled in Young America by 1855; they were largely a mixture of Irish and Germans, with names like Zenzius, Richter, McCormick, and Sweeney. This lack of ethnic homogeneity perhaps explains the name of their village, a striking contrast to its neighbors Cologne, New Germany, and St. Bonifacius. A certain tension, however, was manifested by German resentment at the patron chosen for the community, St. Patrick. Mass at any rate was said in private homes until 1866, when a modest church was built. A decade later, to the immense annoyance of the Catholics of Young America, whatever their national origin, Bishop Grace granted permission that the parish be transferred to Norwood, a few miles to the south. Some gossip at the time suggested that Protestant hostility in Young America was responsible for this relocation, but in fact it came about through the efforts of two young and enterprising Norwood businessmen named John Molitor and Mathias Simonitsch—abetted by the pastor, Gottfried Braun—who argued that since a spur of the Chicago, Milwaukee, and St. Paul Railroad ran through their town, the parish could more readily prosper in such an up-and-coming community. Their boosterism prevailed,

---

28. John Duane et al., *Church of St. Thomas, 1883–1983* (Le Sueur, 1982), and Anon., "The Church of St. Thomas of Derrynane, Le Sueur County, Minnesota" (n.p., n.d. [1938]), 6–10, 3–7. A personal note. This was the parish in which my paternal ancestors settled. My grandfather, William O'Connell (1862–1954), and my grandmother, Hannah Shea O'Connell (1863–1953), were born here. See John D. O'Connell, "The Log Church in Derrynane" (n.p., n.d. [1946]), the author of which was my grandfather's brother.

and so, in the end, did their central European taste in sacred nomenclature: in Norwood St. Patrick had to give way to the Ascension of the Lord.[29]

If the exclusively French and French Canadian character of early Catholicism in Minnesota had been supplanted by a composite of different languages and cultures, that original character nonetheless still manifested itself in several pioneer parishes. Little Canada provides one example[30] and Osseo, the foundation of which still resonates with romantic echoes, another. Pierre Bottineau, son of a French fur trader and his Ojibwe wife, was a throwback to the fast-disappearing *voyageur* tradition. As a young man he had left the Red River settlement in Manitoba and come to Fort Snelling, where he was employed as a guide and interpreter. Later he had lived for awhile near Pierre Parrant's tavern at Pig's Eye Landing,[31] where he gained a reputation for high-stake gambling and overall carousing. In the summer of 1852, Bottineau, now at age forty-two relatively more sober and sedate, joined with Pierre Gervais, Pierre Raiche, and Joseph Potvin in staking claim to a wide stretch of open land just west of what would become the city of Minneapolis. Three years later George Keller, who was fluent in both German and French, celebrated Mass in Bottineau's cabin, with a hundred worshipers crowded inside and spilling out of doors. Shortly afterward, under Bottineau's leadership, a log church, thirty feet by fifty, was built. Money was scarce, but timber was plentiful and volunteer labor readily available. This humble edifice, dedicated to St. Louis de France, was replaced in 1864 by a frame structure put up on a corner of Gervais's farm and renamed in honor of another eminent Frenchman, St. Vincent de Paul.[32]

In the beginning the settlement was called, not unreasonably, Bottineau Prairie. Shortly after it was platted in 1856, it came to be known as Osseo. The preceding November had seen the publication of Longfellow's *Song of Hiawatha,* which achieved immense and immediate popularity. It is said that the poet visited St. Anthony Falls while he was composing his idyllic tribute to the Ojibwe nation. *Osseo* at any rate means "there is light" or, more commonly thanks to Longfellow, "Son of the evening star."

---

29. Anon., "Souvenir of the Jubilee Anniversary, October 5, 1919, The Church of the Ascension, Norwood, Minnesota" (n.p., n.d. [1919]), 7–16.

30. See chapter 4, above.

31. See chapter 2, above.

32. Anon., "Dedication Souvenir of the St. Vincent de Paul Church, Osseo, Minnesota" (n.p., 1922), 3–21.

You shall hear a tale of wonder,
Hear the story of Osseo,
Son of the evening star, Osseo! . . .
Star of Evening, Star of Woman,
Star of tenderness and passion,
All its fire was in his bosom.

One cannot but assume that Bottineau, the old *voyageur* born of an Ojibwe mother, found the change of name acceptable.

Catholics in Osseo enjoyed the services of a resident pastor early on, who, however, had responsibility for several other settlements as well. One of these lay several miles to the north, across the Mississippi. A trading post had been opened on the west bank of the Rum River in 1844. It did not prosper, but ten years later there were cabins on both sides of the river. By 1860 Anoka boasted a sawmill, a gristmill, a lath and planing factory, a stable, two hotels, and a boarding house. Its population stood at a robust 635, of whom as many as fifteen percent were Catholics—mostly Irish, with a sprinkling of Canadians and Germans. In 1864 extension of the St. Paul and Pacific north and west brought Anoka added economic activity.[33] Not till 1866, however, did the Catholics there have a church of their own—purchased from the local Congregationalists for $1,250 and named in honor of St. Stephen—and not till 1873 did a priest reside in their midst.[34]

The first white men to visit the gorgeous valley of the St. Croix were Duluth and his companions in 1680.[35] The *Palmyra*, the first steamboat to ply the river, carried various wares to settlers as early as 1838. Five years later, 400,000 feet of timber, cut farther upstream at Marine and St. Croix Falls, were floated down to Lake St. Croix and collected there, prompting the erection of the first sawmill. By then Stillwater already supported a hotel, a blacksmith shop, and a licensed physician, and by 1849, Presbyterian and Episcopal churches as well as the territorial prison. Beginning that same year Father Ravoux occasionally said Mass in several different private homes of families with distinctively Celtic or Anglo names, like Heffernan, Lloyd, and Brown. In 1853 Cretin

---

33. Blegen, *Minnesota*, 296.

34. Anon., "St. Stephen's Church, Anoka, Minnesota, 1856–1956" (St. Paul, 1956), 5–18. See also Joseph Krause, "The History of Catholicity in Anoka County, Minnesota, 1670–1891" (Master's thesis, St. Paul Seminary, 1954).

35. See chapter 1, above.

assigned the restless Daniel Fisher[36] as pastor of St. Michael's parish, and he, before his return to New Jersey, initiated construction of a church, the task completed on an enlarged plan by his successor, Thomas Murray. Meanwhile, the number of German-speaking settlers increased notably in the Stillwater area, so much so that Grace decided in 1865 that a separate parochial entity was needed to serve them. Accordingly, Father Alois Plut, now transferred for the purpose from St. Wenceslaus in New Prague, and a local entrepreneur named Joseph Wolf mounted a campaign that raised $2,500, of which a third was spent to purchase the Presbyterian church—a rundown frame building on two lots—and the rest on an overall refurbishment of the property. Like so many German parishes, St. Mary's flourished in succeeding years, especially after the Benedictines assumed responsibility for it in 1880; under their direction a handsome brick church was constructed just as Bishop Grace's administration was coming to an end.[37]

To the north and west of Stillwater the Benedictines, out of their priory at St. John's, also came to manage a number of parishes in Stearns County. They had been preceded, however, by the indomitable Franz Pierz,[38] and, due to tensions rife in the old country, they were not always assured of welcome. In October 1854, Pierz, with a heavy pack on his back, appeared at a country crossroads called Clinton after some long-forgotten trapper or hunter. He was greeted by several recently arrived German immigrants, among them John Linnemann and Balthasar Fuchs, who urged him to remain there. As was his wont, Pierz put up a little log shack as a church, bestowed a pious name on the place—St. Joseph in this instance—and then moved on. Another year brought more Germans northward. One of them, Simon Lodermeier, kept a diary.

> We left St. Paul on May 6, 1855. Our party consisted of three families and had a weight of approximately three hundred weights [of baggage]. We hired two conveyances as far as Sauk Rapids, for which we paid thirty-eight dollars. In three days we covered this stretch. I spent one night in a barn, the other in a hay loft. . . . Cheerfully [the blacksmith at Sauk Rapids] took us in for the night. . . . The second day we crossed the Mississippi in quest for land. We traveled as far as St. Joseph. We inquired about

---

36. See chapter 4, above.

37. Reardon, *Diocese of St. Paul,* 605, and Anon., "100 Years, St. Mary's Parish" (Stillwater, 1965), 9–20.

38. See chapter 4, above.

land, but none was to be had. "Everything has been claimed"—we got no other information. In St. Joseph was a small log house, a log church without roof, window, or cross. That was all one could see far and wide. The log house was occupied by the Linnemanns.

Lodermeier, a thin man with a grizzled beard overspreading his chest, and his wife Crescentia, a stout woman but bearing the pallor of chronic ill-health— she died in 1864—both born in Bavaria, ultimately homesteaded in nearby St. Wendel Township.

Father Pierz came back to St. Joseph early in 1856, and at his urging a proper church was built, of logs, to be sure, but with roof, windows, and, presumably, a cross. The old Slovenian missioner had departed before it was finished, leaving regular ministry, as he had intended, in the charge of the Benedictines. This turn of events made some of the residents uneasy; they remembered the great abbeys that had for centuries thriven in the south of Germany and had held in fief vast tracts of the best land. Hence "a petition . . . was sent to St. Paul, begging the bishop [Cretin] not to inflict the monks on them and to keep them out of St. Joseph." But the petitioners had to deal with that most tough-minded of the pioneer Benedictines, Bruno Riess. "A few turbulent spirits," he said dismissively. And probably so: the storm quickly blew over.[39]

One might have predicted early on that heavily Catholic St. Cloud, with St. John's Abbey and University as the jewel in its crown, would one day, were the demographic trends of the 1860s to continue, have a bishop of its own. Such a prediction was not as likely to have been voiced about Winona; yet, as Minnesota triumphantly gained statehood, the population of this southeast river town, set exquisitely among the Mississippi bluffs, approached 3,000, not much less than that of St. Paul and St. Anthony. As years passed, however, it proved more an entrepôt rather than a concentration point for settlers, who either passed upriver on the endless flotilla of steamers from St. Louis or else disembarked on the Winona levee only to board a prairie schooner and head westward toward the open plains. Bishop Cretin, even so, recognized the potential importance of the place, and in 1856 he traveled there in person to organize the handful of Catholics into a parish. But he had no priest to assign as resident to St. Thomas the Apostle, and the fledgling community was served alternately by Thomas Murray from Stillwater and Anatole Oster from Mendota. In 1858 Administrator Ravoux managed to send Michael Prendergast to

---

39. Anon., *A History of St. Joseph, 1856–1956* (n.p., n.d. [1956]), 17–32.

Winona, though that young Irishman, like his colleagues Keller, Sommer-reisen, Berghold, and the rest, had to assume duty over a wide area besides his home base. It was no doubt significant that Bishop Grace included Winona on his very first diocesan visitation, only months after he had donned the miter.[40] In 1862 he sent Theodore Venn to Winona to care for the Germans, Poles, and Bohemians, and nine years later the newly ordained Joseph Cotter, son of a prominent St. Paul civil servant,[41] was assigned to St. Thomas the Apostle, where he remained until 1890, when he was consecrated first bishop of Winona, and St. Thomas church became a cathedral.[42]

St. Cloud attained the same dignity the same year, as did Duluth, whose prospects for such a status, during the early years of Bishop Grace's adminis-tration, would have seemed at best highly implausible. In the mid-1860s the settlement at the head of Lake Superior counted less than a hundred inhabit-ants, a significant proportion of them a remnant of the Ojibwe. By 1870 that number had risen to more than 3,000, of whom nearly two-thirds were for-eign-born immigrants. Most of these were from northern Europe, and they brought with them an almost visceral suspicion of popery. This circumstance made life awkward for the Catholics, who belonged by and large to the lower classes—lumberjacks, sailors on the lakes, small shopkeepers, construction laborers. The community's élites, on the other hand, kept up a drumbeat of hostility to "Romanism" through the popular press. Much of this unpleasant-ness was neutralized by the efforts of one remarkable man. For some years Austrian-born Father John Chebul, in the finest missionary tradition, had en-dured the rigorous apostolic life across northwestern Wisconsin. In 1860 he took up residence in Superior, then a village of five hundred souls, where French and Irish immigrants gave him welcome. From there he had on occa-sion made the seven-mile journey across the bay to say Mass in private homes or stores for the Catholics in Duluth.

By 1869 Chebul concluded that the number of communicants on the western shore warranted the formation of a regular parish. These putative pa-rishioners, however, were mostly poor, and the struggle to raise the $7,000 dollars necessary to furnish an adequate facility was protracted. Meanwhile the prosperity of Duluth and its port grew prodigiously, as did its population. Steadily the numbers increased, until they had reached 25,000 in 1884, the

40. Lucker, "Grace," 59–60.

41. See chapter 5, note 62, above.

42. Anon., *Golden Jubilee, 1856–1906, St. Thomas Cathedral* (Winona, n.d. [1906]), 3–9.

year of Bishop Grace's retirement. His own formal visit in the summer of 1870 from St. Paul, accompanied by vicar general Ravoux, made a considerable impression, but it was Chebul's own sophisticated and cosmopolitan demeanor that tended to neutralize the nativist antagonism which Catholics had had heretofore to endure. Here was a man eloquent in English, German, French, and Ojibwe, one whose old-world manners put him on a plane that none of the local magnates could denigrate. Once the Church of the Sacred Heart, destined to be a cathedral, was securely established—significantly the local Ojibwe had contributed $100 to its construction—Chebul announced in 1871 his intention to return to his missions in Superior and its environs. "We regret exceedingly," commented a local Duluth editorial, "that Father Chebul, the very gentlemanly Catholic priest, will confine his ministrations to [Wisconsin]. He is an earnest, zealous man, popular with all denominations." The cultural environment had changed indeed. Who could possibly succeed such a paragon? Perhaps the only candidate was someone of the stature of George Keller, whom in fact Grace did direct to exchange his strenuous mission in Faribault for a ministry along the scenic western shore of Lake Superior.[43]

Wright County, directly west of what would one day be Minneapolis, was created by the territorial legislature in 1855. Across it ran a great forest of hardwood trees—maple, oak, and elm—broken by a smattering of small lakes. The soil was rich and black. The first white settlers, most of them German, sometimes encountered roving bands of usually inoffensive Ojibwe. A year later a sawmill opened in the hamlet of Monticello and soon after a ferry across the Mississippi was in operation, as well as a thirty-mile stretch of dirt road southwest from there to a tiny settlement of timbermen called Forest City. Also in 1856 a log church dedicated to St. Michael was built, where Mass was said for the first time by the Benedictine Demetrius Marogna.[44] Over the next decade the Benedictines continued to minister to the area fitfully as their personnel permitted. Most memorable among them was a young monk named Alexius Roetzer, six feet tall, strongly built, red-haired, amiable yet strict, "his face long and emaciated, his eye benign and intelligent."[45] By 1865 the Benedictines had pretty well withdrawn from Wright, although, in an

---

43. Raymond Cossette, "The Catholic Church in the City of Duluth, 1869–1890" (Master's thesis, St. Paul Seminary, 1965), 9–14.

44. See chapter 4, above.

45. Quoted in Richard Roedel, "A History of Catholic Settlement in Wright County" (Master's thesis, St. Paul Seminary, 1964), 25. See also Barry, *Worship*, 43–45.

ironic twist, one of their erstwhile brethren, Magnus Meyer, who had fallen out with his superiors at St. John's, was appointed by Bishop Grace first resident pastor in St. Michael. St. Mary's in Waverly, originally a mission of St. Michael, flourished more strikingly than any other parish in the county. A mission in 1876, conducted by the Paulist Fathers, resulted in 460 persons approaching the confessional and communion rail, as well as ten adult baptisms. By 1892 St. Mary's counted 240 families of mixed nationalities.[46]

The road from Monticello to Forest City linked the Mississippi and the Crow rivers and Wright and Meeker counties as well. Among the lumberjacks in Forest City was a Catholic Irishman named Thomas O'Doughertay [sic] whose wife Catherine, on July 14, 1856, gave birth to Sarah Jane, the first white child born in Meeker County. Her early years were rife with unwelcome adventures. As an infant she was kidnapped by Indians, who, however, returned her in exchange for provisions supplied by her father. In 1862, when Sarah Jane was six years old, the O'Doughertays were among the families in peril when the Dakota laid siege briefly to Forest City.

Commerce and immigration, which had slackened in the wake of the recession of 1857 and the Dakota uprising, quickened remarkably once the Civil War was over. The Catholics in Forest City accordingly built a frame church, dedicated to St. Gertrude, where the inaugural Mass was celebrated on Christmas 1867, by one of the peripatetic monks from St. John's, most likely the tireless Cornelius Wittman. Four years later the first diocesan and resident priest was assigned to Forest City in the person of Arthur Hurley, born, educated, and ordained in Ireland. Meanwhile significant economic and social changes had occurred in Meeker County. A railroad link had been constructed between St. Paul and another settlement, some miles south of Forest City. So the county seat was transferred to Litchfield as was the local newspaper and other enterprises, with the conviction that here would be the commercial center of the area. Hurley chose to live there too, though technically he remained pastor in Forest City. This anomalous arrangement made little practical difference, because Hurley, like all his peers at this time, was in essence a circuit rider, constantly on the road, bundling up his Mass kit in order to serve, in his case, congregations as far away as Benson, Morris, and Willmar. The same was true of his successor, Thomas Cahill. Neither of these priests lasted long following this rigorous schedule. Of sterner stuff was John McDermott, a rotund, red-haired, witty man, who in 1874 came to Forest City/Litchfield from Austin. He brought with him the reputation of a ferocious teetotaler, which

---

46. Roedel, "Wright County," 34–55.

may in part explain his appointment in the wake of the "breakdowns" suffered by his two predecessors. One of his first acts at any rate was to found a temperance society in which one hundred members promptly enrolled.[47]

As other priests became available for permanent assignment farther west, Father McDermott's circuit was reduced so that he became in effect pastor of Meeker County only. In 1875 he recorded that he was responsible for about two hundred families, that he performed through the year thirty-six baptisms and witnessed four marriages. In 1878 he saw to the construction of a little church at the station in Darwin and another, two years later, in Manannah. Curiously, though he resided as Hurley and Cahill had done in Litchfield, the prospects of building a suitable facility for that thriving community remained in the realm of rumor. Perhaps for that reason Bishop Grace, in 1882, had McDermott exchange places with the pastor at De Graff. Patrick Kenny, Connecticut born, educated at Collegeville and Montreal, ordained in 1877, immediately set in motion the incorporation of St. Philip's parish, Litchfield. A church was built at a cost of $4,500, and Mass was said in it late in 1883. In September of that year John McDermott returned to Meeker County and became pastor of St. Gertrude's, Forest City, which office, technically, he had held before, but this time in residence there. So, little by little, a measure of permanence and stability was established for the Catholics who lived south of the River Crow. And well it were so, for their numbers continued to swell. Over three early summer days in 1890, 117 were confirmed in Litchfield, eighty in Darwin, and ninety in Forest City.[48]

THE FOUNDATION OF ST. MARY'S PARISH IN ST. PAUL DID NOT FIT the pattern established elsewhere in the diocese, whether in the countryside or in relatively booming towns like Duluth and Winona. It reflected not only a more rapid growth in population—there were more than 40,000 people living in St. Paul in 1880 and twice that many four years later, when Bishop Grace retired[49]—but also the heightened prosperity and sophistication of the capital city. In mid-1865 the project, long considered, to divide the unwieldy

47. Jerome D. Quinn, "The History of St. Philip's Parish, Litchfield, Minnesota, and the Beginnings of Catholicity in Meeker County, Minnesota, 1855–1900" (Master's thesis, St. Paul Seminary, 1951), 4–24.

48. Quinn, "Litchfield," 62–79.

49. Virginia Kunz, *St. Paul: Saga of an American City* (Woodland Hills, Calif., 1977), 52.

cathedral congregation and to set up a new parochial entity to serve Catholics in the so-called Lower Town—that is, at the center of the plateau between Dayton's Bluff on the east and the gradually rising elevation on the west—was launched when Bishop Grace bought a substantial piece of property on Ninth Street for $1,200. French-born Father Louis Caillet, a gentle, self-effacing, but energetic priest, ordained in 1857, was named pastor of the nascent St. Mary's. More than $6,000 was promptly subscribed by Catholics and their Protestant neighbors. Five individuals contributed $500 each. A young Canadian entrepreneur named James J. Hill, a Protestant who had married a Catholic wife, donated $150, while Bishop Grace gave $50. Ground was broken in the autumn of 1865, and the cornerstone laid by Grace, with much fanfare, the following May. The formal opening and dedication of St. Mary's took place on July 28, 1867. Anatole Oster presided (both Grace and Ravoux were then in Rome on diocesan business), Theodore Venn sang the high Mass, and Father John Ireland preached "a stirring discourse."

In contrast to the log huts in Inver Grove and Osseo, and even to the large but barn-like Cathedral of St. Paul, St. Mary's church was widely regarded as "a monument to religion." At a cost of $25,000, it stood 100 hundred feet by 50, built of dressed blue limestone, ultimately adding a campanile 80 feet high and topped by a cross. Inside it featured walls of cream-colored plaster, later frescoed. The sanctuary, fourteen feet deep and semi-circular in shape, was lighted by three windows, a round one flanked by two ovals. The altar, of marbled wood and finished in gold, was the gift of Mrs. John S. Prince. Her husband, a banker and real estate speculator then serving his fifth term as mayor of St. Paul, had been one of those original $500 donors.[50] Mrs. Prince also paid for the sanctuary lamp, and it was she who formally lighted it for the first time in 1867; in succeeding years this Eucharistic flame was regularly tended by her or by one of her daughters. The original communicants at St. Mary's numbered about a thousand, and they included the "élite" of St. Paul's Catholic community. In 1869 a school opened with an enrollment of 250 pupils.[51]

As F. Scott Fitzgerald, himself a St. Paul native, famously observed, "Rich people are different from you and me." St. Mary's relatively well-off parishioners supported their own institutions—particularly the magnificent

---

50. See J. Fletcher Williams, *A History of the City of St. Paul to 1875* (St. Paul, 1876), 385–386, 412.

51. James Reardon, "The Church of St. Mary of St. Paul: The Story of a Pioneer Parish" (St. Paul, 1935), 9–18.

choir—very generously. Besides maintaining the usual societies, typical of
city parishes—Holy Name, Rosary, Perpetual Adoration, Young Ladies Sodality, Knights of the Blessed Virgin, St. Vincent de Paul, each with its own
social as well as religious component—St. Mary's also sought to promote the
betterment of Lower Town over a wider field. The women of the parish were
especially notable in this regard, not least because of the closeness between
the pastor and Mrs. James J. Hill. In the mid-1850s, when Mary Theresa
Mehegan's ne'er-do-well father died, it had been young Father Caillet, fresh
from France, who had assumed the role of protector of her and her impoverished mother. It had been Caillet too who had advised her when the brash but
up-and-coming entrepreneur from Canada, the non-Catholic Jim Hill, had
come courting, and who eventually urged her to accept his proposal.[52] Now,
with her husband's spectacular business success and notoriety, she had succeeded Mrs. Prince as the *grande dame* of St. Paul's Catholic aristocracy. In
1882 a committee chaired by Mrs. Hill presented Caillet with a check for
$12,000 so that the remaining debt could be paid and "so lift from the church
the encumbrance which had been a source of anxiety to him."[53] Two years
later, again under the leadership of Mary Mehegan Hill, twelve influential
matrons in the parish founded and funded St. Mary's Home for Girls, a hostel
for respectable young working women—their number increasing as the city's
economy expanded. Out of this institution, or rather out of this same band of
dedicated women, emerged another Lower Town initiative, a school for deaf-
mutes. And still another, with Mrs. Hill once more to the fore, a day nursery
built adjoining the Home where working mothers could leave their children.
The Ladies Aid Society in the parish dedicated itself to the provision of winter clothing for poor children.[54]

But, though munificent to their own philanthropic ventures, the parishioners of St. Mary's were niggardly when it came to supporting diocesan-wide
projects, much to the annoyance of Grace and Ireland.[55] And Fitzgerald's dictum was verified in another way. On a Sunday morning in September 1884,
Father Caillet told his congregation that John Ireland, now bishop in his own
right, had decided that a new parish was needed—the eleventh in the city—to

---

52. Mary Lethert Wingerd, *Claiming the City: Politics, Faith, and the Power of
Place in St. Paul* (Ithaca, N.Y., 2001), 59–60.

53. Quoted in Raymond Wey, "St. Mary's of Lower Town under Its First Pastor,
Monsignor Louis Caillet, 1865–1893" (Master's thesis, St. Paul Seminary, 1961),
42–43.

54. Wey, "St. Mary's," 48–60.

55. Wey, "St. Mary's," 63–64.

be carved out of St. Mary's territory, in order to serve the rapidly expanding Catholic population in the Mississippi Street district, east of the business district. This news was greeted with a noteworthy lack of enthusiasm, both by those who would remain within the old parish boundaries and those who would now be expected to become members of the new St. Patrick's. Father Daniel O'Reilly, on the cathedral staff, was assigned the unenviable task of initiating the separation. A new public school was being built in the vicinity, and O'Reilly bought the old one from the city for $600, along with $50 for the seats and desks. For another $325 he had the structure moved to the corner of Case and Mississippi Streets. Here the first Mass was celebrated in a single bare room in late October, 1884. Three laywomen opened a school in an adjoining room. It was a bleak, cold place, with hardly any equipment save for a few slates. Pupils and teachers did the janitorial chores.

Perhaps survival was due to the persistence of Daniel O'Reilly, who lived on the upper level of this sad little building. At any rate, opposition within the new parish quickly melted away, and by the end of the year a church 91 feet by 35, valued at $3,000, had been erected. And a goodly amount of money to pay for it was raised through private donations and also through the by now increasingly common means of sponsoring raffles, fancy-article sales, oyster suppers, and the like. The editor of the *Northwestern Chronicle* opined that the more established and prosperous parishes in the city would surely want to help the struggling St. Patrick's. This admonition was clearly directed at St. Mary's; what records survive attest that no such aid was forthcoming. Even so, all seemed to go modestly well until January 1887, when the old school building burned down. By then two sisters of St. Joseph were conducting the school, which was then relocated to the basement of the church, partitioned into four classrooms. Still, the population continued to grow, the church needed and got expansion, the pastor needed and got a house, valued at $2,500. During the 1890s it seemed that the liveliest organizations in the parish were the Church Debt Society and the Temperance Society.[56]

St. Patrick's church did survive, but not, since 1938, on its original Mississippi Street site. The same can be said about the much more affluent St. Mary's. In 1919 its property was sold, including the limestone church where Mrs. Prince and her daughters had guarded the Eucharistic flame, where congregations had listened rapturously as the choir performed masses by Mozart and motets by Palestrina, and where Mrs. Hill told her beads and planned her

---

56. See Grace Schutte, "The History of St. Patrick's Church, 1884–1934" (St. Paul, 1934).

schedule of good works. Jim Hill was dead by then, but, ironically, it was the expansion of the yards of his Great Northern Railway that necessitated the removal to a new location. Times change, and neighborhoods change. The Gilded Age could not last forever.

THESE THUMBNAIL SKETCHES DO SCANT JUSTICE TO THE SUBJECT they address, but perhaps they throw some light on what was the single most important feature of the development of Catholicism in Minnesota. These early parishes—and scores more of them not treated here—represented the determination of the various immigrant groups to maintain the principles of the old religion even as they became citizens in a new land. Preachment of the gospel and administration of the sacraments, particularly the Eucharist, led them, even as they strove merely to survive, also to scour the forests and hack away at the quarries in order to build a church where the sacred rites of passage could be appropriately performed—where Mass could be offered, babies christened, sinners shriven, marriages solemnized, the deceased formally and honorably bade farewell. "With all our prayers and home devotions," said the German farmer settled at Union Hill, "we nevertheless felt like pagans having no church to which we could go to adore God." And as soon as they could these Catholic pioneers put up a school, no matter that the teacher and children met in a little shack or even in the back room of a saloon.

The parish offered social cohesion as well as religious ministration. Round the church and its annual cycle of fast and feast, like-minded people could gather and acquire a focus to their lives in the midst of new and strange surroundings. They could replicate something of the village life they had known in the old country, maintain their customs and preserve their language for a while at least, and thus mitigate to a degree the harshness and drudgery of toilsome days and the occasional nativist antipathy they encountered. In the long run, to be sure, nostalgia would have to yield to genuine assimilation into the American mainstream, and eventually so it did. But for the first generation or so the Catholic pioneers in Minnesota needed to retain a cultural connection between the Old World they had freely departed and the New, in which they trusted that they, their children, and their faith would flourish.

CHAPTER 7

Politics and Pembina

THOMAS LANGDON GRACE WAS IN THE FORTY-SIXTH YEAR OF HIS life when he arrived in St. Paul. He was a portly, round-faced man whose small-lensed spectacles lent him a permanently startled expression, to which, as the years passed, a corona of frizzled hair around a balding pate added a somewhat Pickwickian flavor to his appearance. His placid temperament belied a shrewd and discerning mind. Moreover, his extended experience in Italy during his school days bestowed upon him a cosmopolitan and scholarly air, which he had worn with unaffected ease in Memphis and had brought with him to the upper reaches of the Mississippi River valley. Such an aura would have availed the bishop little in the rough-and-tumble frontier world had he not been a genuinely cultivated man. In his case reputation did not outrun fact. Thomas Grace displayed a refinement, a polish, an elegance of manner and speech that earned him the high regard of his contemporaries, including that of non-Catholics, as "one of the ablest prelates in America."[1] For a community like St. Paul, vital and expanding and yet self-consciously aware of its own coarseness, the presence of this cultured and bookish clergyman—"temperate, courteous, and pious"[2]—offered a measure, a token so to speak, of its own respectability. Nor would he abide any sign of what he perceived to be vulgarity among his own. Once, when a pastor in Minneapolis placarded the town with crude posters advertising the dedication of his new church, the bishop, who was scheduled to preside at the ceremony, stonily

---

1. Williams, *St. Paul,* 390.
2. In the words of the judges at the Propaganda in Rome; see Archives of the Propaganda de Fide, A-222 (1858): 595, 506–607.

refused to attend.[3] There was, in short, nothing flashy about Grace. On the contrary, his strength lay in the careful, understated manner in which he performed the largely humdrum obligations of his office. He was cautious, balanced, always civil, never hasty in his judgments.[4] Above all, he possessed a serene appreciation of his own worth, which kept him preserved from the least pang of jealousy. The success of others did not trouble or threaten Thomas Grace, and, if he were not a leader notable for initiating great projects, he never obstructed a subordinate who did.

Habitually courteous and amiable, the second bishop of St. Paul got on well with most people, even with the likes of the sometimes prickly and imperious Augustin Ravoux, whom he prudently made vicar general. This appointment, aside from acknowledging Ravoux's obvious merit, was also a gesture calculated to soothe the feelings of the no longer dominant French constituency within the diocese. But it should not be concluded that Grace, well disposed as he may have been to the veteran pioneer missioner, exhibited any hesitation to assume the complete control that the papal mandate had accorded him. In other canonical respects, he wasted no time in defining his authority, and doing so in some detail. As early as September 9, 1859, he drew up and issued to his priests the "Constitutions of the Diocese of St. Paul." Besides endorsing the decrees of previous national and provincial councils, held at Baltimore and St. Louis respectively, as well as some of Administrator Ravoux's prior directives, he laid down several highly explicit rules of his own. "We most strictly prohibit in every case whatsoever," he wrote in the monarchical first person plural, "the hearing of the confessions of women in the priest's house, and, if the priest cannot go to the church to hear them, we command that they be deferred to a later date." Confessionals, he added, were to be set up in any station regularly visited by a priest, or, if no chapel has been built in that community, "in homes designated by the bishop for the celebration of Mass." No evidence exists that any scandal had arisen in this regard, but since a staple of anti-Catholic polemic was the accusation that the Romish clergy routinely seduced pious and unsuspecting women when allegedly administering the sacrament of penance, the bishop insisted on the proprieties in order to avoid any such defamatory gossip.

---

3. Reardon, *Diocese of St. Paul,* 166. The offending priest, James McGolrick, later became first bishop of Duluth.

4. For a literary example of these qualities, see Grace's first "Pastoral Letter to the Diocese of St. Paul," dated November 9, 1859, and printed in *A&D* 7 (1935): 196–202.

He was similarly blunt in instructing his priests to observe the proper decorum in their custody of the sacraments, especially the most important of them, the Eucharist: "We strictly enjoin upon the priests of the diocese not to carry the Blessed Sacrament about with them, under any pretext whatsoever, unless actually on a sick call, and we declare those who disobey suspended *ipso facto*." Nor, he directed, was "any priest permitted to administer the sacraments within the territory of another priest, unless invited by him to do so or authorized by us in writing. Each priest has jurisdiction within the district committed to his care." The casual modus operandi of the earlier missionary days had to give way, Grace was saying in effect, to a more settled set of administrative procedures. Even that wellspring of lay piety, demonstrated in the spontaneous formation of so many parishes across the region,[5] needed to be properly channeled: "All the priests of the diocese before the erection of a church [must] obtain the written approval of the Ordinary as well as a deed to the property on which the church or chapel is to be erected." Moreover, every pastor "must procure a book in which to record and describe all the property belonging to the church, ascertaining what portion is subject to taxation and what is exempt, and all the contents of the church of the value of three dollars and over." Finally, and perhaps the greatest sign of anxiety to bring the pioneer Catholic community into conventional conformity, was the draconian (as it would seem to later years) legislation regarding "a marriage contracted before a civil magistrate":

> We decree that . . . if the contracting parties entered into it maliciously and in contempt of church and pastor, they must do public penance. . . . At the Solemn Mass on a Sunday or holyday the pastor will, from the pulpit, announce to all the people the names of the married couple, and in their name and with their consent beg pardon of the congregation for the scandal they gave. Then and only then may they be admitted to the sacraments.[6]

Two months later to the day Bishop Grace signed his first pastoral letter. On one level it was a largely conventional document, addressing to clergy and laity an appeal to live to the full their Christian calling. But it also manifested a candor and adroitness of argument—to say nothing of a literary style—quite remarkable for the genre. Priests, the letter began, must cultivate intense

5. See chapter 6, above.
6. Text (Latin) of the "Constitutions" in AASPM, Grace Papers.

fervor as well as untiring endurance, because "an immense immigration has peopled the vast plains comprised within our state, . . . which, but a decade of years past, were scarcely yet trod by the feet of civilized men." The people in the pews, "the diversity of [whose] nationalities gives beautiful prominence to the unity of the faith," rightfully demand sacramental ministration. But they also have obligations of their own:

> We would, beloved brethren, that you should take a more lively interest in your religion. You should know that you also are the apostles of truth; that God will require of you an account of the good you might do and have not done; an account of how you have used your means and opportunities, your talents, your influence, your advantages of position and association in promoting the interests of His religion, contributing to His honor and glory and to the salvation of souls.

Such duty, Grace added, falls especially upon the relatively few well-to-do Catholics when confronted by "the depressing effects of the great masses of our poor. . . . Be not ashamed, brethren, of the lowly and the poor; think it not a disgrace, but a privilege, to be associated with them. The Church rejoices in the number of her poor. . . . She loves them as Christ loved them." But all Catholic laymen and women, rich and poor alike, are obliged by their moral example—notably, on this hard-drinking frontier, by their temperate behavior—to lead those outside the Church "to a knowledge of the truth. Yet, alas, how little is done." How many are those "who keep their religion hidden, who, if not ashamed of it, fear to obtrude it in their speech or action, who disguise it and dissemble it, and assimilate it with the forms of fashionable error, who, seeing not the weak points of the society in which they move, flatter them, instead of taking advantage of them for the interests of Jesus and of souls."

The polished prose of the pastoral testified to Grace's overall cultivation and habitual studiousness.[7] So did an appeal made in it near the beginning.

> Worthy . . . of consideration are the means furnished by the press for preparing the way for faith in souls. . . . The value and importance of these means can hardly be exaggerated in these times and in this country. The press is equally efficient for good and for evil. . . . It is a power that can be

---

7. See chapter 5, above.

opposed only by itself. It is wielded unsparingly and incessantly against the truth of our religion. We need the same power in defense of that truth. The power is proportionate to the means supplied to create and sustain it; and these means must come from us and the Catholic faithful. If we will have a press such as the necessities of the times demand, a press that will demand the attention not merely of Catholics but of the public at large, we must offer such inducements as will engage and remunerate the best talent and ability.

On this last point the widely read bishop, who knew well both the quantity and quality of current Catholic publications, offered a wry suggestion that many of his readers may not have understood: "Fewer journals and a concentration of talents as of means might be desirable to this effect." Moreover, such practicality could serve usefully for the diffusion of books as well as the promotion of worthwhile periodicals. "How many are there now in the Church who trace their conversion to a chance book mislaid by some poor Catholic on the wayside? . . . Could not a fund be provided . . . from yearly voluntary contributions of the faithful by which . . . arrangements could be made for the distribution of . . . books, and publishers be enabled, through the increased circulation, to issue them at greatly reduced prices?"

Finally, at a time of great political volatility—eighteen months later the nation would be at war—Grace quoted approvingly the single pastoral of his predecessor: "'Brethren, respect the rights and liberty of everyone; but do not suffer your own rights as citizens to be unknown or trampled upon by others. . . . Abstain from party strife; preserve your independence; and do not become mean tools of bold and intriguing men.'" Cretin had delivered his exhortation in 1855, at the height of the bigoted Know-Nothing agitation. But Grace, while admitting the principle, saw a different application. "It is not," he wrote,

> that we ask or seek privileges as Catholics—we ask only that our rights under the Constitution of the country be respected and maintained. The Constitution . . . guarantees equality of rights to all citizens. If that equality be at any time impaired in your regard, . . . it is your duty to stand up as a body and demand that the invidious distinction be removed. The cause of your constitutional and municipal rights is a cause apart and by itself; it should be kept so.

The threat to this "cause," however, came now, he argued, from a different source.

[It should] not have odium entailed upon it by connecting it with the partizan [sic] politics of the day. It possesses sufficient weight in itself, and in the sense of justice and equality of rights of the people of this country at large to insure it a successful issue through a united, firm and manly representation on the part of Catholics. If you will have your rights respected, you must respect them yourselves, and never consent to sink or sacrifice them in the interest of any political organization. Acknowledge vassalage to no party, free master of your own acts, conscious of your rights and firm in the assertion of them, using your own reason and judgment to determine you in your political action and associations, holding your right of suffrage as something sacred, for the common good and for the good of the country—you will [then] command the respect of your fellow citizens of all parties, and will have in all public affairs the weight and receive the consideration to which by your numbers you are legally and justly entitled.[8]

A Whig politician, possibly a British contemporary of Thomas Grace, waggishly described the Church of England as "the Tory Party at prayer." Whatever the merits of this bromide, it would seem that the second bishop of St. Paul felt deep concern that Catholic immigrants—especially the Irish— had fallen thrall to the Democratic Party in the United States. Even before he published his pastoral letter, he had raised this concern in a letter addressed to the *Western Banner,* the Catholic newspaper published in St. Louis. That communication had received considerable notoriety, quite beyond Grace's expectation, and this circumstance had led him to send a copy of the pastoral along with a covering letter to James McMaster in New York. "My dear Sir," he wrote, "I have wished for some time to write to you in reference to a letter of mine which was published early last August in the *Western Banner* of St. Louis, fearing that you might consider the sentiments it contains as reflecting upon the course of the *Freeman's Journal,*" a periodical Grace read regularly and usually with approval.[9]

James Alphonsus McMaster was at the time thirty-nine years old. The son of a prominent Presbyterian minister from upstate New York, he had joined the Catholic Church in 1845. He had tried out a vocation as a Redemptorist, only to decide after a year of novitiate that the life of a religious was not

---

8. "Pastoral," *A&D* 7 (1936): 197–199, 200–202. For an able analysis of the pastoral, see Lucker, "Grace," 66–71.

9. See chapter 5, above.

suitable for him. Back in New York City as a layman, he scoured up enough funds to purchase from Archbishop John Hughes[10] the struggling Catholic newspaper *The Freeman's Journal*. He remained editor and publisher of that periodical for nearly forty years. On matters doctrinal McMaster consistently defended the Church's magisterium, but on social and political affairs, his real interest, he assumed an independent line. He quickly became famous for his acerbic attacks on potentates, ecclesiastical and secular. Inevitably he came into conflict with the autocratic Hughes, who was himself a formidable controversialist, as indicated by the nickname his clergy conferred on him, "Dagger John." McMaster seemed to delight in adopting positions calculated to outrage prevailing opinion. He described himself as an anti-abolition, states-rights Democrat, and during the first year of the Civil War his furious editorial onslaughts against President Lincoln and the federal administration led to his arrest and brief imprisonment and the closing down of his paper for some months.

That the bishop of a frontier diocese, far removed from the vast population centers of the East, felt constrained to assure this stormy petrel of Catholic journalism of his high regard may appear surprising. Moreover, to do so was chancy for a Southerner now located, against his personal wishes, in the North at a moment when McMaster's views on abolition were clearly at variance with the public mood. Not that Grace ever indicated sympathy for chattel slavery. Still, he was Charleston-born and Memphis-bred, and indeed once the war began, grumbling was heard in some quarters around St. Paul about his loyalty to the Union, insinuations the bishop rightly ignored and with his usual *sang froid*.[11] But in fact Grace's communication to McMaster in November 1859 had nothing to do with the impending political and military crisis, and everything to do with two concerns he had raised in his pastoral letter. The first of these included an endorsement that must have been music to the ears of *The Freeman's Journal's* proprietor.

> I hold [Grace wrote] that Catholic papers exclusively religious are comparatively of little service to the cause either of the Catholic religion or of the rights of Catholics. That secular journals animated with Catholic spirit and speaking to the country at large, taking part in the discussion of all public questions and measures, are the kind of papers demanded by

---

10. Irish-born Hughes (1779–1864) was bishop (1842) and first archbishop (1850) of New York.

11. Reardon, *Diocese of St. Paul*, 148.

the times, and they should be free to give their views and opinions upon all subjects, and advocate or oppose the claims of any party or any measures as in their judgment seems to them good. I need not say that these are the features I have admired and recommended in the Freeman's Journal, and for which I regard it as the most efficient paper we have, and I should rejoice to see its material prosperity worthy of its undoubted ability, and such as would enable it to contend with equal advantages against the infidel and anti-Catholic press of the country. Its right to denounce Mr. Buchanan or to advocate the claims of Mr. Douglas and his party or of any other party is implied in its independence, which is all I ask for our Catholic journals and our Catholic people.

This remarkable tribute to the freedom of the Catholic press, relieved of pietism and the dead hand of clericalism, reflected an ecclesiastical tradition in America that was all too soon to pass away. It smacked of the views of that other distinguished Charlestonian prelate, John England,[12] who promoted among the handful of Catholics in his jurisdiction a sturdy sense of lay participation and independence, particularly with regard to the printed word. But the "immense tide of immigration," as Grace expressed it, was to alter radically the parameters of social realities, even in his own lifetime, when there emerged an educated clerisy offering willy-nilly leadership to a largely untutored laity. Meanwhile, there was another matter, also related to the unprecedented inrush of immigrants to the United States, that he wanted to raise with the ardent McMaster, one that at first blush might not have been so welcome to the pugnacious Democratic journalist. It was all very well, as Grace readily conceded, for the *Freeman's* to demonstrate its admirable independence by joining an intraparty squabble to denounce the inept President Buchanan while advocating the ambitious Senator Douglas,[13] both Democrats. For Bishop Grace the much graver issue was the relationship between political party and the American Catholic community.

That our Catholic people—the great controlling mass of them—are independent in the sense just indicated, you will not affirm, or anyone who has given the matter any degree of attention. It is undeniable that the

---

12. Irish-born England (1786–1842) was bishop of Charleston from 1820.

13. James Buchanan (1791–1868), President of the United States, 1857–1861; and Stephen Douglas (1813–1861), U.S. Senator from Illinois from 1847, debater of Abraham Lincoln in 1858, presidential candidate in 1860.

great preponderating body of our people is claimed from the circumstance of its place of birth, as belonging to one particular party denomination in this country, and it virtually and in effect admits that claim by its unquestioning submission and undeviating adherence to the party at all times and under all circumstances, regardless alike of its policy, its principles, its measures, and its men. *This is what cannot be said of any other considerable portion of the people of this country, native or naturalized.*

A century and a half later, the most striking feature of Grace's analysis stands not as a brief against McMaster and *The Freeman's Journal* but rather against those powerful men, secular and ecclesiastical, who would exploit "the immense immigration" of Catholics into the United States, especially in the great sees of the East. What fretted this Dominican heir of St. Thomas Aquinas was the prospect that the integrity of the individual would be sacrificed on the altar of an abstract communal good, attainable, it appeared, only by cooptation by the Democratic Party. Out of prudence, Grace did not name Archbishop Hughes or advert to the precursors of Tammany Hall in New York, but his meaning could not have been clearer.

The basis of the institutions of these United States is the individuality of its citizens. The well-being of the country, the public good and private rights of all depend upon the intelligent political action of the citizens as individuals. Every American feels it not only his right but his duty to examine and discuss all questions whatever of policy and government, to entertain or reject any views, to ally himself with or against any movement according to his own discretionary sense and judgment.

From his newly acquired bastion in the northern wilderness, the second bishop of St. Paul, drawing upon more than two decades of reflection and experience, laid down principles worthy of the sturdiest American constitutionalist.

The mutations of governmental administrations [he continued to argue with McMaster], the changes in national policy, the success or failure of public measures—are all affected, whether for good or for evil, through this free, elastic, untrammeled political action of citizens in their individual capacity . . . [which in essence contradicts] the one same political faction whose hopes of [electoral] success are based mainly upon the blind and unquestioning subserviency of these [Catholic] masses.

But has such obeisance to one political party, the Democrats, afforded the Catholic minority a happy status within the commonwealth?

> The necessary effect of this state of things has been to irritate the minds of all other classes and parties and to engender feelings of hostility against us and our religion, which is blamed as the cause in no small measure of the conditions of things complained of. It deprives us as Catholics of the weight and consideration we ought to have as integral members of the Republic. For, as to us, it is regarded as a foregone conclusion [for the benefit of the Democratic Party]. . . . Little care is had to consult our views and sentiments on any public measure, or regard had for the manner in which it may or may not affect us. Even the party claiming the allegiance of our people hardly feels it necessary to have any particular regard for them, and does not further [their aspirations more] than appearances require, and its promises are generally made with the intent of failure in the fulfillment.

Grace, despite the forcefulness of his argument, intended no disrespect for the equally forthright McMaster. Indeed, "I was sorry to appear to differ with you and desired to explain my reasons. An evil certainly exists which, if it did not affect injuriously our religion and the religious rights of our people, I should be silent upon it." But the facts of the case demand attention: "I need only allude to the demoralizing effects upon our people of this insane partisanship."[14]

McMaster took no offense at the bishop's candor, and of course he was gratified by Grace's endorsement of the modus operandi of *The Freeman's Journal*. Predictably, however, he disagreed that "the degraded political position occupied by Catholics at large throughout the country" was a result of party allegiance. The difficulty arose rather because of a lack of principle or disinterestedness among the Catholic masses, who vote a straight party ticket because they discern some real or potential financial advantage in doing so. This unhappy situation can never be resolved unless they, especially the Irish immigrants, "in their whole conduct, act more as men with individuality and conscience and less like dumb driven cattle." As to Grace personally, "I have rejoiced at your appointment," McMaster concluded, "to a See that, whatever the momentary embarrassments of temporal affairs, is destined in a few

---

14. Grace to McMaster, November 15, 1859 (copy), AASPM, Grace Papers.

years to be so important in numbers and position. I rejoice too in seeing another added to the Hierarchy who is capable of understanding the age and the country."[15]

The bishop took the compliment in stride, while refusing to concede Mc-Master's bovine metaphor with regard to the Irish Catholic population. "Dear Sir," he replied,

> I have given your letter a careful perusal, and I thank you for the candid expression of your sentiments. . . . I can very readily see how your views apply to professional politicians and office-seekers, but not so readily how they apply to that population in general. I have, I must say, a more encouraging opinion of these people than the one your letter seems to express. With all their faults, they possess many sterling qualities, which render them capable of being formed into a valuable and noble body of citizens. And the first step towards this is to bring them out of the thraldom [sic] in which they now are under the domination of those very political tricksters and demagogues among themselves of whom your letter so truly and forcibly speaks.

These ethnic Irish politicians, these "political tricksters and demagogues," are, unhappily, all Democrats. Of course, he protested, "I should be sorry to see the Democratic party, insofar as it is the representation of democratic principles, weakened in any degree." But is it surely a fact that, because of the crisis over slavery, the party "under the existing organization [is] already verging on dissolution." Surely, whatever "the immediate effect" of the "Irish population" exercising more partisan discernment, "the [Democratic] party will lose nothing of their [sic] force and vitality."[16]

The prophecy about the future prestige of the diocese of St. Paul proved accurate, just as the tribute to Grace's astute reading of the times was more than just. In his calm, unflappable and yet straightforward manner, the bishop displayed in this exchange a profound grasp of the realities facing Catholics as they stood upon the cusp of a vast expansion of their numbers and prospects not only in Minnesota but across the United States. But even as he sought to deliver his people from "insane partisanship," he took care not to indulge in partisan pleadings himself. The separation of Church and state was safe in his

---

15. McMaster to Grace, November 26, 1859, AASPM, Grace Papers.
16. Grace to McMaster, December 4, 1859 (draft), AASPM, Grace Papers.

hands. And in stressing the dignity and responsibility of the individual citizen, he stood secure, surely, within the most revered of American political traditions.

The correspondence between bishop and journalist continued off and on over the next fifteen years, and Grace remained a faithful reader of *The Freeman's Journal* until McMaster died in 1886. Much before that, at the end of 1861—the Civil War had begun not too favorably for the Unionist cause—he learned of the editor's arrest and imprisonment. Heedless of any local criticisms that he secretly harbored Confederate sympathies, the bishop sent the editor his condolences. "I found a very great pleasure in receiving today your kind letter," McMaster replied.

> You are right in saying I am no "traitor," nor have I ever been even *suspected* of anything treasonable. My offense was, first, seeing and knowing that *war* can never rewrite [sic] our unhappy country, but that the longer it is continued, and the more that it seems to be the sentiments of the North, the greater the difficulty—after peace—in bringing the *disjecta membra* into any connected or harmonious shape. The second branch [sic] of my offense was that I refused to sucumb [sic] to the reign of terror that has taken from the people their right of speaking and publishing their honest convictions. I knew for weeks what was coming. I had no taste for it, but I could not agree to yield a principle so fundamental to our liberties.

On September 16, 1861, McMaster had been "arrested by a band of men flourishing loaded revolvers and in the pay of [Secretary of State] W. H. Seward. I was arrested without any warrent [sic] or any 'cause shewed [sic].'" He was locked up for five weeks and two days "in an unwholesome and crowded military fort among gentlemen, many of them as innocent as myself. I was set at liberty by order of the same W. H. Seward," who had been "besieged" by many Republicans "who urged that the arrest of a man so well-known to be loyal and honest could work only mischief to his [Seward's] cause." Incarceration at Fort Lafayette in any event served to tone down McMaster's rhetoric and even to temper his more radical instincts. *The Freeman's Journal,* once permitted to publish again, showed a considerable restraint toward the Lincoln administration and the conduct of the war. Its editor did not forget what he conceived to be his confessional and political priorities, but a good deal of the fire had gone out of him. He maintained, however, a good opinion of his thoughtful correspondent in far-away St. Paul: "We have needed all along more bishops like Bishop Grace." By comparison, of the incumbents at the head of the great Eastern sees, like New York, "*many* if not most" have failed to grasp the essential American *esprit*.

> I know how difficult it is to explain what I would say so as not to seem either pietistic or censorious. I do not wish to be either; but, unless the clerical character, in Bishops and in priests, presents a reasonable degree of regard for the proprieties of a Christian behavior—at least in its externals, such as are required of a decent man in any high-toned society— there is poor hope for Catholicity.[17]

The cultivated Thomas Grace was not likely to have confused these views with typical anticlericalism, nor did he ever cease to admire the outspoken if sometimes reckless editor who expressed them. They met only once in person, though their written exchanges continued fitfully. And some years after the Civil War, when the tide of Catholic immigration was, if anything, exacerbating the problems that concerned them both, McMaster sounded a poignant tone in what was probably his final communication.

> My dear Bishop Grace, I hold it a constant regret that I have not had the privilege of seeing you, and having your counsel and conversation, in regard to Catholic interests. I never met you but once. How well I remember the time. But I have always felt that in your advice I could find help that I have not found elsewhere. I do not think this a mere piece of *sentimentality* on my part. I am not given to that. There will be opportunity in heaven for us to understand how it has been that I have, for over twenty years, had so great an admiration for you, and why you so often have shown a friendship for me, of which I have not felt myself deserving.[18]

DURING THE EARLY MONTHS OF HIS EPISCOPACY, AS THE DARK clouds of war gathered ever more threateningly, Bishop Grace had reason to ponder the parlous state of the nation on the word of another Democrat. Not, like James McMaster, an intellectual convert to Catholicism, who carried with him the predictable WASPish baggage of prejudices against vulgar Irish

---

17. McMaster to Grace, November 16, 1861, AASPM, Grace Papers.
18. McMaster to Grace, October 17, 1876, AASPM, Grace Papers.

politicians, but one of the trio of working pioneer politicians—along with Sibley and Ramsey—who had guided Minnesota from territorial status to statehood.[19] Whatever the depth of his commitment to Protestant doctrine, Henry Mower Rice, now a United States senator, had displayed nothing but encouragement for the Catholic mission in St. Paul: his daughter had been the first boarder in the Sisters of St. Joseph's Academy, and it was he who donated the parcel of land upon which the original St. Joseph's Hospital had been built.[20] But, like McMaster, Rice was not of a sanguine temperament, and when Grace appealed to him to mobilize federal financial support promised to the hapless Indian missions in Minnesota—this, two years before the great Dakota uprising—the senator replied bleakly: "To the political troubles[,] we now have to add those occasioned by the recent great robbery of nearly a million of dollars of state Bonds belonging to the Indians but held in trust by the Government." But clearly, though Rice pledged to the bishop to do his best to release the funds, his anxieties were concentrated on the wider "political troubles," occasioned by the election of the Republican Abraham Lincoln to the presidency and the concomitant disarray of his own Democratic Party.

> Reverend and dear Sir, A reply to yours [of December 5, 1860] would sooner have been written had it not been for the many impending difficulties which have arisen. The treasury is empty, our credit gone, our nation disgraced, and dissolution-revolution and bloodshed will probably follow. Thousands will be ruined, and not one honest man of any party or color will be benefited. . . . The troubles in the cabinet have reached you;[21] more will follow, and I fear that this city [Washington] will be in the hands of armed men before the *first* of March. Should such be the case, what a blow will be inflicted upon Religion, morals, liberty. I have refrained from political discussions, have hoped for peace, but, alas, I see my friends cut down pecuniarily, amidst an abundant harvest, all in consequence of disturbances exacted by aspiring men. For the poor I feel deeply, for the misguided I have compassion, but for the *ambitious* who have brought this trouble upon us, I can only pray that they may reform.[22]

---

19. See chapter 3, above.

20. See chapters 4 and 5, above.

21. The reference here would have been to President Buchanan's cabinet; in accord with the older tradition, Lincoln was not inaugurated until March 1861.

22. Rice to Grace, December 29, 1860, AASPM, Grace Papers.

Rice's apprehensions—and no doubt the bishop's as well—did not recede during the tense months that followed. Once more replying from the "Senate Chamber" to a request sent to him by Grace—this time in hopes of securing government approval for entry into the country of a Bavarian-born priest—Rice sent back to St. Paul a copy of his memorandum to the State Department recommending acquiescence on the grounds of "the high position as a Christian and a man Bishop Grace holds in the affections of the people of Minnesota." But again it was the larger issue of national calamity and his gloomy prognostications that took precedence. "The deep and impenetrable gloom that pervades the country puts the future beyond my comprehension. I can only trust in God. Man is mad. Today or within a few days a great battle will be fought within hearing of this building. The result will be horrible to contemplate. I think with you. I see no hope ahead. In any way I can serve you, let me." He signed the letter "Your friend truly" on July 15, 1861, six days before the first battle of Bull Run.[23]

RICE, UNLIKE MCMASTER, WAS A MINNESOTAN, AND HE REALIZED that the bishop's first obligation was pastoral care of his immense diocese—some provision for the hapless Indians, for example, or the procurement of an adequate number of priests, from abroad if necessary. And Grace, however much he shared the senator's sensitivity to larger national and philosophical issues, realized it too. Certain administrative tasks within his see city demanded his immediate attention. Thus only the basement of the third cathedral, begun by Cretin and completed by Ravoux, had been made usable for services. Grace saw to the plastering of the interior of the rest of the building and added two largely ornamental transepts in order to buttress the long exterior walls, lest their weight cause the foundations to bulge inward. Indeed, so anxious did he become over this dire possibility, that he adopted the routine policy of sanctioning in church construction only enough underground space to house a furnace.[24] With the building at the same time of a substantial stone and brick rectory as a residence for the bishop and clergy, the cathedral complex was completed and served until superseded by John Ireland's monumental edifice more than half a century later.

23. Rice to Grace, July 15, 1861, AASPM, Grace Papers.
24. Reardon, *Diocese of St. Paul,* 144.

The new bishop found sufficient space to satisfy the needs of the paro-chial schools at the cathedral and the Assumption parishes, but St. Joseph's Academy was almost bursting at the seams. By contrast, the four-story St. Jo-seph's Hospital was plainly underutilized. In conjunction with the sisters who operated both institutions, Grace arranged to transfer students from the academy to the hospital—in September 1859, sixteen boarders and forty day pupils—while the patients and orphans went into residence in the former school. This interim exchange worked well enough until the mid-1860s, when adequate funding made possible the opening of the new academy on an at-tractive piece of hilly property at Marshall and Western, overlooking St. Paul's commercial district, that Cretin had purchased and had originally intended for a cemetery.[25]

Such managerial tasks were the ordinary coin of a bishop's function, and these Thomas Grace carried out with characteristic calm and decisiveness. But he had come to Minnesota with the reputation of a European-educated sophisticate, and so it is no surprise that the larger community looked to him for some intellectual stimulus. Early in 1860 he received a formal invitation from the directors of the cathedral's St. Vincent de Paul Society to deliver a public lecture, the proceeds from which would be devoted to the society's charitable activities. The bishop agreed to speak on the subject of "Human Rights" on February 23. The local press was all agog. Before the presentation one newspaper described Grace as "distinguished for his learning and elo-quence" and another as "a scholar of high attainments." Afterwards *The Pio-neer* called the lecture "a learned and philosophical production," while *The Minnesotan* reported that "a crowded audience listened to one of the most polished ethical dissertations on Human Rights, such as is seldom heard by the public." Indeed, the speech did create a considerable stir, so much so that the Protestant élite of the city, in a letter printed in *The Minnesotan*, publicly "and respectfully request that, at such time and place as may suit your conve-nience, you will soon favor us with a second lecture containing the illustra-tion and application of the principles so ably enunciated in your first." Grace complied, and the second discourse was given on March 13 "in an easy and fluent manner without any attempt of oratorical display" to "a large and intel-ligent audience," including "besides the Catholic clergy many of the ministers of other denominations and members of learned professions." This second performance was for the benefit of the "ladies of St. Paul's Episcopal congre-gation, in acknowledgment of the relief extended [by them] during the past

---

25. Hurley, *On Good Ground,* 123.

winter to many Catholic poor of our city," an ecumenical gesture that might not have been appreciated by Joseph Cretin.[26]

Throughout his quarter-century episcopate Grace did indeed manifest an intellectual and literary distinction worthy of a son of St. Dominic. But he was a bishop too, and committed therefore to a pastoral function far beyond the reflective quiet of a studious cloister. On one occasion, however, these two often conflicting charges meshed into a single mission and a remarkable document. At the end of 1860, Grace received a letter from a priest at St. Boniface, Manitoba,[27] informing him of the ordeal experienced by Joseph Goiffon, caught in the fierce blizzard near Pembina.[28] This priest, as well as the station he served, was Grace's canonical responsibility, and he determined to pay that most remote part of his diocese a pastoral visit. Circumstances delayed fulfillment of this resolve until the following summer, and not until August 12, 1861—shortly after his latest exchange with Senator Rice—did he set out, accompanied by Father Ravoux, for the far northwest. During this two-month-long journey he kept a diary, written sometimes in the first person, sometimes in the third, but in either case a striking testament to the times.

On the first day Grace and Ravoux traveled by stage from St. Paul to St. Cloud, a distance of about eighty miles, a jolting trip that lasted from 5:30 in the morning till 9:00 at night. Next day they departed for Belle Prairie at 6:00 a.m.

Was met at Little Falls by the venerable Père Pierz[29] attended by four or five waggons [sic] of Canadians who accompanied the Bishop to the Church situated in the middle of the settlement. On entering the Church the Bishop was surprised by the beautiful painting of the Virgin which serves as the altar piece; it struck him as a vision so unexpected . . . to encounter in so distant a place and in so humble a church, a work of art which would be a valuable adornment in any church in any city. The painting was a gift to Père Pierz from a pious association in Germany.[30] Thirty persons were confirmed in this church. The mission consists almost exclusively of French Canadians and numbers about 300 souls.

---

26. Busch, "Coming of Grace," 193–195.

27. Oram to Grace, December 10, 1860, AASPM, Grace Papers.

28. See chapter 5, above.

29. See chapter 4, above.

30. The painting was later donated by Father Pierz to Bishop Grace; it hung in the cathedral rectory in St. Paul for many years.

"Whilst here the Bishop had occasion to witness some of the habits of the Chippewa [Ojibwe] Indians, a band of whom had pitched their tents in the vicinity." Such teepees he thought constructed "in the most clumsy manner . . . and consist simply of a few sticks stuck in the ground, against which sheets of bark of the birch; they are also covered with this bark in winter and rainy weather." As far as Grace could see, these Native Americans—a term that would never have occurred to him—"dwell mostly on river courses and Lakes, and chiefly on fish, the catching of which to supply their immediate want is their only occupation." He observed sourly two "stout young full-grown men who at eventide, kindling a fire with a few dry sticks, . . . wrapped themselves in their blankets and lay down upon the grass." They lay motionless through the night, and, when the sun came up, "they would arise for a moment lazily and heavily and [then] stretching themselves, would wrap their blankets around them and again compose themselves to sleep under the sun." When Grace left Little Falls in the late afternoon, the two warriors were, he claimed, still asleep. An observer after the event may be forgiven for doubting that the busy bishop actually witnessed himself this scene of alleged Native American somnolence.

The journal at any rate records the arrival of the little party at Crow Wing on August 14. Next day, the feast of the Assumption of the Virgin, Grace confirmed fourteen persons there, including three Indians. "This," he noted, "is the residence of Père Pierz—nominally so only—for he is moving about continually, and seems more at home among the wigwams of the Indians than in his cottage in Crow Wing." After passing through St. Cloud, Grace and Ravoux reached St. Joseph on the morning of August 17 and began a review of a string of thriving Benedictine missions.

This town is made up exclusively of German Catholics; it is the most flourishing town in the Saulk [sic] Valley, the lands of which are unsurpassed in the State. A large addition has been made to the Church. Which is used also for schools at which over one hundred children are in attendance. The schools are taught by the Benedictine brothers. Seven and a half miles farther [we] passed St. James' Church, which is really a handsome edifice, built with regard to style and neatly painted. It is to be hoped it will mark a new era in the respect of church-building in Minnesota. After another seven and a half miles [we] passed the new church in Richmond. This also is quite a neat building. The whole of the Sauk Valley is rapidly filling up with German immigrants,[31] mostly Catholics, and

---

31. See chapter 4, above.

at intervals of every few miles churches will be required, and the great fertility of the soil will quickly enable people to build them.

In 1861, August 18 fell upon a Sunday when, the bishop recorded, "[we] started on our way over the worst piece of road between St. Paul and Red River, a road that ran through the 'Big Woods', so-called, [across] twenty-five or thirty miles of swamps, corduroy bridges, holes, and stumps." The "jolting moving and plunging of the coach" was bad enough; far worse was the onslaught of the mosquitoes. "These are larger than the usual size, their bite more painful, their attack more bold and determined, and their number like the atoms in the air. We had covered ourselves with veils, . . . a necessary protection in this emergency." Accommodation at the end of the day at "improvised hotels" delivered the travelers for awhile from the omnivorous insects, but it hardly offered the comforts of home: "The fare was rough and unseemly like the house, but this might have been pardoned if the beds had been as they ought to be." Grace, a veteran pioneer himself and not overly fastidious, nevertheless balked at "the border character" of the victuals routinely placed before him: "Pork innocent of the slightest 'streak of lean' with bread which no stomach could contemplate without a shudder were offered for our morning and midday repast. We were glad to appease our appetites with potatoes and bad coffee." But on that same Sunday, August 18, there rose up, as so often on this journey, a scene of aesthetic grandeur: "[We] passed a beautiful lake, called Pelican, by the neighbors."

Pressing westward, Grace "perceived that we were gradually descending from the higher prairie table lands whose slope receded from us in the blue distance and the beautiful lakes with their fringe of woodland becoming less frequent, announced our approach into the valley which stretches out to the ice fields of the polar regions." At noon on August 19 he and his companions crossed "a stream of considerable volume and rapid current." This proved to be the Ottertail River which appeared to flow southward, but then "swept round on a due westerly course." The Ottertail through its twists and turns ultimately joined, as Grace came to understand it, with another stream, the so-called "Bois de Sioux," which he discerned at first by "a long line of apparent bushes or low trees" ranked from north to south. This juncture of waters formed the great Red River of the North—"great from its associations and relatively only, as it is in reality not more than sixty yards in width; the deep, narrow current is sluggish and crooked, the water . . . turbid and of a whitish color from the washing of the low banks." But even before he confronted the reality of the river, Grace experienced a sight that nothing in his Ohio and Tennessee experience had prepared him for.

After crossing the Ottertail . . . the prairie becomes a flat and level plain stretching out on all sides to the farthest reach of vision circumscribed by the horizon and vaulted by the glorious arch of heaven. No language can convey a conception of the grandeur and sublimity with which this first view of the prairie overwhelms the beholder. The eye seeks in vain to detect some object taller than a blade of grass.

This moment of aesthetic wonder did not last: "Unvaried by lake or grove the prairie became wearisome at length by its sameness." The ennui grew almost palpable as the stage toiled straight northward along the east bank of the Red, from Breckenridge to Georgetown. At this latter village Grace and Ravoux were to board the steamer that regularly plied the river as far north as Winnipeg. But on August 21 they learned that the boat was still far away and could not in any case pass through the rapids forty miles downstream. So they spent the next three tedious days in Georgetown waiting for news. On the evening of the 24th, however, their boredom was somewhat relieved when there

arrived by the stage three English and one French passengers. One of these was an English lord, Lord Milton. The French gentleman was his travelling [sic] companion and no doubt also of distinguished birth. They were on a hunting excursion for pleasure and seemed to have entirely abandoned themselves to the enjoyment of the hour. In the hotel they kept up a continual uproar during the two days and nights that they remained—tricks and pranks of all kinds were the order of the day and carried also far into the night so that there was little or no rest in the house with them.

Even so, the bishop rather liked this quartet of uninhibited young men, especially Lord Milton, "quite a youth, eighteen or nineteen years of age, of [a] pleasing, quiet manner and altogether unassuming." The master of the revels was the Frenchman, Monsieur Lagrange, who "was at the bottom of all the mischief and the leader in all the noise and confusion."

Two days later, word having reached Georgetown that the steamer had finally arrived at the rapids, the clerics and the boisterous hunters hoisted themselves and their baggage on several wagons, which then rattled across the Red into Dakota Territory for the trek northward.

The usual vastness of level prairie without variation of lake or woodland formed the character of the forty miles traveled over—the sameness unbroken save by the narrow skirting of timber that marks the course of the Red River. Our English and French fellow-travellers [sic] enlivened the journey by their shouting and singing and firing at prairie chickens, of which they shot enough to supply the company with a savory dish at dinner, cooked in camp fashion in the middle of the prairie when we halted to rest the horses and ourselves.

In early evening they reached the landing just below the rough water and, after having traveled "nearly 500 miles in stages and waggons [sic]," the bishop and his vicar boarded the steamer that would take them to Pembina and St. Joseph.[32] "The boat is small," Grace recorded, "but the accommodations much better than we expected." It took all of the following day for the muleteers and crew to load aboard the freight that had been carted up from Georgetown, during which time "[we] were amused with the English and French party who gave themselves up to their usual buoyancy of spirit—fishing, hunting, sailing with the boat's yawl, singing, etc., etc." Less diverting were the mosquitoes that "seemed to have congregated from all parts and made the boat their headquarters. There is no describing the annoyance they gave and the variety of exclamations, cries of pain, curses, etc., etc. they called forth from the passengers."

Finally, at five o'clock on the morning of Wednesday, August 28, the boat got up steam and set out from the rapids for parts north. The Red River here was as narrow and hence as difficult to navigate as Grace had first observed it at Breckenridge. "The windings of the tortuous stream were in the form of the letter S continually repeated every three or four hundred yards; the boat in making these short turns frequently ran into the bank . . . and was obliged to have a heavy oar rigged at the bow to turn her head off." This awkward circumstance was much relieved once junction was reached with the Red Lake River (near what is now Grand Forks, North Dakota), and "the channel of Red River expanded to fully double its former width." And more than that, the acute Bishop Grace noted, once union with this great tributary had been effected, "the growth of timber [along the Red] appeared different, . . . being almost exclusively of oak heretofore," and now "it abounded with elm, maple, and cottonwood, the latter of very large dimensions." He continued

---

32. Not to be confused with St. Joseph, the Benedictine mission in Stearns County (see above). The St. Joseph here referred to is the mission of that name opened by Father Belcourt out of Pembina and now known as Walhalla, North Dakota. See chapter 4, above.

meanwhile to indulge "our young hunting party. [They] were perched on the bow of the boat, lower deck, looking out for ducks and gees [sic] which were in great abundance, both in the water and on [the] wing. They killed several which the boat was kind enough to stop to pick up." Late in the afternoon on this first day on the river, Lord Milton and his friends spotted "a large black bear swimming . . . about 200 yards ahead of the boat." No less than four shots rang out, and the bear "was hit but not so badly as to prevent his making his way into the thick bushes lining the bank of the river." Despite the pleas of the hunters, the captain this time declined to pause in the voyage, and so the bishop concluded that "the poor animal was mortally wounded as the distance [of the shooters] was short and two of the guns [fired] carried rifle balls. The boat lay by night," he added laconically, "at the mouth of the Turtle River."

Next morning the boat lifted anchor within a shroud of fog. Grace was astonished, and depressed, by the sight he saw as the mist gradually lifted. "We came upon large districts enclosing thousands of acres on both sides of the river in which nothing but the skeletons of trees were standing, and these mostly very large, extending their leafless and barkless branches far and wide, giving an air of desolation and sadness to the country very difficult to describe, heightened by the thought of great need and great value of wood in this region." What he was witnessing was the result of forest fires: "The cause of this widespread destruction is apparent in the charred trunks and branches of the trees." Whole forests, he observed, are dependent "upon a chance fire on the prairie or the direction of the wind at the time. Three years suffice sometimes to remove every trace that the land had once been darkened with forests of lofty growth." The bishop, alas, like so many of his contemporaries—and their descendants—had no solution: thanks to the prodigious undergrowth that spreads through the woods, "a strolling Indian or an unfavorable wind brings the fire . . . which deadens the trees, [and] the next year the dry trunks and branches are inviting fuel. . . . What was once a forest enriches the black mould [sic] of the prairies."

Finally, on August 30, three weeks after having departed St. Paul, Grace and Ravoux reached their destination. "We took on board," the bishop noted, "four Savages whom we overtook in their canoes on their way from Red Lake to Pembina to sell the maple suggar [sic] they had made the preceding season. These Indians were dressed in their usual fantastic manner and were objects of great interest to our English and French Hunting party." When the steamboat nosed into the crude wharf at about one o'clock in the afternoon, "the landing literally swarmed with Indians and Half-breeds, men, women, and children of all sizes, in all kinds of costumes, semi-costumes, and sometimes none of any kind." The festive hubbub belied somewhat the signs all round of recent desolation—"fences swept away and houses rendered uninhabitable"—the result of spring floods, an all too common phenomenon, as the bishop was to learn, along this stretch of the Red River. Among those pressing forward to welcome him was the indomitable Father Goiffon, "whose tale of sufferings the last winter awakened the sympathies of Europe as well as America. . . . His case has few parallels in intensity of suffering and power of endurance even in this region of exposure and adventure." Then, reverting to the third person, Grace added:

> The meeting between the Bishop and Mr. Goiffon was very affecting. The poor priest had adjusted of himself a rude wooden leg, with the aid of which and the remaining stump of the other foot he was able to get about. His zeal had suffered no abatement, and he was again at his post of duty— traveling from settlement to settlement, preaching, saying Mass, hearing confessions, and attending to sick calls, and was willing and anxious even to continue at his post if it should be the Bishop's pleasure that he do so. The Bishop, however, had already arranged a place for him in which the duties would be less difficult and burthensome.

September 1 fell upon a Sunday, when Grace celebrated "Solemn Mass" in Pembina's church, "a rude logg [sic] building but not without an air of neatness inside." At this service eight persons were confirmed, and Ravoux preached the sermon. Next day the schedule called for a journey "to the village of St. Joseph, at the foot of the Pembina Mountain, thirty miles distant [west] from Pembina," but not undertaken without a measure of irritation. The bishop, for all his sympathy for a zealous, crippled missionary, was nonetheless a bishop and thus given to a certain prelatial imperiousness: "We got on our way," he wrote peevishly, "after considerable delay caused by Fr. Goiffon who seems to have contracted the habit of the Half-breeds in taking four times as much time as other people require to do anything." The denouement, however, was hardly disappointing.

> About five miles distant from the village the Bishop was met by a cavalcade of 200 of the red-sashed villagers, dressed in their costume of Red River hunters. Forming a line from both sides of the road, they descended from their horses and, bending on one knee, received the Bishop's blessing as he passed through. Mounting again and firing a volley with their guns, they followed after the Bishop in full gallop into the village.

Grace was especially edified by his stay in St. Joseph, which lasted for about a week. This crown jewel of George Belcourt's apostolate was composed of about a thousand people, almost all of them "immigrants from the Hudson Bay settlements [in Manitoba] and their occupation chiefly that of hunting. The spring and autumn hunts occupy each about two months, the balance of the year [being] employed in curing and drying the meat and dressing the skins of buffalo robes for the market." It is here, he observed with a kind of wonderment, that one comes into contact with "a wild, free, bold life, . . . and full of thrilling interest. No nobler specimens of physical proportions and manly strength can be found anywhere than among these people. Sickness is seldom known among them." But it was not only such naturalistic virtues that earned Grace's fondness: "The Bishop was greatly pleased with his visit to St. Joseph. The strong faith and piety of the people, their entire devotedness to their religion, their simple manners and kind and affectionate bearing towards their clergy, could not but awaken sentiments of admiration and attachment which will ever be associated with the memory of this visit."

Ravoux and Goiffon conducted a week-long mission of preaching and sacramental administration at St. Joseph, and on the final Sunday Grace offered high Mass and confirmed forty-five persons. "The Church is commodious and very neatly ornamented. The Mass was well sung, accompanied by the Melodion, and the singing of some hymns in the [Ojibwe] language was very sweet." Next day, September 9, the clerics departed overland for St. Boniface in Manitoba, "to pay our respects," as the bishop put it, "to the Reverend Gentlemen [there] and express in person our gratitude to them for their kindly care and truly brotherly ministrations to which we owe the preservation of the valuable life of poor Father Goiffon." The distance was about ninety miles "over a continuous prairie . . . without any object higher than a blade of grass to relieve the view." With nightfall they set up camp, lighted a large fire— "it was chilly"—and ate a meal of cold meat and bread.

> After beguiling an hour or two listening to the narrative of adventures with the Indians and with snow storms upon the trackless plains by our very intelligent guide, we made arrangements for sleep. A buffalo robe doubled on the long, soft grass with a blanket and a second robe of ampler dimensions surmounting these, formed our improvised bed. There were some of the party to whom camping out was no novelty, and sleep came to them fast and deep. With others less fortunate thought kept watch with the stars, and made companionship with the solitude of the prairie and the silence of the night.

Augustin Ravoux, long a veteran of the camps of the Dakota, no doubt slept "fast and deep" in this northern exposure. Thomas Grace, on the other hand, with memories of Perugia and Memphis, "kept watch with the stars."

The following morning they crossed the ill-defined Canadian border, and by evening they arrived in St. Boniface, hard on the shore of the great Lake Winnipeg. "We shall not attempt to express in words the feelings awakened within us by the warm reception we met with from the Reverend Gentlemen . . . and by the kind and delicate attentions shown us by them and by the good [Grey] Sisters during our stay at the settlement." The visitors toured admiringly the educational and charitable institutions that had developed since the days when young George Belcourt had labored there.[33] Grace found the layfolk he met very much like those in St. Joseph, "full of faith and piety and devoted in their attachment to their religion and their clergy," and his departure from them "was like the parting from . . . long-tried friends." Even so, he observed shrewdly, they were also similar to the parishioners in St. Joseph in that "their almost entire reliance upon the chase precludes the cultivation of those habits of industry so necessary to improve and elevate their condition as a people."

After the bishop had concluded a piece of important canonical business—he secured the agreement that the Oblate Fathers,[34] heavily active in St. Boniface and its environs, should assume pastoral responsibility for the missions on the American side of the frontier[35]—he and his party headed homeward. They returned by wagon to St. Joseph, repacked their trunks, and proceeded to Pembina. There they had to wait for two days for a boat, till September 19, but since the Red River had risen sufficiently they were able to pass over the pesky rapids, southward and upstream this time, and to steam without interruption to Georgetown, where they caught the stage for St. Paul. Mercifully, the mosquito plague had somewhat abated—"there had been several severe frosts"—and after a week they arrived in St. Cloud. Ravoux and Goiffon—the latter now to enjoy a less strenuous assignment[36]—continued on to St. Paul, while Grace lingered for a day or two in order to preside at the religious profession of six young Benedictine sisters. He reached home on the

---

33. See chapter 4, above.

34. The Oblates of Mary Immaculate, a religious congregation founded in France in 1816, were active in Canadian missions from 1841.

35. Reardon, *Diocese of St. Paul,* 155.

36. See chapter 5, above.

evening of the last day of the month. The six-week journey, as he meticulously recorded, had cost $289.50, the bulk of which, $219.00, had been spent on stage and steamer fares.[37]

Never in succeeding years did Bishop Grace indulge in so romantic a venture as his journey to Pembina. Not that he ceased to travel round his jurisdiction when his sacramental or administrative duties required it. But the overweening reality of the needs created by the vast immigration into the southern and southeastern parts of his diocese kept him closer to home. And moreover, the arrangement he had made with the Oblate Fathers from Manitoba, to care for the Catholics at Pembina and St. Joseph, held until 1877, two years after the north and northwestern sections of his diocese had been detached to form the vicariate of Northern Minnesota. A similar canonical boundary adjustment occurred in 1880, which created the vicariate of Dakota and so relieved Grace of any pastoral responsibility for any area west of the Minnesota state line.[38] But the well-thumbed diary he left behind remains as an indication that he kept green the memory of what he had experienced along the Red River of the North, the seemingly limitless prairie, the roiling waters, the burnt-out timber lands, the simple piety of a simple people, and perhaps, above all, their "wild, free, bold life" so "full of thrilling interest."

---

37. Grace, "Diary," AASPM, Grace Papers, printed as "Journal of Trip to Red River August and September 1861," *A&D* 1 (July 1908): 166–183. For a descriptive analysis, see Lucker, "Grace," 163–175.

38. A "vicariate" designated a distinct area under the jurisdiction of one in episcopal orders, which however was too diffuse to include in its mandate a see-city. Ultimately the Northern Vicariate gave birth to the dioceses of St. Cloud, Duluth, and Crookston. Similarly the Vicariate of Dakota was mother to the sees of Sioux Falls, Rapid City, Fargo, and Bismarck. See William P. Furlan, "Diocese of St. Cloud," and Leonard Sullivan, "Diocese of Sioux Falls," in Ahern, *Catholic Heritage,* 48, 158.

CHAPTER 8

The Ties That Bind

WHEN BISHOP GRACE RETURNED FROM PEMBINA AT THE END
of September 1861, he found literally on his doorstep John Ireland, who,
thanks to the generosity of Joseph Cretin's patrons in France, had completed
his seminary education. The young deacon's arrival from abroad a month earlier had caused little stir except among his immediate family, depleted during
his eight-year absence by the death of his younger brother, Richard, and the
reception of his sister Ellen into the Congregation of St. Joseph. Much had
changed in the interval. Minnesota was now a state, and St. Paul a lively capital city of eleven thousand. To be sure, because the railroad had not yet crossed
the Mississippi, there remained a sense of isolation among people who could
depend upon river traffic only from April to November; ten miles of lonely
and unused track, running west to St. Anthony and called optimistically the
St. Paul and Pacific Railroad, was as yet only a harbinger of the future. Even
so, the volume of freight moved on and off St. Paul's wharves had multiplied
many times over: more than a thousand dockings recorded in 1861 indicated
a bustling if still somewhat limited commercial activity. And the gaudy, often
evanescent trappings of civilization had come, as they always do, in the wake
of economic expansion. Since Ireland and his companion, Thomas O'Gorman,
had departed in 1853, St. Paul had supported three theatrical companies, a
minstrel show, a circus, a tent show, and an amateur dramatic society. Verdi's
Il Trovatore had been locally produced in 1859. For the presumably larger
number of citizens who did not fancy opera, other forms of entertainment
were available: in March of the following year several thousand St. Paulites
gathered in a yard next to the new jail to witness the hanging of a woman convicted of poisoning her husband. A jail had indeed been built by the time Ireland came back, and a state capitol, as well as a city hall, a dozen more churches
of various denominations, and—thanks to Senator Rice, Bishop Cretin, and

the Sisters of St. Joseph—a hospital.[1] A native Hoosier and physician named William Worrall Mayo, fleeing "from the malarial hell of the Wabash Valley," came to St. Paul in 1854 in search of a more salubrious climate; later he would move on south to Rochester, where his two brilliant sons would create the great medical complex that still bears the Mayo name.[2] In 1856 the restless eighteen-year-old James Jerome Hill, born and raised in Ontario, "took a notion to go and see St. Paul."[3] He stayed there for the rest of his remarkable life, this builder of empires.

John Ireland had divided his French education between two institutions, residing in both in effect as a charity student. He spent the first four years in classical studies at the preparatory seminary at Meximieux, Bishop Cretin's alma mater. Indeed, in later life he romanticized that experience, so much of it enriched by the kindly and watchful concern of Cretin's unmarried sister, Clemence.[4] In a reflective mood many years afterward, he observed approvingly that at Meximieux "our masters exhibited all the piety and regularity which distinguish the better communities of religious. But, at the same time, priests themselves of the diocese [of Belley] in which their pupils would later serve, they were more devoted to the pupils' genuine interests and better equipped to show the proper paths to those aspirants to the priesthood."[5] He moved on in 1857 to the theologate conducted by the Marist Fathers[6] at Montbel, near Toulon, which, despite its name, was a rather dismal spot considering that it lay hardly more than a cannon shot from the western entry to the visual glories of *la Cote d'Azur*. Toward this institution Ireland manifested a strikingly different attitude, an almost hostile one, so much so that he habitually refused to confirm that he had even matriculated there. Later in his career he famously—and sometimes irrationally—harbored a deep antipathy toward male religious orders, which he suspected of regularly undermining proper episcopal authority. Whether such feelings took root during his years among the French Marists, it is impossible to say. In any case he received at

---

1. See Folwell, *History of Minnesota*, 2:22, 64–66; Blegen, *Minnesota*, 195–198; Kunz, *St. Paul*, 23; Williams, *St. Paul*, 388, 393; and chapter 5, above.

2. Clapesattle, *Doctors Mayo*, 32.

3. Quoted in Albro Martin, *James J. Hill and the Opening of the Northwest* (New York, 1976), 27.

4. See chapters 4 and 5, above.

5. Ireland to Theloz, June 15, 1891, AASPM, Ireland Papers.

6. The Society of Mary, founded in 1816 by Jean-Claude Colin at Lyon, dedicated to a missionary and educational apostolate, one of the host of new religious congregations established in post-Napoleonic France.

Montbel an adequate if conventional theological training, and proved to be there, as at Meximieux, studious and sharp-witted. He might have expected to be ordained immediately, once the bishop returned from his northland expedition. But Thomas Grace was not one disposed to hurry. Instead he put Ireland to work as his part-time secretary, while he satisfied himself as to the candidate's intellectual, moral, and liturgical preparation for the ecclesiastical state. Finally he set the ordination for the Sunday before Christmas 1861. On that day began one of the most remarkable partnerships in the annals of the Catholic Church in America.[7]

IT WAS NOT SURPRISING THAT JOHN IRELAND MIGHT HAVE expected to be anointed and raised to the priesthood without any bureaucratic delay, because he, like every thinking Catholic in St. Paul, recognized that the direst need of the diocese was to provide priests and religious to serve the rapidly expanding population. Parishes were springing up spontaneously, churches and schools were going up wherever Catholic immigrants settled, even though the likelihood of pastoral ministry for them remained problematic.[8] Bishop Grace understood the problem too, no doubt more acutely than anyone else, and throughout his episcopate—but especially during the early years—the effort to provide sufficient personnel remained his compelling preoccupation. Indeed, he knew that the missionary bishop's primary obligation was to produce a native clergy. During his tenure Cretin had ordained twelve diocesans and two Benedictines, but virtually all of them were foreign-born. Two more were ordained in Dubuque during the interregnum, while Ravoux was administrator, and both of them were Frenchmen. Grace ordained two Germans in 1860 and Ireland at the end of the following year. From April 1862 till October 1876 Grace elevated to the priesthood forty-one men designated for service in the diocese of St. Paul—among them, in 1865, Thomas O'Gorman—and fourteen Benedictines, subject to the Priory and, later, to the Abbey at St. John's.[9]

In 1862 the bishop opened a school to which he gave the sanguine title "The Ecclesiastical Preparatory Seminary of St. Paul." It was located on the

7. See O'Connell, *Ireland*, 42–65, and the authorities cited there.

8. See chapter 6, above.

9. See Reardon, *Diocese of St. Paul*, 682–683. During this time a forty-second secular candidate was ordained by Grace, one James Schwebach, for the newly established diocese of La Crosse, Wisconsin.

second floor of the old (the second) cathedral and presided over by one William Markoe, an Episcopalian minister recently converted to Catholicism, who was paid twenty-five dollars a month. Father Anatole Oster—the young confidant of Cretin's last years[10]—served as spiritual director. But the institution never attracted more than a handful of students and ceased to exist as a separate entity after 1866. Youthful aspirants to the priesthood thereafter took their studies in company with the lay pupils in the cathedral school. In subsequent years St. Paul sent its senior seminarians to various venues, many to the flourishing St. John's after 1868, others to Milwaukee and Montreal, a handful to Rome, Dublin, and the University of Louvain in Belgium. Not till 1885 did the diocese establish a viable seminary of its own, and by then Grace had retired. But long before that, even as his original preparatory school had foundered, he purchased a forty-acre farm on the shores of Lake Johanna, north of the city. "Some day I hope to build a seminary there," he observed wistfully. More than fifty years later this parcel of land formed the nucleus of the property on which was built Nazareth Hall, the *petit séminaire* that fulfilled his aspirations for nearly another half-century.[11]

Meanwhile, the bishop sought to recruit as many additional clergymen as he could find. The need was compelling, but the practice was risky. The large majority of externs who settled into priestly ministry in St. Paul during Grace's tenure, or who aspired to, were thoroughly respectable, and some proved distinguished. All Hallows College, for example, founded in Dublin in 1842 specifically to train missionaries in English-speaking lands, provided a steady stream of sturdy Irish candidates.[12] By the nature of the case, however, the sprawling young diocese attracted others who were inconstant or eccentric, who had failed for some reason to fit into their native environment, or who—in the most extreme instances—had already manifested unruly or even vicious habits, more often than not due to a weakness for strong drink. An eerie kind of clerical traffic emerged out of this circumstance, which occupied a disproportionate amount of the time and energy of Grace and his brother bishops.

Thus in the late summer of 1863 the bishop of Fort Wayne, John Luers, informed Grace of the strange case of Joseph L. Botti. Five years before, the

---

10. See chapter 5, above.

11. William Busch, "The Diocesan Seminary Project," *A&D* 7 (1935): 62–65.

12. See Fortune to Grace, July 13, 1878, AASPM, Grace Papers. W. G. Fortune, rector of All Hallows at that date, named five to be ordained for St. Paul over the next three years.

archbishop of Baltimore, under the impression that there was a penitential facility for wayward priests in Luers's diocese,[13] had recommended Father Botti to Luers. The priest told the bishop that having been refused incardination into Philadelphia, he had "in despair" gone to Minnesota, where he had practiced medicine. Luers had accepted him, and then, eighteen months ago, suspended him. Botti promptly hired a lawyer.

> He cannot of course gain his suit, but only anoy [sic] me, which to revenge himself he seems determined upon doing. I learned the other day that he had been employed by Bishop Cretin, but suspended having had criminal intercourse with a Squaw. If such is the case, please inform me of it. State that the Rev. gentleman has been in the ministry in your diocese but suspended or faculties withdrawn by Bp. C.[14]

A few months earlier Grace received a peculiar—and, if the truth be told, a comic—pair of communications from a different episcopal source. George Carrell, bishop of Covington, Kentucky, recommended to St. Paul Father Lawrence Spitzelberger who had served in the same parish since his ordination five years before, but who had to be relieved because of the opposition to him "by the leading man in the Congregation." Carrell was not of a mind to reassign Spitzelberger, even though "I always found him sober, attentive, and laborious." He may have been guilty of a "faux pas," but "the man is so humble, obedient, etc., that I cannot help believing that he will be a useful and obedient priest."[15] It has not been unknown, at the time or since, for a bishop to try to pass off a troublesome subject to an unsuspecting brother prelate. But Carrell must have set a record in repudiating that unseemly policy. "I am afraid," he wrote the very next day,

> I was not sufficiently explicit in my letter of yesterday. Until lately I had not heard anything against the priest in whose favor I wrote to you. Some few weeks ago, I understand that his house-keeper was in the family way by him. I rode out to see him. He was candid, humble, penitent. . . . I allowed him a few days to wind up his affairs [sic]. I pity the man. I never

---

13. This was a facility planned and advertised by the Congregation of Holy Cross at the University of Notre Dame. It did not materialize. See O'Connell, *Sorin*, 448–450.

14. Luers to Grace, September 15, 1863, AASPM, Grace Papers.

15. Carrell to Grace, April 6, 1863, AASPM, Grace Papers.

heard of his being addicted to drink, though someone told me he had been seen "tight." I consider it necessary to give you this information.[16]

Apparently a bolt of conscience rocketed through the episcopal residence in Covington one April night in 1863.

The priest shortage nationwide made it tempting for candidates to market themselves, so to speak, and to shop around. Thus Richard Grant, trained for the missions at St. John's College, Waterford, had arrived in Wheeling, West Virginia, at the end of 1864, expecting to be ordained there. Bishop Whelan, however, "had no need" for the Irishman (a suspicious phrase in itself), and so he applied eighteen months later to St. Paul. Grace replied, asking for more information. "In consequence of your Lordship's letter having arrived so late," the bumptious Grant responded, "I have applied elsewhere and am in daily expectation of an answer. But I should prefer your Diocese, it being new and the Catholic population growing. I shall therefore anxiously await your decisive reply."[17] Similarly Francis Nich, writing from Indiana, offered his services to Grace, provided that he would be assured a good assignment, Belle Plaine, for example, "or the German settlements in Carver County"—clearly Nich had scouted out the ecclesiastical terrain in Minnesota.[18]

Nor did that state's notoriously harsh winters necessarily fend off those priests who, for whatever reason, wanted to leave their present location. In 1868 Thomas Kennedy from Philadelphia thanked Bishop Grace for having "granted my application. . . . I hope to be able to winter it out in Minnesota. I do not dread cold climates so much as I do warm climates."[19] Another, one James Cassidy, a twenty-nine-year-old native of Tuam and graduate of the great Irish seminary at Maynooth, had settled for reasons unknown in Arkansas, whose climate he found "deleterious" to his health, and so he offered his "services" to St. Paul.[20] Grace prudently sought the counsel of the bishop of Little Rock, who replied with a cautious warning:

> Rev. James P. Cassidy left this morning for Milwaukee, Wisconsin. He is not a person whom I could recommend for a Mission. But [he] may do well in a college or some such place where he will be under constant su-

---

16. Carrell to Grace, April 7, 1863, AASPM, Grace Papers.
17. Grant to Grace, February 6 and 22, 1866, AASPM, Grace Papers.
18. Nich to Grace, July 2, 1861, AASPM, Grace Papers.
19. Kennedy to Grace, November 10, 1868, AASPM, Grace Papers.
20. Cassidy to Grace, July 30, 1872, AASPM, Grace Papers.

pervision and not have many opportunities of mingling with the world. He was not quite candid or disingenuous in representing bad health as his motive for desiring a change.[21]

Others, like Joseph Clernon, dreaded not dubious weather but perceived ethnic prejudice. After a decade of honorable work in Milwaukee, Clernon hoped to come to St. Paul where he had many friends and relatives. "An experience of ten years of zealous labor has taught me that it's not pleasant for an Irish priest to grow old amongst the Germans."[22]

Sometimes the applications crossed one another or at any rate were related to one another. In 1861 Hugh Kelly, a seminarian from Philadelphia, asked Grace to confer minor orders on him, which would have amounted to formal acceptance of him for clerical service in the diocese of St. Paul.[23] "In case Bishop Wood [of Philadelphia] demands restitution," Kelly told Grace, "I will comply with regard to what you say. I do not consider myself under any obligation to Bishop Wood. This is all I have to say."[24] What "restitution" meant in this context is obscure; perhaps it referred to the monetary investment that Kelly represented after having spent "four or five years" in the Philadelphia seminary and from which he had absconded without explanation. Grace at any rate wrote directly to Wood, and though he granted that Kelly's letters of recommendation were "sufficient," nonetheless "a doubt has occurred to me whether it was with your firm consent that he left your seminary, or whether Rev. Mr. Coffey may not have induced the young man to this step in vindication of his engagements with you."[25] The relationship between Kelly and Coffey—and indeed the two of them with Bishop Wood—remains unclear; Joseph Coffey, once himself a priest in the diocese of Philadelphia, was at the time serving as pastor of the parish in Hastings, Minnesota. Wood replied that though there was no specific charge against Kelly, the very fact

---

21. Fitzgerald to Grace, August 12, 1872, AASPM, Grace Papers. Edward Fitzgerald (1833–1907), bishop of Little Rock from 1867, was one of only two who voted *non placet* to the decree of papal infallibility at the first Vatican Council in 1870.

22. Clernon to Grace, January 22, 1869, AASPM, Grace Papers.

23. As noted in chapter 3, above, ordination to the diaconate and priesthood was preceded by a series of rubrical steps, tonsure (admittance to the "clerical state") and the "minor orders" of porter, lector, exorcist, and acolyte. These have all been suppressed, as has been what was considered a "major" order, the subdiaconate.

24. Kelly to Grace, April 17, 1861, AASPM, Grace Papers.

25. Grace to Wood, April 18, 1861 (copy), AASPM, Grace Papers.

that he had left the seminary under suspicious circumstances strongly suggested that he should not be ordained. As for Coffey, "a most unreliable man," said Wood without qualification.[26] Hugh Kelly came to St. Paul to plead his case, but Grace refused him ordination. He did, however, loan the young man $32 to see him back to Pennsylvania. The bishop also wrote him a letter of recommendation which Kelly judged "sufficiently good." Even so, he had found no diocese interested in his "services." "I therefore, Rt. Rev. Bishop, beg of you in the name of God to give me a more favorable letter or an exeat." He promised to repay the loan within three weeks time.[27] Coffey meanwhile had drifted away eastward. In the summer of 1863 Bishop Whelan of Wheeling once again found himself bound to consult Thomas Grace.

> I took into my diocese, on the recommendation of worthy clergymen, the Rev. Joseph Coffey. I have since ascertained that he resided for a time in your diocese and that you had reason to be dissatisfied with him. Indeed, if I am rightly informed, you found great fault with him. Since he has been here he has not been without blemish, and before I decide his case I would be thankful if you would give me somewhat of his history while with you.[28]

The problem presented by a *vagus*[29] like Coffey has plagued the Church throughout its history. It is hardly astonishing that this predicament should have been felt especially keenly in America during the middle years of the nineteenth century, when the shortage of priests was so taxing. Even so, one can remain legitimately surprised that in this case the bishop of Wheeling should have made inquiries of his confrere of St. Paul only after the priest in question proved to be "not without blemish."

---

26. Wood to Grace, April 26, 1861, AASPM, Grace Papers. The bishop of Philadelphia added a postscript appropriate at the moment when Lincoln had called for 75,000 volunteers to put down the rebellion: "We are all in a fever of excitement here, but united and determined to defend the national flag." Recruitment proceeds "with an ardor and feeling scarcely appreciable except by those who witness it."

27. Kelly to Grace, October 8, 1862, AASPM, Grace Papers. In the canonical context *exeat* (literally, let him go) was a formal document by which an ecclesiastical jurisdiction affirmed that an individual was free to apply without prejudice for acceptance into another jurisdiction.

28. Whelan to Grace, July 28, 1863, AASPM, Grace Papers.

29. *Vagus* means literally "a wanderer." Canonically it referred to a cleric who had no clearly defined ecclesiastical status but who "wandered" without authorization from one jurisdiction to another.

Sometimes an applicant showed himself to be merely odd or maladjusted. John Lyons, a native of Greenwich, Connecticut, spent seven years in the Jesuit seminary in Montreal, and a year more in a seminary in Troy, New York, from which he departed after an undefined "accident." The bishop of Hartford having given him an *exeat*, Brooklyn tentatively accepted him and assigned him to a third seminary, whose superior dismissed him after two years "by reason, I will frankly confess, of my failure to correspond with the regulations as well as was in my power and as was my duty." Now, in 1869, he appealed to Grace.

> I reluctantly consented, at [the superior's] earnest instance, to make a trial in the world. I have remained with my good Parents for the last year and more, and I am still convinced of my Divine vocation to the holy state of priesthood. This is also the conviction of those who know me best. I am now desirous of locating myself far away from home and friends, where I can more freely labor in the duties of my great calling. If you are willing to accept me, . . . I will repair immediately to St. Vincent's Seminary, Pa., and my good Parents will defray all expenses of such [a] trial.[30]

One might hope the bishop couched his refusal in gentle terms.

Some instances, however, did not in Thomas Grace's judgment merit gentleness, including one that confronted him during the first months of his administration. John Mehlmann had been ordained by Bishop Cretin in 1856. He had been assigned to Shakopee and nearby missions, where from the start he was the center of controversy. "I had an adversary," as Mehlmann himself put it, "whom I long ago have forgiven. He listened to the complaints of my congregation and interfered in my own business." After Cretin's death, Administrator Ravoux, "a kind and meek priest and Missionary, was deceived by my adversary and removed me from my Mission in Shakopee, giving them [sic] to the Benedictines." He then turned up at the German settlement at New Trier, where he promptly got into deeper trouble.

> Rt. Revd. Bishop! I confess open [sic] my faults. My faults are caused 1) by a quick temper and 2) by an imprudent zeal. So once I stroke [sic] a man in New Trier in his face; he vexed me so much and so long that I forgot myself and stroke him; immediately after I felt the deepest sorrow about

---

30. Lyons to Grace, September 9, 1869, AASPM, Grace Papers.

it. . . . Considering the fact that I lost my Mission on one side, and the accident in New Trier, I concluded to leave the diocese. Father Ravoux wrote to me . . . [that] I stroke the man without cause; but I concerning [this] matter was wright [sic].

After he departed Minnesota and made his way to Illinois and then to Pennsylvania, Mehlmann "felt never quiet. Bishop Cretin appeared to me often in dreams, reprehending me, and I was anxious the good saintly Bishop must have sorrow having ordained me." Hoping to be incardinated into the diocese of Pittsburgh, he went into residence with the parish priest in Allegheny City. But now, following the advice of "some bishops and my confessor, . . . I beg your Lordship in the most humble manner for the permission to retourn [sic]." He added, as a gesture of inducement, that "the Register of all baptisms, marriages and funerals during my time at Shakopee [and the adjacent stations] are [sic] still in my hands."[31]

Grace could not have found this little piece of blackmail endearing, and he knew from Ravoux that Mehlmann's temper and zeal had been regularly unleashed by his consumption of whiskey. Even so, he dutifully sent off an inquiry to the pastor at Allegheny City, who replied candidly, if cautiously, even though Mehlmann had already wandered away.

[I] received permission [from the diocesan authorities in Pittsburgh] to keep him in my house and to give him such faculties as I thought proper. I had the intention to keep him as an assistant priest. . . . But he being discontented with this situation and for my part observing that he cannot go along without drinking freely every day, [I] was very glad when he moved from Allegheny. If Fr. Mehlmann behaved good himself during his appointment after his ordination, I think that he could become yet a good priest, considering that his propensity for drinking is a consequence of his disappointments.[32]

But Grace was not prepared to accept well-intentioned excuses. "The sorest wounds of religion," he wrote directly to Mehlmann,

are those she receives from the imprudence and evil conduct of her priests. The church in Minnesota is yet in its infancy and struggling to

---

31. Mehlmann to Grace, October 10, 1859, AASPM, Grace Papers.
32. Stiebel to Grace, November 22, 1859, AASPM, Grace Papers.

secure its footing, and can ill afford to incur the risk of new troubles from clergymen of doubtful piety and discretion. Having left the diocese of your own will and received [from Ravoux] your exeat at your own demand, it is no reason to allege for wishing to return that you can find no other Bishop willing to receive you. You have no claims any longer upon the diocese, and the diocese wishes to have none on you.[33]

By the time he received this curt disavowal, Mehlmann was in Dubuque. His rejoinder was scarcely coherent, a self-pitying screed filled with underscorings and misspelled words.

> I think it the grace of God that I always was *too simple* to reach the [level] in meaness [sic] I observed in Colleagues. God knows all, and he is more just and charitable than men. God knows that I had pure intentions, and that I could have missions [in the diocese of] Vincennes and other places, but gave theme [sic] up, driven by an interior inquietude to go back to my mother diocese. . . . I will retire to a monastery till his Holiness the pope will have listened to the voice of the poorest of the servants of Christ. I appeal to his holiness Pope Pious [sic] IX. . . . Should I be refused I will find peace in the destruction of the foundation stone of my faith, like so many men despairing [of] the charity and justice of men.[34]

Over this small frontier drama there hangs an ineffable sadness.

Not so much sadness as conventional exasperation suffused the case of Peter Katzelberger. It began in the spring of 1862, with a glowing recommendation from the prior of the Benedictine community in Atchison City, Kansas. Eight months before, Grace was informed, Katzelberger had immigrated from Germany and had entered the novitiate there. "He is, however, already somewhat advanced in age, for he is a priest for 22 years, and he cannot find [sic] himself in these little things which, although not essential, are nevertheless of importance in monasteries. Old people scarcely find themselves at home in monasteries. . . . It is difficult to break old men of their habits and notions. But why do I speak so to Bishop Grace, who is himself a religious."

> I would request your Lordship to give that priest a situation in your Diocese. He is a good, zealous priest, a good preacher in German, and I am

---

33. Grace to Mehlmann, November 24, 1859 (copy), AASPM, Grace Papers.

34. Mehlmann to Grace, November 29, 1859, AASPM, Grace Papers.

sure he will give you entire satisfaction. He has studied the English with an iron application, and can hear confessions in English. He has preached here twice in English. His English, however, is not the best. There is nothing wrong with him, he never was suspended, he is an exemplary man, but he is too old for monastery.[35]

The following September Father Katzelberger was granted priestly faculties in the diocese of St. Paul.

It might be argued after the fact that Bishop Grace was remiss in not having vetted Katzelberger's application more carefully. But, as the prior had shrewdly observed, "your Lordship needs German priests," and this surely was a fact. Yet questions might well have been addressed. Why, for example, after more than twenty years service in a diocese in Bavaria, had Katzelberger departed for America? And why had he ended up in a monastery in Kansas? Grace, gambling perhaps on the word of the Benedictine worthy, assigned Katzelberger to a parish in the town of Belle Plaine, in Scott County, a "situation" considered at the time something of a plum.[36]

Trouble surfaced almost immediately. "It's with the greatest reverential delicacy," wrote a parishioner to Grace early in October, "that I presume to communicate" the widespread knowledge of Katzelberger's affair with a local "woman of bad repute." She was married to the proprietor of the "Mecanics' [sic] Hotel" in Belle Plaine, "who loudly and boldly accused the Reverend of intercourse with his wife. . . . I heard of [sic] several Catholics that he, Father Katzelberger, is guilty. I know not, but I do know that he took up quarters [in the hotel] in the absence of the Landlord. . . . Our Church is scandalized, so I humbly pray his removal from this place." Whatever stock the bishop put in this accusation may have been affected by a consideration unrelated to the alleged adultery, namely, the ethnic rivalry between Irish and German immigrants living in the same community. "May it please your Grace, you would have been apprised of this long ago, but we Irish Catholics have a great awe and horror to interfere with any clergyman. . . . I would sooner somebody else would do it, but I hope I do no ill by so doing."[37]

---

35. Wirth to Grace, March 15, 1862, AASPM, Grace Papers. In the same depository is a formal document (in Latin), testifying to Katzelberger's *"bonorum morum exemplum,"* dated April 5, 1862, and signed by "Augustine Wirth, O. S. B., Prior."

36. See note 18, above.

37. William Henry to Grace, October 6, 1862, AASPM, Grace Papers.

Katzelberger survived this original complaint, but by the following summer the drumbeat had become too loud to ignore, especially since any reservations Grace may have entertained stemming from nationality issues had been pretty much stilled. "I want to inform you," wrote a parishioner with a German surname, "in regard to Father Katzelberger of this parish."

> In my opinion it would be a great deal Better for Religion that he should be removed from this part of the country, as he does not behave with proper decorum. . . . The Germans of this town are so opposed unto him that they say they will have him prosecuted for libel. The Reason that he libels them was on account of them remonstrating against his actions, which I believe are not very decorous or proper among a protestant community. Your humble servant would be under a lasting obligation to you if you should remove our poor priest and choose us a more circumspect one if you would think well of it.[38]

This appeal had been preceded by an anguished inquiry with regard to Katzelberger's questionable financial demands upon the parish. One of the trustees—"excuse my poor writing, for I am a german [sic]"—wondered whether the pastor had any right to expropriate parochial funds for his own use.[39] But the *coup de grace* may well have been delivered by the prosecuting attorney of Scott County. "Rt. Reverend and Respected Sir," he addressed Grace on September 14, 1863,

> a few days ago I wrote to you about "old Katzelberger" and desire to correct whatever favorable impression my letter may have made in your mind. The facts stated therein are correct, but since that time—which is at this moment—I have conversed with the person who can convict him, not by circumstance but *positive facts* of the most infamous conduct and crimes. The witness of his perfidy and crime . . . is a good Catholic . . . who would *not* tell a falsehood. . . . My own conviction *now* is that [Katzelberger] is a confirmed *hypocrite* and *villain*.[40]

---

38. John Ableih to Grace, July 6, 1863, AASPM, Grace Papers.
39. John Defarr to Grace, February (?), 1863, AASPM, Grace Papers.
40. John MacDonald to Grace, September 14, 1863, AASPM, Grace Papers.

But even before such an explicit avowal of malfeasance, Bishop Grace asked the Benedictines in Shakopee—they who had replaced the unhappy Mehlmann there[41]—to investigate the burgeoning scandal in Belle Plaine. At the beginning of August 1863, one of them was able to assure the bishop that parochial activity there continued apace, including financial support as reflected in the Sunday collections. As for the disreputable pastor: "Father Katzelberger, I was told, arrived the same night I was there and stopped with the known lady. I could not see him, nor could I get the book of baptisms from him."[42] Two weeks later the Benedictine superior in Shakopee, the indomitable Cornelius Wittman,[43] gave Grace a fuller picture.

> I have neglected for a good [time] to write to you about reverend Father Katzelberger for the reason, because I could not find out any more, at least nothing certain. Though a few days ago I received a letter from . . . Belle Plaine saying [the writer] believed the reverend gentleman is married with that widow woman, but could not yet find out exactly, but that is sure, he says, that he has slept with her. I hope that you are informed of that scandal. When the Rev. Father was about leaving that place [Belle Plaine], at midnight with horse and buggy, a sheriff . . . prevented him from doing so. There was a kind of fight amongst them in regard to a settlement.[44]

After such shenanigans, both sexual and financial, Peter Katzelberger could hardly have expected Bishop Grace to grant him an honorable exodus. He tried nonetheless.

> I am and I was always ready to give satisfaction in every respect. I acknowledge that I have committed great faults, and I regret them very much. I ask you for a penance and for compassion and forgiveness. And be persuaded my life will be entirely corrected. I am very respectfully yours.[45]

Peter Katzelberger duly joined the ranks of those called, in a kindly Catholic euphemism, shepherds in the mist.

---

41. See note 31, above.

42. Stuckenkemper to Grace, August 1, 1863, AASPM, Grace Papers. For Meinulph Stuckenkemper, see Barry, *Worship*, 74–76.

43. See chapter 4, above.

44. Wittman to Grace, August 14, 1863, AASPM, Grace Papers.

45. Katzelberger to Grace, October 13, 1863, AASPM, Grace Papers.

Not that those ranks were excessively broad, but such cases necessarily took up a disproportionate amount of Bishop Grace's time and energy and inevitably distorted the records he left behind. And for all the disreputable externs with whom he had to deal, there were contrary examples aplenty. Thus, as a kind of compensation for the ineffable Father Botti, the bishop of Fort Wayne could entrust a letter of recommendation to the hands of Father F. X. Neubrant: "He has been induced to come to your diocese at the urgent solicitation of friends and acquaintances. From all I have heard and seen of him, I think you will have a zealous and faithful Pastor of souls in this young clergyman."[46] Among others, already at work, were the indomitable Valentine Sommerreisen and Alexander Berghold.[47] The latter indeed Grace assigned to troubled Belle Plaine, where he not only repaired the damage done by Katzelberger but soon became the bishop's confidant on recruiting matters. A German-born "Mr. Sterns [sic]" had applied for admission to the diocese of St. Paul. Berghold, asked for his opinion, was restrained in his enthusiasm, because, though he saw some positive signs, the young man "keeps too much our old German customs, not knowing that 'Romae romano more vivimus.'"[48] This judgment perks some interest in the light of Berghold's later career as the charismatic pastor in New Ulm and the champion of German Catholic rights within the diocese of St. Paul. Ferdinand Stern at any rate was ordained to the priesthood by Bishop Grace in November 1865.[49] A few months before, a pastor in New Haven, Connecticut, strongly recommended his acting curate, Father Lambert, "a most respectable young man," whom the bishop of Hartford would have gladly received had he any need for additional clergy.[50] And at about the same time, Grace wrote a prominent layman in Red Wing that he was about to assign an "excellent young clergyman," German-born Christian Knauf, to the pastorate in that town and district.[51]

Perhaps the most impressive of all those priests who came from abroad during pioneer days to serve in the diocese of St. Paul was John Stahira. A Slovenian born in Austrian Carinolia in 1845, he had entered a seminary there and then, inspired to embrace a missionary vocation by the example of his fellow countryman Franz Pierz, he had come to the United States in 1867,

---

46. Luers to Grace, September 10, 1864, AASPM, Grace Papers.

47. See chapter 6, above.

48. Berghold to Grace, October 12, 1865, AASPM, Grace Papers.

49. Reardon, *Diocese of St. Paul,* 682.

50. O'Brien to Grace, August 7, 1865, AASPM, Grace Papers.

51. Grace to Bush, August 11, 1865, AASPM, Grace Papers. Grace had ordained Knauf the previous July 30.

intending to complete his theological education and to learn English. These goals he pursued at the still somewhat primitive seminary in Milwaukee. He had intended early on, so he said, to apply for admission to the diocese of St. Paul, but such plans had been aborted "when we had at the seminary the visit of his Lordship the Right Reverend [Ignatius] Mrak, who enticed me to his Diocese, promising me a German congregation which he thought he would establish in the Copper Region then in full operation." In fact Mrak did not become bishop of Marquette, Michigan—with jurisdiction over the upper peninsula and the adjacent islands in succession to the legendary Frederic Baraga—until 1869, but the young Stahira understood that Baraga would endorse his appointment, "even [though] there is only more or less antipathy from the northern Germans toward the Slovenians."[52] He was ordained whatever the uncertainties and had been assigned as a curate to the parish is Johpening, where he spent nineteen months serving a mostly Irish and French Canadian congregation. This posting was not altogether advantageous, for Stahira, fluent in Slovenian and German and tolerable by now in English, could not speak French. When the copper mines, which undergirded the local economy, went into deep recession, Stahira's hopes for a parish matching his linguistic credentials faded, and he decided at age twenty-six to seek to fulfill his vocation elsewhere. Let me come to St. Paul, he pleaded, and his pastor at Johpening gave him a hearty endorsement.

> I am sorry for me individually for the departure of the good Father from me, because I will lose a friend and also for the good bishop of Marquette who will lose a *good, young, wise,* and *prudent* priest, whose only defect is that he does not speak the french [sic] language which is an absolute necessity in our diocese.[53]

Bishop Mrak reluctantly granted him an *exeat,* and John Stahira went on to become a pastor of extraordinary accomplishment within the diocese of St. Paul. Ultimately he was named bishop in the western reaches of South Dakota.[54]

---

52. Stahira to Grace, May 16, 1871, AASPM, Grace Papers.

53. H. Bourion to Grace, May 30, 1871, AASPM, Grace Papers.

54. Stahira to Grace, May 16, 1871, AASPM, Grace Papers. Stahira was consecrated bishop of Lead, South Dakota in 1902. (The diocesan seat was later moved to Rapid City.) Due to age and ill-health Stahira resigned his see in 1909 and returned to his homeland in Austria. He died in 1915. See Michael Costigan et al., "Diocese of Rapid City," in Ahern, *Catholic Heritage,* 194–195.

LONG BEFORE THAT, HOWEVER, BISHOP GRACE NEEDED TO FIND priests who would oversee the sacramental necessities of the ever-burgeoning parishes across his diocese. Over the years various religious orders and congregations filled some of this need, at least to a degree. Ten members of the Millbank Fathers—a group originally founded in England for missionary activity over the English-speaking world—ultimately committed themselves to the diocesan mission, as did later a number of natives of Prince Edward Island, in eastern Canada. Now and then an individual Dominican or Jesuit far removed, it may have been, from his primal intention, did the same.[55] Among such religious during the early missionary days the most important were the Benedictines, whose exertions in the environs of St. Cloud and Shakopee and even the Twin Cities have been duly noted. Though never so numerous, other religious, at Grace's invitation, assumed parochial duty within the diocese, notably the Dominicans on the south edge of Minneapolis in 1878 and the Franciscans in the parishes in the Minnesota River valley gradually vacated by the Benedictines over the course of the 1860s.

Nevertheless, despite a host of canonical adjustments over the centuries, there has always existed within the Catholic administrative tradition a certain unease between the local bishop and priestly members of congregations whose primary allegiance lies with their order and yet who assume parochial obligations within a particular diocese. Thomas Grace, himself a member of an exempt order and therefore more than most aware of the clout such institutes enjoyed in Rome,[56] appreciated the distinction between those priests who directly owed him obedience as bishop of St. Paul, and those whose allegiance stood, so to speak, one step away, their basic felty to a larger, to an international organization.

On occasion this distinction gave rise to tension. Thus, early on Grace fretted over the internal bickering that appeared to him to be affecting the work of the all-important Benedictine missionaries, whose religious superior was situated at far-off St. Vincent's Abbey in Pennsylvania. The trouble

---

55. O'Neill, "St. Paul Priests," 34–35.

56. See chapter 4, note 61, above. "Exempt orders," in canonical parlance, included the older religious orders—Benedictines, Franciscans, Dominicans, Jesuits—as distinguished from more recent foundations, like the Marists and the Oblates. The "exemption," conferred by Rome, meant that those congregations enjoyed more independence from the local bishop than did their more recently founded brethren. This distinction, however, especially in America, became increasingly blurred over the course of the nineteenth century.

stemmed from the shaky leadership of the community's first prior, Demetrius di Marogna, and from the forceful if somewhat rough personality of Bruno Riess. Father Bruno, to be sure, had been the most effective of all the pioneer monks, but his very strength of temper caused distress among his brethren.[57] Fortunately Abbot Boniface Wimmer was an adept diplomat. Di Marogna he shifted off to the pastorate of the Assumption parish in St. Paul (with Administrator Ravoux's agreement) and then arranged the election of a rather more able prior.[58] To assuage Grace's misgivings Wimmer sent him reassurances along with the gentle reminder that the monks in Minnesota were ultimately Wimmer's responsibility. Canonical prerogatives aside, he expressed confidence that all would be well. "Very likely Father Bruno is to be recalled, or they cannot live in peace, unless the [spiritual] retreat changes things essentially. . . . [I am] ashamed and sorry that we give you such an unfriendly picture of internal discord. I trust nevertheless that in a short time things will give a better aspect, with God's help and your assistance."[59]

At the root of all the difficulties in these early days in Catholic Minnesota was the grinding poverty that beset all foundations, whether parochial or monastic or educational. The passage of time and the growth of population would alleviate such problems, at least to a degree, but at first it remained a constant worry and preoccupation. As often as not, strain between diocesan officialdom and the religious orders turned upon parochial finance and property rights. For example, the Benedictines, in order to consolidate their activities in an area closer to their headquarters at St. John's, by the mid-1870s had departed the missions in Shakopee and the Minnesota River valley. But they continued in charge of St. Boniface in what was then still called St. Anthony Falls, and of St. Joseph, on the northern edge of Minneapolis.[60] They petitioned to have turned over to them as well the even more historic St. Anthony parish (founded in 1851), but Grace refused. This denial annoyed Abbot

57. For background, see chapters 4 and 5.

58. Franchise in the election of prior of dependent houses was vested in the general chapter of the larger community. Di Marogna was succeeded by Benedict Handl and then, in 1861, by the rather more energetic Othmar Wirtz. See Barry, *Worship*, 61–74.

59. Wimmer to Grace, October 18, 1861, AASPM, Grace Papers.

60. In 1976 the original St. Joseph property was acquired by the state of Minnesota for the construction of one leg of the interstate highway system. The parish relocated in the suburb of Maple Grove and was renamed St. Joseph the Worker. See Wright, *Gather Us In*, 67.

Alexius Edelbrock—St. John's had been raised to the status of full-fledged and independent monastery in 1866[61]—concerned, as he needed to be, about securing the income necessary to sustain the Benedictine community's various endeavors. Edelbrock, however, did not possess Abbot Wimmer's smooth diplomatic skills. Why, he demanded angrily, had not the deeds for St. Boniface and St. Joseph been turned over to the Benedictines? "Is not the Bishop's word as good as the Bishop? We have worked hard for both missions in question and have raised them up out of their nothingness, and all this on the promise given us in expectation of the deeds in due time." If the bishop declined to offer them both parishes, Edelbrock concluded, the Benedictines would prefer the one in north Minneapolis, "*provided* you give us charge of all the German Catholics there." "This refused," Grace scribbled in the margin of the abbot's letter, and then added over his signature: "The deeds were given for the present church in St. Anthony and Minneapolis."[62] The bishop had been characteristically playing a waiting game, to see whether he could find his own personnel to staff the two parishes on a permanent basis. In the end, the Benedictines did so, no doubt to the benefit of both the diocese and the abbey.[63]

Of course involvement by a religious order in the financial affairs of a parish could cut both ways, and Abbot Alexius's irritation at Grace's delaying tactics in St. Anthony and Minneapolis was exacerbated by the troubles encountered by the Benedictines' flagship parochial foundation, the Assumption in St. Paul. Thanks to a series of inept and extravagant pastors, the parish debt by 1875 had risen to a staggering $151,000. For years the liquidation of this liability remained near the top of Edelbrock's secular agenda. Prudent management, together with the good will of most of the city's German Catholics—though some had been alienated by the debacle—eventually brought the fiscal affairs of the parish under control, but not without seemingly endless fund drives, fairs, raffles, and any other device, great or small, that might produce income. Even Father Bruno Riess was dispatched back to Minnesota for awhile to help raise funds. But, as the saying goes, it is an ill

---

61. Wimmer to Grace, June 21, 1866, AASPM, Grace Papers.

62. Edelbrock to Grace, March 7, 1878, AASPM, Grace Papers.

63. In staffing parishes religious orders have hoped to derive not only financial support but also vocations. For instance, St. Joseph parish till 1950 had produced one (Benedictine) bishop, eleven other priests, and thirty-eight sisters. See Reardon, *Diocese of St. Paul*, 594.

wind that blows no good. One fruit of the imprudent spending was the hand-some stone church, built in 1871, whose twin spires still adorn the skyline of downtown St. Paul.[64]

Despite Abbot Edelbrock's strong language—characteristic of a man whose tempestuous career ended with his forced resignation in the late 1880s[65]—Bishop Grace's relations with the sons of St. Benedict were by and large cordial. And so, at first, had been the case with the Canadian Oblates of Mary Immaculate, who had undertaken to minister to the Catholics in Pembina and its environs.[66] During the mid-1870s, however, the relationship began to sour. Toward the end of the previous decade, Grace blessed a simple frame church, built on the edge of St. Paul's bustling business district and dedicated to St. Louis, King of France. A few years later, he petitioned the Ob-lates' motherhouse in Montreal to staff this new parish, which was to serve the remnant of the city's French-speaking community. The negotiations, posi-tive at first, soon became muddled by the Oblates' condition that St. Louis church be relocated and then by their proposal that the order assume the pas-torate of St. Mary's instead. There seems little doubt that the bishop would never have acceded to granting jurisdiction over this silk-stocking parish[67] to any but his own diocesan clergy. The Oblates appeared to accept this reality in stride. "Monseigneur," wrote their representative *en scène* to Grace,

> I have seen Father Caillet this morning. I then asked him with regard to St. Mary's Church and Parish; he answered me that if his resignation was in any way required for the general good of the Diocese, he would not stand in the way. But he would be willing to make the sacrifice of his po-sition, provided you yourself in person would ask him to make that sac-rifice for the good of the Diocese.

Louis Caillet, the notoriously gentle and accommodating pastor of St. Mary's, need not have fidgeted himself. Grace had already vetoed the proposition.

> Now [continued the Oblate] as I consider this is too great a sacrifice to ask of [Caillet], and that our remaining under the present circumstances would contribute very little to the general good of the Diocese, I have

---

64. See Barry, *Worship*, 132–133.
65. See O'Connell, *Ireland*, 260–262.
66. See chapter 7, above.
67. See chapter 6, above.

come to the conclusion to let matters stand as they are, and to accept your answer of this morning as a final settlement of the question. In consequence thereof, I have telegraphed your answer to Montreal, asking at the same time for our letters of recall. And as soon as they arrive, we shall in obedience to them make our preparations to take our departure from St. Paul.[68]

But like all frontier bishops, Grace was loath to forgo any likely source of priestly recruits for his diocese, whose burgeoning population was his ever-present anxiety. So, very much against his instincts, he agreed to carve a new parish out of the territory heretofore allocated to the cathedral and St. Mary's and—perhaps moved by the courteous and gracious manner in which they had accepted his previous decision—to assign it to the Oblates. Accordingly, the Church of St. Joseph, at the corner of Carroll Street and Virginia Avenue, was established in 1875. The dénouement was not happy. By 1880 the Oblates had withdrawn from the nascent parish, not without, however, demanding recompense for monies they had expended.[69] This claim brought out the fiercely combative element in Thomas Grace's ordinarily benign modus operandi. "You speak," he addressed the mandarins in Montreal, "of the pain it costs you to write upon this subject of this debt of St. Joseph's Church."

Believe me, Very Reverend dear Sir, when I say that it is not pain alone but a deep sense of wrong I experience in connection with this subject. Your fathers were withdrawn from their pastoral charge in my Diocese without infringement in any manner by me of the terms of agreement upon which they were received in the diocese. To accommodate your fathers the Cathedral parish and the parish of St. Mary's were divided so as to form a third parish without any need therefore, and to the serious detriment and embarrassment of the two former parishes. That embarrassment is still felt. The church of St. Joseph was not needed then, and it is not needed now. It entails a heavy burden upon the poor people to support it. Now, this dividing of the parishes with the consequent disadvantages and losses, was allowed by me in the full confidence that your fathers would remain permanently in the Diocese, and the disadvantages that were felt would be removed in time.

---

68. Magnin to Grace, July 31, 1874, AASPM, Grace Papers.

69. Antoine to Grace, February 14, March 9, and April 11, 1880, AASPM, Grace Papers. J. E. Antoine, O.M.I., was at the time superior of the Oblates in Montreal.

The problem, Grace maintained to the Oblates' superior, was rooted in their original agreement "to serve the parish of St. Louis's church. I could not consent that that church should be removed to a place the effect of which would be the breaking up of the parish and the working of injury and pain to many souls. Neither conscience nor my duty as Bishop, nor justice to the French congregation, would allow me to consent to that. I could not do it." As for St. Joseph's as a kind of recompense:

> I certainly did not give pervue [sic] to the Oblate fathers to erect churches and buildings of unlimited cost and expense to which they would be at liberty to abandon without cause given by other party to the contract, and then demand of this party to the contract [the diocese] in full of the cost and expenditures. The case is further aggravated by the consideration of the losses and embarrassments that have been entailed upon the two parishes in St. Paul by their being divided for the accomdation [sic] of the Oblate Fathers.[70]

The dispute between Montreal and St. Paul proved in the end to be negotiable. The Oblates demanded as recompense for their investment at St. Joseph's parish something over $7,000, while Grace offered the flat sum of $5,000. St. Joseph's in any event remained under the direct control of the diocesan clergy until 1905, when it was suppressed and its relatively prosperous territory given over to provide the site for the construction of a new and spectacular cathedral.[71]

MUCH MORE IMPORTANT FOR BISHOP GRACE IN THE LONG RUN than these minor quarrels with men-religious was the recruitment of their female counterparts. Central to the great Catholic revival in early nineteenth century Europe was the foundation of a multitude of new congregations of women, which now joined the older and more established orders. Many of these institutes—particularly the French, the German, and the Irish—displayed early on in their endeavors a commitment to the missionary project. Such had been the case with the Sisters of St. Joseph of Carondelet who, from their arrival in St. Paul in 1851, had set the local tone in what was considered then a specifically feminine apostolate.[72] Their work in education and

---

70. Grace to Antoine, March 2, 1880 (copy), AASPM, Grace Papers.
71. See O'Connell, *Ireland*, 504–505.
72. See chapters 3 and 4, above.

health care was moreover advanced by the considerable number of young women who over the intervening years had joined their ranks—among them John Ireland's sister Ellen, later the legendary Mother Seraphine, and his cousin, Ellen Howard.

But not even they, prominent as they may have been in St. Paul itself, could answer all the needs of Grace's growing jurisdiction. Most pioneer parishes opened little schools, however primitive, which in the beginning were presided over by volunteers more zealous than proficient and which often as not were located in private homes or, in an extreme case or two, in the back room of a saloon. Often enough ethnic rivalries, so prominent in the immigrant Church, further complicated matters. In the hamlet of Belle Plaine, for instance, the parish of Our Lady of the Prairie, set up in 1860, was divided eleven years later into two, with the Germans building a new church of SS. Peter and Paul, while the rest of the little community, mostly Irish, built one of their own, now dedicated to the Sacred Heart; each parish insisted on maintaining a school of its own.[73] But with or without such a diffusion of resources, clearly a more professional cadre of teachers had become nearly as grave a need for the diocese as was provision of sacramental ministry. In this regard, however, the bishop had to deal with many obstacles besides the competition between "territorial" and "national" parishes. Not least among them was the fact that these nascent parochial schools aspired to provide not only rudimentary teaching in the four Rs—the fourth being, of course, the Catholic religion—but also some meaningful capacity for doing so. Not all the nuns who came to Minnesota in these early days, themselves largely immigrants, possessed significant pedagogical skills, particularly with regard to the literacy and numeracy increasingly demanded in the American social and economic environment. A lesser difficulty—but one which dogged the parochial school system for a long time to come—was the nineteenth-century conviction that women should not be in charge of the instruction of boys. The number of religious brothers always lagged far behind that of available sisters, though in 1871 two Brothers of the Christian Schools took up teaching duties at the cathedral and Assumption parishes in St. Paul and, later, with an expanded community, founded the celebrated high school in that city named for Joseph Cretin.[74]

---

73. See Wright, *Gather Us In*, 36.

74. See Reardon, *Diocese of St. Paul*, 656. The Christian Brothers were founded in France during the late seventeenth century by Jean-Baptiste de la Salle (1651–1719) as an organization of non-ordained religious devoted to teaching both religious and secular subjects, especially to the poor.

Little by little, however, the numbers of religious women increased, as did the thoroughness of their training. The Benedictines, like the Josephites, were already *en scène*. At Grace's urgent invitation, five Dominicans—four of them with Irish surnames—arrived in Faribault in 1865, while the same year four Sisters of Notre Dame, all with German surnames, came from Milwaukee and set up a convent in Mankato.[75] This latter congregation served in a variety of parishes, large and small, some of them Polish- as well as German-speaking communities. In 1868 the first contingent of the Sisters of the Good Shepherd came from St. Louis to St. Paul and began their enduring apostolate among girls and young women who had fallen on bad times. Five years later Bishop Grace welcomed six Visitation nuns, who also traveled upriver from St. Louis and who over the next century and a half would serve a rather more upscale feminine clientele. On at least one occasion internal distress elsewhere indirectly benefited the development of Catholicism in Minnesota. In 1876, Franciscan sisters from Joliet, Illinois, opened schools in Waseca and Owatonna and the next year in Rochester. Their decision to do so resulted largely from hostility some of them had experienced from the bishop of Chicago. His confrere of St. Paul cheerfully seized the moment and authorized a motherhouse for them in Rochester, where a decade later they founded St. Mary's Hospital in cordial conjunction with the young Doctors Mayo, William and Charles.[76]

Sometimes the older orders would serve in the same parish with the men who shared their spiritual heritage: thus Dominicans were stationed from 1878 at Holy Rosary in Minneapolis, Benedictines with their brethren at St. Boniface, also in Minneapolis, Franciscan sisters with Franciscan friars at Union Hill. There was, however, no consistent pattern. The female orders were canonically independent of their male counterparts, whatever their common origin and tradition, and Franciscan nuns taught in the school of the Benedictine parish in Chanhassen. Nor were they necessarily constrained by reason of nationality: German-oriented sisters were at work in Bohemian St. Wenceslaus in New Prague from 1884. Even so, linguistic considerations continued for a generation or more to count for a good deal; it is hardly surprising that the schools of many German parishes were staffed by nuns whose motherhouses were located in Milwaukee.[77]

---

75. See Annabelle Raiche and Ann Marie Biermaier, eds., *They Came to Teach: The Story of Sisters Who Taught in Parochial Schools and Their Contribution to Elementary Education in Minnesota* (St. Cloud, Minn., 1994), 10.

76. See Raiche and Biermaier, *They Came to Teach*, 11–12.

77. See the "Chronicles" in Reardon, *Diocese of St. Paul*, 581–652.

Or, more likely, located in the first instance farther away from Minnesota than that. In the early 1870s, Alexander Berghold, the ever-enterprising pastor in New Ulm,[78] came into contact with a group of nuns residing in Wilkes-Barre, Pennsylvania. His invitation to them to come and teach in Holy Trinity school had to be referred to *their* motherhouse far away in German Westphalia. Bishop Grace's seconding of this request elicited from the noblewoman who was foundress and superior general of these Sisters of Christian Charity[79] a reply not only charming in its idiosyncratic English but also evocative of the spirit that infused these formidable women. "Right Reverend Sir," wrote Pauline von Wallinkordt,

> your episcopal grace will kindly pardon me for taking the liberty to address these few lines to your Right Reverence. I am in want of words to express my thanks to you for the fatherly kindness and friendship with which your episcopal grace entertained two of our sisters introduced to you by Father Berghold; also, more expressly, for the honorary and kind letter that your Right Reverence had the kindliness to address to me. I see in the same and to my utmost joy that your episcopal grace [is willing] to accept [sisters] of our congregation in your diocese and that to the plan regarding the institute at New Ulm you will give your sacerdotal consent and holy benediction. In this I see the will of God, and after having all and everything maturely considered, we have concluded to obey the call of your episcopal grace and send sisters to take charge of the schoolhouse at New Ulm. I will at the same time in the name of our sisters, who will now and later work in your diocese, give you the most sincere promise that they will be, and remain, your episcopal grace's most obedient and humble daughters, who will be ever ready to work, to pray, and to offer to the honor of God and for the sake of the dear youth.

Sister Stephania, "who was introduced to you not long since and who is very much pleased with New Ulm," was to be dispatched immediately as "superioress," along with Sister Sixta "as class teacher etc." Shortly "several sisters from here [Paderborn] . . . will go by way of Wilkesbarre [sic] and from there . . . to New Ulm. Sister Stephania has consulted about all this with

---

78. See chapter 6, above.

79. "Sisters of Charity" was (and is) the designation of many congregations of religious women, often used with a descriptive qualifier (thus Mother Teresa of Calcutta's "Missionary Sisters of Charity"). The term generically applies to uncloistered nuns who engage in various charitable activities.

Reverend Father Berghold, and she has great confidence in him." In return for this commitment Mother Pauline "humbly pray[ed] that your episcopal grace will be to these sisters a kind and willing father and superior, who will graciously grant them counsel and aid, whenever it should become necessary. . . . Holy prayers" she asked for too, "particularly through this hard time of persecution."[80]

Confidence in and amity with the local pastor was always a needful circumstance if the sisters, wherever they came from, were to be his effective co-workers. Most of the time such harmony prevailed, as it did in Winona very early during Grace's administration. There two Irish sisters took up residence in 1861, and before long they were conducting a flourishing school for girls. In this instance the impetus came from their own zeal rather than from the bishop's or the parish priest's initiative. "Right Reverend Sir," their agent wrote Grace in the spring of 1861,

> if you remember, about a year ago the Sisters of St. Bridget wrote to you on establishing a branch of their Order in your diocese. Necessity forced us to locate in Grand Rapids in the Diocese of Detroit. Their [sic] reception has been favorable. The good Bishop of Buffalo gave me permission to aid in establishing the Bridgetines (now that they can get along by themselves). Now, sir, if it meets with your approbation, I shall proceed immediately to your diocese to establish another convent of the Order.[81]

Compatibility between rectory and convent could, under some circumstances, miscarry. In the summer of 1877 Irish-born Francis Quinn persuaded the Ursuline motherhouse in Alton, Illinois, to assign six sisters to serve in his parish in Lake City. It was something of an ecclesiastical coup to obtain the services of this old and distinguished teaching order—founded in sixteenth-century Italy by the canonized Angela Merici and sponsored by other luminaries of the Counter-Reformation, like St. Charles Borromeo. Within months of the nuns' arrival, however, trouble was brewing. The provincial in

---

80. Pauline von Wallinkordt to Grace, January 14, 1874, AASPM, Grace Papers. The date of this letter is significant. The "persecution" to which Mother Pauline referred was the so-called *Kulturkampf,* encapsulated in the repressive legislation sponsored through the 1870s by Bismarck in order to bring the Roman Catholic Church under the control of the state across the newly united Germany.

81. Thomas Brady to Grace, May 7, 1861, AASPM, Grace Papers. The Bridgetines, founded as a diocesan institute in County Carlow, Ireland, in 1807, had been active in the American Midwest since 1851.

Alton complained bitterly to Bishop Grace about the superior at Lake City whom she herself had appointed and whom she apparently now deemed to be in a sinister alliance with Father Quinn to promote a schism within, or even a secession from, the Ursuline congregation.

> Mother Ligouri [Curran] has always shown herself ungrateful and un-faithful to this community. . . . Our dress and customs were never stilish [sic] enough for her proud spirit; she often made ironically [sic] remarks about them. Yet she always blamed the Rules which, had she faithfully observed them, would certainly have sanctified her, as it [sic] has many before her.[82]

Despite such criticism Mother Ligouri survived, prospered, and indeed pro-vided a happy ending to the story. By 1880 she was presiding over the Acad-emy of Our Lady of the Lake which, in subsequent years, was removed to a nearby property in the hamlet of Frontenac, where it was renamed Villa Maria and where it offered the benefits of an education within the Ursuline tradition for more than three quarters of a century.[83]

That tradition represented the gradual redefinition of the status of reli-gious women within the Church. Or perhaps it would be more precise to say the broadening of the definition. Before Angela Merici's time nuns were firmly cloistered and distanced, at least in theory, from activities in the world outside the convent, with the assumption that their lives were devoted to prayerful retirement and contemplation. Whatever teaching, nursing, or other social service the Church undertook was performed by males. By the mid-nineteenth century this situation had dramatically altered, to the extent that, so to speak, the Marthas "busy about many things" far outnumbered the Marys. This did not mean that the active congregations were not committed to a regimen of liturgical and private devotion, or to the observance of a rule that regulated in detail their conduct, or to a domicile apart from the larger society and a distinctive garb. Indeed, such proprieties reflected continuity with the older tradition, even as these new nuns labored in schools, hospitals, and orphanages. Nor did the religious dedicated to strict enclosure dwindle or disappear; groups of cloistered sisters continued to flourish, and their total celebration of prayer in all its forms, even the mystical, remained (and

---

82. Mother Mary to Grace, May 10, 1878, AASPM, Grace Papers.

83. See Reardon, *Diocese of St. Paul*, 673–674. Since 1969 Villa Maria, still under the direction of the Ursulines, has served as a retreat and conference center.

remains) fundamental to the integrity of Catholic spirituality. Mary, after all, had "chosen the better part."

Among the most revered of the contemplative orders was that branch of the Franciscan sisterhood popularly known as the Poor Clares. In 1876 Thomas Grace received notice from Rome of negotiations going on there in hopes of setting up a convent of Poor Clares in St. Paul. As a shepherd of souls he could not but rejoice at such news. His correspondent, however, who identified herself as a Franciscan nun named Mary Ignatius, appeared somewhat rattled and even brash in her presentation.[84] Caution—always Grace's watchword—prompted him to make an independent inquiry. He turned to Ella Eades, an American newspaper woman who acted as Roman correspondent for McMaster's *Freeman's Journal.* A zealous convert, Miss Eades had particularly ingratiated herself with the officials of Propaganda, that Vatican department which dealt with missionary territory, as the United States continued to be defined until 1908. American bishops not infrequently sought her counsel, as Grace now did. Her reply reflected her highly opinionated and often waspish temper.[85] Mary Ignatius Hayes, Miss Eades wrote, was "an adventuress, a swindler, a liar," who had no intention of founding a house of the Poor Clares in Minnesota, though she had a mania about making herself a superior somewhere. Mary Ignatius had moreover "disappeared" from Rome; rumor had it that she may have wandered off to Canada.[86] Whatever the truth of Miss Eades's allegations, many years were to pass before the Poor Clares brought the blessing of their vocation to Minnesota.

In 1924 the then archbishop of St. Paul, Austin Dowling, stated flatly in his quinquennial report to the Roman curia that his diocese depended for its very institutional existence upon the contributions of religious women. Such had been the fact—indeed, such had been the commonplace—for a long time before that. The pattern had been set during Bishop Grace's administration when, in addition to the Carondelet Josephites and the Benedictines, twelve more congregations took up work in Minnesota. Each was distinct by reason of the detailed regimen its members observed and by the habit they wore—black for the Sisters of Notre Dame, white for the Dominicans, brown for the Franciscans. But the characteristics they shared, these "brides of Christ," were

---

84. Sister Mary Ignatius to Grace, n.d., AASPM, Grace Papers.

85. For a brief but telling note about Eades's reputation as a combative gadfly, see John Tracy Ellis, *The Life of James Cardinal Gibbons,* 2 vols. (Milwaukee, 1952), 1:170–171.

86. Eades to Grace, October 7, 1876, AASPM, Grace Papers.

more significant than any formalities that separated them. They all were vowed to poverty, chastity, and obedience, all committed to a rigorously enforced common life, all prepared to embrace self-effacement, signified perhaps most forcefully by the wimple wrapped round their shorn heads, all dedicated to fulfilling, as Mother Pauline of Paderborn put it, a call from God consistent with the bishop's "sacerdotal consent and holy benediction."

Certainly such loyalty to the institutional Church and its governors provided a framework, but in fact these women themselves gave shape and substance to the Catholic community in Minnesota as did no other constituent part of it. It was they who nurtured and spread its ethos, they who guided it day to day from the immigrant beginnings to the solidly middle-class status it had achieved by the 1960s. Sisters in the hospital wards, in the care of the forlorn and neglected, in, above all, the classrooms of small and humble parochial schools—and in "vacation schools" during the summertime for the poorer or more remote parishes—consistently set the norms by which Catholics at large came to define themselves. The local convent was at once a sacred and a mysterious place, and one, incidentally, where a passing vagrant might hope to get a decent meal.

One should take care, however, not to romanticize or sentimentalize the nuns' contribution during these formative years. They shared in the hardscrabble poverty that was the lot of all the pioneers, though this circumstance was mitigated somewhat by discerning in it a spiritual value. They could suffer at the hands of eccentric or tyrannical superiors or the vagaries of the parish priest. They could expect to undergo the stress uniquely to be found in communities shut off from ordinary association with the world outside and constrained by a way of life rigidly imposed and enforced. A calling to the convent presupposed a high level of idealism which perhaps was threatened more by ennui than by chronic overwork. The nuns dealt with children or adolescents most of the time, but they were other people's children, not their own, a status that carried with it a stern challenge to their femininity.

But there is another side of the coin that should be looked at when remembering the heroic sisters who labored so tirelessly in St. Paul and St. Cloud, in Mankato and Faribault and Union Hill. In the social contract as it functioned during the latter half of the nineteenth century and the first half of the twentieth, women were by definition excluded from the decision-making élites. The term "cult of domesticity" had not yet been invented, but the mores that prevailed at the time dictated that a woman's place was in the home, as mother and helpmeet to the male who as her formal master determined the fortunes of both her and her children. A "career" for an unmarried woman was considered an anomaly, except perhaps for the spinster who did, say, seamstress's work in order to help support her aging parents. A Catholic girl, on the other hand, had another choice. She could elude the standing that a male-dominated society consigned her to, if she so desired, by aligning herself with a religious congregation. She then automatically established an independence not granted to her feminine siblings. Such a commitment, to be sure, involved her in a different set of obligations and in a regimen with personal challenges of its own. Nevertheless, this measure of autonomy, however circumscribed, contributed over a century of time to the attainment by the religious congregations of women of a unique prestige, in Minnesota and indeed across the United States. Their remarkable—and deserved—level of influence led young women in their legions to join the orders which, as the years passed, could offer a higher level of education and more opportunities for meaningful social action than could any other feminine association in the country. Primarily, however, their testament, left in numberless bleak classrooms, remained rooted in a peculiarly nineteenth-century spirituality—one with which Joseph Cretin rather than the more sophisticated Thomas Grace would easily identify—that with all its individualistic emphasis, with all its nonscriptural and nonliturgical devotionalism, with all its deep suspicions of the sexual appetite, helped to determine how at a particular time and place the Catholic vocation ought to be lived. Whatever the shortcomings a more blasé generation may lay at the feet of the sisters who accorded gold stars to their more pious pupils, the fact remains that without these women the faith could not, humanly speaking, have survived.

CHAPTER 9

Out of the Toils
of War

IN THE ELECTIONS HELD IN MINNESOTA IN 1859—THE YEAR
Thomas Grace traveled up the Mississippi from Memphis—the young Republican Party swept the board. Alexander Ramsey, narrowly defeated two
years before by Henry Sibley, assumed the governorship, while the two con-
gressional seats and the senatorial one, vacated by the mercurial General
Shields,[1] also went to the Republicans, as had the state legislature. Sibley had
chosen not to run in this contest, and so the only notable Democrat left on
the political scene was United States Senator Henry Rice. Ramsey had readily
shaken off the nativist, Know-Nothing prejudices of his former party, the now
imploded Whigs. Indeed, he recruited a twenty-eight-year-old offspring of
Irish immigrants and a nominal Catholic, Ignatius Donnelly,[2] as his running
mate. But Donnelly as candidate for lieutenant governor made less difference
in the campaign than Ramsey's understanding that fully thirty percent of the
electorate in Minnesota was foreign-born, with the right to exercise the franchise after a brief four months' residence. And he understood as well that
what these refugees from Ireland, Germany, and Scandinavia were most concerned about was squatters' homestead rights to federal land, an issue on
which the Democrats vacillated. His strategy proved decisive: over the next
half century, while Donnelly went on to embrace one grandiose if largely futile cause after another, the Republican hegemony in Minnesota was firmly
established.

---

1. See chapter 6, above.

2. Donnelly's father was a lapsed Catholic, and he himself maintained an ambivalence toward all institutional religion throughout his life. See Martin Ridge, *Ignatius Donnelly: The Portrait of a Politician* (Chicago, 1962), especially pp. 264–266.

The next year saw the national elections. By then the overriding issue across the country was slavery, that "peculiar institution." Threats of secession by the southern states had reverberations even in far-away Minnesota. There was little abolitionist sentiment locally; in fact the more extreme antislavery elements risked open hostility or even, on one or two occasions, a threat of mob action. Nonetheless, the Republican candidate for the presidency, Abraham Lincoln of Illinois, carried the state by an almost two-to-one margin of the popular vote, not least perhaps because he insisted that his primary objective was preservation of the Union, while a lesser goal remained limitation of the spread of slavery, rather than its eradication. At the beginning of 1861, Senator Rice represented the views of most Minnesotans when he proposed a settlement whereby the line of slave state and slave territory as defined in the Missouri Compromise of 1820[3] should extend westward to the Pacific Ocean. But his initiatives and others like his became moot when in mid-April 1861—a month or so after Lincoln's inauguration—the batteries aligning the shores of Charleston harbor opened fire on Fort Sumter. By chance Governor Ramsey was in Washington at that crucial moment; he took the opportunity to pledge to the president the immediate services of 1,000 Minnestoans. Only days later did Lincoln issue his fateful call for the mobilization of 75,000 volunteers.

By the end of what a later commentator termed "the war of the slaveholders' rebellion"[4] Minnesota had contributed eleven regiments to the Union army, a total of about 25,000 men. This was not a negligible number from a state with a total population of only 170,000. The legendary First Regiment of Minnesota Volunteer Infantry took the field at the first battle of Bull Run in July 1861, and served with conspicuous gallantry—and with heavy casualties—in all the campaigns in the eastern theater of operations, achieving a bloody immortality two years later in the Peach Orchard just outside the Pennsylvania town of Gettysburg. The other state units served in the western theater, in Tennessee and Mississippi, in Grant's siege of Vicksburg, in the fierce battles at Nashville and Mobile. The Second Minnesota stood with Thomas at the near disaster at Chickamauga and suffered 150 killed and wounded out of a total complement of 400. Late in 1864 the Second and Fourth marched with Sherman from Atlanta to the sea.[5]

---

3. See chapter 3, above.
4. Folwell, *Minnesota*, 2:76.
5. See Blegen, *Minnesota*, 233–248.

Amidst the patriotic euphoria in the immediate aftermath of Fort Sumter there was talk around St. Paul of organizing a regiment of Irishmen to fight for the Union. Nothing, however, came of this idea. And indeed, after the debacle at Bull Run, overall recruitment slowed appreciably. It took several months, for example, well into 1862, to organize the Fifth Minnesota Regiment. In mid-May, while this unit was drilling at Fort Snelling, Bishop Grace—blandly ignoring whatever few dark rumors still circulated about his southern roots—addressed Governor Ramsey.

> I propose to furnish at my own expense a Catholic clergyman to serve as chaplain for the benefit of the Catholic soldiers of the Fifth Regiment, Minnesota Volunteers, provided the necessary permission is granted to him to act in that capacity. The number of Catholic soldiers, comprising Germans, Irish, and French, . . . forms no inconsiderable proportion of the whole number of Volunteers.

In fact, he maintained, recruitment had been enhanced by the assurance that such a chaplaincy would be constituted. "Promises to that effect made both publicly and in private when it was proposed to organize a Fifth Regiment were received in every part of the State as of a measure just and proper." To fill this post, Grace concluded, he would name Father John Ireland, ordained six months earlier.[6]

The governor replied with a mixture of sympathy and embarrassment. Though Grace had always remained studiedly apolitical, he was the most prominent member of a very large minority of the electorate, and he could not be taken lightly. But Ramsey's hands were tied. A directive from the War Department, he explained, stipulated that a chaplain should be elected by a regiment's field officers, drawn not incidentally from a class unlikely to prefer an Irish Catholic; in the Fifth a Methodist minister from Minneapolis had already been chosen. Nevertheless, the canny governor found a solution of sorts. "Believing it just and proper"—Grace's original words—"that the soldiers of your faith in our armies should be provided for as others are, I cheerfully accept your nomination of the Rev. John Ireland as chaplain and will furnish him with the necessary credentials at once." Those credentials would name him as *state* chaplain to all the regiments serving in the western theater, thus circumventing the federal mandate. As for financial support, "I regret I have not the means at my command for defraying the Rev. Mr. Ireland's

---

6. Grace to Ramsey, May 18, 1862, AASPM, Grace Papers.

expenses, but doubt not the Legislature will certainly provide any advance you may make him."[7]

The governor's Solomonesque compromise was impracticable from the start. "The chaplain's commission," Ireland explained many years later, "was from the State of Minnesota—not formally recognized by the U. S. government. The duty of the State Chaplain was to go from one Minnesota regiment to another," with confidence that "the letters of the Governor [would secure] for him from the federal authorities protection and liberty to travel."[8] With various units scattered over hundreds of miles, to fulfill this assignment was totally unfeasible. Even so, when the Fifth Minnesota Volunteers departed for the south at the end of May, Ireland went with them. A few weeks later his anomalous position was quietly solved; the previously elected chaplain of the Fifth resigned, probably due to illness, and Ireland was chosen to replace him.

He served in that office for barely ten months, though long after the fact he wrote that "My years [sic] of chaplaincy were the happiest and most fruitful years of my ministry."[9] Not unlike veterans of other wars, those who fought to preserve the Union and survived looked back as time dimmed the pain and the tedium, the fear and the loneliness, and, too often, the moral degradation that had been their lot, and remembered instead the noble cause for which they had fought and the camaraderie they had experienced in that uniquely masculine enterprise, an army on campaign. Over succeeding decades, until his death indeed, John Ireland stated the case succinctly at innumerable encampments of the Grand Army of the Republic. "We were the soldiers of Abraham Lincoln," he reminded an assembly of veterans in Buffalo, New York, in 1897. "This the praise we covet; this the memory we yearn to transmit to the coming years."[10]

During Ireland's brief tenure the Fifth Minnesota, incorporated into one of the divisions commanded by General William Starke Rosecrans, operated

---

7. Ramsey to Grace, May 20, 1862, AASPM, Grace Papers.

8. See James P. Shannon, ed., "Archbishop Ireland's Experiences as a Civil War Chaplain," *Catholic Historical Review* 39 (1953): 298–305, esp. 302. Here is printed the text (301–305) of Ireland's lengthiest reminiscence of his time in the army, written (partly in the third person) entirely from memory in 1892.

9. Shannon, "Ireland as Chaplain," 305.

10. See Helen Angela Hurley, "The John Ireland Collection," 120–121, Minnesota Historical Society Archives, Hurley Papers. This typescript is a useful narrative based on press clippings and other secondary evidence.

in western Alabama and northern Mississippi and saw significant action at the battle of Corinth, October 3–4, 1862. The young chaplain—displaying already a gift for lively narrative—described in a dispatch sent back to St. Paul the Confederate assault upon the center of the Union position within that Mississippi town.

> Suddenly a strange commotion arises behind us. We turn around, and great is our surprise. At the lower end of the square the artillery are skedaddling with an astounding rapidity; the infantry rush in through every inlet; the citizens [of Corinth] and all idle gazers-on disappear in a second; the Butternuts emerge from the streets leading into the square. It was a solemn moment.[11]

A vitally crucial moment indeed, and forty-five years later, by then an elderly archbishop, the same John Ireland described it as

> a scene never to be forgotten, rising as vividly now before my mind as on the historic morning of October 4th, 1862—Union soldiers from battery and from infantry rushing wildly across the square, at the opposite side from across the railroad tracks where was deployed the Fifth, and the Confederates soon appearing in hot pursuit. We were no more than three hundred feet from the enemy, who, seemingly not noticing us, continued to thicken their line and hasten across the square, with the apparent intent of reaching at once the center of the town.[12]

Rosecrans himself as he rode into the smoke and firing in the square feared for a moment the destruction of his army: "I had the personal mortification" of witnessing "our wearied and jaded troops . . . scattering among the houses."[13] But a counterattack, in which the Fifth Minnesota played a pivotal role, drove the Confederates back into the woods north of the town; a second

---

11. Ireland, *St. Paul Press,* November 1, 1862. This is Ireland's lengthy contemporary account, dated October 23, 1862, of the battle of Corinth.

12. Ireland, "Response to Hubbard," *Minnesota Historical Society Collections* 12 (St. Paul, 1908): 546–548. This was a formal commentary on a speech by Lucius Hubbard, commandant of the Fifth at Corinth (and later governor of Minnesota), delivered at a meeting of the Minnesota Historical Society, January 14, 1907.

13. *The War of the Rebellion: Compilation of the Official Records of the Union and Confederate Armies,* 128 vols., 17 (Washington, 1880–1901): 166–170.

rebel assault, an hour later, was similarly repulsed, with great loss of life on both sides. "We soldiers of the Fifth," the chaplain wrote exultantly back to St. Paul, "have a special right to pride ourselves in what has been accomplished.... Great is our renown in this army. The other regiments fully appreciate our valor; our praise is on every tongue."[14]

John Ireland over the course of a long career was never a stranger to hyperbole. That the shorthanded Fifth—three of the regiment's companies had been detached to garrison duty in the forts guarding the Indian reservations back in Minnesota[15]—should have enjoyed "a special right to pride" because of the hard-won victory at Corinth would seem open to doubt, since Rosecrans had had to engage in the battle virtually all the 25,000 troops under his command. Nevertheless, the callow farmboys and clerks from Minnesota, mustered into service only a few months before, had fought steadfastly and had contributed meaningfully to the result; credit was surely due them. But beneath young Ireland's verbal exaggeration lay a complex set of emotions and convictions, which extended far beyond the blood-soaked center square of Corinth, Mississippi. He was himself an immigrant to this new land, a refugee from the horrors of the great Irish Famine, who during his schooldays in France had astonished and amused his more sophisticated classmates by his outspoken, not to say aggressive, expressions of fealty to his adopted country.[16] Many of the soldiers to whom he ministered were also persons displaced from old Europe, who had brought with them, as he had, their Catholic faith and their determination to make a new life in the New World. They were not always and everywhere welcomed in America, and not infrequently they kicked against the goad of traditional Yankee values. Yet in the end, at Corinth and at innumerable other battlefields of the Civil War, they earned the right to call themselves Americans in the fullest sense of the term. Men from Maine and Massachusetts, from New York and Pennsylvania—old families which could trace their lineage back to Plymouth Rock or to a Manhattan in thrall to grim Dutch entrepreneurs like Peter Stuyvesant—rallied to preserve the Union and to put an end to that vile "peculiar institution," chattel slavery. But so did the Fifth Regiment, Minnesota Volunteer Infantry, the French and Irish and German Catholics. We, too, John Ireland proudly declared, were the soldiers of Abraham Lincoln.

---

14. Ireland, *St. Paul Press,* November 1, 1862.
15. Blegen, *Minnesota,* 266, 269.
16. See O'Connell, *John Ireland,* 51–52.

ON SUNDAY, AUGUST 17, 1862, AS FATHER IRELAND'S COMRADES in the Fifth kept tedious guard over the rail lines in northwestern Alabama, four young braves of the Wahpeton clan, part of the Dakota or Sioux nation, casually murdered three white men and two women near the hamlet of Acton, a hundred miles or so west of St. Paul. They then stole some horses and galloped off to their encampment located at the junction of the Minnesota and Redwood rivers. Word of what they had done spread quickly through the villages on the reservation, restricted now to a narrow strip of land on the south bank of the Minnesota, stretching into Dakota Territory. The Indians realized full well that retribution for the grisly deed was inevitable, and so the chiefs of the various clans gathered for a council that same evening under the presidency of the most notable among them, Little Crow. One faction argued that the whole tribe should strike the whites before they could mobilize, while another, which included Little Crow himself, took the view that a war launched against so huge a numerical superiority would be futile and disastrous. "The White men," he protested, "are like locusts, when they fly so thick the whole sky is a snowstorm. . . . Yes, they fight among themselves, but if you strike at one of them, they will all turn upon you and devour you and your women and your little children. . . . You are fools. . . . You will die like rabbits." But the younger, hot-blooded element prevailed, and, with whatever reluctance, Little Crow agreed to join them. The next morning he led two hundred painted warriors in an attack upon the trading post and Indian Bureau facility known as the Lower Agency, just north of the scantily garrisoned Fort Ridgely and not far from the town of New Ulm. The great Sioux war had begun.

It lasted little more than a month, and indeed the outcome was determined in scarcely more than a week. When their two assaults on Fort Ridgely were repulsed, the Sioux bypassed the beleaguered fort and headed down the Minnesota valley to New Ulm. There, on Saturday, August 23, upwards of a thousand braves attacked a hastily organized volunteer force which, after fierce fighting, managed to fend them off; the destruction, however, was immense: hardly fewer than two hundred buildings in the town and its environs were burned down, either by the attackers or by the defenders intending to deprive the Indians of cover. Meanwhile, in St. Paul Governor Ramsey called for the mobilization of the state militia, and turned over the command of it to his friend and erstwhile political opponent, Henry Sibley. After New Ulm, other towns, including Hutchinson and Forest City, had to fight off Indian incursions. But the worst and most fearful images that the Dakota uprising left upon the consciousness of the white population were the savage attacks upon isolated farms and homesteads. General Sibley ultimately commanded a force sixteen hundred strong, supported by federal levies, once Ramsey had persuaded Washington that Minnesota on its own ground was embroiled in a "national war." By September 23 Sibley had cornered the largest of the Dakota bands near Wood Lake; there a confused engagement was fought when Chief Little Crow's attempt at an ambush failed and 300 braves were driven off with heavy losses. Instead of pressing his military advantage, Sibley, aware that resistance was crumbling, determined to negotiate for the release of the prisoners still in hostile hands. On September 26, thanks to the connivance of several disaffected chiefs, 269 whites and métis were freed amidst wild rejoicing. After that the Sioux War dwindled into three or four anticlimactic skirmishes. But the "national war" of which Ramsey had spoken had just begun. Over the next two generations the struggle continued to rage across the great plains of the West between the mismatched foes, leaving in its wake bloody symbols like the Little Big Horn and Wounded Knee.

Another symbol stood closer to hand. After Wood Lake Chief Little Crow had fled into Dakota Territory. When he slipped back into Minnesota the following summer he was shot to death by a pair of deer hunters, who were awarded a $500 bounty by the state. With nearly 500 dead at the hands of the Sioux, many more injured, and much property wantonly destroyed, vengeance against the Indians was the order of the day. Nor was this a surprising reaction in the immediate bitter aftermath of six weeks of violence. Indeed, it would seem that only one public man recognized at the time what has been universally admitted in retrospect, that the murders at Acton were merely the sparks, not the cause, that set off the conflagration. As early as 1860, Henry Whipple, Episcopal bishop of Minnesota, warned President Buchanan that the federal government's Indian policies—the outrageous treaties which filched millions of acres of land from the natives for the equivalent of two cents an acre, the incompetence and dishonesty of the political hacks routinely appointed Indian agents, the cynical collaboration between the civil authorities and the crooked traders who preyed upon the naïve natives with trinkets and whiskey—would inevitably lead to trouble. Deprived of their traditional economy, and with no serious attempt made to provide them with a viable alternative, the Indians, squeezed into ever narrower reservations, watched their cultural norms gradually disintegrate and their institutions of law and order decline into anarchy. The bishop—a tall and courtly man, noted for a droll sense of humor as well as a passion for justice, born forty years before of New England revolutionary stock—renewed his plea to President Lincoln in March 1862, months before the uprising. His appeals fell on deaf ears in Washington and in St. Paul, and certainly, if more understandably, in places like New Ulm and Hutchinson, once the fighting was over.

Even as the mopping up of the vestiges of resistance proceeded, Sibley set up a military tribunal to punish the defeated, sullen, and frightened remnant of the warriors who had been captured. By early November, 392 men had been tried, of whom 307 were condemned to death and sixteen to imprisonment. Sibley, strongly seconded by Alexander Ramsey—"The Sioux Indians," the governor had told the state legislature, "must be exterminated or driven beyond the borders [of Minnesota]"—proposed to carry out the executions forthwith. The federal authorities, however, insisted that the matter had to be referred to Washington, because the Indians, by treaty—ironically—could not be judged for capital offenses in state courts. Nor did merely sending the names of the condemned to Washington suffice, as Sibley had hoped. Much to the anger and disgust of most Minnesotans, President Lincoln intervened personally and directed that all relevant documents be forwarded to him. The indefatigable and indomitable Bishop Whipple hastened to Washington, lobbied strenuously the officials of the Indian Bureau, and gained an interview with the president. The upshot was that Lincoln commuted the death sentences of all but thirty-eight of the condemned, whom he agreed had been fairly convicted of murder or rape. They were duly hanged in a single ghastly moment at Mankato, on the day after Christmas, 1862, in the presence of a boisterous crowd of onlookers.[17]

A week before the trap doors at their feet were sprung open, a small and poignant drama began to be played out. On December 19—a Friday—Augustin Ravoux arrived in Mankato. Armed with a letter of recommendation from Sibley, he presented himself to one Colonel Miller, who was in charge of the Dakota prisoners. Miller received him graciously and promptly conducted him to a large hall in the jail where all the detainees had been assembled. There were "over three hundred of them, without counting over sixty other savages who have been acquitted and . . . restored to their families. . . . I spoke to the Indians," Ravoux recalled, "who listened to me with

---

17. The narrative here is a summary of the masterly account in Blegen, *Minnesota*, 259–280. Actually Lincoln designated thirty-nine Dakota for execution, but one was reprieved. In the election of 1864 Lincoln received, as he had in 1860, a majority of Minnesotans' votes, but by a much reduced margin—which may suggest that some resentment lingered among the electorate over the president's decision to temper the extreme punishment imposed by Sibley's court.

great attention." The Monday following—the 22nd—was the fateful day when those condemned to death were segregated from the others. In a smaller room in the prison, at three o'clock in the afternoon, Colonel Miller, flanked by Ravoux, Father Sommerreisen, the parish priest in Mankato, and two Protestant ministers who had labored as missionaries among the Sioux for many years, confronted these unfortunates in a manner that probably could not have been duplicated outside the America of the mid-nineteenth century.

> After reading the sentence in English and in the Sioux language, the colonel told the condemned that no hope remained for them in this life. He advised them to turn their thoughts towards the Redeemer of the world, and to choose, as they thought fit, for their spiritual adviser a Catholic or a Protestant minister. [An adjutant] wrote out two lists: twenty-four had their names inscribed on that of the "black robes" (Among them three metizos, under twenty years of age, who had not yet made their first communion). About a dozen put down their names on the Protestant list.

Father Ravoux was understandably startled by the result of this rather bizarre lottery. "It is true that I . . . passed some time with the Indians; but it is eighteen years since I quitted their deserts [sic], owing to the want of priests among the white population." Perhaps there lingered within the native memory the image of the earnest young Frenchman who had struggled so to master their language and to preach to them the spiritual message so dear to his heart.[18] Or perhaps the tradition among these condemned was a much older one, which recalled in some obscure way how the "blackrobes" had canoed into the midst of their ancestors with Bibles and mysterious sacraments, to be sure, but also with sophisticated tools and with medicines—magical potions almost—and the skills to use them properly. In any event, Ravoux spent the next tense days instructing his "dear neophytes" about the Holy Trinity, about the Redemption Jesus had brought to all mankind, about the Blessed Virgin ("briefly"), about the saints, like Alphonsus Ligouri who had affirmed "in one of his discourses that he who accepts death with resignation desires to repair as much as he can the evil he has done." Ravoux did so fully aware from experience "how difficult it is [even] for those acquainted with the manners and character of the Sioux to bring them to join the Christians in prayer." On Christmas day he administered their first Eucharistic Communion to the three young métis, thereby reconciling them to the Church they had scarcely

---

18. See chapter 2, above.

known before. By the morning of the day of final reckoning, December 26, Ravoux had baptized thirty-one of the condemned Dakota.

> Christmas day I remained with them from two o'clock in the afternoon to one o'clock at night. . . . It was a great pleasure to me to talk awhile to each of them. . . . I discoursed on the happiness of heaven and the glory of the elect, which they should soon enjoy if they continued to render themselves worthy of it by their fervor. . . . This language was most gratifying to them. I considered myself happy in being able to assist to prepare them for the great journey to eternity. . . . [In the morning] I followed the sad train, advancing to meet death without fear. . . . During the few moments they stood on the scaffold, while the executioners were tying the fatal knot round their necks, I remained on my knees, invoking from my very heart the mercy of God in their behalf. The expiation was short, and in an instant they were launched into eternity! May their souls rest in peace! May they rest happily in the bosom of God, and may their supplications obtain the grace of conversion for their unfortunate tribe![19]

In this dance of death there was for Augustin Ravoux a kind of ratification of the original fervor that had brought him across the sea from France twenty years before.

Bishop Grace was not so assiduously nor so flamboyantly involved in the Indian crisis of 1862 as Bishop Whipple, but in his characteristically quiet manner he had worked behind the scenes.[20] A full twenty-five months before the uprising he held a powwow with the leaders of the Dakota, the result of which was a formal request by them that "a clergyman of the order of the blackgowns be stationed amongst us . . . and no other ministers, as we have full confidence in [the blackgowns] . . . to instruct us and to educate our children." This document, with the names of Little Crow, five other chiefs, and thirteen braves appended,[21] Grace forwarded to the Superintendent of Indian Affairs in Washington. "I have received this petition," he wrote in a covering letter, "by the several chiefs . . . of the Sioux or Dakota Indians asking . . . that I would send a clergyman of the Catholic Church to reside among them."

---

19. Ravoux, *Reminiscences,* 72–81. This is the printed version of Ravoux to Grace, December 29, 1862. Due to a mistake in the binding of this volume (1890), there is some confusion in pagination.

20. For a brief treatment, see Lucker, "Grace," 180–182.

21. Memorandum (in longhand), August 14, 1860, AASPM, Grace Papers.

I need not say that the interest I feel in these poor Indians makes me most anxious to comply with their wishes and that nothing would afford me greater gratification than to be allowed to cooperate with the Government in its generous efforts to improve their condition and train them to habits of civilized life. Nothing so much contributes to this result, as has been found by experience, as the influence of religion. No longer engaged in the chase, the Indian needs something to supply that excitement. He needs something to give occupation to his mind, and something . . . to employ his bodily faculties.

To bring about this happy resolution the bishop "propose[d] to furnish a religious community of men and another of Sisters or nuns who will engage not only to instruct the Indians in the principles of Christianity and teach them the essential branches of education, but also develop in them, by encouraging habits of industry, the natural capabilities of usefulness to themselves and each other."[22]

Grace shrewdly discerned the root of the Indians' predicament—the destruction of their traditional hunting economy, their prohibition from ever again "engaging in the chase"—though he may have been too sanguine in predicting that religious and vocational instruction could fill the gap. Nevertheless, it would seem that his proposal deserved some attention in Washington. It received none. At the end of the year he appealed for intercession to his friend Senator Rice, whose efforts were similarly ignored.[23] Fort Sumter fell the following spring, and a year after that, as the war raged ever more intensely, and protests at the treatment of the Indians received no public notice, Grace gloomily decided that the two calamities were not unrelated. "I found your kind note waiting my return from the East," he wrote Bishop Whipple on May 17, 1862.

It occasioned me to reproach myself that I had not, in addition to writing to the Hon. H. M. Rice, written also to yourself, to thank you for your generous appeal in behalf of the Indians of Minnesota and your bold denunciation of the wrongs done them by government officials. There is cause to believe that our country through her present afflictions is but expiating the guilt of a large accumulation of national sins, not the least

---

22. Grace to William Cullen, September 8, 1860, AASPM, Grace Papers.
23. Rice to Grace, December 29, 1860, AASPM, Grace Papers.

among which are the crying injustices inflicted and permitted to be inflicted upon the Indian tribes of this continent.[24]

Four months later came the Sioux uprising.

Three days after the execution at Mankato, Grace, scarcely disguising his
indignation, bearded Lincoln himself. "I would beg leave," he wrote the president, "as Catholic Bishop of the Diocese of St. Paul, embracing the State of
Minnesota and Territory of Dakota, respectfully to call your attention to several communications on file in the Indian Department at Washington, touching the relations between Catholic missionaries and [the] Indian tribes." The
tragedy that had so recently unfolded had stemmed at least in part from the
sad reality "that the sentiments and wishes of the Indians in regard to the missionaries to be resident among them under the authority or sanction of the
Government have never been consulted, and on almost all occasions when
expressed have been wholly disregarded." It is a truism, the bishop argued,
that "the old traditions of the tribes have always determined [sic] preference
in favor of the successors of the missionaries known to the Indians as the
'Black Gowns,' who were first to venture into the recesses of their forests and
announce to their fathers the tidings of the Cross." As for the case at hand,
how much bloodshed might have been avoided had those "old traditions"
been honored.

So late as August 14, 1860, a petition signed by Little Crow and eighteen
other chiefs and head-men of the bands, who were engaged in the recent
massacre of the settlements in Minnesota, was presented to me, together
with another document to be transmitted by me to the Department in
Washington, signed by the same chiefs and head-men, the petitioners
desiring and supplicating in both documents the establishment of Catholic missionaries on their reservations, to have charge of the education
and religious instruction of their people. These documents I forwarded
to Washington under the administration of your predecessor [Buchan-
an], accompanying them with certain propositions on my part and with
such suggestions as I thought advisable in case the Government would be
pleased to accede to the wishes of the Indians. No notice was taken of
these papers, and they went only to swell the bulk of numerous others of
similar terms and import in the Department of Indian Affairs.

---

24. Grace to Whipple, May 17, 1862 (copy), AASPM, Grace Papers.

So now, he asked in conclusion, what is to be done with the pitiable remains of the Dakota Nation?

> The interest I feel in these Indians as well for their material as for their spiritual well-being emboldens me to say [that] I shall be most happy to be allowed to cooperate with the Government in its generous efforts to improve their condition. I flatter myself, not vainly I hope, that with the appliances I can command I shall be able to contribute not a little to the success of those efforts.[25]

It may well be that Thomas Grace exaggerated when he argued that the presence of Catholic priests and nuns on the reservation from 1860 might have forestalled the war that broke out in 1862. In a situation so dire there could have been no easy and quick solutions. Nevertheless, his eloquent indictment of the incompetence of the Indian Bureau appears to have been perfectly valid. At any rate, his protest met the usual blank wall of bureaucratic sloth. Two months after the letter to Lincoln had been dispatched—during which interval Rice had done his best to lobby the Department of the Interior—the senator received a cold communication from a functionary in the Indian Bureau.

> I have the honor to acknowledge the receipt, by reference from you, of a letter of Bishop Grace of 29th Dec. last, addressed to the President. . . . I have to say that the said Sioux have heretofore had such schools as were deemed by the Office commensurate with their wants. . . . In regard to the subjects referred to in your letters aforesaid, it will be necessary to defer all action of this Office till the Sioux shall have been located in the new country [in the west] to which they are about to be removed.[26]

There had been fears among the white population that the Dakota uprising in southwestern Minnesota might prompt other tribes to join in a general insurrection. But the Winnebagoes, confined to their reservation not far from New Ulm, did not stir out of their poverty and wretchedness, while the much more numerous and warlike Ojibwe to the north and east saw no reason to

---

25. Grace to Lincoln, December 29, 1862 (copy), AASPM, Grace Papers. A postscript: "I beg to refer you to Hon. H. M. Rice, Senator from Minnesota, for anything further you may desire to know of the writer of this."

26. William Dole to Rice, March 2, 1863 (copy), AASPM, Grace Papers.

join forces with their ancient enemies. Concern about these latter, however, both in Washington and St. Paul, led to a new treaty in March 1863 which consigned them to reservations at Leech Lake, Lac-qui-Parle, and White Earth, and, of course, in effect appropriated their land and rendered them politically and economically impotent. The following May the Indian Bureau designated Bishops Whipple and Grace, along with another Protestant clergyman, as a board of visitors to the Ojibwe, in order to determine what Christian ministrations would be appropriate for them.[27] Grace accordingly traveled northward with his fellow commissioners,[28] without, however, harboring much hope that anything significant would be accomplished. A year and some months later a similar assignment was proposed to him, this time intended to include clans of the Ojibwe as far west as Pembina.[29] But by then his patience at what was at best an empty formality had run out. These commissions, he wrote to Washington, impose immense physical difficulties, travel over hundreds of miles "by way of Indian trails" and "no conveyance can be got except at great cost," so that one had to proceed "on foot or through lakes and swamps in canoes of bark. . . . The labor and the bodily inconveniences I would willingly undergo, but it is unrealistic to expect that the Visitors should defray with their time [and] allowances the entire material cost of the service. . . . In the expedition last year to the reservations . . . the tent and camping equipage were furnished not [by the federal government but] by General Sibley."[30] After the usual bureaucratic delay, the bishop's withdrawal was accepted, predictably, with "exceeding regret" by the relevant functionary.[31]

Grace, like Cretin before him, conscientiously tried to help the Indians—meaning by "help" converting them from paganism and teaching them European ways. In theory this is what the federal bureaucracy and its local minions wanted too; in practice and policy, however, the government at all levels, dominated by the overweening Protestant culture, preferred that the natives become good Presbyterians or Methodists and, above all, that they just go away. As late as 1873, Grace, though weary at the accumulated rebuffs he had experienced, was at least still going through the motions of securing for the

---

27. I. P. Usher to Grace, May 9, 1853, AASPM, Grace Papers. Usher was an official in the Department of the Interior. The third member of the board was the Reverend Thomas Williamson of Davenport, Iowa.

28. See Grace to Whipple, October 6 and 8, 1863 (copies), AASPM, Grace Papers.

29. Lincoln to Grace, September 15, 1864, AASPM, Grace Papers.

30. Grace to Dole, October 1, 1864, AASPM, Grace Papers.

31. Dole to Grace, December 3, 1864, AASPM, Grace Papers.

Ojibwe a Catholic—and therefore, in his mind, a uniquely positive—presence among the maltreated tribe. "I have received letters from White Earth asking me to intercede with you," he wrote Alexander Ramsey—by this time a United States senator—"that you might use your influence to obtain the appointment of a Catholic Agent at that place."

> I have so often urged the claims of the Catholic Indians and mixed-bloods, and submitted the expressed wishes of the Ojibwe in general before the department in Washington without effect [that] I feel very little encouragement to hope that those claims and preferences will receive consideration. . . . I feel grateful for the kind words you have spoken in our favor on several occasions; perhaps a word now might help obtain what would be a simple act of justice, . . . the appointment of a Catholic Agent at one of our reservations in Minnesota.[32]

Ramsey, by no means a bigot and in any case sensitive to the petition of an important constituent, moved quickly: "I carried [your request] up to the Secretary of the Interior and had an interview with him. . . . He assured me that he would give the subject his fullest consideration." The senator's intervention, however, bore no fruit.[33]

THOMAS GRACE'S FRUSTRATION OVER THE GOVERNMENT'S consistent refusal to grant a favorable or at least a neutral response to Catholic offers to participate in the process of pacifying the Indians was exceedingly painful to him. But, unlike Cretin, he had never committed himself to the missions primarily, to serve as an agent of their conversion. And, like his predecessor, he soon found himself preoccupied by the sheer numbers of the Catholic immigrants pouring into Minnesota. Among many other more prosaic concerns, Grace, given his academic background and his natural predispositions, took seriously an obligation to provide his coreligionists with a vehicle of intellectual inquiry and polemical defense. "Secular journals animated with a Catholic spirit," was what he had in mind, he told James McMaster, "speaking to the country at large, taking part in the discussion of all public questions and measures, are the kind of papers demanded by the times, and they should be free to give their views and opinions upon all subjects.

---

32. Grace to Ramsey, March 24, 1873, AASPM, Grace Papers.
33. Ramsey to Grace, March 28, 1873, AASPM, Grace Papers. See also Lucker, "Grace," 189–194, and Reardon, *Diocese of St. Paul*, 181–182.

And advocate and oppose the claims of any party or any measures as in their estimation seems to them good."[34]

In 1866 the bishop's aspirations came to fruition, thanks to a thirty-five-year-old Irish immigrant named John Crosby Devereux. This native of County Wexford had grown up in Pittsburgh, where in his late teens he apprenticed himself to one of the local newspapers. He held a similar job in Louisville a few years later. There he met by chance the raffish Canon Vivaldi,[35] who claimed to be in Kentucky on a fund-raising tour for Bishop Cretin. The canon's enthusiastic description of the wonders of Minnesota prompted Devereux to try his luck there, and in 1855 he arrived in St. Paul with sixty dollars in his pocket. He worked as a printer for the *Minnesota Pioneer* until the Civil War broke out, during which he served with the Third Minnesota and attained the rank of captain.

A year after the war ended he was approached by Father John Ireland, now rector of the cathedral parish. Bishop Grace, Ireland said, was anxious to have a Catholic newspaper started in his diocese. Would Devereux be interested in such a project? Indeed he would, for he fancied himself potentially a genuine newspaperman rather than merely a mechanic who knew how to operate a printing press. Prudence, however, required some fiscal preparation. Accordingly, Devereux, armed with a letter signed by Ireland, spent the next six months traveling round the diocese in quest of subscriptions. He garnered 640 of them, at three dollars each. Grace supplied rent-free office space, but neither he nor Ireland invested in the enterprise. The actual printing was done at the plant of Devereux's former employer, the *Pioneer*. On November 17, 1866, the first issue of the eight-page tabloid appeared; it was called *The Northwestern Chronicle,* a name suggested by Grace on the grounds that it was "unpretentious."[36]

John Devereux proved a hardworking jack-of-all-trades in getting out the weekly *Chronicle* almost single-handedly and with the scantiest resources. He also wrote prose with a certain flamboyance, which quality, quite in accord with the fashion of the day, he displayed in his first editorial.

We have embarked in [sic] this undertaking not so much from a desire of gain as from a desire to do good. The press is exerting a great influence in

---

34. See chapter 7, above.

35. See chapter 4, above.

36. Stanley J. Maslowski, "Minnesota's First Catholic Newspaper, *The Northwestern Chronicle*: A Survey of Its History and Content, 1866–1894" (Master's thesis, St. Paul Seminary, 1963), 1–4.

the world; "the pen is mightier than the sword." The press has a mission to fulfill no less than the pulpit; and we were fully conscious of that truth when we concluded to enter the field of periodical literature.

He promised to provide "a weekly chronicle of Catholic events" in Minnesota and across the nation. "Foreign matters of Catholic interest will receive due attention," especially events in Ireland. There will be regular translations of French and German material, as well as occasional poetry. As for good causes—and here John Ireland's influence can be discerned[37]—total abstinence will be promoted, Devereux declared, and Catholic colonization in the state encouraged. Finally, he pledged that once circulation had risen sufficiently, the *Chronicle* would award a prize for the best novel written by a local author.[38]

The editor was as good as his word in fulfilling his primary mandate. His pages were filled with information of local concern, interspersed with international news and commentary—particularly with regard to the Vatican Council and the subsequent travails of the papacy[39]—and snippets of history and verse. Bishop Grace used the paper to promulgate his official communications to the diocese. But it did not prosper, its circulation never exceeding 740 subscribers, and so the prize to be awarded a budding novelist never materialized. In 1875 Devereux sold the *Chronicle* to John Ireland for $2,000, which transaction left him eighteen dollars once his debts were paid. Political as well as financial considerations may also have played a part in this change of ownership. Devereux, though careful always to adhere to authoritative Catholic teaching, took his own line in politics and through the *Chronicle* strongly supported the Democratic Party. Grace, as he had explained to McMaster years before, distrusted the Democrats; and Ireland was rapidly evolving into that rarity among Catholic clergymen, a full-blown Republican. In any case, from this date the *Chronicle* became more or less a conventional diocesan newspaper, edited by laymen now and then but firmly under clerical control. It survived until 1900, when its accumulated debts forced its clo-

---

37. See chapter 10, below.

38. *The Northwestern Chronicle* (*NWC*), November 17, 1866.

39. The first Council of the Vatican convened on December 8, 1869. The following July the French garrison preserving what was left of the Papal States was withdrawn, and the council was suspended. By September Rome had fallen to the forces of the newly united Italy, and Pope Pius IX had declared himself "prisoner in the Vatican."

sure.[40] John Devereux lived on in St. Paul and held several minor positions in the municipal government. When he died at age eighty-five in 1916, Archbishop Ireland preached a characteristically fulsome sermon at his funeral.[41]

Several other newspapers were founded under Catholic auspices during Bishop Grace's time. These weeklies addressed almost exclusively ethnic and linguistic constituencies. Two of them, conducted by Irishmen, dealt primarily with the painful politics in the old country—it was the era of the Fenians, the Land League, the struggle for Home Rule—and displayed little interest in local affairs. By far the most distinguished of them was *Der Wanderer,* established by the German Catholics in St. Paul to diffuse in their own language the traditions of their faith and their fatherland. Though initiated by the Benedictine priests at the Assumption parish, *The Wanderer* has flourished under a series of brilliant lay editors and managers, as it does to this day.[42]

AFTER TEN YEARS AS BISHOP OF ST. PAUL, THOMAS GRACE WAS in low spirits. He watched with dismay as the vast territory he was responsible for rapidly filled up with wave after wave of immigrants. He worried about his health and wondered whether he could cope physically with the burdens which every day grew heavier. He said little about his feelings to his entourage—he remained all his life reserved when it came to matters personal—and he gave no sign of a nostalgia for Memphis and the vigor of his young manhood. Nor did he harbor nostalgia for the Rome of his student days: in the summer of 1868 Pope Pius IX announced the summoning of a general council, the first since Trent in the sixteenth century, to convene at the Vatican at the end of the following year. Grace, pleading ill health, promptly applied for permission to excuse himself from attending the council, and Propaganda eventually granted his request, though it took a year for the official document to be issued.[43] He fretted more, however, over the notoriously dilatory congregation's failure to respond to inquiries he had made with regard to serious administrative decisions, an unease he shared with his metropolitan, the archbishop of St. Louis.

---

40. The subscription list and the title of the *Chronicle* were sold to *The Catholic Citizen* of Milwaukee. It ceased publication there in 1935.

41. Maslowski, "First Catholic Newspaper," 21–24.

42. See John S. Kulas, *Der Wanderer of St. Paul: The First Decade, 1867–1877* (New York, 1996), 19–31.

43. "Rescript," dated September 2, 1869, AASPM, Grace Papers.

"The silence of Cardinal Barnabò,"[44] Peter Richard Kenrick replied, "is much to be deplored." But in fact it was all too common an occurrence: "My application for extraordinary faculties, made 4 months since, has not yet been answered." Kenrick, a feisty, outspoken man, was consistently critical of the centralizing proclivities of the Roman curia, in which one vast bureaucracy—Propaganda—was charged with overseeing in minute detail formal Catholic activity in "missionary countries" as radically diverse as the United States and Siam. He tried to reassure Grace that no "personal motive" was involved in Barnabò's apparent inattention.

> The fact is, the Eminent Prelate has a Herculean task to perform, and is obliged to defer the discharge of duties most intimately connected with the interest of Religion. Thus Alton [Illinois] and Covington [Kentucky] are a year without Bishops, and I need not say that Religion loses by such prolonged vacancies. If the American Bishops in Rome [during the coming council] be true to their duties, they will make a movement to have the Ecclesiastical affairs of [this] country placed in some more affective [sic] hands; but I have little hope that they will do so, although nothing appears to me more imperatively called for.

St. Louis was confident that "in the circumstances" St. Paul had "done right" in assuming local initiatives on the justifiably "supposed will of the Pontiff." But as for intervening in Grace's behalf with the prefect of Propaganda, Kenrick refused to do so, not only because of his constitutional convictions but also for an intensely personal reason: "I wish to have as little correspondence as possible [with Barnabò] in consequence of his extraordinary action in the case of the Bishop of Chicago, whose insanity I think mainly attributable to the mistakes made by that Prelate."[45] Kenrick's reference was to James Duggan, a protégé of the archbishop of St. Louis, who, after a tumultuous tenure in Chicago, was removed from office by Propaganda and who spent the last years of his life in an insane asylum. Peter Kenrick was not one to abandon his friends.[46]

For Thomas Grace, whatever his sympathies for the erratic former bishop of Chicago, his concerns remained fundamentally the same. Through the au-

---

44. Alessandro Cardinal Barnabò was by this time the prefect of Propaganda.

45. Kenrick to Grace, September 21, 1869, AASPM, Grace Papers.

46. But for a detailed instance of Duggan's notorious mental instability, see O'Connell, *Sorin*, 416–424.

tumn of 1869 he pondered the diocese's and his own predicament as he saw it. In mid-November he addressed Archbishop Kenrick again, who by this time was in Rome, awaiting the opening of the council. "I think it very necessary," he wrote, "to propose a division of the Diocese of St. Paul."

> The state is filling up very rapidly with people, and it is important to se-
> cure in time landed property in the interest of Religion. This becomes
> every year more difficult—as the lands are being fast taken up and are
> greatly enhancing in value. With the vast area comprised by the Diocese
> at present and the largely increased number of clergy and faithful, I find
> it impossible to give the amount of attention which the interest involved,
> spiritual and temporal, require.

He recommended first the creation of a new diocese which would embrace all of northern Minnesota and the northern portion of what was then Dakota Territory and is now the state of North Dakota. "The See of the new Bishop-rick will be the city of St. Cloud, Stearns County. The district has already twenty-three churches and twenty-one priests. . . . The missions are mostly in the charge of the Benedictine Fathers, who have an Abbey and a college at-tached and three other community houses within the limits of the proposed new Diocese." Grace even nominated in this communication to Kenrick the *terna* who might be elevated to preside over this jurisdiction: the current abbot of St. John's, Rupert Seidenbusch; Alexander Berghold, the charismatic pastor of Holy Trinity in New Ulm;[47] and the no less attractive Joseph Buh,[48] the bearded Slovenian who had taken up the mission in Duluth in succession to the dynamic Father John Chebul, all of them fluent in German. "These priests," Grace observed, "are unexceptionable on all points, but it is very de-sirable that the Bishop should be [Seidenbusch], a Benedictine."

With regard to the rest of the area, the southern portion of Dakota Ter-ritory, Grace maintained that it would be well "to have it erected into a Vi-cariate or attached to the Vicariate of Nebraska or Montana."[49]

---

47. See chapter 6, above.

48. See Robert W. Klein, "Diocese of Duluth," in Ahern, *Catholic Heritage*, 70–71.

49. In ecclesiastical parlance, a "vicariate" was a geographical area which, though presided over by one consecrated by episcopal ordination, was not yet set-tled enough to have been designated a canonical diocese, centered in a particular place.

The settlements [he argued] are along the borders of the Missouri River where many thriving towns are growing up, with due proportion of Catholic inhabitants. The interior of the territory is mostly an arid waste with few or no settlements. There is no way of reaching the settled parts of it from St. Paul except by way of the Hannibal Railroad and Missouri River. I have never been able to visit them. The chief town and west capitol of the Territory is Yankton. In the event of any change as to this territory, the part of it which I have assigned to the new Diocese of St. Cloud, will of course be included in the Vicariate and will not form a part of the new Diocese.

In making this last point Grace apparently foresaw what eventually transpired, the creation of a vicariate for the whole of Dakota Territory. At any rate, he recognized at this moment that such plan should have been brought before a provincial synod, but since none "had been held in St. Louis these past two years, the urgency of the matter induces me to propose it through you in this manner which, I am aware, is informal."

But the bishop of St. Paul had also been moved by an urgency of a more personal nature.

Lastly, I would earnestly beg, Most Reverend Dear Sir, that you will represent to the Holy Father or [the] Sacred Congregation [of Propaganda] that the state of my health is such as to make me feel it a matter of conscience to tender my resignation as Bishop of the Diocese. I suffer from the determination of blood to the head, which causes frequent headache and incapacitates me for anything requiring special mental exertion. I pray and trust that the Holy Ghost will inspire the Sovereign Pontiff what is best for the interests of the Diocese and the good of my own soul.[50]

There was, however, little chance Kenrick's intercession would have served Grace's purpose. Slow in action, Propaganda was long in memory: Barnabò and his colleagues would have remembered that Grace had originally refused to go to St. Paul for similarly vague reasons. But more to the point, Kenrick, in Italy six weeks before the opening of the Vatican Council, had published there two pamphlets in which he stated his reasons for opposing the proposal to endorse by conciliar *fiat* the infallibility of the pope. And once the debates on this burning issue began on the council floor, he stood

---

50. Grace to Kenrick, November 14, 1869 (copy), AASPM, Grace Papers.

among the sternest and most adamant opponents of the definition. It was clear from the start that theirs was a distinctly minority position, and so sixty-one of the "inopportunists," including the archbishop of St. Louis, absented themselves from the final ballot rather than formally voting *non placet,* in order, they said, to spare the pope's feelings. Kenrick and his allies immediately felt intense pressure from the curia to conform. On January 2, 1871, at a welcome-home ceremony in St. Louis, a grim-faced archbishop announced, without specific elaboration, that he accepted the council's decisions. When upbraided for even this indeterminate acquiescence by one of the leading anti-infallibilists, he replied with a genuine *cri de coeur* that he could submit only by invoking "Father Newman's theory of development. . . . This principle removed Newman's great difficulty and convinced him that, notwithstanding the difference [between the primitive and the contemporary Church], he might and should become a Catholic. I thought it might justify me in remaining one."[51] So he did, though for ever afterward he remained a *persona non grata* with the Roman officials. But time in the end smiled upon him; Archbishop Peter Richard Kenrick outlived all his friends and enemies and survived into his ninety-first year.

What stance Thomas Grace might have assumed at the Vatican Council had he attended it remains open to conjecture, though it is not fanciful to suggest that he might well have allied himself with his metropolitan without, however, adopting Kenrick's aggressive style. In any event, Grace's main preoccupation continued to be the immense size of his jurisdiction, and, though he had given up the idea of a vicariate for southern Dakota Territory, he still hoped for a bishop to be enthroned in St. Cloud. He once more applied to St. Louis for counsel. "I would advise you," Kenrick replied toward the end of

---

51. See James Hennesey, "The Bishops of the United States at the First Vatican Council" (Ph.D. dissertation, The Catholic University of America, 1963), 498–513 (published as *The First Council of the Vatican: The American Experience* [New York, 1963]). This remarkable work of scholarship stands as a permanent monument to the late Father Hennesey. The quotation (509) is from Kenrick's response to Sir John (later Lord) Acton, a fierce opponent of the definition of infallibility, and refers to John Henry Newman, *An Essay on the Development of Christian Doctrine* (London, 1845). Most of those who opposed the definition did so on the grounds that it was "inopportune" rather than false, though in Kenrick's case some doubt might legitimately linger about such a distinction. At the final session of Vatican I, 533 voted *placet* vis-à-vis papal infallibility and two voted *non placet,* a bishop from southern Italy and Grace's sometime correspondent, Edward Fitzgerald, bishop of Little Rock.

1871, "to send your application for the division of your diocese, together with the names and *notulae* [recommendations], to Cardinal Barnabò, and at the same time inform him that you have communicated them, the names, to the Bishops of the Province, including myself, and have requested them to express to the Congregation their opinion."[52] Grace did so, and at the same time Kenrick sent Propaganda notice of his own approval of the erection of a new diocese and of the candidates suggested, "especially the Abbot."[53] The result was the dispatch from Rome to St. Paul of a set of new and complex procedures which, when forwarded to St. Louis, aroused the archbishop's bitter vexation.

> Had these requisites been thought of somewhat earlier, it is clear that half the actual sees in the States would not have been erected. Propaganda cares little for us, Papal Vicars, to do than report. This excessive centralization must prove very injurious to Religion, as it leaves no room for the exercise of judgment, enlightened by local experience and knowledge of circumstances, which are necessarily unknown to such a Body as the Sacred College.[54]

But however much disgruntlement, intellectual and practical, Kenrick felt toward Rome, and however suspicious Rome remained about him, straightforward demography—the sheer number of settlers—dictated that they cooperate in a massive reorganization of the Catholic hierarchy in the Middle West. It took two years of negotiation, wrangling, and compromise, but finally, on March 11, 1874, the archbishop of St. Louis and his suffragans met formally to recommend to Propaganda a sweeping modification of existing arrangements. Perhaps the most significant proposal was the division of the huge St. Louis Province by establishing three new archbishoprics, in Chicago, Milwaukee, and Santa Fe. Three vicariates were to be transformed into canonical dioceses in Omaha, Denver, and Leavenworth, "the chief places in these vicariates . . . [with] the present Vicars Apostolic to be made Bishops of such Sees." A new diocese would be erected in Peoria. As for St. Paul, Grace had trimmed back again on his original plan and now proposed simply a vicariate for northern Minnesota. His list of candidates had changed as well:

---

52. Kenrick to Grace, December 1, 1871, AASPM, Grace Papers.
53. Kenrick to Grace, December 20, 1871, AASPM, Grace Papers.
54. Kenrick to Grace, March 2, 1872, AASPM, Grace Papers.

Abbot Rupert Seidenbusch of St. John's remained at the head of the *terna,* but Alexander Berghold for reasons unknown had dropped off in favor a young Father Gregory Koering.[55]

A SUBSTANTIAL PORTION OF THESE RECOMMENDATIONS WAS duly approved by Propaganda, most notably for Thomas Grace the establishment a year later of an apostolic vicariate of Northern Minnesota, with Seidenbusch to head it. Not till 1880, however, was the same entity set up for Dakota Territory. But one item on the agenda—judged perhaps by the attending bishops as the least important—suddenly and unexpectedly raised loud alarm signals in St. Paul: "The Vicar Apostolic of Nebraska asks for a coadjutor on account of failing health, and recommends 1) Rev. Edward M. Hennessy, C. M., of St. Vincent's, St. Louis; 2) Rev. M. Hurley of Peoria, Illinois; 3) Rev. John Ireland, Pastor of the Cathedral of St. Paul, Minnesota." Hennessy, a Vincentian missioner, who appeared to have impressive credentials and Kenrick's support, was judged *dignissimus* (most worthy of promotion to the episcopate), while Michael Hurley, a parish priest of prominence in Peoria, was given the grade of *dignior* (very worthy). Residing in third place on the preferment list as *dignus* (worthy) was the thirty-six-year-old Ireland, and being the third of three suggested strongly that his chances of finding a miter in the wilds of western Nebraska were remote. Then, in mid-February 1875, St. Paulites read the following report in one of their local newspapers:

> The Rev. John Ireland, Rector of the Cathedral Parish and Secretary of the diocese, has been elevated by His Holiness Pope Pius the Ninth . . . to the dignity of Vicar Apostolic of Nebraska, Wyoming, Montana, and part of Dakota. . . . It is currently reported . . . that he has concluded to accept the new dignity conferred upon him and that he will be accompanied to his new field of labor by his father, mother, and other members of his family. . . . While wishing the reverend gentleman every success in his future home, we must say that St. Paul can badly afford to lose his valuable services, and that it may be many years before the void he leaves here can be suitably filled.[56]

---

55. See Kenrick to Grace, March 1, 1874, AASPM, Grace Papers, which is the agenda for the meeting of March 11.

56. *St. Paul Dispatch,* February 16 and 27, 1875.

Among the faults often laid at the door of the American bishops—a mad-dening one to the legalistic officers of Propaganda—was the casual, even hap-hazard manner in which they prepared lists of episcopal nominees, the *ternae*. Such apparently was the case in St. Louis in 1874, at least according to the re-sumé put together by one of Propaganda's clerks.[57] Kenrick and his suffragans duly submitted a *terna* for the vicariate of Nebraska, but they also nominated the same three persons for the proposed new diocese of Peoria. This double submission was clearly an unacceptable procedure. So sometime later a sepa-rate *terna* for Peoria was sent to Propaganda, as well as notice that the prior candidates for Nebraska should be considered for incumbency, since the vicar had died in the meantime. So now the prefect of Propaganda and his col-leagues had the requisite six names for the two positions, but, sticklers for legal niceties as they professed themselves to be, they nevertheless proceeded in a curiously unlegal fashion, lumping them all together as they pondered their decision. Hennessy along with two of the candidates for Peoria were dis-missed from consideration because of unfavorable reports about their fitness for office ("a motivo sfavorevoli notizie"). The third name on the Peoria list was about to be appointed bishop elsewhere, while Hurley, though appearing now only on the Nebraska *terna*, was judged an appropriate choice for Peoria, since he was the resident pastor in that Illinois town.[58] That left Ireland in lonely eminence. "Finally, for the Apostolic Vicariate of Nebraska, no name remains save that of the priest Ireland, about whom there is, besides, suffi-cient satisfactory information."[59] By mid-January 1875, the pope had given his formal approval to the appointments of Hurley and Ireland, and a month later his decision was made public.

So it was that John Ireland first attained episcopal rank through a process of elimination, and a rather sloppy process at that. But the news of his promo-tion had startled Bishop Grace as much as anyone else in St. Paul, and it effec-tively forced the hand of that usually diffident man. He who had evaded attendance at the momentous Vatican Council five years before now rushed off to Rome to try to reverse the decision. By April he was laying siege to the huge black stone palazzo that housed Propaganda on the edge of the Piazza

---

57. Archives of the Sacred Congregation for the Evangelization of Peoples (*Pro-paganda Fide*), *Acta* (APF-A), 243 (1875), 283–285.

58. Hurley declined the appointment, and in 1876 the mercurial John Lancaster Spalding was named first bishop of Peoria. See David Francis Sweeney, *The Life of John Lancaster Spalding* (New York, 1965), 104–107.

59. APF-A, 243 (1875), 284.

di Spagna. He explained to Cardinal Barnabò that he had allowed Ireland's name to appear on the original *terna* only after his colleagues in the province assured him that the appointment to Nebraska would never come to pass. Inclusion had been intended as a compliment to a deserving young priest, nothing more. Grace did not mince words. He expressed his personal displeasure at the turn of events. He warned that Ireland's departure would cause deep resentment in Minnesota and would lead to a host of unspecified troubles. He threatened, finally, to resign.[60]

Barnabò then put his finger on the glaring weakness in Grace's case: was Father Ireland worthy to be a bishop, or was he not? If he was, why did Grace stand in the way of the proposed promotion? If not, why was the priest's name placed upon the *terna* when the bishop of St. Paul could easily have prevented it? Grace replied, rather lamely, that he had always intended to ask that Ireland be appointed his coadjutor. Ireland, he told Barnabò on April 30, "knows intimately the state of my diocese, and is eminently qualified for episcopal rank."

Meanwhile, back in St. Paul, the object of these negotiations had his own role to play, a role carefully orchestrated with that his ordinary was playing in Rome. On April 22 Ireland wrote a letter in Latin addressed directly to Pius IX, in which he petitioned the pontiff to revoke the assignment to Nebraska. He enclosed this letter, together with the papal documents naming him a titular bishop[61] and a vicar apostolic, with another to Grace to whom he wrote: "As you will perceive in reading this letter [to the pope], I enter into no details as to reasons of my resignation, taking the liberty to refer to your statement of the case. . . . I put Nebraska entirely out of my mind and settle down quietly into my old attachment to Minnesota." Then with a docility not altogether characteristic of him, he added: "I never by any direct acting or choosing of my own have fashioned my destiny; it has been always apparently fashioned

---

60. For here and below see APF-A, 243 (1875), 283–285, including a copy of Grace to Barnabò, April 30, 1875.

61. Tradition demanded that a bishop who was not ordinary of a canonically erected diocese should nonetheless have a diocesan title. Thus sites that in ancient times had had a Catholic bishop, but no longer did, were (and are) used to provide titles for vicars apostolic, coadjutors, auxiliaries, curial officials, and retired diocesan bishops. North Africa, the Balkans, and the Middle East abounded in such places. Thus Ireland had been named titular bishop of Maroena *in partibus infidelium* (usually shortened to *in partibus*), that is, bishop of a see in Thrace that no longer had any Catholics living in it. He kept this title until 1884 when he succeeded Grace as bishop of St. Paul.

for me, and it has been all the better with me. . . . In this whole present affair, it would be a hard task for me were I myself to decide alone what I should do. My consolation is that it is all in your hands and not in my own."[62]

By a curious twist of fate the parcel containing the two letters and the accompanying documents never reached Bishop Grace, because the mail steamer carrying it was wrecked off the coast of England.[63] But this accident at sea, as things turned out, had no bearing on the outcome of the case in Rome. Grace had made his argument persuasively enough, and his own prestige within the curia, which stood higher perhaps than he had realized, proved enough to win the day. "There can be no doubt," read the final Propaganda report, "that Mgr. Grace has earned the favor he asks; during the sixteen or seventeen years he has ruled the Diocese of St. Paul he has consistently displayed wisdom, great zeal, and sincere attachment to the Holy See"—this last virtue, it would seem, in marked contrast to his metropolitan, Peter Richard Kenrick. The one legal obstacle that remained Propaganda cavalierly brushed aside: the canonical necessity for a *terna* could be waived in this case, the Congregation decreed, because it was a matter of simply translating a vicar apostolic to another mission, a process done all the more easily since the subject had not only not taken possession of his original assignment but had not even been sacramentally consecrated. On May 9, 1875, Pope Pius IX appointed John Ireland coadjutor bishop of St. Paul, with right of succession.

---

62. Ireland to Pius IX and to Grace, April 22, 1875, AASPM, Ireland Papers.

63. A diver recovered the mail pouch, and Ireland's parcel was returned to him. See Reardon, *Diocese of St. Paul,* 228, and Moynihan, *Life of Ireland,* 13.

CHAPTER 10

Rhetoric and Crusade

JUST AFTER THOMAS GRACE RETURNED TO ST. PAUL FROM ROME in June of 1875, he greeted a large and enthusiastic welcoming delegation from the porch of his residence, and, in the course of an otherwise rambling speech, he said:

> My trip was undertaken mainly for matters connected with the interests of this diocese, but paramount over all was the contemplated removal of Father Ireland from the scene of his labors in this city to a distant See. I thought and I think so still . . . that his departure would be a loss to the interests of the diocese and of the people who loved him so well and so truly.

The pope, he added, had listened kindly to his arguments and "had promised that no change would take place."[1] The papal bulls of appointment duly arrived in mid-October, and on December 21, in the midst of a lengthy liturgical service, John Ireland formally donned the bishop's miter. He was to wear it for forty-three years and to wield as well the bishop's pastoral staff. The preacher for the occasion was, appropriately enough, Thomas O'Gorman, who at the end of his sermon turned to his old schoolfellow and said: "Assume the burden that heaven imposes on your shoulders. Grasp your crozier and rule the flock committed to you." It was an invitation the new coadjutor hardly needed.[2]

---

1. *St. Paul Dispatch,* June 18, 1875.
2. *NWC,* December 25, 1875.

John Ireland had already become a fixture in St. Paul where he had served as assistant and then as pastor of the cathedral parish over the fourteen years of his priesthood. At thirty-seven, he had filled out somewhat from the lanky young man who had returned from brief service as a Union Army chaplain. He stood about five feet nine or ten inches. He had a big-boned frame and large hands. His coarse black hair—touched now by a little grey—which he parted on the left side, grew thick over the tops of his ears and around to the nape of his neck. The sharply slate-colored eyes, the wide and severely drawn mouth, the jutting jaw-line, the high angular cheekbones—all these features combined to give his face an expression perpetually alert. His most arresting physical characteristic, however, was the timbre of his voice: vibrant, resonant, powerful enough to be heard in the farthest corners of the largest hall, honeyed thunder sometimes and sometimes a throaty growl, but always loud, dominant, moving. Indeed, it was the lifting up of that voice that first brought him a local prominence which would evolve over the years into a reputation of almost mythic proportions.

During his tenure at the cathedral, Ireland lived in the bishop's house along with Father Ravoux, once again vicar general, and one or two other priests. The residence was more a missionary headquarters than an ordinary presbytery. Grace was often absent on diocesan visitations or confirmation tours, while the others took duty whenever and wherever needed. Ireland traveled over much of southern Minnesota during the early years of his ministry, to Mankato, Belle Plaine, Le Sueur, Winona, Rochester, and, more frequently, nearby Minneapolis—now, since its incorporation in 1856, assuming predominance over the older settlement at St. Anthony.[3] He recalled later a walking trip from Waverly Mills to Watertown, west of Minneapolis, in the summer of 1866, during which he "got lost on crosspaths and trails," before stumbling on a small wooden structure where he could hear the priestless congregation singing, "En ce jour, O bonne Madonne." Father Ireland listened outside for a while, and then, armed as he always was on these journeys with suitcase and Mass-kit, entered the little church and conducted a Eucharistic

---

3. See several sermons with notations indicating where they were preached, Minnesota Historical Society (MHS), John Ireland Papers (JIP), microfilm roll 2. This collection includes microfilmed papers from the archives of the Catholic Historical Society of St. Paul; the archives of the Archdiocese of St. Paul and Minneapolis; the archives of the Diocese of Duluth; the archives of St. John's Abbey, Collegeville, Minnesota; and the archives of the University of St. Thomas, St. Paul.

service for the astonished gathering.[4] Here was testimony to the late Bishop Cretin's love and cultivation of music, appreciated even by the notoriously tone-deaf Ireland.

The bulk of Ireland's time and energy, however, was spent in St. Paul. These were his apprentice years, the time when he learned about Catholicism not simply as a creed or as a collection of abstract precepts but as a living system. The heart of Catholic life beat in the daily regimen of the parish. The round of priestly duties performed there—the celebration of Mass, the hearing of confessions, preaching, visiting and ministering to the sick, catechizing, charitable endeavors, counseling the troubled, christenings, weddings, funerals—gave substance to that life. There was little drama in this kind of service. On the contrary, it readily turned into deadly routine. Yet without it the Catholic ideal went aglimmering, and the priest himself lost the central meaning of his existence. Indeed, the Catholic people struck an implicit bargain of sorts with their priests: a privileged position among them in exchange for regular sacramental ministration. No grandiose or spectacular activity could substitute for it, not even heroism on the battlefield. John Ireland, who had stood bravely upon a battlefield and would engage in many a spectacular and grandiose project in the future, never forgot this home truth.

This was, to be sure, still the age of deference. Catholics, especially those ill-educated immigrants and their children settled on the American frontier, tended to adopt the motto that the priest knew best, unless he clearly demonstrated otherwise. For one as capable as Ireland—sublimely confident in his own powers, bubbling over with original ideas and plans, robust in health, articulate, energetic, strong-willed—the automatic submission he received in the community gave him an immense advantage over others similarly gifted. He could prove, without a lengthy internship, that he deserved the deference given him. Still, his learning experience as a young priest in St. Paul left him acutely sensitive to the terms of the compact he had entered into with his people. Many years later he jotted down some of the public virtues of priestly demeanor those early years had taught him. A priest, he wrote, must "take an interest in people in their efforts to lift themselves up"; "teach the poor economy: our masses are in many regards no credit to us, [filling as they do] jails [and] poor houses." He should "be affable" to all, "wish to see all, [not] putting them off" or turning them from the door on the plea that there "is no time now." Special care had to be taken of the poor and sick. Ireland insisted that a

4. Mathias Savs, "The Catholic Church in Wright County, Minn.," *A&D* 4 (1916): 222. See chapter 4, above.

priest should *re*visit them. "The sick [deserve] no mere mechanical ministering . . . even if [they are] not seriously sick." One should "talk, exhort, instruct, console. . . . A priest attentive to [the] sick is loved." But an avaricious priest, one who "counts [his] population by the number of those who pay," would earn their abiding dislike. A priest must be polite to everybody, and especially to the poor.

Yet Ireland did not mean that compassion for the humble involved antipathy toward the upper classes. The wise priest "was not so democratic as to despise the rich and persons of influence. The Church needs such." Indeed, the priest himself must be a gentleman, exhibiting "good manners," avoiding all extravagance in dress and style of life. The priest's house ought to be a center of "order [and] simplicity." He should combine affability and approachableness with gravity. Ireland paraphrased Ecclesiasticus: "The clothing of the body, the laughter of the teeth, and the gait of a man tell what he is." The priest's commitment was to be expressed in "truthfulness, politeness; gravity in administering the sacraments; slowness in saying Mass; punctuality; . . . dignity." There should be "no card-playing" for the priest, no "bycling [sic], no cigar in [the] mouth before and after Mass, . . . no gold chains" around his neck. Above all, priests must avoid gossiping, especially about each other and especially in the presence of the laity. They must cultivate mutual esteem and "not [be] jealous of one another," lest the old proverb be fulfilled: "Wolves don't eat one another. Priests do."

But no priestly virtue or combination of virtues came to assume such importance in young Father Ireland's mind as studiousness. "How much depends on our teaching!" he later exclaimed. "Now God does not work miracles to fit us. . . . We must work and study. Take preaching. Study [is] the remote and absolutely necessary preparation. We must be full of a subject to preach upon it. And this filling is not instantaneous. A living fountain, giving water to thousands, fed itself by sources far and wide." And what about the confessional, that awesome place of healing and judgment? "It is fearful to think of so many souls depending for very life upon unskilled physicians." Ireland's conviction that the priest had to be first and foremost a teacher may have been nurtured in the contemplative quiet of a French seminary, but it bore fruit in the mean streets of a backwoods American town. "Children should know the catechism *litteratim,* and then understand it." There should be "private instruction for ignorant adults." In America, where there existed so much misinformed hostility to Catholicism and where secular newspapers loomed so large, the priest had a duty to "make use of the public press [to] contradict false statements, [to] frighten maligners"; he should "let nothing pass" and never "object to having [his] sermons published." But neither child nor adult, neither rough mechanic nor prospective convert nor favored soul in need of special spiritual direction could gain anything from the priest who had "no time" to study. No editor in his right mind would publish the blatherings of a man who had "no time" to study. "How much time is lost," Ireland asked rhetorically, "[reading] newspapers, smoking, card-playing, sleeping?" It was no excuse for one to say he had "no taste for it. Study," Ireland insisted, "brings taste." A priest should build up a good library and subscribe to good reviews; reading more than one newspaper was a waste of time. Worthwhile books should "be gone through systematically" with notes taken down. "[To] preach well [is] to honor God's revelation," and in order to preach well a priest must make himself capable of "deep researches," without which there could be "no fullness, no freshness, no variety."[5]

WITH REGARD TO THIS LAST MONITUM, IRELAND SURELY practiced what he preached. He was all his life an assiduous reader and note taker. During his student days in France he had begun the practice of keeping elaborate files containing excerpts from textbooks, press cuttings, précis, anecdotes, quotations from authors as different as Bossuet and Orestes Brownson, any material, in short, relevant to theological—or, more precisely, to apologetic—exposition.[6] In this practice he assumed a course followed earlier by Thomas Grace while a seminarian in Italy,[7] and over succeeding years, again like Grace, he routinely added to this original cache. His intentions were practical, not speculative. John Ireland was bright and astute, he read French and Latin almost as readily as he did English. But he was not a creative thinker, not an "intellectual" in the rather narrow and desiccated meaning that word has acquired since his time. The lesson he had learned as curate and pastor at the cathedral of St. Paul was that "people flock to hear a priest who has something to say." Here was the key to exerting leadership among a largely rootless people, a kind of clericalism not altogether unsuited for its time and place.

---

5. "Notes," MHS, JIP, roll 1. These twenty-two pages in Ireland's hand are undated, but they were probably written after 1884 and certainly after 1889. They may have been used as an *aide-mémoire* for a priests' retreat or a conference with seminarians.

6. See MHS, JIP, roll 2. Five notebooks have survived and a fragment of a sixth, 375 longhand pages, with various cuttings pasted into the margins.

7. See chapter 5, above.

The bulk of Ireland's influence came undoubtedly through the spoken word. Sunday after Sunday he held forth from the pulpit of the cathedral, and, as his reputation grew, so did opportunities to deliver lectures in various public halls around the town. He paid his congregations and audiences several compliments. First of all, he prepared his addresses with the greatest care, writing them out in longhand and going back over them to rephrase this thought or to clarify that. Secondly, he took pains not to talk down to his hearers. He appeared determined that his speeches should never sound like one peasant addressing other peasants. The result must have been edifying, to be sure, but also perhaps confusing more than once to the simple and mostly uneducated men and women in the pews, as when he told them that "the supernatural state [is] a gratuitous gift," or that the union of Christ with the Church is "a species of assimilation." Nor did he deal with trivial subjects: the list of the extant sermons preached before 1875 reads like the headings of a theological manual.

He scrupulously abided by the formalities then in vogue. He always began with a scriptural quotation and then addressed his hearers as "My dear Brethren." He usually employed the first person plural, thus identifying himself with the congregation—a device recommended by all the books on homiletics. But when the occasion demanded he did not hesitate—he, the clerical leader—to shift to the first person singular, nor to use direct commands like, "you should know" or "understand that." He regarded his sermons as "instructions," and he labored diligently to make them effective teaching instruments. Like most preachers of his generation he seldom spoke for less than forty-five minutes.

As to subject matter, Ireland's sermons were almost all lessons in apologetics, the defense of religious faith through an appeal to other than theological discourse. The "apologist" in this sense does not argue that belief in, say, the resurrection of Christ—the central and most difficult Christian mystery—can be an act of human reason. But he does argue that to make that leap of faith is not itself unreasonable. So the "apologetic" Father Ireland set before his congregation the text of the New Testament, regarded now not as a source of divine revelation but as a source for the history of the first century, a source that examines the evidence of the empty tomb on the first Easter Sunday and the testimonies of witnesses over the next forty days. Thus did the preacher with the vibrant, sonorous voice declaim from the cathedral pulpit in 1871:

> It is to history I appeal. Jesus lived in one of the most luminous historical ages—that of Augustus. . . . The facts concerning him, his declarations, his works, the events subsequent to his death, are transmitted to us by

monuments differing from those which attest all past events only in this much—that they are by far more incontestably authentic and truthful, clear and precise.

Like other great preachers of the nineteenth century—like Newman at St. Mary the Virgin, Oxford, or Lacordaire at Notre Dame de Paris—Ireland framed his sermons in large measure to meet the perceived needs of his congregations. The rigidly anti-Protestant stance he assumed reflected, of course, his own honest view of the matter, but it also took into account the condition of his audience, immigrants and children of immigrants, who lived in a culture hostile—often militantly so—to their religion. The result was a homiletic tone often strongly negative. But this was by no means always the case. The same objective could be achieved if Catholics were persuaded to take pride in the Church to which they belonged. Ireland spared no effort to get them to see themselves as specially blessed even if they did occupy the lower strata of society. "This Church as she exists today," he told a congregation of laborers in Minneapolis in 1873,

> is the most stupendous organization on the face of the earth. She is the most complete, perfect organization, possessing in a supereminent degree, all the elements of corporate life, a well-defined constitution, a powerful hierarchy, clearly-stated laws binding together into one solid body the governing and the governed. Her children number over two hundred millions; she has extended her power over every continent and every isle, [even] the most remote, and, while widespread, still remains everywhere the same, so wondrous is her unity, professing everywhere the same creed and acknowledging everywhere the same governing power.

Such triumphalism might sound extravagant or even embarrassing to sophisticates of a later age, but it was music to the ears of the Minnesota hod carrier of the 1870s, who, hearing it, had reason to straighten his back and look the world straight in the eye.

Ireland's brand of moral exhortation grew naturally out his concern to instruct his parishioners who lived in an often unruly environment. It also reflected his own and his culture's sturdy individualism. Ireland never considered the sermon as part of a larger corporate experience in the liturgy of the Mass. Indeed, while he admitted that fleshly human beings needed to give external expression to their worship, he remained suspicious of "pompous appearances" and placed most of his emphasis upon the cultivation of internal religion. It certainly would never have occurred to him to describe the liturgy, in the words of a later pope—who, incidentally, was to be on other grounds no favorite of Ireland's—as "the indispensable source of the Christian spirit."[8] Ireland tended rather to judge the matter the other way round: the person who approached the altar on Sunday ought to have acted decently during the preceding week. The fulfillment of duty was his constant theme, along with the inculcation of the virtues that enhanced the soul in the eyes of God. The process of salvation began with God's favor, to be sure, but it continued with the individual's practice of those natural virtues like courage and temperance, upon which a genuinely supernatural order could be built.

Ireland was similarly austere in the forms of piety he recommended. He gave clear primacy to devotion to the person of Christ, discoverable in the historically verifiable pages of the gospel. He had little or nothing to say about peripheral matters like indulgences or pilgrimages. He thought the veneration of the saints ought to be more a matter of practical imitation of those giants of virtue than of prayers or shrines. He paid due honor to the Virgin Mary, but usually did so within a doctrinal context—an explanation, for example, of the recently defined doctrine of the Immaculate Conception in its relation to original sin—and he appeared to have little interest in the great revival of popular Marian devotion so marked among Catholics in the nineteenth century. "The Rosary," he pointed out, "is not a dogma we are obliged to believe under the penalty of being treated as heretics. . . . Martyrs have been crowned, confessors and virgins have been received into the celestial courts" without ever telling a bead. "The road to heaven is unrestricted even for those who would not be addicted to this devotional exercise. The Rosary is among the free devotions of the Church."

From the point of view of style Father Ireland's early sermons were very much the product of their time, when pulpit oratory, aside from its directly religious purpose, was expected to display elegance and erudition and a measure of entertainment. To modern ears Ireland's language often sounds overripe, its imagery elaborate. Sometimes the preacher seems guilty of verbal extravagance. "Let the name of Jesus," Ireland declaimed in 1873, "be as a nosegay culled from the gardens of Bethlehem and Calvary, resuming [sic] all the sweet fragrance of the Incarnation." Sometimes too his search for the unusual word led to bizarre results, as when he called the little boat Jesus and his disciples used to cross the Sea of Galilee a "frail embarcation." But such lapses were exceedingly rare, and, though he showed an overfondness for certain

---

8. Pius X (1835–1914). For Ireland's reservations about him, see chapter 15, below.

standard phrases and interjections—"inhabitable globe," "swelling bosoms," "our homages," and "well!" or "oh!" or "alas!" placed after rhetorical questions—Ireland's pulpit prose was by and large clear, well ordered, no doubt compelling and persuasive to the audiences who listened to it, and not infrequently quite beautiful. "Whatever the teaching of science may be," he said in 1866,

> we find deeply instilled in mankind the idea, or the instinct, that the heart is connected with our outward affections; that it is warm in the kind and loving and cold in the selfish and ungenerous; that it is hard in the oppressor, fluttering in the anxious, faint in the cowardly, calm in the virtuous. To speak of the heart is to speak of the passions, of the emotions, the sympathies of man; it embodies our ideas of tenderness, of compassion, of gentleness, of forgiveness, of long-suffering, of every sweet variety of love. The parent, the spouse, the friend finds his specific kind of holy affection. It is the well-spring whence they all gush out, and manifest themselves in action and in word: "For out of the abundance of the heart the mouth speaketh." The heart is the source, at least the symbol, of love; to think of the heart of Jesus is to think of his love; to honor his heart is to honor his love.[9]

YOUNG FATHER IRELAND, NO DOUBT FOLLOWING THE PRUDENT Grace's stern injunction, took care not to address political questions from the pulpit. Thus in a sermon on anger and reconciliation with one's enemies, preached in 1864, he avoided any mention of the war then still raging.[10] A notable exception to this rule—and even on this occasion the doctrinal message had been delivered first—occurred a year earlier, just after Ireland had returned to St. Paul from his tour as chaplain, when it was rumored that local Catholics, especially the Irish, planned to resist, violently if necessary, implementation of the conscription law recently passed by Congress. Anti-draft riots in New York City had resulted in hundreds of deaths and injuries. "My dear friends," Ireland said, "at the request of the Right Reverend Bishop, I shall before leaving the pulpit make a few remarks on a subject which has

---

9. About sixty sermons, written in longhand and, most of them, carefully dated, are in MHS, JIP, rolls 1 and 2.

10. "Homilia de Ira, Verbis Opprobriosis, et Reconcilliatione cum Inimicis, (1864)," MHS, JIP, roll 2.

become one of the most engrossing topics of the day." He minced no words. "In order to restore peace to the country, our Chief Magistrate has thought [it] necessary to make a new levy of men, and, to obtain the requisite number, the system of Conscription is to be resorted to." No doubt the draft would take effect soon in St. Paul, "and it behooves your Pastors to remind you of your duty in such circumstances." "True Catholics" always obey the law, and he expressed confidence that "never by your conduct will you disgrace that Church we all love so tenderly." But "[rumors] that some dissatisfaction towards this measure of the government has been expressed have reached our ears. And it is well to tell you that the Church emphatically condemns such proceedings." Then in that booming voice:

> If a riot should occur amongst us, or any public demonstration against the execution of the laws, we here beforehand repudiate all Catholics who would, by word or deed, partake in or give aid to or countenance the proceedings. Until they would have made retraction of their conduct, the sacraments of the Church would be refused to them, and were they to lose their lives by means of the riot, they would not obtain the benefit of a Christian burial. . . . Take care, my dear friends. Ranting politicians, under the thick cloak of hypocrisy—through an apparent interest in your welfare but in reality to satisfy their own lust for power and riches—may breathe amongst you words of discord. . . . Be led by no one; consult your own consciences, and I know you will do what is right, because your own natures never prompt you but to good and noble actions.[11]

The last clause may have been theologically suspect, yet one may legitimately suppose the "soldier of Abraham Lincoln" in the pulpit delivered this jeremiad with particular fervor. And though not all of his hearers were convinced—"Father Ireland," one woman complained bitterly, "won't support the families if the men go to war"[12]—there were no draft riots in St. Paul. The

---

11. The text is in "The John Ireland Collection, 1838–1959," MHS, Helen Angela Hurley Papers. On the Conscription Law and the consequent disturbances, see Allan Nevins, *The War for the Union*, 4 vols. (New York, 1971), 3:119–124. Irish immigrants played an especially important role in the anti-draft riots in New York, since many of them were strongly anti-black on the perceived grounds that Negro freedmen would prove to be their competitors for employment. The dates here are significant. The bloody confrontations in New York City took place between July 13 and 17, 1863. Ireland made his remarks on July 26.

12. *St. Paul Press*, August 1, 1863.

compact between priest and people, over this thorny issue at least, held firm, probably to the benefit of them both.

St. Patrick's Day orations were exceptions, too.[13] When he spoke to his fellow countrymen on their feast, Ireland ranged over a wide variety of subjects, from romanticized versions of Irish antiquities and standard denunciations of British oppression to contemporary politics and economics, and he also indulged in some of his purplest prose. "Hail then, green flag," he exclaimed on one of these occasions, "hail to thee, within God's consecrated temple. Thou hast taken, this morning, the place that belongs to thee of right—close to the altars of religion. No flag, save the yellow and white of papal Rome, would be here more at home."[14] And on another March 17:

> My dear Brethren, you wish me to speak to you this morning of Ireland, the land of your birth, the land of your forefathers. To speak of Ireland, the lovely isle of the ocean, whose beauty and merits have been the favored theme of so many poets, orators, and sages, whose very name is inspiration, so glorious and precious the memories that cluster around it—to speak of Ireland must ever be especially for those who fondly claim her as their mother, a pleasurable task. I enter, with delight, upon the duty which your presence imposes.[15]

Immigration of the Irish into Minnesota, and particularly into St. Paul, in the early pioneer days bore a statistical significance which, however, did not last. Indeed, the Germans soon outnumbered the Irish, and eventually the Scandinavian influx overwhelmed them both. Of the nearly two million Irish-born who came to the United States between 1870 and 1890, only 1.4 percent settled in Minnesota. During the 1850s, however, they were proportionately numerous enough in St. Paul to make of St. Patrick's Day an observance of considerable civic importance. That fastidious Frenchman, Bishop Cretin, found it "a strange thing" that so many of his flock wanted "to celebrate pompously the day of St. Patrick," but he also shrewdly observed that

---

13. Six of Ireland's early St. Patrick's Day addresses have survived, three complete and three incomplete. Internal evidence suggests that five of them were delivered in the cathedral and the sixth (1871) in the St. Paul Opera House. For an analysis of them, see Charles J. Fahey, "Gibbons, Ireland, Keane: The Evolution of a Liberal Catholic Rhetoric in America" (Ph.D. dissertation, University of Minnesota, 1980), 87–90.

14. "St. Patrick," n.d., MHS, JIP, roll 1.

15. "De Fide Hibernorum," 1869, MHS, JIP, roll 2.

the presence of a large and cohesive bloc of Catholic voters was overall a boon during the territorial run-up to statehood. Another circumstance lent him and his successors no little consolation. If the huge majority of the Irish Catholic immigrants to the United States remained cabined up in their ghettos in the great cities of the East—Boston, New York, Philadelphia—many of those who made their way as far west as Minnesota became self-sufficient and relatively prosperous farmers in Rice and Le Sueur and Olmstead counties and indeed across the fertile valleys of the Mississippi and Minnesota rivers, while others labored productively in the logging camps along the St. Croix.[16]

In the nascent Minneapolis the Irish never achieved any particular civic importance. Those old-stock Americans—largely immigrants from Maine—who controlled the burgeoning industry centered at the sawmills dependent upon the water power at the Falls of St. Anthony, were careful to maintain their Yankee social ascendancy. In neighboring St. Paul, however, the societal situation evolved otherwise. In 1860 roughly half the town's population was foreign-born, with the Irish and Germans in approximate balance. The Irish Catholics clearly occupied the bottom rung on the economic ladder—more than fifty percent of them were engaged in unskilled labor and only twelve percent in trade. By contrast many of the Germans, whether Catholic or not, brought with them to their new homes a modest amount of capital along with skills acquired in the old country, so that twenty-six percent of them made their living in trades and services, twenty-seven percent in manufacturing, and only fourteen percent in manual labor.[17]

Twenty years later, when the city's population exceeded 40,000, the Irish-born proportion of the workforce had, predictably, fallen to about ten percent. Many still labored as hod carriers or railroad gandy dancers, but others had taken up skilled trades like masonry and carpentry. (John Ireland's father was a carpenter.) And, as did their more numerous compatriots in the large cities on the eastern seaboard, still others had secured jobs in some form of civil service, constituting sixteen percent of those who held government jobs. The most notable and visible sign of this phenomenon was the composition of the local police force: in 1878 nine of the twenty-seven St. Paul policemen were Irish-born. As for the professions, the Irish predominated among the immigrant groups in practice at the bar; of the seventeen foreign-born lawyers' shingles on display in St. Paul in 1880, thirty-five percent belonged to

---

16. See Regan, "The Irish," in Holmquist, *They Chose Minnesota*, 130–140.
17. See Wingerd, *Claiming the City*, 35–36.

Irishmen. Perhaps this circumstance came about because the native Irish could speak English—grandiloquently in some instances, even if their brogue aroused a certain Yankee contempt. Lawyering at any rate and commitment to public sector employment combined to involve the Irish disproportionately in politics. Names like O'Brien and O'Connor, Kelly and Doran, figured large among the capitol's dominant Democrats for two generations, and, since rural Minnesota and to a lesser extent Minneapolis consistently voted Republican, the result was that the St. Paul machine and its Irish leadership virtually controlled the state Democratic Party.[18]

Other factors, to be sure, contributed to St. Paul's reputation as an "Irish town," even though neither the immigrants themselves nor their offspring were numerically or economically ascendant. Thus James J. Hill, the future "Empire Builder," married a fervent Irish Catholic girl, which union eventually provided entrée for those like her to the upper echelons of local society.[19] And certainly the leadership exercised for over half a century by John Ireland—whom, incidentally, Mary Mehegan Hill never cared much for, despite their common religion and ethnic origin—played a highly significant role. His program, however, differed from those of other prominent Irish American prelates, in that he cared little about the political turmoil that chronically gripped the old country. Americanization of the immigrants, the Irish first because they were closest at hand but in the end all the immigrant Catholics, was his undeviating goal. Let the land wars rage across the Emerald Isle and the Fenians plot;[20] such events he viewed not with indifference but with the steely resolve that they not distract from bringing refugees like himself and his family firmly into the American middle class. This agenda he laid down with characteristic eloquence very early on, from the pulpit of the cathedral on St. Patrick's Day 1865.

The significance of this very long sermon—forty manuscript pages—lay not in praise for "the darling little isle" or in denunciation of the British penal laws—standard components of March 17 oratory—but in the candor with which Ireland described the problems of the fifteen hundred[21] Irish Americans sitting in the pews in front of him, problems, he said firmly, to some degree of their own making. "Dispirited and broken-hearted" by persecution and exile, some Irish "have been almost necessarily unmanned; they have lost

---

18. See Regan, "The Irish," 142–143, and the authorities cited there.

19. Wingerd, *Claiming the City,* 41–42, 58–59.

20. Ireland called Fenianism "humbug" and "a swindle." *NWC,* December 15, 1866.

21. So reported the *St. Paul Pioneer,* March 19, 1865.

somewhat the pride which is the essential ingredient of manhood; among some of our people there is too great an absence of what is termed respectability—they do not care enough about external decorum." Why must Irishmen "be impulsive, irritable, and noisy? Another unsatisfactory feature of the Irish character is their [sic] hasty and passionate disposition." They quarrel endlessly among themselves, he charged, and, what is especially foolish, they have brought their old-country antagonisms to this new land. The Irish need to cultivate greater self-control to refine their "warm Celtic race."

"I think," he went on,

> there is in our character room for more energy and readiness to devise and undertake projects for our individual and social advancement, and for more perseverance in what we have undertaken. . . . We let our enthusiasm cool down; we fall back if we do not carry our point at the first assault.

He then addressed his listeners directly: the successful person, consistent in applying himself to the task at hand, gives outward evidence of his status; therefore, "wherever you are, be sober, quiet, industrious." This new country has given you a second chance, so you should "take a lively interest in all public affairs." But "avoid excess in politics," and never stoop to selling your precious vote.[22] "Seek every means of instructing yourselves," because in America the informed and educated win the prizes. Above all, do not let yourselves be permanently "unmanned."

> Be ambitious, seek to elevate yourselves, to better your lot; too often we are too easily satisfied. When a man is poor, let him live in a hovel. I esteem him; at any moment I extend him the right hand of fellowship. But if by labor, by energy he can secure to his family comfort and respectability, and does not, then I despise him.[23]

BE MORE DECOROUS AND HARDWORKING, THE YOUNG PRIEST urged his parishioners, but above all "be sober." Indeed, sobriety, he had come

---

22. In the manuscript Ireland originally wrote, "Avoid politics." The words "excess in" were inserted later above the line.

23. "Virtues and Faults of the Irish, at Home and Abroad," 1865, MHS, JIP, roll 2.

to believe, was the necessary prerequisite for any moral or social advancement. Not that forms of vice other than drunkenness did not flourish in St. Paul which, whatever its respectable aspirations, was at the time, after all, a rough frontier town. Father Ireland, like all his fellow citizens, was forcibly reminded of this unhappy reality one November night in 1869 when fire engulfed two contiguous buildings on West Eighth Street. They belonged, as the newspapers gleefully reported, to a certain Mrs. Robinson; one was the brothel presided over by this notorious madam and the other next door was her residence. She proved to be a woman with considerable resources, worth $2,000 in cash and $75,000 in real property. Mrs. Robinson, like the proprietors of the other twenty-seven bordellos in St. Paul, was routinely arrested every month, paid a fine (which amounted to a tax), and then was released to resume her business.[24] The guardians of public morality, with little support from a cynical city administration, had to be prepared to do battle on many fronts.

No doubt the clientele at Mrs. Robinson's establishment included a proportionate number of Irish Catholics. But John Ireland was not unreasonable in arguing—though he did not do so explicitly from pulpit or platform, whatever he may have done in the confessional—that excessive drinking, or indeed any drinking at all, led directly to a host of moral aberrations, sexual and otherwise. The problem, as he saw it, was a deeply cultural one. All too often the Irish in the United States, as they had done in the old country, succumbed to the temptation to drown their sorrows in alcohol and then, perhaps, repair to a house of ill fame. And in Minnesota there was readily available the same cheap frontier whiskey that had helped ruin the Native Americans. As Ireland said at another St. Patrick's Day observance: "There is one fault—I am not comparing [us] with other nations—it exists with us. It has done us fearful harm. Intemperance. The foe to our race today is the saloon keeper. [There are] over sixteen hundred Irish saloon keepers in Chicago."[25] In St. Paul the Irish-born policeman not infrequently had to deal with a drunk and disorderly compatriot. To the Irishman who would drink a teary-eyed toast to his native land, John Ireland retorted:

Alcohol [is] the bane of [your] country and countrymen; but for it Ireland might today be free and an honored member of the sisterhood of

---

24. See Joel Best, *Controlling Vice: Regulating Brothel Prostitution in St. Paul, 1865–1883* (Columbus, 1998), 1–5, 141–142.

25. "St. Patrick," n.d., MHS, JIP, roll 1.

nations; but for it Irishmen would be better, truer, nobler members of society. The man who talk[s] about Ireland and her wrongs with a glass of whisky in his hands [is] an enemy to his country, for he [is] using that which has been her curse and ruin.[26]

Bishop Cretin, despite his upbringing in a wine-drinking country, decided early in his missionary days to endorse the cause of teetotalism. He, like Loras in Dubuque, was genuinely shocked by the ravages caused by strong drink among Indians and whites alike. One of the first organizations he formed in St. Paul was a Catholic temperance society, but, after some initial enthusiasm, it did not prosper. By the time he died in 1857 it had ceased to function. Thomas Grace showed no interest in reviving it or indeed in fostering any kind of organized resistance to the liquor traffic. He attended the national conference of Catholic bishops in Baltimore in 1866 and presumably subscribed to its decree that pastors "for the love of Jesus Christ . . . labor with all possible care and energy for the extirpation of the vice of drunkenness," and to this end encourage total abstinence and form temperance societies.[27] But Grace's natural diffidence and his hesitancy to appear to impose upon his people any obligation that was not strictly and universally applicable kept him from initiating any projects in this regard. He was a man who shrank from even the faintest hint of fanaticism, which was a quality often ascribed to temperance workers. He worried, too, about the close association in the public mind between agitation for temperance and certain varieties of evangelical Protestantism.[28]

Even so, what the bishop did not choose to do himself he would not necessarily prevent one of his subjects from doing, and in 1869 the temperance cause in the diocese of St. Paul did have its rebirth. Many years later Ireland described, with suitably dramatic flourishes, how it happened.

Seven good, generous—too generous—men were assembled together on [a] Friday evening in a very popular saloon on Minnesota Street. They drank and treated one another; but a gleam of good Christian sense

---

26. See the paraphrase in James M. Reardon, "The Catholic Total Abstinence Movement in Minnesota," *A&D* 2 (1909): 59.

27. See Joan Bland, *Hibernian Crusade* (Washington, D.C., 1951), 45–46.

28. See Charles J. Carmody, "Rechabites in Purple: A History of the Catholic Temperance Movement in the Northwest" (Master's thesis, St. Paul Seminary, 1953), 79–83. For Rechabites see Jeremiah 35:2–19.

dawned upon their minds, and one of them said: "We ought to stop lest we be ruined." Another said: "Let us go and see Father Ireland and organize a temperance society." And a petition with seven names upon it was actually drawn up in that saloon, and candidly the keeper of the saloon was one of the signers. The writing was a little tremulous. One was commissioned to bring me the petition, and as he opened the door of my room he was not very steady on his limbs, and he nearly fell, but he soon recovered himself and said: "I have a petition for you." I read the petition and without a moment's hesitation said: "Yes, a society will be organized."

At four o'clock on the following Sunday afternoon an organizational meeting was held in the cathedral clubrooms. "Fifty men signed the pledge, and the Father Mathew Society was born."[29]

Theobald Mathew was the Franciscan friar who had initiated a celebrated temperance crusade in Ireland even before the Great Famine had occurred there. John Ireland claimed a personal connection with him. "When I was a very young boy," he recalled in 1890, "Father Mathew came to my native town to administer the pledge. I served his mass, and he asked me to attend him. He went about everywhere, giving the pledge, and everywhere he administered it, I took the pledge. He used to introduce me sometimes as his little teetotaler. I was not then seven years old."[30] Even so, before the dramatic encounter in his rooms with the agonizing petitioners from Minnesota Street, he gave no public sign that he planned war to the knife with demon rum. Yet the conviction must have been growing upon him for years. He could not but have seen what others saw among the "patches" of Irish immigrants in "New Dublin." "None [of the people] were working," one visitor observed, "and everyone I called to see had plenty of whisky in the shanty. They were a good-natured people until they got drunk, and let me tell you by that time a stranger had better remove himself from the patches."[31]

Once the battle was joined, in any case, Ireland never looked back. Nothing during his long life absorbed him as much as did the cause of total abstinence. He placed all his gifts at its disposal, all his energies. No means to achieve the end of general sobriety were beneath or beyond him. Charm and even humor were useful in dealing with some, high-toned oratory worked

---

29. "Twenty-sixth Anniversary of the Founding of Father Mathew Total Abstinence Society of St. Paul," January 10, 1895, MHS, JIP, roll 5.

30. Quoted in "Ireland Collection," MHS, Hurley Papers.

31. Reminiscences of an old settler, *NWC*, July 3, 1896.

with others, and grim threats of hellfire with still others. Sometimes he took his blackthorn stick to the drunkards in "New Dublin" and chased them from shanty to shanty. He brooked no compromise with the principle that all liquor, whether fermented, distilled, or brewed, was poisonous. He accepted no halfway position. "Remember," he said once, "if you are what is called a temperate man who takes a glass but never exceeds, your example is worse than that of a drunkard."[32]

The Father Mathew Society of St. Paul proclaimed as its object "to encourage total abstinence, and to provide for the temporal relief of its members in certain cases. All persons over fifteen years of age who are willing to abide by its laws and who promise with the divine assistance to abstain from all intoxicating liquors are eligible for membership."[33] Regular meetings were held on Sunday evenings in the basement of the cathedral, which soon gained the sobriquet "Temperance Hall." Ireland, the spiritual director, usually opened the session with reading and commenting on a chapter of the biography of Theobald Mathew. There followed an hour of fellowship during which future social events were planned and candidates for membership discussed. The society offered mutual support in dealing with any problem related to drink, and it grew prodigiously: within three months it boasted of three hundred members and of $125 in its treasury. The initiation fee of one dollar and the monthly dues of twenty-five cents were sufficient to assure three dollars a week to sick members during their illness, and up to twenty-five dollars to help defray funeral expenses to the beneficiaries of brethren who died. The manner of admission to the society was simplicity itself. A candidate was proposed by someone already a member, and, unless five negative votes were cast, the candidate assumed full status. All members were committed to report any violators of the pledge; the latter could be expected to be fined or expelled, depending on the gravity of the infraction.[34] The society remained exclusively male until 1876 when Ireland, by then a bishop, casually mentioned in a speech that perhaps the pledge should be offered as well to the ladies in the audience. "He barely mentioned his idea [when] they all sprang to their feet, and with one full [sic] swoop he made teetotalers of our mothers, wives, and sisters to the utter astonishment of the strangers present."[35]

---

32. At a meeting on January 1, 1871, paraphrased in Reardon, "Catholic Total Abstinence," 59.

33. Quoted in Reardon, "Catholic Total Abstinence," 50.

34. Carmody, "Rechabites," 97–99.

35. Quoted in Reardon, "Catholic Total Abstinence," 91–92.

Not everyone, however, rallied to the cause. Some of the Irish resented the society, because its very existence seemed to them an indictment of their social mores and therefore a blot on their collective reputation. The German Catholics for the most part stood aside, maintaining, with barely veiled contempt, that they—moderate beer drinkers all—did not need to belong to an organization, as the Irish obviously did, to eschew drunkenness. Economic realities moreover also tended to soften the thrust of the temperance movement: brewing was the second largest industry in St. Paul, and there were hundreds of saloons and taverns scattered across the city, their number expanding annually as population increased.[36] Father Ireland was often reminded of the formidable reputation for political clout enjoyed by the liquor interests, visibly symbolized by the string of establishments along Minnesota Street. Once, when visiting a class in the cathedral school, he asked a pupil to define "capital," and she answered that it was a place where laws were made. He then asked her to name the capital of her home state, and the little girl replied: "Minnesota Street." On another occasion one of his parishioners shook his fist in the priest's face and shouted, "You can't touch Minnesota Street!"[37] This was not altogether inaccurate, or at any rate Ireland was not prepared at this early stage of the movement to confront the powerful saloon lobby head on. When in May 1869 a petition was circulated seeking support for an ordinance to close the taverns on Sundays, Ireland, acting for the infant Father Mathew Society, refused to sign it. Voluntarism, not legal intervention, was, he argued, the preferred way to proceed.[38] In later years, after he had changed his tune considerably, he ruefully recalled how on this occasion Minnesota Street had praised him for the "sanity" of the stand he had taken on Sunday closing.[39]

But in the spring of 1869 voluntarism appeared to be working well enough. Temperance groups, in imitation of the Father Mathew Society (and more often than not employing that name), sprang up all over the southern part of Minnesota.[40] In every instance the impetus came from the local priest.

---

36. See Wingerd, *Claiming the City,* 48–49.

37. Reardon, "Catholic Total Abstinence," 49.

38. See Carmody, "Rechabites," 103.

39. "The Saloon," 1888, MHS, JIP, roll 6, a speech delivered in Chicago.

40. A partial list in Reardon, "Catholic Total Abstinence," 53–55. Actually a Father Mathew Society, formed by the two parishes in the village of Belle Plaine, antedated by a few months the one founded in St. Paul. A personal note. The secretary of the society in St. Thomas parish, Derrynane Township, Le Sueur County, was Timothy Shea, my great-grandfather.

In April John Ireland set out on the first of many tours around the southern counties urging parishes to found local abstinence societies.[41] Back in St. Paul, on the Fourth of July, the parent society participated in the town's Independence Day celebrations; the Catholic teetotalers marched in the parade beneath their new four-hundred-dollar banner, "seven feet high and five wide," green on one side and sky-blue on the other, "made of rich . . . silk and beautifully surrounded with heavy gold lace fringe and bullion, with neat cords and tassels," and "an excellent representation of Father Mathew, the Apostle of Temperance."[42] After Mass the members and their banner—it took four men to carry it—proceeded to the outskirts of the town to join in the gaiety of the dry parish picnic. About seven o'clock, "a party of five or six rowdies, partially intoxicated," started a fight in an adjacent picnic grounds where the Lutherans were celebrating the Fourth of July. "A messenger ran to the Catholic picnic and gave the alarm, but by much effort Father Ireland . . . induced the men to remain." Ireland himself and two policemen rushed to the scene and managed to stop "the bloody and disgraceful melee," which had eventually involved more than a dozen men wielding clubs and knives. At least two of the original culprits were drunken Irish Catholics. "It was fortunate," commented a local newspaper, "that the Catholic picnic was a strictly temperance affair or otherwise it would have been impossible to control them [sic] and a much more fearful scene might have ensued."[43]

Ireland's missionary effort continued unabated over the months and years that followed. He repeatedly reminded the parish temperance societies that they were in competition with the local saloon, which, by offering free lunches and other recreational inducements, too easily lived up to its claim to be "the poor man's club."[44] Consequently the parishes began to expand their activities, opening circulating libraries and reading rooms and inviting lecturers to speak about subjects of interest beyond merely the evils of drink. This emphasis on popular education and self-help bore the stamp of the influence of John Ireland, who now began to be referred to as the Father Mathew of the Northwest, a mantle he readily, almost greedily, wrapped around himself. He made room for many able coworkers, clerical and lay, but no peers. Thomas O'Gorman, his lifelong friend and disciple (and by now the pastor of

---

41. Carmody, "Rechabites," 101–103.
42. Reardon, "Catholic Total Abstinence," 55–56.
43. *St. Paul Dispatch,* July 6, 1869.
44. Ireland often disdainfully cited this phrase. See, for example, "The Saloon," 1888, MHS, JIP, roll 6.

the parish in Rochester), stood ever at his side. Notable among the laymen was Dillon O'Brien, a cultured, peripatetic native of County Roscommon, twenty years senior to the pastor of the cathedral, and the latter's aide in a variety of good works until his untimely death in 1882.[45] But how crucial Ireland's charismatic hand was to the health of the movement manifested itself during his absence on a European tour over seven months in 1869–1870. During that short interval the drive to organize temperance groups outside the Twin Cities flagged, and leakage from the St. Paul society moved a testy Bishop Grace, on St. Patrick's Day 1870, to warn an assemblage of two hundred members to avoid political involvement and to cease quarreling among themselves.[46] But Ireland's return two months later reversed the apathy, after he went on the stump to stir up anew fervor for the cause. The time had come, he proclaimed, to set up a statewide organization. With the St. Paul society as host, a rally was called for January 10, 1872, the third anniversary of the day Ireland had sworn in those denizens of the saloon on Minnesota Street.

The convention lasted all day, from high Mass in the morning to "the most sumptuous supper" at nine o'clock in the evening. Twelve of the fifteen Catholic total abstinence societies in Minnesota were represented. All the leading speakers took their turn at the podium—O'Gorman, Dillon O'Brien, and many others—but it was John Ireland's "brief address" that garnered the most attention from the press. "A wonderful impetus," he said, "has been given the temperance cause throughout the whole country," and "Minnesota was moving simultaneously with other parts of the country." He urged upon his listeners the need for coordinated action within the state and the formal association of the local endeavor with the national. He then "made an eloquent appeal in behalf of temperance itself . . . and spoke eloquently of the evils of intemperance and the fearful results which follow its indulgence, of the tears of the widow and the orphans, of the fortunes wrecked, the religion scandalized, and their [sic] country shamed, which lurked in the glass of sparkling liquor." Much of the day had been spent drawing up a constitution and in selecting committees and officers. It must have been with some relief that the four hundred participants finally sat down to their repast in Ingersoll Hall. "After supper, an hour or two was spent in an intellectual entertainment of wit, humor, speeches, and a general good time."[47]

---

45. See Thomas D. O'Brien, "Dillon O'Brien," *A&D* 6 (1933): 35–53, and chapter 11, below.

46. See Carmody, "Rechabites," 105–109.

47. A long account in *St. Paul Press*, January 11, 1872.

The convention of January 1872 marked a turning point in John Ireland's career as a temperance reformer. From that time on he had behind him a stable state organization, which boasted a thousand members and which, within a month, became formally associated with the Catholic Total Abstinence Union of America. His own efforts in the cause began to be directed more and more to a national audience. Not that he neglected his home base or failed to realize the necessity of refining the local movement as it grew in numbers. But when he attended his first national convention late in 1873 and was promptly elected first vice president of the Catholic Temperance Union, the signal was clear that the "Father Mathew of the Northwest" was about to move to a larger stage. He did so with a genuine sense of accomplishment, yet not unmindful of how it had all begun. As he wrote jubilantly to his Minnesota confreres early in 1874:

> Are we not a different people than we were five years ago? How many homes have been made happy? How many wives and children today bless us and pray for us? How many men once forgetful of their manhood and their religion are now redeemed from the thralldom of sin and with prosperity in this world are among the most devoted and earnest children of the Church? If our movement is to be judged by its fruits, by the blessings that have everywhere followed in its wake, we can truly say that the favor of heaven is with us.[48]

---

48. Quoted in *NWC*, January 7, 1874.

CHAPTER 11

The Beckoning
of the Land

IT IS A COMMONPLACE TO OBSERVE THAT THE SURRENDER OF General Lee at Appomattox and the consequent collapse of the southern cotton empire marked the beginning of an unprecedented industrial and commercial expansion across the North and West of the United States. Painful and dubiously successful Reconstruction in places like Mississippi and Virginia—dubious with regard to both the short-lived favorable civil status granted black freedmen in the old Confederacy and that area's economic fortunes—contrasted sharply with the boom that spread across the rest of the country. In Minnesota a foretaste of more plenteous times to come was the arrival in 1861 of the *William Crooks,* which was unloaded from a river steamer on the levee in St. Paul in September 1861. The next year this first railroad locomotive in the state—named for the New Jersey engineer who had fashioned it—made its native run along the twelve miles of heretofore unused and somewhat rusted track to St. Anthony.

Minnesotans had long realized that the key to economic progress was the establishment of a viable railroad system like that already developed east of the Mississippi. During territorial days the legislature had chartered no less than twenty-seven companies with names like the Louisiana and Western and the Lake Superior, Puget Sound, and Pacific that suggested how lofty were the planners' intentions. But the depression of the late 1850s and then the four years of war had shown that such expectations were, to say the least, premature. Once the guns fell silent, however, development and expansion were remarkably rapid: by 1872 upwards of 2,000 miles of track had been laid within the state's boundaries, and fifteen companies were competing for passenger and, much more importantly, for freight business. Not all of these enterprises proved viable in the long run, and control of traffic inevitably contracted by way of merger and bankruptcy into ever fewer hands.[1]

Nonetheless, from this time onward farmers no longer had to depend exclusively on rutted roads and rivers frozen over for half the year to move their produce to market. Results included a prodigious increase in the cultivation of wheat and its industrial metamorphosis into flour. The two million bushels grown in Minnesota in 1860 leaped to eighteen million in 1870 and to thirty-four million a decade later. Not that wheat was the only significant crop produced by this overwhelmingly agricultural society: millions of bushels of oats, barley, corn, and potatoes were also drawn from the fertile ground, as were bountiful gallons of syrup from sorghum grass and maple trees, and dairy products from the ever-swelling herds of cattle. Even so, wheat remained predominant, at least until soil exhaustion manifested itself in the late 1870s and 1880s and led to more prudent diversification—a circumstance that led directly to making Minneapolis the first city of the state in industrial development and population. Though a variety of milling centers had emerged before the railroad era—at river towns, for instance, like Red Wing and Winona—it was Minneapolis, with its water power available at the falls of St. Anthony and its early rail connections, that emerged as the giant flour producer in the United States and indeed in the world at large. Almost as striking was the expansion of the lumber industry. Sawmills at Stillwater on the St. Croix River and at Winona down the Mississippi might flourish so long as the movement of logs depended solely upon water traffic. But once the railways exerted their economic predominance, Minneapolis, with its power and transportation advantages, again asserted its primacy. By 1890 the mills in Minneapolis were producing half a billion feet of finished timber a year.[2]

This railway-driven expansion brought about an almost geometric growth in population, dwarfing the modest immigration of the 1850s. At the end of the Civil War, Minnesota counted about 250,000 inhabitants; fifteen years later that number had tripled, and twenty years after that, in 1900, the state's population stood at 1,750,000, of whom seventy percent were either foreign-born or had one foreign-born parent. Germans remained the single largest ethnic entity, but especially after 1880 Scandinavians considered collectively came to predominance, with large numbers of Swedes settling between the St. Croix and the Mississippi and to the west of Minneapolis, similar aggregates of Norwegians concentrating in the far western counties and along

---

1. See Richard S. Prosser, *Rails to the North Star* (Minneapolis, 1966), 11–25.
2. Blegen, *Minnesota*, 194, 295–297, 320, 325, 340–341, 345–346.

the Red River of the North, and much smaller numbers of Danes collecting in and around the southeastern village of Albert Lea. Though some of these immigrants, Swedes especially, went directly to live in the Twin Cities where they might find commercial or industrial employment—in 1890 Minneapolis's population was 164,000, St. Paul's 133,000—the overwhelming majority were farmers in search of arable land and most of them, except perhaps for the always better-off and more skilled Germans, were as deeply impoverished as refugees have so often been.[3] Thus a combination of overpopulation, a series of poor harvests, and an increased incidence of agricultural mechanization during the 1870s left many a Norwegian head of household prepared to try his and his family's luck in the New World.[4] Similar circumstances prevailed in Sweden at the same time, and so a scattering of Swedish settlers in Minnesota in the 1850s grew moderately during the 1870s, to become after 1880 a virtual flood, which included not only farmers but farmers' sons ready to ply a trade or open a business in an urban environment.[5]

Whatever their ethnic origin, or indeed their ultimate economic orientation, the European immigrants were originally attracted to Minnesota by the prospect of cheap land, title to which was guaranteed by the government. So-called squatters' rights, which played so pivotal a role in the development of frontier St. Paul,[6] were formally confirmed in 1854, and eight years later the congress passed the monumental Homestead Act, whereby an adult male or female could establish ownership of 160 acres of federal land—acquired by treaty, admittedly exploitative, from the Indian tribes—by erecting a livable abode on the claim, dwelling on it for five years, and paying incidental closing costs. So it was that the land west and north of New Ulm was opened to settlement on the most advantageous terms, and especially so once the Dakota war was over and the Indians had been expelled westward. This federal legislation was augmented in favor of the states, which were permitted by Washington to set aside other federal properties for the support of educational enterprises—the University of Minnesota was, and is, one of the great land grant institutions of higher learning—and for the promotion of railroad construction.[7]

3. Lass, *Minnesota,* 145–148.

4. See Carlton C. Qualey and Jon A. Gjerde, "The Norwegians," in Holmquist, *They Chose Minnesota,* 220–221.

5. See John G. Rice, "The Swedes," in Holmquist, *They Chose Minnesota,* 248–258.

6. See chapter 2, above.

7. Lass, *Minnesota,* 136–137.

Railroad companies nationwide routinely encouraged immigration, especially from the countries of northern Europe. Recruiting agents were dispatched to far-flung places like Stockholm and Amsterdam, special passenger rates were secured from steamship lines, and "reception houses" were strategically erected to help ease the orientation of the newcomers. Perhaps the Illinois Central set the pattern: in 1871 alone some 7,000 Scandinavians were persuaded to cross the Atlantic and take up farming in Illinois in proximity to the Central's lines. In Minnesota similar if smaller patterns emerged. But other factors also played a role, not least a religious one. Many Swedes, Lutheran dissidents from the established state church, determined that emigration might allow them more confessional breathing room as well as economic betterment.[8] Among the Norwegian settlers, scattered all over the rural sectors of the state, the first task was to build a little frame or sod church as a symbol of their sturdy Lutheranism; here, in the parish, they were determined to maintain a linguistic and cultural as well as a theological heritage, which in turn served to attract other like-minded fellow countrymen to join them.[9]

As for promoting the immigration of Catholics into Minnesota, Bishops Loras and Cretin during territorial days had mounted modest campaigns which had met with some success, especially among the Irish and Germans. And during the last year of the Civil War—before, that is, the coming of the railroads—Bishop Grace had founded the Minnesota Irish Emigration Society, whose purpose was to establish displaced Irishmen "in homes in lieu of those from which they had been compelled to flee." Young Father Ireland assumed the presidency of the society which, however, was never more than a paper organization, perhaps partly because of Grace's own lackadaisical attitude toward it.[10] Indeed, its only significant activity was taken on by Dillon O'Brien, its titular secretary, who wrote and lectured widely on the subjects of immigration and assimilation.[11] His efforts and those of others similarly minded resulted in a national convention in St. Louis in the early autumn of 1869, convoked to explore the whole knotty question of Catholic colonization in the Midwest. "Of course," a participant remembered with some bitterness, "there were many eloquent speeches and a string of resolutions. There was a

---

8. Rice, "The Swedes," 253–254.

9. Qualey and Gjerde, "The Norwegians," 226–227.

10. Humphrey Moynihan, "Archbishop Ireland's Colonies," *A&D* 6 (1934): 212–231.

11. See, e.g., *NWC*, May 11, 1867. O'Brien served for a time as editor of the *Chronicle*.

banquet and a steamboat excursion, and everything was agreeable and harmonious down to the adjournment. And that was all. Nothing came of it. A committee had been named to carry out the design of the convention. The committee never met."[12]

Thomas Grace's apparent lack of enthusiasm for the society he had founded five years before may have turned upon a question of semantics, upon the meaning of the words "Irish Emigration." He was not indifferent to the plight of dispossessed and harassed Irishmen in their native land—indeed, much of his personal charity was dispatched to Ireland[13]—but he was even more concerned to promote what he stingingly called, "the exodus of the Irish people from the American Egypt."

> I know well the condition of the poor Irish people in our large cities of the East. I have studied the question regarding that condition in all its bearings. It is a terrible thing to contemplate a generous and noble people rotting and dying out from sheer neglect. But more terrible still is the responsibility that rests on the Bishops and the priests, advisers and guardians under God of those people.

There is nothing "providential" in "this state of things," he continued, when "free lands and free homes of the great West [with] ample space [are] easily accessible."

> But the Bishops and priests will not let their people accept [this opportunity]. They have opposed the efforts that have been made to bring their people to these lands. They dissuade the people from going. They discourage the enterprises that are now and again undertaken for that object. They keep the people ignorant of what is essential to their well-being and the well-being of their children, and retain them where they are in an atmosphere of pestilential filth and moral corruption. I say the Bishops and clergy of the East are blamable for this obstruction.[14]

---

12. William J. Onahan, "A Chapter of Catholic Colonization," *A&D* 5 (1917): 70.

13. See, e.g., acknowledgments of contributions, Logue to Grace, March 31, 1880; Conway to Grace, April 4, 1880; and McGettigan to Grace, January 22, 1881; bishops respectively of Raphoe, Killahoe, and Armagh, as well as similar communications from several orders of religious women in Ireland, AASPM, Grace Papers.

14. Grace to Byrne, August 25, 1869, AASPM, Grace Papers. S. Byrne was a fellow Dominican whom Grace had known in the Ohio and Kentucky of his youth. Byrne continued to agitate over the deplorable conditions of Irish immigrants in

This scathing indictment, addressed to a sympathetic priest working in the slums of lower Manhattan, was based upon the fact that among the huge numbers of Irish expatriates in America, only a tiny percentage had ventured away from the Atlantic seaboard, and upon the contention that leading churchmen had encouraged them to remain quiet and content in the slums of New York, Boston, and Philadelphia. Prominent among such leaders was the celebrated archbishop of New York, John Hughes, himself born in Ireland, who scornfully dismissed proposals for migration to the Midwest as "mischievous," because they disturbed "the minds of those . . . already established [in the United States] . . . by a gilded and exaggerated report of theoretical blessings . . . [in] the nominal ownership of . . . uncultivated land, not infrequently teeming with fever and ague," and remote from the ministrations of a parish and a priest.[15] This attitude was monstrously wrong and deceitful in the view of Hughes's episcopal colleague in St. Paul, who hoped fervently that the 1869 gathering in St. Louis might signal a powerful new impetus for the Irish cabined up in the eastern ghettoes to seek out "the free lands and homes" in "the great West." "I send you by this mail," he wrote the similarly outraged Father Byrne some weeks later, "a copy of the Northwestern Chronicle containing the address of the Committee appointed by the St. Louis Immigration convention."

> You will perceive that it covers the whole ground you contemplate. . . . The object of the St. Louis Convention is to do what you wish to be done, and—for all the difficulties in the way of accomplishing the goods proposed—have [sic] been carefully considered in that convention and provision made to meet them. What is needed is the cooperation of the friends of the Irish people in the East; without this cooperation nothing can be accomplished. Indeed, this Movement should have had its commencement where the evil to be remedied has its existence. It *did* commence there years ago, but was put down by *the friends* of the Irish people. . . . I am rejoiced that there is at least one friend in the East who feels in sympathy with the disposal to second the support again inaugurated [at St. Louis], and that friend is yourself. Have no fear as to the concurrence of the Bishops and clergy of the West in this enterprise.[16]

New York through at least the next decade. See Byrne to Grace, August 18, 1879, with clippings from the *New York Herald*, AASPM, Grace Papers.

15. Henry J. Browne, "Archbishop Hughes and Western Colonization," *Catholic Historical Review* 36 (1950): 257–285, especially 271.

16. Grace to Byrne, October 30, 1869, AASPM, Grace Papers.

In fairness it should be admitted that Hughes's strictures were probably a useful corrective to the visionary propaganda put forward by well-intentioned colonizers at St. Louis and elsewhere, who too often depicted farm life in the Midwest as an uninterrupted idyll. Loras and Cretin, for their part, had taken care not to disguise the difficulties settlers in their dioceses could expect, particularly in the early years. Long after the controversy had passed, John Ireland was severely critical of Hughes and his ilk—colonization, he said, "often met with opposition on the part of [churchmen] whose position and intelligence should have promised better things"[17]—but the fact remains that no colonization plan applicable nationwide ever gained significant support within the Catholic community. Ireland's criticism, moreover, was tinged with unintended irony, because what success his Minnesota colonies enjoyed depended to a large degree upon their modest scope and upon the tight clerical control he imposed on them.

Grace's hopes for the St. Louis Convention went unfulfilled, and the local Emigration Society he had established languished, as did other similarly constituted confessional bodies. Then, in 1873, a nationwide financial crisis and its attendant distress dealt a direct blow to any immediate plans for westward colonization, whether inspired by religious or secular sources. The expanding railroad companies were particularly hard hit by the deep depression. Thus the St. Paul and Pacific, in 1873 part of the larger Northern Pacific system, defaulted on its bonds on May 1. Not a few observers, whatever their own plight, took a grim satisfaction in such news. The railroads operating in Minnesota shared during the postwar years the obloquy directed against the industry generally around the country. Accusations of rate fixing, tax evasion, and extortion, laid at the doors of the railway barons, were mostly impossible to refute.[18] Now, with their fiscal base devastated, their immigration offices at home and abroad were promptly closed, reception houses shut down, orders for descriptive pamphlets and brochures canceled. Railroad executives all over the country believed as strongly as before in the benefits to be derived from promoting colonization, but during a period of sharp retrenchment they did not have, or did not want to spend, the money to pay for it.

THE PANIC OF 1873 ULTIMATELY PASSED AWAY, AS SUCH ECONOMIC convulsions always do in time, though not without much pain, recrimination, shaking out of a host of business relationships, and lingering financial

---

17. Ireland, "Loras," 15.
18. Folwell, *Minnesota*, 3:39–57.

274 Pilgrims to the Northland

uncertainty. The more vulnerable railways went under or were absorbed into firms that had proved robust enough to ride out the storm, and construction of new track in Minnesota ground to a virtual standstill. By December 1875, when John Ireland was consecrated coadjutor, the St. Paul and Pacific, not unlike many other such companies, teetered on the verge of bankruptcy. The oils of the sacrament had scarcely dried on Ireland's hands when in mid-January 1876 the *Northwestern Chronicle* reported that the new bishop had had placed at his disposal 75,000 acres of Swift County, Minnesota, about 120 miles west and a little north of St. Paul and Minneapolis. A week later came the announcement that the old Minnesota Irish Emigration Society had given way to the Catholic Colonization Bureau of St. Paul. Ireland, it was further revealed, had signed a contract making him the exclusive agent for all the land in Swift County belonging to the St. Paul and Pacific Railroad.[19]

Politicians of both parties, locally and nationally, recognized that in the long and in the short term, economic development after the Civil War depended in large measure upon a sophisticated transportation system, which meant the need to encourage the availability of track, steam-driven locomotives, and rolling stock, pressing their way into every corner of the Republic. And so railroads like the St. Paul and Pacific had been able to encourage colonization in the first place because of the extensive property they controlled, thanks to the largesse of the federal and state governments. In Swift County, for instance, the St. Paul and Pacific owned alternate sections on each side of its right-of-way for a distance of three to five miles, up to a total of well over 100,000 acres. The intervening sections were still subject to the provisions of the Homestead Act of 1862—which meant the land was free (save for a registration fee of fourteen dollars). Other adjacent public land was available to settlers who pledged to cultivate timber on the treeless prairie (ten acres of tree-plantings for every 150 acres farmed), and even tracts not covered by the Homestead Act could be purchased for only a few dollars an acre. So Ireland was not merely boasting when he said that he aimed at "making a grand total of *one hundred and fifty thousand* acres open to Catholic settlement."

Aside from some differences of detail, the terms that the bishop concluded with the St. Paul and Pacific were consistent with the agreements he would sign later with other rail firms. For a period of two years Ireland's Colonization Bureau was to be the sole agent for the sale of the railroad's property in Swift County. The agent received a flat ten percent commission on all transactions. Moreover, the company agreed to donate a generous number of

---

19. *NWC*, January 15 and 22, 1876.

lots for its agent's exclusive use in the towns that grew up to serve the farmers. Many of these lots eventually provided sites for Catholic churches and schools, but others were put on the market by the Bureau and sold at advantageous prices. Such sales, together with the agent's fees, paid the bureau's expenses. Ireland was not permitted to purchase any railroad land in his own name or for his personal use, although he could—and did—invest in contiguous property.[20]

The cost of the land to the colonist who migrated to Swift County was between five and seven dollars an acre, depending on quality and proximity to the rail line. The down payment amounted to one year's interest at seven percent (or sixty-seven dollars on a tract of 160 acres at six dollars an acre). The balance, principal, and interest had to be paid within ten years. Ireland gained a further concession from the St. Paul and Pacific, which agreed to accept at face value its own land certificates, then selling far below par, as payment; for those settlers lucky enough to take advantage of this provision the already modest price of their tracts could be reduced even further.[21]

On January 26, 1876, the first thirty-two colonists selected their parcels. By September, 800 more had followed suit—seventy-five percent of them of Irish extraction, the rest Polish, German, and French[22]—and 60,000 acres of railroad land had been settled. So quickly did the project move forward that before the end of the year Ireland signed another contract with the St. Paul and Pacific, and eventually, in 1879, the total acreage made available by the railroad to colonists in Swift County came to 117,000. How much additional government land was taken up as a direct consequence of the bureau's initiatives cannot be determined with any certainty, but it was doubtless considerable. The villages of De Graff and Clontarf gradually took shape as the east and west terminals respectively of the colony lands, and then each of them as the nucleus of a colony of its own. A little church in honor of Our Lady of Kildare was built in the former place in 1876; the pastor's name, coincidentally, was F. J. Swift. To Clontarf, seventeen miles away, Ireland dispatched his former colleague at the cathedral and Bishop Cretin's young companion and translator, Anatole Oster, who named the parish he organized there for

---

20. James P. Shannon, *Catholic Colonization on the Western Frontier* (New Haven, 1957), 47–49, 87–91. This remains the definitive study of the Catholic colonies in Minnesota.

21. Moynihan, "Ireland's Colonies," 218.

22. Anon. [Dillon O'Brien], *Catholic Colonization in Minnesota* (St. Paul, 1879), 43.

St. Malachy, a testimony to the Irish character of his congregation rather than to his own Alsatian sensibilities.[23]

Central to Ireland's policy—and of course with Grace's concurrence—was the placing of a priest in each of the ten colonies he founded. One reason was a posthumous acknowledgment of the caveats of Archbishop Hughes. Many potential colonists, Dillon O'Brien wrote in 1879, "feared that if they came West they would be beyond the reach of church and priest." To counter this fear, the Bureau would make certain that "the resident priest and church should go in with our first settlers, be their number large or small. To this good rule we attribute, to a great extent, not alone our success in bringing settlers to our colonies, but likewise their general contentment in their new homes and brave cheerfulness in meeting the trials, hardships and set-backs which are incident to new settlements."

To Ireland's and O'Brien's credit, they did not underplay the difficulties the colonists were sure to encounter, especially during the early years of set-tlement. "If you come from a city, you will, doubtless, feel lonely for a while, until you get accustomed to prairie life; you will miss many immediate com-forts; you will have to put up with discomforts, with disappointments, with trials. The man who feels he can stand up against all such difficulties, and look bravely to the future for his reward, let him come to Minnesota."[24] The presence in the colony of a priest and a church and a school, however humble, would indeed guarantee the settlers spiritual solace, but the parish would also provide them with a sense of social cohesion and of community—much as such institutional support helped to sustain the Protestant Swedish and Nor-wegian immigrants and, indeed, the 50,000 Catholics who had come to Min-nesota before the Civil War.[25]

From Ireland's point of view the resident pastor served another impor-tant function as well. He was the bishop's agent. He acted as facilitator and adviser for the colonists. He was, in effect, an employee of the Colonization Bureau, and in that capacity he smoothed the way for the newcomers in a number of mundane ways. It was the priest who usually met the immigrants at the bleak little station, gave them the necessary initial information, put them into contact with the railroad land office, and remained throughout their early tenure a source of encouragement and support. It was the priest, as one contemporary observer expressed it, "who managed the colony for Dr.

---

23. See Reardon, *Diocese of St. Paul*, 628, 630, and chapter 4, above.
24. [O'Brien], *Catholic Colonization*, 4, 57.
25. See chapter 6, above.

Ireland."[26] And since the priest was the bishop's subject and served only at the bishop's will, he was the ideal instrument by which Ireland and the Bureau in St. Paul were kept informed of the progress of the settlement and could, in turn, assure the railroad that the terms of the contract were being met.

The foundation of the two colonies in Swift County—De Graff and Clontarf—was followed over the succeeding five years by settlements in eight other sites in five other southwestern counties—Big Stone, Traverse, Nobles, Murray, and Lyon—in which upwards of 2,000 families found new homes. (One of the villages that grew out of this expansion—in a gracious gesture to the benign but not directly involved bishop of St. Paul—was named Graceville.) Between 1876 and 1880 Ireland contracted altogether for about 380,000 acres of railroad land, and thereby stimulated settlement on an undetermined amount of adjacent land as well. Throughout this period the railroad companies—anxious to keep the lands along their rights-of-way productive, and no less anxious to restore their tarnished public image—continued to support the bishop's colonizing ventures by granting them various commercial advantages. For example, instead of insisting on conventional mortgages, they extended direct credit to the settlers by simply delaying transfer of land titles until payment was made, and they tended to be lenient with those who fell behind in their installments. When the Swift County colonies were short of winter fuel, the St. Paul and Pacific shipped cordwood to De Graff and Clontarf for sale at cost. Similarly the railroad transported free of charge saplings to any colonist who would plant them on his treeless farm. In response to the grasshopper plague of 1877, agricultural agents employed by the railroad were dispatched to the aid of the farmers, and the road absorbed the cost of sending to the scene the materials used in the attempt to cleanse the fields of the larvae left by the insects.[27]

That this mutual dependence could have personal ramifications was demonstrated in the autumn of 1877. James J. Hill, who had switched his entrepreneurial skills from the steamboat business to railroading, had determined to take over the insolvent St. Paul and Pacific. He and Ireland were exactly the same age, both born in 1838 and both, in their different fields, seen in St. Paul to be up-and-coming men. They were casual acquaintances, and indeed ten years before they had been involved in a comedy of errors. Hill, a Protestant, had won the hand of a fiercely pious Catholic, Mary Theresa

---

26. John Sweetman, "The Sweetman Catholic Colony in Currie, Minnesota: A Memoir," *A&D* 3 (1911): 43.

27. Shannon, *Catholic Colonization*, 59.

Mehegan, and, in accord with the custom of the day, the "mixed" marriage was to be performed in the cathedral rectory. The Mehegan family, left practically destitute after the premature death of Mary Theresa's father, had been much aided spiritually and materially by Father Louis Caillet,[28] who along with Ireland and Anatole Oster was then on staff of the cathedral parish. Hill reserved the appropriate room in the presbytery, and informed Father Ireland that his bride-to-be wished Father Caillet to preside at the ceremony. When the appointed time arrived, a red-faced Ireland came to the bridal party assembled in the parlor and confessed that he had forgotten to deliver the message and that Caillet was out of the city and unavailable. Ireland then offered to witness the exchange of vows himself, but Mary Theresa frostily refused, and asked for Father Oster instead. Thus the first recorded encounter between the two giants of their time and place was an inauspicious one.[29]

Now, a decade later, there occurred an encounter of a different kind. To gain control of the St. Paul and Pacific, Hill needed to attract substantial new capital, since the railway's indebtedness ran to $44 million. One morning in early September 1877, Hill and one of his partners took a potential backer—the president of the Bank of Montreal—on a trip along the line, so that that gentleman could see for himself the rich promise the railroad held for the future. All went well for some distance out of St. Paul, but then as the train rolled farther west, the developed farmland gave way to "wild, untenanted prairie"; the banker shook his head gravely and remarked that no railroad could make any money in such a barren countryside. "At last," as Ireland heard the story years later from Hill's partner,

> the station of De Graff was reached. It was Sunday morning. Around a rude but good-sized structure there were crowds of people; the trails leading toward it were covered with conveyances, most of them drawn by oxen. "What is all this?" inquired [the banker]. "Why," answered quickly his [hosts], "this is but an instance of what is soon to occur along the whole line of the railroad. This is a colony opened by Bishop Ireland one single year ago. Already the settlers brought in by the Bishop are counted by hundreds, and hundreds of others are coming to join them from different parts of America and Europe. This is Sunday morning, and the settlers are going to mass."

---

28. See chapter 6, above.
29. See O'Connell, *John Ireland*, 116–117.

Hill and his partner got their funding, and the latter told Ireland: "In a manner unknown to yourself, you were a friend to Mr. Hill and myself in a moment when we needed friends. Whatever I can do for you is but a return of thanks for what you and your colony once did for us."[30]

IN THE EBB AND FLOW OF HUMAN EVENTS, TIMING, IT HAS BEEN said, is crucial, and certainly for James J. Hill, on his way to the building of a financial empire, that Sunday morning in De Graff was a case in point. But John Ireland in his colonization projects was similarly fortunate. He launched the enterprise at a time when the effects of a severe depression had begun to mitigate, and at a moment when the railroad industry was desperate to reverse its recent misfortunes. He and his colonists were also lucky in the overall agribusiness climate they experienced during the first years, when the settlements were especially fragile. Most of the farmers devoted the bulk of their land to the cultivation of wheat, and the virgin soil responded with hearty yields. Wheat grown in western Minnesota sold at about a dollar a bushel between 1876 and 1880.[31] The railway system, expanding again under the leadership of entrepreneurs like Hill, made shipment to market relatively easy, and the mills to which the farmers delivered their crop were located in nearby Minneapolis, not in Milwaukee or Chicago as heretofore. This is not to say that Ireland's colonists basked in an unrelieved boom, but it does mean that economic conditions were more favorable for them in 1876 than would have been the case ten years earlier or ten years later.

Ireland's preoccupation, echoing that of Bishop Grace, was to offer a better way of life to Catholic immigrants—particularly but not exclusively the Irish—who languished, as he thought, in the slums of the large cities of the eastern United States. It is significant that he did not advertise his colonies in, or solicit recruits from, the land of his birth or anywhere else in Europe. The problem, as he saw it, was not that Catholic immigrants were too few but that too many of them lived in the wrong places and under the wrong circumstances. He doubted that Irish day laborers in Boston and New York who earned a couple of dollars a day and spent their scant leisure time in saloons could be a credit to their adopted country or to their church. In contrast to this sorry state of things Ireland cherished a somewhat fanciful Jeffersonian

---

30. Joseph G. Pyle, *The Life of James J. Hill*, 2 vols. (New York, 1936), 2:205–207.
31. Anon. [Dillon O'Brien], *Catholic Colonization in Minnesota: Colony of Avoca* (St. Paul, 1880), 16–18.

ideal of a sturdy yeomanry that could form the backbone of a stable, productive, and God-fearing society. Men who owned their own land and drew their sustenance directly from it, men who were industrious and sober—the priests who served as agents of the Colonization Bureau were also expected to act as apostles of teetotalism—men who nurtured their families and who lived in harmony with the rhythm of the seasons, these would be good Americans and good Catholics. But the vision had practical limits, as both Ireland and Dillon O'Brien had already learned from experience. However much they may have wanted to succor the poorest of the poor, the foundering of earlier, quixotic colonization projects convinced them that those to be invited to farmland in western Minnesota had to bring with them a modicum of skills and capital. And when at last they deviated from this imperative, their enterprise suffered a severe and humiliating setback

The Catholic Colonization Bureau of St. Paul had no land to give away. Sensibly, in the light of so many prior failures initiated on a grander but unrealistic scale, it was never more than a clearing house that offered a method of obtaining cheap land. Those residents in eastern cities destitute of at least minimal resources could not even get to the colonies in Minnesota, much less survive there. In a series of propaganda pamphlets—folksy tracts that mixed picturesque descriptions of rural life in western Minnesota with carefully researched statistical information—O'Brien candidly stated the need for the prospective colonist to possess some small fund of capital before he ventured West. And he was very specific. Thus in addition to paying train fare—for example, twenty-four dollars per person from New York and Philadelphia—the colonist had to make ends meet until his first cash crop came in, roughly sixteen months after his arrival. "He puts up a very cheap house," wrote O'Brien, sixteen by eighteen feet, "comfortable, warm, and clean—much better than a cheap lodging in a city," which costs him $38.75. Furniture, including a cooking stove at $25.00, came to $43.00, a yoke of oxen and a plow $198.00, fuel and food, including a milk cow, $130.00, adding up to a grand total of $409.75. "This sum," O'Brien warned, "[the settler] will absolutely require when he arrives on the land. To this, in his calculations, he must add his expenses coming here." A family of four, therefore, had to have, by the most optimistic projections, at least five hundred dollars in hand before it fled the steaming tenements. Nor did O'Brien's figures include a down payment on the railroad land, which could range between forty and seventy dollars. Not many of the kind of families Ireland had envisaged as colonists in his more visionary moments could scrape together that much money. As the years passed and their experience broadened, he and O'Brien necessarily revised the estimate upward until a minimum of a thousand dollars became the accepted figure.[32]

But the dream of serving the genuinely indigent died hard. Early in 1877 Bishop Ireland presided at the organizational meeting of the Minnesota Colonization Company, a joint stock company that offered for public sale 2,500 shares at ten dollars a share. Its purpose was "the buying and selling of tracts of land in . . . Minnesota and assisting needy and deserving in settling thereon." Ireland bought ten shares (as did Bishop Grace), and for a while there was a great deal of enthusiasm for the company's prospects.[33] The euphoria, however, did not last. By June the directors had sold only 345 shares, and two years later, when they dissolved the company, they had come nowhere near their goal of twenty-five thousand dollars. The failure did not affect Ireland's Bureau, from which it was entirely distinct, a point Dillon O'Brien was at pains to stress from the beginning: "We are proud to say that we have in Minnesota a chartered stock company . . . [which] proposes to give a poor, industrious, sober man eighty acres. . . . Of course," he added carefully, "this Catholic colonization stock company scheme has no connection with our Catholic Immigration Bureau; our bureau has no capital."[34]

To have no capital had proved in the long run an advantage, because it meant that the colonists who dealt with the Bureau had had to invest resources of their own, however scanty, in the venture, and therefore they tried harder to make it a success. Yet in 1880 Ireland and O'Brien, to their cost, deserted this prudent course in behalf of some fisher folk from the west of Ireland.

Connemara is a peninsular district jutting out of County Galway into the Atlantic. It had always been a poor place whose inhabitants eked out a living from occasional fishing and from little patches of potatoes. In 1879 the district suffered a severe food shortage, so severe that the misery in Connemara rivaled that of the famine days of the 1840s. The dire situation came to the attention of James Nugent, an Anglo-Irish priest already well known for his charitable work in the slums of Liverpool. Nugent collected some money, went to Connemara to distribute it, and concluded that the only permanent solution to the dreadful living conditions there was the emigration

32. [O'Brien], *Catholic Colonization*, 34–35, and *Colony of Avoca*, 16–17. See also Shannon, *Catholic Colonization*, 88–90, 106.

33. Shannon, *Catholic Colonization*, 108–113.

34. Anon. [Dillon O'Brien], *An Invitation to the Land: Reasons and Figures* (St. Paul, 1877), 46.

of a significant proportion of the indigenous population. He wrote to Bishop Ireland—so far had spread the fame of the Minnesota colonies—and begged him to find a place for a community of wretched Connemaras. Ireland, who had once met Nugent and revered him as a leader of the temperance movement, agreed to receive fifty families, though only about half that many actually came.[35]

Ireland having cajoled a steamship company into providing free passage, the Connemaras arrived in due course, 309 of them, in Boston, where Dillon O'Brien met them on the dock. They made a pitiable sight: "The famine was visible in their pinched and emaciated faces, and in the shriveled limbs—they could scarcely be called legs and arms—of the children. Their features were quaint, and the entire company was squalid and wretched."[36] When he saw them, the hard-headed O'Brien, as he later told his son, immediately sensed the impending trouble. "The kindly but visionary Father Nugent . . . chose . . . not the competent but the incompetent, not the industrious but the shiftless; a group composed of mendicants who knew nothing of farming, and were entirely unfitted to cope with life on the American prairie."[37] This comment was made, to be sure, *ex post facto,* many years after the ensuing scandal in which O'Brien did not play an altogether honorable part.

The Connemara caravan detrained in St. Paul on June 26, when Ireland met them with some ceremony. Before the main group proceeded west— needless to say, rail fare was also gratis—the bishop found employment in the city for about seventy young unmarried adults, men and women. He had already set aside for them in Graceville colony, Big Stone County, fifty farm sites of 160 acres each and had urged the colonists already there to lend a hand to the newcomers by "breaking" five acres for planting on each site. (The prairie sod was so tough that to "break" a portion of it was a settler's first and perhaps most arduous task.) To these unprecedented favors were added, at the bishop's expense, a consignment of clothing, farm implements, a year's supply of seed, and credit at the Graceville general store.[38] Established farm-

---

35. On the Connemaras, here and below, see Moynihan, "Ireland's Colonies," 220–222, and especially Bridget Connelly, *Forgetting Ireland: Uncovering a Family's Secret History* (St. Paul, 2003), 3–13.

36. William J. Onahan, quoted in Mary Evangela Henthorne, *The Career of the Right Reverend John Lancaster Spalding, Bishop of Peoria, as President of the Irish Catholic Colonization Association of the United States* (Champaign-Urbana, 1932), 110.

37. Quoted in Thomas D. O'Brien, "Dillon O'Brien," *A&D* 6 (1933): 50.

38. Shannon, *Catholic Colonization,* 159.

ers in the colony were paying something like $2.00 a day for hired hands. Almost all the refugees from Galway had a young relative working in St. Paul or Minneapolis, who might be expected to send regularly a little money to his parents or siblings. All in all, in the glorious summer sunshine, the prospects looked bright.

But the distress started almost at once. The Connemaras arrived in Graceville during the early days of July 1880. (The date is highly significant.) They gazed in bewilderment over the vast, limitless, treeless prairie—"the eye seeks in vain to detect some object taller than a blade of grass, . . . wearisome at length by its sameness," as Bishop Grace had described the landscape during his journey to Pembina two decades before[39]—the likes of which they could never have conceived in their wildest imagination. Homesickness combined with uncertainty and a kind of atavistic resentment at a fate which had brought them thousands of miles in order to live in huts built of sod rendered many of them bitter and apprehensive. Even in this relatively benign time of the year, instead of the bracing breeze off the ocean they felt the scorching winds blowing out of the west from Dakota and carrying with them swarms of repulsive locusts.[40] The existence they had endured in County Galway, bad as it had been, had had at least a familiarity which could soothe the inner spirit, before the interference of Nugent and Ireland. Little wonder that the men among them hired themselves out as casual labor, promptly spent the pittance they earned, and then remarked with a shrug that if difficulty came, "the Bishop brought us here, and he must care for us."[41]

Reports of problems—that the Connemaras were lazy, quarrelsome, dirty, and, most serious, that they were not using the warm summertime to prepare their houses and storage areas for the coming winter—gradually filtered back to St. Paul, but Ireland, who had staked considerable personal prestige on this project, would not countenance any criticism of it. In early September he toured the Graceville colony himself and was only partially reassured. The Connemaras appeared to be faring well enough, but their common mutterings of discontent alarmed and angered the bishop. He lectured them on the absolute need for thrift and hard work and for the measure of sacrifice now

---

39. See chapter 7, above.

40. See Annette Atkins, *Harvest of Grief: Grasshopper Plagues and Public Assistance in Minnesota, 1873–1878* (St. Paul, 1984). Swift County, the locale of Ireland's first colonies, was particularly hard hit by the incursion of locusts (13–25), but Big Stone was not immune, even though the worst had passed by the time of the arrival of the Connemaras.

41. Moynihan, "Ireland's Colonies," 222.

that would secure the future prosperity and respectability of themselves and their children. He told them they should be grateful for this opportunity to improve their lot. And he threatened to cut off credit from those who refused to work.[42]

But the good fortune and happy timing that had blessed the colonization enterprise now ran out. The first blizzard of the legendary winter of 1880–81 struck Graceville in mid-October, and during succeeding months the accumulation of snow and degree of cold rivaled anything the oldest frontiersman could remember. Suffering among the Connemaras, most of whom had neglected to insulate their shanties or dig protective cellars for their potatoes, was intense. Ghastly accounts of their suffering from hunger and frostbite circulated through the area. But so did stories about their inaction, even their indolence in the face of such peril when, it was alleged, a minimal effort on their part could have alleviated at least some of their distress. Ireland sent emergency provisions by rail from St. Paul, and investigative reporters, sniffing a scandal in the offing, soon followed. "The Connemara men," Dillon O'Brien told one of them, "would not take the flour away [from the station], although to them it was a free gift. Some of the other farmers, when a sum was offered them to carry the flour to the homes of the Connemara men, said that they were willing enough to make a dollar, but that they would not turn their hands to benefit such a lazy people."[43]

The adverse publicity that spread out of newspapers in the Twin Cities to those in places as far away as New York reflected negatively, to Ireland's sorrow and fury, upon his whole colonization enterprise. He sent the tireless Dillon O'Brien to Graceville in December, but neither his inquiries nor those of local worthies, Catholic and non-Catholic alike, resulted in any recommendation except the departure of the Connemaras from the colony. So, in the spring of 1881, most of them straggled back to St. Paul, where the bishop tried with some success to find them unskilled laborers' jobs, chiefly in the railroad yards. They settled under Dayton's Bluff, east of the business district in a shanty town, which was known for years as "the Connemara Patch."[44]

John Ireland was not a man who suffered humiliation gladly, particularly when he was convinced that his personal prestige was linked with the overall reputation of the Church. It is not surprising, therefore, that once O'Brien ad-

42. See *NWC*, September 11, 1880.

43. Article in the *New York Sun*, quoted in Henthorne, *Colonization Association*, 113.

44. Reardon, *Diocese of St. Paul*, 242.

vised him that the situation in Graceville was hopeless, he lashed out in the public print.

> I had presumed that no families could come to me from Ireland devoid of all noble qualities. . . . I yet have sufficient faith in the Irish race to believe . . . that the worst specimens can be easily fashioned into the noblest manhood. [The Connemaras] have since their arrival shown an unwillingness to work. . . . During the busy harvest season, many of them loitered around the prairies . . . under the avowed pretext that Bishop Ireland would support them whether they worked or not. Some of them have even gone so far as to invite their children home from St. Paul where they have been earning high wages, telling them that living was free in Big Stone County. . . . The Connemara families are twenty-four in number. Around Graceville are 400 other Catholic families, and I beg the public, when Graceville is mentioned, to remember the latter rather than the former.[45]

The operative word in this statement is "presumed." In the ethical canon presumption is listed as a sin, a species of pride, which in turn, it is said with formidable authority, goeth before a fall. Ireland and O'Brien were clearly guilty of presumption. The success till 1880 of their Colonization Bureau beguiled them into believing that no immigration project was beyond their capacity. But that success had been based upon the requirement that prospective colonists, already attuned to American ways, brought with them some resources of their own and that they understood the hardships they would at first encounter. In their hubris, however, Ireland and O'Brien abandoned that prudent policy and conveyed a gaggle of penniless, illiterate fishermen from the wilds of western Galway—many of whom could scarcely speak English—dumped them on the treeless prairie, and presumed that they could quickly accommodate to a harshly demanding climate and to an agricultural technique totally unfamiliar to them. In retrospect, it seems hardly strange that they should have concluded that "the Bishop brought us here, and he must take care of us."

They were guilty of something else too, the coadjutor bishop and his chief aide. In an attempt, largely successful if not consciously acknowledged, to cover up their presumption, they laid the failure in Graceville exclusively at the feet of the indolent and ungrateful Connemaras. This is not to say that

---

45. *St. Paul Pioneer Press*, December 22, 1880.

allegations of this sort were entirely without merit; so much smoke, discerned by so many witnesses, cannot be dismissed out of hand as though there were no fire beneath. The Connemaras as a group could never have described themselves as busy and attentive farmers. Even so, there was in St. Paul an untoward eagerness to wash the Colonization Bureau's hands of any fault in the handling of the fiasco. For instance, a recent examination of local public records shows that the parish priest in Graceville, for all practical purposes Bishop Ireland's agent there, took at best an ambivalent stance toward the plight of the Connemaras. The hue and cry raised by Protestants in the area over the pitiable state of the colonists, as well as a report commissioned by the governor, were dismissed as instances of bigotry, laced with Masonic malevolence toward Catholics. The most egregious misstatement, however, was Dillon O'Brien's, that had the Connemaras planted the seed that had been given them gratis on arrival in the colony—in those five acres allegedly "broken" by friendly neighbors—and not sold it or wasted it, they could have reaped a plenteous crop which would have preserved them from all their troubles. But in fact the refugees from Galway had not settled into their farm sites till the first week in July at the earliest, a time long after any possibility of an autumn harvest had passed away.[46] What remained for them was casual labor at a dollar or two a day and the necessity to shore up their flimsy houses. Most of them it appears, perhaps understandably, did not do so, and then the blizzards struck them. At any rate, at least five of the original Connemara families survived intact, never left the Graceville area, flourished there, and have ever since borne the stigma that their ancestors were crude and lazy ingrates.[47]

The embarrassment at Graceville did the colonization movement no permanent damage. And John Ireland did not budge from his self-justifying stance. "Many thanks for the kind letter you wrote to me during my trouble

---

46. See especially Connelly, *Forgetting Ireland*, 241–246.

47. See Connelly, *Forgetting Ireland*, especially chapters 4, 11, and 12. Bridget Connelly, Professor Emerita of Rhetoric in the University of California, Berkeley, is a specialist in the field of Arabic folklore. But she is also a descendant of one of the original Connemara colonists, and her book is an able apologia for the Connemaras who remained in the Graceville area. Her research into local records has been particularly impressive and requires extensive revision of earlier accounts of this episode by Shannon (*Catholic Colonization*, 154–166), Moynihan ("Ireland's Colonies," 220–222), O'Brien ("O'Brien," 50–52), and me (*John Ireland*, 149–152). However, Professor Connelly's book also displays much unfounded, sometimes whimsical speculation and uncorroborated testimony which, while not negating her basic point, tends to weaken her overall case.

with my Connemara immigrants," he wrote the archbishop of Baltimore, James Gibbons.

> You did much by your words to cheer me up at a moment when I needed encouragement. I am glad that you at once perceived the important fact that the Connemara people are very distinct from our regular colonists. What I feared was that danger might come to our colonization movement—but this, I am sure, has not been the case. The whole trouble is over. When my "friends" showed themselves in their true colors, I adopted treatment suited to their case, and put a quietus on their complaints.[48]

That he had done so unfairly and without acknowledging his own fault in the matter did not cancel out the overall good that had been accomplished in Clontarf, De Graff, and Graceville north of the Minnesota River, and in Minneota, Ghent, Avoca, Fulda, Iona, Adrian, and Currie south of it.[49] Life was hard for the Catholic pioneers in those outposts in western Minnesota. The climate remained unforgiving, both summer and winter, with nary a tree, at first, to give shade or shelter or even a modicum of fuel. The fertile soil, once the hard prairie crust was scraped away, bestowed abundant harvests of wheat for some years, but then grew spent, and remained so until the nuances of crop rotation came ultimately to be understood. Always, the optimism of spring planting had to be qualified by the possibility of an attack by locusts or by some mysterious fungus that might eat away at the tender shoots the seeds of which had been so painstakingly inserted into the spring ground. Work in the fields was relentless and wearisome, and, with sophisticated mechanization long into the future, the energy to perform it successfully issued from the muscles and sinews of horses and oxen and, most especially, from the men and women who strapped such animals to their plows and harrows. These farmers were invariably at the mercy of the prices of their produce, fixed in

---

48. Ireland to Gibbons, February 21, 1881, Archives of the Archdiocese of Baltimore (AAB).

49. Strictly speaking, the colony near Currie, in Murray County, was not a foundation of the St. Paul Bureau but rather was settled at the initiative of John Sweetman, a wealthy Irishman, who brought colonists there from County Meath. He sought counsel from Ireland and O'Brien, and Ireland arranged for him the purchase of 10,000 acres of railroad land. Of forty-one families originally settled in the spring of 1881, only sixteen remained two years later. See John Sweetman, "The Sweetman Catholic Colony of Currie, Minnesota: A Memoir," *A&D* 3 (1911): 41–64.

the markets of far-off Chicago and New York, and more immediately of the freight charges imposed by the increasingly monopolistic railroad system. Medical facilities were nonexistent, as were the other ordinary amenities of town life. Many babies were born, but many babies died, and the lot of the pioneer woman was, if anything, more fretful and arduous than that of her husband. Even so, despite all the hazards and difficulties and disappointments, Bishop Ireland's colonies survived, and gave to a whole class of persons the dignity and autonomy accorded only to those who attach themselves directly to the land. Their Catholic faith, and their commitment to the parochial culture that Ireland had set up for them, played no small part in establishing a tradition that would last.

From 1882—Dillon O'Brien died in September of that year—the Colonization Bureau wound down its activities and did not initiate any new projects. Its brief tenure, however, had affected John Ireland personally in two unpredictable ways. Promotion of the colonies had given him added national exposure and opened new contacts for him, besides those he had already established as a temperance crusader, outside Minnesota. Gibbons was not the only prominent churchman to lend him encouragement; Archbishop Williams of Boston and Bishop Stephen of Buffalo were similarly supportive, and even Hughes's successor in New York, John Cardinal McCloskey, offered a tepid endorsement.[50] Also, more perilously, it gave him a taste for real estate speculation which was to bring him much grief and humiliation in later years.[51] A paucity of records makes it difficult to know to what extent Ireland invested his own money in rural property during this time. Before 1883 he was restricted by contract from purchasing any of the cheap railroad lands available to the colonists, but this did not prevent him from buying property nearby or from profiting when, as was invariably the case, a thriving colony increased land values substantially in the whole area. Some tracts he kept till the end of his life.[52] Others he sold when the price was right.

BY 1884 THOMAS GRACE, NOT QUITE SEVENTY YEARS OLD, HAD determined to retire as bishop of St. Paul. His episcopate—which he had done his best to evade and which he had hoped to escape fifteen years earlier[53]—

---

50. Henthorne, *Colonization Association*, 50–51.

51. See chapter 14, below.

52. See the real estate inventory attached to Ireland's "Last Will and Testament," MHS, JIP, roll 23.

53. See chapters 5 and 9, above.

had lasted a quarter of a century. In the summer of that year, a week after the celebration of his silver jubilee, he announced his resignation. He was, as always, ungrudging in his praise of his younger coadjutor. "Reference has been made [in earlier speeches]," Grace said at the jubilee banquet, "to the great activity in conducting the affairs of the diocese[,] the enlarged views, the spirit of enterprise, and the energy in carrying forth the works of improvement and reform. How much of this is due to one whom I need not name is not necessary to say; but I will say that in these respects the Bishop and the Diocese of St. Paul have had far more than is implied in the name of the Coadjutor." Ireland's reply was equally gracious, though the discerning listener probably put more stock in the first part of his peroration than in the second. "My past has been through [Grace] secure and happy, and my future suggests to me no fears, because . . . he will for many and long years be still near to inspire and direct my counsels and my undertakings."[54] Bishop Grace at any rate received many verbal tributes on the occasion of his retirement, from civic leaders, including several Protestant ministers and a rabbi, and from scores of ordinary members of his flock. Yet he must have taken particular satisfaction in a few lines addressed to him by one of the commanding figures of early Minnesota history. "My dear Bishop," wrote Henry Sibley,

> I have been honored by an invitation to attend the "Silver Jubilee" today. Having just arisen from a sick bed, I am debarred [from] the privilege, of which I would have gladly availed myself, of witnessing the celebration of the twenty-fifth anniversary of your consecration as a Christian bishop. Permit me to express to you on this occasion the high appreciation I entertain of your personal and official character, and to congratulate you that your arduous labors of a quarter of a century have been crowned with such abundant success. May God preserve your life to the Church and to the Community at large for many years. Respectfully and sincerely yours.[55]

So it was, one pioneer to another.

The pope assigned to Grace in retirement the titular see of Menith.[56] Until 1890 he lived on in his old rooms in the cathedral rectory, and after that

---

54. *NWC*, July 31, 1884.

55. Sibley to Grace, July 24, 1884, AASPM, Grace Papers.

56. Until 1888, when John Ireland was made an archbishop and Grace was given the titular title *ad personam* as archbishop of Sinuia, also *in partibus*.

he went into residence at St. Thomas Aquinas Seminary.[57] On that campus was an artificial pond around which the venerable bishop would take his constitutional every day accompanied by his dog. The students, with their uncanny facility for nicknames, called the pond Lake Menith. For some years he continued to administer the sacrament of confirmation and to perform other ceremonial duties around the diocese, for which he received a stipend of twelve hundred dollars a year.[58] But later on his health, never robust, gradually deteriorated to the point that even such modest exertions were beyond his strength. He was afflicted, too, during the last years of his life by that cruelest of spiritual maladies, scrupulosity. Late in 1896 he sought relief from the obligation of recitation of the daily breviary. "I am now eighty-two (82) years of age," he wrote the apostolic delegate, "and I have great difficulty in reciting the divine office owing to my mind becoming feeble and the annoyance of scruples." He knew that in such cases the authorities usually granted the substitution of the rosary for the breviary, but Grace feared that "the same difficulty would attend.... I would therefore beg to be released from all obligations in this respect."[59] Only a month or two before the onset of his final illness did he manage a nostalgic trip back to his Dominican motherhouse in Ohio, a place he had not seen since the far-off days when he himself had been a young friar. He returned to St. Paul in time to celebrate his last Christmas there, and, on February 22, 1897, Thomas Langdon Grace, of the Order of Preachers, aged eighty-three, died peacefully and in full possession of his faculties. By a curious coincidence it was forty years to the day since the death of Joseph Cretin.

---

57. See chapter 14, below.

58. See Reardon, *Diocese of St. Paul*, 220–223.

59. Grace to Martinelli, November 13, 1896, Secret Archives of the Vatican, papers of the Delegation to the United States. Martinelli replied (November 16) in the kindest tone but told Grace his faculties allowed only permission to substitute the rosary. For a wider exemption, he said, Grace would have to apply directly to the Propaganda in Rome.

CHAPTER 12

Manifest Destiny

THOMAS GRACE'S RETIREMENT AS BISHOP OF ST. PAUL OCCURRED
at a conventionally appropriate juncture of events: in age he had attained the
biblical three score years and ten, and he had served faithfully for a quarter of
a century in a charge he had originally tried to evade. But his timing also reflected the bishop's characteristic tact and his consideration for his successor.
Two years before, in 1882, John Ireland had been named chaplain of the Minnesota National Guard. The appointment came from his old regimental commander during the Corinth campaign, now the governor of the state. "I deem
it a great privilege," Lucius Hubbard wrote,

> to be able to renew in this form the official relations that formerly existed
> between us. . . . I ask you to regard this tender as a token of the very high
> esteem in which I have ever held you personally, and the profound re-
> spect I entertain for your character as a foremost representative of your
> Church.[1]

Pleased as he was at receiving this ceremonial office, as well as at the governor's accolade, Ireland, despite his not inconsiderable accomplishments,
could hardly account himself "a foremost representative" of the Catholic
Church so long as he remained a coadjutor. Grace in retiring saw to it that
Ireland could assume full episcopal authority without any inhibiting ad-
jectives.

And he saw to it that the younger man could do so at what proved to be a
defining moment in the American Catholic experience. Only months after

---

1. Hubbard to Ireland, June 6, 1882, MHS, JIP, roll 23.

Grace's silver jubilee festivities, a plenary council, long in preparation, opened with liturgical pomp and circumstance in the Cathedral of the Assumption in Baltimore.[2] The new bishop of St. Paul joined fully in an assembly whose legislation was to set down institutional parameters destined to prevail till well past the middle of the following century. Ireland, a robust forty-six years of age, already had something of a national reputation, at least within the temperance and colonization movements. The Third Plenary Council of Baltimore, however, provided an occasion for him to expand that reputation, by way of the formal debates in which he took a lively part, and even more so by way of a single speech which attained great notoriety and in which, to a large degree, he set out the criteria that would direct his thinking and action for the rest of his life.

Sixty-two bishops, along with six abbots, thirty-four superiors of male religious congregations, eleven seminary rectors, eighty-one theologians, and a dozen minor functionaries—220 clerics in all—assembled for Baltimore III in November 1884. Thanks to careful preparation of the agenda and to the genial yet firm presidency of the archbishop of Baltimore, James Gibbons, the formal sessions of the council as well as the consultative deliberations proceeded smoothly. Bishop Ireland played an active role in the various debates, and in doing so revealed his predispositions as well as some of the priorities that would preoccupy him over the coming years. Thus, for instance, he strongly opposed the designation of the Ancient Order of Hibernians, a social and mutual benefit organization of ethnic Irish, as a "secret society" and so worthy of condemnation as a pseudo-Masonic fraternity. He spoke out strongly against parish picnics on Sunday or at any other time when liquor might be served. In a similar vein he thought the number of holy days of obligatory Mass attendance ought to be reduced, and indeed that that on New Year's Day be eliminated: too many men, after drinking to excess on its eve, exhibited an alcoholic contempt for the feast. He strenuously opposed parish dances and argued that the musical training of seminarians was a superfluous

---

2. A "plenary" council was a meeting of all the bishops (as well as the superiors of male religious orders) in the United States. By reason of its national scope it was therefore distinguished from a "provincial" council, a meeting of a metropolitan (for example, the archbishop of Milwaukee) and his suffragans. The council of 1884 was the third plenary assembly of the American hierarchy; the others were held in 1852 and 1866.

luxury—neither recommendation surprising from a man for whom music of any kind was merely an incomprehensible jumble of sound.[3]

More substantively, Ireland insisted that each bishop have ultimate control over all Catholic schools in his diocese, whatever the standing of any religious order. He approved in principle—and this was a matter of future bitter dispute—of what amounted to state-sponsored competency examinations for teachers in parochial schools, including teaching nuns. In one of the stormiest sessions of the council, he rose to oppose the establishment of irremovable rectorships within American dioceses, the administrative mandate common throughout the Catholic world whereby a certain proportion of the clergy within a diocese should enjoy permanence of tenure in their parochial assignments unless convicted of some canonical crime. Ireland had no doubt that he, and he alone, had the right in the diocese of St. Paul to determine which priest should serve where and for how long. Although the Church in the United States was still under the jurisdiction of Propaganda, the Roman congregation in charge of mission countries was moving gradually toward granting the United States a more conventional canonical status. But the curia, as was its wont, moved with glacial slowness, and not until 1908 was that status finally established. Meanwhile, at Baltimore in 1884, Ireland argued the issue with characteristic bravura, and during the debate he asked Gibbons, the chair, to express his opinion on this much-controverted matter. The apostolic delegate—the pope's official presider, as the archbishop of Baltimore was—seldom intervened in the conciliar discussions, but in response to Ireland he observed in his mild-mannered way that if the bishops-in-council failed to set aside at least ten percent of the parishes of each diocese for tenured pastors, Rome would do so anyway, to the inevitable embarrassment of the American hierarchy.[4]

JOHN IRELAND'S MOST MEMORABLE CONCILIAR MOMENT, HOWEVER, did not come amidst the give and take of floor debate. As befitted a meeting of religious leaders, time was set aside for formal and public devotions in the

---

3. That Ireland was tone deaf I learned from the late Monsignor Lawrence F. Ryan in a private interview, January 23, 1965. Ireland sang all liturgical texts, whatever their provenance, in the tune of the preface from the requiem Mass. Monsignor Ryan was rector of the St. Paul cathedral during Ireland's last years.

4. *Acta et Decreta Concilii Plenarii Baltimorensis Tertii in Ecclesia Metropolitana Baltimorensi a die IX Novembris usque ad diem VII Decembris A. D. MDCCCLXXXIV* (Baltimore, 1884), xlvii–xlviii, xciii–xcix.

cathedral five evenings a week: the office of Vespers on Sundays and Benediction of the Blessed Sacrament on weeknights, while at each pious gathering one of the prelates in attendance at the council delivered a sermon. Ireland was fortunate in having been scheduled early in the proceedings, on Monday, November 10—the council sat from November 4 till December 7—since by the time of the adjournment the weary participants had been subjected to a veritable orgy of oratory. Bishop Ireland titled his address "The Church—the Support of Just Government."[5] It lasted ninety minutes. It had been memorized, except for the quotations which the speaker read from sheets of paper in front of him. Ireland made his major point near the beginning.

> I love too deeply the Catholic Church and the American republic not to be ever ready to labor that the relations of the one with the other be not misunderstood. It is true, the choicest field which Providence offers in the world today to the occupancy of the Church is this republic, and she welcomes with delight the signs of the times that indicate a glorious future for her beneath the starry banner. But it is true, also, the surest safeguard for her own life and prosperity the republic will find in the teachings of the Catholic Church, and the more America acknowledges those teachings, the more durable will her civil institutions be made.

Here was a marriage contracted in Heaven, Catholicism and America. Far from being mutually antagonistic or exclusive, the two of them, properly understood, were perfectly mated. The evils of anarchy on the one hand, he went on, and of tyranny on the other—"the clamorings and violences of Communists and nihilists" and "the deathly grasp of military Caesarism"—were rooted in modern social theory, inspired "by Hobbes and Rousseau," which asserted that "God counts for nothing in society; He gives nothing to society, and social affairs have no reference to Him." The Catholic Church, guarantor of divine revelation, has "refuted in her teachings absurdities of this kind." The Church alone could effectively guard against that "forgetfulness of the divine origin of society and of government, [which] leaves no choice between anarchy and despotism."

Moreover, Ireland continued—and here he challenged the biases of many of his non-Catholic fellow citizens—the Church has ever been the advocate of

---

5. Text in *The Memorial Volume: A History of the Third Plenary Council of Baltimore* (Baltimore, 1885), 11–32, and reprinted under the title "The Church and Civil Society" in *The Church and Modern Society,* by John Ireland, 2 vols. (St. Paul, 1904), 1:29–65.

liberty. "I lose all patience when I hear prejudice still surviving to the extent to assert that the Catholic Church is not the friend of free institutions." Then, invoking a dubious reading of medieval and early modern history, he asked rhetorically:

> Did not the Middle Ages under [the Church's] guidance gradually emerge from Roman despotism and barbarian feudalism into the possession of political liberty, so that we may truly say she started the nations on the road to the highest forms of liberty? . . . Protestantism did nothing for liberty. . . . If it was anything in civil and political matters, it was political anarchy. . . . Protestantism . . . is not an organized force, and its contribution of positive power to any cause must necessarily be next to nothing. . . . To Americans, then, who love the republic, I fearlessly say, your hope is in the Catholic Church, because she is the mighty power today to resist unbelief and vice.

Some Catholics, for their part, might not share Ireland's "love and admiration for the republican form of government," nor are they compelled to do so by dogmatic commitment or historical precedent. But "this much too, I know, that I transgress no one iota of Catholic teaching when I speak forth my own judgment this evening, and salute the republic as the government I most cordially cherish. Republic of America," he concluded,

> receive from me the tribute of my love. I am proud to do thee homage, and I pray from my heart that thy glory may never be dimmed. . . . Thou bearest in thy hands the brightest hopes of the human race. God's mission to thee is to show to nations that man is capable of the highest liberty. Oh! Be ever free and prosperous that liberty triumph over the earth from the rising to the setting of the sun, *Esto perpetua!*

A passionate and unswerving conviction inspired this speech, however extravagant its rhetorical flourishes might appear to later generations. It was an unabashed assertion of Ireland's personal credo and, in outline, a statement of his permanent policy goals. If the westward expansion of the American people and polity bore the marks of a "Manifest Destiny," so in his mind did the future prospects of the Catholic Church. And the speech was hardly less an avowal of his personal ambition. The young bishop discerned for himself a wider field of action than his relatively modest jurisdiction in Minnesota. America—the whole vast new continent—was good for Catholicism, because its democratic institutions guaranteed the Church a freedom to flourish and expand, which the old regimes in Europe never allowed nor ever would. But Catholicism was likewise good for America, because the Church enshrined and promulgated the very virtues—respect for law, for individual dignity, for family stability, for hard work, for private property—without which those democratic institutions could not prosper or even survive.

But surely the established Yankee culture and Protestant ethic had long promoted these same virtues—had done so indeed with marked success and out of a British tradition inherently hostile to Catholicism and all its works and pomps. Precisely here, Ireland argued, lay the danger that the relations between his Church and his country "be misunderstood." Meanwhile demographic reality had dramatically altered the equation—and had opened the way for enlightened Catholic leadership—because the remorseless influx of European immigrants included literally millions of Catholic citizens who knew nothing of John Locke or of Jefferson and Hamilton, for that matter. Yankee mandarins, like those in Minneapolis who owned the mills and factories and who scoffed at Romish pretensions, could not forever withstand the pressures of a rapidly changing social fabric. But Ireland appreciated that a concomitant obligation fell upon himself and like-minded colleagues, the anointed guides of Catholic refugees from Bavaria, Donegal, and the Abruzzi: they were charged with harmonizing the religious aspirations of these masses with American civic culture. Such had been the objective of his apostolate as parish priest in St. Paul, and even more publicly so in the colonization projects he had initiated in western Minnesota during the late 1870s. Now, as he took the rostrum within a genuinely national setting, John Ireland proclaimed in effect that the doctrine of Manifest Destiny bore a twofold significance, one that attested to the political and economic primacy of the United States, and the other that promised "a glorious future for the Catholic Church beneath the starry banner."

This fusion of patriotism and religiosity sounded unexceptional to many who heard it that evening from the pulpit of the Baltimore cathedral. As one of the more sophisticated listeners noted in his diary: "Sermon . . . on the Church and liberty by Bp. Ireland. An essay good and useful in itself, though entirely lacking in originality." Nor did the diarist estimate very highly the speaker's rhetorical talent. "A dreary thing," he wrote. "Hard to hear. Habit of dropping his voice to be more impressive. Want of naturalness, the besetting sin of those who commit to memory."[6] This rather condescending critique

---

6. Diary of John B. Hogan, November 10, 1884, Sulpician Archives, Baltimore. Hogan was rector of the Sulpician seminary in Boston. I owe this reference to Professor Philip Gleason.

represented a minority view in 1884, and was confirmed as such by the usually enthusiastic reception Ireland's pulpit and platform performances received both in the United States and abroad over the next quarter of a century.
In any case, accolades and brickbats about style aside, the substance of Ireland's manifesto in Baltimore was what mattered in the long run. Homiletic
ends may be often obvious, speculative, and "lacking in originality"—"Do
good and avoid evil!"—while the means to bring them about remain subject
to unforeseen and unpredictable circumstances.

A REMARKABLE AMITY MANIFESTED ITSELF AMONG THE PRELATES
gathered at Baltimore III—remarkable not least because it so quickly faded.
Indeed, almost from the moment of the council's adjournment, twenty years
of strife within the American hierarchy began. Much of the dissension issued
from the challenge laid down in Ireland's speech. Two parties emerged, which
for the sake of convenience have usually been labeled "liberal" and "conservative," and the combatants themselves often employed these terms.[7] This clas-
sification, almost always suspect, is particularly so in this case. Thus, for
instance, the contest did not reflect a theological "liberalism" versus a theological "conservatism." All those involved were doctrinally orthodox, and all
of them were ultramontanes—devoted unreservedly, even slavishly, to the
prerogatives of the Holy See. Indeed, much of their struggle was fought out
along the corridors of the Vatican, where, as they all acknowledged, the ultimate authority resided. Also, distinct issues could on occasion cause shifting
alliances. And as ever in such a lengthy contention, there were many who
sought a middle ground and tried to avoid categorization.

"Americanizer" versus "anti-Americanizer" brings into play a more awkward, but also a more accurate, terminology. John Ireland's wholehearted endorsement of American mores and values aroused fervent support in some
quarters, deep suspicion and unease in others. At root the controversy turned
on a question of pace. Everyone agreed that the masses of Catholic immigrants needed to adjust to the economic, social, and political institutions—to
the overall culture—of the land in which they had chosen to settle. But how
fast should that assimilation occur? Ireland and those who stood with him

---

7. The standard general treatments are Thomas T. McAvoy, *The Great Crisis in
American Catholic History, 1895–1900* (Chicago, 1957), and Robert D. Cross, *The
Emergence of Liberal Catholicism in America* (Cambridge, Mass., 1958).

believed the process should move forward as quickly as possible. This stance appeared to others imprudent, foolhardy, and even dangerous.

Nationalism was the driving ideology of the Western world during the nineteenth century. It reverberated through the soaring strains of the "Marseillaise," it sought fulfillment in the creation of a German *Volk* by way of Bismarck's policy of blood and iron, it found romantic satisfaction in the legendary exploits of Garibaldi's red shirts. Even the rickety old Habsburg Empire had to grant as much status to its Hungarian component as to its Austrian. Yet millions upon millions of Europeans set sail for America during these years—sometimes for religious or political reasons, more often for economic ones. Did they, once landed in New York or Philadelphia, discard their language, their traditions, their folkways, in short their nationality? And did the Catholics among them, faced by a culture created and dominated for two and a half centuries by Protestant Anglo-Saxons and Scotch-Irish, discard their faith? These were the crucial questions confronting the American bishops in the 1880s. And they intertwined to form another: to what degree did the preservation of the immigrants' faith depend upon maintaining the habits and customs of the old country?

The Irish from the Catholic south had come to the United States steadily during the century and, in the wake of the Great Famine of the 1840s, in ever-swelling numbers. Though they were largely impoverished and ill-educated, most of them spoke English, which was an inestimable advantage. There was much nostalgia for the emerald isle among them and considerable interest, especially among the large concentrations of Irish in the eastern cities, in such issues as Home Rule and promotion of the Land League. Farther west, however, such political matters aroused little passion; Archbishop Ireland dismissed the Fenians as rogues and fanatics. Undeterred by a language barrier, the Irish by and large managed to adapt more readily to the American scene, albeit not without suffering discrimination in employment and housing. As for the practice of their religion, they attended the Latin Mass as they always had, were baptized and confirmed and shriven in Latin too, but they listened to sermons and performed their extraliturgical devotions in a familiar tongue, which was the common speech also of the American workplace, the public square, and the saloon.

But after the Civil War the Germans outstripped the Irish and remained the largest single bloc migrating into the United States until 1900, when the massive Italian and southern Slav influx began. Roughly thirty-five percent of the German immigrants were Catholics, and of course they did not speak English, which circumstance automatically rendered them more strangers in the land than the Irish.[8] The same could be said, to be sure, of Czechs and Poles and Slovenians, but the Germans, by reason of their sheer numbers and their social coherence, relative economic stability, and organizational instincts, soon posed the greatest challenge to the Amercanizers.

Ireland himself was no stranger to the prominence and cohesion of the German Catholic community. By the time he returned to Minnesota in 1861 from his schooling in France, the Assumption parish, detached from the cathedral to serve an exclusively German clientele, had been a going concern in St. Paul for several years. Heeding the invitation of that intrepid missioner, Franz Pierz—Slovenian-born but German-speaking—German Catholic immigrants had flocked into Minnesota and settled on the fertile lands on both sides of the Sauk River, in the environs of what would become the lively towns of St. Cloud and Sauk Rapids, and a little later farther south, up and down the Minnesota River valley. In 1856 Bishop Cretin welcomed into his diocese five Benedictine monks, Germans all, who had also responded to Pierz's appeal and had proceeded to establish St. John's priory at Indianbush in Stearns County, an institution that evolved into an abbey, a seminary, and a university. At first, however, they and their immediate successors were preoccupied with pastoral ministry to their fellow countrymen scattered from St. Joseph to Shakopee to Marystown, as well as to the parishioners of the Assumption in St. Paul.[9]

The monks were a godsend to Cretin and Grace, as they sought enough priests to serve their relentlessly growing German constituency. Even so, demand continued to outstrip supply, and young Father Ireland, ever his bishop's confidant, was aware that Grace had accepted, to his ultimate distress, several dicey applicants into the priestly ranks of the diocese simply because they spoke German. But Ireland also knew well the remarkable accomplishments of several of his German-speaking colleagues among the secular clergy, without whose seemingly tireless energies the Church across southern Minnesota might well have languished: George Keller, Valentine Sommerreisen, and, perhaps most notable of all, Alexander Berghold of New Ulm.[10] All his life Ireland kept a soft spot in his heart for pioneers like these; nevertheless, his Americanizing principles led him to the conviction that the glory days of

---

8. See the statistics in Colman J. Barry, *The Catholic Church and German Americans* (Milwaukee, 1952), 5–7.

9. See chapter 4, above.

10. See chapters 8 and 6, above.

Berghold and the others had passed and that they should be honored only in remembrance. He was scarcely home from the council when he provided a small but significant signal that he had resolved to expand that conviction into policy.

The School Sisters of St. Francis, founded in 1874 and composed mostly of German immigrants, had been invited by Bishop Grace to establish their motherhouse in the diocese of St. Paul. By 1884, when they already staffed a dozen parochial schools in southern Minnesota, they had decided to accept Grace's proposal. They purchased property in the Mississippi River town of Winona and put up a modest building in which they intended to house a girls' school and their own headquarters. In January 1885 Ireland, now the bishop, arrived at the new St. Mary's Convent and Academy to preside over the dedication ceremonies. After the Mass he uttered a few conventional pieties: "Inside [this convent] shall reign the peace, the pure joys of the celestial harbor. . . . The world needs more than wealth for its life and happiness. If it had but millionaires, railroads, and stock exchanges, it would be miserable. It needs the refreshing dew of divine grace; it needs the high ideal of moral perfection; and these blessings the religious orders in the Catholic Church give it to a supereminent degree."

Dinner followed the liturgical ceremony and then a tense interview between Ireland and the mother-founder of the order, Alexia Hoell. Were there, the bishop asked, any postulants in the order from Minnesota? A few, Mother Alexia replied. And from Germany? More than a few. Where were the sisters presently teaching? Mostly in predominantly German parishes in Wisconsin and Minnesota. Did not Mother Alexia realize, Ireland said, how important it was that the Church in America shed its foreign image? Mother Alexia, herself German-born, remained noncommittal. He then tersely laid down three conditions to be fulfilled before he would grant permission for the sisters to set up their motherhouse in his diocese: they must accept no more postulants from Europe; no sister could be assigned to teach in a parish without having first attended an American normal school; and finally, the order had to be canonically established as a diocesan community, subject directly to the authority of the bishop.

Mother Alexia, though she may have known little about millionaires and stock exchanges, was a woman of intelligence and spirit. She professed herself ready to compromise and agree to a requirement that young sisters enroll for a time in a teachers' college. But, she said, to acquiesce to the other demands would amount to an unacceptably radical alteration of the order she had founded. Ireland replied with a shrug that in that case he would permit the sisters to operate an academy in Winona but not to locate their motherhouse there. Three years later the sisters had departed Winona for the friendlier climes of Milwaukee. Ireland bought the property they left behind for thirty thousand dollars (they had asked thirty-five thousand) and turned it over to the Sisters of St. Joseph, now governed locally by his sister Ellen, Mother Seraphine, for use as a hospital. This project did not thrive, and in 1894 a different branch of Franciscan sisters purchased the site and began upon it a successful women's college.[11]

The small drama played out in a nuns' parlor in Winona revealed two fundamental elements of John Ireland's Americanist program. "Foreignism" in the American Church had to be eliminated posthaste, and the autonomy of the religious orders had to be curbed as much as possible. Indeed, the confrontation with Mother Alexia showed that the two issues merged in Ireland's mind: it was precisely the independence and the international character of the orders, particularly those dominated by tough-minded Germans, that promoted the continuation among Catholics in the United States of what he considered an unhealthy cultural and linguistic separatism. This conjunction was not new to him, but now that he was master in his own right he could deal with it as he saw fit, even though to do so meant repudiating, as in the case of the Franciscan Sisters, an explicit commitment made by his venerated predecessor.

At roughly the same time Bishop Ireland was reminded that another of his basic principles appeared to be perpetually under German and religious threat. Relations between St. Paul and St. John's Abbey had been largely placid and cordial, and, after 1875 when the vicariate of Northern Minnesota had been erected—Rupert Seidenbusch, the first vicar, had been abbot of St. John's[12]—the likelihood of unease between the two seemed more or less remote. Nonetheless, Ireland was intensely irritated when a monk of St. John's, with the splendidly German name of Othmar Erren, published during the winter of 1885 several articles in which he poked fun at those he called "temperance zealots." Too often, in the view of the new bishop of St. Paul, did German-speaking Catholics spearhead the opposition to the total abstinence movement, dismissing it as needful only for shiftless Irishmen who could not

---

11. See M. Francis Borgia, *They Sent Two: The Story of the Beginning of the School Sisters of St. Francis* (Milwaukee, 1965), 81–84, 92–94. The College of St. Teresa was founded by the Franciscan Sisters headquartered in Rochester, Minnesota, the same group that operated the celebrated St. Mary's Hospital in that city. See chapter 8, above.

12. See chapter 9, above.

control their appetites. It was not a long step for him to place German and religious and anti-temperance into one disreputable category, and he took some satisfaction in denying Father Othmar faculties to function as a priest in the diocese of St. Paul.[13]

Of course a large foundation like St. John's, representing the most ancient and revered order in the Latin Church, was a far more formidable opponent than a little group of nuns struggling to start their congregation. And besides, Ireland was not without sympathy for the Benedictine ideal, at least in the abstract. "Better far, in my opinion," he wrote that same year, "for Religious Orders, and for the Church if the Benedictine Rule had remained more than it has, the type of religious life." The Benedictines, he added, had been content to see themselves as an "element of activity, of strength in the Church," and had not aimed as had the Jesuits and Redemptorists—the two orders for which he cultivated a special antipathy—"consciously or unconsciously to be the whole Church."[14] Even so, he looked with stern disfavor upon the monks' continued missionary activities—"their incursions over Northern Minnesota," as he called them—when such work should now be done by the secular clergy, while the monks confined themselves to tending their farms, lecturing in their classrooms, and chanting the Divine Office in choir. When the abbot of St. John's asked, as "a personal favor," that Benedictine sisters be allowed to staff the school maintained by the German congregation of the Assumption parish, Ireland stonily refused: "The matter," he said without elaborating, "is too important for religion in St. Paul" to accede to the abbot's request.[15]

The German Catholic community, locally and nationwide, was not to be trifled with. This was the case not only because of its relative economic and social stability—alluded to often in these pages—but also because of organizational skills not infrequently designated as characteristically Teutonic. Virtually every German parish, besides promptly opening a school in which the immigrants' children were taught the language and customs of the old country, set up as well a collection of self-help associations, from modest credit unions and insurance programs to reading rooms and athletic clubs. And this penchant for collective action manifested itself on the national level too. As early as 1855 the Catholic Central Verein of America, designed to consolidate

13. Barry, *Worship*, 169–170. See also Bland, *Hibernian Crusade*, 136, 138–139.
14. Ireland to the English Benedictine Aidan Gasquet, quoted in Shane Leslie, *Cardinal Gasquet* (New York, 1953), 34.
15. Ireland to Edelbrock, April 10, 1885, MHS, JIP, roll 22.

local benevolent societies and thereby to present a united front in defense of the German immigrant's religious faith and civic status as he settled in an essentially Protestant and secular culture, was founded in Baltimore. Every year the Verein held a general assembly, and, with the enormous influx of Germans into the United States after the Civil War, its deliberations and policies took on ever more significance. By the 1880s there had evolved out of this organization the Deutsch-Americaner Priester-Verein as well as the annual celebration of *Katholikentage,* a massive congress of clerics and laymen, modeled on the rallies organized by Catholics in Germany during the *Kulturkampf* of the 1870s.[16] Undergirding this manifold assertion of unity and nationalist interdependence was a flourishing German-language press, not only within the so-called (by its adversaries) "iron triangle"—dioceses from St. Louis to Milwaukee to Cincinnati, where German communicants were particularly numerous—but across the country. Indeed, John Ireland had one such newspaper, *Der Wanderer,* published in his own St. Paul backyard.[17]

For those who, like Ireland, were anxious to hasten the process of the immigrants' Americanization, the robust health of the German Catholic community with all its institutional vigor was gall and wormwood. And, to be sure, he was not without allies: John Keane, bishop of Richmond and shortly to be named rector of the new Catholic University of America; Denis O'Connell, at Baltimore III a mere minor functionary but already a supple diplomat with meaningful Vatican connections; and James Gibbons, archbishop of Baltimore and O'Connell's patron, a cautious man who nonetheless was an Americanizer at heart and whose stature was immensely enhanced when he was awarded a cardinal's red hat in 1886. Gibbons saw to it that O'Connell was appointed rector of the North American College in Rome and, for all practical purposes, the unofficial ambassador of the hierarchy of the United States to the Roman curia. But O'Connell was never an unideological arbiter of the views of the American bishops; he was rather a thorough Americanizer, with whom John Ireland formed a very close personal and professional relationship. Perhaps it is not too fanciful to suggest that Ireland played the role of D'Artagnan, while the others were the three musketeers, ever ready—except

---

16. The so-called "culture war" began in 1871 with the passage of anti-Catholic legislation inspired by the great chancellor, Prince Bismarck, on the grounds that the Roman Church was too independent of the newly unified German Empire. The opposition of the Catholic populace, however—predictably well organized—ultimately proved decisive, and by the mid-1880s the objectionable laws had mostly been repealed.

17. See Barry, *German Americans,* 27, 93, 98, and chapter 9, above.

perhaps the ever-prudent Gibbons—to unsheathe their rapiers in behalf of a genuinely American Catholic Church.

On the local front, tension between Ireland and his German subjects remained an ecclesiastical fact of life well into the twentieth century. When approached, for example, in 1888 for approval and a blessing on a Minnesota *Katholikentag,* modeled on the by then well-established national assemblies of German Catholics, the bishop curtly refused, and employed his diocesan newspaper to denounce the project. "These conventions and clerical societies," he wrote, "are based upon lines of foreign races and languages, a most dangerous omen for the peace and oneness of the Church in America. . . . Episcopal approval of the German movement will compel the approval of other national movements as they may arise. And, then, what chaos in the Church?"[18] But the organizers of the event persisted, and the *Katholikentag,* with its festive Masses and parades and innumerable edifying speeches, duly assembled in mid-August at Holy Angels parish in Chaska. And, contrary to his original position, Bishop Ireland was in attendance. His speech to a respectful but skeptical audience candidly put forward the agenda of an Americanizing prelate. He began by extolling the richness of the German literary tradition and by conceding his obligation to provide pastors conversant in the native language of those priests' parishioners. But then, with the skill of an experienced advocate, he focused upon his listeners' most vulnerable sensitivity, their concern for their children.

> Through an exaggerated love of old habits and trans-Atlantic lands, are you to forget the present and the future, and reduce to social inferiority your sons and daughters? Think you, if you follow this course, will they afterwards deem your affection in this regard reasonable and salutary, and will they thank you for services rendered? Your children are Americans; their field for the display of all their activities is America; their hopes and prospects are bound up in the folds of her flag. . . . What I mean by Americanization is the filling up of the heart with love for America and for her institutions. It is the harmonizing of ourselves with our surroundings, so that we will be as to the manner born, and not as strangers in a strange land, caring apparently but slightly for it, and entitled to receive from it but meager favors. It is the knowledge of the language of the land and failing in nothing to prove our attachment to our

---

18. *NWC,* August 10, 1888.

laws, and to adopt, as dutiful citizens, all that is good and laudable in its social life and civilizations.[19]

Notwithstanding this assertion of linguistic priority, Ireland, like all the other American prelates, was obliged to establish "national" parishes in which extraliturgical devotions, sermons, and various social and recreational functions were carried out using the immigrants' native language. One result of this arrangement was a spate of jurisdictional disputes, usually minor, with the "territorial" parishes within whose geographical confines these institutions were located. In 1880 sixteen of the 168 parishes in the diocese of St. Paul were designated as national, mostly German. Two decades later—St. Paul by then a metropolitan see—the number had risen to twenty-six out of 250. The Catholic population during that interval had increased by 100,000, which suggests that Archbishop Ireland impeded the extension of national parishes as much as he could.[20] He also indulged in other administrative ploys in order to curb what he considered excessive nationalism. Thus he routinely appointed German-speaking Slovenians as pastors of German parishes, especially the large and thriving ones within the Twin Cities.[21] But for all Ireland's prestige and forcefulness, the archbishop could not ignore the ethnic facts on the ground. At the turn of the century, for example, St. Agnes parish, in the "Frogtown" section of St. Paul adjacent to the capitol, was comprised of more than a thousand German families, almost all working class and almost all devoted to the religious traditions of their forefathers. By 1909, to be sure, as the older generation of immigrants was gradually passing away, the linguistic divide had narrowed considerably. Even so, when the cornerstone for a new St. Agnes church was laid, Ireland prudently designated a German-speaking bishop to preach at the dedication ceremony.[22]

Ireland's bias may also have manifested itself in the fact that so many of the priests he found occasion to complain about had German surnames.

---

19. For a full treatment of the Chaska *Katholikentag,* see Barry, *German Americans,* 115–120.

20. See the statistical tables in Jay P. Dolan, ed., *The American Catholic Parish,* 2 vols. (New York, 1987), 2:382–401

21. See Reardon, *Diocese of St. Paul,* 260, and Richard J. Schuler, *History of the Church of Saint Agnes of Saint Paul, Minnesota (1887–1987)* (St. Paul, 1987), 21–22.

22. Wingerd, *Claiming the City,* 72–73. The preacher was James Trobec, bishop of St. Cloud. In choosing him for the festive occasion, however, Ireland did not altogether diverge from his general policy. Trobec had been pastor of St. Agnes till his promotion to the hierarchy in 1897; he was Slovenian, not German, by birth.

Father Wenn, for example, the pastor at the hamlet of Loretto, alleged by his parishioners to be an habitual drunkard, used to stand on the back steps of the church and, they claimed, urinate into the cemetery, among the graves of "our beloved dead." Father Keul "ruined three young women" in three years, the archbishop asserted. "The man is radically bad. He brought one woman into the sanctuary, put on his stole, and 'married' himself to her." Father Stultz of Shakopee quarreled with Mr. Schneider, a parishioner, over a contested will. When Mr. Schneider's wife, who spoke only German, became bedridden, Schneider demanded that Stultz come to his farm and hear her confession. "The wife does not care what priest comes, but the old man declares that it must be Stultz, just because Stultz will not come. . . . I requested Father Stultz to go. I commanded. I threatened. . . . Invoking canon law and theology, he said he could not absolve Mrs. Schneider for reasons known only to himself. . . . [They] are both hard-headed Germans," Ireland concluded dismissively, "and neither will give in; each one is bound to conquer."[23] These cases were by no means characteristic of the German clergy, nor did Ireland maintain that they were. Even so, his adamant insistence on rapid Americanization left many a priest in a kind of ecclesiastical limbo. A tragic casualty was that most distinguished of pioneer missionaries, Alexander Berghold.[24] At the end of 1890 he resigned his pastorate in New Ulm in protest at what he considered the undermining of his apostolate to the German-speaking. His priestly life thereafter was spent in a variety of posts around the country, and he even returned to Minnesota for a time, before retiring to his native Austria in 1907. Curiously, he and John Ireland, each so gifted in his own stubborn way, were exactly the same age, having been born and having died within months of each other.[25]

THE DUEL BETWEEN IRELAND THE AMERICANIZER AND THE German Catholic community had, inevitably, national ramifications. The archbishop of St. Paul—as he was after 1888—cheerfully assumed a leadership role in a campaign the parameters of which went far beyond the vagaries of

---

23. Erik to Martinelli, January 18, 1897; Ireland to Satolli, September 5, 1896; and Ireland to Martinelli, January 29, 1897; Secret Vatican Archives, papers of the Apostolic Delegation to the United States (ASV-DASU), St. Paul, fascicles 12, 14, and 19.

24. See chapter 6, above.

25. See the paper by La Vern J. Rippley, St. Olaf College, Northfield, Minnesota (rippleyl@stolaf.edu).

Fathers Wenn and Keul or even the estrangement from the high-minded Alexander Berghold. And, though it may not have been predictable at the time, *l'affaire allemande* led during the 1880s and 1890s into a host of other contentious issues. Among these were the status of the parochial versus the public schools, the definition of what constituted a "secret society" hostile to the Roman Church, the need for and indeed the character of a national Catholic university, the rights and privileges of the religious orders vis-à-vis the diocesan bishop. All these matters stood open to debate, no less than did the German question itself.

Shortly after the adjournment of Baltimore III the battle lines began to form, with strong personalities represented in both factions. On one side stood Ireland and his Americanizing allies Keane, O'Connell, and—more hesitantly—Cardinal Gibbons, along with the new and vibrant American congregation, the Paulists, the foot soldiers of the total abstinence movement, and by and large those both clerical and lay who identified themselves, for whatever reason and with whatever meaning they gave the word, as "progressives." Ranged against them were the German-speaking members of the hierarchy, the old religious orders—especially Ireland's *bête noire,* the Jesuits— and two powerful prelates of Irish extraction: Bernard McQuaid, the feisty bishop of Rochester, and his brilliant sometime protégé, Michael Augustine Corrigan, archbishop of New York. Both of them—McQuaid in the pugnacious manner consistent with his burly character, and Corrigan, more feline, more adept with the stiletto than the broadsword—were imbued with resentment at the aggressiveness, as they judged it, of the Americanizers, at their attempts to set the agenda for the Church in the United States without regard to episcopal prerogatives. And similarly hostile were those thinking Catholics who—again, the definition is elusive—called themselves "conservatives." It need hardly be said that the contest between these élite armies in array, so to speak, held little if any interest for the ordinary man and woman in the pew, who mingled their usually simple and straightforward piety, and their lapses therefrom, with overriding concern about the provision of their daily bread and the well-being of their children.

Which was just as well, since much of the struggle became unseemly as it dragged through the 1890s. Principled positions were too often sullied by personal animosity. The highly partisan and competitive press around the country, gleefully scooping up calculated leaks from both sides, reveled in the seemingly endless disputes. One German-language newspaper confidently announced that the archbishop of St. Paul had lost his faith. Ireland's own organ, the *Northwestern Chronicle,* accused the archbishop of Milwaukee of "collusion" with Bismarck's anti-Catholic government in Berlin, while in private St. Paul, with unconscious irony, remarked that his brother in Milwaukee "was no more American than a Huron" and was "thoroughly unfit to be an archbishop."[26] During the battle for control of the newly founded Catholic University of America, the Americanizers hired a private detective to follow a German-born priest-professor and record his drinking habits.[27]

Conspiracies real and imagined flourished. At one point Archbishop Corrigan asserted that Ireland and his "henchmen" were plotting to capture the Church for the Republican Party.[28] Indeed, Ireland was that rarity at the time, a Catholic bishop who publicly adhered to the Republicans because of their commitment—rhetorically at least—to the cause of temperance. But his advocacy of certain New York politicians, imprudently and in person, brought forth the wrath of the tough old bishop of Rochester. "I contend," said McQuaid from the pulpit of his cathedral, "that this coming to New York by the Archbishop of St. Paul, to take part in a political contest, was undignified, disgraceful to his episcopal office, and a scandal in the eyes of all right-minded Catholics. . . . It was to pay a debt to the Republican Party."[29] Ireland for his part indulged in fantasies of his own. He constantly fretted at the malevolence of the powerful "*Dreibund*," by which he meant the Jesuits, the German American bishops, and assorted German sympathizers in the Vatican. Speaking to seminarians in Baltimore in 1896 in praise of the secular priesthood for which they were preparing, he suddenly lashed out at the Jesuits. "In fact," one of his young hearers recalled, "in the heat of the moment and on the dizzy height of climax [sic], he mentioned the order by name, and . . . with a vigorous thrust of his hand, he took us by storm when he uttered the words, 'Drive them out!'"[30]

To be sure, beneath these rhetorical flourishes and excesses, displayed by exuberant personalities, lay genuinely substantive differences of opinion. But resolution of them or even some sort of compromise was not obtainable *en scène*. Ultimate authority, to which all the contestants were committed, lay with the bureaus and departments of the Roman curia, which by the 1880s

---

26. Ireland to Gibbons, July 2, 1891, Archives of the Archdiocese of Baltimore (AAB).

27. See O'Connell, *John Ireland*, 432–435.

28. Corrigan to McQuaid, October 13, 1892, quoted in Frederick J. Zwierlein, *Letters of Archbishop Corrigan to Bishop McQuaid and Allied Documents* (Rochester, 1946), 152.

29. Quoted in Frederick J. Zwierlein, *The Life and Letters of Bishop McQuaid*, 3 vols. (Rome, 1925), 3:207–210.

30. Copy of Ireland's remarks in ASV-DASU, St. Paul, fascicle 10.

had taken unto itself more direct universal decision making than ever before in the long history of the papacy. Consequently, American bishops' lobbying of Vatican officials was an incessant, and not always edifying, feature of these years. John Ireland had first seen Rome as a wide-eyed tourist in 1870; twenty years later his lengthy visits to Denis O'Connell's seminary on the Via dell'-Umiltà had become routine. Bernard McQuaid, who often chided Ireland for his absences from St. Paul, once spent ten uninterrupted months in that same residence.[31] And in between such personal appearances in the corridors of power, petitions, letters, newspaper cuttings, and, in short, a veritable deluge of American paper inundated the Vatican post boxes.

By and large the Roman bureaucrats handled these volatile personalities and their quarrels with aplomb. They were for the most part well-trained in the arts of administration, and some of them—including the pope elected in 1878, Leo XIII—could fairly be called skilled diplomats. Puzzled as they often were by what seemed to them the heedlessness of the American bishops—and annoyed at their carelessness in observing the precise norms of the canon law—the cardinal-prefect of Propaganda and other ranking officials took care not to try to impose solutions upon the contending factions. They were content rather to see themselves as referees, and, in the venerable tradition of diplomacy, to let the passage of time work out at least some of the contentious issues. That such a policy included a tendency to imply on one occasion that this American party was in ascendancy in Rome and on another to imply the opposite, suggests not so much old-world cynicism as the standard procedure rulers have adopted toward their subordinates since time immemorial.

Nevertheless, it was not insignificant that the pope and his aides, for all their sophistication, were to a man thoroughly European in their intellectual and political orientation. They found it difficult to grasp the essence of the new society that had been created across the Atlantic. For instance, no greater bugbear existed in the minds of Vatican officials than the heinousness of so-called "secret societies." Nor was such a negative judgment uncalled for: the Masonic lodges that had flourished in Italy, France, Austria, and elsewhere since the eighteenth century had been explicitly anticlerical and, in many cases, antitheistic. The lodges had gained great political influence, especially in the Latin countries of Europe, not by reason of their numbers but by their recruitment of large swathes of the ruling classes. In the United States, meanwhile, a plethora of organizations had come into being which did indeed indulge in secret rituals of initiation and in mystic symbolism and cryptic

---

31. Keane to Ireland, December 22, 1888, MHS, JIP, roll 4.

handshakes. As far as Rome was concerned, such societies were equivalent to the aggressive Masonry much in evidence across Europe, and not least in Italy. The American bishops, especially the Americanizers, argued that the "secret societies" in the United States operated without hostility toward the Church and had no political ambitions. These organizations and others like them had cultivated self-reliance and had contributed to a more heightened sense of comity; their ceremonies were harmless, playful. But so adamant was the Vatican on this issue that only the most strenuous efforts of O'Connell, Ireland, and especially Gibbons succeeded in convincing the pope that there was nothing Masonic about the Knights of Labor, that this first national labor union, with its huge Catholic membership, maintained "secrecy" out of fear of vengeful employers, not because of any hostility to religion.[32]

This success, however, did not save the Knights of Pythias, the Odd Fellows, or the Sons of Temperance, to Ireland's dismay and anger. "The members of these three societies," he wrote the papal secretary of state, "Catholics and Protestants alike, see them as nothing more than benevolent associations; they do not find in the constitutions or customs of the societies anything opposed to divine, natural, or ecclesiastical law. . . . I am myself of the same opinion. I have examined with care their charters and official books and interviewed their leaders."[33] His letter was not answered, and the condemnations—tersely worded and without explanation—were duly issued. Ireland was reduced to fuming in private to Gibbons: "In what a ridiculous position [American] bishops are placed, when they, the teachers of Israel, know not why those societies, which they must condemn, are worthy of censure! The Lord save us from the Inquisition and its Sallvos [sic]!"[34]

Perhaps the clearest instance of Roman incomprehension about at least some aspects of Catholicism in the United States occurred in 1891, and, unsurprisingly, was occasioned by the German problem. In December of the preceding year, the St. Raphaelsverein held a conference in Lucerne, Switzerland.[35] This organization, with its chapters across western Europe, had long been active in providing various kinds of assistance to emigrants (named for the Archangel Raphael, patron of travelers). Its leading light and the presider at the Lucerne gathering was Peter Paul Cahensly, a respected German politi-

---

32. For a full treatment see John Tracy Ellis, *The Life of James Cardinal Gibbons*, 2 vols. (Milwaukee, 1951), 1:486–546.

33. Ireland to Rampolla, December 30, 1894, Secret Vatican Archives, Secretariat of State (ASC-SdiS), 1897, fascicle 3.

34. Ireland to Gibbons, December 7, 1894, and March 4, 1895, AAB.

35. For a full treatment see Barry, *German Americans*, 131–182.

cian. Devout and imbued with an unquestionable generosity, Cahensly and his colleagues judged it their duty to see not only to the physical and spiritual well-being of their fellow Catholics about to cross the Atlantic but also to help them once they arrived in America. Central to the Verein's program was the conviction that the faith could best be preserved by maintaining as much as possible the language and customs of the old country; indeed, it claimed that as many as sixteen million Catholic immigrants had given up their religion due to the insufficiency of such cultural support. One of the resolutions in what came to be called the Lucerne Memorial, submitted to the pope for his approval and his implementation, touched directly on the sore point of governance.

> It seems very desirable that the Catholics of each nationality, wherever it is deemed possible, have in the [American] episcopate . . . several bishops who are of the same origin. It seems that in this way the organization of the Church would be perfect, for in the assemblies of the bishops every immigrant race would be represented, and its interest and needs would be protected.[36]

"What is the most strange feature in this whole Lucerne movement is the impudence of the men undertaking to meddle under any pretext in the Catholic affairs of America."[37] And this was probably the mildest remark John Ireland offered on what he derisively labeled "Cahenslyism." And Pope Leo in due course rejected the Lucerne recommendations on the grounds that they were "neither opportune nor necessary." Thus his decision addressed only the concrete proposals submitted by the St. Raphaelsverein without adverting to the ideological basis of those proposals. It was also standard administrative procedure. An able ruler, however absolute his power in theory, seldom upsets the governmental machinery in place for the sake of an abstract principle. Leo XIII, an able ruler in many respects, abided by the maxim that it is far preferable to say too little than too much. He did not challenge Cahensly's assumptions or rebut his arguments; he merely declared authoritatively that the solutions Cahensly suggested were impractical. The assertion that the organization of the Church in the United States would have been "perfect" if nationalist quotas determined the selection of bishops, was dismissed, in effect, out of administrative convenience.

---

36. Full text of the Memorial in Barry, *German Americans*, 313–315.
37. Quoted in the *New York Herald*, May 31, 1891.

The pope's chief aide, his highly accomplished secretary of state, Cardinal Rampolla, unintentionally gave vent to the genuine Roman point of view. When Denis O'Connell confronted him to express the outrage of the American hierarchy that the Lucerne Memorial should even receive consideration in the curia, Rampolla replied lightly, "Ah, they are Irish, and of course they would react that way." (In fact, the bishops' outrage was unanimous and included that of the much-castigated archbishop of Milwaukee.) But when O'Connell pressed him, the cardinal replied in a more serious vein: "When these men come to us and request us to look after the interests of their *connazionali* that they say are losing their faith in America, we are bound to hear them."[38]

But Rampolla's very use of the Italian word meaning "fellow countrymen" revealed an assumption as crass as it was presumptuous: the United States was no more than a collection of displaced Europeans, discrete colonies of Germans and Poles and Bohemians, with no national character of its own. Furthermore, there could be nothing peculiarly American about the Church in America, because America was nothing more than a locale—unhappily overflowing with heretics and Masons—where Catholic settlers went when circumstances forced them to go. Naturally such people preferred to retain the customs and language of the country of their origin, and naturally the composition of the hierarchy, in the muddled if well-intentioned judgment of Peter Paul Cahensly, should reflect this aspiration if it would be "perfect." The Lucerne Memorial was drawn up in Europe by Europeans—not a single American was invited to the conference, nor was any American consulted—and then submitted to other Europeans at the Roman curia. American Catholics, it seemed, were children, incapable of sensibly arranging their own affairs. So proud and patriotic a man as John Ireland found this implication intolerable. "We acknowledge," he said solemnly, "the Pope of Rome as our chieftain in spiritual matters, and we are glad to receive directions from him; but men in Germany or Switzerland or Ireland must mind their own business and be still as to ours."[39]

It appears, however, that his vision of a manifest destiny was not universally shared.

---

38. O'Connell to Ireland, June 11, 1891, MHS, JIP, roll 21, and O'Connell to Gibbons, August 3, 1891, quoted in Gerald P. Fogarty, *The Vatican and the Americanist Crisis: Denis J. O'Connell, American Agent in Rome, 1885–1903* (Rome, 1974), 149.

39. Quoted in the *New York Herald*, May 31, 1891.

CHAPTER 13

The Little Red
Schoolhouse

NO PROBLEM SO VEXED JOHN IRELAND AND HIS ALLIES WHO
sought to promote the rapid Americanization of the Catholic immigrants as
did the status of the grammar school within a local and national context. Involved were so many threads of competing interest all tangled together—
financial, legal, confessional. Out of the early days of the Republic had
emerged the ideal of free and compulsory, and hence state-mandated, primary education, not only for cultural and even pragmatic economic reasons
but also as an important means to promote the Jeffersonian precept that only
an informed citizenry can guarantee the healthy functioning of a democratic
society. That this ideal had become a national assumption was testified to by
the legislature of Minnesota Territory, which promptly established school districts to provide basic education for all children—and this when the total
population numbered only a few thousand scattered over a vast area.[1]

For the Catholic immigrant, however, just ashore from the steamboat
docked at the Jackson Street landing, a difficulty soon presented itself. As he
had to come to terms with a dominant Protestant culture in the workplace, so
his children—highly impressionable as all children are—were forced to do so
every day in the classroom. Nor was his uneasiness without foundation.[2] The
first territorial Superintendent of Education was the Reverend E. D. Neill, a
Presbyterian minister. He proclaimed in his inaugural statement an intention
to maintain a system of genuinely neutral schools, the textbooks employed in
which would be "unobjectionable to any of the various classes of citizens" and

---

1. See chapter 3, above.
2. For what follows see Robert Packard, "Church-State Relationships in Education in Minnesota: 1850–1890" (Master's thesis, St. Paul Seminary, 1958).

313

none of them "calculated to arouse any religious prejudice." But hard-line Protestants were not in the mood for neutrality; these were the days of the bitter if brief ascendancy of the anti-immigrant Know-Nothing Party, and Neill's apparent attempt to appease the French and Irish papists drew sharp criticism. The Catholics, for their part, remained suspicious, and by 1853 they had opened three schools of their own.

The financial strain was extreme, however, and so early that year Bishop Cretin persuaded a friendly legislator to introduce an amendment to the education bill which would allow any parochial school—properly organized, open to inspection, and enrolling at least twenty-five pupils—to petition and receive state support in proportion to the number in regular attendance.[3] If at first the prospects for passage seemed bright, by the spring many voices were raised insisting that the proposal was "un-American." An editorial in a St. Paul newspaper expressed this view without embellishment: "No man who values the permanence of our free institutions, who believes our nation's greatness and prosperity attributable to the prevalence of Protestant principles, should for a moment in any manner countenance any such bill of abominations."[4] Superintendent Neill denounced the amendment too, though in rather more temperate language. From his pulpit he laid out several reasons for his opposition, but fundamental was the ideological conviction—which would be reiterated over and over and long after the preacher had passed from the scene—that denominational schools were fatally divisive and therefore support for them out of taxes was a kind of civic self-destruction that would undermine the integrity of the nation. In a country professing many creeds, the state must be the educator.[5] By no means did this apodictic judgment settle the issue, but the proverbial line in the sand had been drawn.

The controversy erupted again in 1867. By then John Ireland was rector of the St. Paul cathedral, and the fiery John Crosby Devereux was editor of the newly founded *Northwestern Chronicle*.[6] By then, too, St. Paul was no longer a frontier village but a bustling and rapidly growing town with its own school board. Devereux opened the hostilities by a series of editorials in which he complained of the injustice that Catholics should be taxed to support an educational system "from which we gain no benefit. . . . Be it then our business to agitate the matter, and to obtain a change in the school laws. . . . We believe

---

3. See chapter 4, above.
4. *St. Paul Pioneer,* May 5, 1853.
5. Packard, "Church-State," 2–13.
6. See chapter 9, above.

that not a few of the Protestant denominations would assist [in the effort]"—
another line in the sand. Several readers of the *Chronicle* responded favorably; one of them wrote that since the cathedral educated nine hundred
children, all of them citizens of St. Paul, and so relieved the city of considerable expense, it would be only just to subsidize the school at "say, $3000 per
annum."[7] A furor of contentious debate followed and was eagerly taken up by
the fiercely partisan newspapers. To the chagrin of Father Ireland and the delight of that fervent Democrat, John Devereux, it appeared that editors aligned
with the Republican Party were particularly opposed to any change in the status quo.

As the summer began, the dispute moved out of the pages of the papers
toward a more direct confrontation. On June 24 a petition signed by eight
hundred St. Paul Catholics was submitted to the school board. The document
contained the usual arguments: We are being taxed without representation;
our fellow citizens benefit from us paying for the education of a thousand
children of ours while also helping to pay for the education of theirs. So we
shall happily place our schools under the board's jurisdiction for all secular
subjects, and the board may control the textbooks and subject matter in such
courses and examine our teachers for competence. In the light of such concessions the board should recognize our schools, "and give to them, according to the number of scholars, their due proportion of the school fund." This
policy, the petition asserted somewhat vaguely, was not without precedent. As
the editors around town took up the cudgels again, the board appointed a
committee to examine the matter. The result was predictable. The requested
change in funding procedures, read the committee's report—approved by the
full board by a vote of eight to one—"necessarily involves the taxation of the
citizen for the propagation of religious tenets conflicting with his own, a
proposition manifestly opposed to all our ideas of civil and religious liberty."[8]

Two years later the battle was joined again. John Ireland and Clemens
Straub, the Benedictine pastor of the Assumption parish, signed a letter addressed to the school board asserting that "fully one half of the children of
St. Paul can derive no benefit from the present system of Public Education."
Surely, they wrote, some honorable solution can be found with "the rights of
your Board guarded . . . [and yet] no impediment placed in the way of Catholic parents participating in the privileges of the school system." In accord with
the usual procedure, a committee of three was designated to reply, this one

---

7. *NWC,* March 30 and April 20, 1867.
8. Packard, "Church-State," 23–34.

chaired by the redoubtable Henry Sibley. Its recommendation was startling: the Assumption and cathedral schools, Sibley wrote on August 2, 1869, should be transferred to the supervision of the school board, free of rent during school hours, and that "the said schools should be subject, in all things, to the rules and regulations of the Board." A minority report, however, prepared by the superintendent of schools, John Mattocks, raised the familiar objections about subsidizing a particular cult. Once more the newspapers leapt into the fray, the *St. Paul Press* mounting an especially vitriolic campaign. Its editor argued that if Catholics regarded "all adolescent ciphering as sacrilegious which is not duly consecrated by Pater Nosters and Ave Marias, they are at full liberty to indulge in these eccentricities at their own expense. . . . In this country the State regards education and religion as fundamentally distinct."[9] Devereux replied with equal heat, as did, more moderately, other papers. But the *Press* felt the bit in its teeth. This attempt to secure public money locally for Catholic schools

> is but one step of a general, organized, persistent movement . . . under the sanction and by the direction of the Papal See, having for its avowed object the overthrow of our American system of free schools, itself a single cycle of a far larger movement, which aims at the subversion of free government of the State to the always aspiring domination of the Catholic Church.[10]

John Ireland's rejoinder was swift. He ignored the geopolitical fantasies that the *Press* had proffered and adhered instead to the problem at hand. He recognized that resistance to Sibley's majority report among even generally well-disposed citizens of St. Paul sprang from the fact that even if the Assumption and cathedral schools were under supervision of the board, they would still be staffed by Catholics and promote a Catholic ambiance. Nor did he try to evade this crucial consideration.

> A Catholic atmosphere would be thus created, and a Catholic atmosphere you do not wish. Of course you do not wish it. Be, however, consistent. Will you deny that in the public schools as they are the atmosphere is Protestant? The teachers, with scarcely an exception, are Protestants; the children are Protestants; the Protestant Bible is read; a thorough Protes-

---

9. *St. Paul Press*, June 8, 1869.
10. *St. Paul Press*, August 3, 1869.

tant explanation is given of Catholic facts and words; the Superintendent [Mattocks] is a Presbyterian minister; and in your State meetings Catholics are called Papists, Romanists, etc., etc. Do what we will, we can never create an atmosphere as intensely Catholic as this one is Protestant.[11]

Sibley's committee report was rejected by ten votes to four.[12]

In the run-up to the elections to the school board, scheduled for the spring of 1871, there was much partisan maneuvering. Rumors surfaced that Ireland was conspiring to seize the office of superintendent for himself, or at the very least that he was secretly directing the political campaign. The *Press* quoted one "respectable and intelligent Catholic Irishman," a Ramsey County civil servant: "It is no use to talk to me or any of us Catholics about this matter. We are acting under orders from Father John, who is acting under orders from Baltimore. What Father John tells me to do, I will do."[13] This broadside was too much for the more respectable—and staunchly Democratic—*Pioneer*, which labeled the *Press*'s remarks as "the stereotyped ravings of a dirty-shirted Know-Nothing politician of old."[14] And Ireland himself, writing in the third person, used sarcasm in rebuttal:

Father Ireland has far too much to do to dream of outside work. But where is the logic? The horror! A priest in the schools! Have we not a minister in them—ministers in fact in most of our institutions? . . . Or is not a priest equal to a minister before the Law?[15]

On polling day two Catholics were elected to the board, as was the sympathetic General Sibley, but its sectarian composition remained as before.[16]

In succeeding years other local disputes, notably in Anoka and Stearns counties, kept the issue before the public eye, but the result was only continued wrangling. Finally, in 1877, following a national trend, the Minnesota legislature, after much and sometimes ludicrous debate, moved to exclude from public schools all religious teaching and practice, including the reading of the Bible. Some of the solons, however, professed to be alarmed at the moral

---

11. *NWC*, August 7, 1869.
12. See Packard, "Church-State," 37–45.
13. *St. Paul Press*, March 28, 1871.
14. *St. Paul Pioneer*, March 29, 1871.
15. *NWC*, April 1, 1871.
16. See Packard, "Church-State," 47–53.

consequences of this legislation, and so an act passed both houses by large majorities authorizing, but not requiring, teachers to give instruction in the fundamentals of "social and moral science," so as to cultivate among their pupils

> industry, order, economy, punctuality, patience, self-denial, health, purity, temperance, cleanliness, honesty, truth, justice, politeness, peace, fidelity, philanthropy, patriotism, self-respect, hope, perseverance, cheerfulness, courage, self-reliance, gratitude, pity, mercy, kindness, conscience, reflection and the will [sic].[17]

THE LEGISLATIVE MANDATE TO SUBSTITUTE AN INCULCATION of a host of natural virtues—including ones so vague as "reflection and the will"—for the reading of the King James Bible reflected the gradual change in the character of American Protestantism. Even so, certainly most Americans would have agreed that the public schools still advocated, and ought to have advocated, those civic values that were at once an American and a Protestant heritage. For Catholics, however, with their claim to a monopoly upon the fullness of Christian revelation, this solution was no solution. There could be no genuine education without true—that is to say, without their—religion as an integral part of it. So American Catholics, poor as they were, continued doggedly, and increasingly, to build and maintain schools of their own. In 1884, on the eve of the Third Plenary Council of Baltimore, there were twenty-five hundred of these institutions across the country, with an enrollment of half a million pupils. The fathers of the council, with little disagreement as to the substance of the matter, accelerated this process by forsaking the hortatory language of earlier legislation and instead commanding that every parish in the United States open a school within two years.[18] Yet the ideal of every Catholic child in a Catholic school remained beyond attainment. Even in the most prosperous dioceses less than half the potential clientele could be served in Catholic institutions. Had it not been for the self-sacrifice of the religious sisters, who staffed the schools for less than a pittance, the idea could not even have been contemplated.

---

17. Quoted in Folwell, *Minnesota*, 4:172.
18. For a full treatment see Philip Gleason, "Baltimore III and Education," *U.S. Catholic Historian* 4 (1985): 273–306.

For John Ireland the school question involved something of a dilemma. In his jurisdiction as bishop and archbishop he had to face the same fiscal reality he had encountered as a parish priest. He was committed to the mandate of Baltimore III, but in his heart he knew that it could never be fulfilled. In his mind lurked a doubt of another kind, too. He recognized that the little red public schoolhouse was the key instrument in furthering the Americanization process. If the immigrant parents clung to the customs and language of the old country, their children could be weaned away from such anachronisms simply by learning the three Rs in a mixed social setting. Yet, theologically it was impossible for him to overlook the dangers to the youngest in his flock either of old-fashioned Protestant proselytizing or newfangled secular naturalism. And then there was the larger philosophical question: Who was the primary educator of the child? Was it the parent or the state or the Church? Or perhaps a combination of all three? Ireland was finding out in any case how difficult it was to be so fervently Catholic and so fervently American, especially now that he had assumed a position of national leadership.

A stern reminder came in 1890 from the neighboring state of Wisconsin. On March 13, the archbishop of Milwaukee and his suffragans—all three German-born—issued a statement to the press. Purporting to speak in the name of the 350,000 Catholics living in Wisconsin, they raised a formal objection to a piece of legislation popularly called the Bennett Law, which had gone into the state's statute book the year before.

> After calm and careful study of the Bennett Law, we hold that it interferes with the rights of the church and of parents. We, moreover, conscientiously believe that the real object of this law is not so much to secure a greater amount of instruction in and knowledge of the English language as rather to bring our parochial and private schools under the control of the state. And in this attempt, we cannot but apprehend the ultimate intention—gradually to destroy the parochial school system altogether.[19]

The Bennett Law had indeed mandated compulsory school attendance for children between the ages of eight and fourteen as well as classes to be taught in English. Its strong penal provisions—a law "fairly bristling with threats of prosecutions and fines," as the bishops put it—clearly aimed at hastening the

---

19. For quotations here and below, see Robert J. Ulrich, "The Bennett Law of 1889: Education and Politics in Wisconsin" (Ph.D. dissertation, University of Wisconsin, 1965), 214–217.

Americanization process, a goal with which John Ireland could not but sympathize. Perhaps he also noted a hint of things to come when in the midst of their manifesto the three bishops shifted their argument to a different, more ideological ground: the right to educate lay not with the state but with parents who might, or might not, delegate that right to the state. If not, "all the state can demand of such parents for the common good, is that they do not allow their children to grow up in such ignorance or to acquire such knowledge as would make useless or dangerous citizens of their children."

The tone of this proclamation, at any rate, could not have pleased Archbishop Ireland, determined as he was to resolve the school question in a manner that did not open a breach between Catholics and the larger American society. It would have been impolitic for him, however, to have commented publicly, and he did not. Instead, in the early summer of 1890, as the controversy in Wisconsin waxed hotter—the Bennett Law had been the work of a Republican administration, and the Democrats, in an election year, scented an issue in the widespread discontent with it—he sent a private query to the pastor of St. Peter's in Poughkeepsie, New York. Since 1873 that parish had maintained an agreement with the local school board whereby the board rented the parochial school buildings for a nominal fee, operated in them every day a legally recognized public school, appointed and certified the teachers, and paid all ordinary expenses. Control of the facilities reverted to the parish after regular school hours, during which time religious instruction could be given.[20]

The arrangement in Poughkeepsie was only the most notable among not a few similar plans prevailing in various isolated places around the country, and not unlike what Ireland had proposed to the St. Paul board twenty years earlier. The town, the St. Peter's pastor explained, in effect operated two schools in the parish, staffed by five Sisters of Charity and several "Catholic young ladies, mostly graduates of the high school." The nuns were "much respected" in the community, and one of them served as principal of both schools. "There is no Catholic on the Board. There is simply an understanding to employ Catholic teachers. It is hardly in conformity with law to make or expect a contract to this end." The board was apolitical, balanced evenly between Republicans and Democrats. All of Poughkeepsie formed one school district, "so that Catholic children may come [to St. Peter's] from every part."

---

20. See Daniel F. Reilly, *The School Controversy (1891–1893)* (Washington, D.C., 1943), 74–76.

The pastor was convinced that the overwhelming majority of Protestants in the town supported the program, and that a referendum, if held, would prove that contention. For evidence he enclosed for Ireland's perusal testimonials from three prominent citizens.[21]

The timing of Ireland's inquiry about the details in Poughkeepsie was not accidental. The annual convention of the National Educational Association was scheduled to meet in St. Paul that summer of 1890, and the archbishop had been invited to address it. Or rather the local organizing committee had invited him to speak, only to have the president of the association cancel the invitation. This executive intrusion may have appeared prudent to the president, and at any rate it testified to how intensely controversial the parochial school issue had become. But it caused only anger and consternation among the group in St. Paul charged with arranging for the comfort and well-being of the twenty thousand delegates expected to arrive from all over the country. The president was informed in no uncertain terms that John Ireland was the most popular figure in the Twin Cities and probably in the state of Minnesota, and that an insult to him guaranteed a sour local welcome to the convention. The president accordingly hurried off to St. Paul—he was a bureaucrat from Kansas—to repair the damage he had done, and in person abjectly offered Ireland a second invitation, which the archbishop, with no show of irritation, accepted.[22]

The session of the convention to which Ireland delivered his address, "The State School and the Parish School—Is Union Between Them Impossible?", met in the People's Church on Thursday, July 10, 1890, at nine o'clock in the morning.[23] He shared the platform with five professional educators, one of whom also read a prepared paper while the others made up a discussion panel. He spoke for about twenty or twenty-five minutes, far more briefly than was his custom. The relative brevity served him well; the speech, while it displayed its share of rhetorical flourishes, was more tightly drawn and less repetitious than many of Ireland's other famous discourses.[24] It also proved that he could speak effectively before a potentially hostile audience, and not just before docile congregations in his cathedral or adoring throngs at temperance rallies.

---

21. Nilan to Ireland, June 23 and 27, 1890, MHS, JIP, roll 4.
22. Ulrich, "Bennett Law," 365–366.
23. Text in John Ireland, "State Schools and Parish Schools," in *The Church and Modern Society*, 2 vols. (St. Paul, 1904), 1:215–232.
24. See chapter 10, above.

"I beg leave to make at once my profession of faith," he began. "I declare unbounded loyalty to the constitution of my country. I desire no favors. I claim no rights that are not in consonance with its letter and spirit." Then he moved on to reassure his listeners further, but also to stake out the basic grounds of his argument.

> I am a friend and an advocate of the state school. In the circumstances of the present time I uphold the parish school. I sincerely wish that the need for it did not exist. I would have all schools for the children of the people to be state schools. . . . The child must have instruction, and in no mean degree, if the man is to earn for himself an honest competence, and acquit himself of the duties which, for its own life and prosperity, society exacts from its members. . . . Free Schools! Blest indeed is the nation whose vales and hillsides they adorn. . . . No tax is more legitimate than that which is levied in order to dispel mental darkness. . . . Instruction is so much needed by the citizen for his own sake and that of society that the parent who neglects to provide for the education of the child sins against the child and against society, and should be punished by the State.

Then, lifting his fist high above his head, John Ireland spoke the line more often quoted perhaps than any uttered in a long life of public pronouncements: "The free school of America! Withered be the hand raised in sign of its destruction!"

Why then, he asked rhetorically, the parish school? Why specifically have American Catholics placed 750,000 of their children outside the common educational system? "The state school . . . as it is at present organized . . . tends to eliminate religion from the minds and hearts of the youth of the country." No longer did he maintain that the public schools, with ministers either directing or deeply influencing policy, were centers of subtle Protestant proselytizing. The adversaries now were those who had excluded all religion and supplanted it with a curriculum dedicated to the encouragement of industry, punctuality, and politeness, as the Minnesota legislature had decreed. "I am Catholic, of course, to the tiniest fiber of my heart, unflinching and uncompromising in my faith." But "believe me, my Protestant fellow-citizens, I am absolutely sincere, when I declare that I speak for the weal of Protestantism as well as for that of Catholicism. . . . Let me be your ally in warding off from the country irreligion, the destroyer of Christian life and Christian civilization."

Secularists and unbelievers will demand their rights. I concede their rights. I will not impose upon them my religion, which is Christianity. But let them not impose upon me their religion, which is secularism. Secularism is a religion of its [own] kind, and usually a very loud-spoken and intolerant religion. Non-sectarianism is not secularism, and, when non-sectarianism is intended, the secularist sect must not claim for itself the field which it refuses to others.

That distinction, he argued, must form the basis of a solution to the school question. Since the Christians in the United States were so adamantly divided, "a compromise becomes necessary. Is it not a thousand times better to make a compromise than to let secularism triumph and own the country?" In the name of "the spirit of American liberty," Ireland offered two concrete alternatives as means of "putting an end to the constant murmurings and bitter recriminations with which our school war fills the land." One possibility, in imitation of the English model, was to "permeate the regular state school with the religion of the majority of the children of the land, be this religion as Protestant as Protestantism can be." A corollary would necessarily follow, that the state "pay for the secular instruction given in denominational schools," so long as the pupils in them met the appropriate scholastic standards.

In Ireland's judgment, this arrangement did not amount to "paying for religious instruction." Neither, he maintained, did his second suggestion. "I would do as Protestants and Catholics in Poughkeepsie and other places . . . have agreed to do, to the entire satisfaction of all citizens and the great advancement of educational interests." He then briefly described the St. Peter's arrangement. "Do not," he concluded, "tell me of difficulties of detail in the working out of either of my schemes. There are difficulties; but will not the result be ample compensation for the struggle to overcome them?" If other, better proposals were put forward, by all means let them be implemented instead. But until something be done, the basic challenge would remain: "Do the schools of America fear contact with religion? Catholics demand the Christian state school. In doing so, they prove themselves truest friends of the school and of the state."

The audience's reaction to Ireland's blunt speech was mixed, but strong rebuttal came to it almost immediately. Among the panelists scheduled to comment on the session's papers was Jesse Thayer, Superintendent of Education for the state of Wisconsin and therefore the officer in charge of enforcing the Bennett Law. He made it clear from the start that he was in no mood for compromise. His remarks were a bitter attack upon the "sectarians" who questioned "that education which relates primarily to the rights, duties, and needs of sovereignty of citizens" belonged exclusively to the state. "[Ireland's] paper," he said, "has complicated [the matter] somewhat, though it has revealed the practical inherent difficulties involved." He plunged on, increasingly biting and sarcastic. Opposition to the Bennett Law, he said, confirmed the suspicion that "the ultramontane jesuitical element of the Roman Catholics in America" was ready to defy the state. If so, Thayer hurled at them an unequivocal warning: "Unless the question that is now up for discussion is settled in harmony with the principles of this government, there will be conflict between the jesuitical hierarchy of the Vatican, armed with the syllabus [of errors], and the American people."[25]

So John Ireland learned at firsthand that his school plan could arouse hostility and conspiracy theories nationally, just as the *St. Paul Press* had taught him locally years before. Secular newspapers around the country, though generally not so acerbic as Thayer, nevertheless emphasized that in the last analysis this Catholic archbishop was demanding tax support for sectarian schools. What his coreligionists thought of it all took a bit more time to discover. Indeed, judgments did not become entirely clear until Ireland attempted to recreate Poughkeepsie in the land of sky-tinted waters.

IN 1890, FARIBAULT, NAMED FOR THE CELEBRATED PIONEER family that had put up a trading post on the site, was a town with a population of about sixty-five hundred, reflecting a rich ethnic and religious mix. Approximately one-third of the residents were Catholic. The original parish, that of the Immaculate Conception, had been formed in 1858. In succeeding years two national parishes had been established, one to serve the French and the other the Germans. These departures had naturally meant a smaller congregation at the mother-territorial parish and a narrower financial base. Immaculate Conception maintained a grammar school with about 150 pupils staffed by Dominican sisters, who also operated a boarding high school for girls.

---

25. Quoted in Ulrich, "Bennett Law," 374–378. The Syllabus of Errors (1864) was a list of eighty propositions drawn from earlier pronouncements of Pius IX. The most famous alleged "error" was the last, which was regularly cited by opponents of Catholicism as a sign of its anachronistic nature: "The Roman Pontiff can and ought to reconcile and adjust himself with progress, liberalism, and modern civilization."

On August 22, 1891—thirteen months after Ireland's speech to the teachers' convention—the Faribault school board held its regularly scheduled meeting.[26] In attendance was James Conry, pastor of Immaculate Conception. Father Conry informed the board that due to financial difficulties his parochial school would not open for the fall term. This news was received with some consternation by most members of the board, since upon them would fall the obligation of providing staff and facilities for an additional 150 to 200 pupils. One of them, however, a Catholic lawyer named M. H. Keeley, was not surprised, because he and Conry, under the unpublicized direction of John Ireland, were about to propose the Poughkeepsie solution.

Conry went on to say that if thrusting a large number of children into the public system would work a hardship on the community, he was prepared to entertain the idea of placing his school under the control of the board, so long as its "integrity" was preserved. When asked to explain this rather obscure proposition, he offered to rent the Immaculate Conception school to the board, to provide faculty for it, and to guarantee that no religious instruction would take place in it during mandated school hours. The encounter apparently was cordial. The board met again on August 26, and debate raged hotly for several hours, after which by a vote of three to two Conry's proposal was tentatively accepted and the priest was asked to submit a statement in writing. This he did, fixing the yearly rent at one dollar, and when the board met for a third time the next day, the vote to approve the arrangement was unanimous.[27]

The archbishop of St. Paul was not mentioned in the course of these negotiations, nor was allusion made to his speech to the National Education Association the summer before. Ireland's directive role was played entirely from behind the scenes. To shun publicity did not accord with his ordinary mode of action, but he knew how delicate and potentially controversial was the issue at hand. That he intended the promising start of the experiment in Faribault as the first step in a larger program seems clear from a remark made to him by his confidant, Lawyer Keeley: "[The board's decision was] a great victory for us, and if we are discreet and judicious in its enjoyment, it may go far towards working out satisfactorily to all citizens the problem of the education of the masses at public expense."[28]

---

26. For what follows see Timothy H. Morrissey, "Archbishop John Ireland and the Faribault-Stillwater School Plan of the 1890s: A Reappraisal" (Ph.D. dissertation, University of Notre Dame, 1975), 168–178, 196–206.

27. Keeley to Ireland, August 27, 1891, MHS, JIP, roll 4.

28. Keeley to Ireland, August 27, 1891 (the second letter of this date), MHS, JIP, roll 4.

Indeed, Ireland moved in this direction straightaway. Stillwater, the picturesque town on the Saint Croix, was roughly twice as populous as Faribault. It too supported a territorial parish, St. Michael's, as well as separate French- and German-speaking congregations. On August 25, three days after Conry's original approach to the Faribault board, the lay trustees of St. Michael's met with Archbishop Ireland at the latter's residence in St. Paul. The parish's financial situation was parlous in the extreme, due at least in part, they suggested, to the recent and mysterious disappearance of the pastor.[29] Ireland accordingly appointed Charles Corcoran, two years ordained after theological studies at the University of Louvain in Belgium, to St. Michael's. Sometime in the middle of September Corcoran sought Ireland's permission to propose the Faribault plan to the Stillwater board. Because of a diphtheria epidemic, the fall term there had been put off till October 5. Thus, when Father Corcoran, with the archbishop's consent, made his presentation, the members of the board were confronted with a situation not dissimilar to that which prevailed in Faribault. The public schools, due to open in a few weeks, faced the prospect of needing to provide staff, space, and facilities for upwards of 350 additional pupils. A local newspaper estimated that to refuse Corcoran's offer would mean an immediate outlay of fifteen thousand dollars, to say nothing of a substantial and permanent addition to the ordinary education budget. Besides, if the Catholic children were absorbed into Stillwater's common schools, the town would receive a proportionate increase of support from the state of Minnesota. These fiscal realities proved decisive to the board which, on October 13, voted unanimously to accept the plan.[30]

The prospects in Faribault continued to appear promising through the autumn and into the winter. Not so in Stillwater. There opposition from non-Catholic groups was in evidence almost from the beginning. The local ministerial association demanded that the contract between St. Michael's and the city be abrogated. In early November, two of the three school board members standing for reelection were defeated, and the third survived at the polls only by announcing his willingness to terminate the agreement. Various Protestant groups in Minnesota and elsewhere adopted resolutions deploring the Faribault-Stillwater plan as a "subtle encroachment of the Roman Catholic Church on the integrity of our public schools." They pointed to the religious symbols—crucifixes, statues, and the like—that decorated the parochial school classrooms, to the religious garb of the nuns who taught there, and to the sectarian instruction that went on in them every day. Ireland was ready to

---

29. See Morrissey, "Faribault-Stillwater," 201–203.
30. See Ireland to Corcoran, October 4, 1891, MHS, JIP, roll 4.

meet one of these objections. "Adhere to your plan," he directed Corcoran, "to have no prayers in school hours, and take down *all* religious pictures. Pictures are in no manner necessary, and let us do without them. . . . Be sure to fix up the yard properly. Get some maps too for the rooms. Make things look somewhat respectable—even if some money has to be expended. Your school will be visited. Let it not seem to be a 'rat-trap.'"[31] Compromise on the other two complaints, however, remained beyond his reach.

It was a quintessential component of John Ireland's character always to look on the bright side. "With a little prudence," he assured Cardinal Gibbons, "we will in a brief time have the whole school question settled in Minnesota. Public opinion favors us." In this instance his sanguine hopes rested upon the personal relationships he imagined he had with the principals involved. "The Members of the School Board[s] in [Faribault and Stillwater] are personal friends of mine," he protested. This claim was unlikely at best, but the archbishop topped it when he brushed aside as legal niceties certain admonitions affirmed by the Minnesota State Superintendent of Schools, D. L. Kiehle.[32] "Mr. Kiehle is a friend of mine," Ireland observed jauntily, "and many things are done and permitted practically in our favor, through one kind of influence or another, that cannot be elevated into the strictness of law, and that at the same time to all appearances must be within the letter of the law."[33]

Yet for all his optimism Ireland's confidence in a network of "friendships" revealed the fatal flaw in the Faribault-Stillwater plan and, for that matter, in its precursor at Poughkeepsie as well. The edifice was, in fact, a house built upon sand. Its success depended upon a gentlemen's agreement, which presumed a willingness to wink at "the strictness of the law." Even leaving aside the contentious matter of the teaching sisters' clothing—which for many

---

31. Ireland to Corcoran, October 29 and 30, 1891, MHS, JIP, roll 4.

32. Kiehle's office sent out a circular on the Faribault plan on October 21, and on November 7 the superintendent issued a fuller statement. See Reilly, *School Controversy,* 84–86. Kiehle visited Faribault and found nothing amiss. The "experiment," he said, was "wise" and "within the law." But his guidelines included several significant caveats, including this one: "If . . . to any class of patrons [the nuns'] presence is obnoxious by reason of the significance of their religious garb, the [local] board must either retire them or require them to wear the usual garb of teachers in the classroom."

33. Ireland, "Memorial" to Ledochowski, n.d. [late March, 1892] (copy), MHS, JIP, roll 4. Miecislaus Cardinal Ledochowski was prefect of the Congregation of the Propaganda.

non-Catholics summed up all that they disliked about the Roman church— there remained other unstated but crucial particulars about which gentlemen might well disagree. For instance, the plan could not work unless the Catholic children were assigned exclusively to the former parochial school rather than to the public school in their respective neighborhoods. Nor could it work if the particular board were to assign non-Catholic teachers to serve the clientele assembled in the former parochial school. But were not such administrative restrictions, if adopted—not to mention the inconveniences involved—equivalent to a religious test? So it seemed to many citizens of Faribault and Stillwater, who were by no means all "anti-Catholic bigots."

Criticism was hardly restricted to non-Catholic elements. Indeed, the archbishop of St. Paul soon had to heed the threat of a crossfire. "I have found myself," he told Gibbons, "in a singular predicament on this whole Faribault matter. I am between two enemies—one Catholic and one Protestant. . . . The concessions to our school, and its continued identity as a Catholic school, are so important that I dare not fully state them—lest I bring down the wrath of anti-Catholic bigots. If I defend the plan against Protestants, Catholic extremists are alarmed."[34] The Catholic "enemies" and "extremists" were, in Ireland's judgment, the usual anti-Americanization suspects: the powerful New York prelates Corrigan and McQuaid, the Jesuits, the Germans—the "Dreibund" as he liked to characterize them or, in faulty Italian, the "Triplici aleanza."[35]

But the resistance to his ideas was wider than that. Influential members of the hierarchy—like Ryan of Philadelphia and Williams of Boston—recalled the commitment they had made at the Third Plenary Council of Baltimore, to press for the establishment forthwith of a parochial school in every parish in the country. Was not Ireland's plan, as their colleagues Corrigan and Katzer of Milwaukee argued, merely a long step toward the secularization of Catholic schools? Not that St. Paul had lagged behind in fulfilling the mandate of Baltimore III: "St. Paul," Ireland pointed out, "though a new diocese, surpasses in that respect even the older and wealthier dioceses of Boston and New York," with St. Paul educating directly one in fourteen of its population, while Boston's rate was one in nineteen and New York's one in twenty.[36] But such com-

---

34. Ireland to Gibbons, October 17, 1891, AAB.

35. Ireland to Gibbons, February 21, 1892, AAB. Ireland employed these terms in reference to the so-called Triple Alliance (1887) whereby, among other more weighty provisions, Germany, Austria, and Italy agreed to reject any restoration of papal civil authority.

36. See the figures in Morrissey, "Faribault-Stillwater," 341–343.

parative statistics were hardly heartening for the nation at large; that at least two-thirds of American Catholic children attended public schools was a proportion bound to increase despite the best efforts of the hierarchy, and it stood as a paramount reason to consider seriously the claims of Faribault-Stillwater, despite "the combined attacks of the German and Jesuit press throughout the world."[37]

But the press could be friendly, too. A few weeks after the initiation of the Faribault plan a pamphlet was published entitled *Education: To Whom Does It Belong?* The author was one Thomas Bouquillon, a professor of theology at the Catholic University in Washington, who specialized in contemporary social issues. He argued that "the State has been endowed with the right of founding the schools that contribute to its welfare." Secular governments share this right with the family and the church, and, although one might designate it accidental when compared to the role of a parent, nonetheless the state enjoys real "authority over education, . . . the right of watching over, controlling, and directing education." Nor can this power be reduced to something "vague and general": every "legitimate association" must be granted the capacity to preserve itself, and in the field of education this means the state has the right of "establishing schools, appointing teachers, prescribing methods and programs of study. . . . Education belongs to the individual [pupil], . . . to the family, to the State, to the Church, to none of these solely and exclusively, but to all four combined in harmonious working for the reason that man is not an isolated but a social being."[38]

John Ireland had in no way prompted Bouquillon's pamphlet, and Bouquillon himself called his work a speculative exercise with no practical application—like Faribault-Stillwater—intended. But so volatile had the issue become that this academic distinction was bound to go unheeded. Basic to the Faribault plan, as well as to the argument put forward in Ireland's speech to the NEA, were the tenets about the state's educational rights spelled out by Bouquillon. If these assumptions appear, by hindsight, straightforward and unexceptionable, that was not necessarily the case at the time. Indeed, Bouquillon advanced a view that certainly sounded novel and, in the judgment of many Catholics—not merely the episcopal opponents of Wisconsin's Bennett Law—posed a threat to the parochial school system they had sacrificed so much to create.

---

37. Ireland to Leo XIII, March 17, 1892, Archives of the Sacred Congregation for the Evangelization of Peoples (*Propaganda Fide*), APF, SOCG, 1042 (1892), 710–712.

38. Quotations taken from the summary in Reilly, *School Controversy,* 108–112.

Within days the first of many rejoinders to Bouquillon came off the press. *The Parent First* was written by a Jesuit ethicist named René Holaind, who was, ominously, a close adviser of Archbishop Corrigan of New York. He argued strongly the point that Bouquillon (and, by implication, John Ireland) erred in granting the state an *intrinsic* right to educate; any power the state enjoyed was *delegated* by parents who, if they chose, could withhold it. On this difference of opinion turned the controversy that followed, in a veritable storm of articles, brochures, editorials, and reviews, of varying length and quality, which lasted into the following summer of 1892.[39]

In the midst of this war of words Ireland took his case to the only court that mattered when all was said and done. "The Holy father is most anxious to see you," Denis O'Connell wrote from Rome. The pope was studying Ireland's speech at the NEA convention. "I said you would be here soon to give light if necessary, and it pleased and relieved him to hear it. . . . Come on then, and roll back this reactionism forever into its grave."[40] By the first week in February he was in residence in Denis O'Connell's seminary. Ireland was in a feisty mood as he lobbied his way through the papal bureaucracy. "I am busy from morning till night, talking, writing, visiting, etc., etc." One cardinal, "an old doctrinaire, wants us to war constantly against the state," while the rector of a prestigious Roman seminary, on the other hand, "endorses all Dr. Bouquillon's ideas, cordially and fully." Two weeks after his arrival he had his first audience with the pope. It lasted an hour. "He was most affectionate, most eulogistic, most familiar." But the eighty-two-year-old pontiff did not seem overly consumed by interest in the American squabbles over education. "[Only] toward the end [of the audience did] he mention Bouquillon. He evidently had been spoken to by an enemy. I argued mildly, and asked permission to write for him some memoranda. He said he would gladly read them, and then talk to me of the contents."[41]

---

39. For an extensive collection of these materials see the Bouquillon Papers, box 2, Archives of the Catholic University of America. Bouquillon himself contributed two more pamphlets.

40. O'Connell to Ireland, November 10, 1891, MHS, JIP, roll 21.

41. Ireland to Caillet, February 14, 1892, MHS, JIP, roll 4, and Ireland to Gibbons, February 21, 1892, AAB. Father Louis Caillet acted as administrator during the archbishop's absence. Much of Ireland's conversation with the pope dealt with the French political situation. Leo XIII was anxious to reach accommodation with the anticlerical Third Republic, the so-called *ralliement* policy. He wanted to enlist the aid of Ireland, who was much admired among that minority of French Catholics ready to endorse the republican regime. See O'Connell, *John Ireland,* 335–338.

MS page of *Wakantanka Ti ke Tanku* (*The Path to the House of God*), Augustin Ravoux's prayer book in the Sioux (Dakota) language.

Catholic Center,
Pembina,
North Dakota
(c. 1835)

Mendota, Minnesota. Built by Rev. Father Gaultier in 1842. Used as a public school on completion of Stone Church erected in 1866 to extend Minnesota Valley Railroad to West St. Paul. Location: 135 feet west of Faribault House at E. of E line of present Omaha R R depot. Built of logs covered with boards and painted a reddish brown. Drawn from descriptions furnished by old settlers and former pupils. Three rooms to left used as a residence

C. M. Crowley 1917

St. Peter, Mendota (1842)

Galtier's log chapel in 1841 *(opposite, above)*
and 1845 *(opposite, below)* and the first cathedral of St. Paul (1850)

Joseph
Cretin
(c. 1850)

St. Paul, Minnesota
(1850)

(below)
Second cathedral of St. Paul
(1855)

"Give way, give way, young warrior / Thou and thy steed give way."

Thomas Grace
(c. 1880)

John Ireland (c. 1880)

Third cathedral of St. Paul (1870)

Interior of the third cathedral of St. Paul (c. 1890)

Girls' division, Cathedral School, St. Paul (c. 1880)

Church of St. Patrick, St. Paul (1884)

Church of St. Vincent, Osseo (c. 1880)

James Shields,
peripatetic soldier,
politician, and
town-founder
(1862)

Church of
St. Patrick,
Shieldsville
(c. 1885)

Church of
St. Stephen,
Minneapolis
(1885)

Church of the
Holy Redeemer,
Marshall
(c. 1890)

Church of
St. Michael,
Stillwater
(c. 1890)

Church of
St. Stephen,
Anoka
(c. 1900)

Immaculate Conception School, Faribault (c. 1900)

St. Paul Seminary (c. 1900)

Church of St. Mary, St. Paul's silk-stocking parish (c. 1900)

A trio of pioneers:
John Ireland,
Mary Mehegan
Hill, Alexander
Ramsey
(c. 1900)

John Ireland
speaking at the
laying of the
cornerstone of
the fourth
cathedral
(1907)

Henry Lauer
(*left*),
contractor for
the fourth
cathedral, and
Isaac Labisonnière,
one of the builders
of Galtier's chapel
of St. Paul
in 1841, at the
cornerstone
laying (1907)

Raising the cross on the façade of the fourth cathedral (1914)

Fourth cathedral of St. Paul (1915)

Interior of the fourth cathedral of St. Paul (c. 1917)

Church and
School of the
Holy Trinity,
New Ulm
(c. 1920)

Church of St. Mary, Marystown (c. 1910)

Church of
St. Anne,
Le Sueur
(c. 1910)

Basilica of St. Mary, Minneapolis (c. 1920)

Social
reformer
John A. Ryan
(*center*)
and siblings
on holiday
in Ireland
(c. 1925)

Entrance, Nazareth Hall (1925)

Nazareth Hall's founder Austin Dowling and first graduating class (1926)

The marble-clad chapel, Nazareth Hall (1925)

Paul Bussard,
principled
liturgist and
swashbuckling
journalist
(c. 1930)

Louis Gales,
media mogul
(c. 1930)

Rosary procession, Minneapolis (c. 1940)

The emblem
that paid for
the Eucharistic
Congress (1941)

Service at the State Fair Grounds, Eucharistic Congress (1941)

James M. Reardon regularly in charge, Eucharistic Congress (1941)

Francis Missia and choristers, Eucharistic Congress (1941)

John
Gregory
Murray
(c. 1950)

Philanthropist
extraordinaire
Ignatius A.
O'Shaughnessy
(1953)

(opposite)
William O. Brady and other
men of power, Langley Air Force Base
(c. 1957)

(below)
225,000 rally at the state capitol for Father Peyton's Rosary Crusade (1958)

Minor seminarians on the eve of an unpredictable future (1959)

But despite Leo XIII's personal benignity—"He is most kind and paternal to me"[42]—the formalities had to be observed. A panel of five cardinals was appointed by the pope to review the school question. But this arrangement did not prohibit Ireland from addressing directly the source of such a committee's authority. "I wish to extend to your Holiness my absolute assurances that I permit not the slightest interference by the State in the teaching of doctrine or morals" in the Faribault and Stillwater schools, despite what "our enemies— some Germans and Jesuits and certain [American] Catholics reluctant . . . to see any reconciliation between the church and the Republic"—may have claimed.[43] So the Roman procedure continued at its characteristically leisurely pace. But the battle in the end had to be won on its own ground, and as the archbishop made his way from one curial office to another a disturbing element was the continuing bad news from Stillwater. Shortly after his departure for Europe the board transferred teachers and pupils from St. Michael's as a step toward integrating them more fully into the public system.[44] Ireland put the best face he could upon this development and explained to Propaganda that "every morning Sister Hyacinthe goes over [to a public school] with her beads and her habit and her children and teaches school."[45] Privately he expressed great alarm, less, however, with the clear breakdown of the plan in Stillwater than with the possible repercussions in Rome. Administrator Caillet had done right, he said, in directing

> Sister Hyacinthe [to] yield to circumstances. After we have recognized the right of the Board, we will more easily obtain favors. . . . Our enemies— the Germans and the Jesuits—watch all details and send word at once to the Roman authorities, so as to prejudice them against us. The plea is— have nothing to do with the State. It is Protestant, it is infidel. Indeed the cry practically is, have nothing to do with the American people.[46]

Resistance in the United States to Ireland's proposals was growing apace, led predictably by Corrigan of New York and the German-speaking bishops, who were as always the most stalwart defenders of the parochial school. Why

---

42. Ireland to Caillet, March 14, 1892, MHS, JIP, roll 4.

43. Ireland to Leo XIII, March 17, 1892, APF-SOCG 1042 (1892), 710–712.

44. Morrissey, "Faribault-Stillwater," 270–272.

45. John Ireland, "Memorial" to Ledochowski [Prefect of Propaganda], n.d. [March 1892], MHS, JIP, roll 4.

46. Ireland to Caillet, February 14, 1892, MHS, JIP, roll 4.

the archbishop consistently and sweepingly included the Jesuits in his "Dreibund" of "enemies" is not so clear; but he was by no means the first high Catholic prelate to look askance at the Society of Jesus. Toward the end of March at any rate he submitted two formal papers to the cardinals of Propaganda: one a defense and an endorsement of Bouquillon's pamphlet, and the other a "Memorial," in which, he wrote, "I simply wish to treat of an Act of Administration in my diocese whereby, following the dictates of my judgment and of my conscience, I did what I believe to have been best for the cause of Catholic education in the two little towns of Faribault and Stillwater." He reviewed once again the thesis of his NEA address and denied the charge that he had publicly deplored "the existence of the parochial school. . . . I deplored the necessity of the Catholics being obliged after paying tax for the support of State schools to maintain again by voluntary contributions schools of their own." After explaining in some detail the financial workings of the Faribault plan, he closed on a note of personal vindication and of warning lest any decision should disparage that most cherished American institution, the little red schoolhouse.

> Unfortunately today the question has been so much ventilated that public opinion regards me as the representative of the party of the Church in America in favor of the government of the United States, and regards my opponents as those who would combine the foreigners in the United States into a danger for the republic. For myself personally, I care very little; for the country at large in case of mistake I have reasons for alarm. We [Catholics] are only one to eight in the United States without wealth or influence, and a larger proportion than that of wealth and population did not prevent a Kulturkampf in Germany.[47]

Once these documents had been registered at Propaganda, Ireland could do nothing except wait. So he went off on a two-week holiday to Sicily, an indulgence he granted himself, as he put it to John Keane, "only after my guns had been fully loaded."[48] Meanwhile, rumors and claims and counterclaims swirled through the press. Archbishop Corrigan and his allies mounted several strongly worded protests to Rome, and for a moment they appeared to

---

47. "Memorial" [March 1892]. The bitter "Kulturkampf" of the 1870s grew out of Bismarck's legislative attempts to curtail the influence of Catholicism in the newly founded German Empire.

48. Ireland to Keane, April 26, 1892, ACUA, Keane Papers.

have succeeded. In early May Corrigan, at a gathering of bishops and clergy in Albany, waved a cablegram over his head and announced, "Faribault system condemned. Special case tolerated." This interpretation rather overstrained the legalese of the decree issued by Propaganda on April 21: "The arrangement entered into by Archbishop Ireland concerning the schools at Faribault and Stillwater, taking into consideration all the circumstances, can be tolerated [*tolerari potest*]."[49] Not surprisingly Ireland put a different construction on the words. "The so-called Faribault plan," he asserted in a published statement,

> is now formally allowed in spite of Germans and Jesuits. The decision is "tolerari potest," which means canonically "is fully allowed." A letter addressed to me in the name of the Propaganda brings out the full practical meaning of the words. The plan is, of course, a departure from the ideal, and in the case of a departure the canonical language is "tolerari potest." But they imply for practice a full approval.[50]

DIFFERING AVENUES OF INTERPRETATION OF PROPAGANDA'S single sentence guaranteed that the battle was not over. To be sure, Ireland had been disingenuous in his Memorial when he said, almost plaintively, that his concern was simply for "two little towns" in Minnesota. In reality, what he aimed at, and appeared to get, was the setting of a precedent that would permit the plan's implementation nationwide. Corrigan argued conversely that the decree required a discrete judgment in each instance and therefore, since such a procedure would have been administratively impossible, "tolerari potest" applied only to Faribault and Stillwater. "No one can have a higher appreciation than I of the zeal, energy, and courage of the Archbishop of St. Paul," he observed. "His friends and admirers would be only too thankful if he possessed in an equal degree the grace of courtesy, the virtue of prudence, and attention to the value of words."[51] But surely Ireland had the better of this aspect of the dispute: if the "arrangement" were to be tolerated or allowed in Minnesota, why should it not be elsewhere?

The brickbats continued to fly back and forth, and protests and recriminations continued to pile up on the desks of the curial officials in Rome.

---

49. See *Acta Sanctae Sedis* (Roma: S. Congr. de Propaganda Fide, 1891–1892) 24: 622–624.

50. Ireland to Byrne, April 27, 1892, in *St. Paul Dispatch*, May 19, 1892.

51. Quoted in Reilly, *School Controversy*, 174.

Weary of the squabbling, Leo XIII in the autumn of 1892 decided to dispatch a special delegate to the United States in time to attend the annual meeting of the American archbishops,[52] scheduled for November in New York. The envoy—Archbishop Francesco Satolli, a special favorite of the pope—was instructed to present to the assembled prelates a list of authoritative directives aimed at putting a quietus to all the contention, or at least dampening it down. Since there was no doubt as to the major source of that contention, and in order to coincide with Satolli's mission, Propaganda had ordered as first item on the meeting's agenda the status of catechetical instruction for children not enrolled in Catholic schools. Once formally introduced by Gibbons, the delegate told the archbishops that it was "the will of the Holy Father" that they join with him in settling the school question for good and all. To accomplish this much-desired objective he proposed, not for their consideration but for their acceptance, fourteen propositions that, he said, represented the mind of the pope. As Satolli read his prepared statement, the archbishops listened for the most part with equanimity, but they sat up a bit straighter when they heard numbers five and eleven.

> 5. We strictly forbid anyone, whether bishop or priest—and this is the express prohibition of the Sovereign Pontiff—either by act or by threat, to exclude from the sacraments, as unworthy, parents who choose to send their children to the public schools. As to the children themselves, this enactment applies with still greater force.
>
> . . .
>
> 11. It is greatly to be desired and will be a most happy arrangement, if the bishop agree with the civil authorities, or with members of the school board, to conduct the school with mutual attention and due consideration for their respective rights.[53]

Satolli's "express prohibition" of spiritual punishments for those who declined to support or patronize the parochial schools was in harmony with the generally softer line Rome had taken on this question when compared to that

---

52. Baltimore III had commissioned the archbishops to meet as a body in hopes of finding an acceptable solution to the difficult secret societies question. Out of this function had emerged an annual meeting at which the archbishops discussed a variety of matters. Here was the informal precursor of the National Catholic Welfare Conference.

53. Full English text in Reilly, *School Controversy,* 271–276.

of the American hierarchy. At Baltimore III the fathers had threatened parishes that refused to build a school with interdict, only to have Propaganda water down the final decree to the level of episcopal persuasion "by the most efficacious and prudent means possible." And though the council had defeated the motion to refuse confessional absolution to parents who chose public over parochial schools for their children, the vote had been extremely close.[54] As for the delegate's proposition eleven, it clearly stated a generalized endorsement of the Faribault plan. Archbishop Ireland could not have been more pleased, but many of his metropolitan brethren were astonished and alarmed at what seemed to them a direct assault upon the viability of the parochial school system and upon the decrees of Baltimore III.

Ireland's exhilaration did not last; indeed, that blissful moment in the drawing room of Corrigan's house on Madison Avenue marked his high tide. The first small sign of reversal came early in January 1893, when Delegate Satolli circularized the entire American hierarchy to the effect that the pope wanted each bishop to submit in writing an opinion of the fourteen propositions, and furthermore that this communication be sent directly to Leo XIII himself. The result of this poll was overwhelmingly negative. Of eighty-four possible responses, fifty-three bishops signified opposition to Satolli's propositions to one degree or another, while only eleven gave them unqualified approval and six approved with reservations. Among the metropolitan sees only Baltimore, Santa Fe, and Boston joined forces with St. Paul. Gibbons declared that "the doctrine contained in these propositions is so just, so opportune, and is so greatly appreciated by unprejudiced people." He was seconded eloquently by Keane, and not so eloquently by several other bishops who argued simply that supporting an independent parochial school was beyond their fiscal capacity. In his own letter Ireland took the speculative high road, toned down his rhetoric, and attacked nobody by name. There was nothing new for him to say, but he could and did endorse Satolli's propositions "in toto," because they were "true in principle and wise in view of the practical applications which can follow upon [them]."

By sheer weight of numbers, however, the bishops who disagreed with such sentiments dominated the field. Besides stating their objections to the propositions, many of them took the occasion to tell the pope that the imbroglio resulted from the intrigues of Ireland and the "credulity" of Satolli. Not

---

54. The vote was thirty-seven to thirty-two. See Gleason, "Baltimore III and Education," 299–302. "Interdict" would amount to the removal of the priest from the penalized parish, thus depriving it of ordinary sacramental ministration.

surprisingly, Katzer of Milwaukee was particularly severe with Ireland, whom he accused of "unworthy tactics" like falsifying cablegrams, planting vicious articles in the press, and creating the impression that "to dissent from the innovations of the Archbishop of St. Paul is the same as opposition to the Holy See." Corrigan, though recognizing that he was for the time being out of favor in Rome, did not back down from his basic position. He did not name Ireland, but he made the salient point that any "treaty" between public and private education was unconstitutional and therefore unacceptable to the American people: "The schema of our venerable brother Satolli seems to suggest that sooner or later our Catholic children will attend public schools." Patrick Riordan of San Francisco, a sturdy Americanizer and a friend of Ireland, nevertheless subjected each of the propositions to minute analysis and found them, as a whole, wanting and inconsistent with the decrees of Baltimore III.

In sharp contrast to Riordan's analytical approach was the white heat with which John Lancaster Spalding of Peoria addressed the pontiff. The words tumbled from him, chasing each other across the page, with no paragraph divisions and scarcely any punctuation. This erstwhile friend of John Ireland—they had been close allies in the colonization movement and in the founding of the Catholic University—dismissed the propositions out of hand. "The schema . . . has already done irreparable harm to the Catholic schools which are almost the only hope of the Church in this country. . . . I have no doubt that . . . the pronunciomento of Mgr. Satolli . . . has been edited in accord with the interests of Mgr. Ireland and his coterie." The propositions were no more than an "apologia" for the public schools, which were "fatal to all positive religion. . . . The agitation of Mgr. Ireland and his Faribault school plan—which is genuinely absurd, a compromise without any sense, which neither Protestants nor Catholics can accept—has done immense harm to the Church."[55]

On May 31, 1893, Leo XIII addressed a formal and public letter to Cardinal Gibbons, in which he tried to put the school question to rest. It was an ingenious piece of administrative prose. Satolli, the pope said, "this illustrious man, not less preeminent by his learning than by his virtues," had been commissioned "to use all his endeavors and all the skill of his fraternal charity for the extirpation of the germs of dissension developed in the too well-known controversies concerning the proper instruction of Catholic youth." This mission he had accomplished brilliantly. "After carefully weighing the matter,"

---

55. The letters quoted and alluded to are collected in one file in the archives of Propaganda, APF-NS [new series, after 1892] 74:105–386.

the pope solemnly decided in effect that the problem had, as though by magic, disappeared. Anybody who thought the propositions conflicted with the decrees of Baltimore was simply mistaken. But at the same time there remained in force the mandate *tolerari potest*: "Whatever else has been prescribed by the Roman Pontiffs, whether directly or through the Sacred Congregations concerning the same matter, are [sic] to be steadfastly observed." The fight over American Catholic education was officially declared a draw.[56]

But in a sense the fight had been lost ten months earlier, as least so far as Ireland and Minnesota were concerned. On July 15, 1892, the archbishop arrived in St. Paul for a deeply ironic homecoming. He had crossed the sea to do battle in behalf of his school plan and had won a smashing victory, only to have its local manifestation collapse in his absence. The civil authorities in Stillwater had already dismantled the arrangement, and those in Faribault were in the process of doing the same.[57] Nor could Ireland's presence have saved the situation; the Faribault school plan was doomed by its own incoherence and by the publicity that turned it into a cause célèbre. It was a paper theory, and Corrigan and Spalding, whatever their personal animus toward Ireland, were right at least on that score.

---

56. English text in Reilly, *School Controversy,* 226–230.
57. See Morrissey, "Faribault-Stillwater," 270–271, 304–309.

CHAPTER 14

Molding an Elite

UPON DEPARTING ROME AFTER HAVING SUCCEEDED IN GAINING papal approval for the Faribault plan, John Ireland had traveled at a leisurely pace through his beloved France and then on to Ireland. When he arrived in St. Paul in July 1892, he had been gone from Minnesota for nearly six months. In a celebrated malapropism, an ardent admirer used to describe the archbishop as "an international figure both here and abroad." And so he was. That he relished such a role need hardly be said. To play it, however, involved frequent and sometimes protracted absences from home. The journeys across the Atlantic were only one side of the coin: Ireland, in demand as a lecturer on temperance and colonization, often attended sometimes lengthy rallies and conferences in Chicago or New York or other far-flung places. He liked to go to the University of Notre Dame where his speeches promoting Americanization always roused lively applause from the youthful audience. As a prominent member of the group that founded the Catholic University of America, he was often in Washington, and he was not loath when there to lobby the federal government for this cause or that. In 1898, at the request of the Vatican, he hastened off to the capital in a fruitless attempt to avert hostilities between the United States and Spain.[1] The archbishop's credentials as a solid Republican gave him entrée to four presidencies, those of Harrison, McKinley, Theodore Roosevelt, and William Howard Taft. After his victory in the election of 1908, Taft wrote: "No one will receive a more cordial welcome in the White House while I am there than the Archbishop of St. Paul."[2]

---

1. See O'Connell, *John Ireland*, 442–454.
2. Taft to Ireland, November 21, 1908, MHS, JIP, roll 11.

Ireland's opponents within the American hierarchy, notably Bishops Spalding of Peoria and McQuaid of Rochester, were not slow to chide him for this proclivity to busy himself about many matters outside his diocese and to suggest strongly that he would do well to mind his own ecclesiastical business. Such complaints, however, were seldom voiced by Minnesotans, Catholic and non-Catholic alike. His own were proud of the archbishop's reputation as a mover and shaker, as one who walked, head erect, beside popes and presidents. Nor did his coreligionists among them appear to have felt any sense of neglect. It is one measure of John Ireland's immense energy and self-confidence that he managed to combine incessant travel—always slow and often uncomfortable—with a firm and even creative control over his local jurisdiction. And he did so more or less by himself. Elaborate bureaucratic structures lay far in the future. His chancery was an unadorned room in the cathedral presbytery, and later in the basement of his house on Portland Avenue. Not that the archbishop of St. Paul was without able adjutants. As the pioneer generation of Augustin Ravoux slipped into its dotage, stalwarts like Anatole Oster and Louis Caillet, who remembered Bishop Cretin's times, still kept their hand on the plow. But younger men came to the fore too, ecclesiastics all—after Dillon O'Brien's death no layman enjoyed a place in Ireland's inner circle[3]—as was to be expected in the clerical culture of the time.

A sampling of those whom the archbishop came to regard as close collaborators—and those whom he marked out for promotion to high office—tended to display certain basic attributes: they were Irish-born or of Irish extraction, they were strong temperance advocates, they were fiscally prudent, and they were dedicated to the cause of Americanization. Joseph Cotter was born in England in 1844 and as a child was brought to Minnesota by his Irish parents. His father was a ne'er-do-well journalist who ultimately gained a civil service job in St. Paul.[4] Joseph began his theological education at St. Vincent's Abbey in Pennsylvania, but he came back to Minnesota to complete it when, in 1867, he joined the charter class of the newly founded seminary at St. John's.[5] Shortly after ordination four years later, Cotter was assigned as pastor of St. Thomas parish in Winona, the bustling and charming Mississippi River town where he was destined to live out the rest of his life.

---

3. See chapter 11, above.
4. See chapter 5, note 62, above.
5. See Barry, *Worship*, 114.

He finished the brick church begun by his predecessor—a future cathedral—and assumed the usual parochial duties there as well as service to the cluster of missions in the hinterland. Cotter soon earned a reputation as a powerful orator, and in his capacity as president of the Catholic Total Abstinence Union of America during the mid-1880s he achieved a certain national notoriety by delivering no fewer than seventy-three temperance lectures around the country—a feat much appreciated by Archbishop Ireland.[6]

James McGolrick was born in County Tipperary on May Day 1841, the eldest of Felix and Bridget McGolrick's seven children. His father was a tenant farmer and self-described jack-of-all-trades—cobbler, mechanic, tailor, carpenter—and hence the family was relatively well off during the distressful days in Ireland on the eve and in the wake of the Great Famine. Felix set one significant example for his son: he was a teetotaler, a sturdy disciple of Father Theobald Mathew. In 1861 James matriculated at All Hallows, the seminary for missionaries, and two years later he was among the first to respond to Bishop Grace's appeal for recruits from that institution.[7] Ordained in Dublin as a canonical subject of St. Paul, he left Ireland in June 1867. His first assignment placed him at the cathedral as John Ireland's assistant, and though his tenure there was brief, it left its mark on the impressionable young man. For him Ireland's ideals on education, colonization, temperance, apologetics, how to preach, how to deal with people, how to be a successful priest—all these became, as he declared, his own. Early on he secured the approval of his new colleagues: "I am pleased to say," Grace told the superiors at All Hallows, "that Mr. McGolrick is doing well. He has won the affections of all by his amicable disposition. He is not strong in health, but I trust he will improve with our very healthy climate."[8]

McGolrick needed a good deal of physical stamina when, late in 1868, he was charged to start a new parish in Minneapolis. The town at that date was small, muddy, noted for petty crime and violence, its commercial, industrial, and cultural ascendancy still off in the future. The relatively small number of Catholics who had settled there found the environment distinctly unfriendly, even bigoted. They had been served on an occasional basis by the priests at St. Anthony—not incorporated into Minneapolis until 1872—and by a forlorn and insecure little school maintained by a few Sisters of St. Joseph located on

---

6. J. Robert, "Diocese of Winona," in Ahern, *Catholic Heritage,* 90–91.

7. See chapter 8, above.

8. Philip Silvers, "James McGolrick, First Bishop of the Duluth Diocese" (Master's thesis, St. Paul Seminary, 1964), 2–12.

two lots on the east side of Third Street at the intersection of Third Avenue.[9] To this ramshackle frame building, derisively known locally from its unpropitious appearance as "the shed," Father McGolrick first added enough extension along Third Avenue to furnish worship space as well as additional classrooms. The expedient of setting up a "shed church," however, he always regarded as temporary, and by 1872 a church of limestone had been erected on the site: one hundred thirty-seven feet long, sixty-four feet wide expanded in the transepts to eighty-four, a choir gallery, and a square tower ending in a spire with a cross on the top.[10] The parish was named in honor of the Virgin Mary under the title of the Immaculate Conception, and, fittingly, McGolrick offered Mass for the first time in the new building on December 8. He scheduled the formal dedication for New Year's Day 1873, and advertised widely that the occasion would be marked by much fanfare and celebration. But the fastidious Bishop Grace, despite the favorable impression the young Irishman had originally made on him, found the placards scattered about the town announcing the festivities too vulgar for his taste, and he declined coldly to attend. This rebuke, however, seems to have been unique in McGolrick's clerical career. Over the course of twenty-one years he earned the reputation of a hardworking, unostentatious man, punctilious in fulfilling his day-to-day duties, strong on temperance, an able financial officer, good at dealing with an often rootless Catholic youth (among his other accomplishments was the foundation of a boys' orphan asylum). He held forth as a priest in a sometimes hostile social milieu, and he did so without sacrificing principle but also without arousing animosity. When he was elevated to the episcopacy in 1889, the public reception in his honor, chaired by a former mayor of Minneapolis, was attended by most of the city's worthies.[11]

Judging from photographs taken of them in their middle years, Cotter and McGolrick appear to have had, as the saying went, the map of old Erin etched on their faces. John Shanley, by contrast, was a smaller man than they, and darker, with an expression more subtle, more nuanced, even if his Celtic ancestry was as complete as theirs. He was born January 4, 1852, near Albion in northern New York, close to the Ontario border, the youngest of the six children of John and Nancy Shanley, who had immigrated from County Leitrim twenty years before. His father was a stonemason who worked in one or

---

9. Grace had approved the purchase of this property in 1865, at a cost of $1,500. See James M. Reardon, *The Basilica of St. Mary of Minneapolis* (St. Paul, 1932), 6–9.

10. Reardon, *Basilica*, 12–16.

11. Silvers, "McGolrick," 19–31.

another of the quarries in the vicinity of Albion. As he neared the age of fifty, however, John senior decided that he and his family should join the tide westward. After spending a few months in Faribault, they moved on in 1857 to St. Paul. John junior was duly enrolled in the cathedral school and then in Bishop Grace's short-lived minor seminary, where the spiritual director, the gentle and kindly Anatole Oster, made a lasting impression on the youngster. Even as a teenager he manifested a notable precocity. When Grace sent him to the seminary at St. John's—where he met Joseph Cotter—Shanley won all the scholastic prizes.

In the autumn of 1869 Father Ireland sailed for Rome, where he was to act as Bishop Grace's proctor or observer at the Vatican Council, scheduled to open on December 8.[12] Accompanying him was John Shanley, who promptly enrolled in the Urban College of Propaganda to complete his theological studies. This recognition of the seventeen-year-old's academic potential gave him the opportunity to immerse himself in all the wonders of Romanità—the monuments of antiquity, the splendor of Renaissance and Baroque art, the ecclesiastical excitement of the first general council in three centuries. And he was to witness as well events of lasting if, at the time, disturbing significance: the following summer papal Rome fell to the forces of a newly united Italy, ending the pope's civil jurisdiction that had lasted for a thousand years. Meanwhile the notoriously wretched physical conditions at the Urban College posed a constant threat to Shanley's always delicate health, so much so that the authorities, fearful that he might contract the dreaded consumption, granted him a dispensation from the canonical age requirement. John Shanley, only twenty-two years old, was ordained priest in the Lateran Basilica on May 30, 1874.[13]

He spent his entire priestly life at the cathedral in St. Paul, first as curate and then, when Ireland was elevated to the episcopate, as rector. He was an effective, even a creative parish priest. Besides discharging the ordinary obligations of his office, he kept an eye open for other initiatives. He was instrumental in bringing to the city in 1883 the Little Sisters of the Poor, whose special apostolate was to offer care to the aged and infirm. The cathedral routinely sponsored fairs and outings and bazaars, the proceeds from which were used to help support St. Joseph's orphanage. And the rector took up other, rather more unusual projects. There were, for instance, about twenty Italian families

---

12. See chapter 9, above.

13. Gerald Weber, "John Shanley, First Bishop of Fargo" (Master's thesis, St. Paul Seminary, 1951), 1–12.

living in St. Paul. Shanley could speak their language, at least haltingly, and so he set aside for their Sunday worship a basement chapel under the patronage of the Holy Redeemer, where he frequently preached and catechized. This arrangement lasted as long as did the third cathedral, which was demolished in 1914; two years later a modest new Holy Redeemer church opened its doors onto St. Peter Street.[14] Similarly, Shanley made special provision for the black Catholics in the city. Given the racial mores of the time, this endeavor was no doubt partly one of expedience, but the rector gave it more than casual attention. He rented a small, formerly Baptist church on Market Street where services were held and where regular catechetical instruction was given, often overseen by Shanley himself. He also arranged for occasional lectures and concerts to be held there. The congregation was called St. Peter's, and by 1888 enough money had been raised to buy the facility and dedicate it to St. Peter Claver.[15]

Along with his multifarious pastoral duties, Shanley, from 1877 to 1885, acted as editor of the *Northwestern Chronicle*. He made the paper more folksy and more churchly: there was little room in its pages for the political causes that had excited John Devereux.[16] Shanley himself was not without literary gifts. Besides editorials, he wrote many pamphlets and tracts, mostly of an apologetic kind. And he stood among the strongest temperance crusaders, not just in his parish but across the diocese and the state. He was in constant demand as a speaker at rallies. Often he shared the platform with Ireland and would follow the bishop's fierce denunciations of the liquor trade with a softer, almost humorous exposé of the foolish drunkard. His consistent and sturdy advocacy of legislation imposing Sunday closing and high license fees helped the measure become state law in 1887.[17]

The next year the diocese of St. Paul was raised to metropolitan status, and a year after that the ecclesiastical reorganization continued with the creation of five suffragan sees, three in Minnesota and one in each of the two states newly admitted to the Union, North Dakota and South Dakota. Archbishop Ireland, as he now was, used his considerable influence in Rome to secure the appointment of priests he judged suitable to head these new jurisdictions. It was hardly a surprise therefore that Cotter stayed in Winona, now as

---

14. Wright, *Gather Us In,* 102.
15. See Reardon, *Diocese of St. Paul,* 588.
16. See chapter 9, above.
17. Weber, "Shanley," 26–42.

bishop, or that McGolrick went to Duluth and Shanley to Jamestown.[18] It did raise some eyebrows, however, that another intimate of Ireland's—indeed, his closest friend since childhood—was not promoted. This man would eventually get a miter of his own. But not yet.

THOMAS O'GORMAN FIRST KNEW JOHN IRELAND WHEN THE two were schoolboys for a brief time in Chicago. Their fathers were both Kilkenny men, though they had not known one another in the old country. Both had fled the Great Famine, had settled first in New England—Thomas, the eldest of John O'Gorman's four sons, was born in Boston—and then had joined the restless tide of immigration westward. They had met by chance on a Chicago street early in 1852, and by April of that year the two families, nineteen persons in all, set out on the plank road from Chicago to Galena. Once in that Mississippi River town they caught a northbound steamer and arrived in St. Paul in mid-May. They found shelter together for a while, in a shack thrown up hastily near the river—one long windowless room with only partitions of bed sheets separating Irelands from O'Gormans. During the summer the families secured lots and built houses for themselves—John O'Gorman was a stonecutter, Richard Ireland a carpenter—located only a block apart.[19]

The following spring—it may be recalled—Bishop Cretin plucked John Ireland and Thomas O'Gorman out of the cathedral school yard and sent them off to France, to his own alma mater, the *petit séminaire* at Meximieux.[20] This highly significant French connection lasted longer for Thomas than for John: Ireland returned to Minnesota just as the Civil War was breaking out, while O'Gorman, four years younger, did not complete his studies until 1865. But it was a bonding experience even so, as the two of them grew from adolescence into manhood.

O'Gorman followed something of a pilgrim's track after his return from France.[21] He spent the first twelve years of his priesthood as pastor at Roches-

---

18. Shanley's disocesan seat was moved from Jamestown to Fargo in 1891. The diocese of St. Cloud went to Swiss-born Otto Zardetti, who had Roman connections of his own. The first bishop of Sioux Falls was the Benedictine Martin Marty, who had been vicar apostolic of Dakota Territory since 1880.

19. M. Seraphica Marx, "The Life of Thomas O'Gorman, Bishop of Sioux Falls" (Master's thesis, University of South Dakota, 1959), 2–5, and Ann Thomasine Sampson, "The Ireland Connection," Oral History Projects, Sisters of St. Joseph (St. Paul, 1982), 2–4.

20. See chapter 4, above.

21. See Marx, "O'Gorman," 19–32.

ter, ministering to the Catholics in that thriving community as well as to those in four mission stations in the nearby countryside. It was an arduous life, but the stocky, good-natured, bookish O'Gorman took it all in stride and performed the multitude of duties of the frontier missionary with panache. Besides building churches and schools, he founded literary and benevolent societies, and—it need hardly be said—devoted special efforts to the cause of total abstinence. He soon enjoyed the reputation of a gifted pulpit and platform orator who, if he did not possess the riveting rhetorical skills of his former schoolmate, spoke clearly, interestingly, and sometimes eloquently. Testimony that he stood high among the local intelligentsia came from no less a personage than Dr. William Worrall Mayo, who, though not a Catholic, took pains to consult O'Gorman before determining upon the educational program for his sons Charlie and Will.[22]

There was a vein of restlessness in O'Gorman's character, or perhaps he grew bored with life in a small town in Minnesota. At any rate, in 1877 he asked Bishop Grace's permission to resign his pastorate and grant him a leave of absence so that he might join the community of the Paulist Fathers in New York. The Paulists—formally the Missionary Society of St. Paul the Apostle—had been founded in 1858 by the charismatic convert Isaac Hecker. They considered it their special apostolate to evangelize among the English-speaking, largely through preaching and other intellectual endeavors. In contrast to most of the older religious congregations, they were ardent Americanizers. For the next four years O'Gorman toiled as a member of the Paulist mission band all over the northeastern United States. It was said that during this time he became the favorite preacher of New York's Cardinal McCloskey. He indulged his literary interests too, and contributed several articles to the Paulist journal, *The Catholic World*.

Father O'Gorman returned to Minnesota in 1882, probably because Grace and Ireland were contemplating the establishment of a new collegiate seminary in which, it was thought, he might be useful. The plans for this institution had not yet matured, and in the meantime O'Gorman was assigned as pastor to the Immaculate Conception parish in Faribault. His tenure there was brief—three years—but his rather free-spending ways contributed not a little to the chronic financial difficulties of the parish, which led in turn to the proposal of the famous school plan.[23] In due course (1885), Grace being now retired, Ireland threw open the doors of St. Thomas Seminary, and named

---

22. Clapesattle, *Doctors Mayo*, 181.
23. Morrissey, "Faribault-Stillwater," 168–170.

O'Gorman its first rector. It proved to be an unhappy choice. The bespectacled O'Gorman was, to be sure, intelligent, adaptable, and something of a clerical man of the world, but as an educator he was an amateur. He had no scholastic training beyond what he had experienced as a student in France two decades before. He soon discovered that operating an institution of higher learning was a far cry from managing a parish. As for Bishop Ireland, he came to doubt that his old friend even had the proper instincts for the position. "I say to you *confidentially*," he wrote to a prospective replacement during O'Gorman's second year at the helm, "that Father O'Gorman has not the educational experience, nor the educational mind, to secure success. . . . The trouble is simply that I have not the proper man at the head of the Seminary. . . . F. O'Gorman has formally resigned."[24]

The deposed rector displayed no rancor. He readily assumed the post of professor of theology and history at St. Thomas. He had always fancied the latter discipline, and indeed a few years later he produced a hefty volume on the history of Catholicism in the United States.[25] Nor did John Ireland leave his friend in limbo. In 1890, the archbishop of St. Paul, exercising his substantial influence, arranged that O'Gorman be appointed to the chair of ecclesiastical history at the Catholic University. In Washington O'Gorman spent more of his energy working as an agent for the cause of Americanization than as a scholar or a teacher drudging his way through the archives or lecturing in the classroom. His primary task was to keep Archbishop Satolli, who during the early months of his delegation resided at the university as rector John Keane's guest, amenable to Ireland's agenda. As Corrigan of New York bitterly observed, Keane became the delegate's jailer and O'Gorman the subjailer.[26] If anything, O'Gorman showed himself to be the fiercest Americanizer of them all, even contemptuous at times of putative allies who did not strike him as sufficiently belligerent. In the midst of the school controversy, for instance, he told his friend and chief: "The Card[inal] has got his back straightened. He is very brave now, though he was downcast a few days ago. They are a pack of cowards, Gibbons, Keane et al."[27]

---

24. Ireland to McSweeny, May 25 and June 2, 1887, Archives of Mount St. Mary's College, Emmitsburg, Maryland. I owe this reference to my late friend, Professor Joseph B. Connors.

25. Thomas O'Gorman, *A History of the Roman Catholic Church in the United States* (New York, 1895), 515 pp.

26. Robert Emmett Curran, *Michael Augustine Corrigan and the Shaping of Conservative Catholicism in America, 1878–1902* (New York, 1978), 397.

27. O'Gorman to Ireland, December 8, 1892, MHS, JIP, roll 4.

O'Gorman's presence in Washington during these contentious years was an important piece of Ireland's overall strategy. Still, there is no doubt of the archbishop's ultimate intention to see him promoted to the episcopacy. The opportunity came in 1895 when the diocese of Sioux Falls fell vacant. The *ternae* from the bishops of the St. Paul province and from the clergy of Sioux Falls were duly collected, and—hardly a surprise—O'Gorman's name stood first on both lists. "I take the liberty of recommending [O'Gorman] to you in a special manner," Ireland wrote the prefect of Propaganda. For years American public opinion had marked out this brilliant historian for a miter, and now, "as your Eminence knows," the deplorable condition of the diocese of Sioux Falls had need of a man of such prestige and stature. He went on to laud O'Gorman's prudence, judgment, maturity, fluency in languages, and, of course the all-important "devotion to the Holy See." He made no reference to their shared experience as schoolboys, nor to O'Gorman's years with the Paulists, but he may have had in mind some specific events of bygone days when he observed: "As a young man he gave evidence of a certain temperamental inconstancy and capriciousness; with the passage of years this fault has been entirely eliminated."[28]

Satolli endorsed the nomination and sent the relevant documents off to Rome in March. Then, to Ireland's intense irritation, nothing happened. At the end of the summer he asked the delegate to inquire at Propaganda, but no explanation was forthcoming. Clearly the anti-Americanizers still had influence in high curial circles, and for them the outspoken O'Gorman—dismissed by Michael Corrigan as "Dr. Ireland's henchman"[29]—was especially a *bête noire*. Finally, in October, Ireland took up the pen again. Sioux Falls should be filled without delay, he wrote the prefect. Eight months of vacancy had led to "a great detriment to souls and a great confusion of all religious interests." Since O'Gorman had been first choice on both *ternae*, Ireland professed bewilderment at the delay. "It is said that certain ecclesiastics have presented you with objections about his candidacy." What grounds could be advanced, he wondered, to support opposition to so talented a nominee? "I am profoundly convinced that Monsieur O'Gorman is more than any other person the man for Sioux Falls. I would have strong regrets if due to malcontented and unjust critics he were set aside."[30] The archbishop's informant about

---

28. The documents relating to O'Gorman's promotion, including Ireland to Ledochowski, March 18, 1895, are in APF-NS, 97:613–625.

29. Corrigan to McQuaid, October 13, 1892, in Zwierlein, *Letters*, 152.

30. Ireland to Ledochowski, October 17, 1895, and Ledochowski to O'Gorman, December 16, 1895, APF-NS, 97:633–641.

"unjust critics" at work in the curia was none other than John Shanley, just back from Rome, where he had been defending himself against allegations that in Jamestown he had championed the secret societies.[31] Two tense months followed, and then, in mid-December, the good news arrived at last. "It appears," he told Gibbons, "that ferocious attacks were made on our whole list [the two *ternae*] as liberal, semi-heretical, etc. Especially was O'Gorman torn to pieces. But he is all right now."[32] On Sunday, April 19, 1896, at St. Patrick's church in Washington, Thomas O'Gorman was consecrated bishop. Twenty-one years before he had preached the festive sermon at another consecration; on this occasion John Ireland returned the favor.

DURING HIS LONG TENURE AS ORDINARY OF THE DIOCESE AND metropolitan of the province of St. Paul, John Ireland saw to the promotion to the episcopate of fourteen of his priests. Irish names continued to predominate; in 1910, for example, he bestowed the purple in one grand and historic ceremony upon James O'Reilly, Patrick Heffron, John Lawler, and Timothy Corbett.[33] A fifth St. Paul priest, Joseph Busch, was also consecrated on that occasion, the only German American of the fourteen. But he was a highly cultivated man from a solid middle-class background—his father had been a small-town banker—and had worked closely with the archbishop in the chancery. When earlier appointments had been made to sees with a large enough German constituency to suggest that an Irishman might prove problematic, Ireland had offered preferment to German-speaking Slovenes, like James Trobec and John Stahira,[34] the same men to whom he had earlier entrusted large German parishes in the archdiocese.

But this ethnic bias weighed less heavily in Ireland's mind than did another consideration. What he wanted most of all was a native clergy and episcopacy in the narrow sense. No less than seventy percent of the men Rome

---

31. Satolli to Ledochowski, August 15, 1895, APF-NS, 79:542–543.

32. Ireland to Gibbons, January 13, 1896, AAB.

33. The event was unprecedented. Altogether six priests were consecrated in the one ceremony, all for service within the province of St. Paul. The sixth was the Benedictine monk Vincent Wehrle, a veteran missionary in North Dakota. It was occasioned by the deaths of two bishops, the resignation of another, and the creation of two new dioceses. In addition, the aging Ireland required an auxiliary. See Reardon, *Diocese of St. Paul*, 389–392.

34. See chapter 8, above.

selected as bishops within the St. Paul province between 1889 and 1910—all of them Ireland's candidates—were either born in Minnesota or, like Shanley and O'Gorman, had come to the state as children. During this period fully two-thirds of the diocesan clergy had been born and raised elsewhere in the United States or abroad.[35] Here was an important instance of Ireland's Americanization policy expressed on the local level. What Minnesota Catholics needed to serve them, in his view, were Minnesota priests, young men recruited and trained under the archbishop's eye. And so it was from this personnel pool of native sons that he chose his favorites for promotion, a procedure much abetted once he was able to open his own seminary.[36]

But John Ireland was a savvy ecclesiastical politician, and when the opportunity presented itself he took advantage of a means to assuage the feelings of distinguished members of his clergy who were definitely not native Minnesotans. Toward the end of the nineteenth century, the Vatican, partly as a way of raising funds after the fall of the Papal States, instituted the practice of naming individual priests, nominated by their bishops to honorary prelacies of various ranks. Such men were technically attached to the pope's own entourage and hence were entitled to call themselves "Monsignor." The designation gave them no added authority, but it did afford them—by way, for example, of the touch of purple on their ritual garb—a particularly respected position among their priestly peers. The first St. Paul recipient of this accolade was, fittingly enough, Augustin Ravoux in 1887, followed in succeeding years by two other pioneer French missioners, Louis Caillet and Anatole Oster.[37] But Ireland also used this method to reward, at least to a degree, other ethnic groups. Thus in 1906 domestic prelacies were conferred upon Alois Plut, a Slovene, and Dominic Majer, a Pole. Three years later the honor fell to Henry Sandmeyer, a native of Westphalia. And four years after that Wendelin Stulz, a German, and Francis Tichy, a Bohemian, were named monsignors.[38]

Another factor may have contributed to Monsignor Tichy's promotion. As pastor of St. Wenceslaus in New Prague for twenty-six years, he produced more successful recruits for the diocesan clergy than did any of his peers, even those who presided over larger parishes in the Twin Cities. Not lagging far behind him, however, were McGolrick and James Keane at Immaculate

---

35. O'Neill, "St. Paul Priests," 108–109.

36. See chapter 15, below.

37. A full list in Reardon, *Diocese of St. Paul,* 681–682.

38. O'Neill, "St. Paul Priests," 123–124. All eleven priests nominated by Archbishop Ireland (1887–1913) for honorary prelacies were foreign-born, the eight mentioned in the text together with another Frenchman and two Irishmen.

Conception in Minneapolis, and Trobec at St. Agnes and Stahira at St. Francis de Sales, both in St. Paul, all four of whom were elevated to the episcopacy.[39] If Tichy had been a Slovenian name, he might have aspired to higher office. The role of the pastor in discerning and nurturing vocations to the priesthood and religious life was of course crucial, and Archbishop Ireland was not slow to recognize endeavors in this regard and, when he could, to reward them. Between 1885 and 1917 he ordained 334 men to the priesthood; nevertheless, not until the second decade of the twentieth century did the native-born outnumber the externs.

THE TURNING OF THE NUMERICAL TIDE CAME IN 1885 WITH the opening of St. Thomas Aquinas Seminary. The moment was propitious. For one thing, the economic and human growth in Minnesota had continued at an extraordinary rate. The population of St. Paul now approached 120,000, ten times what it had been when Chaplain Ireland returned from the war. But Minneapolis had grown even faster, and for the first time had outdistanced in numbers its sister city. Water systems were installed during the 1880s, sewers laid, streets paved, thousands of homes constructed. James J. Hill built himself a massive mansion on the top of St. Anthony Hill, one sign of the money to be earned in the railroad business in St. Paul, where twelve separate lines converged to make the city one of the major transportation hubs in the nation. By 1890 the state's farmers were shipping thirty-five million bushels of wheat annually over the rails, while its sawmills turned out 650 million feet of timber. The miners of iron ore incorporated, between 1885 and 1890, no fewer than 284 companies.[40]

Catholic growth kept pace. During that same half decade Ireland founded thirty-eight new parishes in the diocese, including ten in St. Paul and four in Minneapolis. In addition a school for deaf children was opened, as well as a boys' orphanage, three homes for "friendless and unprotected" girls, two hospitals, and as many as fifteen grammar and secondary schools.[41] Such signs of overall expansion and confessional vigor were prefaced by Ireland's announcement at the beginning of December 1884.

39. O'Neill, "St. Paul Priests," 35–37.

40. See Blegen, *Minnesota*, 326, 340, 343, and 364.

41. See Reardon, *Diocese of St. Paul*, 585–588, 595–596, 635–640, 658, 665–667, 676.

Taking into account the wondrous development of religion in the diocese of St. Paul, ... we propose with God's help to open in September, 1885, in St. Paul a seminary in which the youth of the diocese whom God may inspire with a vocation to the priesthood, will be enabled to pursue at least their classical studies. ... The diocesan seminary will be the principal work of our episcopate, and from it we expect the most fruitful result.[42]

That this proposal coincided with Thomas Grace's retirement was not coincidental. The old bishop, after several failed attempts to set up a seminary, had grown weary of the project. But he had unintentionally furnished a suitable locale for such an institution. In 1874 he had purchased at a bargain price a farm of 452 acres, located on the western fringes of St. Paul and just across the Mississippi from Minneapolis. Three years later he realized a long-cherished goal when the Catholic Industrial School of Minnesota began operations on the site, with a staff of three religious brothers and a clientele of twenty boys, all housed in a three-storied frame building. The plan was that the Industrial School would provide a haven and a place of vocational training for orphans and the mentally retarded as well as for youngsters in trouble. But it never aroused much interest or support in the Catholic community, and in 1879, the venture clearly a failure, the school was transferred to an uncertain future in Clontarf, one of John Ireland's western Minnesota colonies.[43]

With the generous aid of the original owner of the farm, William Finn,[44] Ireland purchased the building and 280 contiguous acres. The bishop wasted no time. During the hectic spring and summer of 1885 he put carpenters and masons to work adding a new wing to the Industrial School, and then had the whole structure covered with a red brick exterior. The construction and renovation proceeded on schedule and were finished by mid-August, when the priests of the diocese assembled there for their annual retreat. Bringing his clergy together at the new St. Thomas seminary was a significant and calculated act on Ireland's part. He was determined that the institution should forge from the beginning close links with the diocesan priests who, he hoped, would come to identify with it, serving over the long term as recruiters for it in their parishes and offering it moral and pecuniary support. The retreat of

42. *NWC*, December 4, 1884.
43. Joseph A. Corrigan, "The Catholic Industrial School," *A&D* 7 (1935): 3–25.
44. The street that runs south from the center of the St. Thomas campus is named for William Finn.

1885 may have been memorable for another reason: conducting it was the eloquent bishop of Richmond, Ireland's good friend and fellow Americanizer, John Keane.[45]

The morning of September 8—the feast of the Nativity of the Virgin Mary—dawned cool and cloudy. The grounds were wet after a thunderstorm the night before. In the seminary's little chapel the rector, Thomas O'Gorman, celebrated Mass in the presence of his five faculty members and sixty-two students. The rest of the day was taken up with the chores of registration. Classes began the next afternoon, but the sessions were brief. "There being no books, no desks," O'Gorman noted in his diary, "very little was possible." Perhaps such an attitude contributed to Ireland's disenchantment with his old friend, and to his decision to cut short O'Gorman's tenure as rector on the grounds that he lacked "educational experience" and an "educational mind." The bishop always maintained that he had no "trouble" from the seminary faculty, but the enormous turnover in staff at the beginning underscored the basic problems any American bishop faced in trying to create, virtually out of nothing, a viable collegiate or seminary program. During the first three years of its existence, Ireland assigned two dozen different priests to St. Thomas's six or seven faculty positions. They were all willing enough, and a few of them were able. But like O'Gorman they lacked any formal education beyond that attained during their own seminary days and any classroom experience. The occasional lay instructor, who might teach subjects like chemistry or mathematics, was so miserably compensated that he seldom tarried at St. Thomas very long.[46]

If a faculty so unsettled led to an absence of stability and of long-range planning, even the stated purpose of the school and the composition of its student body suggested ambiguity. The word "seminary," it turned out, admitted many shades of meaning. "The studies to be pursued," read a broadside circulated six weeks before the first class was taught at St. Thomas, "will make the young man a scholar, in the true and full sense of the word, ready for the theological seminary, or the schools of law and medicine, or qualified for any social position he may covet."[47] The result was a pedagogical hodgepodge that included—in the terminology of a later, more bureaucratic era—a

---

45. Joseph B. Connors, *Journey toward Fulfillment: A History of the College of St. Thomas* (St. Paul, 1986), 32–33.

46. Connors, *St. Thomas*, 45.

47. Quoted in Connors, *St. Thomas*, 31.

theologate, a preparatory seminary, a junior college, a high school, and a junior high school. Roughly one quarter of the students were seminarians in the strict sense of the word; Ireland ordained sixty-three of them before 1894. Meanwhile, a thirteen-year-old lad, just beginning to learn to parse a Latin sentence, was a schoolfellow of a graduate student in his mid-twenties.

Yet St. Thomas, despite the formidable difficulties of its beginnings, not only survived but, in the long run, flourished. For John Ireland the institution always held a place in his romantic heart suggestive of Meximieux, the *petit séminaire* in the valley of the Rhone in which he had formed his ideals as a man and a priest.[48] But, ironically enough, it was only when St. Thomas ceased to be a seminary that its future success was assured.

THE RELATIONSHIP BETWEEN JOHN IRELAND AND JAMES J. HILL was full of ambivalence. The two of them ultimately became, each in his own sphere, the towering figures in the Minnesota of their era. Born the same year, they had known one another since their youth. But the interests and preoccupations of the railroad magnate and the ecclesiastic differed too widely to have made friendship feasible, nor was it likely that two such strong personalities would have been entirely companionable beyond entertaining a wary mutual respect. In the late summer of 1890 Hill, not a Catholic, gave evidence of his regard by proposing to Ireland that he, Hill, build and endow a major seminary for the archdiocese of St. Paul.

The cleric who played the key role in securing this generous benefaction, however, was not the archbishop but the gentle Father Louis Caillet. Hill's wife was a devout Catholic. Mary Theresa Mehegan was eight years old in 1854 when her ne'er-do-well father died, leaving her, her mother, and her sister virtually penniless. They turned for support to the nuns and priests, chief among whom was Louis Caillet, who had come from France at about the same time. Mary Theresa grew up to be a pretty, grave, self-possessed young woman of independent mind, hardworking—at sixteen she was a waitress in the dining room of the Merchants' Hotel—and fiercely devoted to the tenets of her religion. Among the regular patrons of the Merchants' who found her attractive was an up-and-coming young businessman, a recent immigrant from Ontario, named James Hill. Once they were engaged, he came to have a high regard for Mary Theresa's confidant, Father Caillet, and he pronounced

---

48. See chapter 5, above.

himself content that his wife's religion should also be the religion of their home.[49] The intimacy among the three of them was reinforced during the years Caillet was the pastor of St. Mary's parish and Mary Theresa Hill was his most prominent parishioner.[50]

So the basic reason the "Empire Builder" made so great a contribution to the support of a religion he did not share was touchingly personal. "For nearly thirty years I have lived in a Roman Catholic household, and daily have had the earnest devotion, watchful care, and Christian example of a Roman Catholic wife, of whom it may be said, 'Blessed are the pure of heart, for they shall see God,' and on whose behalf I desire to present the seminary and its endowment." Related to this tribute to Mary Theresa was public recognition of her longtime mentor, Louis Caillet. "I may say truthfully that had it not been for my intimate knowledge of and admiration for his character as a Christian pastor and a personal friend, it is very probable that I would never have thought of assuming the responsibility for [this] work."

Yet Hill did not leave out of account larger public concerns when he decided to provide St. Paul with a *grand séminaire*. Like most men in his position he believed that the masses could stand a good deal of the right kind of religion. But the American Catholic community, "with its large number of working men and women," lacked the financial resources of other denominations, and its people had "little else than their faith in God and those devoted men who have been placed in charge of their spiritual welfare."[51] It was crucial for social peace and prosperity that these "devoted men" be trained not in clerical obscurantism but along the lines of what Hill perceived to be Ireland's progressive ecclesiastical views and patriotic commitment. "An American character," the archbishop assured him, "is impressed today as never before upon the Church in the United States. I know your convictions in this regard, and I am sure you will hear this news with pleasure."[52]

Approval of Ireland's ideology, so far as he understood it, may have led to Hill's cordial agreement to specify in the seminary's charter that "at no time" was the institution to be "under the control of any particular society or [religious] order." But it did not extend to allowing the archbishop carte

---

49. See Mary Christine Athans, *"To Work for the Whole People": John Ireland's Seminary in St. Paul* (New York, 2002), 41–52.

50. See chapter 6, above, and chapter 15, below.

51. Hill's speech at the dedication of the seminary, September 4, 1895 (typed copy), James J. Hill Papers, seminary papers, box 2.

52. Ireland to Hill, May 15, 1892, James J. Hill Papers, general correspondence.

blanche with a half million dollars. Ireland indeed was hardly more than a bystander, as Hill himself oversaw every detail of the construction project, and kept track of every penny of the $240,000 it cost.[53] Nothing was too trivial for his personal attention, and every decision—about plumbing or grading or fire insurance premiums or the quality of brick used or how the students' rooms were to be furnished—was exclusively his own. When the six buildings were completed, Hill determined how the balance of the money was to be invested and how the endowment income was to be spent through a trusteeship to last through the lifetimes of his three sons and for twenty-one years thereafter.[54] Relentless attention to detail and total direction were not notable departures from Hill's ordinary way of doing business, but in this instance he had another excuse to keep control of expenditures in his own hands: he did not trust John Ireland's fiscal judgment. And with good reason.

Late in 1892, as the red brick seminary buildings were going up, the archbishop of St. Paul found himself in acute financial distress. The rather dodgy real estate speculation he had first indulged in among his western Minnesota colonies[55] he had expanded to include properties within the city of St. Paul. As the economic unease of the early 1890s turned into a deep nationwide depression, Ireland was woefully overextended. Land values plummeted, but mortgage payments had to be met, and he had no cash to meet them. He turned to Hill for relief, and it must have been at immense psychic cost for this proud man to have to put on the tattered garb of a beggar.

> I am simply crushed down with this load of debt. My power for work is impaired. The responsibilities of my position, in view of a loss of public credit, take from me all peace of mind. Moreover, I have come to the point when something must occur—for weal or woe. . . . There is no other way out of this dreadful crisis into which I have got but your friendship, and in that I put the fullest confidence. Send me soon word that all is right, and I shall be a happy man.[56]

Such plaintive queries were depressingly part of Ireland's correspondence over the next fourteen years. Not till 1907 was a final quietus written to the

---

53. Athans, *To Work for the Whole People,* 60, citing an 1896 source, puts the figure at $260,000.

54. "Charter," James J. Hill Papers, seminary papers, boxes 1 and 2.

55. See chapter 11, above.

56. Ireland to Hill, April 27, 1893, James J. Hill Papers, general correspondence.

crisis: in January of that year Hill gave Ireland a last gift of $15,000. During that long period Hill was consistently helpful, but on his own terms and in his own way. Ireland received from him at least $110,000 between 1892 and 1897, not enough to deliver the archbishop from the threat of bankruptcy, but enough to keep the wolves from the door. Hill moreover enlisted the aid of his fellow financiers and magnates, and the list of those who contributed money to Archbishop Ireland or who later joined his property syndicate— which essentially amounted to the same thing—sounded like a roll call of the gods of the Gilded Age, also dubbed "Robber Barons" in some unfriendly circles: Henry O. Havemeyer, Jacob Henry Schiff, Michael Cudahy, Marshall Field, Philip Armour, John D. Rockefeller. Only Pierpont Morgan eluded the net, and not for a lack of trying on Ireland's part. At one point, when Hill told him Morgan declined to subscribe, Ireland pleaded by telegraph: "[Though] what you say is very true, . . . could you not put down Morgan for at least fifteen [thousand], because two or three others we have reason to believe will follow his example." Hill responded with a brusque rebuke: "Message received. I have no authority to act for him. This is final."

These lords of the financial universe were not above demanding their pound of flesh. During the presidential campaign of 1896, when William Jennings Bryan, "the boy orator of the Platte," was mesmerizing the country with his assaults on the gold standard, James J. Hill—like Bryan a Democrat, but a "hard money" Democrat who supported the Republican candidate, William McKinley—informed McKinley's campaign manager that "we are giving archbishop Ireland, through a non-partisan letter signed by twenty representative men, an opportunity to state his views fully, which he is prepared to do, and I am sure he will cover the ground, stripping the [Democratic] platform to the bone."[57] And so the archbishop did, in an interview that ran to four columns in the newspapers in which it was published and then was reproduced in 250,000 pamphlets. It did not mention McKinley or Bryan by name, but it accused the Democratic platform of a renewal of secession—"the secession of 1861 which our soldiers believed they had consigned to death at Appomattox. . . . There is the annulment of the union. [And even] worse to my mind . . . is the spirit of socialism and anarchy . . . which has issued from the [Democratic] convention. . . . It is the 'International' of Europe now taking body in America. They are lighting torches which borne in the hands of reckless men may light up in the country the lurid fires of a 'Commune.' The

---

57. Hill to Hanna, September 30, 1896, James J. Hill Papers, general correspondence.

war of class upon class is upon us." McKinley carried Minnesota by 60,000 votes out of 340,000 cast. Whether or not Ireland's appeal, clearly directed to working-class Catholics, had a significant effect upon the result of the election, James J. Hill had taken no chances.[58]

John Ireland at any rate got his seminary, and with it the opportunity to recruit and train under his eye young Minnesotans to serve as priests for the Church in Minnesota. Here was a local expression of Americanization, which promised besides to provide a regular infusion of men, professionally competent, properly motivated and disciplined, into the ranks. The archbishop ultimately ordained 266 of them. Even so, in its early years the institution was often called simply "Mr. Hill's seminary." And it hardly came as surprise when Father Caillet became Monsignor Caillet and was appointed the first rector.

EXPANSION OF THE CATHOLIC POPULATION, AND ITS GRADUAL growth in resources, naturally led to an urgency and, indeed, a demand for more specialized service personnel. One such group that left the deep imprint of its own culture and genius upon generations of Catholic men in the Twin Cities were the Brothers of the Christian Schools, who first came to St. Paul in 1871.[59]

Twenty years before that, however, Joseph Cretin had among his first episcopal acts opened a school for boys in the basement of the second cathedral.[60] According to a later anecdote the event prompted this exchange between the bishop and his vicar general: "Well, there it is," said Cretin. "Our first school for American boys of Minnesota Territory. And what shall we call it?" Replied Augustin Ravoux: "Why, let us call it what young [James] Goodhue, the editor of the *Pioneer*, has called it, Cretin's school."[61] So the terms Cretin's School and the Cathedral School remained interchangeable until 1914. At first various teachers including priests, nuns, seminarians, and layfolk served a mishmash of pupils of different ages and attainments. Enrollment stood at 100 in 1858, 250 in 1861. When John Ireland became rector of the cathedral in 1867, he appealed to the provincial of the Christian

---

58. For the details of Ireland's financial troubles and of his part in the campaign of 1896, see O'Connell, *John Ireland*, 380–386 and 424–428 and the sources cited there.

59. For much of what follows, see Daniel I. Moga, "The History of Cretin High School from Its Establishment to 1928" (Master's thesis, St. Paul Seminary, 1958).

60. See chapter 4, above.

61. Cited in the *St. Paul Pioneer Press*, May 6, 1928.

Brothers—as they were popularly known—to "come to St. Paul where your firm hand is needed in the cause of Christian civilization." He received a courteous refusal. He renewed his application several times during the spring of 1871, with the hope that staff could be sent to St. Paul by September. Two brothers would suffice, he said, though ten could be usefully employed. At this date Ireland clearly shared the common nineteenth-century unease about women teaching boys. Again the reply was negative.[62] Then Providence and Mrs. O'Leary's cow intervened. On October 8, 1871, the great Chicago Fire broke out, and during the conflagration two Christian Brothers schools were destroyed. On November 2, Brothers Jocondian and Diogenius John, both Irish, arrived "to take charge of the boys' department of the Cathedral School."[63]

Their experience in Chicago and elsewhere appeared to put some professionalism into the instruction and management of a gaggle of rowdy boys. Some improvements were made to the facilities, which the local press treated with its routine hyperbole, extolling their "elegance" and "superb ventilation." The next year several more brothers were added to the staff. The curriculum was firmed up, the ordinary grammar school classes augmented by "commercial courses" like bookkeeping and stenography. After Ireland was appointed bishop, he maintained a keen interest in the school, visited it often, and examined himself those pupils who were candidates for first Communion or confirmation. The brothers' overall success spurred other invitations. They taught for considerable intervals at the other two downtown St. Paul parishes—at the Assumption between 1875 and 1882 and St. Mary's from 1876 to 1891. The pastor of the latter, Louis Caillet, prided himself at having been a "Brothers' boy" back in France.[64]

But as the booming 1880s progressed it became painfully clear that the facility required a complete physical makeover. Cretin's second cathedral, long a school and now, on the top floor, the brothers' residence, had once been hailed as an artistic jewel. That judgment, however, had been made thirty years before, in a simpler frontier era. In the heart of the vigorous business district, at Sixth and Wabasha, it stood shabby and inadequate. Urgent repairs were necessary for roof, windows, walls. The bishop put off the brothers' repeated requests for extensive refurbishment, until November 1886, when flames partially gutted the building. A much lesser episode, to be sure,

---

62. Moga, "Cretin," 3–9.
63. *NWC,* October 21, 1871.
64. Moga, "Cretin," 10–13.

than what had happened in Chicago fifteen years earlier, but this fire also determined the Christian Brothers' relationship to the diocese of St. Paul. Their provincial informed Ireland that unless a new facility were provided he would withdraw his men. Construction began fifteen months later, and the second cathedral, which had served so nobly in so many ways, was torn down to make way for a department store.[65]

The new three-story building, with its brick and stone finish and hundred-foot tower, went up at the corner of Sixth and Main. The lower floors were set aside for the conventional classrooms and study halls, while on the third was an auditorium that could hold a thousand people. The cathedral parish raised $90,000 for the project and the other parishes in the city lesser amounts. Still technically Cathedral School, it was sometimes called Cretin Hall (the formal name of the auditorium) or simply the Catholic High School (since enrollment was open to boys from all parishes), but as time passed, most frequently Cretin High School. Through the 1890s a three-year secondary curriculum was introduced, which would ultimately evolve into a conventional four-year program. Even so, well into the twentieth century three quarters of the pupils followed a grammar school regimen, with a smattering of commercial courses added. Not until 1914, when a new cathedral school opened to accommodate the eight lower grades, did Cretin become exclusively a high school.

The Christian Brothers were not a little concerned at the beginning of the 1890s that Archbishop Ireland's celebrated speech before the NEA and his inauguration of the Faribault plan, with the implied ambivalence toward parochial schools, might have suggested a lack of an intention to support institutions like Cretin. They need not have feared; Ireland's pragmatic instincts would never have allowed him to jettison what had proved a marked success. Indeed, in observance of the silver anniversary of the arrival of Brothers Jocondian and John in St. Paul, the archbishop observed with characteristic rhetorical flourish: "I believe the best labors of my life were expended on that school [on Sixth and Wabasha]. I have watched the Brothers at work for a quarter of a century, and this is one of the greatest blessings of God, that we have the Christian Brothers in this city."[66]

And, a few years later, a similar blessing fell upon St. Paul's sister city. In 1900, thanks to a bequest of $10,000 from a prominent businessman and another $15,000 subscribed by the parishes in Minneapolis, property and

65. Moga, "Cretin," 14–17.
66. Moga, "Cretin," 19–25.

housing were purchased on Nicollet Island in the Mississippi. On October 1 the Hennepin Institute opened its doors. Fifty boys were enrolled and were taught by two Christian Brothers; another brother acted as handyman and cook. The next year they were joined by a third brother teacher. In 1902 the name of the institution was changed to De La Salle High School, in honor of the seventeenth-century founder of the congregation, and the following spring John Ireland presided at the first commencement exercises, during which thirteen graduates received diplomas. From these modest beginnings De La Salle emerged as a strong and enduring sign of Catholicism's coming of age in Minneapolis—and a significant unifying factor too—just as Cretin did in St. Paul.[67]

THE DEVELOPMENT OF A MASCULINE ELITE WOULD HAVE GONE for naught had it not been accompanied by similar progress on the feminine side. The expansion of the role played in church life by the congregations of religious women was crucial to the establishment of an orderly institutional structure. Many different orders were committed to teaching and nursing and nascent social work, from the Benedictines who had come to Minnesota in the early territorial days, to the Dominicans in Faribault, the School Sisters of Notre Dame in Mankato, and the Franciscans in Rochester and Winona.[68] But the single most important group were the Sisters of St. Joseph of Carondelet, who in their early days bore an unmistakable Irelandian cast.

The Ireland family that arrived in St. Paul in 1852 was indeed an extended one. Richard and Judith brought with them five children of their own as well as four of Richard's nieces and nephews who had been orphaned during the Famine. These children, named Howard, were more or less the charge of Richard's unmarried sister, Nancy. Ellen Ireland and Ellen Howard were the same age, four years younger than John Ireland. Close friends as well as cousins, they enrolled together in September of that year in the new St. Joseph's Academy. Six years later, over the mild objections of Richard and Nancy Ireland, the two girls, now aged sixteen, entered the Josephite novitiate. In 1860 Sister Seraphine Ireland and Sister Celestine Howard took their simple perpetual vows.

Eliza Ireland, two years the Ellens' junior, followed a different and more deliberate pace toward the convent. She too attended St. Joseph's Academy and was impressed by the nuns she encountered there. After graduation she

---

67. Reardon, *Diocese of St. Paul,* 667–668.
68. See chapter 8, above.

taught school in various places, including at a settlement of Irish immigrants immediately west of Minneapolis, a locale that would one day be called Edina. Eliza was twenty-four when she decided to join her sister and cousin in religion, and assumed the name Sister St. John, perhaps as a tribute to Mother St. John Fontbonne, who had sent the first Josephites to America, or to Mother St. John Fournier, who had led the first contingent of them to St. Paul.[69]

One reason John Ireland proved able to take on so many and such varied activities, to travel incessantly, to project his gravelly voice to the farthest corners of the largest halls, to maintain a mammoth correspondence in English and in French, to oversee to the most minute detail the building of this church or that school, all the while intriguing with the power brokers at the Vatican—one reason was that into his last years he enjoyed robust health. The same could be said of his sister Ellen, who lived into her eighty-ninth year. (Not so Eliza Ireland, who was always delicate and who died of consumption at the age of fifty-three.) Sister Seraphine also resembled her brother in other respects. She had the same kind of questing mind, the same willingness to take risks, the same sublime if sometimes naïve conviction that for the Church in America all things were possible. Her personality, like his, had the capacity to win the sturdy devotion of those with whom she worked. Her faith was firm and uncomplicated, her piety, like her brother's, was genuine if conventional.

Sisters Seraphine, Celestine, and St. John passed through the usual stages of a nun's calling during the last half of the nineteenth century. After postulancy and the novitiate—rife with the almost obsessive attention paid by their superiors to even the smallest infraction of the rule, allegedly meant to prepare them for the vicissitudes ahead—they took up teaching assignments as required. St. John, for example, first resided at St. Joseph's Academy, while she directed the girls' school at St. Mary's parish. Then she was appointed principal of the Academy and, two years later, in 1875, assumed a similar position at James McGolrick's Immaculate Conception in Minneapolis. In the beginning she had to commute from the nuns' residence in St. Anthony by foot or buggy. In 1877, however, a rented house on north Third Street was opened as a convent called from then on Holy Angels. The name was retained through several more moves and expansions through property that seemed always dilapidated—"We'll have all the old shacks in Minneapolis cleaned up before we find a home," Sister St. John remarked plaintively—until a large airy house on the corner of Fourth Street and Sixth Avenue North was purchased in 1882.

---

69. Sampson, *Seeds,* 137–140, 172, and chapter 3, above.

Here Eliza Ireland presided and directed a grammar school and the beginnings of a high school for girls until 1897 when, just before Christmas, her brother, the archbishop, administered to her the last rites.[70]

Her sturdier elder sister moved with remarkable mobility through a series of teaching assignments from the motherhouse in Carondelet, Missouri, briefly, and then back to St. Paul, St. Anthony, and Hastings. In the bleak little classrooms in all these places Sister Seraphine demonstrated extraordinary pedagogical skills. Demanding, yet good humored, she smoothly established good rapport with her pupils. Neither she nor any of her contemporaries could afford the luxury of specialization, and, since her own native curiosity was almost limitless, she cheerfully explored with the girls subjects as distinct as literature and astronomy, history and needlework, and that catch-all discipline combining fundamental mathematics and science called natural philosophy. Meanwhile, within the community her gifts for leadership as directress of several convents came to be recognized and respected. In 1882, when she had turned forty, she was named superior of the St. Paul province of the Sisters of St. Joseph of Carondelet. Ellen Ireland became Mother Seraphine.[71]

She held that position for thirty-nine years. When she took it on, there were 162 sisters in the province, living and working in eight convents—three in St. Paul, three in Minneapolis, one in Stillwater, one in Hastings—and administering ten parochial schools, two orphanages and a hospital. By the time she retired in 1921, Mother Seraphine had overseen the opening of more than two score Josephite institutions and had witnessed the number of nuns in the province edge toward a thousand. Particularly notable was the spread of the sisters' apostolate out of the Twin Cities and into the rural areas of Minnesota and the Dakotas. To be sure, not all of these establishments flourished, and some of them did not survive. But for Mother Seraphine this circumstance was a matter of out of sight, out of mind. Failure was not worthy of a mention; progress was the American Catholic way. Upon her retirement one of her contemporaries succinctly summarized Mother Seraphine's tenure: "Since 1882, the watchword has been 'Progress.' Build, increase in number, spread out, and strive for the means of doing so. This we did, and we are still striving. It is now part of our life."[72]

---

70. Sampson, *Seeds*, 173–175.

71. See Patricia Johnston, "Reflected Glory: The Story of Ellen Ireland," *Minnesota History* 48 (Spring 1982): 13–23.

72. See Hurley, *Good Ground*, 126, 164–172.

The third member of the Ireland family triumvirate displayed a distinct character of her own. Ellen Howard was more cautious and prosaic than her cousin Ellen, tougher than her cousin Eliza. Sister Celestine, perhaps because of these characteristics, displayed early on considerable administrative gifts. After the usual teaching assignments, she was appointed in 1879 supervisor of parochial schools staffed by the Josephites, which meant in effect that she oversaw the training of the sisters who taught in them. Three years later, when her cousin became superior, she assumed a place on the provincial council. In the deliberations of this ruling body Celestine proved a dependable ally of Mother Seraphine, though not without offering candid advice when it seemed to her that Seraphine paid too little attention to internal discipline or indulged in far-fetched plans and projects. Once a decision was reached, however, she adhered to it loyally.

In 1884, with the opening of St. Agatha's Conservatory of Music and Art, Ellen Howard received a fief of her own. It was first located on Tenth Street, near St. Joseph's Hospital, in a house whose owner vacated it when, so the story went, he had been sent to prison for murder. Two years later the conservatory was moved to a more commodious residence on Exchange Street. Here Mother Celestine ruled until she died in 1915. And "ruled" is the operative word. It was her duty to insist that the literally hundreds of young nuns who passed under her charge through the years should develop the decorum she deemed appropriate for religious women. But in doing so she proved to be something of a martinet, specializing, it seemed, in public rebukes and humiliations over trivial matters. When, for instance, she entered the common room, the sisters assembled there were expected to rise and bow; on one occasion a sister did not bow low enough or at any rate in the manner required, and Mother Celestine promptly made her practice the proprieties of bowing on the spot. Another resident recalled a morning when she and a companion were cleaning the superior's office while the rest of the community was eating breakfast. "Mother Celestine [came in] and said, 'Sister, did you have your breakfast?' 'No, Mother,' I said. She repeated the question ten times, and then she asked Sister Juliana, 'Did Sister have her breakfast?' Sister said, 'No, Mother. Thank you.' I didn't say 'thank you.' That is why she asked me ten times if I had my breakfast." Episodes like these stirred up resentment among some of even the best-disposed young nuns, but by and large they took the petty tyranny in stride, confident that the superior was not acting out of malice. A typical reaction came from one who fell under Celestine's sway in 1896: "I lived at St. Agatha's. I always liked it there, but I knew that a number of sisters didn't like it. Mother Celestine was pretty strict, but she had a heart. She would take the sting out of it by saying, 'You don't want to be a half a Sister. Be a whole Sister.' . . . I never found her hard. I wasn't afraid of her."

However ambiguous were the feelings Mother Celestine aroused in those who were subject to her, there is no doubt that St. Agatha's achieved great success under her leadership. The original plan called for the conservatory to furnish a residence for sisters teaching in the parochial schools in St. Paul, serving, that is, in parishes which could not afford convents of their own. But from the beginning Mother Celestine was determined that the institution should also be self-supporting and indeed turn a profit for the benefit of the community as a whole. So a kindergarten was opened on the premises and then, much more significantly, classes across a broad range of musical subjects—from instruction in counterpoint to training in performance on the piano and the zither—were introduced. Next came production by the sisters of fancy needlework and the copying of notable European and American paintings for direct sale. These activities proved especially lucrative and became even more so when incorporated into St. Agatha's curriculum. In 1912 no fewer than 817 students were registered in its various classes, all of which, in accord with the establishment's name, were related to music and art. So flourishing was the conservatory that four years earlier the rather ramshackle collection of structures on Exchange Street had been replaced by a handsome seven-story brick building. The austere Mother Celestine Howard may have been the least attractive member of the powerful Ireland family, but she exerted within her own domain an influence commensurate with that of any of them.[73]

Still, despite all the accomplishments of the pioneer Sisters of St. Joseph, the jewel in the crown remained to be fixed.[74] In November of 1891, at the observance of the fortieth anniversary of the arrival in the diocese of the first four Josephites, Archbishop Ireland delivered one of his patented rousing speeches, toward the end of which he said: "I offer my congratulations to the Sisters of St. Joseph for their promise soon to endow the Northwest with a college for the higher education of young women; and I take pleasure in pointing to this college as the chief contribution of their community to religion during the half century to come." But the panic of 1893—which landed John Ireland himself into such severe financial trouble—rendered the optimistic "soon" moot for the time being. Hope revived with the beginning of the new century. In 1900 the archbishop published a special edition of his col-

---

73. Sampson, *Seeds,* 162–168, and Reardon, *Diocese of St. Paul,* 657–658.
74. For what follows see Hurley, *On Good Ground,* 227–252.

lection of sermons and lectures, *The Church and Modern Society,* the proceeds from which he donated to the collegiate project. The sisters eventually
realized $60,000 from this benefaction, though only at the cost of peddling
the volumes all over the upper Midwest. Two years later a prosperous farmer
named Hugh Derham, in search of a worthy cause, was persuaded by Ireland
to give a further $25,000. In 1903 the cornerstone of Derham Hall was laid.
The first directress of the new institution, which opened its doors in 1905, was
the same Sister Hyacinthe who "with her beads and her habit" had taught
Catholic children under the supervision of the Stillwater school board in
1892.[75] At Ireland's suggestion, it took as its patron St. Catherine of Alexan-
dria, the symbols of whose martyrdom in the fourth century, the wheel and
the palm, had stood for centuries within the Church as signs of learning and
holiness.

In reality, however, the College of St. Catherine remained for at least a
decade no more than a struggling high school, set off on what was then a relatively remote tract of land in St. Paul's Midway district, with farmhouses and
muddy fields all round. Evolution into a genuinely collegiate program was
due to the persistence of Mother Seraphine and particularly to the relentless
efforts of Sister Antonia McHugh, whose dynamism and forcefulness were
reminiscent of the Irelands themselves. As teacher, dean, and, after 1919, president of St. Catherine's, Sister Antonia raised the necessary funds even as she
raised the academic standards that combined to put the college on its path to
becoming one of the most prestigious in the country.

John Ireland died the year before Sister Antonia assumed the presidency
of St. Catherine's. His had been a mercurial career. But whatever ups and
downs he had experienced, the institutional élites he had put together endured within the archdiocese more or less intact over the next forty years.

---

75. See chapter 13, above.

CHAPTER 15

The End
of an Era

A SISTER OF ST. JOSEPH, LATE IN LIFE, RECALLED HOW ARCHBISHOP Ireland, about 1915—the year his cousin, Mother Celestine Howard, died— paid regular visits to St. Agatha's Conservatory.

> The archbishop must have loved St. Agatha's, because he would bring distinguished visitors there. Or he would come himself, and we would all go in to meet him. We would sit on the floor in the parlor, because we did not have enough chairs for eighty-five Sisters who were in the room. Mother Seraphine . . . would also come. She would sit beside him and prompt him if there was something he forgot. He would do the same with her. He would tell about the early days, and so would she. The archbishop would also talk about his journeys, of his trips to Europe.[1]

Toward the end of his life John Ireland, like most old men, increasingly turned his thoughts to the past. He published appreciations of Bishops Loras and Cretin and had hoped to do the same for Bishop Grace. He founded the Catholic Historical Society of St. Paul, and in 1907 he launched its journal, *Acta et Dicta,* whose purpose it was to preserve in print what had happened in "the early days." "We must hurry to gather and to write," he declared in the introduction to the first number, "if much of the sweetest and best of our history is not to escape from us forever."[2] He remained an active member and sometime officer of the Minnesota Historical Society and joined in its ses-

---

1. Ann Thomasine Sampson, ed., "The Ireland Connection." Reminiscences based upon the Oral History Project of the Sisters of St. Joseph (St. Paul, 1982), 15.
2. *A&D* 1 (July 1907): 2–6.

sions with special zest when the subject at hand dealt with reminiscences of the Civil War.[3]

The more recent past held fewer charms for the archbishop. The internecine struggle within the hierarchy over the pace of Amercanization waxed and waned, and then, at the beginning of 1899, it reached a kind of climax. Locally the arena was the venerable German parish of the Assumption in St. Paul, whose pastor, a Benedictine named Alfred Mayer, had long been a thorn in Ireland's side, having publicly opposed the archbishop on matters like the Faribault school plan and the status of secret societies. After efforts lasting several years, Ireland finally prevailed upon the abbot of St. John's, whose subject Mayer was, to remove him from the pastorate. The disgruntled monk organized resistance within the parish, six members of which petitioned the apostolic delegate to reverse the abbot's directive. Mayer's removal, the parishioners argued, was "unjust and tyrannical," "without cause," due to "mere envy, jealousy, and prejudice," and was Ireland's way of "making room for religious liberalism or so-called Americanism . . . [and therefore] pernicious and a danger to Catholicism." The abbot refused to sanction the appeal, and the delegate rejected it out of hand.[4]

This relatively minor dispute was still pending—and so a nagging reminder that the battle had not yet been won even on his home ground—when Archbishop Ireland, in mid-January 1899, took ship to Rome in hopes of heading off a much more serious—indeed, a universal—threat to his program. He was too late. The long-rumored apostolic letter, titled *Testem benevolentiae*, was already in print. In it the pope declared it wrong to assert that the Holy Spirit bestows more charisms in the present day than in earlier ages; that direct inspiration obviates the need for spiritual direction; that natural virtues are preferable to supernatural, because the former prepare the Christian better for action in the world; that therefore active virtues are to be preferred to passive ones like humility, meekness, and obedience; that the vows taken by the members of religious orders inhibit liberty and hence are out of step with the imperatives of the present age. Such views, Leo XIII maintained, constituted a grave danger "to Catholic doctrine and discipline, inasmuch as the followers of these novelties judge that a certain liberty ought to be introduced into the Church," in imitation of "that liberty which, though

---

3. See, for example, Lucius Hubbard, "Minnesota in the Battles of Corinth, May to October, 1862," *Minnesota Historical Society Collections* (St. Paul, 1908), 536–546.

4. See the correspondence in ASV-DASU, St. Paul, fascicle 23.

quite recently introduced, is now the law and foundation of almost every civil community." But "the Church . . . is of divine right, while all other associations . . . subsist by the free will of men." And therefore "the bishops of America should be the first to repudiate [these] opinions," which some people label "Americanism," for otherwise they might fall under suspicion "of desiring a church in America different from that which is in the rest of the world," a Church "one in unity of doctrine as in the unity of government," with "its center and foundation in the Chair of Peter."[5]

John Ireland was quick to offer the repudiation asked for, both in a personal audience with the pope and in a letter published on February 22 in the *Osservatore Romano*, which issue also carried the text of *Testem*. But in doing so he drew a sharp and, to him, obvious distinction.

> I repudiate and condemn all the opinions which the Apostolic Letter repudiates and condemns. . . . [But I] cannot but be indignant that such a wrong should have been done to us—our Bishops, our faithful people, and our whole nature—as to designate, as some have come to do, by the word "Americanism" errors and extravagances of this sort.

Cardinal Gibbons replied similarly, employing, if anything, stronger language than his brother of St. Paul: "This doctrine, which [is] . . . extravagant and absurd, this Americanism as it has been called, has nothing in common with views, aspirations, doctrine, and conduct of Americans. I do not think that there can be found in the entire country a bishop, a priest, or even a layman with a knowledge of his religion who has ever uttered such enormities."[6]

In retrospect it would seem that Ireland and Gibbons were correct. Indeed, the pope himself, in the very text of *Testem benevolentiae*, admitted that the need for papal intervention arose "chiefly through the action of those who have undertaken to publish and interpret [these objectionable ideas outside the United States and] in a foreign language." Or, as Ireland put it more succinctly, a few bizarre notions "set afloat in France." But the harsh rivalries that had soured relations within the American hierarchy for more than a decade guaranteed that some bishops would seize the opportunity to strike a blow at their Americanizing brethren. Corrigan of New York and his suffragans formally thanked the pope, in the most servile tone, for having delivered Catholics in the United States from the "snare of Americanism," which otherwise

---

5. Text in *NWC*, March 3, 1899.
6. Quoted in Ellis, *Gibbons*, 2:71.

"would have taken tranquil possession in our midst, ever increasing its conquests," while Katzer of Milwaukee expressed "just indignation" that "not a few" American churchmen "affirmed that they reprobated the errors, but did not hesitate to proclaim . . . in Jansenistic fashion that there was hardly an American who had held them."[7]

John Ireland's Americanism had nothing to do with the charisms of the Holy Spirit or the relation of natural to supernatural virtues. "Who ever 'preferred' natural to supernatural virtues?" he asked a friend disgustedly. "Who ever taught that the practice of the natural virtues was not to be vitalized and supernaturalized by divine grace?"[8] His views sprang rather from an amalgam of principles, both personal and professional. He believed that American culture was no less unique than the French or Italian variety and deserved to be acknowledged as such, and that if integral Catholicism could be appropriately expressed in a style consistent with the singular genius of the nations of the Old World, so should it be with the nations of the New. Certainly the devotion to "liberty," which seemed to trouble Leo XIII, never meant for Ireland a freedom to question the Church's teachings on virtue and grace or on the prerogatives of the papacy, however some French intellectuals may have interpreted the word. But it did mean that within the American context the state's formal neutrality in matters religious was much to be preferred to the kind of organized hostility to the Church all too prevalent in the countries of Catholic Europe. Ireland wanted, to be sure, a measure of home rule—his autocratic instincts were never far from the surface—but he recognized the limits that an era of triumphant ultramontanism imposed. On a more emotional level, he was himself a successful immigrant and a genuine patriot who wanted his immigrant people to assume their due place in the life of the Republic. Resistance to assimilation into the American mainstream, he feared, far from protecting the faith, would in a generation or two render it irrelevant to the Catholic immigrants' descendants. In their time and place such convictions, if progressive, hardly smacked of the revolutionary; broadly speaking, Americanism appears to have been what an acute French observer dubbed it, "a phantom heresy."[9]

---

7. See Corrigan's correspondence in ASV-SdiS, 280 (1900), fascicle 3, and Katzer's in APF-NS, 147:144–146. In the seventeenth century the French Jansenists accepted a papal condemnation but denied that it applied to their views.

8. Ireland to Deshon, February 24, 1899, quoted in McAvoy, *Great Crisis*, 281.

9. Felix Klein, *Americanism: A Phantom Heresy* (n.p., 1951). Abbé Klein had edited a French translation of the *Life* of the progressive founder of the Paulists, Isaac Hecker, for which Ireland had written an introduction. Klein strongly took the view

Whether phantom or not—and indeed the passage of years has persuaded some that cultural assimilation has been a mixed blessing for the
Church in the United States—the promulgation of *Testem benevolentiae* had
been a bitter pill for Ireland to swallow. It issued from the pen of the pope
whom he believed he had served with more than ordinary loyalty. As a striking instance, less than a year before the publication of the apostolic letter, the
Vatican requested the archbishop of St. Paul to bend all efforts to head off the
impending war with Spain. This commission emanated partly out of Ireland's
own weakness for hyperbole; he had given the impression in Rome that as a
lifelong Republican, and particularly because of his intervention in the presidential campaign of 1896, he stood uniquely high in the counsels of the
McKinley administration. He hastened off to Washington and spent a month
tirelessly lobbying in behalf of a settlement but, in the end, to no effect. In fact
President McKinley listened sympathetically and did all he could to avoid
the conflict, but a hawkish Congress, a jingoistic press, and—perhaps most
significantly—events on the ground in Cuba led inexorably to a declaration of
war on April 25, 1898. Ireland's endeavors received a conventional word of
thanks from the Vatican: "In my name," wrote the papal secretary of state to
the apostolic delegate, "thank Archbishop Ireland for all he has done."[10] Such
faint praise may have sounded hollow, especially months later when *Testem*,
light slap on the wrist as it may have been, cast a shadow internationally over
principles Ireland had espoused throughout his priesthood.

The contest over Americanization at any rate was settled not by massive
rallies, nor the unseemly rhetoric indulged in by both sides, nor by the pope's
writ. It was settled by time. Such at least was the case for John Ireland and the
diocese of St. Paul. German, Czech, and Polish Catholics of the second generation, though they remained members of their national parishes and kept
in touch with traditional language and customs—and the Germans with their
mutual benefit societies—were virtually all English-speaking and virtually all
absorbed into Minnesota's political and economic structure. Moreover, the
vast waves of immigrants that flooded into the Americas from eastern and
southern Europe during the first two decades of the twentieth century touched
only the edges of the state. Thus of more than 2,000,000 Italians who arrived
in the United States between 1899 and 1910, fewer than 10,000 settled in all of
Minnesota, nor did that small proportion increase in succeeding years. In-

---

that the Church in France could do no better than to emulate its sister Church in the
United States.

10. See O'Connell, *Ireland,* 442–452.

deed, in 1912, more Italian-born residents returned to the old country than located in the state. By contrast, at this date 60,000 Italians, all nominally Catholic, were living in the city of Chicago. Poles came to Minnesota earlier and in larger numbers than Italians, but again comparison with Chicago is instructive: Polish Catholics in the Twin Cities in 1915 totaled about 15,000, while in Chicago at that time thirty-four Polish parishes ministered to more than 200,000 communicants, a number that swelled by another 30,000 over the next decade. In 1910 there were just thirteen Czech parishes in the five dioceses that comprised the state of Minnesota. By that time Americanization, at least in Archbishop Ireland's sense of the word, had been pretty much accomplished locally, even if the situation remained far different in the great population centers farther east.[11]

On a more personal level, the struggle within the American hierarchy abated for the same reason. The mitered combatants were older now and frailer—Ireland turned seventy in 1908—and a kind of *fatigue de bataille* had set in. Corrigan of New York died suddenly of pneumonia in the spring of 1902, and when he was buried amidst the splendors of St. Patrick's Cathedral, his implacable foe from Minnesota stood among the thousands of mourners. Ireland's sturdiest Americanist allies, Denis O'Connell and John Keane, lost favor at the Vatican, as did the brilliant but irascible and unpredictable Lancaster Spalding of Peoria, who was delated to Rome for a twenty-year-long and illicit sexual liaison.[12] Ireland, whatever he may have suspected, did not know for certain about this seamy affair, and he was glad to enjoy a reconciliation with one who had been alternately his friend and his enemy before Spalding died in 1916. Just as consoling perhaps—and perhaps the clearest sign that the internecine wars were over—were the three days before Christmas 1905 that Ireland spent as the guest of Bernard McQuaid of Rochester—McQuaid, Ireland's most outspoken opponent and yet, in his strength of character and heedless candor, so much like himself. And over this outbreak of peace and comity presided the genial and cautious, yet firm cardinal in Baltimore.

There was to be no cardinal in St. Paul, though Archbishop Ireland and his surrogates, clerical and lay, lobbied for the promotion over many years. It was neither an unreasonable nor dishonorable ambition: the red hat was the

---

11. For the numbers see Holmquist, *They Chose Minnesota,* 339–340, 364–368, 449–451, and Edward R. Kantowicz, *Corporation Sole: Cardinal Mundelein and Chicago Catholicism* (Notre Dame, Ind., 1983), 68–70.

12. See David Sweeney, *The Life of John Lancaster Spalding* (New York, 1965), 308–312, 347–352.

ultimate badge of papal approval and therefore the highest endorsement a Catholic churchman could receive for his policies and his person. Despite Ireland's stature and national reputation, and despite many hints and winks from Roman officialdom, this ratification never came. One reason certainly was the prolonged strife over Americanization as well as the suspicions fashionably attached to "Americanism." More prosaic was the fact that the archdiocese of St. Paul, in terms of its size and relative importance, did not figure large along the corridors of the Vatican. Indeed, the great sees along the Atlantic seaboard monopolized the American red hats until 1924 when the archbishop of Chicago, George Mundelein, was elevated to the sacred college (and Mundelein was a native of New York City). Ireland never ruled out the possibility that he might attain the prize; as late as 1914 the election of a new pope revived his flickering hopes, and some of his friends assured him the honor would come his way once the European war that began that year was over.[13] But it was not to be, nor did this disappointment unduly disturb the serenity of his latter years.

INDEED, JOHN IRELAND SEEMED CONTENT TO STAY AT HOME. Not since the early 1880s had he devoted exclusive attention to his own jurisdiction, and now it was as though he had found a second wind. A spate of pastoral letters flowed from his pen. He appeared regularly at the speaker's rostrum in the local observances of religious and civic celebrations. His carriage could be seen frequently rolling briskly down Summit Avenue toward St. Thomas and Mr. Hill's seminary, and to these outings he added, after 1905, visits to the young women at the new College of St. Catherine. The archbishop never arrived at these institutions without a bundle of books and journals under his arm, an old man now perhaps, but still anxious to talk to the faculty and students (talk to them, it should be noted, not discuss with them) about literature and history, tell them of his own conversations with celebrities like Julia Ward Howe and the novelist Marion Crawford, and increasingly reminisce about pioneer days. Until 1910, when an auxiliary was assigned him, Ireland performed all the confirmations and parish visitations himself. And in 1916, when the auxiliary was appointed to a see of his own, the archbishop did not ask for a replacement, though Rome quickly offered him one. That year a curial cardinal noted wonderingly that the archbishop was, in his seventy-eighth year, "more active than ever in preaching in the various parts of your

---

13. For details see O'Connell, *Ireland*, 473–498, 508–509.

large diocese."[14] Ireland still took the keenest pleasure in the grandiose gesture that demonstrated how the Church in the Upper Midwest under his tutelage had attained singular distinction. On the occasion of the sixfold consecration in 1910[15] he could not resist a jubilant brag to Cardinal Gibbons: "Six bishops, all of one Province, consecrated on the same day by the one metropolitan, . . . a scene rarely witnessed—never heretofore in America—not even," he added slyly, "in Baltimore."[16]

So, although his stock in Rome had fallen—as it had in fair France, where the church-state conflict flared up anew and the anticlerical government even closed down his beloved seminary at Meximieux—Ireland did not idle his last years away in vain regret over unfulfilled ambition. "The wise mariner," he wrote a French friend in 1911,

> sets his sail in accordance with the wind-currents of the moment. . . . It is quite uncertain when I shall again visit the dear land of the "Tricolore." I am very busy with many things—particularly with my new cathedrals, now journeying fast toward completion. And then the wind-currents across the Atlantic are not just now too favorable.[17]

The archbishop had indeed launched his grandest gesture of all. He was building a cathedral. Or rather, with characteristic bravura, he was building two cathedrals at once.

His ideas had taken a long time to bear fruit. Almost as soon as he became bishop in his own right, he had confided to friends his intention to replace soon the commodious but plain edifice begun by Cretin at Sixth and St. Peter Streets in the St. Paul business district and completed by Grace. In the beginning he, like other civic enthusiasts, entertained the hope that the Twin Cities might merge into one great city called "Paulopolis." Ireland planned therefore to locate the premier church of the archdiocese in the Midway area, not too distant from his college and seminary nor, he assumed, from a relocated state capitol. He accordingly purchased several spacious lots at Summit and Victoria, and, though no official statement was forthcoming, the site was dubbed, informally, the Cathedral Property. Meanwhile he

---

14. Falconio to Ireland, February 2, 1916, MHS, JIP, roll 13.

15. See chapter 14, above.

16. Ireland to Gibbons, May 1, 1910, AAB.

17. Ireland to Klein, December 7, 1911, Archives of the University of Notre Dame, Klein Papers.

assigned Father John Lawler[18] to organize a parish dedicated to St. Luke the Evangelist. By 1888 the energetic Lawler had constructed St. Luke's chapel a block back from Summit, at Portland and Victoria. This "charming ornament," as the local press described it, proved to be mother to the church that now stands majestically at Summit and Lexington Parkway.[19] But the dream of a single federal city faded away during the 1890s, and this, together with the economic depression and his far-flung preoccupations—to say nothing of his personal financial difficulties—led Ireland to one postponement after another. Not until the spring of 1904 did he decide to proceed with the project, which now, however, involved provision of suitable edifice for both St. Paul and Minneapolis.

The choice of sites for the new churches tells much about the personality and philosophy of John Ireland. In each instance the emphasis was upon *visibility:* in St. Paul the cathedral would stand atop St. Anthony Hill and look down magisterially at the commercial center of the city; in Minneapolis the procathedral—as the archbishop incorrectly called it[20]—would bestride an elevated piece of ground just at the edge of downtown and close to the point where Lyndale and Hennepin Avenues, the city's two busiest thoroughfares, intersected. Ireland had spent a lifetime arguing the compatibility of Catholicism and the American ideal, urging his immigrant coreligionists to adapt themselves to this new and wondrous land, protesting to his fellow citizens that Catholics deserved as full a participation in national life as any other group. Now he would leave, as his final testament, permanent statements in stone, more eloquent than all his innumerable speeches combined, which proclaimed that the Catholics had indeed arrived, had put down their roots, and had assumed their rightful place in the American secular city.

The first announcement of the archbishop's plans came on Christmas Day 1903, when he preached the festive sermon at the Immaculate Concep-

---

18. John Lawler (1862–1948), ordained 1885, consecrated auxiliary bishop of St. Paul 1910, appointed bishop of Lead, South Dakota, 1916 (the see was transferred to Rapid City in 1930).

19. Charles O'Fahey, "Pioneer Beginnings," in *Church of St. Luke: A Centennial Memoir, 1888–1988,* ed. Patricia Condon Johnston (St. Paul, 1988), 11–20.

20. Strictly speaking, the term "procathedral" is restricted to the church in a see city which for some reason has no proper cathedral. Minneapolis was not a see city until 1966, and since then the church Ireland built could be designated a "co-cathedral." See Reardon, *Diocese of St. Paul,* 382. The more familiar designation, since 1926, has been the Basilica of St. Mary, of which Reardon himself was pastor for many years.

tion, the largest and most prosperous parish in Minneapolis. He told his startled listeners that given the growth and wealth and prestige of their city it was not only fitting but essential for Catholics to establish their presence in a manner consistent with the contribution their faith made to the well-being of the community and to everyone who lived in it. The best way to accomplish this admirable goal, he said, was to build a structure worthy of the grandeur of their religion and the singular eminence of Minnesota's metropolis. He proposed therefore that the Immaculate Conception evolve into a new parish, a procathedral, which would be distinctly the archbishop's own church, would stand in relation to Minneapolis as did the cathedral to St. Paul. A few months later, at a similarly significant liturgical moment—Holy Thursday 1904— Ireland lamented from its pulpit at the inadequate space his cathedral provided for the crowds who wanted to attend Holy Week services. "Has the time not come," he thundered, "for a great Cathedral in St. Paul?"[21]

The fiscal challenge involved in this twofold project was more than formidable. The proportion of Catholics in the population of the Twin Cities was substantial, but not many of them were affluent. Those who were soon heard directly from the archbishop, who recruited as many prominent business leaders as he could to serve as channels of fund raising, whether as members on one of the network of committees organized to oversee the various phases of the construction process or simply by virtue of their own willingness to contribute or their personal and professional connections to the well-to-do. Thus in St. Paul, James J. Hill's son Louis gave the new cathedral fund $20,000 and acted as treasurer to the executive finance committee. In Minneapolis, Lawrence Donaldson, a leading merchant and a parishioner of the Immaculate Conception, paid $45,000 for property on which the procathedral was ultimately to stand. By mid-November 1905, large donors had pledged or contributed $347,000 for the new cathedral—a good beginning but hardly more than that. Ireland knew that sufficient funds could be raised only by mobilizing support throughout the whole of the Catholic community. To effect this end he was tireless, proclaiming the message—with its catchy slogan, "A Great State, A Great City, A Great Cathedral!"—to congregations, rural and urban, across the diocese. He published a pamphlet in German, French, Polish, and Bohemian, as well as English.

All will give [he wrote] as God permits them to give. There should be no one who, entering the Cathedral, is not able to say—it is mine. I have put

---

21. See Reardon, *Diocese of St. Paul,* 382, 373–374.

into the making of this great monument a stone that is mine. The stone, perchance, is small, but there it is; and, since it was the measure of my best will, God will reward it, as the earnest of my faith and love.[22]

But the archbishop was not content merely to persuade. To support construction of the new cathedral a direct assessment was imposed on all the parishes in the diocese—except those in Minneapolis and its hinterland, which instead were obliged to contribute to putting up the edifice at Hennepin and Lyndale. In the end this method proved substantially successful, but it did not always proceed at the pace Ireland desired. "Why, I beg leave to ask," he wrote with some impatience in 1911, "should there be among the parishes of the Diocese of St. Paul those that dispute among themselves the strange honor of being the latest arrivals at the goal of glory?"[23] Nor was he above practicing a little clerical extortion in behalf of the good cause. When that same year the golden jubilee of his ordination occurred, Ireland allowed no formal celebration, but, as he told Cardinal Gibbons, "I am tolerating the substantial substratum [of an] offering from the priests of the Diocese of $100,000."[24] The archbishop even mounted a kind of children's crusade. In the spring of 1906 little metal saving boxes were distributed to every child, and even before that, when he went to a parish to administer confirmation, he urged these youngest in his flock to offer their pennies to help complete a project of which, he promised, they could be proud all their lives. "My dear Child," he wrote one of them in the autumn of 1905,

> I thank you very cordially for your pretty letter of September 19 in which you tell me that you are going to set aside your savings for the benefit of the new Cathedral. This is a splendid idea. I pray God to bless you very richly. Sixty or seventy years from now it will be a great pleasure for you to read your name in the Memorial Volumes. They will contain the names of all the subscribers to the Cathedral. I pray that you may live at least that number of years, and that, meantime, you will always be dear to the heart of our blessed Savior. I shall try to have your example imitated by many children of the diocese.[25]

---

22. Quoted in Eric C. Hansen, *The Cathedral of Saint Paul: An Architectural Biography* (St. Paul, 1990), 27.

23. Ireland to pastors, April 8, 1911, MHS, JIP, roll 11.

24. Ireland to Gibbons, April 8, 1911, AAB.

25. Ireland to Esther O'Connor, September 25, 1905, Archives of the Cathedral of St. Paul.

On Sunday, June 2, 1907, amidst a fanfare of bands, banners, marching units, speeches by the governor of Minnesota and a United States senator, then more bands and marching, by Civil War veterans, old settlers, and uniformed cadets from the College of St. Thomas, the cornerstone of the new cathedral was laid. Almost exactly a year later a similarly resplendent if somewhat smaller ceremony took place in Minneapolis. The blueprints for both buildings were the work of Emmanuel Louis Masqueray. A bearded, forty-three-year-old French bachelor, who affected a cane, yellow gloves, and occasionally a cape, Masqueray was an alumnus of the prestigious Ecole des Beaux-Arts in Paris. He had settled in New York, and, after working for several notable architects, opened his own firm in 1901. Three years later he acted as chief designer of the Louisiana Purchase Exposition in St. Louis, and it was there that Archbishop Ireland contacted him and offered him the position of architect for his two cathedrals. Masqueray promptly accepted the commission. He spent the summer and autumn of 1905 touring the cathedrals of France, and then came to St. Paul where he spent the rest of his life. The trust placed in this relatively young man was amply rewarded; his gifts proved prodigious and varied, as testified to by the renaissance-basilica elegance of the Co-Cathedral of St. Mary and the neo-baroque grandeur of the Cathedral of St. Paul.[26]

Masqueray and Ireland worked well together, a circumstance abetted no doubt by the latter's francophile tastes. Both men spent a great deal of time at the two construction sites. But their joint enterprise proceeded slowly and painfully. And it was haunted all through its course by financial worries. Cash contributions frequently failed to match pledges; in 1908 workmen nearly had to be called off the job for lack of money to pay them or to pay for the materials they needed.[27] Five years later it appeared that the great dome of the cathedral could not be fixed to the edifice because of a lack of funds. In response to the crisis, a citizens' committee was organized, and at the end of January 1913, a delegation came to the archbishop's residence and presented him a purse of $100,000. The money, the spokesman explained, was contributed by people of all faiths and all classes, and included gifts as small as a dollar and as large as $2,500. It was intended to pay for the dome, but even more, he said, to represent a personal tribute of the people of his city to John Ireland himself. The old man responded with a poignancy he rarely indulged in.

---

26. See Hansen, *Cathedral,* 7–8.

27. See Smith to Ireland, July 28, 1908, and Ireland to Smith, August 1, 1908, Archives of the Cathedral of St. Paul. Prominent St. Paul businessman Charles H. F. Smith was chairman of the subcommittee on finance.

I would be unworthy indeed if I were not profoundly moved by this donation and these sentiments. Of all you have said, your declaration of esteem for me has pleased me most. I am an old settler in St. Paul. It was in 1852 that I came up the Mississippi and settled here. My whole life and work have been for St. Paul. It would be hard indeed if after all this I could not say I had friends here.[28]

And so the dome was lowered atop the vast church which, when completed, could seat 3,000 worshipers.

On Palm Sunday 1915, Mass was celebrated for the first time in the Cathedral of St. Paul, and in Minneapolis a few months later John Ireland solemnly dedicated what he continued to call the Procathedral of St. Mary, filled to its capacity of 1,400 people. The total cost of about $2,500,000 had been essentially met—$1,630,000 for St. Paul's, $775,000 for St. Mary's.[29] The interior decoration and permanent furnishing of both buildings were tasks left for the future, but the archbishop took justifiable pride in crowning his career with an achievement doubters had said could not be done. "Ah, your Grace," one Irish priest is reputed to have asserted before a shovelful of dirt had been turned over, "the socialists will make a hay loft of your fine building." But the socialists never came, and over the century that has passed since John Ireland thanked the little girl for her pennies, the two granite monuments he raised in homage to the faith have stood serenely amidst the turmoil of ever-changing times.

STILL, FOR ALL HIS PREOCCUPATION DURING HIS LAST YEARS with the erection of these two quite magnificent visual testimonies, Archbishop Ireland remained at heart a verbal man, a crafter of words, one who believed wholeheartedly in the power of the voice and the pen. It was therefore a distressful moment for him when in 1900 the mounting deficits of the *Northwestern Chronicle* forced him to close the paper and sell its subscription

---

28. Quoted in the *Catholic Bulletin* (CB), February 1, 1913.

29. See the figures in Reardon, *Diocese of St. Paul*, 378–379, 385–387. Comparing monetary values of different eras is a risky business, but it seems safe to speculate that to reach equivalence in dollars a century later one would need to multiply the amount expended on building the cathedral and the basilica by twenty or thirty times or perhaps even more. In 1913 a night's lodging in a respectable hotel in downtown St. Paul cost $1.50.

list to a publishing house in Milwaukee.[30] For a decade the archdiocese was without a journalistic voice. Then in the summer of 1910, at the annual retreat for the clergy, Ireland announced his intention to found another newspaper. Editorial space was rented in an office building at Fifth and Minnesota Streets in downtown St. Paul and a printer contracted. The first issue of the *Catholic Bulletin,* an eight-page broadsheet, came off the press dated January 7, 1911. Thanks to the archbishop's active promotion, it was mailed to twenty-five hundred prepaid subscribers.[31]

The founding editor of the *Bulletin* was thirty-eight-year-old James Michael Reardon. One among several young men recruited from Prince Edward Island in Canada for service in the archdiocese of St. Paul—"Pie Eyes," some waggish clerical colleagues dubbed them—Reardon was ordained in 1898. He joined the faculty of the St. Paul Seminary and then was appointed head of the archdiocesan Mission Band, a small group of priests who conducted spiritual retreats in various parochial and other institutional venues. He did not cede his editorial position even in 1916, when he became pastor of the venerable St. Mary's parish in St. Paul's Lower Town. Only in 1922, a year after he had assumed the pastorate of the misnamed Procathedral in Minneapolis—the Basilica of St. Mary—did he pass the direction of the *Bulletin* to other hands.

Reardon remained in charge at the Basilica till he died, aged ninety-one, in 1963, intriguingly fourteen months after the opening of the Second Vatican Council. Intriguing, because he typified perhaps better than anyone else the clerical culture that John Ireland had created which, in the wake of the Council, was swept away. Reardon idolized Ireland, and in some respects mirrored him. He too was a man of words who spoke well and wrote well, mixing a baroque formality with a touch of traditional Irish fluency, just as the archbishop had done so successfully. He too took a lively interest in local history, and, though he had no professional training, his work in that field—much of it cited in these pages—was thorough, careful, and remains valuable to this day. He too was intent to demonstrate that Catholics were good Americans who through sobriety and industriousness deserved their rightful place in the respectable middle class. Though he lacked Ireland's fabled charm, Reardon was like his mentor in demanding total and strict adherence to the rules he established within what he regarded as his area of responsibility. Generations of curates at the Basilica of St. Mary could testify to his conviction in this

---

30. Reardon, *Diocese of St. Paul,* 173.

31. Reardon, *Diocese of St. Paul,* 304–305.

regard. Duty was his byword, and like Archbishop Ireland he believed that his priesthood, so long as he abided by *its* rules, entitled him to a position of moral leadership within the Catholic community. James Reardon was, all in all, a formidable figure.[32]

He would not have been had he lived into the post–Vatican II era. In part this would have been a matter of style: Reardon's, like Ireland's, was imperious, without the latter's affability. Such a posture could not be sustained amid the profound societal changes that emerged out of the tumults of the 1960s and put a quietus to the age of deference. Among Catholics the adage that the priest knows best was no longer persuasive. Indeed, the men and women in the pews on a Sunday morning, so much better educated and more acclimated to the larger American culture than their uneasy immigrant forebears had been, often wondered whether the priest knew as much as or perhaps even less than they did. After the Council, the familiar feudal trappings fell away with astonishing swiftness. An archbishop now extended his right hand to be shaken, not to have the ring on it kissed. And the Roman pontiff no longer entered St. Peter's hoisted in a sedan chair, flanked by men carrying enormous fans made of ostrich feathers, and wearing a royal tiara on his head.

But of course Vatican II and its aftermath did much more than simply diminish the automatic authority enjoyed by the likes of James Michael Reardon. The Council occasioned the raising of a host of issues of supreme importance to the life of the Church, not all of them by any means treated in the formal conciliar documents. And the changes that resulted swept across the ecclesiastical board: changes in the execution and meaning of the liturgy, in the norms of personal piety, in the understanding of the priesthood and the religious life, in the appreciation of the collegial character of church authority, in an intensified awareness of the apostolate of the laity, in a troubling ambiguity about the nature of human sexuality. It is safe to say at this distance in time that the bishops assembled in Rome between 1962 and 1965 did not foresee how radically different the Catholic Church would become as a consequence of their deliberations, nor the bitter contentions that later erupted. Even safer to say is that Monsignor Reardon could not possibly have comprehended what has happened since Vatican II in the Church he had served as a priest for sixty-five years.

---

32. In the mid-1940s my parents were members of the Basilica parish. As a student in the minor seminary, I was required every September to obtain a letter from my pastor testifying to my good behavior during the summer holiday. So, as a teenager, I gained an insight into the meaning of fear and trembling when I rang the bell of the Basilica rectory and asked to see Monsignor Reardon.

Therefore his witness to the lives led by Catholics in Minnesota during Ireland's last years (and the early years of his successor) manifests a certain poignancy. Much of what he and the readers of his *Catholic Bulletin* took for granted has passed away. Not the sacraments, to be sure, or the formal creeds or the primacy of the gospel. But surely the emphases have changed, the priorities have been scrambled, the very definition of "Catholic" has undergone reexamination. Just as surely, however, this circumstance should come as no surprise. As Newman famously observed: "In a higher world it is otherwise, but here below to live is to change and to be perfect is to have changed often."[33] With all due respect to the great English cardinal, perfection in that growing organism, the Body of Christ, remains as tantalizingly elusive as ever. But what at any rate Newman really argued throughout his *Essay* was that lines of legitimate development—legitimate in the sense that they were not inconsistent with the original testament—can be discerned in the teachings and practice of the Church across the centuries. Father Reardon, in his capacity as editor of the *Catholic Bulletin*, was in a unique position to provide insight not only into the substance and flavor of Catholic life at a particular point in time but also, quite unconsciously, to impart a measuring stick for later generations to judge if and how, as the rather cynical French dictum has it, The more things change, the more they remain the same.

"The *Catholic Bulletin*," the editor wrote in the inaugural issue, "has no other cause to subserve [sic] than that of the Catholic Church, particularly in the Northwest, by ministering to the intellectual needs of her children in all that appertains to their spiritual welfare." This statement of policy appeared on page four. In this and succeeding numbers Reardon maintained a consistent, even rigid, pattern of presentation, reflecting perhaps the orderliness of his own mind. On page three, for example, there was always a section devoted to matters "Doctrinal, Devotional, [and] Liturgical"; here too the reader found the "Saint of the Week." Snippets of news from each diocese in the province were printed on page five; for instance it is noted that in St. Paul forty new students had matriculated at the College of St. Thomas, bringing the total enrollment to 650, many of them to be housed in a new dormitory which would cost $125,000.[34] Page six was devoted to reports from Catholic missionary endeavors in Asia and Africa. Every week, on page seven, one could find "Gleanings by the Wayside: Select Reading for the Family," short,

---

33. *Essay on the Development of Christian Doctrine* (London, 1845), 242.

34. This was Ireland Hall, still in use at St. Thomas. I lived there between 1966 and 1972.

inspirational pieces of fiction and poetry. Included in the "Gleanings" was "The Children's Hour," often featuring a poem like this one, author anonymous, which began: "Be something in this living age. / Prove your right to be / A light upon some darkened page, / A pilot on some sea." A question-and-answer column regularly appeared on page eight; not untypical was this query: "What is meant by saying that a person gains fifty days indulgence by performing certain acts?" Also on page eight was "Secular News of the Week," a smattering of dispatches local, national, and international.[35]

The *Bulletin* carefully refrained from discussing American politics, except in the most tangential manner. It appeared worthy of comment that the notorious Chauncey De Pew was succeeded in the United States Senate by a Catholic—the only one in that august body—and that a Catholic was appointed head of the Brooklyn Navy Yard.[36] But the anticlerical politicians in other countries received censure regularly. These miscreants were usually lumped together as "radical socialists" who, along with the Freemasons, worked their evil way through Italy, France, and Austria. The paper wondered darkly whether the increase in illiteracy among recruits to the French army was the product to be expected of "the infidel Republic."[37] Reardon published the full text of Pope Pius X's encyclical condemning the separation of church and state in Portugal.[38] In 1917 he reprinted Archbishop Ireland's article on the church-state crisis in Mexico. Characteristically the old Americanizer seemed more concerned about the effect that struggle might have in promoting anti-Catholic propaganda in the United States than about the situation in Mexico itself. Nor did he manifest any multicultural sympathies: he defended the Mexican bishops, many of whom had been exiled or imprisoned, because, he wrote, they had been striving "to uplift the people of Mexico, so far as they have been permitted to do so by the native peculiarities of the people themselves."[39]

Other features were gradually added to the weekly intellectual fare provided by the *Bulletin*. By 1913 signed "Letters to the Editor" began to appear; those Reardon chose to print were notably uncontentious in tone and substance. Reviews of edifying books also turned up now and then, furnishing as often as not warnings to avoid heretical or immoral literature. That same year a new department of "Domestic Science" was introduced on the grounds that

---

35. *CB*, January 7, 1911.
36. *CB*, April 8, 1911, and August 24, 1912.
37. *CB*, January 28, 1911.
38. *CB*, June 24, 1911.
39. *CB*, April 14, 1917. The article appeared originally in *Extension*.

too many "untutored girls" think it easy to become good housewives till problems arise. The first brief article was titled simply "Food," in which a comparison is drawn between the needs of a locomotive and a human body, along with a fairly sophisticated treatment of fats, oils, proteins, carbohydrates and the like. Two weeks later came "Stoves: How to Build a Fire, Starting a Fire, Air in its Relation to Fire," and the week after that, "Dish Washing."[40]

Of course every issue of the *Bulletin* contained local news. One number in 1917 might serve as an exemplar as to how the paper chronicled some of the variety and vitality of parish activities within one wintry week. In St. Paul, St. Andrew's Drama Club performed "The Man of Mystery"; admission was fifty cents for adults, twenty-five cents for children, proceeds to support the parish school. A few nights later, also at St. Andrew's, a local judge addressed the meeting at which forty-eight enthusiastic volunteers set up a chapter of the St. Vincent de Paul Society. At St. Michael's, a branch of the Propagation of the Faith was instituted; a hundred people attended the initial meeting. At St. Luke's, 126 young men and women gathered to organize a society "for their religious and social advancement," the officers of which included a spiritual director (the pastor) and a treasurer; an "entertainment committee" was promptly appointed. At St Mark's, a professor from the University of Minnesota lectured on "Bees" to the pupils in the school; on the evening of the same day a musical performance was presented in the parish hall by soprano and tenor soloists, with a "reader" and a pianist. At St. Lawrence, in Minneapolis, a Junior Holy Name Society was established, with the aim of enrolling all the boys of the parish. At St. Stephen's, "a large and appreciative audience filled the hall" for the Dramatic Club's production of the comedy "Cranberry Corner." As for parishes outside the Twin Cities, there was a ladies' card party at Watkins; a basket social at Murdock; a Father Mathew Temperance Society inaugurated at Belle Creek; and an installation of new members of the Ancient Order of Hibernians in the parochial school in Montgomery.[41]

The subscription price of the *Catholic Bulletin* was $1.50 per annum, "payable in advance." (For comparison's sake, it should be noted that in 1911 the Merchants' Hotel in St. Paul—where more than half a century earlier young Mary Theresa Mehegan had waited on tables and met the up-and-coming James Jerome Hill—charged in accord with its "European Plan" one or two dollars a night, with fifty cents added for a bath.)[42] But like all

---

40. *CB*, January 4, 18, and 25, 1913.
41. *CB*, January 13, 1917.
42. *CB*, July 1, 1911.

newspapers the *Bulletin* needed to supplement its income by selling advertising. In the early years, prominent among advertisers were Catholic schools, from which little revenue could be expected, and banks, one might assume rather more promising. By 1917, though the schools continued to appeal to readers, representation of the banks had virtually disappeared. Plenty of firms and professions, however, found it advantageous to advertise in the *Bulletin*, and in doing so they painted a picture of the kind of consumers the Catholics of the Twin Cities had become. The most faithful advertiser was the Rasmussen Practical Business School, its message on display in every issue. The caption was always the same—"Don't go to School 'to have a good time' but to be useful and successful!"—as was the accompanying photo of a stern-looking man, presumably Mr. Rasmussen, pointing a finger at the viewer. Among other ads were those for the St. Paul Milk Company; Prendergast Plumbing, Heating, and Tinning; St. Paul Gas Light Company; Henderson and Company, Stock, Bond, and Grain Brokers; a Minneapolis wholesale grocery business; a dentistry firm with offices in both St. Paul and Minneapolis; a funeral parlor in Minneapolis and a chiropodist named Edwin Murphy in St. Paul; McCluskey Clothiers, selling "silk-lined topcoats" valued at $25 for $15. And this fetching announcement: "Dr. Margaret Whalen has opened offices in the New York Life Building. Exclusive Catholic Osteopathic Physician in St. Paul." Almost as loyal as Mr. Rasmusssen, and destined to remain so long after he was gone, was this advertiser: "The E. M. Lohmann Co. Church Goods. Religious Articles. 385–387 St. Peter Street." Appended to this plain statement was a list of the ten altar wines available, among them sauternes and clarets. "All our wines are more than four years old."[43]

Running like a leitmotif through the pages of the *Bulletin* during these years—the last decade of John Ireland's life—was a concern to show that Catholicism was not only compatible with American culture but also a guarantor of American values. This perspective is hardly surprising, since it was at the heart of the policy that Ireland had always advanced and that Reardon heartily endorsed. The alacrity, however, with which the editor pounced upon any testimony even remotely favorable to the Church reveals an uneasiness in himself and in the community his newspaper served. Had Catholics really been accepted by the larger American community? Had they received from their fellow citizens the respect they and the tenets of their religion deserved? Any scrap of outside approval was eagerly seized upon. The cordial relationship between Theodore Roosevelt and Archbishop Ireland was duly noted.

---

43. *CB*, March 17 and June 9, 1917.

But so was the assertion, prominently displayed on the front page, of an obscure Presbyterian minister in Minneapolis that the divorce rate in Ramsey County was half that in his own Hennepin, due, he said mournfully, to the greater influence of Catholicism in St. Paul and its environs.[44] It seemed important to stress any secular success or recognition a Catholic might achieve, however little its relation to the local scene; not untypical headlines included "Catholic Wins Scholarship to Edinburgh University" and "Governor Appoints Catholic as Health Officer of the Port of New York," adding with satisfaction that this gentleman would receive the handsome salary of $12,500 a year.[45] At the beginning of 1917 Father Reardon initiated a new series called "Protestant Tributes to Catholicity."

In April of that year the United States entered the First World War. The *Catholic Bulletin* up till then had paid scant attention to the hostilities raging across Europe. Now that policy changed dramatically. John Ireland set the tone. Under the headline "Nation's Life is at Stake" he wrote: "How much there is at stake! There is at stake the dignity, the honor, the life of America, and all the sublime things symbolized in the word America. . . . The flag is now unfurled: it must float before the nations of the earth in the sunshine of triumphant victory. The call to each and every citizen of America is to do his best for America," not merely to those "privileged" to cross the sea and engage in battle.[46]

The war stories that henceforth dominated the *Bulletin*'s pages showed much of the same disquiet that had prompted the introduction of "Protestant Tributes to Catholicity." The war could be an occasion for Catholics to prove they were genuine patriots, indeed more patriotic than most others, more dedicated to enfold Old Glory "in the sunshine of triumphant victory." So there were accounts of gallant chaplains—warmly welcomed by the War Department—and of nuns ready and willing to serve in conjunction with the Red Cross as nurses for the armed forces.[47] Much attention was paid to the endeavors of the Knights of Columbus, who, among other good works, pledged a million dollars to "provide for the spiritual and social welfare of the Catholic troops."[48] Lively descriptions were printed of military drills now carried out with heightened earnestness by the cadets at the College of St. Thomas. A hastily organized "Civilian Auxiliary" composed of "business

---

44. *CB*, February 11, 1911.
45. *CB*, March 2 and 9, 1912.
46. *CB*, April 28, 1917.
47. *CB*, June 30 and July 21, 1917.
48. *CB*, June 30, 1917.

men, professional leaders, and tradesmen" from St. Paul and Minneapolis soon joined them.[49] In October the archbishop formally recommended the purchase of war bonds.[50] A month later it was asserted that the membership of the first American unit to move into the front lines in France—a battalion of engineers—was forty percent Catholic. Indeed, the *Bulletin* claimed, Catholics made up fully one third of the manpower in the United States army. Moreover, Catholic soldiers performed much better in situations requiring physical stamina than did their comrades of other faiths. "Shall we conclude that Catholics are more patriotic because they lead cleaner lives?"[51]

Hyperbole there may have been in many such stories, but that detracts nothing from the gallantry of those who rallied to the colors at a moment of world crisis. Nor was the *Bulletin's* reiteration of the devotion of Catholics to their country in the midst of war misplaced. First of all, it was perfectly true,[52] and, besides that, it reflected a necessary step in a rite of passage whereby the Church moved out of its immigrant past into a genuinely American setting. Conditioned as Catholics were by a commitment to a worldwide communion, this was an on-going process—and perhaps it still is. But John Ireland in 1917 had no doubt of the significance of the moment.

> All are ready for the self-same service—that of America. With good reason I am entitled to pronounce judgment in this matter. I have peculiar opportunities to know the several elements in our population—and I stand up at all times to bear testimony to the loyalty of all of them. . . . All are Americans, and Americans all will be. Where today are the Irishmen? Only in far-off Ireland; none today on the soil of America; none west of the Atlantic Ocean. Where today are the Germans? Only in far-off Germany; none west of the Atlantic Ocean. Here all are Americans. . . . It is wonderful. . . . It is the accomplished fact.[53]

The old veteran of the battle of Corinth, one of "the soldiers of Abraham Lincoln," sensed that this new war, whatever its tragedies, would at least bring with it a victory for Americanization.

---

49. *CB*, April 21 and June 2, 1917.

50. *CB*, October 13, 1917.

51. *CB*, November 3 and 10, 1917.

52. Three of my uncles, Catholics from the Archdiocese of St. Paul, served in the First World War. One of them suffered a bayonet wound that permanently impaired his health.

53. *CB*, April 28, 1917.

But he had little time to savor such thoughts. Even as he voiced them he was seriously ill of arteriosclerosis. His doctors insisted that he avoid the rigors of a Minnesota winter, and so in January 1918, he went to St. Augustine, Florida. He celebrated his eightieth birthday there, and reported to friends back home that "progress there is, but more slow than I would like it to be." By the end of April, however, back in St. Paul, he took to his bed. He lingered through the summer, growing ever weaker, and by early September the death watch had begun. Constant at his bedside were his sister Ellen—Mother Seraphine—and Thomas O'Gorman, his closest companions and confidants over the whole of his tempestuous career. A few minutes before four o'clock in the morning of Tuesday, September 25, 1918, he died.[54]

Not least among James Michael Reardon's contributions to the well-being of the archdiocese of St. Paul was his editorship of the *Catholic Bulletin*. He provided his fellow Catholics with a wide-ranging, literate weekly which informed and, no doubt, often inspired them. And he succeeded also in a business sense. By the time he stepped down in 1922, he left a subscription list that had increased by a factor of ten, to 25,000, "twelve hundred dollars in cash and bonds, a well-equipped office, and no obligations." Upon reflection he was careful to point out that Archbishop Ireland had in no way tried to influence the *Bulletin*'s policy. "At no time did he insist that his views be made the views of the paper. In this regard the editor had fullest freedom and his fullest confidence."[55] But in fact Ireland did not need to interfere; he knew full well that Reardon shared his own vision down to the last jot and tittle. Indeed, through his powerful personality, his gifts for leadership, and his immense moral and physical stamina—no doubt abetted by the circumstances of a particular time and place—Archbishop Ireland had fashioned the Catholic Church in the Upper Midwest to a considerable degree in his own image and likeness. So much was this the case that anyone who followed him would only with great difficulty emerge from the great man's shadow. An anecdote that has circulated for eighty years has it that Reardon, featured speaker shortly after Ireland's death at some clerical function, concluded his remarks by quoting a line from the gospel: There was a man sent from God whose name was John. Then, looking down at the new archbishop, he said: And when shall we see his like again?

Perhaps the story is apocryphal. Perhaps not.

---

54. See O'Connell, *Ireland*, 516–518.
55. Reardon, *Diocese of St. Paul*, 394–386.

CHAPTER 16

The Travails
of Austin Dowling

FOUR MONTHS AFTER JOHN IRELAND'S FUNERAL, WORD REACHED
St. Paul that his successor had been appointed. The editor of the *Catholic Bulletin* was not particularly impressed. Shortly after Ireland's death, James Reardon wrote,

> speculation arose in many quarters as to who would succeed him. The
> Diocese of St. Paul has been for many years both intrinsically and extrinsically important. Intrinsically, by reason of its size, its institutions, and
> its large and growing Catholic population. Extrinsically, St. Paul may be
> said to have been one of the most important sees in the Catholic world,
> because it was the home of the great Archbishop Ireland. For these reasons, rumor began to attach itself at once to the names of various prelates
> throughout the country who were looked upon as big and progressive.
> Rome, however, has a custom of discounting rumors of this nature. The
> various bishops mentioned for the Diocese of St. Paul were men of great
> worth and ability. The appointment of Bishop Dowling being confirmed,
> St. Paul may well congratulate itself upon the acquisition of a young, vigorous prelate and able leader.[1]

Thus was Austin Dowling welcomed to Minnesota with a tribute of faint
praise.

In fact the appointment was as much a surprise to the new archbishop as
it was to those who had expected a "big and progressive" man—"I'm dis-

---

1. *CB*, February 8, 1919.

mayed at having to succeed so great a personage," Dowling confessed.[2] So dismayed, in fact, that the palpitations of his heart led him to hurry off to Chicago and consult a celebrated cardiologist. After a thorough examination the doctor said, "That heart can work ten years longer." Never a robust man—as early as 1902, when he was thirty-four, he had spent six months' sick leave in Germany—the heart actually kept beating, though sometimes irregularly, for eleven years.[3]

But Dowling in any case never failed to acknowledge straightforwardly the challenge involved in succeeding an iconic figure like Ireland. When the train carrying him and his party from southern Iowa entered the confines of the archdiocese, at Faribault, he spoke briefly from the rear platform to the crowd of more than eighteen hundred who had come to the station to greet him. They saw a short, plump man, only weeks away from his fifty-first birthday, with scanty graying hair, a fair complexion, and delicate features. They heard a strong, confident voice, but one quite unlike the honeyed thunder of Archbishop Ireland in his prime.

> My dear people, to you all I am a stranger. The only tie that binds us is our common faith. I am come to follow in the footsteps of your late Archbishop, one of the greatest men of the past century. It shall be my constant endeavor to carry out his plans and the traditions he has bequeathed.[4]

Daniel Austin Dowling[5] was born in New York City on April 6, 1868, the son of an Irish immigrant couple, Daniel and Mary Santry Dowling. While still a small child, he moved with his parents and sister—two other sisters died in infancy—to a new home in Newport, Rhode Island. Austin was a frail, bookish lad who did well in the schools conducted by the Sisters of Mercy in Newport. Upon graduation from their St. Mary's Academy, he was deemed

---

2. Frances Boardman, "In Remembrance," in *The Commonweal* 7 (January 7, 1931): 261–262. Boardman was a reporter for the *St. Paul Dispatch* who interviewed Dowling in Des Moines on the eve of his departure for Minnesota.

3. M. Antonie Dowling, "Biographical Sketch, Most Rev. D. A. Dowling, D.D., Archbishop of St. Paul," AASPM, Dowling Papers. This affectionate memoir by Dowling's sister, fifteen typed pages, recalls the events of his childhood and career as a priest in Rhode Island.

4. *Faribault Daily News*, March 24, 1919.

5. See Marvin R. O'Connell, "The Dowling Decade in St. Paul" (Master's thesis, St. Paul Seminary, 1955), 3–6.

too young to begin a collegiate career; instead he was tutored intensely for a year in Greek and Latin by his parish priest. This pause in his formal education proved propitious, because, when he enrolled in Manhattan College in New York, Austin's preparation in the classics so impressed the Christian Brothers who conducted the college that they assigned him to the sophomore class. He was barely nineteen when he received a bachelor's degree with high honors. He then entered St. John's Seminary in Brighton, just outside Boston, to prepare himself for the priesthood. There he was a fellow student of James Walsh who was later to found the Maryknoll Missioners.[6] After three years at Brighton, Dowling was sent by his bishop to the Catholic University of America in Washington to complete his theological studies. He was ordained for the diocese of Providence on June 24, 1891. Father Dowling spent the first year of his priesthood in graduate study at Catholic University. His chosen field was history, which remained his primary intellectual interest all his life. One of his professors at Catholic University was Thomas O'Gorman. A year of parochial work in Providence was followed by two and a half years teaching church history at Brighton, a seminary that served all the dioceses of New England. From 1896 to 1898 he edited the *Providence Visitor,* "and during that period he was probably the most widely quoted Catholic editor in the country."[7] A year before the turn of the century Dowling returned to the pastoral ministry, and in 1905 he was appointed rector of the Cathedral of SS. Peter and Paul in Providence, a post he held for seven years. In mid-January 1912, he learned that he had been named first bishop of Des Moines.

And so it was that Dowling—in the words of a flowery accolade offered him at the end of his tenure in Des Moines—left "the splendor and affluence of the East," and came to the Midwest, "where he readily and effectively put his hand to the plow in the humbler surroundings of Iowa."[8] Humble indeed: the young bishop found in his new diocese a small Catholic population—numbering hardly 25,000—and limited physical resources. Certainly his experience as teacher, editor, and pastor in New England stood him in good stead, and though he had little to work with he performed the tasks at hand diligently. His unassuming and modest manner won him regard in the wider, overwhelmingly Protestant community. He demonstrated that his first con-

---

6. Antonie Dowling, "Biographical Sketch."

7. *CB,* December 6, 1930. The *Bulletin,* Father Reardon no longer the editor, was kinder to Dowling in its obituary notice than it had been at his unexpected appointment in 1919. But the unlikely plaudit here quoted expressed the kind of bravado Dowling himself most disliked.

8. Quoted in *CB,* March 15, 1919.

cern, as it was to be throughout his episcopal life, was the establishment of as strong a program of Catholic education as possible. His greatest single achievement in this area was the founding of Des Moines Catholic College, which opened its doors in September 1918.

Circumstances, in short, determined that his record in southern Iowa was worthy but necessarily modest and hardly a warrant for promotion to the much larger responsibilities in Minnesota. There he was to become pastor of a flock more than ten times as numerous as the one he left behind. There his professional collaborators would include 350 priests, instead of sixty, and 1,200 nuns. There in excess of 31,000 children and young people were enrolled at all levels in Catholic schools, considerably more, that is, than all the Catholics living in the diocese of Des Moines.[9] It is a doctrinal truism that the Holy Spirit breathes where he wills, but not without the involvement of human agents. Clearly Austin Dowling had friends in high places.

He was installed as second archbishop of St. Paul on the feast of the Annunciation, March 25, 1919. The ceremony, with its usual pomp and circumstance, took place in John Ireland's cathedral, a massive and imposing edifice on the outside but, as Dowling surely noticed, bare, cold, and undecorated within. Once enthroned he listened to the welcoming speech of Father James Byrne, pastor of St. Luke's parish in St. Paul and administrator of the archdiocese during the interregnum. Byrne, a pulpit orator very much in the Ireland mold, concluded his rambling remarks in the flamboyant style so long in the ascendancy.

> In this ferment of ideas and conflict of interests, were you to bring genius and learning alone, you would only add one more voice to the discordant tumult. But besides genius and learning you bring a kindly, benevolent, charity-inflamed heart for all; and in a democracy like ours, charity, if it can only be discerned, wins the victory—whether prophecies be made void and tongues cease and all knowledge be destroyed.[10]

Dowling's response provided perhaps the first clear sign, to priests and people at large, how different the new ecclesiastical regime was going to be. He was eloquent, to be sure, but his was the eloquence of simplicity and directness. "My first thought," he began in accord with ultramontane convention, "is reverence and loyalty to the Holy See." He paid due tribute to "the

---

9. For statistics see Reardon, *Diocese of St. Paul,* 423.
10. Full text printed in *CB,* March 29, 1919.

revered and wonderful Archbishop Ireland," and went on to enumerate some of the manifold works of his predecessor, and to praise them and him. His evocation of the Renaissance may have startled some of his more rough-hewn listeners: "In appearance large and majestic," said the diminutive Dowling—he stood at five feet, five inches—"[Ireland] reminded me always of nothing quite so much as of those wonderful figures that Raphael used to draw." He ended on a sober note.

> I pray God to give me the courage to do the things that must be done here. . . . I pray for the assistance of the clergy and laity. What great men like Archbishop Ireland could do alone, I do not presume to attempt to achieve without the help, assistance, and cooperation of all the people.[11]

After the formal installation, the new archbishop offered solemn pontifical Mass. Among the thousands in attendance was Dowling's sister, Mother Antonie of the Sisters of Mercy, who sat proudly in the front pew. A banquet was served for the clergy following the Mass in the spacious Knights of Columbus Hall, at the end of which, in accord with clerical custom, came the inevitable after-dinner speeches. Each of the eight suffragan bishops took a turn, except O'Gorman of Sioux Falls, who was ill. Their talks were much alike, all mercifully brief, all full of compliments for the new archbishop and expressing confidence in a glorious future. But amidst the good cheer and ecclesiastical hyperbole there were several snide references made to Dowling's eastern origins. Thus Patrick Heffron of Winona, one of Archbishop Ireland's sturdiest disciples, observed that when Dowling learned of his appointment to Des Moines "he knew not where the place was." Beneath this seemingly innocent jibe lay a vein of resentment which was to dog Dowling throughout his eleven years in St. Paul. Joseph Cretin had come as a missioner from France and Thomas Grace from Memphis, and the heroic John Ireland had been singularly one of their own. Six of the suffragans were local priests, molded in Ireland's image, while the seventh, the Benedictine Vincent Wehrle of Bismarck, had been a veteran missioner in North Dakota and had been made a bishop, not coincidentally, in Ireland's celebrated sixfold consecration ceremony in 1910.[12] Only the Dominican John McNicholas of Duluth stood outside the Ireland orbit, and his appointment had occurred a few scant

---

11. A copy of this speech, in Dowling's own hand, is in AASPM, Dowling Papers.

12. See chapter 14, above.

months before the old archbishop's death.[13] None of these men—and not a few unmitered priests of the archdiocese as well—believed they were less worthy of promotion to the great see of St. Paul than the little man from Rhode Island who had spent seven obscure years in Des Moines.

Dowling, if he sensed such undertones, paid no heed to them. As ever the gentleman, he replied with the courtesy and straightforwardness that were to become the hallmarks of his episcopate. After a gracious reference to the absent O'Gorman—"Thirty years ago I sat at his feet in the halls of the Catholic University and took notes in his history course. Today the absence of Archbishop Ireland makes St. Paul a lonely place for dear Bishop O'Gorman. Nevertheless, I am grateful for his heartfelt and tender wishes for my welfare"[14]—he thanked the friends who had come to help him celebrate this happy day by "the impulse of their affection, and without any special invitation. Throughout life," he added somewhat wistfully, "I have ever been fond of friends and their friendships." He paid special tribute to the priests of Des Moines, half of whom were present for the festivities; through their personal kindness and cooperation the "apprehensions" he had experienced when he had first come among them had soon faded away. He closed his remarks with a thought, and a plea, for the future.

> I ask all of you to take this thought home with you. I invite confidence, cooperation, and sympathy. I need your hearts as well as your heads; sympathy and wisdom. If given in full measure, this will accord me full confidence.[15]

DURING THE WEEKS AND MONTHS THAT FOLLOWED DOWLING inevitably spent much of his time and energy acclimating himself to a new environment. He paid inaugural visits to archdiocesan institutions, chiefly in the Twin Cities, received formal greetings from various civic groups, and, a little later, moved outside the metropolitan area on the annual confirmation tours, which brought him into regular contact with the Catholic communities across his jurisdiction. On all these occasions he was required to speak, and he did so in the unassuming yet cultivated style reminiscent of Bishop Grace. When administering the sacrament of confirmation or presiding at other

---

13. Robert Klein, "Diocese of Duluth," in Ahern, *Catholic Heritage,* 73.

14. A priest from Sioux Falls named Daniel Desmond spoke for O'Gorman.

15. Partial texts in *CB,* March 29, 1919.

liturgical functions, these addresses were straightforward sermons on some appropriate gospel theme.[16] In the immediate aftermath of his installation, however, Dowling was more or less reduced to exchanging platitudes with the likes of the student chosen to deliver a welcoming discourse when, in early April, he visited St. Thomas College for the first time: "Your sterling Americanism has kindled our admiration. Your advice to the immigrant to let not the love of the mother country overshadow the land of his adoption makes for a loyalty that is undivided."[17]

But at other times the archbishop gave a broad indication of his personal priorities and assumptions. Ten days after listening to the harangue at St. Thomas—and replying in kind—he spoke to a meeting of the Arts and Letters Department of the Guild of Catholic Women, held in the "spacious home" of Judge Willis on Summit Avenue. We need, he told an "overflow crowd," to insist that the principles of genuine art be applied to urban planning, public buildings, and especially our own churches. "In former times churches were centers of real art, while at the present day we seem to aim at the utilitarian in our church structures."[18] He paid the requisite compliment to John Ireland's cathedral, even as he pondered how artfully to decorate its bare and drab interior. And perhaps the thought crossed his mind that he himself might one day raise a building of rare beauty, both inside and out.

Even more telling were his remarks a month later to the Catholic Students Association at the University of Minnesota; indeed, they sounded the theme of Austin Dowling's career.

> A complaint is usually made by you, who endeavor to set forth the Catholic position, that there is no support from Catholics. The intellectual life of the Catholic Church in this country is only in its beginning, and we trust we shall soon see the Church as a student of culture and of all things of the mind. . . . It is an embarrassing thing to know that fifteen to twenty million people, representing a complete and whole philosophy of life, as does the Catholic people, are without adequate literature, without either a means of expressing its thought or a demand on the part of the Catholics that that thought should be presented to them.[19]

---

16. Dowling was also in demand as a speaker at important events outside the archdiocese. See John McNicholas, ed., *Occasional Sermons and Addresses of Archbishop Dowling* (Paterson, N.J., 1940).

17. *CB*, April 12, 1919.

18. *CB*, April 26, 1919.

19. *CB*, May 24, 1919.

ALREADY FORMING IN DOWLING'S MIND DURING THESE EARLY DAYS in St. Paul were the outlines of a plan that might promote an appreciation among the Catholic people of the Church's age-old "complete and whole philosophy of life" and its cultural significance. A sweeping enhancement and, to some degree, overhaul of the educational structure within the archdiocese could, he believed, initiate such a process locally. This is not to say that the archbishop's ordinary duties were neglected; indeed, every season brought its complement of heavy, routine work. Thus, for example, in one six-week period—from mid-October to the end of November, 1927—Dowling visited forty-three communities across the archdiocese, from Marshall in the southwest to Cannon Falls in the east, and administered confirmation to more than 4,000 children and adults in fifty-three parishes. Such parochial visitations involved, even if informally, a serious inquiry into the spiritual and material well-being of the parish, an examination of its physical plant, and a close inspection of its financial registers. Interspersed in this particular semiannual tour he preached the sermon at the funeral of his good friend, Bishop Peter Muldoon of Rockford, Illinois;[20] preached also at the episcopal jubilee of another friend, Archbishop James Keane of Dubuque; and preached finally at the funeral of his not particularly friendly suffragan, Patrick Heffron of Winona. He presided at three clergy conferences, two in St. Paul and one at Benson, 175 miles away. He addressed a luncheon gathering at the College of St. Thomas and a Knights of Columbus Armistice Day observance in Minneapolis. He conducted moreover a retreat for Catholic social workers and delivered a formal speech to the Seton Club of Minneapolis, a home for Catholic working girls.[21] This daunting schedule was by no means unusual.

Nor could the archbishop fancy that the era of brick and mortar was over. The parish was as ever at the heart of the Catholic enterprise, and so the provision of sacred space for its liturgical and devotional ministrations remained a priority. Although the Catholic population increased only modestly—from 265,000 to 281,000—some forty churches were built and dedicated during Dowling's eleven-year tenure, many in the metropolitan area of Minneapolis and St. Paul but many also in Minnesota hamlets hardly larger than dots on a map. In August 1919, the archbishop blessed the newly completed St. Mark's, as well as the basement of St. Luke's, where Mass was said till completion of the superstructure in 1926; these two splendid buildings still dominate the

---

20. See chapter 17, below.
21. O'Connell, "Dowling Decade," 44–46.

west-central residential district of St. Paul. A year later he blessed the "commodious" Church of the Incarnation in south Minneapolis. St. Lawrence parish, staffed by the Paulist Fathers since 1915, which served among others the Catholic students attending the University of Minnesota, completed its new church in March of 1922. In the countryside, the parishioners of St. Michael's in Prior Lake built a new church in 1921, which, if smaller and less imposing than the structures just named, was not less important or permanent. The same could be said for the Church of St. Mary in Bellechester, which was built new in 1926 and dedicated by Dowling in July of the following year. Some of the oldest parishes in the archdiocese, whose beginnings went back to pioneer days, put up new churches, like St. Mary's in St. Paul and St. Vincent's in Osseo, both blessed by the archbishop in 1922. But new parishes were abuilding as well. St. Mary's in New Ulm, founded in 1911, welcomed Dowling and his blessing of their new church in July of 1923; and later that year he performed the same ceremony in the new church-school combination of the parish of the Nativity of Our Lord in St. Paul, organized only eleven months before.[22]

Many of these ventures in parochial construction were undoubtedly, and necessarily, "utilitarian" as far as their artistic merit went, but several other projects, in which Austin Dowling intimately involved himself, gave better scope to his aesthetic ideals. Among these, as will be seen, the most spectacular was the splendid edifice he called Nazareth Hall, the preparatory seminary. Another, less grandiose, was the completion of the interior of St. Mary's chapel on the campus of Mr. Hill's major seminary. The six buildings put up by the railroad magnate in the early 1890s did not include a distinct chapel; some services were held in the residence halls, and all-school liturgies in the *aula maxima,* the spacious auditorium on the second floor of the classroom building. In 1901 Mary Mehegan Hill—whose Catholic piety had inspired her husband's generosity in the first place[23]—determined to fill this obvious void. With her gift of $40,000 construction was begun, and the handsome chapel of grey sandstone—in marked contrast in form and color to the functional blood-red brick structures which dominated the rest of the campus—was completed in 1905. Inside, St. Mary's, with its long nave and deep circular apse, emulated the noble Roman basilica style, but for lack of money it remained visually drab and undecorated.

---

22. See O'Connell, "Dowling Decade," 25–28
23. See chapter 14, above.

At first Dowling, preoccupied with the construction of Nazareth Hall and with a host of other commitments, local and national, paid scant attention to St. Mary's. But in the latter years of his episcopate his commitment to architecture as spiritual rhetoric came to the fore. He raised enough money to provide the chapel with an adequate organ, with a completion of the horizontal choir stalls which made feasible the traditional antiphonal chanting of the Church's solemn offices, with the appropriate carvings for the capitals on the columns that stood like sentinels guaranteeing the building's longevity, and, perhaps most movingly, with the painting over the apse of the post-Resurrection Jesus on the shore of Galilee inquiring whether Peter did indeed "love him more than these." Throughout the process of refurbishment Dowling attended meticulously to every detail. And, poignantly, he recruited as his chief adviser in this enterprise one whom he had known since childhood. Bancel La Farge was the son of John La Farge, the celebrated artist who made his home in Newport, Rhode Island. Dowling, as Bancel's brother recalled, "had been a next door neighbor of ours in Newport. Archbishop Dowling took a great interest in my brother Bancel, the mural painter, and invited him out to St. Paul where he did some work . . . on the Cathedral and on the chapel of the St. Paul Seminary."[24] This younger John La Farge, a Jesuit priest, went on to gain fame as a formidable editor of the prestigious *America* magazine and as a leader of social reform during the 1940s and 1950s. St. Mary's chapel meanwhile remained intact until the 1970s when a different liturgical ethos indicated a need for sweeping changes to its interior design.

But Dowling took an earlier and even more intense interest in the completion of his predecessor's cathedral. A suitably spacious sacristy was built in 1925 and a three-story rectory as well. At the end of that year work began on refurbishing the sanctuary. It was a long and tedious process, and no detail was too small to elude the archbishop's attention. "I enclose the observations of Father Ryan," he wrote the architects in 1928,

> on the altar cards. He has arranged a new (or at least to me new) order for the prayers on the central altar card. I do not know that these will balance. Thus the middle column seems to me to have less in it than the first column. That will have to be proved. The suggestion of legs is one that will have to be considered before you accept it. On a thing so small they might very well be fragile and, in handling, create a situation that would

---

24. Athans, *To Work for the Whole People*, 61, 110–113, 154–163.

call for frequent and expensive repairs. Then again, can the middle card be raised without affecting the appearance of the other two?[25]

Father Lawrence Ryan, rector of the cathedral since 1916, was Dowling's zealous coadjutor in the task of overseeing the project. Indeed, it was he who was in charge of the day-to-day operation. A man of impeccable taste, and utterly devoted to the ideal of the beautification of the archdiocese's principal house of worship, he—though his suggestions about the altar cards may have appeared problematic—and his archbishop proved to be a dynamic team, their work carried forward by Ryan even after Dowling's death.[26] In the end, all the effort and expense resulted in a boon for them and for all the people of the archdiocese since. The superb marble high altar set beneath the towering baldachin, the subtle mosaic, the grand statuary—all this and the harmony achieved among them led Dowling to observe early in 1928: "It is all finished, the last addition being the throne, which, like all the rest, is simple but magnificent."[27] A cherished aspiration of John Ireland Dowling also made a reality. In the cathedral's original plan, space was set aside for a series of "Chapels of the Nations," honoring those saints whose cults were practiced by the various national groups within the archdiocese. After some modification, the work was begun, and by the summer of 1928 the chapels were finished. Situated in the ambulatory behind the high altar, they stood in honor of St. John the Baptist, St. Patrick, St. Boniface, SS. Cyril and Methodius, St. Anthony of Padua, and St. Thérèse of Lisieux.[28] "All that I ever proposed to do [is] done," Dowling said, "and, unblushing I say it, it [has] been done well. . . . I have no expectation that in my lifetime we will resume operations."[29]

---

25. Dowling to Maginnis & Walsh, March 14, 1928 (copy), AASPM, Dowling Papers. In the Tridentine Latin liturgy, three cards, containing appropriate prayers for each venue, were placed at the right end of the altar, at the left, and in the center.

26. See Eric C. Hansen, *The Cathedral of St. Paul: An Architectural Biography* (St. Paul, 1990), 51–52.

27. Dowling to Clara Lindley, April 11, 1928, AASPM, Dowling Papers. Mrs. Lindley was the daughter of James J. Hill and a generous donor to the refurbishment of the cathedral's interior.

28. Hansen, *Cathedral,* 51–78. Besides its useful text, this book contains a host of wonderful illustrations in color.

29. Dowling to Clara Lindley, March 15, 1928, AASPM, Dowling Papers. But further embellishment was still Dowling's intention. Plans were already afoot for the decoration of the interior of the dome and the design and production of the stained glass windows.

The archbishop took justifiable pride in thus carrying forward the embellishment of John Ireland's great monument to the viability of Catholicism in the Upper Midwest. And he bristled at what he considered trivial criticism. On one occasion, during Sunday Mass, he and his guest, the apostolic delegate, Archbishop Pietro Fumasoni-Biondi, stood at the edge of the ambulatory after just having toured the Chapels of the Nations. All well and good, remarked the delegate with an hauteur not unknown among high Roman officials, but—pointing at the main altar—do you not see that the antependium is not the proper color for this liturgical season? "Antependium!" retorted the diminutive Dowling. Then, grasping Fumasoni-Biondi's arm, he pointed to the crowded nave. "Do you see them, your Grace? Do you see all those people? Do you see all those men? Not just a handful of women as in every Italian church this morning. Antependium indeed!" Austin Dowling, aesthete as he genuinely was, had never miscalculated the priorities of his office.[30]

ARCHBISHOP IRELAND HAD LAID DOWN THE PRINCIPLE THAT THE cathedral, as the church of all the people, should be paid for by all the people. He intended the application of this tenet to include the ultimate completion of the building's interior. But in 1920 Archbishop Dowling reversed this policy, and from then on the financial responsibility devolved upon the parishioners of the cathedral and an occasional generous donor.[31] He provided a strong hint as to why on October 8, 1919, when he celebrated a Mass marking the first anniversary of Ireland's death.[32] It is proper on this occasion, he said from the cathedral's makeshift pulpit, to call attention to the fitness of commemorating the career of Archbishop Ireland in an appropriate manner. The suggestion had been made, and duly considered, that a statue of the great man in heroic proportions be placed "on one of the pedestals that crown and accentuate the broad flight of stairs leading up to the main entrance of the cathedral on Summit Avenue." Then too, Dowling continued, he had thought of naming some building in Ireland's honor. But these ideas and suggestions had seemed somewhat petty as adequate memorials "for a man who loomed

---

30. This anecdote was told me by the late Monsignor John Sweeney, a close student of Austin Dowling's life and career.

31. Hansen, *Cathedral,* 52.

32. Ireland had died on September 25, 1918, but on that date a year later Dowling was attending a meeting of the National Catholic Welfare Conference in Washington, D.C.

so large in the history of our country as did Archbishop Ireland and who wrought so well and so enduringly for the Church in the Northwest as he did." Little by little, Dowling went on, it had been growing upon him that there was a tribute that the late archbishop's friends, admirers, and spiritual children might pay him congruent to his greatness and in harmony with what would have been his own desires. That tribute was the consolidation, the unification, and the perpetuation of his most notable work in life. But this might not be too readily discerned; John Ireland had done very many notable things during the half century of his active ministry. However,

> for my part, if I must choose that portion of my venerated predecessor's career which will endure, that which is most characteristic of a great shepherd of souls, and that in which he found most satisfaction at the end because it represented his sacrifices, his devotion and his highest hopes, it will be the great educational system that he inaugurated, the institutions that he established but which he had neither time nor strength nor means to coordinate, unify and consolidate.
>
> My suggestion, then, is that we, the heirs of his great desires, distinguished throughout the Church by our association with his life and illustrious name, take up this work where he left it, and with filial piety devote ourselves to a plan which, while systematizing our educational effort on a scale of grand proportions, will show from what spiritual stock we sprang and in what school of sacrifice we received our training.[33]

"Grand proportions" require a great deal of money, raised from far-ranging sources; the expense of beautifying the interior of the cathedral would have to be borne by those most closely associated with it.

During the weeks that followed the October sermon, Dowling outlined his ideas to various individuals and small groups. Then, on Friday evening, November 28, in the assembly room at the cathedral, a meeting of St. Paul pastors was held at which he aired his plans in some detail. A similar gathering of Minneapolis pastors was convened the following Monday in the school library of the procathedral. On both occasions there was "general discussion, much enthusiasm and an almost unanimous agreement that the plan was timely, necessary and worthy of the great name with which it [was] to be associated."

---

33. *CB*, October 11 and December 6, 1919. The sermon, referred to simply as an "eloquent discourse" in October, was published in December.

The archbishop's talks at these two meetings emphasized the unique opportunity for progress in Catholic education which Ireland had left as his testament. No diocese in the country, he said, has a more complete material preparation for a thorough and comprehensive educational system than has St. Paul. Here almost the whole educational effort is in the hands of diocesan authorities. Our parochial schools and our high schools "of various kinds and qualities," our diocesan colleges and our seminary "are all at the service of the diocese without any other than diocesan direction or inspiration"—an observation music to the ears of these disciples of John Ireland, suspicious as he had been of male religious orders. The moment has come, Dowling concluded, to attempt "a work of consolidation such as has not been attempted elsewhere, but such as must be attempted everywhere sooner or later if we are to be allowed a part in educational work."[34]

The apparent enthusiasm that greeted his still fluid plans was for Dowling a source of encouragement. During the early months of 1920 he seized on every opportunity to sound the same theme in hopes of stirring up a similar reaction. At nearly every archdiocesan function, he invoked what had become for him almost a mantra, that the survival of the Catholic educational system depended on fulfilling the need "to coordinate, to unify, to consolidate." Although he spoke in general terms, no one doubted that the archbishop was thinking hard about the details of his program. On February 12, he was the featured speaker at the Cretin High School Alumni Association banquet, and "during the course of his address he enlarged on his plans for a greater Archdiocese of St. Paul in the educational field; and he appealed for sincere sympathy and great understanding." In the middle of May, speaking this time to the St. Thomas College Alumni banquet in Minneapolis, Dowling "pointed out the wonderful future St. Thomas [was] destined to achieve. With frank openness [sic], His Grace told of the financial conditions that always hamper the full development of a Catholic college. . . . He then unfolded his own ideas, his hopes and his plans for the upbuilding of the educational institutions of the diocese in the near future."[35]

Indeed, the ideas were maturing. In July the wheels began to turn more swiftly if quietly. Father Thomas Welch, archdiocesan chancellor, assumed full-time direction of the operations preliminary to a capital campaign. Office space was secured in a downtown St. Paul bank building, and a full clerical staff was engaged. An accurate census of the Catholic population was the first

---

34. *CB*, December 6, 1919.

35. *CB*, February 21 and May 29, 1920.

order of business, and it was "no easy task."[36] Next, from this more or less complete list, information was sought about "who the individuals are and especially such things as will make possible a successful method of approach to them. . . . Everything so far has been working smoothly and silently. Soon the silence will be broken."[37]

And so it was. On September 7 a giant meeting was held at the armory of St. Thomas College. More than seven hundred men, including all the priests of the archdiocese and two lay representatives from each parish and mission, sat down to luncheon at 12:30. It was a festive affair, with orchestra music in the background as the guests ate their midday meal in the gaily decked hall. Once the plates and cutlery were cleared away, Austin Dowling ascended the speakers' platform, where "he was greeted with a spontaneous outburst of applause which lasted for some considerable time." When the hall had fallen silent, the archbishop thanked those assembled for their presence and for the interest which they thus demonstrated. He wasted no time in informing them that he hoped from this meeting to launch "a campaign for education" whose prime purpose would be "the unifying of Catholic thought and interest in the diocese." Such "unifying" was "the next logical step the Church must take in any area after she has done what she always does first: set up her altars, administer the sacraments." This exclusively spiritual ministration, though of first importance, nevertheless is not enough, particularly at this time and in this country. "This spirit [which] has continued down to the present day" has tended to make "the Church here . . . parochial. It has no public opinion." As a result, "so far as the country at large is concerned, the Catholic Church is a silent church." She has been without a voice simply because she has lacked organization. But, said Dowling, looking over the crowd with an approving smile, the recognition of the need as expressed by this enthusiastic meeting is a promise that "the Church in America will move forward to a larger vision, . . . that it will divest itself of the strictly parochial idea that is insular and work together into a happy combination of efforts." This assembly, here at our own college, he continued, is important for another, very fundamental reason. For the men gathered in this hall "represent the various nationalities from which the parishes of the diocese have sprung." Now, instead of considering each parish a little nation, those who have come together here have indicated by their presence their willingness to cooperate with him in creating

---

36. A copy of Dowling's letter to all the pastors in the archdiocese is in AASPM, Dowling Papers.

37. *CB*, August 28, 1920.

a "united diocese." And the best method of guaranteeing this happy result is an organized and expanded school system. To be sure, "we have a great educational force, but as it exists today it is disorganized."

It may be assumed that the gentlemen present at the meeting, clerical and lay, listened carefully to the archbishop's words. They knew he was a person to respect, they realized he spoke good English and spoke it very well. But perhaps they also thought a little wearily that they had heard all this before, perhaps many times, or at least they had read it before in the columns of Father Reardon's weekly. They were interested primarily in finding out what their new archbishop wanted of them; specifically they waited for him to tell them what he wanted to "coordinate" and "unify" and "expand" and how he proposed to do it. Above all, they wondered how much money he was going to need and how he planned to raise it.[38] They did not have to wait long. For after almost a year of hints and generalizations, Austin Dowling was now ready to lay all his cards on the table.

His first recommendation could not have been a surprise to many in his audience. Supervision, and not merely titular supervision, was the basic crying need of St. Paul's Catholic schools.

> A good work always becomes better through supervision. . . . We Catholics have a habit of coming together in groups and of praising ourselves and our achievements. A business man gets together his groups of supervisors not for personal praise but to discover flaws, the causes for loss, the reasons for possible inefficiency, and he is consistently planning the betterment of his affairs through supervision. This supervision will get us out of the rut of self-praise. It will build up a real system of organization.

One of the first "flaws" supervision will uncover, promised Dowling, is the lack of standardization in the archdiocesan system. Unity of outlook, of textual material and technique saves money and it turns out better products as well. And this fact, he said, leads to the second objective of the educational campaign: we need a diocesan normal school, simply because there can be no unity without homogeneity of teachers. "There is a real place for the Christian system of Normal training where the chief stress is Christian. As for methods," he went on, "we may copy them from any lawful source; as for

---

38. In his sermon of October 1919, Dowling had appeared to hint at a goal of raising two million dollars.

motive, the chief characteristic of our work must be Christian. . . . The time has passed when we can turn to any religious community and say, 'Here are our schools; you find the money and the subjects, and then train them.'"

Next Dowling outlined for his now very attentive audience his plans with regard to the provision of Catholic secondary education, a critical matter indeed. Children are more than willing to attend Catholic high schools, he maintained, but there are so few of them that only a handful can do so. New large secondary schools are acutely needed in both the Twin Cities, and, no less important, consolidated institutions in the rural districts.

Another pressing requirement, Dowling continued, is the establishment of a minor seminary and the maintenance of the major seminary. After all, a native clergy is necessary for the proper functioning of the Church in any area, and, he pointed out, it is a disturbing fact that hardly one third of the archdiocese's secular priests had been born in Minnesota. We must be aware that while vocations to the priesthood are nurtured within the bosom of the Catholic home and family, they must then be given the proper incentive and environment in which to flourish, which is what a minor seminary is uniquely constituted to do. And as for the St. Paul Seminary, Dowling reminded his hearers that, though the institution had been founded and endowed by James J. Hill and largely maintained by members of his family, such beneficence could not go on forever.

Finally, the two diocesan colleges, under the patronage of St. Thomas and St. Catherine, have "rendered splendid service" to the people of this area, the archbishop observed. But like most Catholic colleges in the United States they have had to lead a hand-to-mouth existence much too long: "We propose to see just what they need, and then give it."

Dowling paused and looked across the floor of the armory. The seven hundred men present now had a definite picture in their minds of how widely the archbishop intended to "expand" and "consolidate." How much money such a program would cost they probably had no idea, nor is it likely that Dowling himself could have offered a precise estimate. At any rate, most of them recognized that here was a serious proposal to meet needs within their community which they had intuitively sensed without having it spelled out in their own minds. Perhaps too they were even a little flattered at the very ambition and scope of the plan, and when they heard their spiritual leader tell them that the campaign he hoped to mount soon and vigorously would have as its aim the raising of five million dollars "as a good beginning," they remained relatively unruffled.

"We have the means," insisted the archbishop in conclusion, "and if we bear in mind what we accomplished in the past when we had nothing, we can do the task." This must be a community effort, he said, and all Catholics must cooperate in it.

> We now propose to put this question to every Catholic in the archdiocese. We have the names and data concerning our Catholic people. . . . We do not wish to embarrass those who cannot give in a material sense, but we intend to appeal to those who can give. We desire our people to give all they can, prayers, moral support, and money. We have fifty thousand names, and each should represent a generous donor. . . . In a short time our campaign will develop and an effort will be made to secure the sympathetic interest of every Catholic in the archdiocese. Meanwhile, I commend this whole project to the prayers of all our people. We are going to save our children through Christian education and to see to it without let or hindrance they may go to Christ and be his loyal followers. We place this matter, then, at his blessed feet.

When he stepped down from the platform, Austin Dowling received a standing ovation.[39]

There was more speech making at the meeting, though little more of substance was said. At any rate, amidst applause and oratory—Judge T. D. O'Brien emphasized the role Catholics could play in American life if their educational system were placed "on a broad, solid footing"—the Archbishop Ireland Educational Fund was born into what must have seemed a cheery world. How the child would mature remained another question. Indeed, with the wisdom of hindsight one might suggest the possibility of a reverse of the psalmist's maxim: those who sow in joy may well reap in tears. It is difficult to grasp, more than eight decades later, just how enormous a sum $5 million represented in 1920; and it was to be solicited from a populace, numerous as it may have been, which except for a few successful entrepreneurs was working or lower middle class.

YET THE ORGANIZERS OF THE FUND EXHIBITED FROM THE START a surprisingly sophisticated methodology. Nor was there a lull in activity: scarcely a month intervened between the rally-meeting at St. Thomas and the

---

39. *CB*, September 11, 1920.

formal opening date of the campaign, October 10. The first task was to set up a workable timetable by which every Catholic family in the archdiocese might be acquainted with the drive and its purposes. To achieve this objective, the jurisdiction was divided into five districts of varying sizes. District one comprised the Twin Cities and their suburbs, where more than fifty percent of the Catholic population was massed. The second district included the parishes lying directly north and west of St. Paul. District three was by far the largest topographical section, embracing more than half of the archdiocese's fifteen thousand square miles; it was a strip one hundred forty miles long and sixty miles wide, extending west to the South Dakota border. Directly south of it and running parallel to it, though only half as broad, was district four. Finally, the fifth district was a half-moon shape which took in the communities south of the Twin Cities.[40]

Meantime the all-important grass roots organizational effort kept pace. Each parish provided for itself a permanent campaign committee composed of the pastor and two prominent laymen. These three men in turn selected a larger committee whose mandate it was to oversee and coordinate campaign activities in that parish. Oversight and coordination in this context meant the indispensable task of establishing personal contacts. To add incentive to each parish endeavor, form letters over Archbishop Dowling's signature (which he very likely wrote himself[41]) were sent to each Catholic family, outlining the needs of the local educational system and the manner in which they were to be met through funds acquired from the campaign.

The same informative character of the drive was demonstrated by the manner in which the people of the archdiocese were approached from the pulpit. On Sunday, October 10, a visiting priest addressed each congregation in district one, dwelling upon "the general plan of the campaign . . . and the purpose for which the funds were to be used." He continued this message the following week, on October 17, while on the same day the first of these instructive sermons was preached in all the churches of district two. Then, on October 24, the priest visiting a parish in the Twin Cities and their suburbs made the actual appeal for funds; at the same moment, in district two, the second series of sermons was being delivered and in district three the first series. So it proceeded until every parish in all five districts had heard three explanations of the Fund and its goals, the last of which signaled the actual solicitation of money. By Sunday, November 28, 1920, every attendee at

---

40. Reardon, *Diocese of St. Paul*, 451.
41. Copies of these communications are in AASPM, Dowling Papers.

Mass in the archdiocese had been thus appealed to from the pulpit of his own church.[42]

The next phase of the campaign rested in the hands of the parochial committees. It was up to these workers to make the actual door-to-door canvass of the relevant neighborhoods. In the rural areas and in the parishes in smaller communities, this final step could be taken with relative smoothness. But in the large, sprawling parishes of the metropolitan district, it posed certain difficulties. As a result, in Minneapolis and St. Paul general committees were formed, composed of "prominent business men" in each city. These groups were, so to speak, the nerve centers of the campaign, and they dispatched two or three young men to each parish for the purpose of instructing the local committee in methods of solicitation.[43]

Though the organization of the campaign was not so cumbersome that it cannot be described in a few paragraphs, it was nevertheless an affair complex enough to demand much close supervision. This was the responsibility of the managers, under the overall direction of Father Welch, but it need hardly be said that Dowling was "in constant touch with every feature." Wherever it was thought that the archbishop's presence might help the campaign, there he went. And "wherever" meant just about everywhere in the archdiocese before the two-month drive concluded.[44]

A description of how Dowling spent his evenings (after having already put in a full day) during the campaign's first week might give some idea how "constant" his "touch" was. On Saturday, October 9, the eve of the formal opening, at the campaign headquarters in downtown St. Paul, he addressed some sixty young men who were to help the parish committees train workers for solicitation. On the Monday following, at 8:00 p.m., he spoke to the delegates of the Minnesota Federation of Catholic Women's Clubs in convention at the St. Paul Hotel. In Minneapolis on Wednesday, October 13, Dowling was the dinner guest of the city's general committee, and after the meal addressed the members "on the purpose of the campaign." Next evening he met with and "instructed [the young men] who will proceed at once to train the active workers and solicitors in each parish in Minneapolis." There was a meeting of St. Paul's general committee at campaign headquarters the following evening, and again Dowling presided and spoke.[45]

---

42. *CB*, November 27, 1920. A sixth district was later carved out, embracing a few scattered parishes in the southeastern part of the archdiocese.

43. *CB*, October 16, 1920.

44. *CB*, November 13, 1920.

45. *CB*, October 16, 1920.

All this elaborate planning, all this marshalling of squads of eager young persons, all this apparent enthusiasm for a noble cause seemed at first to promise sweeping success. As early as November 3, after only a week of direct solicitation, the pledges had reached the $1,800,000 mark; this figure represented an average of almost $150 a contributor, no small sum for anyone and a very large one for many. Ten days later the pledged amount passed $2,500,000. But the pace was not maintained, and the $5,000,000 goal was never reached, not even on paper. The totals published several years later revealed that $4,392,872.50 had been pledged by 45,551 persons.[46] Had all such individuals honored their commitments the drive could have claimed a decisive if modified victory. They did not. All pledges included the provision that the sums promised would be paid by the end of 1925. The first installment of payments in the first three geographical districts came due on December 1, 1920, and that in the other districts a few weeks later. Throughout that month and into the new year money poured into headquarters at the rate of $5,000 a day. One day, in fact, early in January 1921, receipts totaled $23,000.[47]

This rate of contribution, however, was not sustained. A soft national economy at the end of 1920 posed a deterrent to many who no doubt had made their pledges with good intentions. Still, the dismal reality was that at the end of 1925—when all payments were scheduled to have been honored—nearly 22,000 of the 45,551 who had promised to contribute had paid nothing, amounting to a shortfall of $1,700,000. Dowling attempted to resurrect the campaign in 1922 and again in the summer of 1923, when students of the St. Paul Seminary, armed with file cards recording names and addresses, provided by the campaign headquarters, spent their summer holiday going door to door. A last desperate effort was mounted in 1925 to reignite the heady atmosphere of October 1920. The results were meager. In the end, although the final figures were never revealed, it is a certainty that hardly more than $3,000,000 ever entered the coffers of the Archbishop Ireland Educational Fund.[48]

On the eve of the last ditch attempt to salvage the campaign in 1925, Dowling addressed his people lengthily, and somewhat wistfully.

> We feel we have done our part. If we had the money we would like to build or assist more high schools for Catholic boys and girls. If we had the $1,700,000 that was pledged five years ago, on which we securely

---

46. Reardon, *Diocese of St. Paul,* 452.

47. *CB,* January 15, 1921.

48. See O'Connell, "Dowling Decade," 69–81.

counted and which has not been paid, we could, [together] with what we have, do many things. We feel we can say we have kept faith with you. Have you kept faith with your promise? . . . Are you one of those who could have subscribed and didn't? Can you resist doing so now? . . . The great things that have [already] been accomplished [by the Fund] have not yet received the appreciation that is their due. Some day we will awaken to the fact that our diocese has taken a long step towards a complete educational system, such as will be found in few other parts of the country. . . . If you believe in the Church of God, you must believe in the means that will, with God's grace, sustain it; you cannot stand aloof, fault-finding, critical, hostile, and at the same time consider yourself a practical Catholic.[49]

Four years later, in a speech to the Catholic Mothers' Club in Minneapolis, Austin Dowling, already ailing with the heart disease that would kill him a year later, rendered his final verdict. "The Archbishop Ireland Fund," he said, "undertaken some years ago, which, despite some reverses, was a great success, shall be a chapter in the history of the diocese that will make those who come after us shed tears because of the sacrifices that united so many people in one great desire. . . . Not long ago I talked to the chairman of the Rockefeller Fund [sic] about it, and he said to me, 'I never heard of such a thing, that you should lay a problem of this kind before the people, not the wealthy but the little and the big. I never dreamed anything like that could be done and succeed.'"[50]

In retrospect the claim of "great success" appears to be a considerable exaggeration. To be sure, the Fund endowed the archdiocesan Bureau of Education, and so set in motion that work of supervision and professional organization which Dowling deemed essential. In 1927 the archbishop blessed the new Normal School, housed in the James J. Hill mansion, which had been donated by the Empire Builder's four daughters. The Educational Fund partially subsidized this institution, designed through a summertime curriculum to meet "the needs of Sisters teaching in grade schools who have heretofore found it difficult to obtain special instruction in their field under Catholic auspices anywhere in the middle west." In 1923 some eighty percent of the cost of a new building for De La Salle High School in Minneapolis was paid

49. *CB*, September 12, 1925.
50. Text in Dowling's hand, AASPM, Dowling Papers.

for by the Fund, and five years later, when Cretin in St. Paul put up a structure that cost $625,000, the Fund contributed about one third of the total.

But many of the grandiose projects put forward as goals of the Archbishop Ireland Educational Fund never materialized. No new secondary schools were provided for boys or girls in the Twin Cities area, nor did the chain of consolidated high schools Dowling had intended for the rural parts of the archdiocese ever come to be. As for the Colleges of St. Thomas and St. Catherine—"We propose to see what they need, and then give it," the archbishop had said at the opening of the campaign in 1920—these institutions received no significant support for much needed buildings and equipment. True, the Fund gave St. Catherine's $200,000 so that the college could collect a matching grant of half that sum from the Rockefeller Foundation for its fledgling endowment. But, equally true, St. Catherine's had cancelled a scheduled fund drive of its own in deference to the archbishop's campaign. There is little doubt that under the vigorous leadership of Sister Antonia McHugh the college would have raised the required amount on its own.[51]

IT CANNOT BE DISPUTED THAT THE JEWEL IN THE RATHER tarnished crown of the Ireland Educational Fund was Nazareth Hall. Yet the founding of this minor seminary was as well the source of much controversy. Debate about how best to train young men for the priesthood has gone on within the Catholic Church since seminaries were first mandated by the Council of Trent in the sixteenth century. In a rough oversimplification it might be said that two models emerged. The first mandated that seminarians be segregated totally from the ordinary social environment, from "the allurements of the world," as pious tracts would have expressed it, and in this splendid isolation pursue an intellectual curriculum and a program of spiritual development appropriate to the station to which they aspired. The second—following a venerable European collegial tradition—recommended that candidates for the priesthood should indeed live in a discrete setting and follow a distinctive spiritual regimen—should form, that is, an independent "college"—but should, at the same time, accept and follow the academic norms of a larger university community. But, as European universities during the nineteenth century became ever more secularized, and faculties of theology and philosophy either disappeared or increasingly offered courses un-

---

51. Reardon, *Diocese of St. Paul*, 448–452. For Sister Antonia, see chapter 14, above, and Dowling to Clara Lindley, December 2, 1927, AASPM, Dowling Papers.

acceptable to Catholics, the need for separate venues for those engaged in these so-called sacred sciences was glaringly apparent. And so arose the great major seminaries, dedicated to rigorous training in philosophy and theology as well as to a no less meticulous emphasis upon spiritual and ascetic development, the most notable among such institutions being, perhaps, Saint-Sulpice in Paris, where Joseph Cretin had been a student.

So, it would seem, the first alternative had trumped the second, at least with regard to the upper reaches of clerical education. But what about those of more tender years, what about those adolescents who, in the midst of all the hormonal uncertainties characteristic of their age, felt an impulse to answer affirmatively a calling to the priesthood? The solution, as the nineteenth century passed, seemed to be the establishment of minor or preparatory seminaries, *petits séminaires,* institutions in which, as Dowling put it, "we may receive young candidates for the priestly state—a boarding school wherein vocations may be strengthened in a wholesome ecclesiastical atmosphere— wherein the heads and hearts of these favored sons of Providence may be fashioned, while yet impressionable, according to the ideal of the Christian priesthood."[52] In putting forward this proposition he was by no means introducing an idea novel to the American scene; lively debate over how best to recruit and train young men for the priesthood prior to their theological studies had been going on since the 1840s.[53] Bishop Grace in the early days of his episcopate had attempted to set up on the second floor of the old cathedral the kind of preparatory institution Dowling had in mind, but a lack of candidates and resources had soon written finis to the venture.[54]

John Ireland had treasured his own experience in a *petit séminaire;* indeed, he had had the ethos and regimen of Meximieux in mind when he founded the St. Thomas Seminary in 1885. But that institution had evolved into a conventional college (in the American sense of the word) and a military academy for high school boys, once the munificent Mr. Hill had established the St. Paul Seminary. Ireland was satisfied that younger aspirants to the priesthood could receive their preparatory training at St. Thomas, though he recognized that a distinct facility for them was desirable. This deficiency was apparently remedied when, a few months after the archbishop's death in

---

52. Quoted in a campaign pamphlet, "What We Have, What We Need: Seminaries," AASPM, Dowling Papers.

53. See Philip Gleason, "Boundlessness, Consolidation, and Discontinuity between Generations: Catholic Seminary Studies in Antebellum America," *Church History* 73 (September 2004): 583–612, especially 596–599.

54. See chapter 8, above.

1918, Timothy Foley, a local construction magnate, offered to give St. Thomas $100,000 provided that the college raise $150,000 more within three years, the money to be used to build a separate dormitory for young seminarians.[55] Thus it would seem that the second of the models described above was to prevail in St. Paul: the boys and young men who wanted to try their vocations to the priesthood would receive spiritual training in a distinctly clerical environment while following the same curriculum as the lay students.[56] But Ireland was ill throughout 1918—he died in September—and no formal action was taken; even so, Foley's proposal remained in force.

This plan, however, did not suit Archbishop Ireland's successor, who wanted "a boarding school wherein vocations may be strengthened in a wholesome ecclesiastical atmosphere," and who thought he had located an ideal site for such an institution. In 1866, Thomas Grace, troubled by the recent failure of his *petit séminaire,* had paid $800 for forty-two acres of largely wooded land on the shores of Lake Johanna, some few miles outside the St. Paul city limits, where, he said, he hoped he could "someday" open a seminary. In 1915 Ireland purchased an adjoining forty-seven acres for $3,525, and here, in February 1921, construction of Nazareth Hall began. The vast and stunningly beautiful building was completed by the late summer of 1923—except for the Chapel of the Annunciation which, with its walls of Numidian marble, took a year longer. The great tower, which stood one hundred five feet above the main entrance, almost immediately became a landmark.[57] Dowling was in constant touch with the architects, builders, and decorators throughout the process; as was the case in refurbishing the sanctuary of the cathedral, no detail was too small to merit his attention. The result was a splendid symphony in brick, limestone, and marble. As one quite independent authority expressed it: "Perfect. Perfect in design, beauty and architecture; a magnificent thing."[58]

---

55. *CB,* November 9, 1918.

56. Joseph Connors, *Journey Toward Fulfillment: A History of the College of St. Thomas* (St. Paul, 1986), 185–186.

57. In 1970 Nazareth Hall, after a decade of falling enrollment, was sold to Northwestern College, an independent Bible college founded in 1902. An undated brochure, "The History of the Roseville Campus of Northwestern College," 23 pp., briefly summarizes the history of the property and describes the physical appointments of the building in some detail. A copy in AASPM, Dowling Papers.

58. Charles J. Connick, quoted in *CB,* February 26, 1927. Connick, a distinguished specialist in stained glass designing (and not a Catholic), had come to Minneapolis on a commission from the Hennepin Avenue Methodist Church, still one of the most beautiful churches in the Twin Cities.

The architectural triumph notwithstanding, the new preparatory seminary did not win universal approval. One hostile critic, with withering sarcasm, implied that Nazareth Hall distracted the obsessive archbishop from
other, more important concerns.

> Nazareth Hall was the apple of [Dowling's] eye and woe betide the priest
> or layman who dared to utter an uncomplimentary syllable about the
> institution, its architecture, location, purpose, faculty or product. Every
> other institution in the diocese was a step-child, seldom visited except of-
> ficially. At Nazareth Hall a suite of well-furnished rooms was set apart for
> him to which he retired from time to time to rest and recuperate and
> breathe the invigorating suburban air.[59]

The precedent for establishing a *petit séminaire* outside the urban area
may have been set by the venerable Bishop Grace, but the implementation of
that idea in the 1920s gave rise without much ado to controversy. The estimated cost of the project had at first been set at $500,000; the final figure bal-
looned to $1,250,000, a million more, that is, than had been envisioned if
Timothy Foley's gift had been put to its donor's original purpose at St. Thomas. Moreover, Foley's offer of money, still pending when Dowling arrived in
St. Paul, had probably been the spark that ignited in the new archbishop's
mind the idea of establishing a corporation to support Catholic education in
the archdiocese and, concomitantly, of the massive monetary campaign to
initiate and then support it. Or, at the very least, Foley's generosity amounted
to the first substantive contribution to the Archbishop Ireland Educational
Fund.[60] A deeper irony was that a measure of legal legerdemain had to be employed to secure Foley's money. "In executing the terms of this [Foley's] trust,
it has seemed wise for the present that the preparatory seminary should be
held by the Corporation of St. Thomas College, though its management will
be quite separate from that of the existing college."[61] In other words, the Fund
gave St. Thomas $150,000 in order to secure the Foley grant, but the money
was spent at Lake Johanna, not on Summit Avenue between Cleveland and
Cretin.

---

59. Reardon, *Diocese of St. Paul*, 452.

60. Foley's philanthropy was not entirely altruistic. By the terms of the agreement, Foley Brothers Construction would receive the contract to build the preparatory seminary at St. Thomas.

61. *CB*, February 19, 1921.

Besides the resentment felt at St. Thomas—whose alumni, it must be re-membered, included most of the priests in the archdiocese and many promi-nent businessmen—was the widespread feeling that the construction and partial endowment of Nazareth Hall had been extravagant. The entire cost of the preparatory seminary, debt free from the opening of its doors in 1923, had been paid for by the Fund and had absorbed at least one third of the total revenues garnered by the campaign. The erection of the "Marble Halls," as one derisive cleric habitually referred to it, had left other and, it was argued, worthier causes to go a-begging. Again, it was St. Thomas that appeared to have been the primary victim. Among the improvements the college "vitally needed" were a dining hall, a dormitory, a science hall, and a power plant.[62] None of these physical enhancements came to pass, nor any relief of the insti-tution's debt burden, despite Dowling's pledge on the eve of the campaign "to see what [the colleges need], and then give it." But perhaps even more hurtful was the immediate transfer of more than a hundred students, a tenth of the student body—and including arguably many of the liveliest and most talented undergraduates—to the shores of Lake Johanna.

The worst was yet to come. The fortunes of the College of St. Thomas reached their nadir during the 1920s. Under the direction of well-intentioned but ill-educated and inexperienced administrators—parish priests who wanted nothing more than a return to a pastoral apostolate—the college's academic standing fell disastrously. Crucial to its viability was the accredita-tion it received from the University of Minnesota. Just after Christmas 1927, citing poor performance along the whole spectrum of conventional peda-gogical requirements, the university official in charge of such matters in-formed the acting president, John Foley, that formal approval of St. Thomas's program would be terminated, effective at the conclusion of the 1928 spring semester. "I may say," Father Foley[63] replied poignantly, "it is not a very en-couraging reception into the office to which I have been recently appointed." He offered the usual assurances of amelioration that such circumstances de-mand, as the gloomy prospect of investigating committees from the univer-

---

62. "What We Have," AASPM, Dowling Papers.

63. Monsignor Foley (as he later became) was appointed pastor of Immaculate Conception parish in Faribault after his unhappy experience at St. Thomas. As a child I was his parishioner, and I recall that there was no one at the time—in the depths of the Depression—in the town or the region more beloved than he. He died in October 1964, aged eighty-nine.

sity loomed across the immediate future. On May 19 the announcement appeared in the press that the college's accreditation had been formally revoked.[64]

A month before this doleful news, Foley glanced out his office window one day and saw several priests, unknown to him, touring the campus in the company of an official from the archdiocesan chancery. He thought nothing of it at the time, but soon enough he learned the import of this mysterious visitation. Indeed, he might have found a clue in the fact that he held office only in an "acting" capacity. On July 7, 1928, Archbishop Dowling—the signs of his last illness all too apparent, "a pathetic figure," one acquaintance described him at the time—convened a special meeting of St. Thomas's board of trustees. He informed the members that he had invited the Congregation of Holy Cross to assume control of the administration of the college. The contract between the archdiocese and the congregation, which was to be signed two days later, stipulated that the agreement should be in effect for a five-year trial period, after which it was assumed by both parities that the arrangement should become permanent and that all of St. Thomas's property, except Nazareth Hall, should pass into the unfettered possession of the Indiana Province of Holy Cross. He took this step, Dowling said, "with extreme reluctance and out of no want of respect" for his predecessor, who had solemnly enjoined that the college never be placed under the control of a religious order.[65] He cited as first among his reasons the loss of accreditation. Hardly less important, in his mind, was the fact that the archdiocese lacked the priestly manpower to staff the St. Paul Seminary, Nazareth Hall, and St. Thomas. Moreover, the priests teaching at the college, for all their good will, lacked the advanced degrees necessary and the means to procure them. Finally, he said, chronic problems—coping with up-to-date methodology and appropriate curriculum, no less than with inadequate facilities and personnel—required aid from a religious order with long and varied experience in Catholic higher education. Certainly the Holy Cross fathers qualified in this regard, with their successful enterprises at Notre Dame as well as at Austin, Texas, and Portland, Oregon.

The board—five of the seven members were present, four of them priests, including, for the first and last time, poor Father Foley—unanimously endorsed the archbishop's proposal. Whether they really agreed with him on the

---

64. *St. Paul Pioneer Press,* May 19, 1928.

65. The revised articles of incorporation (1908) stated explicitly that St. Thomas "be at no time under the control or management of any particular society or order of the Roman Catholic Church." In 1928 this statement had to be waived.

substance of the matter has not been recorded, though one of them acknowledged afterward that he had been deeply moved when Dowling, so visibly ill,
pleaded to be delivered from so great a burden. Another faction, however,
was not so sympathetic. "It came as a complete surprise to priests and people,"
wrote the implacable James Reardon more than twenty years later.

> The transfer was resented by the clergy, alumni and laity as contrary to
> the constitution and tradition of the institution and its best interests, a
> direct challenge to the diocesan priests who had administered its affairs
> and taught in its class halls since it was founded in 1885, built it up to its
> prosperous condition, and were quite able to continue the management
> of it. . . . The change in administration alienated in large measure the in-
> terest and support of the diocesan clergy and many friends of the institu-
> tion, and the breach was widened by the attitude of the newcomers who
> professed to be able to found a new Notre Dame in the Northwest and
> make it a success without the aid of the priests of the diocese.[66]

How widely shared this judgment was remains unclear. Certainly a
goodly number of priests did agree—especially those who had had close ties
with St. Thomas over the years or who, like Reardon, were fiercely loyal to
John Ireland and his memory. For them, the little man from Rhode Island,
whom they had never much appreciated, had now shown his true colors, and
by betraying their alma mater had also besmirched the testament of their
hero. There is scant evidence, however, that the transfer disturbed large sections of the laity. It is not too far-fetched to suggest that many of them, including some alumni, found the prospect of an association with Notre Dame
rather exhilarating. Indeed, appointing Knute Rockne "non-resident athletic
director" at St. Thomas may have charmed more than a few.[67]

But at the heart of Reardon's indictment was a patent absurdity. Far from
being in a "prosperous condition," St. Thomas was in desperate straits, on the
verge, in fact, of collapse. It is significant that in making his case Reardon did
not even mention the loss of accreditation. And *l'affaire* Nazareth Hall was
another factor, if not explicitly acknowledged, that figured in his condemnation of the transfer. Had the original terms of Timothy Foley's gift of 1918
been honored, then the preparatory seminary would have been located on the
St. Thomas campus, the vast amounts of money spent at Lake Johanna would

---

66. Reardon, *Diocese of St. Paul,* 480.
67. *CB,* September 1, 1928.

have been saved, and the demand for diocesan priest-staff would have been reduced by a third. There may have been some justice in this hypothetical reconstruction of events. But there was none in the assertion that Dowling had not had St. Thomas's interests at heart. Indeed, it could be argued—also admittedly hypothetically—that when the Great Depression began a year after the transfer, the college might have gone under had the Holy Cross administrators not been on the scene. For they proved to be, despite Reardon's dismissal of them as ambitious "newcomers," able men who guided the institution through five exceedingly difficult years.[68]

One of Monsignor Reardon's charges, however, was undeniable. Dowling's arrangement with Holy Cross was arrived at in complete secrecy. He consulted no one, not even those most intimately involved, like John Foley. For those who disliked the decision, its clandestine character made it the more intolerable. This was no doubt a tactical error, though bureaucratic complexities—the agreement had to pass prior muster with the various councils within Holy Cross—and Dowling's own concern about possible rumors spreading—particularly one that suggested St. Thomas would be given to the Jesuits, an eventuality which would have infuriated Reardon even more—might serve as partial explanations for it. But at a deeper, more poignant level, was the reality that Austin Dowling had no one around him whom he cared to consult. "Throughout life," he had said at his installation banquet, "I have ever been fond of friends and their friendships." In St. Paul, as time was running out for him, friends were scarce on the ground. There was one notable exception. The aged Ellen Ireland—Mother Seraphine in religion—assured him that her brother would not have disapproved of the transfer.[69]

---

68. In this brief narration of the transfer of St. Thomas to Holy Cross, I have followed entirely the account in Connors, *Journey*, 214–225. Professor Connors judiciously and gently corrects Monsignor Reardon's flawed and angry indictment.

69. Connors, *Journey*, 223.

CHAPTER 17

Americanism
Redivivus

THE DECADE DURING WHICH AUSTIN DOWLING PRESIDED OVER
the archdiocese of St. Paul has been labeled the Roaring Twenties, the Jazz
Age, the era of the "flappers." Fashionable women shortened the hemlines of
their dresses, and fashionable men applied lots of oil to their hair. On formal
occasions—and even on some less formal—everyone wore a hat or, in the
case of working-class men, a cloth cap; women de rigueur wore hats, more
or less resplendent depending on their means, whenever they went into a
church. The law forbade the distribution of alcoholic beverages—thanks to
the Eighteenth Amendment to the Constitution—but people did not seem to
drink less than before, and a legion of gangsters flourished by slaking the nation's unabated thirst. The decade was by and large a prosperous time for
Americans, and very much so when compared to what followed. Getting and
spending was the order of the day. "The business of America is business," proclaimed President Coolidge; he like other Republicans, who remained in firm
control of the federal government, tended to campaign on slogans like "a car
in every garage and a chicken in every pot." And indeed the automobile did
become a commonplace—from the unpretentious Model-T Ford to the sumptuous Packard—thus providing an unprecedented measure of mobility and
hence a deepened sense of freedom to people of all classes. Meanwhile,
Charles Lindbergh flew the *Spirit of St. Louis* across the Atlantic to Paris. The
Georgian Bobby Jones reinvented a game that had originated in Scotland.
And if golf was still the preserve of the leisured well-to-do, baseball was for
everybody; the exploits of George Herman Ruth, "the King of Swat," reverberated across the nation. It was a heady time to be an American.[1]

---

1. For a scholarly but lively depiction of the 1920s, see Marshall Smelser, *The
Life That Ruth Built* (New York, 1975).

But there were other straws in the wind. The sheer horribleness of the 1914–1918 war and its aftermath had provoked a severe reaction against the ideals and value systems that had prevailed before. The disillusionment of the "lost generation" was deeper in Europe than in the United States, simply because Europeans had fought longer and suffered much more grievously than Americans. In fact, however, the shifting of the cultural ground had begun before the war. As the twentieth century dawned, that collection of traditional moral and intellectual assumptions, called not altogether inaccurately "Victorian," was coming under increasing attack from scientific and artistic and even religious sources. A signal that would ultimately prove immensely significant was the publication in 1900 of *The Interpretation of Dreams* by an up-till-then obscure Viennese neurologist named Sigmund Freud. Over the next couple of decades theories about relativity and evolution and astronomy combined to bring into question truths that had seemed timeless and universal. In aesthetics too—in poetry and painting, in music and architecture—a definition of beauty radically different from that which had held sway for so long thrust itself to the fore. Nor did the old economic and political order escape challenge. Anarchists in Spain and socialists in Germany might debate the intricacies of Karl Marx's teachings, but they agreed that the exploitative financial structures of conventional capitalism had to be eradicated. The war, with its ghastly and seemingly pointless bloodletting, appeared to confirm the bankruptcy of the Western tradition. The victory of the Bolsheviks in Russia eloquently made the same point.

Cultures are always subject to change and development. Romantic music, like romantic poetry, was different from the classical. Robert Schumann's mid-nineteenth century compositions do not sound like those of Haydn or Mozart. But the atonal system adopted and propagated by Arnold Schoenberg represented more than merely horizontal progress from an agreed starting point. It was, in a way, an intellectual and artistic revolution. Similarly, the poetry of Ezra Pound and T. S. Eliot—both Americans who lived in Europe—appeared entirely detached from the work of Tennyson or John Greenleaf Whittier. Not that these esoteric artists had an immediate effect upon the European masses, any more than did Einstein in his explanation of the space-time continuum. But it is a truism that the dominant themes adopted by societal élites filter down ultimately to the people at large.

In America, a younger, less sophisticated society, the process at first displayed a more directly pragmatic character. Observers stood in dismay as the agricultural depression of the 1880s and 1890s led to a massive flight from the farms to the cities, there the rural dispossessed to mingle with the hordes of new immigrants from southern and eastern Europe. Anxiety had already risen across the country at the ease with which a set of entrepreneurs—the so-called "robber barons"—manipulated the conventional financial system to accumulate out of railroads, steel manufacture, and oil production vast and unprecedented wealth and political influence. The campaign by various "progressives," most notably Theodore Roosevelt, to expose their ruthless style and curb their power was only partially successful. A sign of the times was the bestselling novel *The Jungle* (1906), Upton Sinclair's cautionary tale about the horrors of those who labored in Chicago's meat-packing industry. A year later there appeared an equally searing fictional indictment of the American industrial climate, Theodore Dreiser's *Sister Carrie,* which described the ruin of a young woman of good will caught up in the amoral atmosphere of a brutally competitive capitalism. The happy rags-to-riches stories of Horatio Alger no longer conformed to literary fashion.

All these trends toward reordering society did not move in lockstep, but eventually, for the sake of semantic convenience, they were lumped together and called "Modernism." The term, since it applied to so many fields of endeavor, was necessarily imprecise. For Catholics, however, it had a specific meaning, a movement among some intellectuals that cast doubt upon the reliability of scriptural texts and upon the philosophical foundation of belief. Catholic Modernism was a European, mostly French, phenomenon and had little resonance in the United States.[2] Even so, its condemnation by Pius X in the encyclical *Pascendi* (1907) as "the synthesis of all heresies" had a wider significance than simply the particular doctrines it anathematized. The whole of modern culture, the pope seemed to be declaring, was losing its respect for objective truth, for universally accepted moral standards, for hierarchical order. God's word—indeed God himself—was in the dock.

If this gloomy assessment were correct, then the position of the old-line Americanists like John Ireland fell under dire threat. For their basic argument had been that the United States embodied the very best of traditional values in the secular arena, and that Catholicism, far from being at odds with the spirit and aspirations of the Republic, actually bolstered them. American Catholics therefore should shed their immigrant ways and embrace wholeheartedly what was the best political, economic, and social system ever devised. They need sacrifice nothing of their faith by accommodating themselves to that system. Pius X's predecessor had already checked some Americanist enthusiasms, though Leo XIII's rebuke in *Testem benevolentiae* had been mild,

---

2. See Marvin R. O'Connell, *Critics on Trial: An Introduction to the Catholic Modernist Crisis* (Washington, D.C., 1994).

and Ireland and his associates had been able to argue successfully that no specific denunciation applied to them.[3] But what if the grand American experience was faltering? What if, under its various guises, "Modernism" was eating
away at the fabric of the traditional American ethos, undermining the qualities that had made the nation great and unique? An avowed socialist garnered
more than a million votes in the presidential election of 1920. Two years later
an American poet living in England published a long and intricate poetic
treatise, whose title, *The Wasteland,* encapsulated the view that war and the
collapse of the Victorian hegemony had left modern men and women adrift
in a moral wilderness. In 1925 *The Great Gatsby,* written by one raised a
Catholic in St. Paul, testified to the same sense of loss and chronicled, if unintentionally, how money, fast cars, sexual obsession, and alcohol could not fill
the vacuum. Another American novelist, also (at times) a Catholic, expressed
his despair at the prospects of the human enterprise by mocking the Lord's
Prayer: "Our nada who art in nada, nada be thy name."[4] And all the while psy-
choanalysts and mathematicians and physicists posed explanations about the
nature of man and the universe that appeared to contradict the wisdom accumulated over thousands of years.

The growing conviction that this was so ushered in what has been called
"the second phase of Catholic Americanism."[5] This phenomenon represented
a curious turn of attitude. Not by any means a reversal of attitude, however;
these new Americanists did not repudiate their forebears' dedication to personal liberty, the separation of Church and state, the worth of individual economic initiative, or any of the other civic virtues enshrined in the American
pantheon. But total accommodation to the larger culture could no longer be
entertained as a goal, because that culture, it was argued, had in many respects begun to forfeit its principles. Paradoxical as it may seem, preservation
and restoration became the watchwords. By their unity of faith and their concomitant commitment to tradition, to natural law, to a philosophy grounded
in realism, to a sexual code fixed within a wholesome theology of the
family—such attributes made it feasible for Catholics to preserve what was
valid in the American dream and to restore what had been lost. This is not to
say that a program sprang forward full blown or all at once; even the consciousness of it developed slowly through a series of incremental steps and

---

3. See chapter 15, above.
4. Eugene Debs, T. S. Eliot, F. Scott Fitzgerald, Ernest Hemingway.
5. My narrative follows, quite inadequately, the perceptive and detailed account
in Douglas J. Slawson, *The Foundation and First Decade of the National Catholic
Welfare Council* (Washington, D.C., 1992), 1–25.

missteps. But it progressed relentlessly so that by the time Dowling became archbishop of St. Paul, a new Catholic subculture was fast becoming a reality. While John Ireland had told the immigrants and their children to be good Catholics by adjusting to the American way, Austin Dowling told them that by being good Catholics they could save their souls, to be sure, but they could also reinvigorate the Republic as the Founding Fathers had conceived it.

The practical result within the subculture was a proliferation of initiatives aimed at separating Catholics—the paradox deepens—from the larger society. But the object of such segregation was to achieve distinctiveness, not isolation—a distinctiveness designed to preserve the best that was Catholic and the best that was traditionally American. Catholic schools therefore had to be nurtured at all costs, not only to maintain the faith but also to bolster national values under threat from an increasingly secularized public education system. Archbishop Ireland had always been ambivalent in this matter, because in his heart he accepted the argument that the public school was a formidable instrument in the Americanizing of the immigrant. His successor entertained no such reservations. "This country is the melting pot of nations, we are told," Dowling wrote in 1920.

> Very true. But what is its mold? That may be difficult to answer, but one thing we know—it is not a Catholic mold into which the Americanized foreigner will be poured. It is possible that it will be a socialist mold; it might very well be in many cases a Protestant mold; it is frequently a materialistic, anti-clerical mold. But apart from what we ourselves do at this dangerous period of transition for the children of the foreigner in our schools nothing will be done. . . . The influence of the public school in stemming the tide of immorality, of bad faith among men and of no faith in God is scarcely noticeable.[6]

What was needful for the children was not less so for their elders, learned or not. And the principle of fruitful exclusiveness demanded more than a parochial scope. "Our conditions have unduly emphasized the role of the parish unit which, however necessary, is ordinarily a principle of narrowness and exclusion."[7] This widely shared conviction had led in 1904 to the establishment of the Catholic Educational Association. In 1910 the National Con-

---

6. *CB*, October 14, 1920.

7. Austin Dowling, "The National Catholic Welfare Conference," *Ecclesiastical Review* 79 (October 1928): 337–354. The quotation is from 340.

ference of Catholic Charities came into existence, the Catholic Press Association a year later, and the Catholic Hospital Association two years after that.
An instructive example of this process was the organizing of academic and
intellectual societies parallel to secular ones already in place. By the mid-
1930s there were distinct Catholic organizations for historians, anthropolo-
gists, poets, sociologists, biblicists, artists, litterateurs, and economists.[8] One
objective of such groups was to support and encourage the professional competence of their members. But there was more to it than that. Thus, when
the American Catholic Historical Association was established in 1919, Peter
Guilday, the distinguished editor of *The Catholic Historical Review,* founded
four years earlier, explained that the new organization was necessary "if the
Church is to be recognized in her true position as the sacred and perpetual
mother of all that is best in modern civilization." And the association's first
president added, "Blessed with the true faith," Catholics were bound to refute
the false history cultivated by "their less fortunate brethren. In American history, theirs is the glorious page. The history of the Church offers the best patterns for the correction of the social evils of our day."[9]

This claim may have been extravagant, even fanciful, but it encapsulated
the buoyant spirit of optimism that pervaded American Catholic leadership
after the First World War—a mood labeled, not unfairly, a species of "boosterism."[10] And no one expressed it more loftily or eloquently than Archbishop
Dowling.

> We all know that the spirit of the world today is not the spirit of Christ.
> We Catholics, at least, are not deceived by the Christian phraseology
> in which neo-paganism in some places clothes its hard, materialistic
> thought. What we fail to realize, however, is that now is the acceptable
> time, if ever, for us to take our stand as a formative, constructive influ-
> ence in the community; that we can exert a beneficent Catholic influence
> only by comprehending our world program as distinguished from our
> parochial program; and also that methods of publicity and of education
> that have advanced the cause of every wild system among us are open
> to us in our advocacy of the principles and the policies which, as they

---

8. Philip Gleason, "The Search for Unity and Its Sequel," in *Keeping the Faith:
American Catholicism Past and Present* (Notre Dame, Ind., 1987), 140–142.

9. Quoted in Slawson, *Foundation,* 15.

10. Jay P. Dolan, *The American Catholic Experience* (Garden City, N.Y., 1985),
349–351.

underlie the Christian civilization we know, must be the most effective restorative of its declining powers and its departing faith. Christian men, can there be a more inspiring apostolate than that of bringing this salutary evangel to the land we love and live in?"[11]

THOSE CRITICS WHO CLAIMED THAT AUSTIN DOWLING IN 1928 had transferred control of the College of St. Thomas to the Congregation of Holy Cross thoughtlessly—or, even worse, frivolously, in hopes of trading on the national reputation of the University of Notre Dame, Holy Cross's flagship institution—chose to ignore the plentiful evidence that the archbishop had been engaged for many years in a larger educational enterprise outside his immediate jurisdiction. He had been from its inception one of the leading lights of the infant National Catholic Welfare Council and the head of its Department of Education. In this capacity he was familiar with, as he put it, "the leading educators of the United States": indeed, the executive committee of his department was coextensive with the executive committee of the Catholic Education Association. Notable among those who served on these bodies was James Burns, formerly president of Notre Dame, who had radically reformed that university's structure to bring it into line, really for the first time, with national academic norms.[12] Another member was Matthew Schumacher, who had rescued St. Edward's University in Austin, Texas, from serious financial and academic problems when he served as its president between 1919 and 1925. Their colleague in religion, William Cunningham, was a scholar widely published across a range of issues related to higher education, particularly those dealing with collegiate curriculum, planning, relationships between Catholic colleges and accrediting agencies, standards of admission, and faculty development. In 1928 Father Burns was provincial of the Indiana Province of Holy Cross, and it was he with whom Dowling negotiated the transfer. And in September of 1928 Father Schumacher assumed the presidency of St. Thomas and Father Cunningham became dean of studies.[13]

The emergence of the National Catholic Welfare Conference (as it was later renamed), in which Dowling ultimately played so large a role, was the

---

11. Dowling, *Occasional Sermons*, 30. The quotation is taken from a speech delivered to the Chicago Holy Name Society Union, January 2, 1921.

12. See Thomas T. McAvoy, *Notre Dame, 1919–1922: The Burns Revolution* (Notre Dame, Ind., 1963).

13. Connors, *Journey*, 224–225.

result of an untidy process of evolution. Because the Third Plenary Council of Baltimore (1884) had concluded without resolving the vexed problem of how the hierarchy should view the status of the so-called "secret societies," a committee was set up composed of the archbishops—twelve at the time—to meet and explore the question further.[14] Even as the urgency of the secret society issue waned, the members of the committee continued to gather annually and informally—it had no legislative authority—to discuss matters of mutual concern. This apparatus proved useful in bringing forward broad questions of common interest among the metropolitans themselves and their suffragans, as well as in keeping Rome regularly apprised of developments on the American scene. Once the Catholic University of America was established (1887), these same archbishops became members *ex officio* of the institution's board of trustees, thus further codifying to a degree their collegiality.

This loosely representative body proved inadequate, however, when in 1917 the United States entered the war that had already been raging in Europe for three years. The vast majority of the nation's bishops urged their people to support the American intervention. A few prelates—Irishmen who instinctively disliked an alliance with Great Britain and Germans unwilling to consider relatives in the old country as enemies—felt otherwise, but their doubts were largely muted. In rallying to the Allies' just cause, so the prevailing argument went, Catholics could at the same time demonstrate most clearly their patriotism and so their right to be accepted as full-fledged citizens, whatever their immigrant background. And indeed Catholics did respond positively to the call in numbers and enthusiasm across a wide range of war-related activities—the percentage of the armed forces who were Catholics, for instance, was much higher than their percentage in the overall population. The archbishops' committee was too diffuse a mechanism to coordinate all the undertakings necessary, and so there emerged under its auspices the National Catholic War Council, with an executive of four bishops who directed the necessary bureaucratic structure set up to handle the day-to-day business. This arrangement met with the approval of the hierarchy as a whole. It by no means always worked smoothly, but by and large it succeeded in mobilizing and sustaining the American Catholic contribution to the victory of November 1918. The Council's achievement also convinced many within the ecclesiastical leadership that a similarly constructed national organization should be constituted once the war was over. Among their number was James Gibbons of Baltimore.

---

14. Ellis, *Gibbons*, 1:449–450.

On February 20, 1919, in Washington, the aged cardinal celebrated the golden jubilee of his episcopal consecration. No fewer than sixty-eight American bishops attended the festivities, along with many foreign dignitaries. Most notable among the latter was a Vatican diplomat dispatched by Benedict XV to bring Gibbons the pope's personal congratulations. More than that, Archbishop Bonaventura Cerretti also brought with him the pope's urgent appeal that the American bishops join the Holy See in working to promote a just and lasting peace in accord with Christian ethical principles, particularly in the fields of labor and education. This plea was music to the ears of those prelates eager to institute a formal successor to the War Council. Their plan was basically simple: "We have urgent need now of organizing on broad national lines for the welfare of the whole Church; . . . the organization to be formed should have the authority and support of the whole Hierarchy and be subject to its direction and control. The departments of the organization [should] follow the broad lines of the Church's work and needs in this country." In other words, a permanent secretariat should be established with distinct departments charged to act at a national rather than a diocesan level. This bureaucracy would be under the supervision of an episcopal committee representative of the body of the American bishops as a whole. At the proposed annual meeting of the hierarchy the activities and initiatives of the secretariat, as overseen by the committee, would seek from the plenary session "authority and support" as well as "direction and control."[15] With Gibbons in the lead, these straightforward proposals were presented to the first annual meeting of the hierarchy in Washington, September 24, 1919, and after some debate were approved. The next day the ninety-two bishops in attendance elected by secret ballot seven of their number to serve as members of the administrative committee of the newly constituted NCWC. Among them was Austin Dowling.[16] The archbishop of St. Paul, reelected every year till his health failed in the late 1920s, may have lacked friends among the clerical élite back home; not so, apparently, among his episcopal peers, over whom the memory of John Ireland cast no shadow.

The organization of the NCWC[17] and the consolidation of its institutions took a painful decade to accomplish. Binding together 101 dioceses, many of

---

15. Muldoon et al. to the archbishops (copy), AASPM, Dowling Papers. Peter Muldoon of Rockford was the leading light on the provisional committee Gibbons appointed, with himself in the chair, to prepare the agenda of the bishops' meeting.

16. Ellis, *Gibbons*, 2:298–304.

17. In the wake of Vatican Council II, the National Catholic Welfare Conference in 1966 was replaced by the United States Conference of Catholic Bishops (USCCB),

them headed by strong personalities who tended to be jealous of their prerogatives, was no easy task. The most formidable—and disreputable[18]—of such
men was the archbishop of Boston, William Cardinal O'Connell, who, after
Gibbons died in 1921, tried to seize control of the fledgling Conference and,
when that failed, tried to destroy it. O'Connell cultivated his Roman connections[19] and played upon the Vatican's unease at any corporate group that might
usurp its authority and presume to enact legislation—indeed, the curial officials, with their long memories, recalled the conciliar struggles of the fifteenth century and insisted that the word "Conference" replace the original
"Council." There was little danger of such a development; no such pretensions
existed in a hierarchy that was steadfastly, even supinely, ultramontane. Nor
was there any intent to create a permanent organization with powers like
those exercised at the Plenary Council of Baltimore in 1884. "Council" in
the context of 1919 meant simply and innocently that the American bishops
should take "counsel" with one another on a regular basis.[20] The change of
name, however, was not good enough for the imperious O'Connell, who fancied that he embodied in himself true *romanità,* the genuine Roman ecclesiastical spirit. In 1926, when Dowling, as head of the NCWC's Department of
Education, proposed a rather sophisticated approach to impending federal
legislation, O'Connell brushed it aside. Dowling had had no Roman experience, he said. Dowling's education had been confined to the United States.
"To know the Catholic Church and to have those Catholic traditions that
enable one to keep the faith intact, one must have been to Rome, have had
international experience." The likes of Dowling were always too ready to

a canonical body with some (if limited) legislative authority, and the United States
Catholic Conference (USCC), a civil entity designed to foster collective action on
the interdiocesan level in areas of concern to the American Church, like education
and social action. In effect the USCC purports to be the bureaucratic arm of the
USCCB.

18. O'Connell's influence in Boston was immense. But dubious financial practices over a long career undermined his prestige and his legacy. As early as 1920 a
scandal erupted involving misappropriation of funds by the cardinal's priest nephew,
who also, it was discovered, had been secretly married for eight years.

19. O'Connell was educated and ordained in Rome. He served as rector of the
North American College there before his appointment as bishop of Portland and
then (1907) archbishop of Boston.

20. See Elizabeth K. McKewon, "The 'National Idea' in the History of the
American Episcopal Conference," in *Episcopal Conferences: Historical, Theological
and Canonical Studies,* ed. Thomas J. Reese (Washington, D.C., 1989), 23.

compromise with the heretical state. "America is a Protestant country, expressive of Protestant traditions, not Catholic."[21]

After Benedict XV died in 1922, the NCWC was in fact suspended by the Vatican, due largely to the intrigues of O'Connell, but the administrative committee, including Dowling, mounted a swift and effective rebuttal to Boston. The new pope, the shrewd Pius XI, quickly recognized the need to meet the legitimate concerns of the vast majority of the American bishops, and the ban was lifted after a few months.[22] It had to be acknowledged, in Rome as everywhere else, that since Catholics, seventeen million of them, now constituted the largest single religious denomination in the United States, a permanent national leadership organization was a necessity. Certainly Austin Dowling subscribed to this view. From the beginning of his tenure in St. Paul he had emphasized the need for overall diocesan regulation of the educational structure, of charitable and philanthropic endeavors, and of missionary or outreach activities.[23] He brought the same persuasions with him to Washington in 1919 and was ready to apply them to a larger field. In retrospect he put succinctly and with admirable and characteristic candor the problem that faced him and his episcopal colleagues who were trying to put together the NCWC.

Catholics have the name of being highly organized and obedient and responsive to their leaders; but they are not easily organized nor responsive to their leaders, except in following the doctrine and sacramental life of the Church. Even those among us who listen to the compliments about our leadership know this to be true. . . . There is no group so hard to convince as a Catholic group. There is a tremendous timidity among Catholics, a fear whenever they attempt anything. . . . Catholics, however, have a great tradition of power. When civilization would seem to be disappearing, then the Church is marvelous. . . . [But today] one difficulty is [Catholics'] parochial mindedness. The most successful organization is a small organization, a parish organization. . . . Now this belittles us and makes it difficult for Catholics to organize as it is manifest we should be organized. We have no public opinion. We are at the mercy of anybody who says anything about us. To create a public opinion, you must have a

---

21. Quoted in James Hennesey, *American Catholics: A History of the Roman Catholic Community in the United States* (Oxford, 1981), 240.

22. For an excellent overview of the juridical development of the NCWC, see Gerald P. Fogarty, "The Authority of the NCWC," in Reese, *Episcopal Conferences.*

23. See chapter 16, above, and O'Connell, "Dowling Decade," 48–50.

Catholic viewpoint and think with the Church. The sense of the Church, which looks out upon life and interprets its values in accordance with the teachings of Christ, must be your sense. . . . There is in the Church a certain physical detachment from church service, beyond the reception of the sacraments. It is a coolness, and because of this coolness there is a lack of Catholic influence in our country.[24]

The NCWC set itself the task of countering this "parochial mindedness." The secretariat duly took up quarters at 1312 Massachusetts Avenue N.E. in Washington. Operating on a skimpy budget, its small staff of clerics and laymen and women—the very presence of the latter an affront to the likes of Cardinal O'Connell—worked through its discrete departments to put a face on a national American Catholicism. Archbishop Dowling and his six associates on the administrative committee were in constant touch with Washington, but they had their own dioceses to run and so had to carry a double burden. In Dowling's case, moreover, the organization of the NCWC's Department of Education, of which he was named the head, occurred just as he was mounting in St. Paul the campaign to establish the Ireland Educational Fund and planning the construction of Nazareth Hall. For a man of delicate health these combined endeavors took their toll. One strong consolation to him and his colleagues was the hearty cooperation, in money and personnel, the Conference received from the newly founded National Council of Catholic Women, the first president of which—not incidentally as far as Dowling was concerned—was Gertrude Hill Gavin, a daughter of James J. Hill.[25] (Nor was it perhaps incidental that Dowling's regard for women's civil rights was well known; even as bishop of Des Moines he was regarded as the foremost advocate within the American hierarchy of women's suffrage.[26])

From its inception the NCWC—secretariat, administrative committee, and plenary body—strenuously maintained that its activities should not be construed as lobbying in the usual sense of that word. Perhaps this assertion was true as to ends, but hardly so as to means. If the organization could legitimately distinguish its objectives from those of private interests, like the American Federation of Labor or the National Association of Manufacturers, it nevertheless employed the same devices as did these groups to influence public policy. For Austin Dowling, as head of the Education Department, this

---

24. *CB,* November 27, 1926. Dowling was addressing the annual convention of the Minnesota division of the National Council of Catholic Women.

25. McKewon, "The 'National Idea,'" 25.

26. See Hennesey, *American Catholics,* 233.

meant using the techniques of pressure no less than persuasion to assure the status of Catholic schools. Nor was such a course of action unnecessary. The 1920s saw the resurgence of hostility toward parochial schools on the part of some Masonic groups and particularly of the revived Ku Klux Klan, which directed its spleen, if not its violence, as much against Catholics as against African Americans.[27] There was always a threat that the federal government might revert to traditional nativist prejudices, and Archbishop Dowling kept a sharp eye, and successfully so, on possibly unsympathetic educational legislation pending in Congress.[28] But it was the prosecution of a state case—with, ultimately, national implications—that brought him his greatest satisfaction and marked out his standing as a national leader.

In 1922 Oregon's legislature enacted a statute which amended the state's fundamental law with regard to primary and secondary education.

> Any parent, guardian or other person in the state of Oregon, having control or charge or custody of a child under the age of sixteen years and of the age of eight years or over at the commencement of a term of public school of the district in which the child resides, who shall fail or neglect or refuse to send such child to a public school for the period of time a public school shall be held during the current year in said district, shall be guilty of misdemeanor[,] and each day's failure to send such child to a public school shall constitute a separate offense.

Some exceptions were incorporated into the statute: unreasonable distance from the closest public school; private tutoring, so long as the child were examined by the county school superintendent every three months; and the physically disabled, as well as, in the statute's less than sensitive words, "the abnormal and subnormal." The penalty for noncompliance was to be "a fine of not less than $5, nor more than $100, or to imprisonment in the county jail not less than two nor more than thirty days." The act was to take effect September 1, 1926.

The NCWC, under Dowling's lead, sprang into action. An appeal alleging the law unconstitutional under the Fourteenth Amendment[29] was filed

---

27. For a spirited confrontation between Klan members and students of the University of Notre Dame, see Robert E. Burns, *Being Catholic, Being American: The Notre Dame Story, 1842–1934* (Notre Dame, Ind., 1999), 306–346.

28. See Slawson, *Foundation*, 85, 87, 101, 250, 253–254.

29. The Fourteenth Amendment reads (in part): "No state shall make or enforce any law that shall abridge the privileges or immunities of citizens of the United

forthwith. But in order to be sure that religious animosity should play a less than prominent role, the brief of the "Society of Sisters"—specifically, the Sisters of the Holy Names of Jesus and Mary, an order founded in 1880—was shrewdly conjoined with that of a nonsectarian private institution, the exclusive Hill Military Academy, which, with its hundred or so students between the ages of five and twenty-one and its considerable property, could reasonably seek redress under the aegis of that same amendment. The lower courts sustained the sisters and Hill, but the state in its turn appealed. Finally, the cases reached the Supreme Court of the United States, where they were argued before the justices on March 16 and 17, 1925. The unanimous decision in *Pierce v. Society of Sisters*[30] and *Same v. Hill Military Academy,* issued on June 1, was written by Justice James C. McReynolds. Its summation:

> [In fact] the Compulsory Education Act of 1922 required parent or guardians to send children between the ages of eight and sixteen to public school in the district where the children resided. The Society of Sisters was an Oregon corporation which facilitated care for orphans, educated youths and established and maintained academies or schools.
>
> Did the Act violate the liberty of parents to direct the education of their children?
>
> Yes. The unanimous Court held that "the fundamental liberty upon which all governments in this Union repose excludes any general power of the State to standardize its children by forcing them to accept instruction from public teachers only."

Among the nine justices who subscribed to this verdict were luminaries like William Howard Taft, Louis Brandeis, and Oliver Wendell Holmes, Jr. And, to Archbishop Dowling's great satisfaction, also the sole Minnesotan on the bench, the Honorable Pierce Butler.[31]

The Oregon case was a landmark because it established definitively the priority of parental rights in the field of education, a matter that had vexed American society for at least half a century. Catholic schools were safe now

---

States; nor shall any state deprive any person of life, liberty, or property without due process of law."

30. Walter Pierce was the governor of Oregon.

31. Citation: 268 U.S. 510 (1925). The full text of Mr. Justice McReynolds's decision can be found in *NCWC Bulletin,* July 1925.

from the long arm of state or federal legislation. Not that all their problems were solved, especially their financial ones, as Dowling knew all too well: even as he rejoiced in reading Mr. Justice McReynolds's decision he had to ponder the faltering Ireland Fund campaign back home. Nevertheless, the victory achieved in Washington represented a significant moment in the development of the second phase of Americanism.

ON A SUNDAY IN MID-SEPTEMBER 1923, AUSTIN DOWLING mounted the pulpit in his cathedral to preach at a Mass celebrated by a silver jubilarian. John A. Ryan had been ordained to the priesthood twenty-five years before, at a time when the great building on Summit Avenue was only John Ireland's aspiration. That Dowling was an eminent preacher, who had cultivated a more nuanced and less bombastic style of oratory than his storied predecessor, was attested to by the numerous invitations to speak that came to him from every corner of the country. On this occasion, however, those in attendance sensed a certain ambiguity. Canonically, Ryan was Dowling's subject, but he had left St. Paul in 1915 to serve in a broader apostolate and so had never served directly under the archbishop. They were colleagues, so to speak, at work in the fledgling NCWC—Dowling as a charter member of the administrative committee and episcopal director of the Education Department, and Ryan a driving force within the Social Action Department. But their styles were thoroughly dissimilar: Dowling diffident, measured, much preferring action behind the scenes; and Ryan aggressive, often abrasive, reveling in controversy, and—it was said in some high Catholic circles—a radical if not an out-and-out socialist. Such differences, however, did not prevent Dowling from lauding in his sermon the jubilarian's priestly virtues and congratulating him for the honor he had brought to his archdiocese and to the American Church at large. Afterward Ryan sent the archbishop a letter of thanks, pulsed with his deeply Irish sentiment. Many criticisms, he wrote, had been leveled against him because of his so-called advanced, "even dangerous," views, nor was he by any means indifferent to such negative judgments. "I am concerned about my standing among my fellow priests and before the ecclesiastical authorities. . . . [But] when my own archbishop thus honors me in his cathedral, 'I should worry' over the criticisms and misunderstandings of small minds."[32]

---

32. Quoted in Francis L. Broderick, *Right Reverend New Dealer: John A. Ryan* (New York, 1963), 155. "The Right Reverend New Dealer" (Ryan was made a monsi-

John Augustine Ryan was born in Vermillion township, Minnesota, on May 25, 1869, the eldest of the eleven children[33] of William and Mary Elizabeth Luby Ryan, both Irish immigrants. William had left impoverished Tipperary to seek his fortune in the New World, and after disappointment in the gold fields of California had come to Minneapolis, where his sister had already settled and where he met the woman soon to be his wife. With a smattering of cash and a hefty mortgage, he purchased 160 acres of rich prairie land in Vermillion, seven or eight miles out of St. Paul. William Ryan was a high-principled man, hardworking, humorless, strict with his children and himself—he never smoked or took a drink or played cards—displaying all the admirable and yet chilling traits characteristic of Irish Jansenism. The Ryan household was intensely devout; morning prayers were always said before breakfast, and during Lent the rosary was recited every evening, while every member of the family was expected to take on an explicit penitential practice and to read each day from some spiritual book. The high point of the week was Sunday Mass, celebrated once a month at nearby St. Agatha's, Coates Station; on the other Sundays the Ryans traveled seven miles to Rosemount and joined the congenial, mostly Irish congregation there.

As the eldest son John learned early the strenuous labor required on a family farm, from planting to harvesting to everything in between. Even after he went off to boarding school, he returned home every summer and worked in the fields. He was a clever lad, who, thanks to his doting mother's tutoring, could read when he was six. He excelled in the somewhat chaotic public school, during whose seven-month term forty or more children between the ages of five and eighteen were taught by a single teacher. But as the eldest John also fell most directly under his father's withering discipline, so much so that at sixteen he ran away to Minneapolis and took a job piling laths for twenty-five cents a day. The hiatus was brief, however; Mary Elizabeth quickly fetched her son back to Vermillion. Still, a separation of sorts seemed prudent, and shortly afterward John enrolled in Cretin High School in St. Paul, located then in the old cathedral,[34] and lodged with his uncle's family in the city. He

---

gnor in 1933) was originally intended as a term of abuse, coined by Charles Coughlin, the famous "Radio Priest," whose broadcasts from Detroit in the 1930s attracted audiences in the tens of millions. His notions of social justice were far removed from those of Ryan, with whom he often jousted. By the end of the decade Coughlin's demagogic attacks on Roosevelt's New Deal and his barely latent anti-Semitism had undermined much of his appeal. He died in 1979.

33. Ten of whom survived into adulthood, six boys and four girls.

34. See chapter 14, above.

found the regimen and pedagogy of the Christian Brothers far from challenging, and, thinking he might have a calling to the priesthood, he transferred to St. Thomas Seminary in 1887. The tuition, board and room, and fees, $200 in all, were paid by his Grandfather Luby. Among the seventy-five students, about half were aspiring seminarians and the rest were preparing for other careers. Young John flourished on the spacious twenty-acre campus, still in those days surrounded by farmland. During the five years of the "classical" course he stood at the head of his class, and on the playing field was a stellar first baseman. In 1892 he entered the "clerical" course which was transferred two years later to Mr. Hill's new major seminary a few hundred yards away.[35] On June 4, 1898, John Ryan was ordained priest in the seminary's class building, his parents and nine siblings in attendance. On this joyous occasion William Ryan sternly ordered that from that moment on every member of the family had to address the number one son as "Father John," a formality honored long after the old man was gone.[36]

But the young man did not only experience his father's grave Irish courtesy toward the clerical estate or simply remember with resentment his sometimes harsh demeanor. William Ryan was a member in good standing of the local chapter of the National Farmers' Alliance, organized up and down the Mississippi River valley to combat the monopolistic railway system, whose freight rates combined with steadily declining grain prices were driving many a farm family into penury. Growing up, John was witness to many conversations in the Ryan kitchen in which disgruntled friends and neighbors shared their anger at the wickedness of the railroads and, by extension, of the other massive cartels in oil and steel. The more radical—and perhaps knowledgeable—among them pointed to the need, they argued, to inflate the rigid currency linked indissolubly to gold and to nationalize at least part of the country's transport system. The Alliance, like similar organizations in industry, did not fare well during the 1890s, as testified to by the defeat of William Jennings Bryan in the presidential election of 1896. As for the large Ryan family in Vermillion, it could not in the end sustain itself on the land, and eventually the farm had to be given up.

It was out of this populist tradition, with its stark personal ramifications, that John Ryan the seminarian first read Leo XIII's encyclical *Rerum novarum* (1891). This papal document, "On the Condition of Labor," quite literally changed his life, or rather set him in a direction from which he did not swerve

---

35. Connors, *Journey,* 60–61.
36. Broderick, *Right Reverend,* 1–25.

for half a century. Leo posited as a "first and fundamental principle" the inviolability of private property, thus rebutting the basic tenet of socialism. Nor did the pontiff accept the inevitability of class struggle as envisioned by Karl Marx. Employers and employees need not, and indeed should not, be placed in a status of mutual antagonism: "Each requires the other; capital cannot do without labor, nor labor without capital." By natural law the laborer had a right to enough of this world's goods to maintain himself in "reasonable and frugal comfort." At the same time he owed the entrepreneur who hired him an honest day's work. But, if the employer could always expect a worker to produce a fair output, reciprocally under no circumstances could he deny that worker a reasonable wage. In fact, however, working men have been systematically exploited, "so that a very small number of very rich men have been able to lay upon the masses of the poor a yoke little better than slavery itself." Therefore, the pope asserted, employers must reflect upon the obligations imposed upon them by the natural law, and must in practice accept labor unions, so that for the common good just wages, decent working conditions, and wide access to private ownership of property be open to all. And finally—and here young John Ryan took special notice—"Whenever the general interest of any class suffers, or is threatened with evils which can in no other way be met, the public authority must step in to meet them."[37]

After ordination Ryan was sent to Catholic University in Washington for graduate studies in order to prepare himself to teach moral theology at the St. Paul Seminary. Once there, he encountered professors who encouraged him to approach that rather broad field with questions of social justice principally in mind. His doctoral dissertation, called *A Living Wage,* was published in 1905. "The first attempt in the English language to elaborate what may be called a Roman Catholic system of political economy," as one admirer called it, received brickbats as well as accolades. Too many gratuitous assumptions, declared one reviewer; edging toward socialism, said another. Some high ecclesiastics found the book and its successor, *Distributive Justice* (1916), unsettling. John Ireland apparently was not among them; all his life the archbishop had been a sturdy Republican, but a "progressive" one—he counted among his personal friends Theodore Roosevelt and William Howard Taft. Ryan duly took up his duties on the staff of the seminary until 1915, when Ireland released him, due perhaps in some measure at the behest of some of Ireland's less "progressive" Republican friends, and he joined the faculty of Catholic University.

---

37. Claudia Carlen, ed., *The Papal Encyclicals, 1878–1903* (New York, 1981), 241–261.

In both institutions Father Ryan was considered by his students an amiable enough fellow out of class but an indifferent teacher at best. His lectures seemed to them dull monologues; it never occurred to him to invite them to engage in discussion. He was always in a hurry, intensely anxious to tell the students what they ought to know. Nor did his faculty colleagues find him particularly congenial.[38] Neither the classroom nor the common room was ever John Ryan's métier. There was a messianic streak in him which worked itself out in the millions of words he published and in the battles he fought over so many years—he died in 1945—as the heart and soul of the NCWC's Social Action Department. What is pertinent here, however, is that though he wrote sixteen books and literally hundreds of lesser pieces, harangued an often reluctant national public in every possible forum, and dealt on equal terms with all the politicians, intellectuals, and social reformers of his time, the principles upon which he acted took shape in his Minnesota years, and he never deviated from what he set down in *A Living Wage* and *Distributive Justice*. His was an amalgam of Midwest populism and papal teaching as found in *Rerum novarum* and in the confirmation of that encyclical forty years later, Pius XI's *Quadragesimo anno*.[39]

In retrospect much of what Ryan proposed as practical applications of those principles seems old-hat now, so completely have they been woven into the texture of the American body politic: the right of both skilled and unskilled workers to organize, the minimum wage, the eight-hour day, unemployment insurance, legislative protection for peaceful picketing, protection of women and children in the workplace, a progressive income tax. Indeed, so old-hat that some of what was taken for granted as desirable when he died has failed to materialize or has been abandoned: public ownership of forests and mines as well as of utilities, a progressive inheritance tax, and prohibition of stock market speculation.[40] After the crash of that stock market in 1929 and the onset of the Great Depression, Ryan's reforming agenda took on a new impetus. By and large he supported, sometimes perhaps exorbitantly, the programs of the New Deal initiated by President Franklin Roosevelt four years later. But he always justified himself by invoking that pregnant line from *Rerum novarum*, insisting that when "any class suffers . . . [from] evils which can in no other way be met, the public authority must step in to meet them."

---

38. Broderick, *Right Reverend*, 37.

39. See Claudia Carlen, ed., *The Papal Encyclicals, 1903–1939* (New York, 1981), 415–443. The subtitle of the encyclical is "Reconstruction of the Social Order."

40. See Broderick, *Right Reverend*, 52–64, 88–92.

After 1915 Monsignor Ryan (as he became in 1933) no longer lived in Minnesota.[41] But his roots ran deep, and for many years he kept in contact with those individuals and institutions—like the editors of *The Union Advocate* and, by contrast, the members of the mostly conservative Saturday Lunch Club in Minneapolis—that had helped form his social ideas. As his national reputation grew, the *Catholic Bulletin,* and the secular press as well, gave him much local notoriety. The most important link with home, however, was that with his family. The farm at Vermillion, to be sure, was in other hands now, with the elder Ryans taking up residence in St. Paul and their children dispersed. Two of them, Mary Jane and Katherine, joined the Sisters of St. Joseph. Another, Lawrence, was ordained in 1910, and was appointed rector of the St. Paul cathedral in 1916. Eleven years John's junior, Father Lawrence became his brother's closest confidant. The two of them appeared to be, in many respects, an odd couple, the elder chubby and aggressive, the younger lean, ascetic, and unfailingly courteous. But the really significant difference between them lay in the divergence that their career paths had taken: John Ryan was an academic throughout his entire priesthood, without a day spent in parochial ministry, while Lawrence was the pastor *par excellence* and, not incidentally, the manager of his cathedral's splendid interior decoration.[42] Even so, they maintained a fraternal bond of mutual affection and respect. While Lawrence scoffed at those ultraconservatives who hinted that his brother was a dangerous radical and a socialist at heart, he did on occasion act as a restraining influence on some of John's more rambunctious initiatives. When in 1940 John Ryan wrote his autobiography,[43] he submitted the original draft for his brother's examination. He had devoted six vitriolic pages to a frontal assault on Father Charles Coughlin, the famous "Radio Priest," with whom he had jousted for years over the latter's hostility to the New Deal, as well as his alleged anti-Semitism and softness on European fascism. Lawrence urged John to omit the lengthy passage, arguing forcefully that to "adopt the vehicle of silence" would be "a thousand times more eloquent than all the words of a Shakespeare." John, very reluctantly and after much grumbling, agreed.[44]

---

41. It is sadly noteworthy that Ryan is not mentioned in Clifford E. Clark, Jr., ed., *Minnesota in a Century of Change: The State and Its People since 1900* (St. Paul, 1989), a book more than 600 pages long.

42. See chapter 16, above.

43. *Social Doctrine in Action: A Personal History* (New York, 1941). As the title suggests, this book dealt more with the author's life as a public man than with his private relationships.

44. Broderick, *Right Reverend,* 76–78, 249–251.

The polemical pace inexorably slowed as the sands of time began to run out for John Augustine Ryan. His secular hero, Franklin Roosevelt, died in April 1945, prompting from him a heartfelt eulogy for "a supremely great American, a supremely great President, a supremely sincere lover of his fellow men." A month later Ryan was hospitalized in Washington with severe influenza, and a month after that he was flown back to St. Paul; he wanted to die at home, he said. At St. Joseph's Hospital he was under the constant care of Sister Constance, née Mary Jane Ryan, who knew that her ministrations were for her brother's comfort, not his recovery. In mid-September he told his doctors he would like to see the old farmstead at Vermillion one last time. Father Lawrence[45] duly drove him there, and he gazed out over the fields in which he had labored as a boy without saying a word. A few days later he died.[46]

Though John Ryan expounded on the arcane intricacies of economics, and regularly and purposefully strode along the corridors of political power, he always did so as a priest and as a moral theologian. "The law of progress for the human race," he wrote when a young man, "is the moral law. The better the moral law is observed the greater will be the meaning of human advancement. And every violation of the moral law, every sin that is committed, is a check to humanity's onward march." The point in all his polemic was that infractions of social justice—especially the plight of the worker in the industrial age, exploited and therefore degraded—were *sins*. He was a perfectly conventional Catholic, firmly in the tradition of the First Vatican Council and

---

45. After a long tenure as rector of the St. Paul Cathedral, Monsignor (as he ultimately became) Lawrence Ryan served as pastor of St. Mary of the Lake parish in White Bear Lake, a bustling suburb of St. Paul. After that, in his seventies, he was appointed spiritual director of the St. Paul Seminary, a post he held while I was a student in that institution from 1950 through 1956. He gave conferences to the student body twice a week, presentations which amounted, in essence, to a course in ascetical theology. His demeanor was stern, even forbidding, and his rhetorical gifts were limited, so that his conferences made less of an impression than perhaps their substance deserved. I do not recall exchanging a single word with him during my time at the seminary. After his retirement, he took up residence in the early 1960s at the College of St. Thomas, when I was a junior faculty member there. While at St. Thomas he took an active and very effective part in the work of the campus ministry, and, to my surprise, proved a charming and delightful companion at the common table in the priests' dining room. I am pleased here to testify to the merits of this holy and cultivated man, whose worth eluded me during my callow student days. He died in 1974, aged ninety-four and sixty-four years a priest. Lawrence Ryan, like his brother, was a *sacerdos magnus*.

46. Broderick, *Right Reverend*, 1–3, 276.

its insistence upon the double testimony of faith and reason. "Our faith is based upon knowledge," he explained. "We have faith in Christ, because we have knowledge of the Resurrection." He was adamant on the importance of "public service to God, penance, sanctification; to those ends the observance of festivals, abstinence and fasting are very conducive. Similarly [with regard to priests] . . . celibacy, the recitation of the breviary, the celebration of the Mass." "We cannot live upright lives without God's grace, and grace is given principally through the sacraments. If we do not approach the sacraments frequently, we are neglecting one of our principal duties."[47] Sometimes his religious and metaphysical commitments brought him into sharp contention with those who were ordinarily his allies on public policy; thus, for example, he was a fierce and uncompromising opponent of artificial contraception, which he labeled "a perversion of nature and not merely unnatural."[48] But none of these principles, in Monsignor Ryan's judgment, was incompatible with American tradition nor, indeed, with the Americanist vision of John Ireland. On the contrary, they aimed to help preserve what was best in American life in the face of new challenges: a greedy and runaway capitalism and its grotesque half-brother, socialism, as well as a godless and hedonistic rationalism.

---

47. Quotations from Joseph P. Chinnici, *Living Stones: The History and Structure of Catholic Spiritual Life in the United States* (New York, 1989), 140, 139, 143.

48. Broderick, *Right Reverend*, 148–150. The debate in the early 1930s turned on legislation permitting the dissemination of birth control information through the mails.

CHAPTER 18

Prayer and People

ALL POLITICS, THE CONVENTIONAL WISDOM HAS IT, IS LOCAL. And so in the last analysis is the mission of the Catholic Church. The local school or hospital, and particularly the local parish, provides the venue wherein the baptized man and woman work out their vocation. While he recognized the truth of this adage, Austin Dowling often found the fact narrow and constraining. This was why he instituted centralized organization and direction of the school system within the archdiocese of St. Paul, why he encouraged broad associations of lay people like the Knights of Columbus and the Daughters of Isabella. The same conviction led him to participate so actively in the national endeavor to bring the ethos of Catholicism to bear on the larger American scene. He applauded the proliferation within the United States of exclusively Catholic societies in the professions, so long as that exclusivity was geared to promote rather than depart from what he saw as genuine American ideals—the Catholic "mold" was the surest instrument to guarantee that what emerged from the melting pot would preserve the best of the American tradition. His considerable contribution to the work of the fledgling National Catholic Welfare Conference was inspired by the same strong commitment to the "second phase" of Americanism.[1] His attitude was an amalgam of the religious, the cultural, and the conventionally patriotic.

Even so, Archbishop Dowling knew that his primary responsibility lay within his own jurisdiction. Indeed, he realized that any national aspirations he and other Catholics in leadership roles might hope to fulfill would depend at the end on the character of the local churches. In 1923, in preparing the re-

---

1. See chapter 17, above.

quired quinquennial report to Rome, he set down with characteristic candor his analysis of the state of the archdiocese of St. Paul, which, in his mind, was a microcosm of Catholicism in America.[2]

Dowling had no doubts about the basic faithfulness of his flock. "There is a most admirable frequentation of churches," he wrote, "an extraordinary willingness to receive the sacraments. . . . It may be truthfully said that our people love the Church." But that was not the whole story. In the somber temper that he so often displayed, the archbishop confessed that much of the manner in which Catholics lived out their calling remained "unsatisfactory" to him.

> There often seems to be little depth to their piety. There is the very large number of mixed marriages, there is the dearth of vocations, there is the very slight evidence of Catholic thought or discipline upon the public life of the community. There are many reasons for this condition. . . . In the first place, our people are all immigrants or the children of immigrants. They were poor a short while ago. The only thing they have of their past is their religion. All the things they have to remember are associated with poverty and the disadvantageous position of a foreigner. As they progress in wealth and station, they frequently strive to hide their origins, to change their names, and to affect manners that do not belong to them. Even when they keep up the practice of their religion, they are frequently ashamed of it. Then the overwhelming majority of the population is non-Catholic and frequently prejudiced against the Church. A Catholic could not be elected governor of this state no matter what his good qualities. The Church is very unpopular with a large number, and this unpopularity affects the practice of religion by many Catholics. Americans do not like to belong to an unpopular party, one that has no chance of winning. A third party has never been possible in the political alignment of this country. This sentiment weakens the religion of many Catholics.

---

2. For what follows, see *Ad Limina* Report, 1924 (copy), AASPM, Dowling Papers. Every five years each diocesan bishop is required to submit a report to the Roman curia, usually in person and always in writing, on the spiritual and material condition of his jurisdiction. The technical term is *Ad Limina Apostolorum,* to the doorsteps of the apostles, that is, to the Rome of SS. Peter and Paul. Dowling spent the early months of 1924 in Europe. He was received in audience by Pius XI on January 31.

True as many of these observations may have been, they clearly lacked the boisterous optimism of John Ireland. Nor did they hew a strictly consistent line: Catholics loved their Church and yet were ashamed of it. And it must be said too that Dowling, also in contrast to his magnetic predecessor, enjoyed little social interaction with lay people, and so his sweeping judgments about them might require a measure of circumspection. He was not a recluse, and by reason of his confirmation tours and other official functions he was visible enough across the fifteen thousand square miles of the archdiocese. Visible but somehow remote, even isolated, standing alone in a pulpit or in cope and miter sprinkling holy water on a new building. He was by nature shy and physically frail, and by choice a scholar who needed a modicum of time and space for his books.[3]

The archbishop's views about the clergy, whom he certainly knew better, were rather more positive. By and large he was proud of them. "There is no grave disorder among them," he reported to the Roman curia, in regard to the obligations of sacerdotal piety; they appeared to accept the obligation of sacramental confession, daily meditation, visits to the Blessed Eucharist, the recitation of the rosary. There was no abuse, so far as he knew, in the matter of celibacy. The obligation to recite the Divine Office each day was fulfilled "with scarcely an exception." Priests in the archdiocese of St. Paul dressed "decently in accord with the custom of the country in black clothes and Roman collar." Furthermore, "they do not frequent theaters," Dowling wrote almost loftily, nor engage in secular business, nor mix in politics. For the most part they had enough means to live "quite comfortably" though without affluence; indeed, the pastors of some small rural parishes found it difficult to make ends meet. They were "a happy breed of men," friendly to one another regardless of ethnic or linguistic background. They were faithful to the Holy See and obedient to their ordinary. Over the five years covered by the report, there had been but two serious lapses among them, one of which, Dowling was convinced, had been due to mental illness. These conclusions—which applied, he said, as much to the sixty or so religious priests serving in the archdiocese as to the 360 seculars—were based on the "visitation of clerics," informal and yet "quite searching." His procedure, as he expressed it, consisted "in the confidential and fatherly discussion of the cleric's spiritual life, without taking notes, etc."—a method he deemed "more prudent" than a strict canonical examination.

---

3. See O'Connell, "Dowling Decade," 42–44.

Despite his own leaning toward books and study, however, Dowling had to admit that "our priests have not for the most part habits of study. They are not given to speculation." If this lack of speculative interests among his closest associates piqued him at all, the archbishop took some consolation in the fact that, as a result of this deficiency, "there is no suspicion of errors against the faith among them." This reassurance to Rome was significant, because the ghost of the Modernist crisis of less than two decades before still haunted the corridors of the Vatican.[4] Nevertheless, Dowling—as had Ireland before him—had taken what concrete steps he could to guarantee that his priests maintained an acceptable level of theological competence. In accordance with canon law, he attended "conferences dealing with moral and liturgical topics held twice a year in six different parts of the diocese," and these he personally supervised. All priests who had the cure of souls had to attend them too.

Whatever reservations Dowling might have entertained in 1924 about the laity and clergy, he had none with regard to the religious women serving in the archdiocese. Over 800 sisters, representing eleven congregations, taught in the schools, managed and staffed the hospitals, cared for the orphans and the aged. His tribute to them was unequivocal: "The utility of religious women is so great that it may be said to be indispensable." This assertion would no doubt have been echoed by virtually all the Catholic people of the archdiocese, not in a bureaucratic sense but in an almost mystical one. The local convent seemed a place of awe, where those who lived there, young and old, shared a mysterious calling which required the sacrifice of the individuality so much prized by Americans. But beyond the mystery was the service routinely and selflessly given to all who required it. For every overbearing nun, for every nun with a streak of meanness, a score were on hand to bind up wounds of all kinds. The honor accorded them was, by and large, richly deserved.

Dowling's tribute applied to the various orders of nuns, but it had special resonance with regard to the largest and most venerable of them, the Sisters of St. Joseph of Carondelet. The archbishop, only months before his own death, had an occasion to give special and highly personal testimony to this fact. On June 25, 1930, Ellen Ireland, Mother Seraphine, was buried from the mighty cathedral her brother had built and dedicated fifteen years before. Her religious career had spanned seventy-two years as a Josephite, thirty-nine

---

4. See chapter 17, above. From 1910 all clerics, prior to receiving the order of subdeacon, were required to swear an oath against Modernism. This obligation was rescinded in 1967. The subdiaconate itself was suppressed five years later.

years as the congregation's provincial superior. At the funeral Mass the large congregation listened respectfully to the little prelate from New England who had taken Archbishop Ireland's place in Minnesota, as he eulogized, with rare spontaneity, the great man's younger sister as "our first parishioner and most distinguished Catholic who was mother to the city of St. Paul."

> Mother Seraphine was ever the friend of priests; whether she knew them or not, she prayed for them. To me she was like a mother. I came when her heart was broken after the death of her brother. He was an old man who had done his work. He could not live without great pain, but she had known him as a little boy, and she could not think of him as aught else, and clung devoutly to her memory. Yet although her heart was breaking, she was as faithful and devoted to me as if she was my own sister. She thought only of the Church, and I was the Church's representative. She did not know me, and I was neither kith nor kin, but I was the representative of the Church, and she worked with me with a human affection which makes her memory particularly tender to me.[5]

THE REMARKABLE AND ADMIRABLE DEVOTION THE CATHOLIC laity in the archdiocese of St. Paul displayed toward their sacramental obligations was a consolation to Archbishop Dowling, even though he maintained doubts about the "the depth to their piety." In his report to Rome he did not spell out precisely what he meant by this caveat, except in terms of what he discerned to be among them a kind of civic timidity. Nor did he propose a solution that would deepen his people's practice of their faith. This may well have been because when outward forms within a society are observed with near unanimity, inquiry into the internal dispositions of its members can appear irrelevant or even disloyal, at least in the mind of an administrator. To be sure, Dowling was too wise and sensitive a man to subscribe to so simplistic a view; nevertheless, he was willy-nilly an administrator, busy about many things.

The piety of American Catholics during the 1920s—and for decades beyond—was framed within a canonical or legal context. They were obliged, needless to say, to observe the biblical Ten Commandments, as were all votaries of the Book, Jewish, Christian, or Muslim. In addition to these precepts, however, was an additional set of rules, dating from the sixteenth century, de-

---

5. *CB*, June 28, 1930.

bated and refined often since then, and given formal status for Americans by the Third Plenary Council of Baltimore (1884) in six propositions:

(1) To keep holy Sunday and holy days of obligation by hearing Mass and refraining from servile work.
(2) To keep the days of fast and abstinence appointed by the Church.
(3) To go to confession at least once a year.
(4) To receive [Eucharistic] Communion at least once a year at Easter time [i.e., between Easter Sunday and Trinity Sunday].
(5) To contribute to the support of one's pastor.
(6) Not to marry within the third degree of kindred or to solemnize marriage during forbidden times [i.e., Advent and Lent].[6]

Along with predictable moral and doctrinal subjects, these norms were regularly presented from the pulpit to the pew. This is not to say that works of mercy within that Sunday morning ambience were ignored: the corporal works, which included feeding the hungry and clothing the naked; and the spiritual, with an emphasis on counseling the doubtful and forgiving the guilty.[7] But perhaps the most meaningful clue to understanding the modes of piety cultivated by Catholics in Minnesota into the 1960s can be found in the use of a particular verb: the obligation, as expressed in the first proposition cited above, to "hear" Mass on Sundays and certain festivals. The implication was that the Eucharistic sacrifice—the celebration of the death of the Lord until he comes to earth again—was, except for the priest, a formal exercise in "listening." And this inference is confirmed by concomitant terminology: it was the function of the priest-celebrant to "say" or to "read" Mass. There was of course a sense in which such idioms were quite literally true. The Mass was "said" in Latin, a language understood by scarcely anyone in the congregation. Nor could it be presumed that most priests, despite their education which featured classics written by Cicero, Virgil, and Horace, and yet which was not always rigorous, could necessarily be accounted accomplished Latinists. Perhaps the greatest anomaly in this arrangement was the moment when the priest at the altar, his back to the congregation, read the scriptural

---

6. See Regina Coll, "Commandments of the Church," in *Encyclopedia of Catholicism,* ed. Richard P. McBrien (San Francisco, 1989), 334–335. *The Catechism of the Catholic Church* (1992) makes no mention of the sixth of these propositions.

7. See Patricia M. Vinjie, "Mercy, corporal works of" and "Mercy, spiritual works of," in McBrien, *Encyclopedia,* 854–855.

proclamations assigned for that day to the rear wall of the apse, in a language nobody understood. This latter mode was adjusted on Sundays, when the priest ascended the pulpit and, before delivering his sermon, read a translation into English of the "epistle" and "gospel" he had just recited in Latin.

In a parish of average size two or three "low" Masses were celebrated on a Sunday morning—Saturday evening observance lay far in the future— followed by a "high" or sung Mass, which was required to begin before noon. At a low Mass the people in the pews turned the pages of a devotional book, like the venerable *A Key of Heaven,* or quietly plied the beads of their rosaries, or in some other way tried to maintain reverent thoughts about the mystery unfolding before them. If priests were in attendance, garbed in cassock and surplice—at a particularly festive Mass, say, said by a bishop in the cathedral, or at a fellow priest's funeral—they routinely and silently recited the breviary as the mysterious Eucharistic action proceeded; concelebration was unknown. On an ordinary Sunday, while parents kept a wary eye on restless children, and the ushers took up the collection at the Offertory—and not infrequently a second one for some special need, after the Communion— silence pretty much prevailed until the priest raised his voice to recite the Pater Noster. After that he consumed both the consecrated species and then dispensed the Eucharist under the form of unleavened bread alone on the tongue of those laity who came to kneel at the communion rail.[8] By no means did the whole congregation press forward to receive the sacrament as has become commonplace in later times. Despite the injunction of Pope Pius X (d. 1914) about the need for more frequent Eucharistic communion among the mature and the very young alike—"the indispensable source of the Christian spirit"—most Minnesota Catholics, in awe at the sublimity with which they had been taught to embrace the doctrine of the Real Presence, remained cautious. Communion received once a month, after absolution granted in sacramental confession the Saturday evening before, if not a norm, was certainly a common practice. It was taken for granted that at a high or sung Mass no one except the celebrant partook of the sacred species. Some older Catholics, reflecting perhaps the Jansenist principles that unconsciously invigorated so many of the French and Irish immigrants into Minnesota, found it hard to accept that the radical sinfulness of the human condition was congruent with

---

8. The debate about whether the proper reception of the Eucharist required that communicants receive the sacrament under both species goes back to the Reformation and beyond. The official Catholic position was that each species, bread and wine, contained independently and completely Christ's "body and blood, soul and divinity."

a frequent approach to the Holy of Holies.[9] Indeed, individual and corporate sinfulness and its consequences preoccupied much of the pulpit oratory of the time and reached a kind of climax in the funeral Mass, during which the priest, garbed in somber black, prayed, to be sure, that eternal rest be granted to the deceased, but this prayer was tempered by the doleful chant of *Dies irae*, the day of judgmental wrath when all accounts would have to be settled. No one received Communion at a funeral.

Such restrictions and hesitations may seem strange in the light of the almost universal fidelity, as acknowledged by Austin Dowling, of Catholics in his archdiocese in fulfilling the obligation to attend Mass on the prescribed occasions, solid evidence that the Eucharist was at the core of their devotional life, as it had been for Catholics since time immemorial. But the richness and profundity of the Eucharistic doctrine admitted, as it always has, of varying interpretations and emphases. The Mass is at once the representation of Christ's sacrificial death, the bringing down upon the altar literally the Body and Blood of Christ under the forms of bread and wine—in a repetition of what Jesus himself did at the Last Supper—and, through the consumption of the species in Holy Communion, a holy meal, which spiritually sustains the believer and unites him intimately to Christ and, at the same time, also to his brothers and sisters who have shared the sacred feast with him. None of these three aspects of the Eucharistic mystery is by any means exclusive of the others; indeed, every theological manual since the Middle Ages would testify to the validity of each of them and, in the name of integrity, would insist upon the acknowledgment of all three together.

But theological manuals do not always determine the course of popular piety. Among Catholics in Minnesota during the years between 1920 and 1960—and across the United States at large—the deepest Eucharistic devotion was reserved for the Real Presence of Christ effected by the words of consecration spoken in hushed Latin by the celebrant at the most solemn moment of the Mass—"this is my Body, this is the cup of my Blood"—succeeded by the solemn elevation by the priest of the Host and then of the Chalice, as an altar boy tinkled a small bell—at the sight and sound of which the traditional response was a bow of the head and a threefold striking of the breast.

---

9. My paternal grandfather, William S. ("Big Bill") O'Connell (1862–1954), was a lifelong resident of Le Sueur County, Minnesota. He was a successful farmer and community leader and, not least significant, a leading member of St. Thomas parish, Derrynane township. In this latter capacity he performed a host of works of charity and munificence. His sacramental commitment was attendance at Mass each Sunday and holy day, and confession and Communion at Eastertide.

Through this sacramental action, God Himself had condescended to come down from the highest Heaven and, moreover, to dwell permanently and palpably with his people. For once the Mass was over, and the worshipers had filed out of the building to return to the burdens and joys of their daily lives, the Divine remained in the church, cabined behind the golden doors of the tabernacle situated at the center of the altar. There were seven sacraments, to be sure, but the Eucharist was uniquely the Blessed Sacrament. Witness to this conviction were various devotional practices, like the brief and formal Benediction when the priest raised the Host in its gilded monstrance in blessing over the assembly; or the lengthier Forty Hours Devotion, much like the old parish mission, when adoration of the Eucharistic presence mingled with instruction and exhortation to the faithful that they might appreciate the grandeur of the Divine within their midst and live their lives accordingly; or the processions—some quite elaborate—on the annual springtime feast of Corpus Christi, which triumphantly proclaimed with songs and flowers that in the Blessed Sacrament God is truly with us. And so there had evolved the folk customs that marked the ordinary Minnesota Catholic's behavior: the deep genuflection when coming into the Presence at any time; the total fast from midnight preceding the morning that Communion was to be received; the persuasion that the hands of the unordained must not touch the sacred Host and, indeed, the teeth not chew it.

This rather narrow interpretation of the Eucharistic culture—if one may call it so—contributed much to the way in which the faithful defined their priest and, hardly less, as to how he defined himself. He was first of all the agent by whom was effected the Real Presence and the defender of the Host preserved in the tabernacle. From these functions flowed all his other obligations and prerogatives. To be sure, as pastor he was financial manager of the parish, supervisor of its school (if there was one), sole legitimate preacher and interpreter of the Gospel, moral judge in the confessional box, counselor to the troubled and distressed, celibate father of all his people, young and old, rich and poor, a unique witness to the loftiest ideals of the faith. But he was an *alter Christus,* another Christ, and so able to satisfy all these roles, precisely because of his intimacy with the Real Presence.[10] Practice, it need hardly be said, did not always mesh with theory; it never does. Even so, unless the parish priest were deemed guilty of egregious moral fault—a rarity and even

---

10. See the excellent analysis in Joseph P. Chinnici, *Living Stones: The History and Structure of Catholic Spiritual Life in the United States* (New York, 1989), 148–151.

more rarely acknowledged in public when it did occur—his people, since he remained custodian of the Blessed Sacrament, were by and large prepared to indulge his eccentricities. He may have been a curmudgeon[11] or a dilettante or a hopelessly inept keeper of the parish's fiscal accounts, yet he was also the means, averred the men and women in the pew, by which Jesus himself came to dwell among them.

This doctrinal emphasis, rooted in a Latin liturgy, left plenty of room for other forms of piety consistent with it, forms usually expressed in the vernacular. Some of these were offshoots, so to speak, of devotion to the Real Presence, like private "visits" to the Sacrament, or "holy hours" when the Host in its monstrance was placed on the altar for adoration. One especially popular practice resulted from the linking—based on revelations afforded to a seventeenth-century French visionary[12]—of devotion to the Sacred Heart of Jesus with reception of Communion on the first Friday of each month; indeed, some overly enthusiastic devotees suggested that one who participated in nine consecutive "First Fridays" might almost count on attaining salvation. Other nine-day observances of prayer for a particular intention—novenas— some parish-wide, some private, were also common. Devotion to the Virgin Mary remained a hallmark of popular piety, as did veneration of the saints, some of recent vintage like Thérèse of Lisieux, the Little Flower, who personified the "little way" of achieving spiritual perfection through the dutiful acceptance of each day's humdrum duties; others more remote in time, like Anthony of Padua, who helped find things that had been lost, big and small; and still others the consequence of antique legend, like St. Christopher, the protector of travelers. The great religious orders promoted among the laity, as they always had, pieties indigenous to their own genius; there continued to be a uniquely Franciscan approach to the sacred, inspired by the memory of "the poor man of Assisi," and an appropriately more cerebral Dominican style, while the aggressive Jesuits advocated the sturdy virtues to be found in *The Spiritual Exercises,* formulated by their soldier-founder. Nuns in the schoolroom, even as they drilled the children through the question-answer format of the *Baltimore Catechism,* also assured their charges that each of them was watched over by a guardian angel. Messages from the pulpit reminded the faithful of indulgences to be gained, of souls in Purgatory to be prayed for, of pious sodalities and associations to be joined, of stringent

---

11. Like the pastor of St. Mary's, Waverly, who regularly preached during the 1950s on Mother's Day on the evils of "Momism."

12. "Alacoque, St. Margaret Mary," in McBrien, *Encyclopedia,* 26.

Lenten rules on fast and abstinence to be adhered to, of the penitential Ember Days to be observed (in a scarcely comprehensible liturgy) marking the beginning of each of the four seasons.[13]

In short, the spirituality on offer to Catholic Minnesotans during the 1920s and for several decades after presented a rich and varied set of practical initiatives, centered always in the doctrine of the Real Presence of Christ in the Eucharist. It need hardly be said that some adopted one or another of these practices with genuine enthusiasm, others viewed them with relative indifference, and most fell somewhere in between. It has ever been so. But it is not without significance that these forms of popular piety, whatever their more ancient roots, were directly traceable back to the Counter-Reformation and the Council of Trent of the sixteenth century, and therefore to a degree they represented a reaction against Protestantism. In the America of the first half of the twentieth century, when the Protestant culture was still in the ascendancy, such spiritual norms inevitably exhibited a defensive character. "Mixed" marriages were sternly frowned upon and could be sanctioned only if the non-Catholic party formally agreed that any children born of the union be raised Catholic; and even then the ceremony had to be held not in the church but, with a minimum of pomp, in the parlor of the parish rectory, as had been the case with James J. Hill and Mary Theresa Mehegan.[14] There was a tribal element at work, too. Fish on Friday was not only a penitential practice for immigrants and the children of immigrants; it was also a meaningful statement of the group's self-identity in a new land (and thus more rigorously observed in the United States than in the more relaxed Catholic countries of Europe). Since they aspired to disport themselves as real Americans—and, perhaps paradoxically, as the most reliable supporters of the best in the American tradition—Catholic Minnesotans did not on the whole, despite Austin Dowling's misgivings, fail to see a connection between their religiosity and their place in the national life.

CERTAINLY THERE WAS A MAJESTY AND SPLENDOR IN THE LATIN liturgy, developed and elaborated over nineteen centuries (and frozen in place, so to speak, by the Council of Trent), which inculcated a genuine appreciation of the sublime mystery unfolding among the worshipers who par-

---

13. "Ember days," in McBrien, *Encyclopedia*, 463. The Ember Days observance was abolished in 1969.

14. See chapter 11, above.

ticipated, however passively, in it. This happy circumstance was realized more readily in some venues than in others; in large, prosperous parishes which could support good choirs, in cathedrals, most of all perhaps in flourishing Benedictine monasteries—where the sublime tones of the ancient Gregorian chants bore witness to the sacramental action at the altar. For good music indeed, or the lack of it, was a kind of measure of the liturgical status of a Catholic parish during the 1920s and thereafter. Commonly there lurked a suspicion of congregational singing; that, after all, was an emblem of Protestantism. The result was the formation in most parishes of a volunteer choir, whose devotion and musical aspirations more often than not outstripped its talent.

One site where the music matched the sublimity of the liturgical occasion—not only at Mass but also at the "hours" of the Divine Office, from Matins in the very early morning to Compline at nightfall—was St. John's Abbey and University in Stearns County. And here, in this traditionally German-American Benedictine community, sprang up a different approach to the doctrine of the Eucharist—not new, its proponents insisted, as ancient indeed as Christianity itself, but muted over recent centuries. A fuller approach, they added, one that took into account all the elements and consequences of the mystery of the altar. Its most tireless and dedicated advocate was a monk of St. John's.

George Michel, born in 1890, was the second of the fifteen children of a prosperous St. Paul businessman who had immigrated to Minnesota from Westphalia. Young George was sent to St. John's for preparatory school and then enrolled in the university. He was bright, energetic, a considerable baseball and tennis player, as well as a writer of poetry and fiction. These literary efforts may have been amateurish—not unlikely for even a gifted teenager—but they signaled an enduring characteristic, an obsession almost, to put words on paper.[15] When he entered the novitiate in 1909, he chose the name Virgil. He was professed in 1913 and ordained in 1916. He celebrated his first solemn Mass at the church of the Assumption, the old German parish in downtown St. Paul.

One consideration that had given George Michel pause before he committed himself to St. John's was the sense that the abbey was not adequately fulfilling the Benedictine ideal. Why should one join a monastic community,

---

15. See the enormous bibliography in Paul Marx, *Virgil Michel and the Liturgical Movement* (Washington, 1957), 421–434. All this from a man who died at age forty-eight.

be ordained in it and for it, and then spend one's priestly life administering a parish? During the ages of faith monasteries had been centers of spirituality and learning which had vitalized a whole culture, while St. John's missionary past had necessarily shaped a different ethos.[16] But a sympathetic abbot, recognizing the young man's intellectual worth, reassured him that his yearning to be a religious scholar would be given full scope. As though in confirmation of this pledge, Dom Virgil after ordination was sent to the Catholic University in Washington, where in two years he earned a doctorate in English, with a minor in philosophy. He was not much impressed by these groves of academe. "It may seem strange to you," he confided to his sister, "if I say that I do hardly any work for [my] classes." But he read voraciously, and he was stirred by the lively debates about modern educational theory and social action—outside his areas of concentration—that absorbed the university at that time. Between 1918 and 1921, back at St. John's, Michel taught courses in English and philosophy, the former more successfully than the latter. He showed himself impatient with ancient and medieval philosophers, and, when it came to the moderns, he was fascinated but self-taught and often confused. The result was a classroom full of befuddled students. A new abbot, Alcuin Deutsch, grew concerned that his predecessor's young protégé had too slender a grasp on the scholasticism which was the de rigueur foundation of all philosophical and theological inquiry at Catholic institutions of higher learning. So, in the late winter of 1924, after a couple of years of administrative duty in addition to his teaching load—director of the preparatory school, dean of the college—Virgil Michel was sent to Rome in order to learn to become a docile disciple of St. Thomas Aquinas. It proved to be a fateful decision.[17]

By this time Michel was thirty-four years old and at the height of his powers of observation. Europe had by no means recovered from the ravages of what was called simply the Great War. Nor had the young monk from St. John's discovered within himself a vein of sympathy for Thomism. His professor at the International Benedictine College of St. Anselm was "really a lovable personality, no teacher, really deep in metaphysical questions, . . . Scholastic with a vengeance. . . . Scholastic philosophy here does not sally forth to make conquests. It shuts itself within its stronghold (whatever that is), it shuts all the loopholes with airtight theses and corollaries—and the result is that outside philosophies can shed no light on our present problems."

---

16. See chapter 4, above.
17. Barry, *Worship*, 262–268.

In a darker mood he complained that to follow the course of his "lovable" teacher "you must literally study him [and his book on metaphysics] by heart, . . . must be an intellectual slave."

But it was neither Rome nor what was for him a barren classroom that changed Virgil Michel's life. Remarkably talented linguistically, he talked to everyone and anyone. Incessant travel across Austria, Germany, France, Spain, and, especially, Belgium brought him face to face with a continent sunk in deep despair. It had lost its soul during the recent awful conflict and was trying to recover it in a gaudy materialism, but also in a burgeoning movement which might herald a new spiritual dawn. The dichotomy startled him, particularly in Spain. There he found the clergy lax, louche, and almost totally alienated from ordinary people. And yet, especially in the Basque country in the north, he was edified by a genuinely devoted Catholic family life free from an intimation of anticlericalism. (Still, he was not surprised in 1936 when bloody persecution of the Church became a prime policy of the short-lived Spanish Republic.) At the University of Louvain, where he spent the better part of a year, and at the great German monasteries of Maria Laach and Bueron, Virgil Michel was introduced to a Pauline doctrine virtually unheard of in the United States at the time, which in turn implied a radically different Eucharistic piety: "The blessing cup that we bless is a communion with the blood of Christ, and the bread that we break is a communion with the body of Christ. The fact that there is only one loaf means that, though there are many of us, we form a single body, because we all have a share in this one loaf."[18]

Michel came away from his European experience a man with a mission. He had discovered, as his biographer puts it,

> the reality of the Church as the Mystical Body of Christ . . . and the official life and prayer of that Body, the liturgy, which he now saw as the indispensable means of instilling the true Christian spirit into society by first permeating the lives of Christians. He began to perceive that a properly worshiping people, realizing that oneness in the Mystical Christ and actively contacting the living realities of the liturgy, could in time transform a whole society. If Catholics could be brought by active participation in the liturgy to think and pray and work with the Church and to live with her the life of Christ, they would soon also have the answers to many social problems, which in their roots . . . were so often spiritual

---

18. 2 Corinthians 10:15–17.

problems. Thus, as early as in 1925, Virgil Michel considered the doctrine of the Mystical Body, the liturgy, and the non-individualistic liturgical movement as the providential means to counteract the new paganism compounded of individualism, naturalism, and secularism.[19]

It was the corporate character of what came to be called the Liturgical Movement that appealed most to the monk, Virgil Michel. And as the years passed he came to realize the many seemingly, at first, tangential consequences such a character could involve. There must be concern about the daily lives of this worshiping people, about their financial and social problems, about their leisure activities. Social structures could not be ignored, nor deep questions about war and poverty. Though he differed from that other remarkable Minnesota priest, John A. Ryan, because he thought the latter's solutions to the economic crisis of the Great Depression were "too statist" in their orientation,[20] Michel nevertheless acknowledged Ryan's analysis of the ills of unfettered capitalism. Until his premature death in 1938, he remained, out of a fierce devotion to the doctrine of the Mystical Body, a champion of the distraught, the distressed, the marginalized.[21] He was an early and enthusiastic supporter of Peter Maurin, Dorothy Day, their houses of hospitality, and their Catholic Worker movement.[22]

Virgil Michel returned to his abbey in the late summer of 1925, and a year later, sustained by the support of his abbot and most of his monastic brethren, launched at St. John's the Liturgical Library, the Liturgical Press, and the journal *Orate Fratres*.[23] It was an exhilarating moment, but the road for the Liturgical Movement proved rocky indeed—the status quo is never easily circumvented—and even the ultimate dénouement may not have altogether given Michel solace, had he lived to experience it.

---

19. Marx, *Virgil Michel*, 36.

20. Marx, *Virgil Michel*, 216–217.

21. See the website http://www.saintjohnsabbey.org/worship/worship/page1. htm. Accessed May 20, 2008.

22. See Louise and Mark Zwick, "Virgil Michel, Benedictine Co-worker of Dorothy Day and Peter Maurin: Justice Embodied in Christ-life and Liturgy," *Houston Catholic Worker* 20 (January–February 2000), available at cjd.org/paper/roots/ rmichel.html.

23. "Pray, my brothers [and sisters], that my sacrifice and yours. . . . " The prayer said at the end of the offertory of the Mass and just before the "secret." In 1951 the name of the journal was changed to *Worship*, an indication of the growing impetus toward the vernacular in the liturgy.

NOT SINCE 1875, WHEN THE VATICAN HAD SET UP THE VICARIATE of Northern Minnesota, had St. John's monastery had any formal connection with the diocese of St. Paul. This canonical division was refined in 1889 when, in a general realignment of ecclesiastical jurisdictions—including St. Paul being designated a metropolitan archbishopric—the diocese of St. Cloud was instituted. Still, the relationship remained more or less cordial—Archbishop Ireland, famously disdainful of most religious orders, professed a wary respect for the Benedictines—and before there was a local seminary system, not a few St. Paul seminarians were trained at St. John's. Thus even before Dom Virgil Michel initiated his liturgical crusade, there was already in St. Paul a constituency anxious to enroll under its banner.

Indeed, one could say more. Even Michel's biographer concedes that William Busch was the first in the field, that "it would be difficult to overrate Busch's role in the founding and guidance of the American liturgical apostolate."[24] Busch, born in Red Wing in 1882 (and so eight years Michel's senior), was ordained at the St. Paul Seminary in 1907. After three years as an assistant at St. Luke's parish in St. Paul, Ireland sent him for graduate studies to Louvain in Belgium, where he earned a degree in ecclesiastical history. While there, he came into contact before the Great War with some of the same theological currents Michel was to encounter in an even stronger form after the conflict. Returned to Minnesota and assigned to teach history at the seminary,[25] Busch amidst his various duties pondered the practical implications of what he had learned in Europe. In 1919 Busch's first published result of such ruminations took an interestingly and unsubtle aesthetic point of view that might not have meshed with the rather more grandiose notions of his new archbishop, Austin Dowling.

> When will the Catholic Church in the United States rid itself of the kind of altar which Ralph Adams Cram has well called a "glorified soda

---

24. Marx, *Virgil Michel,* 117.

25. Monsignor Busch (as he ultimately became) spent two terms as professor of church history at the seminary (with a pastorate in between). I was his student during the second of those terms (1954–1955). I found him to be a gentleman of considerable elegance and charm, though somewhat remote. He was in his early seventies by that time. He also taught a one-semester course in the liturgy, which was, predictably, a source of great illumination. But as a teacher of history he was far less successful; over four semesters of dull lectures, his course ended *before* considering the history of the Protestant Reformation. His teaching career perhaps confirms the biblical saw: "Where your heart is, there your treasure will be." Or perhaps he was the victim of the pedagogical system in the seminaries of his time. He died in 1971.

fountain?" Will things actually go from bad to worse until we have added mirrors for additional glittering effect? Are we convinced once and for all that a beautiful church can only be secured through the use of polished marbles (or imitations thereof)? The lobbies of theatres and hotels are beginning to break away from the rule, leaving the white marbles for the barbershops, moving picture houses—and Catholic churches.

It was simplicity he was pleading for, and directness, so that the liturgical celebration be seen not as some convoluted Byzantine exercise, reserved for a clerical élite, but as a participatory event in which all the faithful present played a part. A solid start would be to use "a simple table of good solid wood, with four substantial columns actually forming 'legs' of a table," for is not an altar, he asked rhetorically, the table from which is served the uniquely sacred meal?[26]

It is difficult at this distance in time to overemphasize how far-fetched such an argument appeared in the early 1920s. But William Busch was young and strong and committed. If local allies were lacking, he could look north-ward toward St. John's, where Michel's patron, Abbot Deutsch, maintained a basic if as yet inchoate sympathy with the project of liturgical reform. (Nor was it a disadvantage in terms of ecclesiastical politics that Joseph Busch, William's much older brother, was at this time bishop of St. Cloud.[27]) The first order of business was to cultivate "understanding," and it is significant that Busch in 1925 gave an address entitled "The Liturgical Movement" at a meeting of the Catholic Educational Association.

> The heart of the liturgical movement is understanding, first of all, and then the right celebration of the holy Sacrifice, not by the priest alone, but by all who are present, in the fullest possible expression of the *Ecclesia Orans,* by the general participation which Pope Pius X has said is "the primary and indispensable source of the Christian spirit."[28]

Some weeks after delivering this speech, Busch wrote excitedly to Virgil Michel, recently returned to St. John's.

---

26. William Busch, "Construction of an Altar," in *Ecclesiastical Review* 61 (1919): 439–440. For this and for much of what follows, see the excellent analysis of Athans, *To Work for the Whole People,* 398–402.

27. Joseph Busch, born in 1866 (and thus sixteen years William's senior), was consecrated bishop of Lead, South Dakota (the see transferred to Rapid City in 1930). He was appointed bishop of St. Cloud in 1915. He died in 1953.

28. Quoted in Athans, *To Work for the Whole People,* 399.

During the past months while you were in Europe I had taken up with Abbot Alcuin both by letter and conversation the subject of the presentation to priests and people in this country of some of the excellent European literature on the liturgical movement. . . . The abbot told me that my first suggestion to him in this regard came to him just at the time when a similar one was made to him by yourself.[29]

Thus was the partnership formed, and frequent after that were the journeyings between Collegeville and St. Paul. There was no doubt that Dom Virgil, with his boundless energy and wide-ranging interests, was the leading light in this association. But Father Busch played a crucial role, and did so in a much less supportive institutional setting. As Michel himself put it to him, "In my notion you always had the position of chief worker and consulter." And indeed the unflappable Busch was often a steadying influence on his more fiery friend, who was prone to speak or write without concern for consequences.[30]

TO PROMOTE THE NECESSARY "UNDERSTANDING" OF INTEGRAL liturgical worship proved a daunting task. Busch wrote articles for *America* and *Commonweal*—semi-popular magazines catering to the educated and more or less progressive Catholic laity—which stirred hardly a response. Frustration was inevitable. As late as 1935, in touching upon the proposed Catholic censorship of the motion picture industry, he gave vent to it.

We would not be where we are in this movie business, we Catholics, if we had been well-schooled in the liturgy, in the chorus of divine praise, in the enjoyment of divine life, in the drama of our public worship. . . . There is this difficulty in my present argument, that those who really know what the liturgy is do not need to hear what I am saying, while those whom I would like to persuade may, from their inexperience of the liturgy, not understand what I mean.[31]

The movement gradually took on a national character, but in St. Paul William Busch was its lonely if unrelenting advocate. Even before his association with Virgil Michel and *Orate Fratres* he began a series of articles in the

---

29. Busch to Michel, September 28, 1925, quoted in Marx, *Virgil Michel*, 38.

30. See Marx, *Virgil Michel*, 117.

31. William Busch, "The Legion of Decency," in *Orate Fratres* 9 (1935): 303–305.

local diocesan weekly on liturgical subjects.[32] And yet, as it turned out, he was not entirely alone. His first duty was that of a seminary professor, and he knew full well that if future priests could be imbued with a devotion to the liturgy much of the battle could be won. Indeed, he said as much in his 1925 speech to the Catholic Educational Association. "The liturgical movement is of immense importance, and I am tempted to say of supreme importance in the life of the Church in our country, and particularly in seminary life." During the 1920s, if he found scant support among his faculty colleagues, a handful of students were more amenable.

The most remarkable of them was Paul Cornelius Bussard. Born on an Iowa farm in 1903, and raised on one in southwest Minnesota, Bussard spent three listless years at the College of St. Thomas but apparently came into his intellectual own when he entered the St. Paul Seminary in 1923.[33] He won most of the scholastic prizes awarded by the philosophy department and showed similar acumen when he moved on to theology. He read widely and not only the books prescribed by the courses he was taking. Indeed, his singular brilliance over a lifetime was largely self-directed and he seldom saw the need to disparage his talents. Upon ordination in 1928 Archbishop Dowling assigned him as curate in the cathedral parish.

Young Father Bussard had absorbed much of what Father Busch had taught him about the liturgy. From 1926 he had studied the articles in *Orate Fratres* and perused the books coming from the Liturgical Press at St. John's. And he had come to appreciate, surely better than most of his contemporaries, the theological basis upon which the Liturgical Movement was built; while still a student he had been invited to read to the seminary community a paper he had written entitled, "The Church, the Mystical Body of Christ." He must have left many of his listeners puzzled. There was an attraction, too, for one of Bussard's temperament, in that the movement seemed in a sense daring, innovative, a challenge to the stodgy status quo.

The single most important objective of the Liturgical Movement in its early days was to wean the people in the pews away from their private devotions during the celebration of Mass and to persuade them to make use of a missal instead. In following in the vernacular the prayers the priest was saying in Latin, they could begin to participate, at least intellectually, in the ac-

---

32. See *CB*, September 27, 1924.

33. For most of what follows—including quotations not otherwise cited—I am indebted to my friend Professor Anne Klemjent, of the University of St. Thomas in St. Paul, who is writing a history of the *Catholic Digest,* and who generously shared with me an unpublished research paper.

tion going on at the altar. Several Catholic publishing houses had marketed missals, but to little effect; to the uninitiated they were bulky and awkward to handle, since the reader had to flip back and forth from one section of the book to another in order to follow the "ordinary" and "proper" (changing) parts of the Mass. Still, the more fundamental problem was simply unfamiliarity. Father Bussard aimed to address this last difficulty by offering at the cathedral a six-week training course in the use of the missal. That about thirty people attended his class was gratifying, but he soon realized that at such a pace the "understanding" that William Busch had insisted upon as the movement's necessary first step would be restricted to a very small number.

A solution lay at hand. Edward Jennings, born in Chicago in 1896, the son of Irish immigrants, was Paul Bussard's classmate. He had come to the seminary after spending several years as an undergraduate at St. John's where he had fallen under the spell of Dom Virgil Michel, with whom he stayed in close touch. In St. Paul he predictably responded with enthusiasm to Busch's teaching, and in Bussard he found a soul mate. In some respects the two of them formed a study in contrast: the smoothly handsome, reserved Bussard, the burly, rugged, affable Jennings; the one a blooming intellectual, the other with the soul of an entrepreneur. But in the task they took upon themselves, the partnership worked surprisingly well. Jennings revered Bussard's mind, and Bussard never doubted Jennings's organizational skills. Indeed, he watched in admiration how Jennings, still a seminarian himself, acted as a sales agent for Michel's *Orate Fratres* and the Liturgical Press in seminaries across the Midwest.

In 1929 Father Jennings suggested a way to get around the missal problem. Why not, he said to Bussard, print a little pamphlet, a leaflet, which would incorporate the text of both the ordinary and proper of the Mass, along with descriptive notes about the rubrics and other explanatory material, for a particular Sunday or feast day, a throw-away bit of paper, cheaply produced and priced and easily distributed. So, with the blessing of Michel, Busch, and, perhaps just as importantly, Archbishop Dowling, was born in January 1930 the *Leaflet Missal*. A room was set aside for the project in the basement of the chancery Dowling had built six years earlier, on Dayton Avenue, directly behind the cathedral rectory. Bussard acted as editor of the enterprise and Jennings as business manager. The success of the venture was prodigious. Soon monthly issues of the *Leaflet* were counted in the tens of thousands. As one admiring bishop put it, "[The *Leaflet Missal* is] a practical method for bringing our people into intimate and intelligent contact with the Mass."[34] A

---

34. Quoted in Reardon, *Diocese of St. Paul,* 488.

similar reflection came from Paul Bussard, as he tended toward the sardonic in his later years: "[The *Leaflet Missal*] supplied the woman or man in the pew with the English of the Mass that the priest was uttering, or muttering, with his face turned to the far wall of the church." There can be little doubt, at any rate, that the Jennings-Bussard initiative eventually revolutionized popular piety among Catholics in Minnesota first and then across the United States.[35] For every person who read the articles in *Orate Fratres,* untold numbers came ultimately to enrich their worship by employing the fragile pamphlet that issued out of the basement room on Dayton Avenue.[36] A patron, Austin Dowling, expressed it best.

> The Leaflet Missal is a work of liturgical propaganda, undertaken by two young priests of this archdiocese, after the pattern of similar attempts in Germany and France. It hopes to present the text of the Sunday masses in so simple a form and at so reasonable a price that nobody can hereafter complain of the complexity of the Missal or the difficulty of finding the place in it. The language will be the vernacular, so that all may follow a translation carefully collated with the best versions. The elect, who prefer the Latin, have already become familiar with their missals, and if they love them as they should, will only be too glad to further the progress of this movement.

And the covenant between these two liturgical pioneers was far from over. Six years after the first number of the *Leaflet Missal* came off the press, Jennings and Bussard participated in the founding of the most successful publishing venture the American Catholic community has ever known.

FIRST, HOWEVER, BEFORE THEY COULD TAKE CREDIT FOR helping to launch the *Catholic Digest,* they needed to be introduced by one of

---

35. The original project has evolved three quarters of a century later into The Leaflet Missal Company, "one of the largest Catholic book and Catholic gift stores in the Midwest," with its headquarters on Minnehaha Avenue in St. Paul. See on the internet http://www.leafletmissal.org.

36. When I was ordained in 1956, my first assignment was, briefly, as acting pastor of St. Mathias parish in Wanda, Minnesota. I was astonished and edified that in this tiny village the people had been taught to participate in the Mass so fully, by joining in its Latin hymns and responses. This so-called *missa recitata* had been cultivated by a previous pastor, Father Frederick Barthleme, a contemporary at the St. Paul Seminary of Edward Jennings and Paul Bussard.

their contemporaries into the wider field of popular education. Louis Gales was born into a working-class family in Racine, Wisconsin, in 1896, and so was of an age with Edward Jennings. After grammar school Louis took a series of jobs and managed at the same time to accrue some high school credits at the local commercial college. While thus in the real world of the workplace and the business college he came to appreciate the importance of the skills needed to market a product. Still, ever since he was a small boy he had wanted to be a priest, and so, at nineteen, he entered St. Francis Seminary in Milwaukee. His spotty and largely pragmatic academic background had not prepared him very well to follow the classical course there, and, besides, his real desire was to be a missionary rather than a diocesan priest. In 1918 he accordingly transferred to St. Paul's College, the Paulist seminary in Washington, D.C. The ideals of the Paulists which had attracted Thomas O'Gorman so many years before[37]—with their emphasis on up-to-date methods of reaching out to the marginalized American Catholic, the non-Catholic, and even the unchurched—suited young Gales's aspirations admirably and indeed guided him throughout his life.

His formal association with the Paulists, however, ended prematurely in an incident that might have been termed hilarious had it not been so sad for him. Louis's brother, Willard, had moved to Washington to start a business enterprise. Louis, who since his days at the Racine College of Commerce had proved himself adept at writing short and pithy descriptive material, agreed to provide advertising copy for the new company. But the rigid rules that governed seminaries in those days forbade such "worldly" activities and contacts. To get round this prohibition the brothers devised a strategy whereby they maintained contact by hiding their messages under a rock on the campus. This ruse was in due course detected, and the upshot was that Louis Gales returned to Wisconsin.

But the inner fire had not burned out. In 1923, after long and strenuous efforts, a former Paulist named Peter O'Callaghan founded what he called the Home Mission Society to meet "the spiritual needs of Catholics in neglected regions of America." He opened a seminary in New Jersey to train prospective priests who would serve in these areas under the jurisdiction of the local bishop. Father O'Callaghan's departure from the Paulists had risen out of tactical, not philosophical, differences, and the Paulist ethos very much prevailed in this new institution. Gales applied for entry and was accepted. The project, however, soon encountered a variety of canonical difficulties, and

---

37. See chapter 14, above.

after several rounds of confusing claims and counterclaims, Rome intervened and quashed it. O'Callaghan then needed to find places for the seminarians who in all good faith had joined him. One of his sturdiest supporters had been Austin Dowling, to whom O'Callaghan recommended Louis Gales. And so the peripatetic ecclesiastical career of the boy from Wisconsin came to a tidy conclusion. He was incardinated into the archdiocese of St. Paul and ordained in 1926.

Gales was appointed assistant pastor to the great German parish of St. Agnes in St. Paul—hardly a cannon shot from the cathedral where Paul Bussard was shortly to be assigned—and he remained in that position for a decade. But from the beginning this short, slender, dark-haired man, thirty years old now, brought wider purposes to his duties than did most newly ordained curates. The missionary spirit had by no means diminished in him, nor had a conviction—in the best Paulist tradition—that a modern apostolate demanded the utilization of modern means. And in the United States of the 1920s, a revolutionary time in the expansion of mass communication, those means appeared to be necessarily linked to the new media. This was the era when radio came into its own, when movie-going became an American obsession, when the purveyors of information and cultural hegemony in print geared themselves for a universal audience: the first issue of the *Readers Digest* appeared in 1922.

Within a couple of years of his arrival at St. Agnes, Father Gales founded the Cooperative Guild—renamed in 1933 the Catechetical Guild—whose purpose was to publish and distribute to Catholics of all ages "teaching aids, books, games, puzzles, projects," as he explained toward the end of his life. He even designed a catechism game which evolved later into a richly illustrated book. Indeed, providing suitable material for children became and remained a major part of the Guild's activities. Later years saw the appearance of the instructive cartoon magazines such as *Topix* and *Timeless Topix,* as well as several series of easily read books written for youngsters of different ages: *Wopsy* for toddlers and *Tales of Valor* for the ten- to fourteen-year-old set. But adults were not neglected. During the early 1930s the Guild established a Catholic Library Service, which loaned books to study clubs, twenty books for three dollars. Once the downtown headquarters were established, a reading room stocked with a thousand wholesome volumes was open to the public. Still later Gales moved the Guild into radio broadcasting and the production of films and audio materials. The achievement of the Guild was extraordinary as it spread its work across the country and across the ocean; and there was no better testimony to its success than the number of imitators that flourished in its wake.

Such expansion, needless to say, could not have been foreseen in 1929 when Louis Gales, with the help of a few underemployed parishioners, set up shop in the basement of the parish rectory. But neither could it have been clear then how determined this young priest was to contribute to the spiritual sustenance and instruction of ordinary people—the same people to whom the more cerebral William Busch and Paul Bussard wanted to bring the full richness of the liturgy. After he left St. Agnes, Father Gales, besides continuing to direct the Guild's ever larger and more complex operations, acted for a quarter of a century as chaplain at Ancker Hospital and at the hospice conducted by the Little Sisters of the Poor. In time his diminutive, seemingly shy figure became almost an icon in downtown St. Paul, always garbed, it seemed, in a simple cassock and always smiling. But little did these externals reveal of the relentlessness with which he followed the missionary call he had heard in his youth, to serve the needs of the modern American Catholic. Only his accomplishments could do that, the single most significant of which, the jewel in the crown, was the founding—with Bussard and Jennings indispensably at his side—of the *Catholic Digest* in 1935.

IT MAY BE WORTH OBSERVING THAT GALES, JENNINGS, AND Bussard were all born outside Minnesota. That they came together in the seminary and later formed their fruitful alliance was, to a degree, fortuitous. Archbishop Dowling supported them, but he did not recruit them. The case was quite otherwise with regard to three other externs destined to exert much influence within the archdiocese of St. Paul. William O. Brady, James Connolly, and Francis Gilligan all hailed from Fall River, Massachusetts. Through his New England connections Dowling learned that these talented students were about to complete their course at the Sulpician Seminary in Washington, D.C., and learned too that the bishop of Fall River, with little need for priests to staff educational institutions, was prepared to grant them an *exeat*. Accordingly, after their ordinations—Brady and Connolly in 1923 and Gilligan a year later—they were incardinated into the archdiocese, with the explicit commitment from the archbishop that they would be appointed to the faculty of the St. Paul Seminary.[38] Dowling promptly sent them off for higher studies: Brady to the Angelicum in Rome for dogmatic theology (to his

---

38. See Brady's letters to Dowling, cited and quoted in Athans, *To Work for the Whole People*, 204–206. Most of what follows is taken from this book. See especially 173–180, 390–394.

dismay upon his return he was assigned to teach moral theology—so relaxed then were the pedagogical norms); Connolly to Louvain for church history; and Gilligan to the Catholic University of America for moral theology, with an emphasis upon questions of social justice. By 1927 the three of them had assumed their professorships at the seminary.

Predictably, Brady, Connolly, and Gilligan were soon dubbed by the local clergy "the three wise men from the East." Nor was this phrase uttered with playful intent. Why should John Ireland's seminary be staffed by men from New England? Were there not young indigenous priests willing and able to take on teaching responsibilities in the archdiocese's most prestigious institution, Mr. Hill's seminary? Why should these "foreigners" be automatically given the privilege of advanced education in Europe and in Washington? This sour, even derisive, point of view was heightened at the end of Dowling's decade in St. Paul when he "gave away" the College of St. Thomas to outsiders. Moreover, from their shared Sulpician experience, the three of them introduced into the seminary ethos a narrow rigor which had heretofore not been prevalent—no newspapers, no radios, no overt contact with the "world" outside, an *esprit,* so it was said, far removed from Archbishop Ireland's liberal ideal. However just such complaints may have been, the fact remains that two of the "wise men"—Connolly's less forceful personality left a milder mark— exerted a profound influence on the fortunes of the archdiocese, because they were so much involved in forming its priests over several generations.

William Brady, who taught moral and pastoral theology until 1933, when Dowling's successor named him rector of the seminary, was a man of utter decisiveness. This characteristic was no doubt admirable in its way, and it surely contributed to his achievements as an administrator. He was besides a good if, predictably, doctrinaire teacher, articulate in the spoken and written word, energetic, and possessed of much social charm. Some of his students and colleagues, however, found his self-confidence almost abrasive, almost a species of brashness. Even his good friend, Francis Gilligan, observed toward the end of his long life that Brady "was never unsure of anything." His presence at the seminary was in any event formidable, one which was bound to affect the sensibilities and aspirations of the young men who took their formation in the ministry under his aegis. He departed the seminary in 1939 when appointed bishop of Sioux Falls, but his strong-willed leadership was destined to revisit the archdiocese. Seventeen years later he returned to St. Paul as coadjutor and, shortly afterward, as archbishop in his own right.

During much of Brady's rectorship, James Connolly served as the seminary's spiritual director. "Gentleman Jim," as the students nicknamed him, was a man of considerable sophistication, but the seminarians found his conferences on ascetical theology decidedly humdrum. Such negative judgments, however, did not intrude upon Connolly's path of ecclesiastical preferment. In 1940 he was named rector of Nazareth Hall—where he earned the dubious distinction of expelling over a short span of time a record number of students—and three years later he came back to the St. Paul Seminary as rector. And two years after that, in 1945, he was named coadjutor of his home diocese, Fall River, and ultimately its ordinary, a goal, his critics claimed, that had been his all along. He retired in 1970 and then fell into the shadow zone of senile dementia until he died in 1986.

Of "the three wise men from the East," the one with the most enduring impact upon the archdiocese of St. Paul was Francis Gilligan. Born and raised as were his confreres in Fall River, Gilligan, orphaned at an early age, followed a conventional educational pattern for an aspiring ecclesiastic—classical studies at the Jesuit college in Worcester, philosophy at St. Mary's in Baltimore, theology at the Sulpician Seminary in Washington—with summers spent laboring on the steamship line, with its largely Negro crew, plying between Boston and New York. Once at Catholic University, he became a graduate student of John A. Ryan, who challenged him to write his doctoral dissertation on the morality of the color line. Gilligan did so, and thus began a long and fruitful apostolate in the field of race relations. He followed Ryan's lead in other respects, too, investing much energy, for instance, in support of the right of laboring people to fair wages and decent working conditions. He differed from his mentor, however, in that he was less bookish than Ryan and instead applied his principles of social justice directly in the community at large, sometimes as a strike mediator, sometimes simply by dining ostentatiously with African Americans at an elegant restaurant. More formally, he served on a host of civic bodies concerned with racial and labor questions and for many years directed the archdiocese's labor schools, where workers could learn how to organize and their employers could ponder the teaching of *Rerum novarum.*

But it was as a seminary professor for nearly thirty years that Francis Gilligan made his greatest impact, because he engendered in many generations of archdiocesan priests—in some cases very strongly—a sense that moral issues of the most serious kind undergirded the quest of ordinary people for economic security and racial equality. Here was a curious turnaround: Ryan, the fiery man from Minnesota, instilled in the man from Massachusetts a fierce determination to promote actively the cause of social justice, and that man brought that passion back to Minnesota and pressed it upon the young men in his classroom. Classes with Father Gilligan were always memorable, not only for the reasons already noted, but also for his verbal and physical eccentricities: the raspy voice, which never quite lost its New England twang, the choppy hand motions, the ruddy face beneath (in his later years) a shock of white hair, and the remarkably beautiful smile which, however, did not always intimate good humor.

AUSTIN DOWLING DID NOT LIVE TO WITNESS FRANCIS GILLIGAN'S appointment to the Labor Committee of the National Association for the Advancement of Colored People. But the archbishop had given the idealistic young seminarian his start and had never ceased to support and encourage him. The same could be said with regard to those other five externs—Bussard, Jennings, Gales, Brady, Connolly—who brought their gifts, perhaps providentially, to the service of the archdiocese of St. Paul. The seamless robe that is the Catholic Church possesses a chronological component, so that decade after decade—indeed, century after century—where one sows, another reaps. Dowling sowed much good seed, the fruit of which grew and flourished until the Second Vatican Council, thirty-five years after his death.

The physician whom Dowling consulted when he learned he had been named archbishop opined that his heart had a good chance of functioning adequately for another ten years.[39] The doctor was only a year or so off the mark. Early in January 1928, Dowling checked into Mercy Hospital in Chicago suffering from chest pains and shortness of breath.[40] From there he was transferred for further treatment to the Mayo Clinic in Rochester.[41] By the summer he had resumed his ordinary duties—which included the final, stressful negotiations involved in placing the Congregation of Holy Cross in control of the College of St. Thomas—until a year later when he was put to bed with pneumonia, caused, his doctors said, by fatigue from overwork.[42] He seemed to rally somewhat after that, but it was universally noted that he was growing increasingly frail. On October 7, 1930, after administering confirmation to a large class in Glencoe, a town fifty miles west of the Twin Cities, the archbishop collapsed. He never really recovered, though he lingered for nearly two months. In the forenoon of Saturday, November 29, 1930, Austin Dowling, aged sixty-two, died.[43]

39. See chapter 16, above.
40. See "Report" of Mercy Hospital, January 27, 1928, AASPM, Dowling Papers.
41. Dowling to Mrs. E. C. Lindley, March 15, 1928, AASPM, Dowling Papers.
42. *CB,* June 22, 1929.
43. *CB,* December 6, 1930.

In Washington, on September 24, 1919, at the first annual meeting of the American hierarchy, the ninety-two bishops in attendance, after some lively debate, voted to set up the bureaucratic structure of the National Catholic Welfare Conference. It was a fateful decision for the Church in the United States in which—it may be recalled—Archbishop Dowling played a pivotal role then and over the next decade, as head of the Conference's Education Department. The day before, also in Washington, he preached the festive sermon at the dedication of a new building at the Sulpician Seminary. He spoke with his usual understated elegance, and, though history had always been his favored intellectual discipline, it was the future that occupied his mind and his rhetoric on this occasion.

> The old order passeth giving place to the new. . . . So far the Church in this country has been singularly sustained by the momentum of spiritual agencies that were derived from other lands and other times. In the new day there will be no such powerful auxiliary to supplement our own normal activity. It will be the American Catholic Church, or it will be nothing. Against that day we must prepare.[44]

---

44. AASPM, Dowling sermons. This file contains both manuscript and mimeographed material. See also McNicholas, *Sermons of Dowling*. For an analysis of Dowling as a preacher, see O'Connell, "Dowling Decade," 99–129.

CHAPTER 19

Mea Omnia Tua

ON THE DAY AFTER NEW YEAR'S, 1932, THE BISHOP OF PORTLAND, Maine, took pen in hand. "My dear Monsignor Byrne," he wrote, "as soon as my bulls came, I renewed an invitation I had given to the Apostolic Delegate personally in Washington in November to come to St. Paul to preside at the ceremony. His answer came only yesterday, stating that His Excellency would be pleased to act on Wednesday, January twenty-seventh." The letter went on to explain to James Byrne, administrator of the archdiocese of St. Paul since the death of Austin Dowling fourteen months before, that now that the required papal documents had arrived in Portland and the delegate's presence at the installation confirmed, the bishop had proceeded to engage Tiffany of New York to prepare a thousand invitations. These would be forwarded to the chancery in St. Paul for mailing to various ecclesiastics and institutions around the country. If Byrne should determine that more than this number was called for, he need only say the word. Meanwhile, the bishop would send out some personal invitations directly from Portland. "They will not be engraved," he added, "only printed."

Tiffany would guarantee a measure of appropriate elegance, but in this instance not its most expensive variety. The bishop, it would seem, recognized the grim economic realities of the moment. The proposal had been made in St. Paul

> to organize a reception committee to come by train to some specified place to meet me. Frankly, in the present condition of the country and the state of mind of the people, my coming, in my opinion, ought to be as modest as possible, in fact so unobtrusive that my first appearance should be at the door of the cathedral on the morning of the installation, after a

previous meeting with you and the board of consultors in the chancery office to present my credentials and have them accepted.[1]

But despite this prudent suggestion, a group of priests and prominent laymen from the Twin Cities met the bishop in Chicago, and when the party arrived at the St. Paul Union Station at 9:20 p.m. on January 26, 1932, fifty-four-year-old John Gregory Murray was greeted by a goodly crowd of well-wishers.[2] He moved easily and genially among them, thus displaying a trait that would characterize his social manner over the next quarter of a century.

He duly appeared the next morning at the door of the massive cathedral John Ireland had built and Austin Dowling had beautified. He was greeted by Administrator Byrne with a sprinkling of holy water and a whiff of incense. With the usual pomp and circumstance the ministers of the Mass proceeded down the center aisle toward the sanctuary where thirty-six bishops and abbots were already gathered. Across the vast expanse of the church 5,000 worshipers (nine of whom fainted during the lengthy ceremony) strained to catch sight of the diminutive Murray, partly obscured by "the tall aristocratic" Archbishop Pietro Fumasoni-Biondi, the apostolic delegate, who walked next to him. Then most eyes turned upward as "a flock of birds flutter[ed] overhead," not doves indeed, but "three flights of pigeons [which] circled the cathedral dome in bright sunlight during the episcopal procession and installation." Neither a good omen nor ill in the mind of the new archbishop, a practical man and "a genial prelate who was once a newsboy on the streets of Waterbury, Connecticut."[3]

After the required liturgical functions, the reading of papal documents, and brief addresses by the administrator and the delegate, John Gregory Murray rose to speak to his people for the first time. He began conventionally enough, with thanks and pledges of loyalty to the Holy See and a wish that they would consider themselves "devoted children" to a dedicated father. But toward the end of the speech he entered upon less traditional ground and touched upon more directly contemporary concerns. There existed, he said, an "explicit commission" that "our united efforts would produce constant increase from day to day in the domain of the spiritual and the temporal."

---

1. Murray to Byrne, January 2, 1932, AASPM, Murray Papers.

2. Reardon, *Diocese of St. Paul,* 510, called it "an immense throng."

3. *Time* 19 (February 8, 1932): 32–33. This report says the crowd in the church numbered 6,500; Reardon, *Diocese of St. Paul,* 510, distinguishes between 5,000 inside and 1,500 more on the steps and street outside.

The Church cannot be indifferent to any fact or circumstance that affects the welfare of men, even though it has only an indirect bearing on their spiritual development. [Therefore Pope Pius XI] has called for the reconstruction of the social order; he has proclaimed the sanctity of the well springs of family life as the unit of the social order; he has directed the organization of the crusade of charity to provide an equitable distribution of worldly wealth, . . . [in order] to relieve the distress of multitudes who are victims of maladjustment in [the] prevailing order. . . . Such a program, outlined by the Father of all the faithful indicates wherein our activities in the temporal order will fortify the life of all in the spiritual. At no time in history has there been such widespread perplexity as to the outcome of our existing systems in the economic and political fields. No era has furnished greater opportunity for the enlightened and self-disciplined Catholic layman to contribute his share to the redemption of society at large.[4]

Less than ten months later, even as the economic "maladjustment" widened and deepened, Franklin Delano Roosevelt was elected president of the United States.

During the days and weeks that followed, however, the gloom of the Great Depression was temporarily lightened somewhat by the round of events welcoming Murray to the archdiocese and to Minnesota. The reception was markedly warmer than that afforded Dowling in 1919; this may have been because the episcopal throne had been vacant for more than a year and because Murray did not experience the misfortune of succeeding the iconic John Ireland. Ceremonial visits to the Basilica of St. Mary in Minneapolis, to the St. Paul Seminary, to the colleges of St. Thomas and St. Catherine followed a predictable pattern. So did luncheons and banquets held in Murray's honor by the Knights of Columbus and other Catholic organizations, as well as similar events hosted by civic and business groups.[5] The most remarkable of these events took place the evening after the installation, January 28, when 14,000 people gathered in the St. Paul Auditorium to witness a formal and almost political welcome. The mayors of both Twin Cities were in attendance. But the dominating presence was that of handsome, mercurial, eloquent Floyd B. Olson, the first candidate of the Farmer-Labor Party to be elected governor.

---

4. *CB*, January 30, 1932.

5. For a comprehensive list of these festivities, see Reardon, *Diocese of St. Paul,* 512–514.

In his remarks Olson stressed his "happiness" at the emphasis in Murray's installation sermon on dealing "with the maladjustments of our economic situation, . . . in which children are in want and men and women in despair." The archbishop, the governor said, has admirably pleaded for the molding of better citizens who then can solve "the maladjustments" in accord "with the teaching of Christ." Murray, for his part, responded to the tributes with echoes of the long-standing Catholic community's aspiration to be seen as having emerged from its immigrant beginnings: "The greatest human privilege and distinction that has fallen to my lot is the possession of American citizenship."[6]

JOHN GREGORY MURRAY, THE SON OF IRISH IMMIGRANTS, WAS born February 26, 1877, in Waterbury, Connecticut.[7] He attended public schools in Waterbury and then enrolled at the College of the Holy Cross in Worcester, Massachusetts, from which he was awarded the baccalaureate in June 1897. Later that year, having been accepted as a candidate to the priesthood for the diocese of Hartford, he was sent to the University of Louvain in Belgium for his theological studies. He was ordained there in April 1900, barely twenty-three years old. This relatively tender age suggests that Murray was a superlative student, and there is no reason to conclude otherwise. It smacks, however, of the apocryphal that more than thirty years after his departure from the university he was still remembered there as "good John Murray" and "the pearl of Louvain."

Back in Hartford, Father Murray served in a variety of posts, including prison chaplain and professor in the minor seminary, until 1903 when he was appointed diocesan chancellor, a position he held for nineteen years. This broad experience in administration was expanded further when he was named auxiliary bishop of Hartford in 1919, and six years after that he became the fifth bishop of Portland. His predecessors included James A. Healy

---

6. *CB*, February 6, 1932. For a brief synopsis of Olson's career as governor, see John E. Haynes, "Reformers, Radicals, and Conservatives," in Clifford E. Clark, Jr., ed., *Minnesota in a Century of Change* (St. Paul, 1989), 375–378.

7. For what follows, see Reardon, *Diocese of St. Paul*, 507–510. Reardon says that "biographical data" was furnished by Murray himself (706). This is a perfectly credible assertion, because the account is so dry and spare—nothing, e.g., about the Murray family. It would be hard to imagine a man more guarded about his personal life—outside the circle of a very few close friends—than the third archbishop of St. Paul.

(1878–1900), whose mother had been a black slave in Georgia before the Civil War, and William O'Connell (1900–1906), later cardinal archbishop of Boston, whose career there was tarnished by family scandal and his own imperiousness.[8]

Murray's tenure in Portland witnessed a whirlwind of activity. The number of priests increased over six years from 167 to 216. Parishes with a resident pastor replaced missions, schools and churches were built at a heartening pace. But if the economic times were good when he arrived in Maine, they were not so when he departed, and one result was the considerable debt accrued by the diocese, with which Murray's successors had to contend.[9] Overall, however, youthful and sprightly, he was popular both inside and outside the Catholic community.

John Gregory Murray chose as the motto for his episcopal coat of arms the phrase *Mea Omnia Tua,* which translates, "All that is Mine is Yours." But, in accord with the peculiarities of the Latin language, it can just as legitimately be rendered as "All that is Yours is Mine." This verbal ambiguity appeared to be reflective of the man's personality and of his mode of operation. Unfailingly courteous and accommodating, punctilious to a fault in carrying out the duties of his office, never afraid to adopt a principled position whatever the opposition to it, not above displaying a playfulness at times, he nevertheless guarded the bastion of his inner self so assiduously that a kind of mystery enveloped him. He was immensely popular with the people at large. In speaking to reporters after his installation, the "genial prelate . . . declared that he preferred walking or trolley-riding to automobiling. 'I do only the things I'm supposed to do and then only at the last minute.'"[10] He soon became a legend in the Twin Cities as he rode the streetcars and walked briskly along the busy streets. In his high-pitched New England twang, he would talk to anybody and everybody. But his familiarity was not so much egalitarian as a gesture in *noblesse oblige:* this very important personage, this short, plump, ruddy-faced, bespectacled figure, garbed in his Prince Albert coat with his soft black hat, brim upturned, fixed on his head, mingled freely and cheerfully like the old-school gentleman he was. Nor would he take liberties with them. During his last months, when everyone knew he was dying, he continued to trudge up the hill from downtown St. Paul to the cathedral, causing a

---

8. See chapter 17, above.

9. The Internet provides much useful information about the history of the diocese of Portland. See http://www.portlanddiocese.net/info.php?info_id=43. Accessed May 20, 2008.

10. *Time* 19 (February 8, 1932): 33.

virtual traffic jam, as the well-intentioned drivers in passing cars stopped to offer him a ride. He smilingly waved them on.

The ambiguity was much more evident in Murray's dealings with the clergy. He was, certainly, by and large supportive of them and appreciative of their work. But he could be sharp with them, too, as for instance when they nervously blundered in assisting at the arcane and exceedingly complicated pontifical ceremonies that still prevailed in those days. Nor was he above occasional sarcasm. About 1946 a priest applied directly to the archbishop for promotion to an assignment more desirable, in his view, than his present one. "But Father," said Murray, "that's a *good* parish."[11] A rebuff could be administered in a more public setting. A new church built in Minneapolis during the early 1950s reflected in its design and decoration the pastor's commitment to the principles of the burgeoning Liturgical Movement[12] and hence stressed the physical and symbolic centrality of the sacrificial altar; in the sermon he preached at the building's dedication, the archbishop spoke almost exclusively about the importance in any church of the tabernacle and the Real Presence.[13] Clerical jokesters claimed that at festive liturgies at which he presided but did not himself give the sermon, Murray routinely mounted the pulpit at the end of the ceremonies and explained to the congregation, in long sentences that always seemed to be looking for a verb, what the preacher of the day had *really* meant to say.

Anecdotes abounded about how the archbishop thus kept his priests off balance, often in quite incomprehensible ways. Once in the late 1940s he traveled by trolley to assure the pastor of a large parish in Minneapolis that, contrary to rumors, one of his curates would not be removed. A week later the young priest was reassigned.[14] At about the same time a dispute arose at Nazareth Hall, the minor seminary, between the rector and the professor of music, the rector complaining that too much polyphony and too little Gregorian chant was being sung during liturgical functions. The priest-professor, an accomplished musician, demurred. The rector then took his case to the archbishop, who asserted that by all means chant (pronounced with a broad "a"), in accord with papal directives, must be the exclusive musical style followed "in my seminaries." But once informed of this sweeping dictate, the professor, a feisty man, went in his turn to the "trembling room" in the chancery at 244

11. Interview with Rev. Harold Green.
12. See chapter 18, above.
13. Interview with Rev. Richard V. Berg.
14. Interview with Archbishop John R. Roach.

Dayton Avenue. Murray's reply to his protest: "I said no such thing to the rector. And even if I did I didn't intend him to tell you."[15] A few years later a seminarian wearing his de rigueur black suit and riding on a streetcar found to his alarm the archbishop sitting next to him. And what courses are you following? Murray asked him. The seminarian went blank, and stammered, "Your Excellency, I'm so nervous I can't remember." "Nonsense," replied the archbishop. "You're not nervous. Why, if the men teaching you were teaching me, I wouldn't remember the classes either."[16] The multitude of such stories, though perhaps embellished in the telling, strongly suggests that not all of them were apocryphal.[17] Nor were they in any case necessarily unedifying. One evening in the late 1940s a call came to the cathedral rectory—where Murray was in residence—from a woman in Minneapolis whose husband had

---

15. Interview with Rev. Walter H. Peters.

16. Interview with Rev. Leo J. Dolan.

17. My own brief encounter with Archbishop Murray confirms my view that not all the anecdotes were apocryphal. A few days before my ordination to the priesthood (June 2, 1956), the archbishop, as was his wont, came to the seminary to interview individually the men to be ordained for the archdiocese of St. Paul. It had been determined that I was to do graduate work in history beginning the following September. When I entered the room, I could plainly see bulging in his neck the tumor which would shortly kill him. He said—I paraphrase—I understand you are going to study history. Now tell me your view of the discipline of history. Is history the gathering of isolated facts? Or is it the construction of a general overview? Thirty seconds after I left him I could not in my nervousness remember how I had answered. I went in distress to my mentor, Father Patrick Ahern—who had gone to a great deal of trouble to secure for me a fellowship at Notre Dame—to confess that I had bungled the interview. Don't be concerned, Ahern replied with a chuckle, this is the Murray *modus*. He put that dilemma to you, because you could not solve it. If you said the accumulation of isolated facts, he would have replied, where will you locate them? If you had said the general overview, he would have asked, how can you construct it?

During the interview the archbishop also said that he would tell no one of my fellowship and advised me to do the same—because, he added, if the pastor to whom I assign you for the summer knows you are leaving in September he may not treat you very well. But in fact he assigned me as "acting pastor" of the Church of St. Mathias, in the western Minnesota village of Wanda. A week after my arrival in that charming place, the archbishop came to a neighboring parish to dedicate a new building. I was in attendance. When he noticed me he said, "How did you find Wanda?" "Wonderful, your Excellency (as indeed it was)." "That's not what I meant. How did you find it?" "It's on the map," I replied. "Oh. I wasn't aware of that."

I never saw John Gregory Murray again. A few months later he died with great fortitude.

been suddenly stricken ill. The staff by chance was all engaged, and so the archbishop answered the ring, though in general he disliked conversing on the telephone. The woman explained that her pastor forbade any calls after 9:00 p.m. So Murray, noting her address, secured the holy oils, boarded the streetcar, and in due course administered extreme unction to the sick man. Afterward he walked to the nearby rectory and rang the bell. When the pastor in response leaned out of a second-story window, the archbishop shouted up to him, "Father, you needn't worry about Mr. Doe. I just anointed him."[18]

IN THE AUTUMN OF 1956, AS HE LAY DYING IN ST. JOSEPH'S Hospital in St. Paul, John Gregory Murray was visited by an old friend. Francis Cardinal Spellman, archbishop of New York and at the time the most influential churchman in the United States, made the trip on a private plane, with no publicity or fanfare. What the two men talked about is of course unknown. No doubt the cardinal, a priest who had attended many deathbeds during his long career—and who in any case was as astute a judge of the sensitivity required in a one-on-one exchange as anybody of his generation— offered the conventional assurances of prayer for the dying; and no doubt either that the archbishop received such pledges with his usual stoical courtesy. Still, it would not be presumptuous to conjecture that much of their conversation dwelt upon persons and events that went back twenty-five years and more. The fact is that Murray came to Minnesota from New England with weightier connections than those of Austin Dowling. Hartford, so to speak, out-trumped Providence.

On January 18, 1932, Father Rudolph Nolan, chancellor of the archdiocese of St. Paul, received a telegram from Portland: "Please make reservations for Tuesday [January 26] at best hotel. One large sitting room, four double bedrooms with four individual baths, all in suite. To be held for Mrs. Nicholas Brady." The thirty-eight-year-old Nolan—a tall, burly, handsome man— replied by wire the next day: "The 'State Suite' has been engaged for Mrs. Brady and her party at the St. Paul Hotel." Three days after that Bishop Murray sent off another telegram: "My luncheon party will number twelve [relatives and friends from Portland]. Brady party will lunch either in their suite or at my home, if you can arrange it."[19] Nolan had been dealing with the details of the arrival of a new archbishop since the preceding November, when

18. Interview with Msgr. John P. Sankovitz.
19. Telegrams, as dated in the text, in AASPM, Murray Papers.

the appointment was made public. He took pains, for instance, to convey assurances that the financial books would be in order: "Reports are in preparation that will give you the present status of the various trusts, Chancery funds, etc." But more mundane matters also had to be seen to, like the preparation of the archbishop's residence. "I do not want to give the impression that the house is falling down or that it has been neglected. Neither is true." Still, because of Dowling's protracted illness, and the reluctance of staff to cause him any unnecessary inconvenience, some maintenance had been postponed. "Your bathroom," Father Nolan wrote in his breezy style.

> This is very old-fashioned. The fixtures are not in the best of condition. There is no shower. The bathtub is a relic—a huge swimming pool. I am sure a carnival high-diver could do a forty-footer into it without injury. The lavatory is an 1890 fixture. I propose new fixtures—combination tub and shower and new tile. This will make a messy job and should be done before any general cleaning is undertaken.[20]

"As to the archbishop's quarters," Murray replied, "there need only be such improvements as you think will make them neat and simple. A shower would be much appreciated."[21]

It is doubtful that Rudolph Nolan, preoccupied with ledgers and showers and tiles, knew much about Mrs. Nicholas Brady, but he was shrewd enough to see to it that she and her party received royal treatment when they arrived for the installation. Or aristocratic at least, for after all Genevieve Brady was a Papal Duchess. Her fame may not have penetrated into the upper Midwest, but her celebrity and influence in Catholic circles in New York and Rome were prodigious. This was largely due to her generosity; long indeed was the list of the Catholic charitable organizations to which she and her late husband had contributed substantial sums of money.[22] Indeed, only days before Murray's installation she had been feted in New York as the founder and endower of a home for Catholic working girls. Among those offering tributes to her on that occasion was "the Reverend Doctor Fulton J. Sheen of Catholic University."[23]

---

20. Nolan to Murray (copy), November 15, 1931, AASPM, Murray Papers.

21. Murray to Nolan, November 23, 1931, AASPM, Murray Papers.

22. See, for example, the list printed in *The New York Herald Tribune,* January 29, 1941.

23. *CB,* January 13, 1932.

Nicholas Brady inherited a thriving pharmaceutical business which prospered even more during and after the First World War. He and his wife kept luxurious homes on Long Island, on Fifth Avenue in Manhattan, in Dublin, and up the Janiculum on the Via Aurelia Antica in Rome, the "Casa del Sole," which overlooked the Piazza di San Pietro and the basilica. They spent a good deal of time at the Casa, especially at the great religious feasts of Christmas and Easter and more generally during the spring of the year when Rome's climate was (and is) at its most benign. Nick got his exercise on his tennis court—he was uninterested in golf, ordinarily the rich man's sport—while he and Genevieve regularly socialized with the other wealthy American expatriates and tourists. But their most significant contacts, more rather than less fashionable, were with high officials in the Roman curia. Both were fervent Catholics—especially Genevieve, who attended Mass daily and who seemed constantly on pilgrimage to, among other holy places, the home of the German stigmatic, Teresa Neumann: "I shall never forget my visit to her."[24] And Nick was scarcely casual about his religion. Commenting on the death of Cardinal Bonzano (who had once been apostolic delegate to the United States), he wrote: "Rome seems a little empty to me. . . . Our friend died as he had lived, simple in manner, great in soul, a Saint of God. I feel a certain sure faith these days."[25] No cynicism or self-interest there, nothing unseemly that this affluent American couple should cultivate, and be cultivated by, the movers and shakers within the Vatican.

And here is where Francis Joseph Spellman makes his entry. After a theological education, such as it was, at the North American College in Rome—when he became proficient in Italian—Spellman was ordained in 1915 for the archdiocese of Boston. After ten years of clerical drudgery at home under the baleful eye of a hostile Cardinal O'Connell, he managed to wangle a job in the Roman curia as a translator.[26] From the first, affable and accommodating,

---

24. Genevieve Brady to Murray, July 27, n.d. [probably 1932 or 1933], AASPM, Murray Papers. In most of the letters of Mrs. Brady that Archbishop Murray preserved, dates are incomplete or entirely missing. Internal evidence, however, suggests that the bulk of them were written in 1932–1933, and sometimes such evidence makes possible tentative dating.

25. Nicholas Brady to "John" (copy), December 11, 1927, AASPM, Murray Papers. Genevieve sent this copy to Murray, May 16, 1932, with the notation: "Isn't it beautiful and so like him?"

26. Much of what follows is taken from John Cooney, *The American Pope: The Life and Times of Francis Cardinal Spellman* (New York, 1984). This book must be regarded with great suspicion. Its bias against Spellman is venomous. Its

young Father Spellman made himself useful to his curial superiors and, increasingly, to the affluent American Catholic community in Rome. Indeed, he became in time the chief liaison between these two groups. Shortly after his arrival in 1925, in attendance at a function in St. Peter's, he spied an obviously distinguished American couple sitting at the rear of the vast basilica. He immediately arranged to have them moved to the very front area. Nicholas and Genevieve were grateful for this kindness, and from then on "Father Frank" was a familiar at the Casa del Sole, playing tennis with Nick and regularly a presence at the glittering parties Genevieve gave for the *crème de la crème* of Roman society.

Much of Spellman's activity had to do with helping to channel American money to good causes—as the Bradys were always willing to do—though not necessarily to explicitly pious ones. In June 1926, for example, Nicholas Brady took Pietro Cardinal Gasparri for a drive in the country in his luxurious automobile. Not surprisingly, Spellman was also a passenger, and at luncheon, never one to vacillate, he said to Brady, "Will you give Cardinal Gasparri a limousine?" "Sure," Brady replied. In due course the car was delivered to the secretary of state—the second most important personage in the Vatican—and so delighted and obliged was Gasparri that, during his initial ride in it, he insisted that Spellman accompany him. Also in due course Nicholas Brady was created Knight of the Supreme Order of Christ and his wife a Duchess.[27]

There were other similar interventions on Spellman's part, many of them, curiously enough, also involving gifts of automobiles to high-ranking prelates. It seems hardly a sinister occurrence that, if aged and highly traditionalist Italian gentlemen should take pleasure in owning newfangled horseless carriages, the go-getter American priest should be ready to gratify them. Spellman was undeniably ambitious, as many of his contemporaries were not slow to point out. But that ambition was moderated by a scrupulous personal honesty, a conventional piety, a relatively simple lifestyle—no Renaissance prelate he—and, above all, by a recognition of his own gifts and limitations. And he was shrewd, and not only in money matters; he proved over a long career to possess keen judgment in dealing skillfully with people and events

---

documentation fails every criterion of historical standards. However, since there is no other credible treatment of the cardinal's career, certain facts and chronology can be discerned here to a degree unavailable elsewhere. The official biography—almost a hagiography—is no help: Robert Gannon, *The Cardinal Spellman Story* (Garden City, N.Y., 1962).

27. Cooney, *American Pope*, 37–38.

in order to further, as he conceived it, the ultimate triumph of the Catholic Church in this world and the next.

Nor should it be assumed that Spellman during his Roman days had earned the regard of his ecclesiastical superiors only by trivial pursuits. One indication of the increasingly substantive role he was beginning to play in church affairs was the abiding friendship he formed with the cerebral and deeply spiritual Eugenio Cardinal Pacelli, Gasparri's successor as secretary of state. Pacelli appreciated Spellman's practical acumen, while Spellman valued what he considered the cardinal's broad sense of the universality of the Church; most curial officials, he said impatiently (and in private), were bogged down in Italian parochialism. But the most spectacular testimony to the trust the highest officials placed in Spellman came in the summer of 1931, and it involved that very parochialism. Pope Pius XI, vexed by Mussolini's harassment of various Catholic organizations in Italy, wrote a stinging rebuke of the Fascist regime in the encyclical *Non abbiamo bisogno*. The document was remarkable simply for having been written in the vernacular, which, however, also suggested that it would have been imprudent to have it published in Italy. Francis Spellman was commissioned to take the text secretly to Paris, publish it there and arrange for translations, which he did with panache.[28]

JOHN GREGORY MURRAY ALSO KNEW THE BRADYS, BUT HIS relationship with them was very different from Spellman's, as indeed the two priests were cut from very different cloth. Educated in Louvain, not in Rome, Murray never manifested the personal devotion to *romanità* that characterized Spellman (and Cardinal O'Connell). To be sure, his relations with the Roman curia were always proper and dutiful, but they remained formal and even a little remote. He seldom visited Rome, and through his long tenure in St. Paul he rarely sent priests there for advanced studies. Without for a moment challenging the pope's universal jurisdiction, Murray manifested perhaps a hint of Belgian Gallicanism.[29] He had no taste at any rate for the Roman

---

28. Cooney, *American Pope*, 42–44. The English text of *Non abbiamo bisogno* is readily available on the Internet. The pope was particularly hurt and angry, because only two years earlier, in 1929, the church-state stand-off prevailing since 1870 had apparently been settled by the famous Lateran Treaties.

29. During the nineteenth century the "Gallicans" were those Catholics who wanted to curtail the increase of centralization in the Catholic Church's governance, while the "ultramontanes" were those who wanted to further it. The First Vatican Council (1869–1870) appeared to settle the matter in favor of the ultramontanes.

camaraderie with its intricate network of clerical alliances that was lifeblood to Spellman.

Genevieve Brady was not a complicated person. Tall, stout, and plain-faced, she was good-hearted and pious and very rich, but despite all her worldly advantages she was also childless, and this circumstance seemed to spur her on to many benefactions. Especially after her husband's death, she came increasingly to look upon Murray as a confidant, counselor, and friend. Whenever and wherever they had first met—Hartford, perhaps, or Newport—by the late 1920s a mutual sympathy had been firmly established. "Dear Archbishop Murray," she wrote from shipboard on her way to Rome,

> I hope you received my wire. I wanted you to know immediately how grateful I was for the thought which prompted those beautiful roses. You are always so kind to me. I have been thinking a lot about you and praying for your health too. You know how much you mean to me, Archbishop Murray. You and Nell and Agnes[30] seem to be all my world just now. All I have left.

"There are 51 priests aboard," she added, "going over for the jubilee of the [North] American College. . . . So we have Mass from 5:30 till noon."[31]

The bouquet of roses she received from Murray as she boarded the ship was in tune with the courtly, old-world manners with which he always treated her. On this occasion, however, she had already revealed her own solicitude for him. "I am afraid," she wrote from her house at 910 Fifth Avenue, "you might be thinking of coming on before I sail. You must not, because I know how busy you are."[32] But other bouquets came to her too, for instance on her name day (the feast of Ste. Genevieve, January 3): "How very kind you were to me during the holiday season. The lovely flowers at [illegible] and then the beautiful red roses over the feast of St. Genevieve. Thank you, dear Archbishop, for your many thoughts of me."[33] He remembered her too in her sor-

---

30. Mrs. Agnes Garvan Cavanaugh of East Norwalk, Connecticut. See *New York Herald Tribune*, January 29, 1941. "Nell," though mentioned frequently in this correspondence, is otherwise unidentified.

31. Genevieve Brady to Murray, May 16 [1932], AASPM, Murray Papers.

32. Genevieve Brady to Murray, n.d. [late April, 1932], AASPM, Murray Papers.

33. Genevieve Brady to Murray, n.d. [January 1933], AASPM, Murray Papers. The illegible word in the text was the name of the "novitiate" where Mrs. Brady had made a pre-Christmas retreat.

rowing widowhood: "Thank you for your wire on Nick's name-day [the feast of St. Nicholas, December 6]. You are always so thoughtful."[34] Again on shipboard on a later occasion she found consolation in Murray's remembrance of happier times:

> We have had a good trip and are now in the blue Mediterranean, expecting to land tomorrow. Thank you, Archbishop Murray, for the beautiful red roses and for your Mass on the 27th. I feel Nick and Cardinal Bonzano are always so near us. . . . Thank you for your goodness and for all you do to guide me. I would be in such a different frame of mind if it weren't for your help, Archbishop Murray.[35]

Mrs. Brady seldom alluded to her health—a short bout with the flu now and then—but she fussed over Murray's, constantly chiding him for working too hard. When his sister underwent surgery, she wrote from Fifth Avenue: "How are you feeling? Was the strain too much for you?"[36] Even when he protested that he felt well, she remained unconvinced. "Thank you for your letter about your health," she wrote again from her New York town house. "I am glad things were not quite so serious. I am afraid we will have to talk about *you* a little when you come [here later in the month]."[37] In the summer of 1933 she tried to persuade him to join her in Rome and then accompany her to the celebrated health spa at Carlsbad on the Czech-German frontier. The idea apparently did not appeal to the archbishop. "Of course I am terribly disappointed about your not coming to Carlsbad. I do feel you need it so badly. What about later in the summer[;] even if I am not there you could really have a cure."[38] What ailment the waters of Carlsbad were intended to alleviate is unclear.

When in residence at the Casa del Sole, and even after husband's death, Genevieve kept in touch with powerful personages in the Vatican. "I have been in Rome three days," she told Murray in the spring of 1932,

---

34. Genevieve Brady to Murray, n.d. [December 1932], AASPM, Murray Papers.

35. Genevieve Brady to Murray, n.d. [Spring 1933], AASPM, Murray Papers.

36. Genevieve Brady to Murray, n.d. [1933?]. AASPM, Murray Papers. For the only time in this correspondence did she invoke her privileges as a Duchess; she signed the letter, "Affectionately, Excellenza," a misspelling for the Italian "Eccellenza."

37. Genevieve Brady to Murray, n.d. [1934?], AASPM, Murray Papers.

38. Genevieve Brady to Murray, June 18 [1933], AASPM, Murray Papers.

and am so happy to be here. Everything is serene, and yesterday Cardinal Gasparri celebrated his 80th birthday. It was quite a day, at six o'clock a Te Deum was sung in San Lorenzo, his titular church. In the evening I had a little birthday dinner for him. Besides the Cardinal and Monsignor Beruarduici, Cardinal Pacelli came, as also the nuncio [to Italy] and Archbishop [Giuseppe] Pizzardo and two other monsignori. . . . It was very colorful, and I know they had a good time. They are like children, so easily pleased.[39]

Nor was Archbishop Murray the only man whose state of health worried her. "None of my friends seem to care for themselves. Cardinal Pacelli is working so hard and really looks so frail. He has been wonderful to us this year. We go to his Mass about twice a week, and he has come over to dinner with us so simply."[40] She fretted also over "Father Frank," though with somewhat less warmth. "I do not believe Spellman will be here much longer. There are many rumors." This tidbit she shared with Murray from Rome in early May, but from Carlsbad, on July 27, she suggested another scenario. "I am afraid they are going to keep Dr. Spellman in Rome for a while yet. The Holy Father seems to think he needs him so much. I think it is a great disappointment to Monsignor [Spellman]. He is all worn out since the [Eucharistic] Congress [in Dublin]. I am afraid he will have a nervous breakdown."[41] But Spellman himself, nervous or not, knew better; the man who had smuggled *Non abbiamo bisogno* out of Italy was not to be denied. Two days before, on July 25, 1932, Pacelli informed him that he had been appointed auxiliary bishop of Boston. At this news the American colony in Rome, Mrs. Brady among them, proved more than ready to cheer the pope's decision. Over the days before his episcopal consecration at St. Peter's on September 8, Spellman, now aged forty-three, lodged at the Casa del Sole, where a spiritual counselor came regularly to direct his meditations.[42] And the following spring, Pius XI gave the new bishop a glowing testimonial: "The Holy Father spoke so beautifully of Bishop Spellman at our audience. He said he personally loved him."[43]

---

39. Genevieve Brady to Murray, May 5 [1932], AASPM, Murray Papers.

40. Genevieve Brady to Murray, June 18 [1933], AASPM, Murray Papers.

41. Genevieve Brady to Murray, May 5 and July 27 [1932], AASPM, Murray Papers.

42. Cooney, *American Pope*, 54–55.

43. Genevieve Brady to Murray, June 18 [1833], AASPM, Murray Papers.

What role John Gregory Murray played in assisting Francis Spellman to secure the miter cannot be stated with precision. But by the latter's own acknowledgment it was not negligible, and it perhaps helps to explain that visit to Murray's deathbed in 1956. "My dear Friend," he wrote,

> Cardinal Pacelli has informed me that the Holy Father has named me Auxiliary Bishop of Boston.
>
> I want to thank you from the bottom of my heart for all of your great kindness to me. I shall never forget your goodness, and I shall never cease to be grateful.
>
> I have made no plans, and I shall make none. I shall leave the decisions about the place and time of consecration to my superiors.
>
> In the meantime I commend myself to your prayers that I may not fall too far short of what the Church and my superiors and friends expect of me.
>
> Affectionately yours, Frank Spellman.[44]

When Murray telegraphed his congratulations, Spellman replied in the same almost obsequious tone as before, and in doing so offered a tantalizing hint as to why he should have felt so much gratitude.

> I am so grateful for your telegram. I wrote you at once to tell you of my appreciation for this nomination, and to express my recognition of my indebtedness to you. I shall never forget your kind trip to Boston when you had so much to do. I should be delighted to have you at the consecration, but I know that is impossible. I hope to see you soon after my return.
>
> Devotedly, Frank Spellman.[45]

One wonders about the purport of Murray's "kind trip to Boston" when indeed he "had so much to do," settling into his new duties in St. Paul. But even before Spellman's promotion some New England–Roman intrigue appeared to be afoot. During the spring of 1932, two sees in O'Connell's Boston province were open, Portland and Manchester, New Hampshire. On May 5, when she wrote Murray about the Roman "rumors" regarding Spellman, Mrs.

---

44. Spellman to Murray, n.d. [late July, 1932], AASPM, Murray Papers.

45. Spellman to Murray, n.d. [before September 8, 1932], AASPM, Murray Papers.

Brady had added, "What do you think of the Bishop of Portland and also of Manchester? Just announced here." A Boston auxiliary had been appointed to Manchester and a priest from Hartford—an old friend of Murray—to Portland. Four days later, at the end of a letter dealing with minor administrative matters (informing the new archbishop that certain canonical faculties had been granted and arranging for the conferral of the pallium[46] *in absentia*), Spellman spoke again of his indebtedness to Murray.

> I can never thank you enough for what you said to the [Apostolic] Delegate. At least the first part of the affair, the Bishop of Manchester, seems to be going through. Of course I do not know how His Eminence [O'Connell] will regard the second part, but whatever happens will be tremendously interesting, at any rate.
>
> I shall be glad to see a Hartford man going to Portland. I do not know how long it will be before the nominations are made, but it will not be very many more days at any rate.
>
> Thanks from the very depths of my heart for everything.
>
> Affectionately, Frank Spellman.[47]

A trip to Boston and a word to the apostolic delegate. Murray, during his six years in Portland, had been O'Connell's suffragan and knew well that man's turbulent temperament. He knew too the cardinal's intense dislike of Spellman. As treasurer of the National Catholic Welfare Conference,[48] Murray routinely visited Washington and so had occasion to encounter the delegate, Fumasoni-Biondi, who had his own part to play in the appointment of American bishops. The full picture of all these maneuverings can never be known, partly because of John Gregory Murray's habitual caution and reticence.[49] It may have seemed in any case ironic that for all the "indebtedness" Spellman may have felt he owed the archbishop of St. Paul for his elevation, he spent seven miserable years under the sway of the hostile O'Connell. But he was patient, and his reward came in due course. Eugenio Pacelli was elected Pope Pius XII March 2, 1939; six weeks later Francis Spellman learned that he had

---

46. A strip of lamb's cloth worn around the neck, which symbolizes an archbishop's status. The conferral by the pope need not be in person.

47. Spellman to Murray, May 9, 1932, AASPM, Murray Papers.

48. See chapter 20, below.

49. In the Archives of the Archdiocese of St. Paul-Minneapolis there are no copies of Murray's own correspondence with the Bradys, Spellman, or Fulton Sheen.

been promoted to the great see of New York, vacant since the preceding September. In his triumph he was gracious to his old benefactor. "Dear Archbishop Murray," he wrote,

> I am so grateful for your letter. I shall depend on you so much for many things. *But I do not want you to go to all that trouble to come to the installation.* I shall take the will for the deed, and I know what the will is. *So please spare your health and energy for the Church and also for me.*
>
> Devotedly, † F. J. Spellman.[50]

Seventeen years later he was gracious again.

GENEVIEVE BRADY DID NOT RESTRICT HER MORAL AND FINANCIAL largesse only to clerics of high station. She was particularly generous to one who would not attain episcopal rank till long after her death, but who would nevertheless rival Cardinal Spellman—though in a very different way—for influence among American Catholics at the middle of the twentieth century.[51] "Archbishop Murray," she wrote from Rome, "I do wish you could give Dr. Sheen a few moments some time. I think it would help him tremendously and perhaps be a little help to you. This is my own suggestion, not his."[52] Born in 1895—and thus six years Spellman's junior—Fulton John Sheen was ordained for the diocese of Peoria in 1919, after studying theology at the St. Paul Seminary: "The food was meager, and I developed an ulcer which required an operation. The courses were extremely good."[53] He was sent for further studies first to the Catholic University in Washington where he made another St. Paul contact: "Some of the teachers were excellent, . . . such as the famous Dr. John A. Ryan, who was a leader in this country in the field of social ethics."[54] After that he went to Louvain where he earned a doctorate in 1923.[55]

Upon his return from Belgium Father Sheen spent a year in a slum parish in Peoria, and then he was assigned to the School of Theology in the Catholic

---

50. Spellman to Murray, May 15, 1939. The installation took place on May 23.

51. The two men eventually became alienated. See Myles P. Murphy, *The Life and Times of Archbishop Fulton J. Sheen* (New York, 2000), 84–88.

52. Genevieve Brady to Murray, n.d. [early 1932], AASPM, Murray Papers.

53. Fulton J. Sheen, *Treasure in Clay* (New York, 1980), 20. This is Sheen's embarrassingly self-serving and sentimental autobiography.

54. Sheen, *Treasure*, 22.

55. Kathleen L. Riley, *Fulton J. Sheen: An American Catholic Response to the Twentieth Century* (n.p. [New York], 2004), 3–11.

University. It did not prove to be an altogether comfortable fit. From the first, Sheen's most remarkable gift was a kind of mellow eloquence which enjoyed a very wide appeal. Handsome and urbane, blessed with a rich and melodious voice, he quickly became in great demand as a preacher, and the books he wrote, even as a young man, displayed the same combination of wit, polish, verbal dexterity, and warm spirituality so effective in his sermons. He had a knack for choosing the right metaphor, the appropriate anecdote, the telling piece of arcane information to make his point persuasively. Sheen nourished these talents with ever increasing success, until in the 1950s he achieved the extraordinary feat of television stardom, along with the likes of contemporaries Sid Caesar and Milton Berle. His was a species of high religious populism which won the hearts of millions, including that of Mrs. Nicholas Brady.

Not so among his colleagues at the Catholic University. That institution, hardly more than thirty years old in 1920, was still struggling for intellectual respectability, for administrative coherence, and, particularly, for reliable financial support. Sheen's popularity did not appear to redound much to the university's benefit. It was widely suspected, moreover, that Sheen's frequent absences from campus left him scant time and energy to teach his courses properly. Though he "has the best will in the world," observed the rector in September 1931, "[Sheen] has become so accustomed to the feverish life of a public speaker that it is going to be extremely difficult to tie him down to the more or less drudgery of preparing men for the kind of work he is doing [in the classroom]." Sheen for his part claimed, unconvincingly, that his candor had entangled him in a nest of squabbling academics.[56] He also more than hinted that criticism of him sprang from jealousy of his notoriety rather than from any dereliction on his part. John A. Ryan, ever ready with an acerbic retort, brushed this contention aside: "The charges of jealousy etc. all emanated from Dr. Sheen's vivid imagination."[57]

This tense situation reached its climax during the tumultuous spring of 1932. By that time Sheen was a familiar in Genevieve Brady's household, whether in New York or in Rome. That good lady was upset at the toll the simmering dispute was exacting on her protégé, even if she didn't fully understand the academic circumstances. "Dr. Sheen has been ill in St. Vincent's for a week," she wrote Murray from Fifth Avenue early in the year. "I suppose

---

56. See Sheen, *Treasure*, 42–47 on the faculty quarrels, and 51–54 on his teaching. He claims that he spent six hours to prepare one class lecture.

57. See Riley, *Sheen*, 12–17, quotations 15.

the University will put him off the faculty if he gets sick again. Poor man." And then she added, significantly, "Monsignor Beruarduici[58] was in New York over last weekend."[59] Significant, because Mrs. Brady ultimately decided that this official in the Roman curia—and a frequent dinner guest at the Casa del Sole—was the *bête noire* in what she conceived to be the persecution of Fulton Sheen. As she explained to Murray at length:

> Father Sheen was here [in Rome] for a week. I have had my talk with Archbishop Beruarduici. Of course a point of view makes such a difference. I do not think he gives Father Sheen any spiritual motives at all. He says his [Sheen's] preaching is getting poor and he needs more professional study. What do you think?

But had the wily Italian already undermined the possibility of Murray's beneficial intervention?

> B. said that you said you could not finish anything Dr. Sheen wrote or listen to the end of his talks. I am sure that is a little exaggerated. Dr. Sheen is coming to talk over his plans for the future with you and says he will take your advice. You see, B. spoke to him here. I had him [Sheen] meet Card. Pacelli here at dinner and then talk quite a little with the Cardinal. He [Pacelli] said his first duty was to his classes. That if he felt he conscientiously prepared his class work, then he should go on preaching. You see, Cardinal Pacelli likes preaching himself and so appreciates what good can be done. They have all heard of Dr. Sheen's preaching here. Of course the Cardinal said no one should preach without much preparation. You see, B. advised Sheen not to preach at all for a year.
>
> I am telling you all this so you will know why Dr. Sheen is coming to you for advice. I think B. is very hard on him and does not understand him at all. I have prayed so hard over it all as it seems just wrong to lose such a preacher, but I do know he (Dr. S.) is doing too much. If he was only in an order where he had a spiritual superior. James Ryan [rector of Catholic University] does not seem the right superior for a man like Dr. Sheen.[60]

---

58. I have been unable to identify this individual. Neither Sheen's own autobiography nor any of his biographers mention him. But then they don't mention Mrs. Brady either.

59. Genevieve Brady to Murray, n.d. [early 1932], AASPM, Murray Papers.

60. Genevieve Brady to Murray, n.d. [March, 1932?], AASPM, Murray Papers.

It may well have been that Archbishop Murray found Sheen's rather cloy-ing style not to his taste, but it is just as likely that he disapproved of a Roman bureaucrat appointing himself spiritual director to a young American priest. Sheen at any rate was ready to follow Mrs. Brady's advice. "Your Grace," he wrote Murray in mid-April 1932, "last evening I was in New York to bid au re-voir to Mrs. Brady before she sailed for Rome, and in the course of our con-versation I mentioned a problem concerning me at the present time, and for the solution of which I am appealing to you." The "problem" had nothing to do with Beruarduici, whose opinions apparently bothered Sheen much less than they did Mrs. Brady. "During the past week the University tabled all pro-motions, mine included. . . . Despite the fact that I have been here for six years, and have written six books since being affiliated with the University, the promotion was indefinitely postponed." A few days ago, he went on, a top administrator "asked me to go through the country for a week, interviewing bishops in an endeavor to interest them in the University. In answer I told him the relationship between University and professor should be reciprocal, and if the University thought me worthy to present their [sic] case, they should have given me recognition of the work I have already accomplished."

The official responded sharply in writing, and Sheen quoted him: "'It is my firm conviction that your ecclesiastical future will depend not merely upon your personal qualities, . . . nor by the special gifts of training which en-able you to tower over most of the priests of this country, but whether or no you become "an organization man." . . . I have no doubt but what your influ-ence in your ecclesiastical circles some day will not be dependent upon your gifts of mind and of voice. Most geniuses have been rather erratic and, in common parlance, have not known how to "play ball" with others.'" Sheen went on:

> My problem, Your Grace, is this: I do not wish to offend the authorities of the University by refusing to become what they call an organization man, and yet I do not want to have any success which has been mine turned into a "racket," even though it would mean something for my ecclesiasti-cal future. I have always thought that ecclesiastical futures were deter-mined by the Providence of God, and now I learn that they are deter-mined by "playing ball" with the organization.

It is hardly surprising that the university wished to use Sheen's already con-siderable influence and popularity—he had begun his successful radio broadcasts in 1928[61]—as a tool for raising money. But the rising star was not in an accommodating mood. "In all confidence, I tell you that I could not work up sufficient enthusiasm for certain departments as they are presently conducted. And even though I could, I wish to keep my priestly and academic life clear from all tinge of commercialism."[62]

Murray's counsel, evidently that Sheen should use his fabled charm to lessen the tension, "I have followed to the letter, and there has been a general good understanding all around. I have been freed from taking on any more obligations without in any way having my loyalty doubted." The archbishop also sent a check to help defray the expenses of the house in which Sheen now lived. "Your Excellency, I am overwhelmed. I know you do not care for profuse thanks, but please believe me when I say that I shall breathe them daily in prayer. . . . May God reward you. Thanks. Thanks. Thanks." He concluded with one of those verbal ornaments for which he became famous and which—if Archbishop Beruarduici was correct—Murray himself found distasteful: "Last week I received one of the most-desired gifts of my life: the privilege of reserving the Blessed Sacrament. The Guest has arrived, and the Guest is the Host! I am so very happy."[63]

The International Eucharistic Congress in Dublin, June 21–26, 1932, briefly brought together all the principals in this story. "Mrs. Brady tells me you are to be in Dublin," Frank Spellman wrote Murray, "and I am so pleased, because I will be there too."[64] And Fulton Sheen: "I am sailing for the Congress on [June] 7th and will go almost immediately to Dublin where I shall stay with Mrs. Brady. On the 25th of June I am to read a paper, 'Calvary on Irish Altars,' at the American section."[65] It must have been a particularly happy occasion for Genevieve Brady, though Archbishop Murray stayed only for a few days. And a month later, the pious euphoria having passed, she was still worrying about Sheen.

Bishop Murray, will you be a good friend to Dr. Sheen. He needs an older priest so much, I think. You already are such a good friend[;] how wonderful your counsel would be. He has just finished his six day retreat at Lourdes and is now in Belgium, but sailing on the Leviathan July 30th.

61. Sheen, *Treasure*, 63.
62. Sheen to Murray, April 20, 1932, AASPM, Murray Papers.
63. Sheen to Murray, May 16, 1932, AASPM, Murray Papers.
64. Spellman to Murray, May 9, 1932, AASPM, Murray Papers.
65. Sheen to Murray, May 16, 1932, AASPM, Murray Papers.

He is so wonderful, it would be a shame if he was not guided right. Do please, dear Bishop, be a friend to him. He does not know I feel this way.[66]

But Fulton John Sheen now stood on the cusp of a spectacular career which had a guidance system all its own.

IN 1936 EUGENIO CARDINAL PACELLI, VATICAN SECRETARY OF state, journeyed for the first and only time to the United States. He conferred with President Roosevelt at Hyde Park and then took a tour of Catholic centers around the country, including St. Paul. Archbishop Murray's contribution to the marked success of the visit was considerable, as the cardinal readily acknowledged.

The airplane trip which Your Excellency so thoughtfully and generously organized and provided for me has now been happily completed, but I wish to assure Your Excellency that it will always remain for me a pleasant memory. It really seems incredible that I could have seen so many places of such long distances apart and so many of the great natural beauties of the United States in such a short space of time.[67]

At Pacelli's side throughout the trip was, predictably, the auxiliary bishop of Boston, Francis Spellman. Murray was invited too, but, aloof as always, he "felt compelled to remain" in Minnesota in order to honor prior commitments.[68] One who saw the cardinal only for a fleeting moment was Genevieve Brady. She was bitterly disappointed, because she had assumed that the distinguished visitor, who was an old friend, would spend goodly time at her Long Island estate. She put the blame that he did not do so squarely on Spellman, whether fairly or not, and she never forgave him.[69] The coolness persisted till her death two years later when, instead of the $100,000 he had expected from her will, Spellman received nothing.[70]

---

66. Genevieve Brady to Murray, July 27 [1932], AASPM, Murray Papers. This letter was written from the health spa in Carlsbad.

67. Pacelli to Murray, November 5, 1936, AASPM, Murray Papers.

68. *CB*, March 4, 1939. Murray's refusal was thus made public shortly after Pacelli was elected Pope Pius XII.

69. Cooney, *American Pope*, 64–71, especially 67–69.

70. Cooney, *American Pope*, 330.

There is another possible explanation, or rather one which if true would have intensified the lady's antipathy. There is no documentation to sustain it, but taking into account the personalities of the persons involved, it is not incredible. At the time of Cardinal Pacelli's visit to America, Genevieve Brady was in love. The object of her affection was William J. Babington Macaulay, Irish minister to the Holy See. He was many years her junior. Spellman, fearful that this interloper would drain away the Brady fortune, made strenuous efforts to prevent a marriage. But when Genevieve asked Murray for advice, he told her to follow her heart.[71] So she did; she married Macaulay in 1937, and the next year, on November 24, she died in Rome. The net worth of her estate was $6,300,000, an enormous sum in the midst of the Great Depression. Macaulay, as Spellman had feared, inherited the lion's share, but more than $1,700,000 went to Catholic organizations, charities, and individuals. Pacelli and Sheen each received $68,824, John Gregory Murray $172,061.[72]

Spellman bore no ill will. "'Shocked' is no word to describe my emotions in learning of Mrs. Brady's [sic] death. . . . *She was one great person.* No one meant any more in my life than did she."[73] And even when he was excluded from the will, he put a good face upon it. "Hearty congratulations," he wrote Murray, "on receiving such a splendid remembrance. I am glad, in fact delighted, that you received it. I thought the will was wonderful. No other Catholic to my knowledge ever did so much good. May God bless and reward them both."[74]

And no doubt they were both remembered, Nicholas and Genevieve, during that last conversation between Francis Spellman and John Gregory Murray.

---

71. Interview with the late Msgr. Florence D. Cohalan, author of *A Popular History of the Archdiocese of New York* (Yonkers, N.Y., 1983).

72. *New York Herald Tribune,* January 29, 1941. The odd figures reflect the fact that the inheritances were in the form of securities.

73. Spellman to Murray, n.d. [November 1938], AASPM, Murray Papers.

74. Spellman to Murray, n.d. [January 1939], AASPM, Murray Papers.

CHAPTER 20

Hard Times

W. H. AUDEN CALLED IT "A LOW, DISHONEST DECADE." WHAT THE poet had in mind were the machinations of European politicians—some of them malevolent, some merely weak and indecisive—that led to the cataclysm of the Second World War. The poem was titled "September 1, 1939," commemorative of the day German panzers crossed the Polish frontier. For Americans, enclosed and, it was taken for granted, protected by two oceans, the events of the 1930s abroad—the savage civil war in Spain, the Italian aggression against Abyssinia, the calculated murder of millions of Ukrainian peasants by the Stalinist regime in Russia, the rearmament of Germany under the aegis of the racist Nazis, the rape of Nanking by the Japanese—all seemed far away, psychically as well as geographically. For Americans had profound worries of their own. Economic downturns had occurred before, many times, but nothing in the past matched the disasters that followed upon the stock market crash of October 1929. The boisterous and relatively prosperous 1920s gave way to a time of bleak prospects and, in many cases, utter despair. The decade in the United States may not have been "dishonest" in Auden's sense, but it was most certainly "low." The new president, elected in 1932, introduced a plethora of programs that mitigated the worst effects of the Great Depression, and insisted with remarkable eloquence that "the only thing we have to fear is fear itself." Yet, though the flurry of New Deal legislation staved off the dissolution of the economic system that many had predicted, in fact the malaise of mass unemployment, soup kitchens, bank closings, violent labor unrest—exacerbated by dust bowl drought in the middle of the country—did not end until, ironically, the United States was drawn into the war Auden had both celebrated and deplored in his poem.

The suddenness with which the Great Depression fell upon the American people was dizzying. No element of society was spared, except perhaps motion picture stars or the likes of Mr. and Mrs. Nicholas Brady—and many people even in that lofty status became paupers almost overnight. In Minnesota, agriculture, still the most important statewide industry, felt the catastrophe almost at once. Between 1929 and 1932, prices for farm goods fell drastically. Income declined by sixty percent. Farmers became desperate to meet their obligations, to pay their taxes as well as interest and principal for loans on land and machinery—desperate enough, in many cases, to promote nonproductive "holidays," withholding, that is, primary commodities from the market in hopes of securing a better price. Nor was this strategy enough to prevent violent protests. But credit dried up anyway, and foreclosure loomed for many unable to meet payment on mortgages; in 1933 sixty of every thousand farm families filed for bankruptcy. The statistics, however, cannot themselves chronicle adequately the rural distress. Development of domestic and commercial electricity and indoor plumbing, by now more or less commonplace in the towns, was put off for most of the decade even in relatively well-off farming areas. Mining on the Iron Range, the staple of the economy in the northeastern part of the state, recorded an overall decline in production (and profits and jobs) of thirty-six percent over the decade; in 1932 the great digs in Hibbing and Chisholm virtually shut down. The human costs of this decline to ordinary workers in terms not so much of comfort as of survival can be measured only with difficulty seven decades afterward. The same could be said for those whose livelihoods depended upon the vigor of the manufacturing sector; but the catastrophic decline in the demand for farm machinery, road-building equipment, and overall heavy construction meant that the workers in such industries faced an increasingly perilous situation. Firms that hired such employees were very heavily hit. In 1931 sixty-one percent of such companies reported losses; a year later the figure had risen to eighty-six percent.

One in four employable men was without a job, with the result that the wages of those who did find work—always fearful of being laid off—were kept appallingly low. The unionization that had flourished at the beginning of the century languished during the 1920s, when technological advances and the tendency of business interests to coalesce into distinct pressure groups— like the Citizens' Alliance in Minneapolis, for example, an almost sinister organization of bankers and employers dedicated to maintain at all costs the principle of the open shop[1]—combined to render some workers redundant

---

1. See William Millikan, "Maintaining Law and Order: The Minneapolis Citizens' Alliance in the 1920s," *Minnesota History* 51 (Summer 1989): 219–233.

and others frightened into acquiescence because resistance to the bosses might thrust them and their families into penury. The overarching workers' organization, the American Federation of Labor, had come to have only a tangential effect on these economic realities; the decline in its membership was calamitous and, anyway, it traditionally represented the kind of skilled craftsmen whom the modern assembly-line industry had less need of.[2]

The universal distress caused by the Depression changed the ground rules, and Minnesota was in the forefront of a profound transformation of economic and political relationships throughout the country. In November 1933, the workers at the George A. Hormel meatpacking plant in Austin, after long, agonizing, and fruitless negotiations with management, simply took over the premises and occupied it for three days, staging the first sit-down strike of the era. They had been careful beforehand, however, to garner local support. Certainly, "If you don't like [your pay and working conditions] you can quit. There are fifty guys across the tracks waiting to take your job for less than you are being paid." But there was another side to the coin: "How can a merchant expect a man to walk into his store and buy when he is making only $10 a week?" No mere rhetorical question was this to the small businessmen essential to the functioning of the economy in this southern Minnesota town. The strategy succeeded, and in the end Hormel—the creators of that famous Depression and World War II delicacy called Spam—granted its workers an increase in wage from three to five cents an hour.

The real test, however, came the following year in Minneapolis, a noto-riously anti-union city—"scab town" as some bitterly labeled it.[3] Teamsters Local 574 was formally associated with the AFL, but its leadership was far more radical than that of the national body. Such was hardly a surprise, since, while wage increases for industrial and manual labor across the nation during the 1920s had averaged eleven percent, the figure for Minneapolis workers stood at barely two percent. Following the model adopted by the meatpackers in Austin, the Minneapolis truck drivers cultivated support among the local

---

2. See David L. Nass, "The Rural Experience"; D. Jerome Tweton, "The Business of Agriculture"; Ronald A. Alanen, "Years of Change on the Iron Range"; Kirk Jeffrey, "The Major Manufacturers"; John E. Haynes, "Reformers, Radicals and Conservatives," in Clifford E. Clark Jr., ed., *Minnesota in a Century of Change* (St. Paul, 1989), 144–145, 263, 158, 238, 375–377.

3. For an overview of the teamsters' strike of 1934, see Irving Bernstein, *Turbulent Years* (Boston, 1970), 217–317; Arthur Schlesinger, Jr., *The Coming of the New Deal* (Boston, 1958), 385–396; and Thomas E. Blantz, *A Priest in Public Service: Francis J. Haas and the New Deal* (Notre Dame, Ind., 1982), 107–124.

population—relatively easy to do, since almost everybody was enduring some level of economic misery—even as they significantly increased their numbers by recruiting into their union workers from auxiliary occupations, from loading docks, that is, and warehouses, taxi fleets, and delivery services of various kinds.

This show of muscle had an exhilarating effect upon other, largely dormant unions, and it gave heart to the legion of men who had no jobs at all, and to their harried wives as well. So when the teamsters' inevitable confrontation with the bankers and employers who made up the Citizens' Alliance came in the spring and summer of 1934, the two sides were not unevenly matched. A strike in May—over the usual problems, to be sure, of wages and working conditions, but also and perhaps more elemental over contractual recognition of the union and the closed shop—quickly turned ugly; a gunfight in downtown Minneapolis left two police officers dead. Two months later a wider strike stoked up hotter feelings, and on July 24 the police fired on a truckload of unarmed pickets, killing two and wounding dozens. This violence assured a teamsters' victory, because it aroused widespread public revulsion—as many as 100,000 people marched in the funeral procession of one of the dead strikers—and because it necessitated the direct intervention of the state and federal governments, both inclined to support the workers' basic demands. President Roosevelt and Governor Olson were very much in tune with one another.[4] By the time the strike ended, after fifty-six days, four people had been killed, hundreds injured, and all told it had cost the city $50,000,000. But from then on Minneapolis was a different kind of place,[5] as indeed were Minnesota and the nation at large.

DURING THE WHOLE STRESSFUL TIME OF THE TEAMSTERS' STRIKE one of the two arbitrators, dispatched from Washington by the newly created National Labor Board, was Francis J. Haas. Haas, a forty-five-year-old priest who had come to Minneapolis directly after having performed similar mediation duty during a strike against the utility companies in his home town of Milwaukee, was director of the National Catholic School of Social Service, affiliated with the Catholic University. More to the point, Father Haas—a big,

---

4. See Peter Rachleff, "Turning Points in the Labor Movement," in Clark, *Minnesota Change*, 206–210.

5. See Raymond L. Koch, "Politics and Relief in Minneapolis during the 1930s," *Minnesota History* 41 (Winter 1968): 153–170.

stocky man whose smile had a steely glint to it—had been appointed a member of the Labor Board precisely because he was a fervent follower of John A. Ryan. He represented the new generation of social activists that Ryan and his colleagues at the university had trained and inspired and that the Roosevelt administration found especially useful. So it appeared that Ryan's influence came home once more, so to speak, in the person of this articulate and strong-willed disciple.[6]

Indeed, the dire circumstances of the time gave a new relevance and impetus to Monsignor Ryan's clarion call for economic reform, raised throughout the 1920s and echoing the refrain he had heard round his father's kitchen table in Vermillion township so long before that.[7] As the prophet Jeremiah of old rebuked the hard-headed Israelites whose apostasy had brought them defeat and exile, so Ryan excoriated the élites—"the economic royalists," in Roosevelt's telling phrase—who had committed a secular apostasy by refusing, at immense human cost, to acknowledge the obvious failures of the current economic system. Twelve million unemployed, and six million with only part-time jobs, showed, he said in a speech in New York, how "desperate" the situation had become.[8] And the desperation could not be measured simply in terms of dollars and cents. Think of the mental anguish, he argued, think of the permanent damage done to the character of men who "face another day of worry, monotony, and blasted hopes. Such has been their life day after day, night after night, these two years and more." Five hundred thousand boys "are roaming the country, qualifying themselves for enrollment in the army of bums, tramps, and vagrants." The financial system had collapsed, and Catholics who denounced government intervention as socialism should bear in mind that "thousands of our churches and parochial schools are in imminent danger of bankruptcy." This courting of catastrophe is unnecessary, he continued: within the United States physical and human resources abound, hampered only "by the greed of the few." The business community remains "intellectually bankrupt," maintaining in the face of all the evidence that a balanced federal budget will solve the problem. On the contrary, a "massive program of public works, six to eight billion dollars worth," must be pumped

---

6. In addition to Blantz, *Haas,* see, in synopsis, Thomas E. Blantz, "Father Haas and the Minneapolis Truckers' Strike of 1934," *Minnesota History* 42 (Spring 1970): 5–15 (with its enthralling illustrations).

7. See chapter 17, above.

8. It should be noted that these unemployment figures occurred within a population of about 120,000,000.

into the economy. Any cutbacks in government spending (aside from the elimination of waste) "will not only destroy useful public services but [also] reduce purchasing power and the demand for goods."[9]

It need hardly be said that this manifesto, like many others in subsequent years, though it dealt explicitly with an economic state of affairs, reflected also a political—indeed, a partisan—point of view. Ryan remained, to be sure, canonically a priest of the archdiocese of St. Paul; but as a professor in far-off Washington, D.C., and someone viewed widely as a resourceful and eloquent tribune of the masses at a time of deep and almost universal discontent, he enjoyed a remarkable measure of independence in expressing his opinions. This was a luxury not available to administrators, clerical or otherwise, *en scène*. Back in Minnesota, John Gregory Murray, who stood as an obvious representative of the lower middle-class status typical of the second generation of Irish Catholic immigrants, could not but sympathize with Monsignor Ryan's passionate indictment of the malevolent greed of the traditional élites. But he, Murray, also appreciated the fact that Minnesota, until the recent and spectacular emergence of the populist Farmer-Labor movement, had been a conservative and Republican stronghold. In contrast to a gadfly like Ryan, the archbishop needed to tend to the spiritual needs of all the local Church's members, whatever their class or partisan persuasion. Moreover, even the slightest perception of political interference by Catholic priests could stoke the fires of the lingering nativism so evident during the presidential campaign of 1928. And so Murray, in the first year of his administration, dispatched a strong ukase to his clergy. No political discussion, he wrote, was to be held on church property, because "complaints have come from the laity concerning activities of members of the clergy who have undertaken to meddle in political affairs, and in some instances to commit the members of their parishes to an expression of opinion on questions that have no direct bearing on the life of the Church or on the ethical and doctrinal principles essential to the spiritual welfare of the flock." In accord therefore with the canons of the Third Plenary Council of Baltimore,

> we forbid any priest, secular or religious, to discuss in public any question dealing with legislation of a political nature or affecting candidates for political office or concerning persons holding political office. If in relation to such a topic there seems to be any matter involving a religious or moral problem which a clergyman thinks should be discussed in

---

9. *CB*, February 11, 1933.

public, he must first obtain the permission of the Ordinary of this archdiocese. . . . This regulation applies to all church societies, parochial, diocesan, and national. It also applies to all property, owned or occupied,
by any Catholic Church corporation within the archdiocese. . . . Violation of this legislation will subject the delinquent, whether clerical or lay,
to appropriate punishment.[10]

But this prohibition did not mean that the local Church should remain
aloof from the misery brought on by the Depression or should not try to alleviate it. Early on Murray urged his priests and people to contribute generously to the Community Chest in both Minneapolis and St. Paul, the precursor in each city of what would become the United Way.[11] And even before
instructing his priests to keep out of politics, he had set out his own plan of
relief. Prayer, he said, must be the starting point, and so an archdiocesan-
wide novena began on June 3, 1932. Catholicism, however, is not a religion of
faith alone, and so positive good works needed to augment pious appeals to
Heaven. The archbishop therefore initiated what he called a "charity crusade,"
a rather sophisticated organization designed to seek out resources that might
lessen the plight of the most deprived. Each parish was to institute a relief
committee whose task was to solicit funds aggressively from everyone—even
those of modest means—who lived within the boundaries of the parish, of
whatever creed. The solicitation was to be followed by evaluation and careful
judgment so that help could be dispensed "intelligently, in the form of employment, food, hospitalization, or other institutional service rather than in
the form of money." The pastor was the immediate overseer of the process,
but he was bound to report in detail to the chancery every six months "so that
imbalances from one district or parish to another can be corrected. . . . As the
solicitation—recommended to be one day's wages a month—does not consider creed or class or race, neither should relief."[12]

Nor was Archbishop Murray slow to cooperate with other nongovern-
mental institutions with programs that addressed specific needs. Early in 1933,
for example, at the invitation of the Red Cross he made appeals on the two
most prominent local radio stations (WCCO and KSTP) to Catholic women

---

10. Murray to "Reverend Father," March 17, 1933, AASPM, Murray Papers. This
three-page copy is in essence a draft, much worked over, with clarifying clauses and
phrases introduced in longhand. Partially quoted in *CB*, March 25, 1933.

11. Murray to "Reverend Father," November 8, 1932, AASPM, Murray Papers.

12. *CB*, May 28, 1932.

to help provide clothes for the destitute. The Red Cross, he explained, would supply the material if the women would lend their time and sewing skill. "It is more blessed to give than to receive," he intoned predictably, as he praised the voluntarism that the economic crisis had aroused. The harsh reality in this instance was that 37,000 such garments were required within the Twin Cities alone.[13]

But care for the extremely disadvantaged did not exhaust the responsibilities of the local church, nor monopolize its fiscal anxieties. As John A. Ryan warned, if the Depression deepened, parishes might well have to declare bankruptcy, and schools and other institutions might have to close down. The ordinary rhythms of Catholic life could be endangered. Most Catholic Minnesotans belonged to the lower middle class, and their resources, limited to begin with, fell sharply with the onset of the Great Depression. But limited too was the kind of economic expertise among the laity that would become commonplace three or four decades later, by which time a large number of Catholic laymen and women had assumed a professional status undreamed of by their immediate forebears. The ecclesiastical culture of the 1930s, however, continued to take it for granted that "the priest knows best," so that leadership in the struggle to contain the worst effects of the financial crisis had to belong to the pastor of the parish, the rector or the principal of the school, the administrator of the hospital or orphanage, and, at the directive center, the archbishop, clerics all.[14]

John Gregory Murray, who had left the diocese of Portland on the verge of bankruptcy, knew full well the dimensions of the problem. He knew too that, aside from an occasional benefaction, the bulk of the monies needed to meet the obligations of the archdiocese of St. Paul came from ordinary parishioners, many of whom worried about providing food and shelter for their families next week or even next day. The envelopes placed in the collection basket at Sunday Mass (and the separate envelopes dropped there by the children, because no penny or nickel was too small a contribution) determined to what degree the Church in the upper Midwest might effectively carry out its apostolate in a world beset with economic anxiety. And, finally, Archbishop Murray also knew that some pastors, even under the severe difficulties now commonplace, were adept at organizing the parish's resources—in

---

13. *CB*, March 18, 1933.

14. Technically the administrator of an extra-parochial institution—a nun or a religious brother—was not a "cleric"; but her or his distinction from the laity remains clear enough.

some instances introducing imaginative methods of census taking and bill paying—and others were not. Indeed, sixty-one parishes (out of a total of 227) were so strapped for cash that they could not pay their priests' modest salaries.[15] Priests could generally get by with Mass stipends—normally five dollars for a sung Mass, one for a low—and other stole fees; or at any rate a pastor could, since by canon law he had a right to all offerings given for weddings, funerals, and baptisms performed in his church, no matter who the ordained minister was.[16] This, to be sure, was (and is) a delicate matter, at least of perception; the danger always lurked that the "offering" would seem to amount to a "charge" for service rendered, and thus edge into simoniacal practice. By and large, most people accepted the distinction as valid.

During the fat years of the mid-1920s a schedule of assessments had been drawn up to indicate how much each parish should contribute to support diocesan-wide activities and, in some instances—for example, assistance to the foreign missions or financial provision for the pope—even broader special needs. The technique used to raise such funds was usually an additional collection at Sunday Masses, and indeed the lean years of the 1930s ushered in the golden era in American Catholicism of the second collection. But clearly, as Murray understood, the realities imposed by the Great Depression required a reexamination of the assessment procedure. Special collections notwithstanding, the situation was dire. Even so, one overarching principle had to be honored: "The disposition of [the money must be] in harmony with the purpose specified when the contributions were received."

> Hence no part of any collection received for the Holy Father, for the missions, for the Catholic University, for the seminary, for the orphans or any other specified purpose may be reserved for parish purposes. . . . On the other hand it is not within the discretion of the pastor or the lay trustees to decide that out of the contributions made by the faithful for parish support any part may be assigned to the Holy Father, the missions, the university, the orphans, the diocesan college or other worthy projects.

---

15. For much of what follows, including all statistical material, see Murray to "Reverend Father" (copy), August 31, 1934, AASPM, Murray Papers. This document—six single-spaced typed pages—was sent to all the pastors. Its primary purpose was to address the question of assessments of parishes in support of diocesan-wide activities.

16. When I was a student at the St. Paul Seminary during the 1950s, the canon law professor liked to remark amiably that the only right granted assistant pastors was "the right to Christian burial."

The only exceptions to this rule are those made by the Holy See. In this country there are three specified purposes for which funds may be drawn from the parish treasury to meet other than parochial needs: the diocesan seminary, the cathedraticum, and the support of infirm clergy.

This careful delineation of the rules governing the disbursement of parochial funds was characteristic of Murray who, throughout his years in St. Paul, always insisted in public that the norms of canon law be strictly observed (though in individual cases he was sometimes benign or, perhaps, neglectful in applying them). So it was important to him that the three exceptions just mentioned be understood within the appropriate legal context. In each instance the picture was bleak. "The total amount contributed to the seminary fund during 1933 was $28,806.07. The expenditures during the same year for board and tuition of ecclesiastical students were $49,951.97. This item shows a deficit of $19,145.92." As for the cathedraticum—the fund assessed and supposedly sufficient "to provide support for the archbishop, the living expenses of the chancellor and members of the household of the archbishop, to care for the maintenance of [his] home, to furnish transportation"—it too limped badly, which fact Murray of course felt personally. "The contributions to the cathedraticum fund in 1933 amounted to $17,700. Fifty-three churches," he added somewhat sourly, "gave nothing, and eighty-three gave fifty dollars or less. The deficit in the cathedraticum account for 1933 was $5,847.94."[17] And for the infirm clergy? "This third tax authorized by canon law was devised by the Third Plenary Council of Baltimore [1884] for the support of infirm priests.... The total amount received for the Fund for Infirm Priests or Clergy Fund in the year 1933 was $6,613.00. The total expenditures were $13,770.23." If these and other imbalances were to be corrected, a new fiscal regime was clearly needed. Murray and the chancery staff spent eighteen months poring over reports and statistical tables, until the archbishop, after shifting the percentages assessed one or two points in either direction, could announce that "160 parishes will pay less [in assessments] and sixty-seven parishes must pay more."

---

17. In the mid-1930s Murray moved across Summit and Selby Avenues into rooms in the cathedral rectory, thus alleviating to a degree the strain on the cathedraticum. Another reason for vacating the house at 226 Summit was "to provide [there] accommodation for sisters attending the summer school of the Diocesan Teachers' College," located next door in the Hill mansion. See Reardon, *Diocese of St. Paul*, 515, and chapter 16, above.

Far from apologizing for the already formidable "multiplicity of collections," Murray was prepared to expand the number for other than financial reasons. Indeed, he wrote,

> eliminating all collections except the usual weekly contribution to the [parish's] budget also eliminates all motives for giving except the sense of duty. It gives as much enthusiasm as the tax bill. If pastors would wish to create personal, intimate consciousness of the sacred relationship between their people and themselves, their assistants, and their coworkers, in the method of giving they would set aside a particular Sunday each month for a specific parish need, . . . [like] the salary of the Sisters . . . or the support of poor children in the parish.

So twelve additional collections a year, if carefully explained and deftly managed, could be a source of deeper unity and commitment within the parish. But if this recommendation were adopted, one danger had to be avoided.

> The announcement made to explain the appeal should not take more than a minute and a half in each case, so that abundant time may be left for an orderly exposition of the truths of religion. Any talk on money problems becomes detrimental to the cause for which it is made when it extends beyond three minutes. If the multiplicity of collections even in behalf of diocesan necessities tends to increase the time allotted to the discussion of finance and decreases the time available for the methodical, conscientious, zealous exposition of divine truth, it were better that we abolish all our material equipment, close our buildings, and set ourselves the task of preaching in the fields or the street corners after the example of Christ, rather than permit the mechanization for the spread of the gospel result in the elimination of the gospel from the lips of the preacher and the hearts of his hearers.[18]

HARD TIMES WAS THE UNIVERSAL LOT DURING THE DISMAL 30S, but the Catholic community in the archdiocese of St. Paul and its institutional framework survived, thanks to scrimping, cutting financial corners, employing some skillful management, and haranguing from the pulpit on Sunday

---

18. Murray to "Reverend Father" (copy), August 31, 1934, AASPM, Murray Papers.

that often exceeded Murray's "three minutes"—but thanks most of all to the sacrifices of the religious sisters, who, in addition to their pitifully compensated work as nurses and teachers, sold candy bars, gave piano lessons, and spent their summers catechizing children in rural parishes that had no parochial schools. Not far away, however, survival appeared far less likely.

The metropolitan province of St. Paul included eight suffragan sees across Minnesota and the Dakotas.[19] This hierarchical arrangement was (and is) more a matter of administrative convenience than of substance. The metropolitan archbishop had no direct jurisdiction in any diocese but his own. He stood, so to speak, as *primus inter pares*, who, except for a few minor appellate functions,[20] operated for the most part as a kind of committee chairman in dealing with concerns of common interest within the region. Nevertheless, as the head of the ordinarily largest and, from an economic and political point of view, the most important population center in the area, the archbishop was often the conduit of direct relations with, or at any rate the source of crucial information to and from, the Roman authorities with regard to province-wide issues. So it proved to be in the late winter of 1935.

Early in March the archbishop of St. Paul returned home from a trip to New York and found a letter, marked personal and confidential, from the apostolic delegate in Washington.[21] Fumasoni-Biondi[22] by this time had given place to Archbishop Amleto Giovanni Cicognani, a genial and shrewd Vatican diplomat, appointed in 1934 and destined to hold the prestigious American assignment for the next twenty-five years. (Why his mother had named the prelate after the indecisive Prince of Denmark remains unclear.) His note was as brief and to the point as Murray's reply was lengthy and discursive.[23] "Your Excellency, Upon my return I found your inquiry concerning the problem of the Diocese of Sioux Falls. Since that time I have endeavored to obtain information about conditions in South Dakota without direct communication and without any intimation to any person as to my purpose." The situation there "is truly deplorable from the point of view of agricultural and commercial possibilities." The ravages of the Depression have been

---

19. At the time Crookston, Duluth, St. Cloud, and Winona in Minnesota; Bismarck and Fargo in North Dakota; Sioux Falls and Rapid City in South Dakota. New Ulm, Minnesota, was erected in 1957.

20. For the odd case of the deceased bishop of Fargo, see below.

21. Cicognani to Murray, March 2, 1935, AASPM, Murray Papers.

22. See chapter 19, above.

23. Murray to Cicognani, March 11, 1935 (copy), AASPM, Murray Papers. This remarkable document covers four single-spaced typed pages.

compounded by "a plague of grasshoppers similar to the plague of locusts in Egypt [which have] devoured every blade of grass and every leaf on the trees in the southern section of South Dakota."

> The farmers were obliged to exhaust all their resources to buy feed for the cattle both in the summer and in the winter. Last year there came a drought so that most of the cattle had to be driven across the border into Nebraska to find anything to eat. Many of them died, and most of the rest were sold for almost nothing. Last week one of my priests reported to me that there is nothing left of a top soil to grow anything during the coming season, and in anticipation of lack of fodder the price of hay has risen from fifteen to fifty dollars a ton at present, so that there is nothing left for the farmers who have any cattle but to kill them off. Hence the future is even darker than the past.

In an economy as closely—one might argue almost exclusively—integrated into agriculture as eastern South Dakota's was, these blows of nature were cataclysmic. Of the two dioceses in the state, Rapid City in the west had experienced financial trouble early on, but nothing so shattering as the present crisis in Sioux Falls. John Lawler of Rapid City was recognized as a tough and resourceful administrator—"he ruled the diocese with determination," as a local historian tactfully put it.[24] "When I first came here," Murray explained to Cicognani, Lawler and one of his priests "with my permission" canvassed several parishes in the archdiocese "with the result that the only menacing obligation on the Diocese of Rapid City was wiped out by funds collected in the Archdiocese of St. Paul."

> Of course Rapid City had no such problem as Sioux Falls, because it had no institution to carry, and the bishop was so tenacious of conservatism in the matter of debt that practically no priest got a full salary. Moreover, in that territory is the richest gold mine in the world, and there were other resources than agriculture to sustain the population.

Besides his tenacity and determination to stay out of debt, Lawler was a known quantity when he came begging to Minnesota. He had been rector of

---

24. Michael Costigan et al., "Diocese of Rapid City," in Ahern, *Catholic Heritage*, 196.

the St. Paul cathedral and, after his consecration in 1910,[25] had served as John Ireland's auxiliary for six years. Famously brusque and abrasive in manner, he nevertheless had close connections with the senior clergy across the province. Bernard Mahoney of Sioux Falls enjoyed no such advantage. A priest of the diocese of Albany, he had served for many years as spiritual director of the North American College in Rome. With this background, and the clerical expectations that often accompanied it, "he came [to South Dakota] with a sense of being exiled," in the words of a not unsympathetic observer.[26] Sioux Falls fell vacant in 1921 with the death of Thomas O'Gorman, Archbishop Ireland's lifelong friend and confidant, and the forty-seven-year-old Mahoney, a small, slender, nervous man, was installed the following year.

The burdensome "institution" Murray referred to pejoratively in his letter to Cicognani was Columbus College, founded in 1909 in Chamberlain and transferred to Sioux Falls, where it was housed in a new and expensive building just days before O'Gorman died. The college had been a pet project of the bishop, who shared many of the grandiose assumptions of his associate and mentor in St. Paul: if Ireland had his St. Thomas College, why should not O'Gorman have his Columbus? For Murray in 1935 this sort of hubris appeared to have reaped a whirlwind. With a consistently small enrollment, Columbus's books never displayed anything but red ink, and the whole project was based on a false premise, assuming, argued Murray, the permanence of "a time when the agricultural activities of the United States were stimulated beyond all reasonable proportions by the war in Europe, and the impression prevailed that the agricultural districts of the Middle West were to be the New Paradise of the United States."[27]

Columbus College, under a debt that grew eventually to $850,000, staggered on until 1929, when it finally shut its doors. But physical closure did not erase the obligation owed by the diocese, nor the concomitant need to pay eviscerating interest charges every year in an atmosphere that grew ever more parlous as the Depression and the agricultural crisis deepened. "Under the circumstances," said Murray, "I can readily see that the promise made by Bishop Mahoney in May, 1934 [to pay enough interest on the diocesan debt to avoid the foreclosure on his residence, scheduled for March 14] failed of

25. Lawler was one of the six consecrated in the celebrated ceremony of May 19, 1910. See chapter 14, above, and Reardon, *Diocese of St. Paul,* 390–392.

26. Leonard Sullivan, "Diocese of Sioux Falls," in Ahern, *Catholic Heritage,* 162–164.

27. Murray to Cicognani, March 11, 1935 (copy), AASPM, Murray Papers.

fulfillment in November of the same year, and I do not think that it is possible for the Bishop to look forward to the season of 1935 with any hope to discover resources from within his own territory to meet the obligation arising from the debt on Columbus College."

Nor had Mahoney's desperate attempts to find some kind of relief from the ever burgeoning crisis done more than involve other religious entities in the calamity.

> The Bishop [of Sioux Falls] has endeavored to transfer the burden of the College from the diocese to a religious community. At present the Franciscan Sisters,[28] who have St. Mary's Hospital in Rochester and St. Teresa's College in Winona, are conducting a normal school in the [Columbus] college building. I know nothing of the details as to whether the community of the Franciscans offer any hope to the Bishop [Mahoney] to assume the burden. Personally I do not see how they can do so, because I am given to understand by bankers in St. Paul that there is a debt of three million dollars on St. Teresa's College and a debt of one million dollars on St. Mary's Hospital, obligations that were so crushing as soon as the Depression came that they have proved intolerable for that community.

Five hundred patients, Murray explained to the delegate, were wont to "pass through the Mayo Clinic each day, and most of them sought hospitalization in St. Mary's Hospital, which was furnishing abundant surplus to the Franciscan community to take care of St. Teresa's College." The Depression "has caused the daily number of applicants to the Clinic to fall to fifty," driving the celebrated Doctors Mayo to the brink of bankruptcy, and also inevitably "cut[ting] off the revenue of St. Mary's at a moment when a new building costing more than a million dollars was just finished." Perhaps the sisters could manage nearly five million dollars in debt "if the thousands of patients returned to Rochester, . . . but I doubt whether the future will justify any such expectation."

The fever to expand and its unhappy consequences were not restricted to the dioceses of Winona and Sioux falls.

> In my own archdiocese the Sisters of St. Joseph contracted a debt of $750,000 on the new Academy of the Holy Angels, and $500,000 on St. Catherine's College, both of which institutions are in such straits that

---

28. For the arrival of these nuns in Minnesota, see chapter 8, above.

their total income is insufficient to meet their interest items [sic] with the result that they have to mortgage their institutions in Minnesota and North Dakota in order to raise money to pay interest. Only last Saturday I was in conference with them to help them refinance $250,000 at a lower rate of interest to save $15,000 interest alone each year.

But Minnesota, hard hit by the Depression as may be, still stood on a different level from South Dakota. "In Minnesota there is still enough confidence left for people to buy notes at 4% on Catholic institutions because there is some credit left." But in South Dakota "the hopelessness is so widespread that no low interest-bearing securities could be sold, whether within or without the state." So the $850,000 debt—along with the $34,000 a year needed to service it—hung over not only the defunct college and the nuns who had rashly associated themselves with it, but over all the institutions of the diocese of Sioux Falls.

"The outlook for Sioux Falls is so depressing that I do not think Bishop Mahoney has the heart to carry the burden which he has found so heavy for the past thirteen years." Indeed, the metropolitan archbishop felt impelled to speak to the apostolic delegate in even stronger terms. "Frankly, I think Bishop Mahoney should be given a less burdensome task. His place may be taken by one who has the courage and temper to be a beggar among his brethren of the hierarchy for the rest of his life." The impending seizure by creditors of the episcopal residence in Sioux Falls "will furnish the best possible psychology for appeals to be made outside the Diocese of Sioux Falls. . . . If any plan is formulated to go direct to the people in behalf of Sioux Falls, I shall be happy to participate to the limit in seeking aid for the Ordinary whoever he may be, as well as for Bishop Mahoney if he is disposed to let the loss of his home be made an occasion to appeal to all the people of the Northwest [sic]."

The larger issue, in Murray's mind, was the need to "reestablish the confidence of the public in the disposition and the ability of the Catholic population in this country to pay all obligations in full." Sioux Falls, whose financial problem "has been of such long-standing and of such general knowledge," might well provide a good place "to begin the rehabilitation of the credit of the Church." If Bernard Mahoney was not up to the assignment—and Murray clearly did not think he was—then who might best take it on?

If Your Excellency thinks that I might contribute to the solution by personal service in that field, I shall vacate St. Paul for some one who is more fit to fill the place, and I shall go to Sioux Falls in any capacity the Holy

See may designate in order to clear the accumulated debt. Perhaps I may be presumptuous in thinking I can do better than others. I do not think that I can do better than others, but I do think that some kind of relief should be given to Bishop Mahoney and some concerted effort made to rehabilitate the finances of the Church in that territory.[29]

This remarkable offer of course received no serious consideration. The apostolic delegate replied promptly and thanked the archbishop of St. Paul for the information. "As Your Excellency states, the situation [in Sioux Falls] is acute." A plan for recovery was being formulated, Cicognani wrote, but—not uncharacteristic of Vatican policy, ever suspicious of any local initiatives— no details were provided to the metropolitan *en scène*. "Of course Your Excellency's offer relative to Sioux Falls is out of the question, but I know it was prompted by a truly Apostolic heart."[30] It also, by happenstance, opened an unusual vista from which to view the personality of that fiercely private man, John Gregory Murray. He had come from settled Hartford and Portland to the wild west, and now, in the midst of chronic financial crisis, he offered to go farther west still, hoping to help "to rehabilitate the finances of the Church."

For Murray believed that the problems in Sioux Falls were indicative of a much deeper malaise, and as treasurer of the National Catholic Welfare Conference from 1931 to 1935 he was in a good position to make that judgment. In carrying out the duties of this office, he was constantly reminded of the hand-to-mouth existence the secretariat in Washington—where beat the heart of the Conference's work[31]—had to endure. Thus in the autumn of 1933 he received an anxious plea from the secretary general for $4,300 in order to pay staff. Six weeks later another entreaty: "We shall need at least two thousand dollars to meet our immediate obligations."[32] Murray found the money in this instance,[33] but time after time he had to send out appeals to fellow bishops, like this one:

29. Murray to Cicognani, March 11, 1935 (copy), AASPM, Murray Papers.

30. Cicognani to Murray, March 21, 1935, AASPM, Murray Papers.

31. See chapter 17, above.

32. Burke to Murray, October 11, 1933, and Ready to Murray, November 22, 1933, AASPM, Murray Papers. John Burke, a Paulist, was the first general secretary of the NCWC (1919–1936), and Michael Ready, a priest of the diocese of Cleveland, was Burke's assistant and successor (1936–1944).

33. Burke to Murray, December 4, 1933 (telegram), AASPM, Murray Papers.

Your Excellency, In closing the accounts of the National Catholic Welfare Conference for the fiscal year 1934, the outstanding obligations of the treasurer were $63,291.32 of which amount $25,000.00 was in the form of a bank loan on which the treasurer has been paying interest personally since June, 1931. Against the above amount were sums expected from various dioceses for the year 1934 and previous years amounting to $63,635. Of that amount I am still living in hope that you may be able to pay me [the sum pledged]. . . . Only the ultimate payment of the expected quotas still in arrears will enable me to clear my obligations in favor of another who can demonstrate better financial ability than myself. May I still look to Your Excellency for aid in my distress?[34]

Or this one:

Your Excellency, You have been so consistently helpful in aiding the Treasurer of the National Catholic Welfare Conference to meet his obligations that I have deferred asking you for a contribution to the 1935 budget till I had no other recourse. As my treasury is empty and credit exhausted, I am hazarding the hope that Your Excellency may find it possible to send me either all or part of the sum you have been accustomed to give.[35]

Archbishop Murray surprised at least some of his colleagues by maintaining his good humor during these difficult negotiations. "I wish indeed," wrote one of them, "I could do something to lighten your burden in collecting the necessary funds to keep our organization moving. I think you have the hardest and least appreciated task of any member of the Conference, and yet you are so cheerful and generous about it."[36] But a pleasant demeanor did not quite conceal his distress at the failure of so many bishops to support their own association. And in his final communiqué as NCWC treasurer a measure of sarcasm emerged. "The enclosed printed report indicates all contributions made

---

34. Murray to Schrembs, April 10, 1935 (copy), AASPM, Murray Papers. Joseph Schrembs (1866–1845) was bishop of Cleveland. In longhand at the top of this document: "25 copies mimeographed of this."

35. Murray to Boyle, April 11, 1935 (copy), AASPM, Murray Papers. Hugh Boyle (1873–1950) was bishop of Pittsburgh. In longhand at the top of this document: "70 copies mimeographed of this." Clearly Schrembs and Boyle were not the only laggards.

36. McNicholas to Murray, December 4, 1932, AASPM, Murray Papers. John T. McNicholas was archbishop of Cincinnati.

to the treasurer up to the ninth of November, the day on which the report went to press. The report shows a balance of $1.17 which will be turned over to the new treasurer." It was, he continued, "a source of keen regret that I was unable to collect the balance due on the budget" for the last two months of the year. "In view of my delinquency in this respect I presume on the kindness of my brethren in the hierarchy to come to the aid of my successor . . . that he may not be embarrassed by my failure to collect this item of $12,100, as well as by my failure to collect the amounts due on the budgets from 1931 to 1934, totaling an additional item of $35,432.32."[37]

But there was nothing whimsical in the language Murray used when sharing his concerns with the apostolic delegate. "I can see no other way" to solve the finite Sioux Falls problem than to move it to a bigger stage, "to seek resources on a large scale from the public at large" outside Sioux Falls, and "thus make the financial world conscious of the solidarity of the members of the Church in meeting every obligation in full."

> That consciousness has disappeared in recent years, so that the old adage "The Catholic Church never defaults" is no longer accepted in the world of finance. To reestablish the confidence of the public in the disposition and the ability of the Catholic population in this country to pay all obligations in full, a concerted effort should be initiated among all the hierarchy who seem to have become demoralized by their problems. My experience as treasurer of the National Catholic Welfare Conference convinces me that in many instances the sense of responsibility to moral if not legal obligations has been submerged in a sea of self-pity, with the result that I have had to pay $8000 in interest out of my own pocket during the last four years [in order] to carry obligations of the bishops to their own organization, and the burden of $25,000 in a personal note may have to be carried for years to come, just because the bishops will not rouse within themselves the consciousness of the fact that the Church is a divine institution by profession and her leaders ought to come to the fore in demonstrating her divine character at a moment when every system expressive of materialism is in disgrace.[38]

---

37. Murray to "Your Excellency," November 27, 1935 (copy), AASPM, Murray Papers. Murray's successor as treasurer was the celebrated Francis Clement Kelley (1870–1948), bishop of Oklahoma City.

38. Murray to Cicognani, March 11, 1935 (copy), AASPM, Murray Papers.

As was often the case with Archbishop Murray, the prose is cluttered and untidy, but the anxiety no less than the annoyance shines through clearly enough. Hard times indeed. Bernard Mahoney survived the moment of crisis in 1935 and two years later even showed enough gumption to initiate a debt-reduction program within the diocese of Sioux Falls. Not much progress had resulted by the time he died in 1939, but then not much financial progress of any sort had happened in the United States by that time. The Depression stubbornly continued to hold the nation in thrall, alleviated only by the indispensable if limited programs of the New Deal.[39]

COMPARED TO THE DISTRESS IN SIOUX FALLS DURING THE mid-1930s, the scene in another of St. Paul's suffragan sees, Fargo, appeared tranquil. The bishop there was James O'Reilly who, like Lawler of Rapid City, was one of the six famously consecrated by John Ireland in one fell swoop in 1910. Over the nearly quarter century of his tenure in North Dakota, O'Reilly, a handsome Irishman, oversaw the organization of thirty-four new parishes and the construction of fifty-six churches, twenty-four schools, and seven hospitals.[40] Then, a week before Christmas 1934, at the ripe age of seventy-nine, he died, and Archbishop Murray found himself involved in a set of bizarre circumstances.

In accord with the Code of Canon Law in force since 1917, the death of a bishop automatically set in train a defined series of actions. The duty fell first of all upon the board of consultors—the six priests who composed the deceased prelate's *ex officio* advisers—to appoint, *sede vacante*, a temporary administrator. But from the beginning of their deliberations—and no doubt distracted in the bustle and confusion of the festive season—the consultors in Fargo were hopelessly deadlocked: after six ballots, three candidates enjoyed two votes each. They then addressed a letter to Murray in his capacity as metropolitan and asked "'for a decision or advice.'" He replied that he would come to Fargo the day before O'Reilly's funeral, at which time he would "endeavor to offer them advice," but that early in the process "I had no authority to intervene to make a decision." And so the senior member of the board

---

39. Sullivan, "Sioux Falls," in Ahern, *Catholic Heritage*, 163–165.

40. A. A. A. Schmirler and Gerald W. Weber, "Diocese of Fargo," in Ahern, *Catholic Heritage*, 186.

called a meeting for four o'clock, and prior to the meeting I permitted each consultor to ask questions as to the various ways they might solve the deadlock, either by another ballot or by compromises. . . . I made it clear that each must follow his conscience, that I had no authority to be present at their meeting or to make any suggestions as to a choice [of administrator], but that if they had not made a decision in two days time [i.e., eight days since O'Reilly's death became publicly known] . . . I should have the exclusive power for the following eight days to make a choice, but not before.

Listening to this arcane bit of canonical lore apparently persuaded the consultors that they preferred to retain the local option. "Later in the afternoon they came to me as a body to announce that Reverend Vincent Ryan had been chosen as administrator."[41]

Which should have been the end of a not particularly significant tale, but not so. "This week Father Ryan called on me and informed me that he had failed to find any will after a search in all likely places in Minnesota[42] and North Dakota. He said further that he had found check deposits in the name of James O'Reilly personally, but none in the name of the Diocese of Fargo or in the name of James O'Reilly as bishop." Stacks of currency, largely one thousand dollar bills, had been stuffed into drawers and cupboards in the bishop's house in Fargo. "[Ryan] also found negotiable securities, mostly bonds of the United States." Altogether the administrator estimated that "the total amount of all holdings in the name of James O'Reilly comes close to $400,000. The heirs of the bishop are a priest in the Diocese of Pittsburgh and nieces and nephews in Ireland."[43]

That, of course, was the rub. O'Reilly's incredible carelessness opened the strong possibility that funds presumably belonging to the diocese of Fargo—the freewill offerings of Catholic people of no great wealth—could be legitimately claimed by the bishop's surviving relatives. Or as Murray put it: "The amount of income tax paid last year by Bishop O'Reilly indicated that he considered about $20,000 his personal estate, but as he held everything in his own name, all the courts and government will presume everything to be personal."

---

41. Murray to Cicognani, January 5, 1935 (copy), AASPM, Murray Papers.

42. Before his promotion to the episcopate and appointment to North Dakota, O'Reilly had been the pastor of St. Anthony's parish in Minneapolis.

43. The final audit set the figure at $450,000. See Murray to Cicognani, May 28, 1935 (copy), AASPM, Murray Papers.

At present no one except Father Ryan, one member of the board of consultors, and myself know of this financial condition. I told Father Ryan to take everything that was lying around loose, about $300,000, and put it into a safe-deposit box in the name of the Diocese of Fargo. I then told him to begin to set up a claim at the banks for all the rest of the deposits he could get control of in the name of the diocese, beginning with the largest of $23,000 in the Fargo bank where diocesan monies had been deposited for years in the name of James O'Reilly . . . [and] against which he wrote checks for both diocesan and personal items. Starting with this account [Ryan] could prove from vouchers that it was primarily a diocesan rather than a personal account, and thus endeavor to obtain consent immediately from the bank, with the consent of the judge of probate, to write checks as administrator of the diocese.

Establishing "this precedent with the bankers of Fargo and the probate court" could allow the diocesan administrator to get control of the funds before the blood-heirs moved to assert their testamentary rights, if indeed they chose to do so. "Otherwise [hypothetically] only a long legal process in court could be attempted to save the money of the diocese from the heirs who meant nothing to Bishop O'Reilly, from the state of North Dakota which would claim a large portion for inheritance taxes, and from the Federal Government which could claim double penalty for unpaid income taxes over a period of twenty years."

The advice was shrewd—"sage" was the word Cigocgnani used in endorsing it—and in following it the diocese of Fargo was spared a financial disaster.[44]

CLOSER TO HOME ARCHBISHOP MURRAY FACED A PROBLEM which was at once financial and, so to speak, political: what to do about the College of St. Thomas. More than two years after coming to Minnesota he confided to a brother bishop that this institution "has given me more concern since the day I arrived than any other single item . . . in my experience. Even during the dinner at my installation twenty hours after I arrived in St. Paul it was the chief topic of conversation."[45] The financial picture was indeed stark. "The debt of $580,000," he explained to the apostolic delegate,

---

44. Cicognani to Murray, January 11, 1935, AASPM, Murray Papers. One of O'Reilly's Irish heirs asked for an accounting.

45. Murray to Noll, June 16, 1933, quoted in Connors, *Journey*, 252. John F. Noll (1875–1956) was bishop of Fort Wayne.

contracted before I came here, destroyed the credit of St. Thomas's [sic] College to such an extent that I had to encumber the Archdiocese with the debt in order to safeguard the accrediting of the college with the North Central Association and thus keep the college open. By assuming the principal and interest as a diocesan obligation, I have enabled the college to barely meet its expenses, whereas when I came it had $180,000 in floating bills. I was told it was useless to make an appeal to the people to meet our obligations, and so I made an appeal to the diocesan clergy who have given me $125,000 since last August [1934], but in some instances the clergy used their credit to borrow money so as to give me a contribution.[46]

This description of the state of affairs at St. Thomas was roughly accurate, though it might have been better to say "fully restore" accreditation rather than "safeguard" it. And the diocesan clergy did indeed contribute an amount in six figures in support of the college. But what in fact Murray had asked them to raise among themselves was $250,000, which constituted the mortgage portion of the total indebtedness. The minimum amount required from pastors was $1,000, from other priests $500.

It has appeared that some priests have had such difficulty in financing their parish obligations that they must forego part or all of their yearly living from the parish. Under the circumstances it may seem unreasonable and inconsistent to ask the clergy to meet the immediate necessity of clearing the mortgage in order to have the college in a favorable condition when its status as to eligibility for accrediting will be subjected to investigation. . . . This appeal is not a matter of choice. It has been forced on us by the very circumstances which make it all the harder for those solicited to find the resources necessary to respond to the request. The only satisfaction to be found in the conditions necessitating the appeal is the conviction that in the sacrifice exacted is to be found the assurance of renewed life within the Church and the activities which she must maintain in the face of humanly insuperable difficulties to prove her divine origin, her divine mission, and her divine destiny.[47]

---

46. Murray to Cicognani, March 11, 1935 (copy), AASPM, Murray Papers.
47. Murray to "Reverend Father," August 14, 1934 (copy), AASPM, Murray Papers.

By the summer of 1936 the clergy had contributed $154,292.95 to the St. Thomas College Debt Fund.[48]

It is no surprise that this response, coming as it did during the darkest days of the Great Depression, fell short of the goal. Nevertheless, it represented in part the priests' fulfillment of an implicit contract between them and their archbishop. Exactly a year before issuing his appeal for funds, Murray had restored St. Thomas to diocesan control. The agreement between the archdiocese of St. Paul and the Congregation of Holy Cross[49] was scheduled to expire on July 17, 1933. The five Holy Cross administrators—headed by a richly experienced academic, the affable and eloquent Matthew Schumacher as president, and the deeply learned educational philosopher William Cunningham as dean—fully expected that the congregation's direction of St. Thomas would then become permanent. And they had reason for this confidence. Despite the harsh economic circumstances and the chronic mismanagement the institution had endured for decades, a genuine recovery was clearly underway. Accreditation was restored to the academy and partially— for freshman and sophomore courses—to the college. Between 1928 and 1931, the year of Murray's appointment, enrollment in the college department rose to nearly seven hundred, an increase of thirty percent. Morale was high. When the old and ramshackle administration building was condemned and had to be torn down, Father Schumacher and his aides skillfully planned and arranged the funding for what they called the Liberal Arts Building—long since renamed Aquinas Hall—a handsome stone edifice set along fashionable Summit Avenue to house offices, twenty-eight classrooms, and the library, exclusively for collegiate use.[50] Its durability and utility have been amply demonstrated over the seven decades since.

The Holy Cross administrators at St. Thomas took care to cultivate friendly relations with Archbishop Murray, and at first they sensed no indication of hostility or coldness. They might, however, have felt some unease

---

48. See AASPM, Murray Papers, for a copy of the printed statement in which each contribution is listed by name. Murray could thus publicly praise some and embarrass others. Only three pastors gave more than the minimum: St. Luke ($2,000), St. Mark ($2,000), and Nativity ($1,500), all in St. Paul and all relatively prosperous parishes. James Reardon, pastor of the Basilica of St. Mary in Minneapolis, gave the minimum. Murray himself contributed $5,000. The younger priests understandably had less to give, but the widow's mite seems to have been reprised by Father Eugene Moriarty ($10), who was ordained in 1932 and who later was professor of canon law at the St. Paul Seminary.

49. See chapter 16, above.

50. Connors, *Journey*, 232–241, 251.

about which way the wind was blowing when, at the dedication of the Liberal Arts Building in the late winter of 1932, Murray in his speech, while lavishly praising the institution's alumni, made no reference to Schumacher and his colleagues.[51] These alumni included virtually all the senior and most influential priests in the archdiocese, who had never liked or approved of Austin Dowling and who considered the intrusion of Holy Cross into St. Thomas a betrayal of their hero, John Ireland. Then Schumacher and his provincial superiors at Notre Dame made a serious tactical error. The policy of accrediting agencies routinely includes a requirement that academic institutions have an endowment. One way for American Catholics, as a community never rich, to provide such a permanent resource was to link the school or college to a parish, the steady income from which would be a guarantor of the institution's solvency. This had been standard procedure for Holy Cross ever since the missionary congregation had come to America from France in the middle of the nineteenth century.[52] Now Holy Cross proposed that the chapel at St. Thomas should become a parish church and, staffed by the college's priests, should include in its parochial responsibility the surrounding area, yet to be determined in detail.[53] But the "surrounding area," however defined, could not but encroach upon the territory, and therefore the income, of the parishes of St. Mark, St. Luke, and Nativity.[54] One can readily appreciate how this scheme would, if anything, intensify the clerical animosity toward the religious order now in charge of St. Thomas, despite the explicit prohibition of that institution's fabled founder.

Archbishop Murray did not share his great predecessor's almost paranoid dislike and suspicion of religious orders. But in the debate over the future of St. Thomas he was confronted with a genuine conundrum. All the evidence at hand indicated that Schumacher, Cunningham, and their associates were doing a superlative job in rescuing the college and academy from imminent collapse. Yet at the same time, the diocesan priests with whom he had to work were adamant in their opposition to Holy Cross. Murray understood the dilemma in which he found himself, and he chose to solve it by in-

---

51. *CB*, March 12, 1932.

52. For instances of parish-as-endowment (among many possible), see O'Connell, *Edward Sorin*, 583–584 for Watertown, Wisconsin, and 633–635 for Austin, Texas.

53. Reardon, *Diocese of St. Paul*, 527–529. On this subject Reardon is reliable only as to the documented facts. His bias spoils his overall account. See note 68, chapter 16, above.

54. See note 48, above, for those pastors who contributed an amount above the minimum to the St. Thomas Debt Fund.

dulging in a touch of mendacity.[55] Not until a trustees' meeting in late April 1933, he said incredibly, had he become aware that Archbishop Ireland had, in 1908, explicitly and in writing decreed that St. Thomas or any "such college . . . be at no time under the control or management of any particular society or order of the Roman Catholic Church."[56] Since that was in fact the case, obviously the college must revert to the control of the archdiocese.

And so the men of Holy Cross departed, bitter and disappointed, and not at all mollified by the lavish praise the archbishop heaped on them in a press release some weeks later.[57] The dilemma had been resolved by means of a lapse in candor, which, Murray seems to have judged, did not figure large in the long-term scheme of things. "I am in the comfortable position," he wrote ironically to Bishop Noll, "of all the clergy against the renewal of the contract [with Holy Cross], and all the laity who have boys at the college a unit against me if I permit the congregation to withdraw. In this enviable position I am disposed to look forward fifty years and try to decide what the generation of that day would wish to have decided."[58]

Fifty years on, and more than that, appear to have validated Archbishop Murray's decision, however dodgy his explanation at the time. The public at any rate were given a hint about the imminent change at St. Thomas when the diocesan clergy appointments were published in the early summer of 1933. Of the fifty-six priests given new assignments, no fewer than fifteen were sent to the University of Minnesota to pursue graduate degrees in a variety of fields and so to prepare themselves for academic careers.[59] A sweeping shake-up of clerical officers occurred simultaneously. Monsignor Humphrey Moynihan—as a young man John Ireland's secretary,[60] and then, in sterling Irish baroque fashion,[61] professor and administrator at the seminary and the college—was

---

55. Connors, *Journey,* 259, overly charitably describes Murray's denial of knowledge of Ireland's views as "a puzzling aspect."

56. Quoted in Connors, *Journey,* 92.

57. Text in *CB,* July 22, 1933.

58. Murray to Noll, June 16, 1933 (copy), AASPM, Murray Papers.

59. See the list dated June 24, 1933, AASPM, Murray Papers (partially quoted in *CB,* July 1, 1933). Among those so assigned were James J. Byrne, later auxiliary bishop of St. Paul and archbishop of Dubuque, and Roger Connole, for many years superintendent of the diocesan schools. Also William O'Donnell, Bernard Coughlin, Walter LeBeau, and William Orzeszak (Ozark), all of whom spent their priestly careers at St. Thomas and all of whom were valued colleagues of mine between 1958 and 1972.

60. O'Connell, *Ireland,* 1–3.

61. "Irish baroque" is a term of my own invention. By it I mean to specify a cleric who manifested a certain clear but limited level of cultural achievement,

appointed pastor of the Incarnation parish in Minneapolis, while William O. Brady became his successor as rector of the St. Paul Seminary. Humphrey Moynihan's younger brother, James, reluctantly assumed the presidency of St. Thomas, abetted by Donald Gormley as director of the military academy and the brilliant and tireless Joseph Schabert as dean of the college.[62]

The interlopers from Notre Dame had gone back to Indiana, and the diocesan clergy were once again in charge. But such administrative juggling did not solve the financial crisis. Indeed, not till the vast economic changes that came in the wake of the Second World War did St. Thomas find its way out of crippling debt. In the short term, however, expansion of the student body was the crying need. And so, to encourage a wider enrollment, costs in the college department were slashed by $200 per annum: tuition was fixed at $150, while board "and all other items" came to $450, for a total of $600. To attend the academy would cost $100 more: tuition at $125, full dress uniform at $100, and "all other items" at $475. The archbishop urged pastors to devote four consecutive Sundays over the late summer to encouraging enrollment of young men at St. Thomas. "It is suggested that an appeal be made to the members of the parish to set up a fund that will provide at least the cost of tuition for deserving students from the parish."[63]

St. Thomas, the apple of John Ireland's eye, had, so to speak, come home again.

---

characterized by an acquaintance with classical authors and with some medieval, notably Dante, and who wrote a diligent if somewhat overripe prose. The best representatives were the two Moynihans and James Reardon, all, significantly, ardent disciples of Archbishop Ireland.

62. *CB*, July 22, 1933. For a fulsome but justifiable account of Father Schabert's contribution to the well-being—indeed, to the survival—of St. Thomas, see Connors, *Journey*, 239, 268, 279–281. Professor Connors euphemistically speaks of the "strain" imposed by overwork upon Schabert which led to his removal from St. Thomas and to a series of dismal parochial appointments. The last of these was St. Elizabeth's, a slum parish on the edge of downtown Minneapolis (long since closed down and swallowed by the Hubert H. Humphrey Metrodome). Between 1959 and 1964 I was Father Schabert's weekend assistant at St. Elizabeth's, and I came to honor him because, though old and frail and ill, he never ceased to care for the marginalized people who were his parishioners. Only once in my time in his parish did he mention his career at St. Thomas. "They would not let me be president of St. Thomas," he said, "because I wasn't Irish." How complex the immigrant reality was as it affected those most intimately concerned. Joseph Schabert died in 1965.

63. Murray to "Reverend Father," August 7, 1933 (copy), AASPM, Murray Papers.

CHAPTER 21

In Defense of Jews
and Public Decency

DURING THE EARLY YEARS OF JOHN GREGORY MURRAY'S episcopate in St. Paul, as economic circumstances grew ever more straitened and, in many cases, more desperate, the Catholic people, like Americans generally, took what consolation they could from events in the greater world outside. In the spring of 1933, for example, Pope Pius XI told a group of priests visiting the Vatican that the end of the Depression "was not far distant."[1] Alas, the pontiff's infallibility did not extend to matters of this sort, and the economic distress dragged on worldwide till the end of the decade. Wishful thinking may well have been a palliative for dismal times, both at home and abroad. A year earlier Benito Mussolini and Pius XI had met for sixty-five minutes, also within the confines of the Vatican palace. "Il Duce . . . was much impressed and delighted with his visit, . . . and announced . . . that he plans to return there often."[2] The fascist dictator had made, as it was said, Italian trains run on time and also had exhibited appropriate respect for the Holy See. Catholics could not but be pleased.

At home Franklin Roosevelt was duly inaugurated in March of 1933, and his address on that fateful occasion earned from the National Catholic Welfare Conference praise for "its fine spiritual outlook," a rather vague accolade within a rush of breathless prose.[3] But there was chagrin too, rooted in that insecurity which still stalked the American Catholic community. The new president had appointed one Catholic to his cabinet—the consummate political operator James A. Farley, and him to the relatively unimportant office of Postmaster General. A gloomy researcher moreover went to the trouble to

---

1. *CB*, March 4, 1933.
2. *CB*, February 7, 1932.
3. *CB*, March 11, 1933.

tabulate the statistical inferiority members of the Roman Church had borne in this regard over the lifetime of the Republic. Of the 301 individuals who had served as members of the cabinet, only five had been Catholic—two Democrats, three Republicans—the most recent in 1908.[4]

Two days after Roosevelt's inauguration, elections in Germany had resulted in a large plurality for the National Socialist Party, whose leader, Adolf Hitler, had been appointed chancellor on January 30. Between those events the German bishops had raised some questions about compatibility between the Nazi platform and Catholic doctrine. They did not mention race.[5] Then, after the election, a series of reports came out of Berlin from the National Catholic News Service correspondent that suggested a softening of the bishops' nascent hostility. German Catholics "are not alarmed at Hitler's strength, despite the party's recent electoral successes." They are heartened that Franz von Papen, "a very good Catholic," is involved in the negotiations leading to the formation of a cabinet. Only "urgent necessity," like the emergence of a credible Communist alternative, "would prompt" the Center (Papen's Catholic party, active within the Reich since 1870) to form a coalition with the Nazis, "for the purpose of safeguarding the present [anti-Communist] foreign policy and the guarantees of international peace." The former prohibition forbidding Catholics to join the Nazi Party had been revoked. According to one "impeccable source," Hitler regularly "goes to Mass and receives the sacraments." And finally, reports of the persecution of German Jews "are greatly exaggerated."[6]

Such observations, particularly the last one, seem in retrospect almost grotesque, as they must have seemed at the time to the "Pearl of Louvain." Long before he came to power Hitler had made clear, in the ranting pages of *Mein Kampf* (1925–1926) and in countless tirades in beer halls and at outdoor rallies, his hatred for the Jews. And to depend upon the good offices of a time-serving hack like Papen was to lean on a slender reed indeed. So, in a characteristically wily fashion, Archbishop Murray instructed the editor of the *Catholic Bulletin* to publish the misinformation from Germany, outlandish as it was outrageous, while he himself, in the same number of the paper, issued a stinging rebuttal. The immediate occasion was a rally to which he was invited, sponsored at the end of March by the venerable Temple Israel[7] in Min-

---

4. *CB*, March 4, 1933.

5. *CB*, February 25, 1933.

6. *CB*, April 1, 1933.

7. In 1878, twenty-three founding members of Temple Israel rented a hall at Nicollet and Washington Avenues for Friday night services in the Reform tradition.

neapolis, to protest the plight of German Jews. Warmly congratulating the organizers, Murray explained that a three-month standing commitment in Pennsylvania prevented his presence at the event. And then he wrote a message which was read out from the platform by the Paulist chaplain of the Catholic students at the University of Minnesota.

> Permit me to unite with you and all our right-minded citizens in protest against political action which adopts as its principal purpose the annihilation of the Jewish people and all other liberty-loving groups in the great country of Germany, who are opposed to the chauvinistic and narrow-minded program of the Nationalist [Socialist] Party. With my fellow bishops of that great land, I lift my voice to beseech a civilized world to make articulate the conscience of humanity in behalf of those who have committed no other crime than to be members of a race which has given to the world the priceless boon of the most enlightened culture in antiquity and was divinely chosen to cradle the forces which have made Christianity possible.
>
> With assurance of my sympathy to your effort to maintain the essential rights of all men to follow the voice of conscience, I remain very faithfully yours.[8]

This was a remarkably strong and prescient statement, since the really savage persecution of German Jewry still lay in the future, and the horrible "final solution," the *Ha-Shoah,* had not yet taken hold even in Hitler's sick and fevered psyche. But implicitly the archbishop had more than just Germany in mind, as did, for that matter, the members of often embattled Temple Israel. American society was not without its dark veins of anti-Semitism during the years before and during the Great Depression. Minneapolis—already notoriously anti-union[9]—was one of the cities where flagrant discrimination against Jews in housing, education, and employment was particularly conspicuous.[10]

Two years later the first synagogue was opened, a modest wooden structure at Fifth Street and Marquette Avenue. In 2007 Temple Israel's congregation numbers more than two thousand families, one of the largest in the United States. See http://templeisrael.com/history.html. Accessed May 20, 2008.

8. Quoted in *CB,* April 1, 1933.

9. See chapter 20, above.

10. See, among a large literature, Laura E. Weber, "'Gentiles Preferred': Minneapolis Jews and Employment, 1920–1950," *Minnesota History* 52 (Spring 1991): 166–182, and Hyman Berman, "Political Anti-Semitism in Minnesota during the Great Depression," *Jewish Social Studies* 38 (Summer/Fall 1976): 247–264.

Nothing so violent or vicious as would unfold in Germany, but a blight upon the local community just the same.

Still, as the German situation grew ever more appalling Archbishop Murray remained outspoken about it, without forgetting the local bigots. In the summer of 1937 he ordered a special collection for a fund to provide support for "converts from Judaism to Christianity and the descendants of such converts who have been forced to leave Germany and come to America, for no other reason that they have in their veins the same blood as was shed on the cross of Calvary for the redemption of the human race."[11] At the beginning of 1938 he urged the Catholic people to support a huge rally at the St. Paul Auditorium intended to give Minnesotans "an opportunity . . . to manifest their sympathy for the pathetic condition of their brethren within German territory who are victims of unusual measures that are designed to suppress civil and religious liberty." The demonstration, Murray added, "aims to invoke the power of the God of the Christians to safeguard not only the flock of his divine Son, but also all the men and women and children of every denomination and every racial blood within that country." Therefore, Sunday, January 16, the day of the rally, "at all the Masses in all the churches of the archdiocese will be observed as a day of expiation for the crimes committed against the rights of God and the rights of man in a country that has enjoyed our common heritage of Christianity." The Germans "are a noble people, now assailed by the plague of a new species of paganism that recognizes no characteristic of human dignity and acceptability except the type of material blood that courses in the veins of insane leadership."[12]

The "unusual measures" reached an infamous climax on January 9, 1938—the *Kristallnacht,* the night of broken glass—which proved far worse than an ordinary pogrom. The rampages of the Hitler Youth and the *Schutzsaffel* (the SS) left ninety-one Jews dead, hundreds injured, 7,500 shops and businesses gutted, 177 synagogues destroyed. This barbarity moved John Gregory Murray to a higher level of eloquence than he was normally capable of.

> The savage persecution of our brethren of the Jewish race demands united effort to put an end to the barbarism into which a once noble

---

11. Murray to "Reverend Father," August 16, 1937 (copy), AASPM, Murray Papers.

12. Murray to "Reverend Father," January 8, 1938 (copy), AASPM, Murray Papers.

people have been dragooned by the most diabolical leadership exercised in modern times. The disappearance of the last vestige of humanity from a nation which has made remarkable contributions to science and civilization can be explained by no other process than unconscious reversion into the diabolism from which this people was delivered by Saint Boniface, their apostle of the eighth century. . . . The recurrence of outrages against the members of that race, which is known in sacred history as "the chosen people of God," has gone to the extreme of ruthlessness against man and blasphemy against God, when the very temples in which they assemble to pray are put to the torch, and the sacred vessels are desecrated.

Beginning next Sunday, he directed, a second collect "Against Persecutors" [number eleven in the Tridentine liturgy] was to be recited in English by priests and people together, this to be done at all Masses "until the present inhuman German leadership is crushed."[13]

It was altogether fitting that Archbishop Murray should direct his people to prayer as an antidote to the manifest evil of anti-Semitism both in the orgy of violence abroad and in the subtle discriminatory winks and nods at the expense of "kikes" and "hebes" at home. But he was anxious at the same time to mold public opinion on this crucial issue. Perhaps he had Minneapolis more in mind than Nuremburg when, commenting early in 1939 on the plight of the Jewish/Christian refugees, he said:

How hypocritical of any Catholic, who unites with the priest at the altar in commemorating "the sacrifice of our Patriarch Abraham," to repudiate the common spiritual heritage of the chosen people of God by fostering either hostility or indifference to the descendants of Abraham, just because they are the children of Abraham! An obligation rests primarily on those who are members of the Mystical Body of Christ to exemplify his mercy and his love by extending to the members of his race the type of charity begotten in his Sacred Heart for the salvation of the world.[14]

On the greatest moral issue of his time, the little man from Hartford had come down squarely and courageously on the right side. He deserves in his way as

---

13. Murray to "Reverend Father," November 14, 1938 (copy), AASPM, Murray Papers.

14. Quoted in *CB*, January 24, 1939.

much credit as his chief, Pius XI, who had to speak to the world at large, tee-tering on the edge of war, and who said simply, We Christians are all really Semites.

Whether Archbishop Murray—and other influential persons who spoke out as he did—contributed significantly to tempering the relatively mild yet offensive local anti-Semitism cannot be determined with any certainty. It may well be that only in the aftermath of the Second World War, when the un-speakable crimes committed at Auschwitz and the other camps came to be known, did the ugliness of any such prejudice manifest itself unequivocally. Collective Western guilt over the Holocaust made possible the creation of the state of Israel; it also placed anti-Semitism of any kind beyond the bounds of civilized behavior.

AND, TO BE SURE, THERE WERE OTHER SOCIAL EVILS TO CONFRONT. Indeed, at least one prominent prelate, the archbishop of Cincinnati, believed that so dire a situation required the convening of a fourth plenary council.

> I feel that we Bishops are in a period of transition. We have dealt with the old order of things. We now see a modern paganism literally destroying the very foundations of religion and morality. Can we remain silent? Can we refuse to write a sensible page of legislation in a Fourth Plenary Coun-cil? Can we withhold a Pastoral Letter as part of the Council, which may be so helpful to our successors in future generations?[15]

On present trends, the *Catholic Bulletin* warned darkly in 1933, "one of every five or six marriages" contracted in the United States will be dissolved. Clearly two of the four institutions that influence community behavior are declining—the family and the Church—while the two others—government and industry—flourish more than ever.[16] How industry's societal clout had in-creased in the midst of the Great Depression the editors did not explain. But at any rate a couple of generations later a putative divorce rate of between fif-teen and twenty percent—a statistic, it should be noted, emerging from the till then unprecedented sexual liberality of the 1920s—appears almost Victo-rian. There has been of course no such thing as an Age of Innocence. Still, from the rather jaded retrospect of seventy years, the moral culture that

---

15. McNicholas to Murray, October 26, 1934, AASPM, Murray Papers. Nothing came of this idea.

16. *CB,* January 7, 1933.

Catholics in Minnesota—and indeed across America—confronted during the 1930s looks remarkably simple and straightforward compared to what has come since.

Archbishop Murray early in his episcopate laid out the broad principles of the Church's responsibility vis-à-vis the social order.

> Since the Church cannot remain isolated in the current of everyday life, it is quite important that her voice should be made articulate in the decisions of our great social organism, whenever those decisions affect the moral integrity of the home, the school, the Church, and various groups within the Church that through adversity or misfortune have become dependent on the governing powers of society.[17]

The last clause of that statement had direct reference to the current economic crisis and to the steps, still unsure and faltering, that the Roosevelt administration was taking to ameliorate the situation. While careful to insist that their clergy eschew even the appearance of partisan politics,[18] Murray and his episcopal colleagues nevertheless tended to support the president's initiatives. Thus the NCWC formally endorsed the National Recovery Act of 1933, one of the earliest achievements of the New Deal.[19]

But the Church's commitment to promote the nation's "moral integrity" could not be restricted, in Murray's judgment, simply to helping repair the damage done to the nation's political and economic infrastructure, important as that may have been. Surely there were other issues that reflected just as much the need for a Christian vision if society were to be redeemed. Indeed, the archbishop argued, economic recovery "will be fruitless without a recovery in the field of Christian manhood and womanhood." Degradation has become so widespread and so linked to criminal enterprise that it amounts to "commercialized kidnapping." Pastors must educate their flocks to "flee the tide of nudism, race-suicide, and commercialized vice." Roadhouses and dance halls "sow the germs of self-destruction." At the same time, the archbishop wanted his people to be sophisticated enough to deplore acts which, while not immoral, "disregard the proprieties arising from a sense of Christian culture and Catholic decency." He was particularly distressed by one such.

---

17. Murray to "Reverend Father," March 28, 1933 (copy), AASPM, Murray Papers.

18. See chapter 20, above.

19. *CB*, September 9, 1933. For the text of the Act, see http://www.civics-online.org/library/formatted/texts/recovery_act.html. Accessed May 20, 2008.

In our agricultural fairs the spectacle of marriages even between those who are not Catholics as a feature of activities to increase the gate receipts should lead to a withdrawal [by Catholics] of participation in exhibits, attendance at the fair and membership in any board that is responsible for the program. Marriage was instituted by God as a sacred source of life for society at large, and, while those who are not members of the Church may marry when and where they please, Catholics by their presence should not condone or approve a violation of common decency. The next stage in the development of barnyard ethics may become more revolting to those who have any sense of decency left to cover the exhibition of degradation and degeneration.[20]

It seems a far stretch to include rustic weddings held at fairs when compiling a list of pressing moral concerns. But on matters of public morality—and particularly matters sexual—there was more than a hint of official paranoia in the regulations Catholics between the wars were expected to abide by. Dancing was another activity that appeared, with small justification, to stir the celibate hierarchy's Jansenist juices. A Vatican decree of 1917 confirmed a directive of the Third Plenary Council of Baltimore (1884) that forbade any dancing on any church property, even for "pious causes" like parochial fund raising, and, moreover, all priests had to absent themselves from dances held elsewhere.

These regulations must be observed in the spirit in which they were made. Therefore the laity should not embarrass the clergy by demanding the use of church buildings, schools, or other property held by the church for social gatherings which they desire to assemble, with dancing as part of the program. This holds true whether the gathering is for the entire community, for the members of the congregation only, or for family groups that sometimes request the use of church property for wedding parties.[21]

But to suggest a measure of overreaction in legislation of this sort is not to deny that Murray was right to insist upon vigilance, particularly with re-

---

20. John Gregory Murray, "Moral Recovery" (a pastoral letter), August 8, 1933, AASPM, Murray Papers.

21. Murray to "Reverend Father," March 25, 1933 (copy), AASPM, Murray Papers.

gard to children, "Two incidents have come to light recently," he declared at
the beginning of 1934, "which we think might profitably be brought to the attention of pastors and teachers." The first was information given to the archbishop by the principal of a parochial school who, her suspicions aroused by
some of her pupils' smirking allusions to the neighborhood movie theater, directed them to write down descriptions of the conduct they witnessed there
by grade and high school students, "especially on Saturday and Sunday afternoons when hundreds of children attend movies." The principal of a neighboring school made a similar experiment.

> The information conveyed in the written statements was shocking. Kiss-
> ing, hugging, necking, swearing, cursing and drinking stood out as rela-
> tively minor offenses; there was unmistakable evidence of immoral prac-
> tices among the boys themselves as well as among the boys and girls,
> during the showing of the picture.[22] So serious, in fact, was the state of af-
> fairs revealed by these statements that I am requesting all the pastors to
> investigate conditions prevailing in the theaters within their parishes.[23]

The second finite "incident" was not unrelated to the first, though it also
represented a perennial conundrum faced by American Catholics in their relationships to the secular city. The archbishop had been informed that a questionnaire had been sent out "by the State Board of Preventable Diseases and
the State Board of Education to the teachers in the public high schools." The
document brought forward "thirty two topics on Sex Education which might
be divided into three groups." First, "those dealing with adolescence and
courtship; [secondly] those dealing with the psychology of the generative or-
gans, procreative act, and pregnancy; [and thirdly] those dealing with such

---

22. I was a grade school child during these years, regularly in attendance on
Saturday afternoons (not on Sundays, very much an adult preserve) for a Western
starring Hopalong Cassidy or Dick Foran, and a chapter of a serial about the masked
Lone Ranger or perhaps Flash Gordon's contest with Ming the Merciless. I have no
recollection of the immoral goings-on as described by Archbishop Murray and his
informants.

23. Murray to "Reverend Father," February 14, 1934 (copy), AASPM, Murray
Papers. This document is a typewritten draft vetted in pencil at various points. Thus
the quotation in the text beginning "requesting all the pastors" is a correction for
"requesting that the whole matter be turned over to the Morals Division of the police and to the Department of Juvenile Delinquency." Murray apparently decided the
original proposal was too draconian.

problems as masturbation, prostitution, venereal diseases, etc." The questionnaire asked the teachers "to suggest into which branches of the high school
curriculum these various topics might be incorporated."

> You can readily see, dear Father, what will be the ultimate results if men
> and women without any ethical or moral convictions are permitted to
> handle these questions. Several visits to the State Capitol brought out the
> information that this project was initiated by the State Board of Edu-
> cation over a year ago, that all the Superintendents of public high schools
> [sic] in the State had received a similar questionnaire and had already
> made a report. Although the project is still in the inquiry-stage, there ap-
> parently is nothing to prevent a particular high school from putting it
> into effect, if it so desires. Since almost every parish in the Archdiocese
> has classes or discussion clubs for students attending the public high
> schools, I am requesting the priests who are in charge of high school stu-
> dents be on the alert for any evidence of the penetration of such immoral
> procedures into the educational program, and to send to the chancery of-
> fice any information which would help us to meet and solve a problem
> which is confronting us on such a large scale.[24]

And what about mass entertainment? In his message deploring the behavior of schoolchildren in movie theaters, cited above, Murray concluded:
"It occurs to me that similar conditions would be uncovered in other localities if an investigation were made. At any rate, we have here undoubtedly an
example of the influence exerted on our youngsters even by the type of recreation found in our theaters." The moral impact of moving pictures, so it was
argued, went beyond any prior vehicle of entertainment, and, in the eyes of
the conventional Catholic leadership, it was mostly deleterious, and for a specific reason. "While all agencies of evil are to be condemned and avoided
equally, the reading of bad books, magazines and periodicals, the listening to
vulgar broadcasts over the radio, and attendance at crime-breeding night-
clubs are all under the control of the individual." Not so the motion picture
industry, with regard to which the individual "is confronted with the problem
of a mass movement for pleasure into which he is enmeshed with seventy
million other persons," the number of tickets sold each week at movie theaters across the United States.

---

24. Murray to "Reverend Father," February 14, 1934 (copy), AASPM, Murray
Papers. In this second section the draft is modified only in minor ways.

Clearly some supervision is needed if Hollywood is not "to pander to the degraded taste of the American public." "An organization known as the Legion of Decency has been in the process of development under the auspices of the [American] bishops."[25] Archbishop Murray was a zealous supporter of the Legion throughout his time in St. Paul, and from 1935 the lists of movies, labeled morally acceptable or objectionable, duly appeared in the pages of his diocesan weekly.[26] Over the years the categories grew more nuanced, but the basic principle was honored throughout the Legion's existence. In the beginning taking a formal pledge to condemn bad films and to try to persuade the public at large to do the same meant that a person had permanently "enrolled" in the Legion. In 1938 the procedure was altered, and the pledge was renewed each year at Masses celebrated on the feast of the Immaculate Conception. It was in the original sense of membership that justified Murray, in his own mind at least, to "speak for the 150,000 citizens enrolled [locally] in the Legion of Decency" in protest to the mayors of St. Paul and Minneapolis at the upcoming production, in 1935, of *Tobacco Road,* "a foul, degrading, vile, lewd, blasphemous spectacle."[27]

A more jaded age no doubt finds such preoccupations of marginal importance. So too with a diktat of 1939. Because saloons stayed open till the early hours of Christmas morning, drunks regularly staggered into churches during the celebration of midnight Mass. "There is [therefore] no alternative," declared the archbishop, but "to forbid the saying of midnight Mass anywhere in the Archdiocese of St. Paul . . . notwithstanding permissions or privileges heretofore granted to any priest, church, chapel, convent or institution within this jurisdiction." The first Mass of the feast could not begin before four a.m.[28]

---

25. Murray to "Reverend Father," August 28, 1934 (copy), AASPM, Murray Papers. This document, six typed pages long, came from the Legion's headquarters in Chicago. It is clearly not written in Murray's literary style.

26. See, e.g., *CB,* January 5 and March 9, 1935, which stated: "This listing of current films, adopted by the Legion of Decency of the Archdiocese of St. Paul, is prepared by the Motion Picture Bureau of the International Federation of Catholic Alumnae.

27. *CB,* December 21, 1935. The pledge and "enrollment" had taken place at Masses on Sunday, December 8. Murray was objecting to Jack Kirkland's dramatization (1933) of the Erskine Caldwell novel (1932). The motion picture *Tobacco Road* appeared in 1941.

28. Murray to "Reverend Father," December 11, 1939 (copy), AASPM, Murray Papers.

But another anxiety voiced by Murray did not prove to be so transient, an issue in fact that to this day haunts the Catholic community. It was not just "the tide of nudism" and "commercialized vice" that alarmed the archbishop; it was also "race-suicide." Pope Pius XI's encyclical on matrimony, *Casti connubii,* was published at the end of 1932. In it the pontiff reiterated the traditional teaching that "frustrating the marriage act" was a "pernicious error." But the virtual unanimity that had prevailed on this matter since Old Testament times had long since been eroded. Indeed, other Christian communions were at that very moment in the process of altering their views about artificial contraception. In 1930, for example, the Lambeth Conference of Anglican bishops resolved that for serious reasons a couple could legitimately limit or avoid parenthood by means other than abstinence. And such certainly was the position long held by the secular culture.[29] Catholics in Minnesota, like Catholics everywhere, were told otherwise in no uncertain terms. "Archbishop Warns Against Birth Control Propaganda," rang out a headline in the *Catholic Bulletin.*[30] Murray instructed his priests to inform their people that they must not associate with organizations supporting birth control or sterilization, both contrary to the natural law. Medical personnel and social workers who disseminated birth control information or who participated in any related action must be denied the sacraments "until they have agreed to repair as far possible the injury done and [to] guarantee to refrain from cooperation in such evil." And a sharp eye must be kept on tax-supported institutions, national and local.

> The small bands of vicious propagandists who have captured the fancy or destroyed the morale of our social leadership do not represent the great body of American thought and morals. The propaganda within private and public welfare groups must find an antidote in the organized force of sane thinking and sound ethics. For that reason further information will be sent you in the near future to enable you to set in motion a movement to restore the code of correct philosophy to its proper place in the government of social welfare agencies.[31]

---

29. See *Time* 18 (July 14, 1931): 34–35.

30. *CB,* August 10, 1935.

31. Murray to "Reverend Father," August 6, 1935 (copy), AASPM, Murray Papers.

The official policy was unambiguous, but the trifling increase in the population of the archdiocese of St. Paul during the 1930s suggests that perhaps not all Catholic couples followed the prescribed line.[32]

A CLERICAL DISPUTE, RELATIVELY TRIVIAL IN ITSELF AND chronologically well into John Gregory Murray's years of administration, provides an insight into his style of governance. In 1940 the pastor of Guardian Angels parish in Hastings[33] contested the claim of the pastor of St. Joseph's in nearby Miesville for territorial jurisdiction, on the grounds that St. Joseph's had been founded to serve Germans exclusively. If the claim were conceded, the practical affect would have been to consign to Miesville some Catholics of non-German descent living between the two towns, along with their boxes of envelopes for the Sunday collection. The complainant, the priest in Hastings, was Rudolph Nolan—the same Father Nolan who, as chancellor, had overseen the refurbishing of 226 Summit Avenue prior to Murray's arrival in St. Paul and who had arranged housing and other accommodation for Mrs. Nicholas Brady and her entourage at the time of the installation ceremony.[34] The disagreement was referred to Murray, who, in turn—because the competition between national and territorial parishes had so vexed the American Church over so many years that the Vatican required notification of such cases—had to inform the apostolic delegate.

The archbishop of St. Paul was clearly irritated. Immigration had "diminished virtually to nothing," he wrote, and so adjudication in matters of this sort ought to have vanished. And he was personally miffed as well. "Father Nolan, who had been chancellor under Archbishop Dowling and was still chancellor when I came, requested appointment to the vacant parish of Guardian Angels in Hastings the week after I arrived in January, 1932."[35] But

---

32. According to the *Official Catholic Directory*, the Catholic population of the archdiocese of St. Paul increased from 281,298 in 1932 to 301,768 in 1939.

33. In 1987, Guardian Angels merged with the German national parish in Hastings, St. Boniface, to form St. Elizabeth Ann Seton. See Wright, *Gather Us In*, 223.

34. See chapter 19, above.

35. In 1942 Father Nolan was named pastor of St. Stephen's parish at 22nd and Clinton Avenue South in Minneapolis. Between 1948 and 1952 my parents and I were parishioners at St. Stephen's. During these years I was a seminarian, first at Nazareth Hall and then at the St. Paul Seminary. St. Stephen's was in those days the prototypical pre-Vatican II urban, blue-collar, lower middle-class parish—seven Masses on Sunday and multiple devotions through the week and the parochial

Murray was annoyed most at his predecessors. John Ireland had laid down no distinct boundaries between the two venerable parishes—Hastings founded in 1856, Miesville in 1873[36]—except to endorse "a middle line," decided by informal negotiation between pastors a generation or two earlier. Dowling had simply ignored the issue. But "Father Nolan, with knowledge of the conditions in the chancery office, would not accept the principle of a 'middle line' as regards the parish of St. Joseph in Miesville." No data exists "to determine whether the former archbishops . . . set up so-called German parishes as territorial parishes in localities where all [sic] residents were German."[37]

How this disagreement was settled—if indeed it was—is not known. But what emerges from Murray's account of it—aside from pique at the personal disloyalty of Rudolph Nolan—is the archbishop's annoyance at the administrative carelessness of his two predecessors. Without data, precedent could not be established, and informal negotiation to "a middle line" was hardly an adequate substitute for precise delineation. John Gregory Murray's managerial instincts ran toward conformity and centralization, and such a stance inevitably led to an expanded bureaucracy. Witness how very early in his time in St. Paul he decreed that parochial societies associate themselves formally with the National Council of Catholic Men and the National Council of Catholic Women, and he laid out in detail the steps necessary to expedite the accomplishment of this objective. Characteristically he also drew careful distinctions. His directive, he said, did not apply to various organizations—the Knights of Columbus, the Daughters of Isabella, the Ancient Order of Hibernians—which, though made up of Catholics, "are designed to provide some form of intellectual or social advantage for the members themselves, and at the same time contribute to the welfare of others. Thus they establish relations with other agencies that are not religious in character and yet play a very important part in the development of forces which necessarily react on the Church in her contact with the outside world."[38] With all due respect,

---

school the most important auxiliary activity. Nolan presided over a bevy of gifted curates: Harry Majerus, Donald Eichinger, William Bullock (later bishop of Des Moines and of Madison) and, on weekends, the director of the St. Thomas Military Academy, John R. Roach (later archbishop of St. Paul). My father, a simple but astute man, delighted in his time as a parishioner at St. Stephen's, where, he said, he never heard a bad sermon. Rudolph Nolan died in 1952, aged fifty-eight.

36. See Reardon, *Diocese of St. Paul*, 607, 626.

37. Murray to Cicognani, November 4, 1940 (copy), AASPM, Murray Papers.

38. Murray to "Reverend Father," March 25, 1933 (copy), AASPM, Murray Papers. See also *CB*, April 19, 1933.

Murray appeared to be saying in effect, belonging to the Knights of Columbus included, besides Catholic witness, the availability of an advantageous insurance policy, a clubroom for camaraderie and games of pinochle, and, for the fourth degree, the right on ceremonial occasions to don a cape and sword.

It seemed as though the archbishop could never garner enough information. "As already announced," he wrote on September 1, 1934, "the parishes of the archdiocese will begin taking an individual census of each parish and mission church by September 15, if such action has not been taken before that date." Cards for this purpose had been sent from the chancery. Other means of gathering data may be used in accord with taste, the directive continued, but all information must be recorded on the cards, which were then to be returned to the chancery.

> If a pastor wishes to arrange for a rapid preliminary survey by members of the laity, organized in groups to cover small restricted areas within his parish in order to list Catholics or supposed Catholics or prospective Catholics by just taking names and addresses, there is no objection. But the real spiritual work of the census must be done by a priest who alone has the knowledge and the right to obtain the intimate personal details that furnish the basis for healing invalid marriages, reconstructing shattered family life, and coming into contact personally with prospective converts.

And four other sets of cards were also being dispatched to the pastors, on which were to be entered the records of parishioners' baptism, confirmation, marriage, and death. Since his arrival in St. Paul, Murray said crossly, no such material had been delivered to the chancery—the implication being that it had not been delivered before 1932 either, and so another negative reflection upon the administrative styles of Dowling and Ireland. "It is quite necessary that I have this information in preparation for the quinquennial report which I must take to Rome for the ad limina visit before the end of the year."[39]

Nor was he reluctant to set out the norms of public worship, even in considerable detail. The last Mass on Sunday, for example, always *pro populo,*[40] must be sung from the first of October till the end of June, it must not

---

39. Murray to "Reverend Father," September 1, 1934 (copy), AASPM, Murray Papers.

40. The Mass offered weekly by the pastor specifically, and without stipend, "for the people" of his parish—"the parish Mass," Murray called it.

commence later than eleven a.m., and "on all Sundays throughout the year instruction will be given for not less than twenty minutes over and above all announcements and the reading of the gospel." And what should that instruction consist of? Murray's chancery was ready with an answer. Sermons should be preached in accord with the teaching and the order of the *Catechism* of the Council of Trent, a copy of which was sent to all priests "as a personal gift of the Archbishop." A printed schedule was sent as well, which provided the preacher with his precise subject matter, beginning (October 7, 1934) with "The Nature and Necessity of Faith" and ending five years later with "Amen," as the summation and last word of the Lord's Prayer, with the relevant pages of the *Catechism* in each instance duly cited.[41]

It is doubtful in the extreme that these directives, and many like them, were always or even often carefully observed. That the chancery should assign formally and officially the date when a parish should hold its annual Forty Hours Devotion in honor of the Eucharist, was in fact a convenience for a busy pastor.[42] But to set up an elaborate timetable of sermons to be prepared over a five-year period would have seemed to most priests an addled notion. And indeed, a review of John Gregory Murray's episcopal career gives off not seldom the impression that what he ordered to be done he really thought of as something good to be done, or something required to be done by canon law, without, however, expecting the ideal necessarily to mesh with practical reality. But in one area, thanks to the energy of a dedicated subordinate, an initiative bore fruit almost immediately.

The Confraternity of Christian Doctrine traces its existence—and its commitment to bring adequate catechesis to the Catholic man, woman, and child in the pew—back to the sixteenth century and the era of the Council of Trent.[43] The organization had lain dormant for a century and more, but to its credit the American hierarchy had given the confraternity a renewed life. In St. Paul Archbishop Murray initiated the program in 1935 and appointed as its director Father Rudolph Bandas, a much degreed academic whose primary assignment was professor of theology at the St. Paul Seminary.[44] The aims of

---

41. Printed "Schedule," October 7, 1934–December 7, 1939, AASPM, Murray Papers.

42. See, e.g., *CB*, January 12, 1935.

43. For an overview, see http://www.newadvent.org/cathen/03711b.htm. (Accessed May 20, 2008.) For a brief treatment of the confraternity from a national perspective, see Jay P. Dolan, *The American Catholic Experience* (New York, 1985), 256.

44. Bandas earned the degrees from Rome and Leuven. For his career at the seminary—culminating in the rectorship, 1945–1958—see Athans, *To Work for the Whole People*, 180–184.

this restoration included the formation of study clubs to advance the knowledge of their faith among adults, vacation schools for youngsters, particularly those living in rural areas or not enrolled in parochial schools, and the training and support of teachers of public school pupils in the Twin Cities during the weekly release-time for religious instruction permitted by statute in Minnesota.[45] In his opening directive on this matter Murray, while speaking specifically of vacation schools, encapsulated the whole spirit and purpose of the revived confraternity.

Such a program does not view religious instruction merely as a preparation for the reception of the sacraments. Religious instruction is designed not for academic knowledge but for perfect participation in the life of God through activity in the Church, the Mystical Body of Christ. Hence the vacation school should enroll all the children whether they have received the sacraments or not, and create within them a taste for the things of the soul that they will be eager to pass into our study clubs and then into the broader field of higher Catholic culture and Catholic Action.[46]

Statistical achievement came quickly. In January 1935, Murray had called for the parishes to organize study clubs; by April, Bandas could report that about five hundred such clubs were already functioning, their schedules established, and their texts (on the life of Christ) determined. Similarly, the confraternity's vacation religious schools, a hundred of them, were ready to convene between June 15 and July 14; seven orders of nuns had been recruited to teach in them.[47] The Confraternity of Christian Doctrine flourished in succeeding years as well. An administrative center near the chancery was eventually set up, and Catholic Youth Centers, under the confraternity's aegis, were founded in St. Paul and Minneapolis. It seems safe to say that no initiative undertaken in John Gregory Murray's time was more successful than this. And one must give due credit to Rudolph Bandas, especially since his reputation among the generations of priests he helped train as a seminary professor and rector is mixed at best.[48]

---

45. Reardon, *Diocese of St. Paul,* 530–532.

46. Murray to "Reverend Father," February 15, 1935 (copy), AASPM, Murray Papers.

47. See *CB,* January 5, April 13, and April 27, 1935.

48. Athans, *To Work for the Whole People,* especially 180–184 and 215–216. Father (later Monsignor) Bandas was rector of the seminary during my years as a student there, 1950 to 1956.

THE SUCCESS OF THE CONFRATERNITY OF CHRISTIAN DOCTRINE
provided one sign that, despite the hard times, the Catholic community in the
archdiocese of St. Paul during the 1930s possessed plenty of vigor. And there
were other signs, many of them, that pointed to the same conclusion. The
parishes and institutions manifested a robust life that gave rise to a variety of
activities which were rooted in religious commitment, to be sure, but also
spoke to social and cultural concerns. And economic ones too, precisely because the hard times necessitated any legitimate means of raising money. Indeed, it would be more accurate to say that all these currents melded together,
as a sampling of events taking place in parishes outside the Twin Cities in the
late spring of 1935 might demonstrate.

On Sunday, June 2, the baseball team made up of men from St. Columb-
kill parish, Belle Creek, played a game against Bellechester; afterwards a
chicken dinner was served in the church hall. Holy Trinity in Goodhue unfurled its new parochial banner, purchased by the Holy Name Society, and
congratulated two of its high school students who had won honors in an
essay contest sponsored by the National Catholic Rural Life Conference. At
St. John's in Jordan thirty-five first communicants were enrolled in the Arch-
confraternity of the Scapular of Mount Carmel. Also on June 2 the women of
St. Philip's parish in Litchfield put together a day long "celebration," with dinner at noon and a buffet from 5:00 p. m., in order to raise needed funds. There
were a wedding and a baptism the week of May 26 at St. Timothy's in Maple
Lake, and on May 27 baccalaureate services were held in the church for parochial and high school graduates; "Father William Wey of Winsted preached
the sermon."

One hundred three children received first Communion on the feast of
the Ascension, May 30, the largest class ever at St. Edward's, Minneota; breakfast prepared by members of the Mothers Club followed in the church hall.
On May 19, at St. Michael's parish, Morgan, forty-eight young men and
women were initiated into the St. Michael and St. Ann Club. Beginning with
Mass and Communion for the new members, the program lasted throughout
the day and included dinner at noon and a roster of speakers in the afternoon. A "Silver Tea," arranged by the Altar and Rosary Society of Our Lady of
the Lake parish in Mound, was held from 2:00 p.m. on June 9 to mark the
opening of the new rectory. A week before that, in New Trier, "members of
the St. Mary's [parish] Ladies Society and the St. Teresa Society sponsored a
card party in the subauditorium [sic] of the church. Bunco and 500 were
played." On the same day, "the Dramatic [sic] Club" of Sacred Heart in Rush
City performed, "under the auspices of the church of St. Gregory," North

Branch, a three-act play entitled, "Brown's Shady Past," in the North Branch auditorium. Ten women were inducted into the Christian Mothers Sodality of St. Mathias parish, Wanda; continuing members renewed their pledges. J. P. Spiess served for forty-two years as secretary of the St. Peter Society, a group named for his parish and his town. An informal party was held in his honor on May 28, at which he was given a cane with an inscription on its silver band: "J. P. Spiess at the St. Peter Society, 1892–1934."[49]

A similar selective chronicle of activities in Minneapolis and St. Paul parishes toward the end of that summer tells much the same story. St. Paul first.

On the afternoon of Sunday, September 8, the Parents and Friends Club of St. Agnes parish held its second annual Sauerkraut and Wiener Festival at the Como Park picnic grounds. Games were organized for the children, and music was provided by the Humboldt High School band. That same evening, at Blessed Sacrament, the five boys from the parish scheduled shortly to enter Nazareth Hall preparatory seminary were honored at a reception. The Fortnightly Club of St. Columba's opened its fall season with luncheon and cards in the school auditorium on September 10; two days later Father Charles Carty, a noted missionary, began a three-day retreat for the women of the parish. Sponsored by the Rosary Sodality and the Young Ladies Sodality, the parishioners of Holy Redeemer were invited to a lunch and "entertainment" in the church hall on the evening of September 11. At the same time St. Luke's Parish Council was meeting in the school to lay out a schedule for early autumn activities, beginning with a "bridge luncheon" on September 24. "Mrs. G. N. Burg, 2122 Iglehart Avenue, opened her home on Monday, September 9, at 2:00 p.m. for the first fall meeting of the St. Mark's parish Fortnightly Club. Mrs. P. J. Bruce, president, presided." And while Mrs. Burg's guests sipped their coffee and munched their cookies, the Rosary Society of St. Vincent's parish assembled for its regular meeting in the school hall; three days after that the Holy Name Society there held "a card and bunco party" in the church hall.

And Minneapolis.

The Ascension Club with its athletic facilities was reopened for the use of parishioners and others in the area; the schedule drawn up for the winter season highlighted swimming lessons for children and adults. On Wednesday, September 11, the Young Ladies Sodality of Holy Cross parish hosted a 500, bridge, and bunco party, with "entertainment and prizes"; the "chairman" of the affair was "Miss Adeline Smuda," aided by the names upwards of

---

49. *CB*, June 1, 1935.

twenty-five others, all clearly of Polish descent and thus witnesses to the eth-
nicity of northeast Minneapolis, not reluctant to have their names recorded
in the public print. The eleven o'clock Mass at Holy Rosary on September 8
was offered for the members of the Third Order of St. Dominic; the Holy
Rosary chapter "attended in a body." Father Donald Gormley, Director of
St. Thomas Military Academy, addressed the Woman's [sic] Club of Incarnation parish on September 13; this was the first business meeting of the club for
the current year and was followed by luncheon. The same evening a keno and
card party, sponsored by the Mothers Club of St. Stephen's parish, was held in
the school auditorium.[50]

Over the years of the Murray episcopate a comparable pattern could be
discerned among archdiocesan institutions and organizations not limited by
parochial boundaries. Thus on January 15, 1939, the De Paul Club observed
its fifteenth anniversary at a dinner in the Radisson Hotel in Minneapolis.
Featured among the speakers was Father Thomas Meagher, director of the
Catholic Welfare Association. The club had been founded to promote the
education of talented Catholic girls with limited financial resources; money
raised was disbursed by Meagher's Association. Three days later, at the Seton
Guild's residence and cafeteria on South Ninth Street in Minneapolis,[51] Father
Francis Schenk of the St. Paul Seminary gave the second in a series of addresses to "the marriage clinic for Catholic women," his topic "Rights and Duties of the Married Couple." By this time the guild—devoted like the De Paul
Club to the service of Catholic girls and young women of slender means, but
much more elaborately so—had put in place its midwinter program, including fiction and poetry readings, drama classes, Christian doctrine studies,
physical education courses, as well as speech therapy and training in crafts,
first aid, and hygiene.

On January 19, the third Thursday of the month, the Catholic Order of
Foresters, St. Paul court number 89, now formally "affiliated" with St. John's
parish in St. Paul, convened its regular meeting in the church hall. That same
evening the Si-Ho-Chi [sic] Club organized a card party at St. Bridget's parish
in Minneapolis, the proceeds from which were designated "for the benefit of
a Catholic mission in China." And two evenings before that "Division 9, Ladies Auxiliary of the Ancient Order of Hibernians met in the Teachers' Federation Building, St. Paul." The Newman Hall Auxiliary announced that two
rummage sales and a card party would in coming weeks be held in support of

---

50. *CB*, September 7, 1935.
51. See Reardon, *Diocese of St. Paul*, 609.

the apostolate to Catholic students at the University of Minnesota. On Sunday, January 15, the Black Friar Guild, Twin Cities' chapter, received Communion "in a body" at St. Albert the Great, Minneapolis, with breakfast afterwards. The guild met again on January 18 at the Diocesan Teachers' College in St. Paul, in order to entertain tryouts for the guild's second play of the season, titled "Catherine the Great."[52]

Nor were the institutions of learning in the archdiocese behindhand in giving expression to a varied and lively Catholic cultural experience. A few months after the amateur thespians had trod the boards at the Teachers College, the administration of the College of St. Catherine—having survived the calamitous economic circumstances of the early and mid-1930s[53]—announced that the opening of "the Little Theatre," after year-long construction, would occasion a conference of the heads of the drama departments of all the colleges in Minnesota. It began on May 1, 1939, when Dr. Lowell Lees, chairman of the speech department at the University of Minnesota, delivered the keynote address. The annual May Fete lay just ahead, when each class played a distinct role in diverting the rest of the college community; the seniors this year pledged to stage a particularly sparkling variety show. Later in the month the St. Catherine's School of Dramatics would present, under the direction of the department's chairman, Mabel Frey, a production of Milton's "The Masque of Comus" on a simulated, three-level Greek amphitheatre. And given "St. Kate's" growing eminence, it appeared more than appropriate that the Minnesota Council of Catholic Women should have chosen the college as the venue for its spring assembly.

The likes of rummage sales and card parties by the Newman auxiliary were afforded heightened legitimacy each year, when the alumnae of the Newman Club—who themselves had been students at the University—hosted a Communion breakfast. In 1939 the event took place on Sunday, April 30. After Mass celebrated at St. Lawrence church on Southeast Fifth Street in Minneapolis, and breakfast afterward at Newman Hall, participants were treated to a speech by Father Richard Doherty of the St. Paul Seminary, entitled "Troubled Europe Today." Doherty purported to have been an active newspaper correspondent who had had extensive professional contacts both in Europe and in the United States prior to his ordination, which experience gave the discussion (at the Newman breakfast) its relevance. Some weeks later, on May 21, 1939, the Alumnae Association of St. Margaret's Academy

---

52. *CB*, January 14, 1939.
53. See chapter 20, above.

in Minneapolis, in concert with the governing Josephite nuns, arranged a mothers/daughters breakfast, followed up on June 3 by a festive observance at the Radisson Hotel in downtown Minneapolis of the academy's thirty-second birthday.[54] At the banquet on that occasion the speaker was the archdiocesan vice-chancellor, Father Silverius Hauer. At Cretin High School in St. Paul the cadets who belonged to the Dramatic Club presented on May 7 and 8 a three-act mystery entitled "The Tiger House." And on those very days the senior class at St. Joseph's Academy, also in St. Paul, gave to the theatergoing public its version of "The Cradle Song." One academy freshman homeroom mounted a candy sale in the lobby to raise money for a large portrait of Pope Pius XI, who had recently died.[55]

Indeed, Achille Ratti, the Milanese librarian who had ascended to the throne of St. Peter in 1922 as Pius XI—the old lion, *il leone vecchio,* as his admiring compatriots dubbed him, who had, to a degree at least, tamed Mussolini and challenged Hitler—died February 10, 1939. The demise of the Holy Father came somewhat as surprise to Catholics in Minnesota. The news out of Rome early in February reported that the pontiff, in his eighty-second year, was suffering from a cold, nothing serious; a week later appeared a description of his internment in the crypt of St. Peter's Basilica in the Vatican, as well as, locally, an account of the pontifical service at the St. Paul Cathedral, at which the late leader of the Catholic world was eulogized by Archbishop Murray.[56] Eugenio Cardinal Pacelli was duly elected as Pius XII on March 2, and five weeks later Francis Spellman, an obscure auxiliary bishop in Boston, was appointed to the great see of New York. Murray, who knew these people well,[57] was perhaps less surprised than many by this remarkable promotion.[58]

---

54. See Reardon, *Diocese of St. Paul,* 668.

55. *CB,* April 29, 1939.

56. *CB,* February 11 and 18, 1939.

57. See chapter 19, above.

58. Patrick Cardinal Hayes of New York died September 4, 1938. Clerical rumor had it that had Pius XI lived, John McNicholas, archbishop of Cincinnati (and bishop of Duluth, 1918–1925), would have been promoted to New York. McNicholas was a close friend of Austin Dowling and of John Gregory Murray. See, for example, McNicholas to Murray, September 20, 1932, and November 28, 1933, AASPM, Murray Papers.

CHAPTER 22

A People Set Apart

CATHOLICS IN MINNESOTA DURING THE 1930S TOOK LITTLE interest in the higher reaches of ecclesiastical politics; whomever the Holy Father decided to send to New York was perfectly agreeable to them, but the matter did not really concern them. Even their own bishop was a somewhat remote, august figure. Their commitment to their faith, and their practice of it, centered on their parish, with its variety of activities and its specialized personnel: the pastor and, if the parish were large enough, his assistants in the rectory and, if there were a parochial school, the sisters in the convent. Social and familial bonds could be strengthened, to be sure, by joint participation in organizing card parties or engaging in amateur dramatics or sponsoring a learned lecture. But of course the truest measure of a parish's spiritual health was the quality of its sacramental and devotional life.

The promotion of that life admitted of no admixture from the outside. Indeed, the rigidity with which exclusivity was imposed upon the Catholic people during Archbishop Murray's tenure in St. Paul—and upon Catholics everywhere, for that matter—reveals an almost primordial fear of putting the faith, particularly that of young people, at risk. It reveals also the continuing dichotomy that had bedeviled American Catholics from the beginning: immigrants and the children of immigrants, they desperately wanted to be accepted as genuine Americans, and yet they recognized real danger in the temptation to accommodate without demur to a still largely Protestant culture. This was the same tension, the same ambivalence, that had troubled John Ireland when he confronted the competition between parochial and public schools.[1]

---

1. See chapter 13, above.

There was hardly a trace of ambiguity in Murray's position: it would be hard, in fact, to imagine a more sweeping list of the rules of disengagement than the one he promulgated early in 1940. "The various activities carried on in public schools, public institutions, and social organizations," the archbishop said, "demand the scrutiny of the pastors throughout the Archdiocese to offset the penetration of subversive influences in the associations into which the children of the Church are thrown by circumstance of necessity, indifference, or a perverted sense of freedom from Church discipline." He was especially exercised by "the formation of musical organizations in the schools and state institutions, . . . glee clubs and school choirs of which Catholics may be members." What if such a singing group is invited to perform in a program of worship in a Protestant church?

> Of course no Catholic may take active service in any ritual that is not Catholic, by singing or acting in a program religious in character, or designed to provide support for non-Catholic religious activities. Devotional services under auspices that are not Catholic do not permit of participation by Catholics. If they are required to be present, their presence may be only passive, without any expression of adherence to the form of worship conducted in the school or institution within which they are enrolled. . . . Catholics may not attend graduation exercises or be present at baccalaureate addresses in non-Catholic churches, but must absent themselves and receive their diplomas in private, if attendance is imposed upon the entire class.

And "subversive influences" were not restricted to heretical ceremonies. Catholics must not be participants in organizations whose activities "imply a profession of faith," such as "the YMCA, the YWCA, the HiY, the Girl Reserves, the Salvation Army, the Volunteers of America,[2] nor may they enroll in the De Molay, the American Youth Congress, the Young Pioneers, and a score of similar communistic organizations designed to alienate them from the Catholic religion or all religion."[3] Moreover, adult Catholics must avoid

---

2. At this point in the typed list "the Camp Fire Girls" is crossed out with a pencil.

3. Murray's term "communistic" is extravagant. DeMolay International was (and is) a youth organization with formal ties to Freemasonry. See http://www.demolay.org. (Accessed May 20, 2008.) The American Youth Congress was indeed during its brief existence during the 1930s a far left grouping, but its major patron, Eleanor Roosevelt, stoutly denied it had any communist connections. It disbanded

public lectures and public forum discussions, unless they are advised by their pastors of the safety of participation, nor may they take part in Bible reading, Bible interpretation, religious functions, devotional exercises, initiation ceremonies, chapel services, religious purpose [sic] programs, moral problem discussions under any auspices other than that of the Catholic Church.

"The responsibility of the clergy" in this regard "is extremely grave, and constant supervision of associations formed by the laity and especially by our youth must be exercised by the clergy, with the cooperation of parents and teachers."[4]

This harsh and sweeping repudiation of so many denominations and organizations, all of them in the public mind geared toward the amelioration of society at large, aroused a good deal of local resentment, once the content of the archbishop's ukase became widely known. The result was a luncheon meeting arranged by a group of Protestant ministers, at which Murray deftly— so one highly biased witness claimed—refuted with an easy clarity all the objections raised.[5] It is perhaps not too late after the fact to suggest that the archbishop's rejoinder to his critics on that occasion may have had more to do with stabilization than with refutation.

In any event, this was not, needless to say, an ecumenical era.

MUCH OF THE PIETY OF THE ERA SEEMED TO REST UPON repetition, seemed to require a quantitative measure. Recitation of the rosary provided one instance of this and reception of the Eucharist on nine consecutive "First Fridays" another.[6] Litanies with their invocations of the sacred and the studied responses—"Have mercy on us," "Pray for us," "Free me, O Lord"—spoke to the same conclusion, as did the so-called Divine Praises at Benediction, with priest and people alternating—"Blessed be God," "Blessed be God," "Blessed be his holy Name," "Blessed be his holy Name," and so on

---

in 1940. See http://en.wikipedia.org/wiki/American_Youth_Congress. (Accessed May 20, 2008.) The Young Pioneers was a Soviet organization, established by Lenin, with no American counterpart.

4. Murray to "Reverend Father," March 25, 1940 (copy), AASPM, Murray Papers.

5. Reardon, *Diocese of St. Paul,* 543–544.

6. See chapter 18, above.

through a modest list of doctrinal commitments. But this numerical and re-petitive characteristic showed itself most clearly in defining those good works related to the granting of indulgences. A spectacular example occurred early in the episcopate of John Gregory Murray. "Notwithstanding the hardships of worldwide economic collapse," he wrote, "and even as a consequence of such disaster, devout souls who find it possible to journey from home will throng about the sepulcher of our Savior and the throne of his Vicar, to be united more intimately to God and each other in the common cause of our sanctification."

A Holy Year[7] had been promulgated to begin April 1, 1933, and Catholics who traveled to Rome or the Holy Land over the succeeding twelve months could reap a rich spiritual reward. The pilgrims

who visit the basilicas[8] at Rome three times the same day or on subse-quent days may gain a plenary indulgence for themselves or for the souls in Purgatory, provided that they receive the sacraments of Penance and the Holy Eucharist and recite the following prayers before the altar of the Blessed Sacrament: the Our Father, Hail Mary, and Glory be to the Father five times in memory of the Passion, and once for the intention of the Holy Father; before the image of our Lord crucified the Apostles' Creed three times, and once the ejaculation, "We adore Thee O Christ and we bless Thee, because by thy Holy Cross Thou hast redeemed the world"; before the statue of the Blessed Virgin the Hail Mary seven times in honor of our Blessed Mother's sorrows, and once the petition, "Holy Mother, pierce me through, in my heart each wound renew, of my Savior crucified"; finally, before the high altar [of each basilica] the Apostles' Creed once. The indulgence may be gained each time that the threefold round of visits is made.

The overwhelming majority of those who could not go on such a mission "may gain the indulgence of the Holy Year during the same period, provided that they receive the sacraments of Penance and Holy Eucharist, visit their own parish church twelve times or their own chapel twelve times in the case of religious communities, and say the same prayers . . . enumerated for those

---

7. The first "Year of Jubilee" or "Holy Year" was proclaimed by Pope Boniface VIII in 1300. From the late Middle Ages the event occurred, with a few exceptions, every twenty-five years.

8. I.e., the four "major" basilicas: St. Peter's, St. John Lateran, St. Mary Major, and St. Paul's Outside the Walls.

making the visits to the basilicas in Rome." During the Holy Year the customary indulgences can be gained for the departed, "but all indulgences for the living, save the indulgence of the Holy Year, are suspended." An exception to this last provision was to be routinely made in behalf of the dying and for those receiving the sacrament of Extreme Unction.[9]

This obsession with precise numerical measurement in the spiritual realm can be discerned from other angles. For instance, in the spring of 1942 Murray directed that the people of the archdiocese be asked to prepare a spiritual bouquet for Pius XII in honor of the silver jubilee of the pontiff's episcopal consecration. The result was an edifying outpouring of good will, but remarkable also by the exactitude with which it was computed.

2029 Masses offered by the clergy; 5325 Masses offered at the request of the laity; 299,075 Masses heard [sic] by the laity; 173,538 Holy Communions received; 93,276 stations of the cross; 369,578 rosaries recited; 63,371 hours of adoration of the Blessed Sacrament; 1,048,555 [sic] hours of labor and suffering; 51,871 visits to the sick; 10,393 visits to the poor; 893,503 ejaculations; 24,900 litanies; 497,728 other prayers; $7455.35 alms to the poor; $6811.07 alms to the missions.[10]

A similar "manifestation of devotion" was tendered in the spring of 1950 to Archbishop Murray himself, when he celebrated the golden jubilee of his sacerdotal ordination. "The thousands of prayers, Masses, and acts of sacrifice offered for my intention which was [sic] directed in thanksgiving, reparation, and supplication to Almighty God not only in behalf of myself but of all the flock of Christ, became a gift transcending in value all the treasure that I have received from friends on any other occasion."[11]

---

9. Murray to "Reverend Father," March 24, 1933 (copy), AASPM, Murray Papers. For the striking contrast between the Holy Year observance of 1934 and that of 2000, see http://www.vatican.va/jubilee_2000/index.htm. Accessed May 20, 2008.

10. *CB*, April 11 and May 16, 1942.

11. Murray to Cullinan, May 24, 1950 (copy), AASPM, Murray Papers. The archbishop was also presented a purse of $67,333.00—$134.52 specifically from children—"towards my personal outstanding obligations in the form of notes amounting to $117,933.06" incurred since his arrival in St. Paul eighteen years earlier. So, with his debt reduced to $50,600.06, "for this relief I am most grateful." Monsignor John J. Cullinan was at this time pastor of St. Luke's parish in St. Paul. See also Reardon, *Diocese of St. Paul*, 555.

Keeping track of spiritual activity—putting a number to it—is by no means an ignoble thing to do. And repetition in one's prayer life is to a large extent a necessity; after all, as philosophers since Aristotle have insisted, it is precisely by repeating a good work that a virtue is formed, and surely following the Pauline injunction "to pray always" involves employing a large dollop of familiar verbal or mental formularies. Indeed, a good deal of unease was generated among Catholics when the sweeping changes introduced into the liturgy after the Second Vatican Council altered the fixed pattern of their common worship. The point here at any rate is not to disparage the commitment to quantification characteristic of the spirituality of an earlier time, but to position it within the larger context. This was the era when American Catholicism, having shed its immigrant clothes, measured its success within the contemporary culture, at least to a degree, in terms of the numbers of faithful it could muster: the tens of thousands, for instance, who marched in the annual rally of the Holy Name Society at the Minnesota State Fair Grounds or in the Rosary Processions held each May in St. Paul and Minneapolis. Little wonder, then, that laymen and women, who wanted to honor their spiritual mentor, the pope, should judge they had done so most appropriately by having "heard" Mass 299,075 times for the pontiff's intention.

But perhaps a highly significant expression of this mind-set proved to be also the most spectacular single event during John Gregory Murray's time in Minnesota.

ONE CONSEQUENCE OF THE INTENSE DEVOTION TO THE REAL Presence of Christ in the Eucharist[12] was the spread of the so-called Eucharistic Congress. In one sense this phenomenon can be traced back to the Middle Ages, as can most Catholic pious practices, but not until the religious revival of the nineteenth century did it assume a formal and regular place in the institutional life of the Church. It came in different sizes and shapes; there were local and regional congresses, and, from 1881 in Lille, France, international congresses, very elaborate and lengthy affairs—like the one attended by Murray in the company of Mrs. Nicholas Brady, Francis Spellman, and Fulton Sheen, in Dublin in 1932.[13] In between, so to speak, were the national congresses. In the United States the series began during the 1890s and continued every two or three years. The Eighth National Eucharistic Congress convened

---

12. See chapter 18, above.
13. See chapter 19, above.

in New Orleans in 1938. Next in turn was St. Paul or, more precisely in this case, St. Paul and Minneapolis.

An examination of the planning and execution of the Ninth National Eucharistic Congress, June 23–26, 1941, deserves a suitably careful analysis, because, while it predictably tells much about the spirituality of Minnesota Catholics—and indeed that of Catholics across the nation on the eve of the Second World War—it also reveals how a local church had developed its bureaucratic structures so that it could mobilize its personal and physical resources to meet a wider challenge—a far cry from the simpler days of Galtier, Cretin, and Grace. As general chairman, Murray appointed James Michael Reardon, pastor of the Basilica of St. Mary in Minneapolis, and former editor of the *Catholic Bulletin*.[14] It proved to be an auspicious choice; Reardon's organizational skills were considerable, he enjoyed the good opinion of the Catholic community, and his resolute, not to say imperious, temperament fitted him to see through a complex project. Assisting him was Father William Brand, chaplain of the Catholic Boys' Home, also in Minneapolis, as secretary, and Mr. Frank Delaney, vice-president of the First National Bank of St. Paul, as treasurer. Nineteen distinct committees were formed to deal with matters ranging from liturgical ceremonies to rail transport, publicity, and traffic. The chairmen—twelve priests, seven laymen, and, of course, no women—formed the congress's ultimate governing board, the General Committee, which met monthly.[15]

The arrangements began in detail with a directive from Archbishop Murray, dated a week before Christmas 1940. Each pastor received a sheet "on which you are asked to list the officers of the various committees that will be organized in each parish to cooperate with the diocesan committees, which are already in process of formation, so as to begin weekly meetings after the first of January." Then he added a caveat: "In the selection of officers, it is quite important that the pastor give consideration to those who are zealous Catholics, with particular devotion to the Blessed Sacrament [and] in the frequent reception of the sacraments, rather than [to] individuals who enjoy some degree of social distinction." Some delay may be necessary in this process, but it must not occur in "the organization of the most important committees, which require long preparation for their work. This is especially true of . . . the committees on music and banners as well as uniforms."

14. See chapters 15 and 16, above.

15. Minutes, General Committee, January 6, 1941, AASPM, Ninth Eucharistic Congress Collection (NECC).

Music for the congress merited special and prompt attention. In overall charge was Father Francis Missia, choirmaster at the St. Paul Seminary. The first steps had been taken. "The special Mass composed by Professor Pietro Yon for the occasion has just come from the press." Missia had prepared the "Eucharistic Hymnal,"[16] containing traditional Latin and English hymns and ordinaries of the Mass (including the Missa de Angelis, but not in Gregorian notation). Thousands of copies had been sent out by the archdiocesan Bureau of Education, so that the children could be prepared for the processional singing they were to do antiphonally (boys, girls, boys, girls). "That Father Missia and his committee may succeed in the great task undertaken, to make liturgical music the feature of the Congress, there is need for cooperation from every pastor, priest, choir director, organist and school principal in the Archdiocese." Adults were to familiarize themselves with the Hymnal, because they too were to sing in the processions. Moreover, "every pastor with a trained choir will accept the responsibility and the privilege of having his choir members participate in the singing of the Mass on Tuesday, June 24, and Thursday, June 26, the last day of the Congress," when 150,000 people were expected to assemble at the State Fair Grounds. On those two occasions Missia aimed for a mass chorus of 3,000, and he was precise as to how he wanted to balance the timbre of the singers' voices: 1,050 sopranos, 700 altos, 550 tenors, and 700 basses. Finally, Murray laid down the rules for gender segregation: At the holy hour for men at the Fair Grounds (June 24), only male singers allowed; at the holy hours for women at the St. Paul and Minneapolis auditoriums (June 25), no men or children.[17]

As for financing, it was estimated that the venture would cost about $100,000. Earlier national congresses had been supported by taxing the clergy and assessing the parishes. Reardon came up with an ingenious alternative.

> I have designed [he wrote all the pastors] the official emblem of the Congress [pictured] at the top of this page, and I propose to issue it as a souvenir in oxidized silver, and sell it for fifty cents through the parishes, allowing them a commission of five cents on each sale. Towards the end of Lent a consignment of these souvenirs—one for every person in your parish, according to Chancery Office records—will be shipped to your address, and you will be asked to remit at the rate of forty-five cents

---

16. A copy in AASPM, NECC; 170 pp., copyrighted by Fischer and Bro., St. Gregory Guild.

17. Murray to "Reverend Father," December 18, 1940 (copy), AASPM, NECC.

apiece, the ten percent commission to be retained by the parish for any purpose designated by you.

In the meantime—"and this is where the shoe pinches for, of course, you know there is a catch in it"—funds were needed immediately to sustain the preliminary work, and so each pastor was requested to send half of the eventual total in advance. To be certain he was understood, the chairman provided an example: in a parish of 6,000 persons, at forty-five cents, the whole amount would be $2,700, of which $1,350 would be due in the chancery by February 10. This arrangement had been approved by Archbishop Murray.[18]

Father Reardon elaborated on his plan at a meeting of the General Committee a few weeks later. Besides the parochial scheme, the emblems, along with other souvenirs, were to be put on sale at the National Eucharistic Center (as the State Fair Grounds were renamed for the congress), the auditoriums in both cities, hotels, and department stores. The emblem was to be duly copyrighted so that no unauthorized vendor could sell them. "Also," he announced elatedly, "the head of the State Tourist Bureau has agreed to send out a booklet with the Congress emblem on the cover, describing the advantages of visiting Minnesota in the summer, to every priest in the United States, free of charge."

At the same meeting other possible sources of revenue were discussed. For example, it was determined that food and soft drink concessions should be awarded to competing companies. Murray suggested that the Agricultural Building be set aside for exhibits, at a charge of a dollar per square foot.[19] The plan worked handsomely, and Reardon's emblem was a roaring success. Cash on hand on January 31, 1941, totaled $10,267.77. By February 28 the figure had reached $56,837.30 and by April 30 $79,197.64. In the end, from all sources, support for the congress came to $160,000, of which about $120,000 resulted from the sale of the emblem. Disbursements amounted to $118,000, including $12,034.16 for rental of the Fair Grounds and $4,000 for the pope's representative and "his suite."[20] The balance, roughly $42,000, was used to endow a Minnesota Eucharistic Society.[21]

---

18. Reardon to "Reverend Father," January 24, 1941 (copy), AASPM, NECC.

19. Minutes, General Committee, February 12, 1941, AASPM, NECC.

20. Included in the "suite" was the local philanthropist Ignatius A. O'Shaughnessy for whom Murray requested appointment to the papal honor of Private Chamberlain of Cape and Sword. See Murray to Cicognani, April 19, 1941 (copy), AASPM, Murray Papers.

21. Financial Reports, signed by William Brand, AASPM, NECC, and Reardon, *Diocese of St. Paul*, 545–547.

The money was raised locally, but the "national" character of the congress was not ignored in the planning stage. Indeed, one might say international or at least intercontinental: Murray personally invited all the bishops in North America, and he reserved the whole of the St. Paul Hotel to house the 150 who actually attended.[22] Along with the invitation, each bishop was sent a pink index card on which he was to enter the name of the priest he appointed "Diocesan Chairman for the Ninth National Eucharistic Congress" and then to mail it back to St. Paul. Even those who did not attend protested their support and typically requested copies of the congress's official prayer[23] for distribution within their dioceses—for instance, 1,000 imprints went to Fargo.[24] Each bishop furthermore was asked to submit a copy of his coat of arms which would be displayed at the Eucharistic Center; the brash William O. Brady sent two from Sioux Falls, one black-and-white and the other in color.[25] Direct episcopal participation in the work of the congress was also put in place; twenty-six sessions aimed at discrete groups—employers, charity workers, young adults and the like—were scheduled at the center, over which one bishop would preside and another act as inaugural speaker and discussion leader.

---

22. E.g., Brand to Toolen, April 1, 1941 (copy), AASPM, NECC. T. J. Toolen was bishop of Mobile.

23. "O Jesus, Thou art really, truly and substantially in the Most Blessed Sacrament of the Eucharist. Every day Thou dost offer Thyself anew to Thine Eternal Father in the adorable Sacrifice of the Mass for the salvation and sanctification of men. In Holy Communion Thou dost make Thyself the nourishment of our souls, and in Thy abiding Presence dost remain with us in this valley of tears to be our never-failing source of consolation and spiritual strength during these days of distress and affliction.

"Deign, O Jesus, to bless with richest fruitage the Ninth National Eucharistic Congress, to crown its work with success, and to make it a medium for the diffusion of a fuller knowledge of Thee, our Eucharistic Lord, and a source of increasing love for Thy Sacramental Presence. Amen.

"Sacred Heart of Jesus, bless the Eucharistic Congress.

"Dearest Mother Mary, teach us to love Jesus according to thine example.

"St. Pascal Baylon, St. Juliana Falconiere, Blessed Imelda and Blessed Peter Julian Eymard, pray for us."

Three hundred days indulgence were granted for reciting the prayer and performing any good work in favor of the congress or making an offering for its success.

24. Reardon to Muench, February 15, 1941 (copy), AASPM, NECC.

25. Brady to Reardon, February 6, 1941, AASPM, NECC.

All lay groups of any national significance received special communications about the congress. More than 5,000 descriptive folders were dispatched to organizations like the Knights of Columbus, the Central Verein, the Foresters, the Hibernians, the Association of Catholic Trade Unionists, the Guild of Catholic Lawyers, the Alliance of Catholic War Veterans, even the University of Notre Dame Alumni Association.[26] Invitations were also sent to the superiors of the various orders of religious women all over the country. Most of them, while promising prayers, declined to attend, either because of the rules of cloister or because of prior commitments, usually to summer catechetical schools. One notable exception were the Franciscans in southern Minnesota. "About four hundred of our sisters will attend. Each morning large groups will go to St. Paul from Rochester and Winona, but will return the same evening."[27] And finally—it need hardly be said—all the priests in the archdiocese were mobilized for whatever supportive tasks necessary, not least for the distribution of Communion to the anticipated crowds.

So the planning for the congress was thorough and detailed. Every constituency was contacted, every resource sounded out, every possible future contingency taken into account. Very little was left to chance. Perhaps the single most eloquent testimony to this almost fevered commitment to assure an adequate preparation took place in the areas of the archdiocese outside the Twin Cities. Over the two months prior to the opening of the congress in late June, Archbishop Murray and Father Reardon visited, on a carefully publicized Sunday schedule, each of the rural deaneries, where a pontifical Mass was celebrated in that jurisdiction's principal parish—Faribault, for example, or New Ulm or Redwood Falls—and followed afterward by a Eucharistic procession made up of "marching units from all the parishes in the deanery. . . . Throngs of between 3,000 and 8,000 participated in these events."[28]

On Monday, June 23, the religious and civic greetings offered to the papal legate,[29] the bulky, seventy-six-year-old Dennis Cardinal Dougherty, archbishop of Philadelphia, marked the formal opening of the congress. The latter

26. "Report" to the General Committee, June 16, 1941, AASPM, NECC.

27. Mother M. Aquinas to Reardon, May 9, 1941, AASPM, NECC.

28. Thomas J. Shanahan, ed., *Ninth National Eucharistic Congress, St. Paul and Minneapolis, June 23–26, 1941, Official History and Record* (St. Paul, 1941), 114–117. This book, 293 pp., included all the relevant addresses made during the congress, as well as other contemporary anecdotal material. Several copies are preserved in AASPM, NECC. It earned a modest $6,000.

29. "Legatus a latere [papae]," "representative from the pope's side," that is, personal representative. For this favor $5,000 was sent to Pius XII. See Murray to Cicognani, July 26, 1841 (copy), AASPM, Murray Papers.

event, held in the Minneapolis auditorium and presided over by Monsignor (as by then he was) Reardon, was graced by the presence of Mayor John Mc-Donough of St. Paul, Mayor George Leach of Minneapolis, and Governor Harold E. Stassen. The politicians' addresses were, as usual, predictable evocations of conventional public piety, but it was the presence of the Republican Harold Stassen that carried the most significance. Though Cardinal Dougherty could hardly have been aware of it, the election of Stassen as governor in 1938—when he was only thirty-one years old—had amounted to a sea change in Minnesota politics. The charismatic Floyd Olson[30] had died in 1936, and his Farmer-Labor Party, racked by internal divisions and by credible allegations of corruption and of Communist infiltration, could not compete with an attractive "progressive" Republican, who had endorsed the economic achievements of Roosevelt's New Deal and had embraced an enlightened internationalism. Reflecting perhaps his Minnesota heritage, Stassen brought to politics what one observer called a secular Lutheranism.[31] Invoking Sir Walter Scott, Reardon introduced the governor as "a young Lochinvar [who] came out of the west and startled the most astute of the older statesmen with his daring disregard for traditional tactics."[32]

The next three days were rife with hectic activity, but, so careful had been the preparation, the multiple events for the most part proceeded smoothly. Pontifical Masses, attended by 50,000 and out of pious nostalgia using Bishop Cretin's chalice, on Tuesday and Thursday mornings; a midnight Mass for men; holy hours for men and women; a children's Mass at the Fair Grounds on June 25 with a choir of 10,000 parochial school children, directed by Father Missia; the eight or nine discussion groups that met each day; a Byzantine-Slavonic–rite Mass at the basilica—in short, an elaborate public tribute across both cities to Catholic Eucharistic doctrine and practice. One particularly striking ceremony occurred at the cathedral on the morning of June 26, a blazingly hot day, when the Right Reverend P. F. Assemani, pastor of St. Maron's church in Minneapolis, sang Mass in the venerable Maronite rite, supported by his parish choir; the sermon, entitled "The Catholic Maronite Church Through the Centuries," was preached by Father Joseph Eid, pastor of St. Anthony of the Desert, Fall River, Massachusetts.[33]

---

30. See chapter 19, above.

31. See Haynes, "Reformers," in Clark, *Minnesota Change*, 379–383.

32. Quoted in Shanahan, *Eucharistic Congress*, 25. The first two lines of Scott's poem: "O, young Lochinvar is come out of the west / Through all the wide border his steed was the best."

33. Text in Shanahan, *Eucharistic Congress*, 114–117.

The great climax of the congress took place that afternoon, a half-day holiday proclaimed by both mayors and the governor. Archbishop Murray carried the sacred Host, in its monstrance and under a canopy, from St. Andrew's Church in St. Paul to Como Park a mile away, where an altar of repose had been set up. There a crowd of 80,000 assembled and passed in review, and then marched, 25,000 official banners and pennants fluttering above them, another mile to the Fair Grounds, with the apostolic delegate, Archbishop Cicognani, bearing the monstrance. Once arrived at the Eucharistic Center, the papal legate, Cardinal Dougherty, presided at the sacramental Benediction of an estimated 125,000 people, soaked to the skin. But the late afternoon downpour did not appear to dampen the crowd's spirits. Indeed, Reardon claimed afterward that the rain was "a blessing in disguise, though not realized by those in charge of the ceremonies. It helped to emphasize the outstanding feature of the Congress—the abiding, deep-seated faith of the participants in the Real Presence and the ardor of their devotion to the Eucharistic King under trying circumstances."[34]

All in all, the chairman, even if he could not control the elements, had done superlatively well. This fact was acknowledged by those whose interests in the congress were hardly religious. "Using your own expression 'not to gild the lily,'" wrote Mayor Leach,

> I hardly need tell you what a thoroughly good job you did in handling the greatest gathering the people of Minneapolis have ever had the privilege of entertaining. I hear it from all sides, and from certain creditable quarters you might not come in contact with, such as the police department, the management [of] the Fair Ground Board, and the employees at the Auditorium. It certainly was well done.[35]

Reardon was no doubt pleased by this courteous statement, even if it sprang from a non-Catholic politician's appreciation of the commercial advantages for the city in bringing to it "the greatest gathering of people." And also because he had become a booster of Minneapolis in the perpetual, if inconsequential, competition between the Twin Cities. A small witness to his bias was revealed in a somewhat plaintive note sent to him by Cardinal Dougherty a month before the congress. "I received some time ago information regarding Minneapolis and the growth of the Church there," the legate wrote, "but

---

34. Quoted in Shanahan, *Eucharistic Congress*, viii.
35. Leach to Reardon, July 1, 1941, AASPM, NECC.

nothing regarding St. Paul and its growth, civilly and ecclesiastically. Please be sure that I appreciate your courtesy; and if you will please take the trouble of sending me some kind of booklet or folder regarding the city of St. Paul I shall be very grateful."[36] There was recognition too from the Church he had served so assiduously in so many capacities. A few days before the convening of the congress, Father Reardon became Monsignor Reardon, with moreover the highest rank—Protonotary Apostolic—of all those priests elevated to honorary membership in the pope's household.[37]

The chairman of the congress's publicity committee, Father Thomas Meagher, proved a tireless campaigner with the media. He arranged for Reardon to deliver on June 15 an explanatory address on the local radio station WCCO, with its CBS hookup. During the congress there was coverage by NBC and even more by Mutual. Before the rains came on the afternoon of June 26, Pius XII spoke directly to the crowd at the Fair Grounds by way of Vatican Radio. Along with his doctrinal message, the pontiff observed gracefully: "We had once the pleasure of visiting our venerable brother, your devoted archbishop."[38]

One of Meagher's press releases has particular relevance, because it touched ever so lightly upon the tension within the promulgation of the Catholic Eucharistic doctrine, that between emphasis on the Real Presence and on a more participatory liturgy. "Directed at the promotion of layman [sic] participation in ceremonies [sic] of the Catholic Church," the chairman wrote inelegantly, "a special sectional meeting for liturgists will be conducted during the Ninth National Eucharistic Congress.... The Most Reverend James A. McFadden, D.D., Auxiliary Bishop of Cleveland, will preside over the meeting [to be] held from 2 to 5 p.m. on June 25 in the southeast annex of the Agriculture Building at the Fairgrounds.... An address on the group's Congress theme, 'Christ Glorified in the Sacrifice of the Liturgical [sic] Mass,' will be given by the Rt. Rev. Alcuin Deutsch, O.S.B., Abbot of

---

36. Dougherty to Reardon, May 20, 1941, AASPM, NECC.

37. Reardon was invested with his new rank on June 18, 1941, and from that date could sign himself, James M. Reardon, P.A. Father Francis Missia, so active (as the text suggests) in the musical work of the congress—which Archbishop Murray said was to be its "feature"—routinely referred to Reardon as "Monsignor *per accidens*," that is, P. A. meaning accidental promotion. Missia was famous for the bluntness of his pejorative comments about his fellow priests. Perhaps in this instance he believed that he should have received "a touch of the purple" himself for all the largely successful work he had done at the congress. Missia died in 1955, aged seventy-one.

38. Text in Shanahan, *Eucharistic Congress*, 125–128.

St. John's Abbey, Collegeville, Minnesota, and President of St. John's University." In due course, Abbot Alcuin spoke eloquently in tone and substance much in accord with the pioneering evangel of Dom Virgil Michel, who had been at once his protégé and his mentor, and who had died in 1938.[39] Another voice, calm and steady amidst all the marching and counter-marching within the congress—legitimately so, given its nature—pleaded for a more measured and traditional response.

"Excessive individualism [Meagher's release went on] prevalent in modern times has inclined many toward a preference for private devotion to the detriment of their understanding of official liturgical worship," said the Rev. William Busch, St. Paul, chairman of the committee in charge of the meeting. "However, there is now a period of revived interest in the liturgy, and it is this fact that determines the purpose of a special sectional meeting [at the congress], to concern itself with the ways and means for the fostering of this liturgical revival," Father Busch said.[40]

There is no inherent contradiction—the point warrants repetition—between the theology of the Real Presence and the theology of the Mystical Body of Christ, which puts a premium on corporate worship. Nevertheless, within the family of the Church, debate on such issues sometimes waxed very warm indeed. Plainly a Eucharistic congress emphasized transubstantiation and the reality of the presence of Jesus—"body and blood, soul and divinity," as the catechism put it—in the species of visible bread and wine. William Busch did not of course deny this assertion, but in his characteristically understated manner he gently indicted the "excessive individualism" that led worshipers—lay people who said the rosary and priests who recited the breviary during Mass—to neglect the corporate participation in that sacred action which, as Pius X had said, was "the genuine source of the Christian spirit." To have insisted upon this line of reasoning in the midst of a vast public witness to the divine Presence in the sacrament of the altar—to have assumed, in other words, a more nuanced view of a venerable doctrine—took a measure of intestinal fortitude.

---

39. See chapter 18, above. Text of Deutsch's speech in Shanahan, *Eucharistic Congress*, 214–220. For the abbot's long and fruitful service to the Liturgical Movement, see Barry, *Worship*, especially 256–277.

40. Press release, n.d., AASPM, NECC.

THE EUCHARISTIC CONGRESS OF 1941 WAS ITSELF AN ASSERTION of Catholic exclusivity, and so was the mild qualification of its central emphasis suggested by liturgical reformers like William Busch and Alcuin Deutsch. But that exclusivity had other, more sweeping, manifestations. Despite the difficult economic circumstances, the 1930s witnessed a resurgence of buoyancy within the Church. Under the broad aegis of Pope Pius XI's call for "Catholic Action," an unprecedented mobilization of the laity took place with highly significant consequences. The movement had literary and intellectual roots: the philosophical certainties offered by neo-scholasticism brought a burgeoning self-confidence to the Catholic élites, while the English-speaking contingent experienced an intellectual revival of its own, initiated by the writings of the likes of Newman and Orestes Brownson. But it manifested itself besides across the whole gamut of society. Notable, for instance, was the lifelong work of the Belgian Canon Cardijn,[41] who instituted the famous methodology—"see, judge, act"—as an instrument for social change which ultimately inspired such worldwide organizations as the Young Christian Workers and the Young Christian Students.[42] The impact of this program was far-reaching, extending even to the formation after World War II of Christian Democratic political parties across Western Europe.

Cardijn's precise intentions had less direct influence upon the American Catholic scene than it did in Europe, where the alienation of the working masses from the Church had been much more pervasive and severe. Nor did the rampant anticlericalism that characterized Italy, France, and Canon Cardijn's Belgium enjoy much currency in the United States.[43] To be sure, the American participation in the revival was largely derivative, and it depended primarily upon literary sources. Significantly the English publishing house of Sheed & Ward opened an office in New York City in 1934. Frank Sheed, tireless Australian-born polemicist—author among many other publications of the immensely influential *Theology and Sanity* (1947)—and his wife, Maisie Ward, granddaughter of one of the prominent converts to Catholicism to

---

41. Joseph Cardijn (1882–1967), a national hero through two world wars, formed the first cell of the Young Christian Workers in 1924. Pope Paul VI created him cardinal two years before his death.

42. Consult http://www.ycw.ie. Accessed May 20, 2008.

43. During the mid-1920s, James J. Walsh (1865–1942)—American medievalist and Catholic polemicist, author of *The Thirteenth, Greatest of Centuries* (New York, 1907, 1952)—published a book called *These Splendid Priests* (New York, 1924).

come out of the Oxford Movement[44] and author of the magisterial biography of G. K. Chesterton (1943), represented both the cerebral and practical faces of the Catholic revival.

But the English roots of the phenomenon went back further than that, to Gerard Manley Hopkins and Patmore and Alice Meynell, to Chesterton's allies and drinking companions Belloc and Maurice Baring, and, in the next generation, Evelyn Waugh, Christopher Hollis, the self-taught historian Christopher Dawson and the publisher Tom Burns, the ascetic Vincent McNabb and the economist and environmentalist Barbara Ward:[45] most of them converts, though not all, and only a few of them clerics. An American Catholic dependence upon such French revivalists as Claudel, Leon Bloy, Mauriac, Gilson, Jacques and Raissa Maritain—all lay persons—was obviously less direct and widespread, but not without significance even so. If one were permitted to indulge in whimsy, one might posit that for every American reformer like Dorothy Day there were two or three French Peter Maurins; for every spectacular and articulate American convert to Catholicism like Thomas Merton, English artists of equal or perhaps greater stature who took the same fateful step—Ronald Knox, say, or Robert Speaight, or Alec Guinness—seemed to abound.

While it may have been that Catholics in the United States could not boast so lively and prominent an intellectual revival as had occurred overseas,[46] they did possess one unique advantage. The educational system they had built up, at the cost of so much sweat and so many tears, had produced a mass literate society with no equal in Europe or anywhere else in the Catholic world. In the archdiocese of St. Paul tens of thousands of children and adolescents crowded the parochial schools. The College of St. Thomas, emerging gradually from its deep financial and administrative travails, was providing for local young men an ever-improving curriculum, which was imbued at once with Catholic values and with a solid initiation into the wider culture. More striking still was the accomplishment of the Sisters of St. Joseph, who over a few decades had transformed a girls' high school into the vibrant College of St. Catherine, which in 1937 was awarded a chapter of the prestigious Phi Beta Kappa Society—only the third institution of higher learning in

---

44. See Marvin R. O'Connell, *The Oxford Conspirators A History of the Oxford Movement, 1833–1845* (New York, 1969, 1990), 323–325.

45. No kin to Maisie Ward.

46. See the celebrated indictment in John Tracy Ellis, "American Catholics and the Intellectual Life," *Thought* 30 (Autumn 1955): 351–388.

Minnesota to be so honored, and the first Catholic one in the United States. Under the prodding of Archbishop Dowling, the two seminaries, major and minor, had begun to upgrade their faculties and thus over time brought into being a more cultivated secular clergy.

The products of these élite establishments were surely prepared to delve into the loftier insights of their European coreligionists. But what about the vast numbers of middle- and working-class Catholics who did not (and could not) cross into the groves of academe? The very essence of the American way called for literary instruments whereby such persons could be introduced to a broader appreciation of the multiple facets involved in the living out of their faith. *The Commonweal, America, The Catholic World*—such publications served the educated minority admirably. But should the rest of the Catholic community be restricted to reading flaccid diocesan weeklies or journals devoted almost exclusively to an ethnic assertiveness no longer relevant? Surely there was room for a middle-brow journal that could promote rather than compete with other Catholic magazines. Or at least so it seemed to Father Louis Gales, that populist entrepreneur, who, through his Catechetical Guild, had already launched a series of programs in popular education by imaginative use of the mass media.[47] Consistent with that experience, in 1936, five years before the Eucharistic Congress, he founded the *Catholic Digest*. Associated with him were those two young and energetic priests, Paul Bussard and Edward Jennings.

The *Digest*, inspired by the immense success of the *Readers Digest*—which by 1936 enjoyed a monthly circulation of more than a million—was one more sign of Catholic exclusivity. Indeed, it might be seen as a logical development of the learned societies which had begun, twenty years earlier, to distinguish formally Catholic philosophers, sociologists, and other academics from their secular colleagues.[48] The three priests and a staff of devoted and articulate laymen began publication of the *Digest* with the scantiest possible financial backing, a circumstance familiar to Gales from his earlier endeavors, but one which never appeared to have disturbed his serenity. Archbishop Murray granted his verbal approbation to the venture—the highly bureaucratic and paper-dominated administration of the archdiocese still lay in the future—and allowed the *Digest* office space in the basement of the chancery, where Bussard and Jennings already edited the *Leaflet Missal*. The archbishop even contributed $1,000 from his personal funds as seed money for the proj-

---

47. See chapter 18, above.
48. See chapter 17, above.

ect, but at the same time and characteristically, he insisted that the priests be identified by their primary parochial or institutional assignments. The *Digest* was a good idea, no doubt, but it went beyond the apostolate of the archdiocese; it belonged to the three men who owned it, not to the archdiocese, the implication being that if the undertaking failed the financial liability would be theirs.[49] An anecdote has it that during the mid-1950s, when the *Catholic Digest* was at the height of its success and Father Bussard had consequently attained national prominence, inquiries received by the chancery about him were directed to whatever parish the priest happened to be serving at the time as a weekend assistant—and, it was said, Murray always pronounced the name as "Buzzard."

For Bussard, endowed with remarkable intellectual and literary gifts, was clearly the single force that carried the *Digest* from its humble beginnings to a unique position as an arbiter within American Catholic popular culture. In recruiting him as editor, Louis Gales had shown himself once again a shrewd facilitator, but although he assumed for a time the title of publisher and continued as the company's majority owner until it passed into other hands in 1962, he took little or no part in the magazine's day-to-day operations. Edward Jennings, as the *Digest's* business manager, reprised the role he had so ably played since 1929 with the *Leaflet Missal.* The latter enterprise apparently remained his first love, because in the early 1950s he assigned his shares in the *Digest* to Bussard in exchange for full control of the *Missal.* The result was that Gales held sixty-five percent of the *Catholic Digest's* stock, Bussard thirty-five percent.[50] The first pressrun in October 1936, amounted to 15,000 copies; ten years later, at the end of the Second World War, that figure had swelled to 550,000. By then the magazine's headquarters had moved to more commodious space in downtown St. Paul, and an auxiliary office had been opened in New York City.[51]

Paul Bussard came to his task as the original editor (later the publisher and, ultimately, for all practical purposes the sole and unchallenged chief of the *Catholic Digest*) as a liturgical reformer.[52] In 1936 he was thirty-three years old and had been ordained (like Jennings) for only eight years, but already he had established an impressive literary and academic record. Between March

---

49. See Anne Klejment, "*Catholic Digest* and the Catholic Revival, 1936–1945," *U. S. Catholic Historian* 21 (Summer 2003): 89–110.

50. I owe this information to my friend Professor Anne Klejment.

51. Reardon, *Diocese of St. Paul,* 488–489.

52. For much of what follows, including quotations, I owe once more to Professor Klejment, who kindly allowed me the use of two unpublished papers.

and August 1931, two years after the successful launch of the *Leaflet Missal,* Bussard published no fewer than twenty-five articles in the prestigious local Catholic weekly, *The Wanderer,*[53] under the overall title "The Layman and His Missal." They were remarkably mature pieces, carefully connected to one another to formulate a coherent argument, the gist of which was that liturgical practice provided a far better way for the men and women in the pews to learn about their faith and give witness to it than the "pedagogically incompetent" *Baltimore Catechism,* with its tedious list of questions and pat answers. Here was a point of view capable of upsetting many vested interests—from the *Catechism*'s publishers to the nuns accustomed to using it every day in the schoolroom—a consideration of small import to Bussard. He could happily salute the work of a confrere, Father John Gruden, the learned pastor of St. Agnes parish in St. Paul, who was busy providing a solid theological underpinning to his own position. But when Gruden's *The Mystical Christ* was published a few years later—a hefty, scholarly tome—Bussard became even more convinced of the need for a populist approach.[54]

He wrote the *Wanderer* articles during the interregnum, between Dowling's death and Murray's arrival in St. Paul. The former had recognized the young priest's talent and had planned to assign him to higher studies abroad, provided he learn German, but the chronic bad health that marked the archbishop's last years left many a promise unfulfilled. Archbishop Murray did indeed send Bussard off to graduate school, but—in accord with the Murray-esque practice of keeping his subjects off balance—not to Europe but to the Catholic University in Washington, and not for a doctoral degree in theology or liturgy but, to the priest's "dismay," in "education," that most amorphous of academic disciplines. Bussard was intensely unhappy in Washington; the program of study he thought "deplorable," so much so that he readied himself to return to St. Paul, "since I was learning nothing." Murray then relented, at least to an extent, and allowed Bussard to spend the 1933–1934 academic year in Germany, where he studied at the University of Munich and at Maria Laach Abbey, one of the primary centers of the European liturgical renewal. The fruit of these happy months of research was a dissertation published under the title *The Vernacular Missal in Religious Education,* which cleverly satisfied the dubious standards of Catholic University's Education Department while

---

53. *Der Wanderer,* founded in 1867 (see chapter 9, above), began publishing an English edition in 1931. The German-language edition ceased publication in 1957.

54. John Gruden, *The Mystical Christ: Introduction to the Study of the Supernatural Character of the Church* (St. Louis, 1946).

at the same time it argued credibly by way of a kind of sociological survey that use of the missal promoted a fuller faith experience.

Back at home, with his degree in his pocket, Father Bussard was assigned to teach Latin at Nazareth Hall, the preparatory seminary (a duty hardly relevant to his graduate study), even as he assumed the editorship of the new *Catholic Digest*—this last, as far as Archbishop Murray was concerned, an extracurricular activity. Then in 1938 one more strong reminder was given to Bussard and others that the business of the archdiocese came before any private initiative. Due to a series of surprise illnesses among its curates, the rapidly growing parish of the Nativity of Our Lord, organized in 1922[55] and located in the middle-class Groveland section of St. Paul, suddenly stood in need of the services of another priest. Murray dispatched Bussard to the scene. But here the angels smiled upon the young reformer. At that moment Nativity, under the direction of its famously authoritarian sixty-nine-year-old founding pastor, Father Terrence Moore, was going through the construction of its new church, a soaring gothic edifice estimated to cost, during those harsh depression years, a daunting $350,000. Gothic was never Paul Bussard's favorite mode of church architecture—too prone, in his view, to lure the worshipers' gaze and attention upward to its gilded arches rather than to the altar upon which the sacred Sacrifice was taking place. Yet Bussard, a man of consummate charm, cajoled Moore into considering that the adornment of the upper church—its stained glass windows, in depicting the hours of the Divine Office and the seasons of the liturgical year, its stations of the cross in portraying at their culmination a victorious and risen Christ rather than the conventional bloodied and suffering One—ought thus to reflect what recent research, like Bussard's own, had established as the *modus* of the ancient Church. The tough-minded Father Moore and his parishioners were impressed and convinced by the charismatic temporary assistant. It took time to complete, but long after Bussard had gone on to other things—indeed, after the Second World War—the final decorative scheme was faithful to his inspiration.

Prudence required that, given Nativity's burgeoning population, more than the conventional sacred space be provided. And so a lower church was also constructed, a crypt seating a thousand people. Here Paul Bussard scored his greatest coup. "The one thing necessary," he had argued, "is to unite the faithful closely with Christ. Can that ever be done by a priest who stands with this back to them and reads Sacred Scripture to a wall?" He persuaded Father

---

55. See Reardon, *Diocese of St. Paul*, 591.

Moore—and, more surprisingly, Archbishop Murray—to allow the altar in the crypt to be free standing, so that at Mass the priest faced the congregation and the worshipers could see and follow his action at the altar and pray with him from their vernacular missals. What could be better calculated to encourage, through the most sacred of Christian ceremonies, a unity and even an intimacy with Jesus and with God's people? Bussard contended that such an arrangement was common in the ancient Church and had changed—had been corrupted he did not quite say—during the Middle Ages. "We have, then, in Nativity church an altar placed facing the people as was quite common for the first thousand years of Christianity, and one [in the upper church] placed as has become the fashion in the second thousand." And, ever jaunty, he added: "The [altar] on which the Holy Father says Mass in the greatest church in all Christendom, St. Peter's, is placed just as is ours [in the crypt] of Nativity parish."

Seldom can one describe a person as ahead of his times. In one respect at least Paul Bussard was such a person.

YET IN ANOTHER SENSE HE REMAINED VERY MUCH A MAN of his times. It was an era when the mass print media flourished as never before or since. The astonishing early success of the *Catholic Digest* testified to the presence of a huge public eager to be informed and entertained. The excerpts printed in the *Digest* by and large aimed to do both, while at the same time revealing for all to see, according to the magazine's motto, "the golden thread of Catholic thought." A roster of the authors represented in the issues of its first ten years of publication appears to bear out this contention: Frank Sheed, Vincent McNabb, Christopher Dawson, Georges Bernanos, and the Americans John La Farge, Dorothy Day, and Ade Bethune, among many other notables. Bussard became increasingly absorbed in all aspects of the *Digest,* from article selection to circulation to overall financial management, so much so that he gradually lost interest in the Liturgical Movement that had so invigorated his youthful priesthood. Or perhaps by the early 1960s he discerned that much of the renewal he had promoted with such éclat had been, or was about to be, accomplished. In any case not all the credit for the success of the *Catholic Digest* belongs to Bussard. Louis Gales may have continued to be a remote if benign figure in the background, and Edward Jennings may have never become quite attuned to Bussard's increasingly obsessive style.[56] But

---

56. Jennings died in 1974, Gales in 1978, Bussard in 1983.

others—like Joseph Connors, Edward Hartigan, and Father Kenneth Ryan—contributed mightily to the project, out of sense of vocation and at considerable personal cost.

Still, it must be said that the two most influential Minnesota Catholics during the middle third of the twentieth century were Paul Bussard and John A. Ryan.[57] And indeed their influence spread far beyond the confines of their native state. Their approach to events and their manner of dealing with challenges, no less than the theaters in which they played out their roles, were very different. But a "golden thread of Catholic thought" did bind them together to a degree. Bussard's crusade for liturgical renewal—its insistence on the unity and participation of the whole worshiping community—possessed an unmistakable collective component, while Ryan's tireless drive for social and racial justice derived directly from his conviction that Jesus had called for a communal solution for the problems of the ages.

---

57. See chapter 17, above.

CHAPTER 23

War and Revival

IN THE LATE SUMMER OF 1939, AS EUROPE MOVED INEXORABLY toward war, Pope Pius XII issued an appeal for further negotiations among the quarreling nations, much as his predecessor, Benedict XV, had done in 1914. That neither succeeded does not distract from the nobility of their efforts. And there was also, according to one observer, a hint of the romantic in Pius's attempt, or so Catholics in the archdiocese of St. Paul were informed on the second day of the Second World War. "When the Supreme Pontiff decided to broadcast to the world his earnest plea for world peace, Rome was overcast by a cloudy, rainy day. Immediately before the Holy Father's moving message was read, there appeared in the skies a resplendent double rainbow."[1] A sign, it seems, to endure contradiction over the next six ghastly years.

The secular politicians fared no better. At the end of September 1938, Neville Chamberlain returned to London from Munich. We have achieved, proclaimed the British prime minister to thunderous applause, "peace with honor, peace for our time." Less than a year later, even as the pope was speaking—Prague having already been seized by the Germans—Hitler's panzers crossed the frontier into Poland. Shortly after that the Soviets, linked now to the Nazi regime by the infamous nonaggression pact, occupied the eastern part of that unhappy country. Thus came the fulfillment of Marshall Foch's gloomy prophecy of 1919 with regard to the Treaty of Versailles. "This is not peace," he said. "This is a truce for twenty years."

As the Second World War began, Minnesota Catholics, like most Americans, assumed a thoroughly isolationist stance. Polish Americans certainly had no sympathy for the German aggressor, nor, as the Nazi juggernaut swal-

---

1. *CB*, September 2, 1939 (attribution only to the NCWC News Service).

lowed up much of Western Europe, had those of French, Belgian, or Dutch extraction. But the quarrel, they believed, was essentially a European one, the decadent Old World up to its bloody old tricks again, a vast ocean away. Only a generation before, young Americans had had to strap kit bags and rifles on their backs and go "over there"—to the strains of Catholic vaudevillian George M. Cohan's patriotic ditty—and bring about a dubious victory at enormous cost. Never again. As for the violence besetting the Far East, separated from the United States by an even broader ocean, it appeared more remote still: inscrutable little yellow men slaughtering one another for no discernible reason. To be sure, over the next two years, public opinion was deeply moved by the heroism of the British people standing alone and sustained by little more than Churchillian eloquence. No one who heard him can ever forget the gravely mellow voice of Edward R. Murrow reporting back to America by radio as the bombs were falling all around him during the Blitz: "This, is London."

But other voices were also heard during these years of ambivalence, none more frequently and stridently, particularly among Catholics, than that of Father Charles Coughlin, the Michigan populist whose Sunday afternoon broadcasts were listened to, it was claimed, by as much as one third of the national radio audience. Coughlin was an early and ardent supporter of Franklin Roosevelt—"The New Deal is Christ's Deal" he famously asserted—but as the 1930s progressed his views took on a different emphasis. Whether or not radical anti-Semitism became his obsession remains a matter of dispute; the fact is that his growing contempt of "Jewish-dominated capitalism" led him to remarkable misjudgments—that, for instance, the vile Nazi *Kristallnacht* of 1938 was "a persecution of the Jews only after Christians had been persecuted." Minnesotan Charles Lindbergh made no secret of his admiration for German efficiency and industrial capacity, while Roosevelt's ambassador to Britain, the Irish Catholic Joseph P. Kennedy, loudly supported Chamberlain's policy of appeasement, and once the war began he doubted, just as loudly, that Hitler could or even should be defeated. The civil war in Spain contributed much to this mixed picture. Most Americans sympathized with the Republic despite its reliance on the military aid of the Comintern and the Soviet Union, but, though atrocities abounded on both sides, Catholics by and large identified with General Franco's Nationalists who, whatever their connection to the fascist dictators, did not shoot priests and rape nuns.

The pages of Father Paul Bussard's *Catholic Digest*, since it excerpted material from a wide variety of publications, testify to the range of opinion among Catholics during these crucial years. From the beginning, however, the editors themselves assumed a strong anti-Nazi stance, which must have pleased Archbishop Murray.[2] Dorothy Day and her disciples from the Catholic Worker movement adopted a consistent pacifist line, arguing, for example, that a foreign war should never justify initiating a draft, a matter widely debated during 1938 and 1939; much better for Congress to enact neutrality legislation and to nationalize the American arms industry, thus depriving the merchants of death of their unholy profits, than to adopt a policy that "dehumanize[ed] men into dumb cattle." More nuanced, and perhaps therefore vaguer, was the opinion of the celebrated Jesuit pamphleteer, Daniel Lord, who wrote in late 1940 when a conscription law had been passed—the first in peacetime in United States history—and thought that participation in any war effort depended on an individual's "reflective conscience" as a genuine follower of Christ. More easily said than done, wrote another *Digest* contributor. The Selective Service Act of 1940 had indeed provided for conscientious objection, he granted, but American Catholics, who intended to take advantage of that clause had failed to understand that the nation had the right "to keep . . . itself strong and alert," and so they needed to acknowledge "the clear duty of serving their nation in defense of its just rights and dignities."

The attack by the Japanese on Pearl Harbor in December 1941 swept away most of the doubts among American Catholics, but not all of them. Fulton J. Sheen, whose work appeared frequently in the *Catholic Digest,* even in 1942 judged involvement in the world war as "morally ambiguous." Characteristically invoking a neo-scholastic methodology with a certain clumsiness, his position wandered into cosmic questions about why God willed this terrible conflagration and what its relationship might have been to the essential freedom of will of the human person. Not surprisingly he offered rhetorical rather than substantive explanations. More concretely he addressed the problem of how morally justifiable it was to carry on the conflict as an ally of the godless Communist Soviet Union (which Hitler had invaded seven months before Pearl Harbor). Sheen's answer was that the American people must consider themselves as allies of the Russian people rather than of the odious Soviet regime—a distinction made implicitly by the likes of Winston Churchill. In any event Father Bussard made it clear early on where the *Digest*'s editors stood: Let Catholic "readers [of the magazine] fold their hands in prayer and open them to buy [U.S. savings] bonds," ran the recommendation on the back cover of the June 1942 issue. Dorothy Day's views on social issues continued to find exposure in the *Digest*'s pages, but not her pacifist ones.[3]

---

2. See chapter 21, above.

3. For the material in the text, including the quotations, see Klejment, "*Catholic Digest,* 1936–1945," 102–103.

DURING THE TIME IMMEDIATELY PRIOR TO THE DISASTER AT
Pearl Harbor, the people of the archdiocese of St. Paul, like Americans everywhere, watched uneasily as the clouds on the world scene grew ever darker,
even as they hoped and prayed their country might be spared. Meanwhile,
life, as it always does, went on. The economy showed signs of modest recovery, not least because of apprehension over the cataclysm abroad. Firms
like Honeywell and Minnesota Mining and Manufacturing, destined for massive expansion, were already exhibiting a technological sophistication which
would soon be put to good use in the fledgling defense industry. The farmers
and the great grain companies also experienced an improving market not unrelated to present and possible future conflict.[4] In one of the gloomiest of iro-
nies, the horrors of war wrote finis to the horrors of the Great Depression.

The institutional church of St. Paul expanded too. In 1939–1940 three
new parishes—St. Rose of Lima, Transfiguration, and Corpus Christi—were
founded in the city of St. Paul, and two more in the suburbs, St. Jude in Mahtomedi and Holy Trinity in South St. Paul. During the same time span four
more were added in Minneapolis: Christ the King, St. Olaf, St. Leonard, and
St. Martin. The latter two were designated to serve African American Catholics in the southern and northern sections of the city respectively, and in
this apostolate they joined, rather late in the day perhaps, in a specifically ethnic ministry which had flourished at St. Peter Claver parish in St. Paul since
1888.[5]

A personnel change of some significance also occurred during this time.
In 1939 the forty-year-old William O. Brady was appointed bishop of Sioux
Falls, where he remained with some impatience until he returned to St. Paul
seventeen years later. The promotion involved many varieties of expense,
Archbishop Murray said, and so he imposed a tax on the clergy to pay for
them: $100 for pastors, $75 for priest-teachers, and $50 for assistants.[6] To suc-
ceed Brady as rector of the St. Paul Seminary, Archbishop Murray named his
own fellow University of Louvain alumnus, Lawrence Oscar Wolf. Father
Wolf's track to this eminence moved along some unprecedented byways.

---

4. See Kirk Jeffrey, "The Motor Manufacturers: From Food and Forest Products to High Technology," in Clark, *Minnesota Change*, 223–259.

5. See Reardon, *Diocese of St. Paul*, 591–592, 600–601, 650–651, and Wright,
Gather Us In, 106, 171–178. St. Martin's parish was closed in 1958.

6. Murray to "Reverend Father," June 24, 1939 (copy), AASPM, Murray Papers.

Born in Minneapolis in 1896, he became a teenage convert to Catholicism under the inspiration of the Christian Brothers, when he attended their De La Salle high school in that city. After some hesitation about his future, he followed the classics course at St. Thomas College and then the philosophy and theology program at the seminary. Following his ordination in 1924, Archbishop Dowling sent him to Louvain, where he received his doctorate in philosophy five years later. His seminary students remembered him as a demanding professor and rather rigid in his principles, though they often found consolation in his refined manner and unfailing courtesy. As rector, however, the rigidity proved his undoing, not only in his day-to-day relationships with students and staff but also with higher authority. When the exigencies of wartime required that the seminary share some of its facilities with lay students from St. Thomas, Wolf was adamantly opposed. It did not soften his resolve when the archbishop characteristically endorsed the arrangement without bothering to inform him. This first seminary alumnus to become its rector duly resigned the office in 1943 and returned to his earlier position as professor of philosophy. Much of Wolf's career turned upon his frail physical constitution—it was widely believed that he suffered from incipient tuberculosis, although he lived into his seventy-seventh year.[7] James Connolly, Brady's fellow "wise man from the east," succeeded Wolf until 1945 when he was named bishop of his native Fall River.[8] Then Father Rudolph Bandas assumed the office he was to hold for thirteen years.

That summer of 1939 the archdiocesan-wide collection (on the third Sunday in July) for support of the St. Paul Seminary amounted to just over $34,000, and two months later that for Nazareth Hall totaled $8,122.86, down $600, Murray ruefully noted, from the year before.[9] But neither of the seminaries, major or preparatory, presented in these difficult times anything like so prolonged a financial anxiety as did the College of St. Thomas. Ever since the expulsion of the Congregation of Holy Cross,[10] the struggle to liquidate the institution's corrosive debt and to establish for it a firm fiscal footing had been unrelenting. And not without a positive result. Over the five years before 1939, the archbishop reported, 292 priests had contributed to St. Thomas's

---

7. See Athans, *To Work for the Whole People*, 175–177. In 1951 I took a course in philosophical psychology from Father Wolf. I recall mostly his genial demeanor and elegant speech rather than any substantive insight or information. Even by that date he was considered something of a recluse.

8. See chapter 18, above.

9. *CB*, September 9 and December 16, 1939.

10. See chapter 20, above.

coffers $155,000, while laity in the parishes had added $291,000 more, leaving a relatively manageable debt of $278,000. This level of generous giving was truly admirable, he granted, given the economic circumstances of the day; but only when the considerable number of parishes that had not yet responded affirmatively to the appeal did so, could the college, so essential to the overall mission of the Church in the archdiocese and, indeed, across the Upper Midwest, liquidate its indebtedness and so fulfill its providential mission.[11]

But besides these diocesan-wide efforts in its behalf, an angel had appeared on the scene whose personal benefactions would in time make possible the emergence of the modern St. Thomas. His name was Ignatius A. O'Shaughnessy, class of 1907. At first a restless entrepreneur, he turned after the Great War to oil exploration and brought in a successful well in Oklahoma on his very first attempt. The gushers multiplied in subsequent years until, by 1938, he was head of the largest private petroleum company in the world. That year he joined the St. Thomas board of trustees—he had maintained a residence in St. Paul, had kept up an interest in his alma mater, and had sent his three sons to the academy and college—and at an early meeting of that body offered to underwrite the construction of a fully equipped recreation building. (As a student he had been a star on the football field.) O'Shaughnessy Hall was ready for use at the beginning of 1940 and, with its courts and swimming pool, its bowling alleys and lounges for formal and informal gatherings, proved an inestimable boon for the institution. The handsome building of yellow Mankato stone was but the first of the O'Shaughnessy monuments to grace the St. Thomas campus; a stadium, a library, and a teaching complex were erected over the years that followed. The College of St. Catherine also benefited substantially from his generosity, as did the University of Notre Dame. Indeed, no individual in its history contributed as much to the support of Catholic higher education in the United States as did Ignatius O'Shaughnessy.[12]

He was a simple man in many respects, direct and even laconic in expression. "My dear Archbishop," he wrote Murray as O'Shaughnessy Hall was opening its doors, "I believe that the enclosed checks will take care of the balance due on the new building at St. Thomas. Sincerely yours." The archbishop, in his somewhat wordier style, sent heartfelt thanks for the $30,000 and

---

11. Murray to "Reverend Father," November 1, 1939 (copy), AASPM, Murray Papers.

12. Connors, *Journey*, 299–302.

added: "May the fruit of the sacrifice you have made in this cause be a consolation to you as well as a source of edification to others! Only God can bestow fitting recognition of your contribution to His glory."[13]

The relatively good results in securing support for a local institution of higher learning were not, however, repeated in the case of a national one. In the autumn of 1939 the Catholic University of America launched its "Golden Jubilee" fund drive, which aimed to raise $2,000,000 as the school entered its second half century. The quota set for the archdiocese of St. Paul was $150,000. A team of solicitors came to the Twin Cities from Washington, headed by Monsignor Fulton J. Sheen, who had apparently relented from his former reluctance to tour the country seeking money for his university.[14] But despite the best efforts of Archbishop Murray and his chancellor, Father Donald Gregory, the response to the campaign was tepid at best: only $66,000 was contributed, or forty-five percent of the clearly unrealistic goal.[15]

"WITH CONFIDENCE IN OUR ARMED FORCES, WITH THE unbending determination of our people, we will gain the inevitable triumph, so help us God." Thus did Franklin Roosevelt conclude his address to the congress and the nation on Monday, December 8, 1941. Four wearisome years later, when the triumph had indeed been gained—and "the day of infamy," as the president characterized the Japanese attack on Pearl Harbor, avenged— more than 400,000 Americans had been killed.[16] Roosevelt too was dead, not from battle wounds but surely in part at least from the stress of carrying the enormous burden of wartime leadership. Eventually American young men fought in North Africa, in Italy and France, and in the especially bloody conflict across the vast stretches of the Pacific, in places they could hardly pronounce, like Guadalcanal and Iwo Jima. On the home front the war meant first of all the mobilization of heretofore untapped economic resources of the country to produce the guns and tanks, the ships and planes, needed to sustain the men in the field. It meant priority for the armament industry to which workers were recruited with deadly seriousness—workers of both

---

13. O'Shaughnessy to Murray, February 17, 1940, and Murray to O'Shaughnessy, March 9, 1940 (copy), AASPM, Murray Papers. The archbishop was away in late February and early March; hence the delay in the acknowledgment.

14. See chapter 19, above.

15. Reardon, *Diocese of St. Paul*, 539–540, and *CB*, October 21, 1939, with its photograph on the front page of Sheen in his monsignorial garb.

16. The population of the United States in 1941 was about 140,000,000.

sexes: "Rosie the Riveter" became a folk heroine. It meant buying U.S. Savings Bonds and, for children, Savings Stamps that, once bought, were proudly pasted in a small paper booklet. It meant major and minor annoyances like ration books and travel restrictions, and it meant, for many, the dreaded telegram from the War Department and the subsequent gold star in the window.

In the old liturgy every low Mass ended with the recitation, in the vernacular, of a prayer that began, "St. Michael the Archangel, defend us in battle." It might have been said with added fervor and more secular intent in the wake of Pearl Harbor. Catholics at any rate with few exceptions rallied to the flag as they had in 1917. Quite literally so in one sense. As early as January 1942 Archbishop Murray definitively answered queries as to the appropriateness of displaying Old Glory in a church or of draping it over the casket of a fallen soldier. A nineteenth-century Vatican decree, he explained, had forbidden these practices, but that document had been modified so that "therefore the national emblem of the United States may be used in church." It did not follow, added this feisty hater of the Nazis, "that the emblems of Communism or Nazism, even though considered national emblems, could be introduced into the church, inasmuch as the Holy See has condemned both systems, and their emblems fall under the condemnation."[17] It is not unlikely that most of his pastors had anticipated the archbishop's clarification of the canon law.

But of course the rallying occurred also at a much more profound level. Early in 1942 Murray ordered that each parish prepare and send to the chancery a printed roster listing its men and women serving in the armed forces and attach to it a filled-out questionnaire indicating each individual's date and place of birth and baptism, marital status, and branch of service. By late summer the total number of men had reached 10,598, along with a smattering of women. The largest single contingent, 348, came from St. Mark's parish in St. Paul.[18] By the end of the war the figures had swelled to 32,015 men, of whom 997 were killed, as were three of the 1,151 women who served.[19]

The Catholics in the archdiocese, like Americans everywhere, had to adjust their lives to the new reality. The archbishop sent out a flurry of directives and recommendations. "Every pastor, every parish, every individual Catholic," he proclaimed, "must cooperate with the civil authority in every way." As long as the conflicted lasted, special prayers *in tempore belli* were to

---

17. Murray to "Reverend Father," January 22, 1942 (copy), AASPM, Murray Papers.

18. *CB*, April 11 and September 5, 1942.

19. Murray to "Reverend Father," December 5, 1945 (copy), AASPM, Murray Papers.

be said in every church. He endorsed the sale of Savings Bonds and Stamps on church property. For the duration of the war, persons who worked past midnight in the production of material needed for the national defense were permitted to drink non-alcoholic beverages up to within one hour of receiving Holy Communion and to eat solid food within four hours; this authorization, however, bore a Delphic, Murrayesque mark in that "the fact of these actions must remain secret lest anyone be scandalized."[20] At first the archbishop hesitated to require that the major seminary go into a twelve-month schedule, but, with universal conscription the order of the day for young, unmarried men, he insisted that the students with their deferrals from the draft keep a low profile, accept no paying summertime jobs, and overall keep out of sight. Priests too "should eliminate themselves from the public forms of recreation and sociability."[21] By 1944, however, the seminary had adopted an "accelerated" year-round program, broken only by brief holidays in January and June.[22]

"St. Paul Priest with First Troops to Europe," read the headline in the *Catholic Bulletin* on January 31, 1942. Father Neil Cashman, ordained in 1935 and formerly an assistant pastor at St. Mark's in St. Paul, was assigned as Catholic chaplain to the token contingent of American soldiers dispatched to Northern Ireland during the weeks immediately after Pearl Harbor. Five other archdiocesan priests were on active duty when the war began. But now, with the new emergency and with each diocese being asked to release ten percent of its men to serve as chaplains to the vast armies being feverishly organized, Archbishop Murray invited "all the assistants in the Archdiocese to volunteer for service with the Armed Forces of the United States." He pledged that those who did so and met the requirements of the War Department would be given leave to join the chaplain corps. And, to add further motivation to their patriotism, he assured them that when they returned after the "inevitable triumph," they would be granted parishes of their own—a consummation devoutly to be wished by any assistant pastor. More than fifty priests accepted this proposal, most of whom saw hazardous duty overseas and three of whom were severely wounded.[23] The first to accept the challenge was John J. Buchanan, an assistant at Incarnation parish in Minneapolis.[24] He eventually

---

20. Murray to "Reverend Father," December 10, 1941, January 28 and February 11, 1942 (copies), AASPM, Murray Papers.

21. Printed circular, June 5, 1942, AASPM, Murray Papers.

22. Athans, *To Work for the Whole People*, 179.

23. Reardon, *Diocese of St. Paul*, 550 and 686–687 for a complete list.

24. Murray to Buchanan, February 5, 1942 (copy), AASPM, Murray Papers.

served with George Patton's famous Third Army in its push across Normandy, and was awarded the Silver Star for heroism in an action on August 26, 1944, when he dressed the wounds of his fellow soldiers while under direct enemy fire.[25] Father Buchanan was discharged from the army in September 1945, and six months later John Gregory Murray, true to his word, named him founding pastor of the church of the Holy Childhood in St. Paul.

Under the rules of the old liturgy a priest was not allowed to celebrate Mass more than twice a day (except on All Souls Day and Christmas). Now permission was given for three Sunday Masses to be offered by one priest in every parish from which a chaplain had been taken. And, Murray warned, the requirements of the chaplain corps might mean that in the larger parishes the priestly staff would have to be reduced to one or two and perhaps to none at all in the smallest ones. He made no apology. "TO DEPRIVE THE MEN IN SERVICE OF THE MINISTRY OF THE CLERGY," he wrote in upper-case vehemence, "WOULD BE A CRIME WHICH WILL NOT BE FORGIVEN BY GOD OR COUNTRY."[26] The situation became grave enough that it was decided in September 1942 to ordain eleven fourth-year theologians to the priesthood—almost a full year before the conventional date—who on Sundays would leave the seminary and offer Mass in designated parishes. They did not, however, receive faculties to hear confessions. Notable among them were David Dillon, George Garrlets, and Stanley Srnec.[27] The next year Rome confirmed the three-Mass policy and granted a dispensation from the Eucharistic fast to the priest after he celebrated the second one.[28]

Anticipating the wartime changes in the academic schedule adopted later by the St. Paul Seminary, the College of St. Catherine introduced a year-round program as early as January 1942.[29] At St. Thomas the outbreak of war and the call-up of young men to the colors sent enrollment plummeting—the college was "shot to pieces," in the doleful words of its president, Father James Moynihan. But salvation of an admittedly disrupting sort came in 1943 when the United States Navy contracted with the college one of its so-called V-12 programs, whereby over the next two years upwards of 700 men followed a basic curriculum that would equip them to enter officer candidate schools. And so

---

25. *CB*, February 17, 1945.

26. Quoted in *CB*, July 11, 1942.

27. *CB*, September 26, 1942. Father (later Monsignor) David Dillon preached at my first Mass, June 3, 1956.

28. Cicognani to Murray, March 18, 1943, AASPM, Murray Papers.

29. *CB*, January 31, 1942.

the faculty at St. Thomas was held together, just barely, though, as at St. Catherine's and the seminary, summer vacation was ruled out for the duration.[30]

Meanwhile, the ordinary business of the archdiocese had to proceed, though the war and its vicissitudes were seldom out of mind. One hundred twenty-five largely rural vacation catechetical schools opened on schedule in the early summer of 1942, with eleven congregations of nuns participating. But simply promulgating and launching such an important educational endeavor was not enough. In August Archbishop Murray convened representatives of the ten deaneries outside the Twin Cities to discuss their administrative concerns with regard to the "graded instruction" the children might have achieved in public schools and its relationship to the religious vacation schools and to the Saturday and Sunday instruction undertaken by some parishes. Other meetings and rallies took place that summer, like the one in June at the village of Morgan, where the Southern Minnesota District of the Federation of Catholic Societies assembled to "mobilize" the twenty branches of "the units of the state Catholic Women's Union in behalf of God and country."[31] At the end of that month activists from around the country gathered at the St. Paul Hotel to participate in "a summer school in Catholic Action under the auspices of the National Central Office of the Sodality of the Blessed Virgin Mary"; the purpose of the conference was to examine how the war effort could be supported by cultivating within it "a Catholic mentality, a Catholic morality, and a Catholic sense of social justice."[32] When Governor Stassen designated October as "Metal Salvage Month," the archbishop heartily endorsed the project, expressing himself in the capital letters he apparently reserved for patriotic utterances: "NO ONE CAN HOPE TO LOOK TO THE FUTURE WITHOUT QUALMS OF CONSCIENCE IF HE FAILS TO DO HIS DUTY NOW."[33] And toward the end of 1942 he asked his people to join the nationwide "Crusade for Victory," a day of prayer on the feast of the Immaculate Conception, prayer for "a victory that will remove forever the menace of war from both the conquerors and the conquered, and a peace that will be acceptable to God."[34]

But even war could not divert the Church from its obligation to perform the corporal works of mercy. There had been departments of Catholic chari-

---

30. Connors, *Journey*, 309–310.

31. *CB*, August 15, June 6 and June 13, 1942.

32. Murray to "Reverend Father," July 4, 1942 (copy), AASPM, Murray Papers.

33. *CB*, October 10, 1942.

34. *CB*, December 5, 1942.

ties in each of the Twin Cities since Archbishop Ireland's time, but no formal apparatus existed to serve people in the rural areas of the archdiocese. To correct this imbalance a centralized Bureau of Charities was established and incorporated under Minnesota law in 1943 as a child-placing and family-support agency. At first it functioned almost exclusively on matters related to adoption, but it soon took on broader areas of rehabilitation. Governed by a twelve-member board of trustees, the bureau's first director was Francis Curtin. Father Curtin, a genial, warm-hearted man, sowed seeds that were destined to bear much fruit—the Bureau of Catholic Charities ranks with the promotion of the Confraternity of Christian Doctrine as the most lasting successes of the Murray episcopate.[35] Father Frank himself became something of a legend, pestering business men to buy bicycles for orphans and bringing professional football teams to play benefit games in the old Parade Stadium in Minneapolis.

Nor did the war excuse Archbishop Murray from duties his rank imposed outside his immediate jurisdiction. He continued to sit on the Administrative Board of the National Catholic Welfare Conference—expanded to seventeen from the seven members of Austin Dowling's time—not anymore as the beleaguered treasurer, but as head of the rather less demanding Catholic Press Department.[36] Then too, though he had no direct authority over his suffragan bishops, occasionally he was called upon to deal discreetly with matters affecting them.[37] The notoriously imperious John Lawler—consecrated in 1910 and briefly John Ireland's auxiliary[38]—had been bishop of Rapid City since 1916. Now at the beginning of 1945, aged eighty-three and no less domineering than before, the Vatican had determined to ease his way into retirement. The apostolic delegate in Washington, Archbishop Cicognani, asked Murray to travel to western South Dakota and urge Lawler to accept a coadjutor with right of succession. If he did so, Cicognani said, he would receive "the honor of Assistant to the [papal] Throne"—the title, that is, of archbishop in his own person, *ad personam,* as had been the case with Bishop Grace at the time of his retirement. But, the delegate continued, the awarding of such an honor was "contingent on [Lawler] requesting a coadjutor," the choice of whom would be strictly Rome's and not Lawler's. "I hope that with your wonted tact Your Excellency will be able to reach a happy conclusion to your visit to Rapid

---

35. Reardon, *Diocese of St. Paul,* 550–551.
36. *CB,* April 25 and June 27, 1942. See also chapters 17 and 20, above.
37. See chapter 20, above.
38. See chapter 14, above.

City."[39] Apparently Murray's "wonted tact" did indeed achieve the desired objective. In June of 1946—the mills of the Vatican ground more swiftly in this instance than usual—a coadjutor *cum jure* was appointed to Rapid City. John Lawler died two years later.[40]

Throughout the war there lingered some of that traditional eagerness to demonstrate that Catholics practiced an intense level of patriotism, the residue of the tension the immigrants had felt in keeping their alien faith and still being good citizens in a largely Protestant land. This characteristic was not nearly so marked as it had been in 1917–1918, but, though the fixation seems sixty years after the fact almost quaint, the passing of a generation had not eliminated it entirely. Readers of the St. Paul archdiocesan weekly were reminded regularly of the extraordinary contribution Catholics were making to the war effort. As early as January 1942 the *Bulletin* happily announced that "Catholics were among the first to receive War Honors"—five of sixteen recently decorated with the Distinguished Service Cross were Catholics. And a week later, months before the fall of Corregidor and the Bataan death march, a featured story was headed by "Catholic Philippines Lauded for Valiant Defense." Still with an eye on the conflict in the Pacific, readers were informed that "the Minister of War in Australia is a Holy Name man." When Vice President Henry Wallace gave a speech to delineate "what we are fighting for," the *Bulletin* observed in a headline, "Nation's War-Aims Talk Reflects Pope's Views." Enemy atrocities, especially those against religious personnel, received special attention. "Priests and Nuns Slain by Japs in Solomons," rang out one headline, and the story that followed recounted how four missionaries had been bayoneted by Japanese troops on Guadalcanal. Shortly afterward appeared the report that a Jesuit priest had died as the result of "tortures in a Nazi prison camp." And the *Bulletin* did not hesitate to discern the role played by patriotic Catholics in the higher realms of diplomacy: "The liberation of French Africa," the editors wrote, "has been attributed to the brilliant work of a U.S. Catholic diplomat." The reference was to Robert D. Murphy, a veteran State Department operative who did indeed orchestrate "behind the scenes" (as the *Bulletin* put it) the diplomatic prelude to the expulsion of Axis forces from Algeria and Tunisia. When President Roosevelt died, it appeared notable that his successor should choose Matthew J. Connelly, "a graduate of Fordham," as his "confidential secretary," and laudable that Mr. Truman, in

39. Cicognani to Murray, February 2, 1945, AASPM, Murray Papers.

40. Michael Costigan, Thomas Faulkner, William O'Connor, and Robert White, "Diocese of Rapid City," in Ahern, *Catholic Heritage*, 196–201.

his first address to Congress, should express views "similar to the [American] bishops' ideas on peace," specifically "eschewing power politics" in the relations between large nations and small.[41]

Also throughout the war Catholics were uneasy about the alliance with the Soviet Union. Most subscribed to Fulton Sheen's debatable distinction between the Russian people and the Communist regime, though some old-line isolationists, as they saw with some satisfaction the ever-increasing savagery of the fighting on the Eastern front, wished a plague upon both combatants. When Anthony Eden, after a trip to Moscow, said in a speech that there "was no real conflict of interest" between Britain and the USSR, American Catholic opinion was highly critical of the British Foreign Secretary. Similarly negative assessments, more or less muted as the war dragged on, reached a crescendo when the agreements reached at Yalta and Potsdam were made public. In March 1945 the *Catholic Bulletin* covered one of its front pages with a series of anguished headlines: "Scotland's Hierarchy Condemns Yalta Edicts; Grievous Act of Injustice against Christian World; Bishops Say Big Three Deal on Poland Involves 'Murder of a Nation.'" And in August, after the last of the wartime conferences between the leaders of the victorious allies: "Potsdam Edict Makes Poland Soviet Vassal." There was disquiet too, if not so explicit, about the negotiations in San Francisco aimed at establishing a United Nations Organization (in which former Governor Stassen was a leading participant). "Secular opinion seems to be prevailing in the discussions at San Francisco," observed the *Bulletin*'s editors. "There are many Catholics among the delegates to the conference, but a spirit of co-ordination has eluded them."[42] Unlike the Communists, they might have added.

The war in Europe ended in the spring of 1945, and Archbishop Murray ordered special prayers of thanksgiving to be said in all parishes. In June the Holy Name Societies of the archdiocese organized holy hours in the cathedral and the basilica for the same purpose. The Polish parishes launched a fund-raising campaign to bring relief to devastated Poland; the early returns were encouraging. Then, in August, amidst the choking fumes of the mushroom clouds hanging over Hiroshima and Nagasaki, the Japanese surrendered. Among Catholics, and for that matter among people everywhere, of whatever faith or none, debate over the morality of the use of atomic weapons began almost immediately. The world at any rate was finally at peace, though it proved to be a very troubled peace.

---

41. *CB*, January 3, January 10, March 28, May 30, October 24, October 31, and December 5, 1942, and April 28, 1945.

42. *CB*, January 31, 1942, and March 19, August 11, and May 5, 1945.

AND INDEED IT PROVED TO BE A VERY DIFFERENT WORLD. HEAPS of ruins disfigured much of Europe and Asia and reconstruction appeared to be a despairingly intractable task. Yet, in accord with the best in the human spirit, the job was undertaken, and in a remarkably short span of time it achieved, through a predictable series of ups and downs, a surprising measure of success. Much of the accomplishment was due to private initiatives, like the modest efforts undertaken by the Polish parishes in the archdiocese of St. Paul and more extensive ones by better-endowed foundations and institutions. But in the last analysis only a massive intervention by all the king's horses and all the king's men could put the broken world back together again. At the end of the war, the economic and industrial base of the United States, despite the Herculean strains put upon it over four years as the "arsenal of democracy," stood if anything stronger than before, while its conquered enemies and even its erstwhile allies lay almost prostrate physically and politically. In 1947 the European Recovery Program, the Marshall Plan—a characteristically American combination of altruism and self-interest—began the process of renewal which sooner than anyone could have predicted brought Western Europe back to an economic and social viability that rivaled prewar levels.

So there flourished a national feeling of optimism, of expansiveness, a conviction that a brave new world was coming into being in accord with American values. The Great Depression, a sad and cautionary memory, had given way to unprecedented prosperity. By no means was everyone rich, but almost everyone was better off than he had been a decade before. Technological advances made ordinary tasks easier, brought entertainment into the humblest home by way of a graceless screened box, supplied a host of new treatments and therapies to the never-ending battle against pain and illness. This overall sense of well-being—what critics would later call smug and narrow self-satisfaction—lasted throughout the 1950s. Not that the times were without their national traumas: the ever-darkening shadow of the Cold War, the bloody stalemate in Korea, labor disputes, ideological combats, Truman versus MacArthur, Alger Hiss versus Whitaker Chambers, and, much more to the point, the daily vicissitudes all men and women endure far from the glare of the public arena. Even so, the American mood on the whole remained upbeat.

Perhaps the single most important reason why was a piece of legislation signed by President Roosevelt a year before the war ended. After lengthy and often contentious debate in the Congress, the Servicemembers' Readjustment Act, better known as the G.I. Bill of Rights, became law in June 1944. Designed to bring veterans back smoothly into civilian society, it guaranteed them, in recognition of their sacrifices, substantial financial aid in education, housing, and unemployment compensation. What it did in effect—and perhaps unintentionally—was to destroy the traditional American class system. People who had never dreamed before the war of going to college or owning their own homes—these were privileges of the well-off—now had open to them a new range of possibilities. The result was dramatic. By the mid-1950s, when the provisions of the original Act terminated, 7,800,000 World War II veterans had participated in an education or training program, and 2,400,000 had secured home loans guaranteed by the federal Veterans Administration. In 1947, the peak year, veterans composed forty-nine percent of those who applied to college admissions offices.[43]

When the soldiers and sailors came home, American Catholics shared in the general euphoria. Their contribution to the war effort seemed to have done away with feelings of uneasiness about their place in the nation's life; the grandchildren of the immigrants had little reason to worry about nativist prejudice. And thanks largely to the G.I. Bill, young Catholics in unprecedented numbers entered the professions and the managerial élite, and so participated fully in the expanding economy, as they moved their big, bustling families into secure new homes. In short, Catholics achieved what John Ireland had striven so hard for: they became part of the great American middle class. And in 1960 one of their own was elected president of the United States.

Reflective of this burst of confidence was the physical expansion of the institutional Church. Statistics make dry reading, and they often fail to illuminate factors not susceptible to numerical scrutiny. Nevertheless, they serve a real if limited purpose, and applied to the archdiocese of St. Paul they show a remarkable development between 1945 and 1950. At the end of World War II 527,000 Catholics lived in Minnesota, 294,000 of them in John Gregory Murray's jurisdiction. He presided over the endeavors of 532 priests in 267 parishes, of 1,740 nuns, and of fifty religious brothers.[44] Five years later a rather more detailed exposition of the figures manifests a striking growth in most categories. To be sure, the number of priests, 527—443 diocesan and 82 regular—declined slightly, and that of the brothers remained constant, but the number of sisters, belonging to thirty-three congregations of religious women, increased to 1,978. Fifty-three thousand pupils in Catholic primary and secondary schools, together with 24,000 catechized in vacation schools or release-time programs, and combined with the 2,600 enrolled in

43. See http://www.gibill.va.gov. Accessed May 20, 2008.

44. *Official Catholic Directory* (New York, 1945). The total number of Catholics in the United States at this date stood at 24,000,000.

the colleges of St. Catherine and St. Thomas, all sharp increases, meant that nearly 80,000 young people experienced some variety of formal Catholic education. This figure did not include the 533 students receiving ecclesiastical training at the St. Paul Seminary and Nazareth Hall. These institutions were staffed by sixty-two priests, 1,404 sisters, forty-four Christian Brothers, and 328 lay teachers. Five general hospitals, two added since 1942, cared for 41,000 patients annually. The number of infant baptisms in 1950 almost doubled, to 14,600, pointing up the rise in the post-Depression birthrate—a demographic phenomenon that lasted, at least among Catholics, well into the 1960s. And the overall population of the archdiocese shot up to 370,000 in a mere half decade.[45]

Aside from mere numbers, there were other signs of renewed vigor. Late in 1945 the Oblate Sisters of Providence, an African American congregation headquartered in Baltimore, agreed to take on duties as catechists at St. Peter Claver parish in St. Paul and to staff the school when it subsequently opened— as it did in 1950; this proved an occasion for archdiocesan and civic celebration of an admittedly edgy state of racial harmony. In the summer of 1946 the Family Guild was formed, whose purpose was to vitalize Christian family life by way of retreats, conferences, and days of recollection. Under the direction of Father Richard Doherty of the St. Paul Seminary, this endeavor was strengthened by the Cana and pre-Cana retreats for married and affianced couples. Not unrelated was the launching under the aegis of the Archdiocesan Council of Catholic Women of the so-called Nazareth Conferences, which were meant to train parents to deal specifically with the inculcation of Catholic values in their children. The next year saw the founding of the Guild of St. Francis de Sales for Catholic journalists, also directed by Father Doherty (himself a sometime newspaper man). Meanwhile, in 1947 Mr. Hill's Seminary secured accreditation from the North Central Association of Colleges and Universities and so the right to grant B.A. and M.A. degrees. Crowning this success, the seminary's new and splendid library, named for Archbishop Ireland, opened its doors three years later.[46]

Also on the institutional side, even the long nagging financial problems of the College of St. Thomas limped during these postwar years toward a resolution. Not, however, due to the campaign launched in the summer of 1945 to raise $3,830,000 for debt relief and expansion of facilities. Much to local distress, an expensive outside fund-raising firm was contracted and then

45. See Reardon, *Diocese of St. Paul*, 576–577.
46. Reardon, *Diocese of St. Paul*, 552–558.

proved so inept that the effort had to be abandoned. Once again Archbishop Murray turned, however reluctantly, to an assessment of individual priests and parishes. Still, the viability of the college, thanks mostly to the G.I. Bill of Rights, was at the same time firmly established. Enrollments soared in a helter-skelter fashion, and so did grants from the Federal Public Housing Authority, which supplied gratis temporary and makeshift residences for students and faculty, as well as a cafeteria and a student activity building. And, under the leadership of the new president, the forceful and magnetic Father Vincent Flynn, the chronic and notorious ill-management of St. Thomas—especially when compared with the skillful stewardship of the Josephite Sisters down Cleveland Avenue at St. Catherine's College—came to an end. In March 1948, the long-planned science building, facing Summit Avenue and constructed of the same yellow Mankato stone as the abutting administration building, was dedicated appropriately under the patronage of Albertus Magnus—appropriate because St. Albert was considered something of a medieval scientist and in any case had been a mentor of St. Thomas Aquinas, whose name was popularly associated with the administration building.[47] By the end of January 1949, thanks to the generosity of the people of the archdiocese, ninety-three percent of the college's obligations had been met.[48]

But the most important sign of revival was the foundation of twenty new parishes during this short span of years, six in St. Paul (including St. Stephen's of the Ukrainian Rite), four in Minneapolis and, significantly, ten in the burgeoning suburbs of the Twin Cities.[49] The impetus was different from the days of the pioneers, when logs were dragged into the nearest clearing, a rude building put up, and then a petition sent to Bishop Cretin or Father Ravoux to send a priest to minister in it a few times a year. In the urbanized mid-twentieth century a more sophisticated and centralized system that called for long-range planning necessarily prevailed. But, as always, the parish was the beating heart of Catholic life, and, as always, it took the stamina and sacrifice of many people to start one anew.

St. Leo the Great, carved out of territory from Nativity, Holy Spirit, and St. Therese parishes in St. Paul, began even before the war ended. On June 24, 1945, Father Bernard Murray, the founding pastor, celebrated Mass for the

---

47. Connors, *Journey*, 321–324. In 2000, Albertus Magnus was renamed, quite inappropriately, Roach Hall, in honor of the sixth archbishop of St. Paul/Minneapolis, John Robert Roach (1921–2003).

48. Murray to "Reverend Father," January 31, 1949 (copy), AASPM, Murray Papers.

49. See Wright, *Gather Us In*, 185–204.

first time in the Highland Theater, just off Ford Parkway. The first baptism, of Matthew Claude Christensen, was administered that same day. Shortly afterward a vacant store was acquired to serve as a chapel. Ground at the corner of Cleveland and Bohland Avenues was broken in December for a combined church and school. By Christmas Eve 1946 the building was ready for use, and the school opened the following September. In 1951 a portion of St. Leo's territory was detached to establish St. Gregory's parish.[50]

On May 28, 1946, Archbishop Murray appointed John V. Ryan as pastor of the new parish of St. Pascal Baylon on the east side of St. Paul. A few weeks later Father Ryan said the first Mass in the Ramsey County Correctional School for Boys, better known as "Totem Town," in nearby Highwood; eighteen families were in attendance. Sunday liturgies were later conducted in parishioners' homes, until a temporary building was constructed at the corner of White Bear Avenue and Conway Street. This remarkable edifice was put up by the men of the parish out of two army surplus Quonset huts which Ryan had purchased for $35 each. It seated 275 persons on pews donated by St. Genevieve's parish in Centerville. To bolster the parish's morale and sense of identity—and, not incidentally, to raise badly needed funds—the pastor from the beginning of his tenure organized "block parties," regular social gatherings in each block across St. Pascal's neighborhoods. Not till October 1949 was the cornerstone laid for a church-school combination, which was complete enough by the following June for Mass to be said there. The school opened in September.[51]

On Sunday, June 14, 1946, at eight o'clock in the morning and again at ten, Father John Phelan offered Mass "on an ordinary square table covered with bedding-linen, a single doily, and a crucifix." A total of eighty-nine persons, representing forty-eight families, attended the services, held in the basement of the administration building of Glenwood Hills Hospital. So began the spiritual journey of the parish of St. Margaret Mary in Golden Valley, the suburb west of Minneapolis. After offering daily Mass in the home of a parishioner, Father Phelan routinely tramped about the area knocking on doors, taking census, and soliciting funds. He was a genial, gregarious man who always looked on the bright side. Once, when a parish picnic was deluged by rain, he said: "This isn't rain, it's holy water; we're being blessed by the Lord himself!" On January 12, 1948, "a bitterly cold day," members of St. Margaret

50. Anon., "St. Leo's Church" (n.p., 1965), no pagination. Father Murray and Archbishop Murray were not related.

51. Anon., "Do You Remember? Highlights of the History of St. Pascal's Parish" (n.p., 1986), 2–5.

Mary's 122 families gathered for the dedication of the new basement church on the corner of Golden Valley Road and Wirth Parkway. After that ceremony thirty-two children received the sacrament of confirmation.[52]

Archbishop Murray did not forget the pledge he had given to the younger clergy at the outbreak of the war; the pastorates of many of the new parishes were assigned to priests who had served in the armed forces. This did not necessarily mean, however, that these men had been given easy duty. Indeed, the clerical joke at the time was that the archbishop handed an ex-chaplain a streetcar token and a map with the territory of his canonical jurisdiction shaded in. Within weeks of his discharge from the army in January 1946, Raymond Rutkowski, who had spent the war years in the Pacific theater, was named pastor of the Church of the Presentation of the Blessed Virgin Mary, to be established in Maplewood, on the northeast edge of St. Paul. His parishioners were mostly truck farmers and returning veterans "who purchased the tract homes being speedily built all over the area." The first Mass was said in the Gladstone School on Frost Avenue on January 27. Through the rest of 1946 a large house functioned as a rectory and a chapel. Early the next year Father Rutkowski bought a nine-and-a-half-acre parcel of land at the corner of Larpenteur Avenue and Kenard Street for $1,850, and construction of the usual church-school combination began immediately. Enough of it was completed by Christmas to celebrate midnight Mass there. Two years later the school opened under the direction of the Franciscan Sisters of Sylvania, Ohio.[53]

Mark Farrell served as an army chaplain in the Pacific theater for twenty-six months. On December 5, 1944, in the battle of Leyte Island in the southern Philippines, his unit came under a fierce Japanese artillery barrage. He was struck by shrapnel on the left side of his body while administering the last rites as well as caring for and helping to evacuate the wounded. For his deeds that day he was awarded the Silver Star and the Purple Heart. He spent many long months recuperating, the last of them in a military hospital in San Francisco.[54] He never recovered the full use of his left arm.

Back home in the summer of 1946, Father Farrell was assigned as temporary assistant at St. Jude's parish in Mahtomedi. There, on the shores of White

---

52. Anon., "The Dedication and the History of St. Margaret Mary's Church" (n.p., 1959), no pagination. Good Shepherd parish had been established in Golden Valley the year before St. Margaret Mary.

53. Anon., "Church of the Presentation of the Blessed Virgin Mary" (n.p., 2002), 1–3.

54. *CB*, February 24 and July 14, 1945.

Bear Lake, John Gregory Murray arrived by trolley one day in July, and explained to Farrell that the sprawling parishes of the Incarnation and the Annunciation in south Minneapolis needed to be reduced in area by the foundation of a new jurisdiction. On August 27 the parish of St. Joan of Arc was formally incorporated. The choice of saintly patron was Mark Farrell's—the tribute of one soldier to another. While Mass was offered in the gymnasium of Eugene Field School, funding plans—about which Father Farrell was particularly astute—were quickly developed, including the issuance of bonds "handled by Keenan and Clary." Property was secured at 46th Street and Clinton Avenue South, and, though the church was not entirely finished, Christmas midnight Mass was celebrated there in 1947. Six months later the parishioners of St. Joan learned happily that the Sisters of St. Joseph of Crookston would staff the school to be opened in September. And two years after that, in June 1950, the newly ordained Wallace Hermes was appointed assistant pastor. He and Father Farrell made a remarkably effective team.[55]

ON JULY 19, 1950, EXACTLY ONE HUNDRED YEARS HAD PASSED since the creation of the diocese of St. Paul by Pope Pius IX. There was no intent to let such a milestone pass without a duly suitable observance. But a logistic difficulty immediately presented itself: in midsummer schools were not in session, and hence thousands of students could not be mobilized to take part. It was determined therefore to bring the celebration to its climax the week of October 15. Before that, however—before the gaudy commemoration reached its apogee in the Twin Cities—a series of events took place across the eleven rural deaneries. Beginning on May 7, a pontifical Mass of reparation and thanksgiving was offered in turn in each deanery with an appropriate sermon on the significance of the centenary, delivered by a specially chosen preacher. Large if not overwhelming congregations participated.

The fête moved on the morning of Tuesday, October 17, to the St. Paul auditorium, where Bishop Thomas Welch of Duluth—the senior suffragan in the province and once Ireland's secretary and chancellor and Dowling's vicar general[56]—offered Mass with a choir of more than 6,000 youngsters who,

---

55. Frank Murray, "St. Joan of Arc, Parish History" (n.p., 1951), no pagination. During the 1950s my family lived in St. Joan's parish. I offered my first Mass there in 1956 and my father's funeral Mass in 1959. Father Farrell was very kind to us. He died in 1990, and I cherish my memories of him.

56. But Archbishop Murray had not been thoroughly convinced of Welch's suitability for promotion. When asked by the apostolic delegate in 1937 whether the

reminiscent of the Eucharistic Congress of nine years before, sang sweetly under the direction of the indefatigable Father Francis Missia.[57] An overflow crowd of more than 5,000 was in attendance, including a half dozen bishops and scores of clergy and religious. In the evening, at the same venue, a "reception" was held at which addresses and various musical numbers entertained and informed a lesser number of listeners. The next day and evening, similar events took place in the Minneapolis auditorium. On Thursday, October 19, the commemoration moved on to the St. Paul Seminary, where after the Mass and sermon—delivered by James Moynihan, the biographer of Archbishop Ireland[58]—the assembled clergy, hundreds strong, moved across campus to witness Archbishop Murray's dedication and blessing of the new Ireland Memorial Library, which he performed with his usual "ritualistic exactness." Afterwards, in the new library's spacious reading room, he conferred the first five of the seminary's recipients of the master's degree, including one upon Richard Moudry, whose dissertation on Galtier's first chapel in St. Paul has already been cited in these pages.[59]

Predictably the *Catholic Bulletin* heralded the commemoration in bold capitals: "100th Anniversary Celebration Rated Great Success." A later generation of critics, however, has dubbed these centenary events as a species of "triumphalism" and especially of "clericalism." Such allegations are not without merit. Still, there was much to celebrate over all that had happened since Augustin Ravoux, when he learned in July 1850 that St. Paul was soon to have its own bishop and cathedral, proceeded to purchase all that property with money he did not have.[60] An uninterrupted existence for a century is no mean acomplishment.

---

bishop of Duluth should be considered for appointment to the see of Detroit, Murray replied: "[Welch's] personal qualities, . . . his discretion, his patience, his experience in St. Paul, make him a worthy candidate for any position of honor within the Church. But I hesitate to place on him the tremendous burdens which must be carried by the future Ordinary of Detroit, without respite for the period of a generation or more." Murray to Cicognani, March 12, 1937 (copy), AASPM, Murray Papers. In May of that year Edward Mooney, bishop of Rochester, was named first archbishop of Detroit.

57. See chapter 22, above.

58. James H. Moynihan, *The Life of Archbishop Ireland* (New York, 1953). By this time Moynihan was pastor of Incarnation parish, Minneapolis. The text of his sermon at the seminary printed in *CB*, October 21, 1950.

59. For details of the observance of the centennial, see Reardon, *Diocese of St. Paul,* 573–575. For Moudry, see chapter 1, above.

60. See chapter 2, above.

CHAPTER 24

The End of the
Counter-Reformation

ARCHBISHOP JOHN GREGORY MURRAY WAS ABLE TO PARTICIPATE
more or less fully in the centenary festivities of the summer and autumn of
1950. For some lengthy time before then, however, his activities were limited.[1]
At about nine o'clock on the evening of March 31, 1947, returning to his rooms
in the cathedral rectory from a meeting of the Board of Trustees at the College of St. Thomas, the seventy-year-old archbishop was struck down by a
passing automobile as he crossed the street at the corner of Summit and Selby
Avenues. Characteristically, he wanted no fuss made about his person, and
so a press release was issued which stated that he had not been seriously hurt.
A week later a correction had to be circulated: originally undiscerned and
now unspecified internal injuries necessitated entry into St. Joseph's Hospital,
St. Paul, "for treatment and observation." No visitors.[2] The "treatment and observation" apparently did little good, because by the middle of May, though
he was now permitted to walk in the hospital's corridors and to attend Mass
daily in the chapel, still no visitors were allowed. This injunction apparently
applied to everyone, including Hilary Hacker and Gerald O'Keefe, who had
come into office two years earlier as, respectively, vicar general and chancellor. Fathers Hacker and O'Keefe would implement archdiocesan policy with
a certain unimaginative literalness, till they were rewarded with dioceses of
their own: Bismarck for Hacker in 1957, Davenport for O'Keefe in 1967.

After eleven weeks at St. Joseph's, Murray was tentatively released to the
care of his two unmarried sisters, Miss Jane and Miss Mary, still residing in

---

1. Reardon, *Diocese of St. Paul,* 521, exaggerates when he asserts that Murray refrained from "all public functions until 1950."
2. *CB,* April 5 and 12, 1947.

the old family home in Waterbury, Connecticut. His other sibling, brother James who lived in New York City, was a frequent visitor to Waterbury during these tense weeks. But in the end tender, loving attention was not enough to alleviate the archbishop's condition. On July 19, the symptoms and the discomforts associated with them brought him back to Minnesota, this time to Rochester and the celebrated Mayo Clinic. There ten days later he underwent surgery to remove a "displaced" kidney. Convalescence proved to be long and difficult.[3]

Meanwhile, in mid-May announcement came from the apostolic delegation in Washington that for the second time the archdiocese of St. Paul was to receive an auxiliary bishop. Given the deliberate pace of the process the Vatican employs in the appointment of bishops, the short time-span between the end of March and the middle of May strongly suggests that this one was close to implementation before Murray was injured. James Joseph Byrne in any case, aged thirty-nine—a tall, slender, prematurely silver-haired man with a seraphic smile—was born in St. Paul, educated at Nazareth Hall and the St. Paul Seminary, and sent after his ordination in 1933 to Murray's favorite institution of higher learning, Louvain University in Belgium, where he earned a doctorate in theology, writing a dissertation on Cardinal Newman's theory of doctrinal development. Upon his return from Europe, he joined the faculty of St. Thomas College, became dean of the college in 1941 and then, in 1945, was assigned professor of dogmatic theology at the seminary. His reputation for a deep personal piety appeared confirmed, at least to many observers, by the exquisite and fastidious manner in which he celebrated the old Tridentine liturgies. He was consecrated on July 2, 1947, and immediately assumed responsibility for the archbishop's public commitments. The following January he was appointed pastor of Nativity parish in St. Paul.[4] For the next eight years, as Murray's health waxed and waned, Byrne served loyally and effectively to lighten the older man's burden; the very ideal of an auxiliary bishop.

ARCHBISHOP MURRAY WAS WELL ENOUGH BY CHRISTMAS 1947 to pontificate at midnight Mass at the cathedral and, the following Eastertide, to preside at services there.[5] He had long proved himself relentless in fulfilling

---

3. *CB*, May 31 and July 19, 1947.

4. *CB*, July 5 and 12, 1947. John Lawler in 1910 was the first auxiliary in St. Paul. John Ireland in 1875 was Grace's coadjutor with right of succession, a very different canonical status.

5. *CB*, December 20, 1947, and March 20, 1948.

what he conceived to be the obligations of his office, and little by little, as he regained his strength, he worked himself back into as full a schedule as a man of his age, recovering from serious injuries, could possibly have taken on. Still, there were signs that even as indefatigable as he had always appeared to be, his pace had necessarily slowed. He now shared with Bishop Byrne the onerous task of parish visitations, which included administering the sacrament of confirmation, reviewing the parish's financial records, and interviewing its personnel. (A clerical anecdote of the 1950s suggested that when on these occasions Murray talked to the sisters in the local convent, he inquired whether they thought they were adequately housed, fed, and given sufficient recreation time, while Byrne wanted to know if the nuns were satisfied about their spiritual progress as religious.) Perhaps more significantly, never after the automobile accident did Murray take on the long and laborious ceremonies involved in ordinations.[6] In the summer of 1949 Bishop Byrne made the required *ad limina* visit to the Vatican.[7]

Expansion continued during the early 1950s, though not as rapidly as in the preceding half decade. Over his last years Archbishop Murray founded four more parishes. Among them was one slated for the east side of St. Paul, St. Thomas the Apostle, in order to relieve the crowded conditions at Blessed Sacrament parish. In 1954 land with a two story frame house on it was purchased at 213 Stillwater Avenue. Father Thomas Robertson, just discharged from the army—after his second tour of duty—was assigned as pastor. Plans were laid for the construction of the usual church-school combination. Meanwhile services were held in the basement of a parishioner's hardware store. Altar, pews, and other essential fixtures were donated by surrounding parishes. The first Mass was offered there on October 17, 1954, as were the first baptisms, those of Peggy Ann Mullaney and Thomas Gregory Murphy. The permanent building was completed in September 1956, at which time the school opened its doors.[8]

Another former military chaplain received his first pastorate in 1954. On June 19 Ambrose Filbin said the first Mass in the new parish of St. Pius X, White Bear Lake, in the auditorium of the Gall Public School on White Bear Avenue and County Road C. About 100 people were in attendance, and the collection totaled $111.38. Father Filbin wasted no time in organizing his

6. Athans, *To Work for the Whole People*, 201–202.

7. *CB*, August 20, 1949. Byrne traveled by way of Dublin where he was the guest of his cousin, Mrs. Sean O'Kelly, wife of the president of Ireland.

8. Anon., "St. Thomas the Apostle Parish" (n.p., 1979), no pagination.

charge. The parish was duly incorporated on June 25, with lay trustees Donald Behr and George Huth. A women's group was formed on June 30 and a
men's a week later. A temporary rectory, also on White Bear Avenue, was purchased for $18,600. Kenneth Bacchus, a local contractor, donated a parcel of
land at the intersection of Cedar and Highland Avenues for a church-school
combination. Construction began on October 7, and Mass was offered in the
completed building on Pentecost Sunday 1955. In the autumn a school of six
grades began classes with a teaching staff of five nuns and about 300 pupils.[9]

That all these new ecclesial foundations—like the ones cited earlier in
these pages—included a school in their original planning went without saying. Such had been the pattern from pioneer days. Often enough these pledges
remained only aspirations, at least for a goodly span of time. But the relative
prosperity of Catholics during the 1950s offered fresh vistas and fuelled further physical expansion of the parochial educational system, and not just in
the Twin Cities and their suburbs. Thus Holy Redeemer parish in Marshall,
established in 1881, had operated a school since 1900, but in September 1950 it
opened a much larger and better-equipped building on another site. Similar
were the developments at Stephen's in Anoka, St. Mary's in Shakopee, St. Joseph's in Montevideo, and St. Martin's in Rogers. In the metropolitan area
Immaculate Heart of Mary in St. Paul, whose founding pastor was another
ex-chaplain, Father Raymond Reed, inaugurated its school that same September with five Benedictine sisters. And in Minneapolis, Father James A. Troy,
who had established St. Austin's parish in 1936, finally managed to a start
school fourteen years later. There were at work in this last instance an anomaly and a bit of nostalgia. St. Austin's church was located at 41st Street and
Thomas Avenue North, while the school went up at 40th Street and Bryant
Avenue North. And it was called Archbishop Dowling School. Evidently, unlike many who had been ordained by John Ireland, Troy was an admirer of
the great man's successor.[10]

CHRONICLING THE ALMOST FRANTIC INSTITUTIONAL EXPANSION
of the immediate post-war years tempts one to overlook what all the archdiocesan churches, schools, seminaries—in the autumn of 1950 Nazareth Hall

---

9. Anon., "St. Pius X Church" (n.p., 1978), no pagination.

10. *CB*, September 2, 1950. Father Troy was ordained in 1907. In 1950 Anoka
and Shakopee would not have been considered part of the metropolitan area.

reached its physical capacity, 234 students[11]—clubs, youth centers, summer camps, workshops, summertime catechetical instruction, conferences, Holy Name rallies, and rosary processions were calculated to accomplish. The success in nurturing the interior life of the spirit cannot, needless to say, be measured by listing a large number of activities. Even so, there might be applied here a kind of sacramental principle, the use of external signs to indicate internal reality. Corporal works of mercy would surely furnish one such sign, like the archdiocesan-wide drive that collected 3,400 cartons, 114,000 pounds, of clothing for refugees; or, more modestly but not less significantly, like the annual tea sponsored by the Daughters of Isabella to help fund the Hawthorne Dominican sisters who heroically served the terminally ill in Our Lady of Good Counsel Free Cancer Home in St. Paul.[12]

Sunday Mass attendance remained high, as did the devotion of the First Friday. Lines outside the confessionals in every parish church during the Easter season were very long. The yearly Forty Hours devotion to the Eucharist, frequent parish missions, Lenten stations of the cross (televised on WCCO television for the first time on Good Friday 1952 from St. Olaf's Church in Minneapolis[13])—these and other pious exercises attracted considerable numbers. The penitential order stood intact and, if not universally observed, it was nonetheless accepted as the norm. The rules as reiterated by Archbishop Murray, though somewhat simplified, still seem exceedingly severe to a later, more relaxed generation. Abstinence from meat was required for all over the age of seven every Friday and Ash Wednesday, on the vigils of the feasts of the Assumption and Christmas, and on Holy Saturday morning; partial abstinence (meat once) was expected on Ember Days and the vigils of Pentecost and All Saints; and fast, meaning one full meal, for those between the ages of twenty-one and fifty-nine on every Lenten weekday, Ember Days, and the vigils of Pentecost, Christmas, Assumption, and All Saints.[14]

Pius XII proclaimed 1950 a Holy Year, which reached its climax on November 1 when the pope invoked his prerogative of infallibility (for the first and to date only time) to define the Assumption of the Virgin Mary as a revealed dogma. The procedure whereby the faithful could gain the Jubilee in-

---

11. *CB*, September 23, 1950. Of the total 184 were studying for the archdiocese, the rest for eleven other dioceses.

12. *CB*, February 5, 1955, and November 27, 1954.

13. *CB*, March 28, 1953. The telecast was sponsored by the Knights of Columbus.

14. Murray to "Reverend Father," January 12, 1952 (copy), AASPM, Murray Papers.

dulgence was rather less rigorous than had been the case in 1933,[15] but its esprit was the same: those unable to go on pilgrimage to Rome were to visit certain churches four times, say the prescribed prayers, and receive the sacraments of penance and the Eucharist; this favor could be won till the end of 1951.[16] The dogmatic definition of the Assumption demonstrated how central devotion to the Virgin continued to be to Catholic piety, and the so-called Marian Year that began on May 1, 1954, was a further indication of the same. In the archdiocese the most visible manifestation of this veneration was the growth in participation in the yearly rosary processions in each of the Twin Cities; by the late 1950s, upwards of 40,000 people in St. Paul prayed their way to the steps of the cathedral where Benediction of the Blessed Sacrament closed the ceremony; similarly in Minneapolis on the same Sunday in May, 35,000 marched to the Basilica of St. Mary.[17]

Another sign of spiritual vitality was the burgeoning retreat movement. The Jesuits of the Missouri Province purchased an estate on Lake Demontreville, near North St. Paul, in 1948, and the next year a series of retreats for laymen was begun, preached by two permanent staff members and an occasional guest master, always consistent with the principles of St. Ignatius's *Spiritual Exercises.* The response was enthusiastic, so much so that a Laymen's Retreat League was formally organized, directed by four counselors from Minneapolis and four from St. Paul. At the same time the Religious of the Cenacle, at the invitation of Archbishop Murray, established a house in Minneapolis in order to provide space and the appropriate setting for retreats for women. The demand for this service was reflected in the schedule the sisters set up: forty-nine weekend retreats each year, accommodating thirty persons, and an average of two days of recollection each week. The largest and most elaborate of these facilities was Christ the King Retreat Center in the town of Buffalo, a short distance northwest of the Twin Cities, and located on the shore of the lake of the same name. The Oblate Fathers, aided by an ever growing staff of religious and laity, offered a year-round schedule of retreats for diocesan priests, laymen and women, young people, married and engaged couples, the bereaved, the disabled, and almost any other conceivable constituency. During these years other religious orders found the archdiocese an agreeable place to situate important institutions: the Franciscans opened a

---

15. See chapter 22, above.

16. Murray to "Reverend Father," January 6, 1951 (copy), AASPM, Murray Papers.

17. *CB*, May 5, 1959.

seminary in Chaska and the Congregation of Holy Cross its novitiate in Jordan.[18] In 1951 the Foreign Mission Society of America, better known as Maryknoll, secured property on Gerard Avenue South in Minneapolis.[19]

And there were stirrings on the liturgical front that would develop over time into reforms that would have the most profound effect on the Eucharistic practice, and therefore the piety, of Catholics in Minnesota and everywhere else. In 1951 an Easter Vigil service was introduced experimentally in Rome and other widely separated places throughout the world. In the United States six such liturgies took place, one of them in the Cathedral of the Sacred Heart in Winona. Traditionalists reacted to this possible innovation with some misgiving, but they could hardly object when, two years later, Pius XII gave a sweeping authorization for Mass to be celebrated in the evening so that working people could more easily attend.[20] Then in 1955 came a radical revamping of the Holy Week liturgy. Instead of the numbingly long and complicated services held in a virtually empty church on the mornings of Holy Thursday, Good Friday, and Holy Saturday, somewhat shorter and simpler ceremonies were to be celebrated in the late afternoon or evening on the first two of these days, while the Easter Vigil became de rigueur on Holy Saturday night. And reception of Holy Communion by the faithful was to be permitted on Good Friday.[21] For the likes of William Busch and Paul Bussard it was the first glimmer of dawn.

ON FEBRUARY 26, 1956, JOHN GREGORY MURRAY CELEBRATED his seventy-ninth birthday with his sisters in Waterbury. Back home in April he addressed the convention of the Serra Clubs of Minnesota at the College of St. Thomas. On May 8 he inaugurated a $3,000,000 fund drive in behalf of St. Joseph's Hospital in St. Paul with a television appearance. It was his first experience with that medium, and it would obviously be his last, for he was desperately ill with "glandular cancer of the neck"—throat cancer. But though the tumor was clearly visible, he refused to slow down or modify his schedule. On Sunday, June 10, the archbishop administered confirmation to three classes, traveled west to the hamlet of Sanborn where he blessed a

18. Reardon, *Diocese of St. Paul,* 670–671 and 676–677.

19. *CB,* March 3, 1951.

20. *CB,* May 31, 1951, and January 17, 1953.

21. Murray to "Reverend Father," January 30, 1956 (copy), AASPM, Murray Papers.

new parish social center,[22] and then back to the Twin Cities for the Holy Name rally at the State Fair Grounds. It was a scorchingly hot day, but the only concession Murray made to the heat was to agree to sit as the thousands of Holy Name men—the largest rally ever, with 203 parishes represented— marched past the reviewing stand. The following week he confirmed in nine parishes, and at the end of the month he dedicated a new church in Dawson, in the western extremity of the archdiocese, not far from the South Dakota border.[23]

But before that, on June 20, a momentous announcement was issued by the apostolic delegation in Washington: William Otterwell Brady, bishop of Sioux Falls, had been appointed coadjutor archbishop of St. Paul, with right of succession, and Auxiliary Bishop James Byrne had been named ordinary of the diocese of Boise, Idaho.[24] On Thursday, June 22, Brady paid a courtesy call on Murray to whom he wrote three days later: "I do much appreciate your kind and gracious reception." Their discussion dealt mostly with the provision of an appropriate residence for the new coadjutor. Brady declined to live in the cathedral rectory, as Murray had done for so many years, because, he said, there was not enough room there "for the furniture which I have from my mother's home." Other possibilities were explored, including temporary housing at the College of St. Catherine. Brady wondered if this might be "a tactical error" in making him "obligated to the Sisters." This difficulty was apparently set aside since in August he did settle into rooms on the campus where his sister, Sister Mary William Brady (neé Leonora), was president.[25]

During this brief visit to St. Paul Archbishop Brady gave his first news conference. For the most part his statement followed the conventional line— gratitude to the Holy See, praise for Archbishop Murray, high hopes for the future—and his answers to questions were necessarily noncommittal. But at the end there came a Brady flourish, a gesture of that flamboyance which charmed many and irritated others. I am, he said, fifty-six years old, I stand six feet tall and weigh 205 pounds, forty-five inches across the chest, forty across the waist, forty-four across the hips, sixteen and a half collar, seven and a half hat size, and size eleven shoes. These measurements have remained constant for many years, he maintained.[26]

---

22. It was at Sanborn on that day when I had my exchange with Archbishop Murray as recounted in chapter 19, note 17, above.

23. *CB*, February 23 and June 16, 1956.

24. Byrne was named archbishop of Dubuque in 1962, and he died there in 1996.

25. Brady to Murray, June 25, 1956, AASPM, Murray Papers.

26. *CB*, June 30, 1956.

On August 3 John Gregory Murray embarked on his last journey.

The archbishop is losing ground [the vicar general, Father Hilary Hacker, reported to Brady]. Even though he preached and said Mass yesterday at the hospital, he is no longer able to bounce back and recover his strength. When I took him to the hospital last Friday, I felt that he might have to stay there. This morning I talked to the doctor and he felt that we ought to plan on the Archbishop's staying in the hospital. He will receive better care there. The doctor also felt that we ought to consider the possibility of an alternate for the twenty-first [of August, the scheduled date of Brady's induction]. I do not wish to be an alarmist, but the Archbishop may not be strong enough to preach on the 21st, and there is a possibility that he may not even be able to take part in the ceremony. If you come to town next week, you can judge for yourself. The doctor also mentioned that they are not going to give him any more x-ray therapy.[27]

The archbishop never did emerge from St. Joseph's Hospital, and there he remained until he died on October 11, 1956. A day or two later President Dwight Eisenhower, campaigning for reelection, came to the Twin Cities and, well briefed on the popularity of the deceased prelate, paid strong tribute to him in a much abbreviated political speech. And such recognition was richly deserved. To the very end the little man from Hartford had given all that was in him, every fiber of his being, to the service of the people whom, he believed, Providence had assigned to his spiritual care. It would seem that the episcopal motto, whatever the ambiguity in the Latin, really did mean "All That is Mine is Yours."[28]

The formal induction of the coadjutor took place as scheduled, on August 21, the apostolic delegate, Archbishop Cicognani, presiding. Among the great and the good invited to the ceremony was Fulton Sheen, since 1951 an auxiliary bishop of New York and a television star. There was for a while, however, some confusion about the celebrity's plans. "Bishop Fulton Sheen," Hacker wrote Brady, "mentioned in a telephone conversation with one of our priests that he was going to give a lecture at the Leamington Hotel in Minneapolis the evening of August 20. He will make his own hotel reservations and provide his own car. So far we have had no word from him that he was going

---

27. Hacker to Brady, August 6, 1956, AASPM, Brady Papers.
28. See chapter 19, above.

to attend the ceremony at the Cathedral."[29] But all ended well. "Delighted," wired Sheen, "to be present for pontifical Mass and luncheon on August 21. Greetings."[30] Archbishop Murray could not be present, and so Brady preached the sermon himself, a quite brilliant performance in its simplicity and appropriateness. It was characteristically brief, ten or twelve minutes; besides his natural and easy eloquence, a key to Brady's popularity as a public speaker was his habitual brevity. "If Archbishop Murray could be present this morning," he said at one point,

> I think he would turn to his own clergy, religious, and people of the Archdiocese of St. Paul, and he would say to you, as he has said so many times in the last year or so, in his letters and his casual conversations—he would say to you, "We have worked together a long time; I am thankful for what we together have accomplished. Today we take in a new hand, a new helper to carry on the work of the Church here."[31]

Two days later James Byrne bade farewell to Minnesota with a pontifical Mass followed by a festive luncheon attended by several hundred priests at St. Thomas College. And so an era ended.

THE NEW ERA, THOUGH IRONICALLY DESTINED TO LAST BUT A busy five years, began that same day and in that same place. As the celebration for Bishop Byrne was breaking up, a junior member of St. Thomas's history department was summoned to the president's quarters. There he found the recently inducted coadjutor. "Have you had much experience in administration?" Archbishop Brady asked the young man. "None," was the reply. "Well, you're going to get a lot of experience, because you're the new president of this college." The untimely and unexpected death of Father Vincent Flynn in mid-July—he was only fifty-four—had created the vacancy now to be filled by Father James Patrick Shannon. Perhaps, said the startled Shannon, the archbishop was confusing him with someone else, someone older and more seasoned; or perhaps it would be well to consult with the college's faculty and the archdiocesan clergy before a final decision was reached. But Brady brushed such reservations aside; he had consulted, he said, widely enough. "I assure

29. Hacker to Brady, August 2, 1956, AASPM, Brady Papers.
30. Sheen to Hacker (telegram), August 5, 1956, AASPM, Brady Papers.
31. Typed text in a folder of sermons, AASPM, Brady Papers.

you that although this is Archbishop Murray's last appointment, it is my first appointment. You are as much my man as his man."

It may well have been Archbishop Brady's single most important appointment. Over the next twelve years James Shannon and his mystique were to exert a powerful influence not just on the College of St. Thomas—which under his direction flourished as never before—but upon the life of the archdiocese as a whole. His triumphs were many, though finally some species of disappointment caught hold of him and laid him low. To have been elevated to a college presidency at the age of thirty-five may have surprised some people; not those who had come into contact with him, even from his adolescence. From his earliest years he showed extraordinary promise. Valedictorian of his class at St. Thomas Academy, he completed the four-year course at the college in three and graduated *summa cum laude* with a double major in classics and history. Ordained in 1946, he was assigned to the cathedral and so came into daily contact with Archbishop Murray. He taught English literature at Nazareth Hall for two years and at the same time earned a master's degree in that subject from the University of Minnesota. At Yale his prize-winning doctoral dissertation—a study of Archbishop Ireland's colonies in western Minnesota—was published by Yale University Press (and has already been cited in these pages[32]).

One should not conclude from these academic achievements that young Shannon was a bookish recluse. On the contrary, his outgoing personality, natural friendliness, and geniality won as much applause as his intellectual gifts. In high school he was commander of the crack drill squad of cadets. In college he was a superb debater on a team that competed successfully all over Minnesota and beyond. As a senior the St. Thomas student body elected him "Mr. Tommy," an award made annually since 1931 to the man who best embodied the qualities held in special esteem at the college. And now, fifteen years later, he was leader of all the Tommies. The heartache would come still later.[33]

---

32. See chapter 11, above.

33. Connors, *Journey*, 355–359. James Shannon was appointed auxiliary bishop of St. Paul in 1965. In 1968 he resigned from the episcopate, and the next year he contracted a civil marriage. He earned a law degree from the University of New Mexico in 1973. The following year he returned to the Twin Cities, where he was active in philanthropic administration, first at the Minneapolis Foundation and later (1980) at the General Mills Foundation. He died in 2003, aged eighty-two.

A personal note. James Shannon was my instructor in English literature at Nazareth Hall, 1948–1950. Between 1958 and 1966, during his presidency of St. Thomas, I was a member of the history faculty. I preached the sermon at his episcopal consecration, St. Paul Cathedral, March 31, 1965.

That first meeting between Shannon and Brady at the very beginning of the latter's episcopate—indeed, even before it formally began—was indicative of the nature of the leadership the archdiocese of St. Paul would experience over the next five years. William Brady's decisiveness, his willingness to exercise his authority to the fullest and to cut through conventional red tape, in short, his unalterable self-confidence extended to every facet of his administration. But this imperiousness was justified to a degree by his ferocious work habits—no one in his entourage knew as much about the details of this problem or that program as he did. And, in another sense, this autocracy was tempered by his broad good humor and wit. A more clubbable man than any of his predecessors, he moved easily among the upper middle classes whose support was essential for the multitude of the projects he had in mind. He smoked cigarettes and drank Scotch whiskey—always in moderation—and doted on chocolate which proved in the long run bad for his digestion. He drove a big black Lincoln. He joined the St. Paul Athletic Club in January 1957. He cultivated the local Knights of Columbus and especially the Serra Clubs, not only because of the funds they might help to raise, but also because of the camaraderie they promoted among influential Catholic laymen. Similarly, he urged the amalgamation of the various local women's groups into the Archdiocesan Council of Catholic Women with its close relationship with the National Catholic Welfare Conference. His instrument in this regard was the charming and formidable Florence (Mrs. Fred) Kueppers. "Again," she wrote at the end of 1957,

> in answer to the call of our archbishop, we are asking you to affiliate with the federation provided for all Catholic women's organizations in the Archdiocese of St. Paul. . . . Only a few, for some reason, have failed to realize the importance the Archbishop places on this federation in the Archdiocese. This year we would like to achieve one hundred percent affiliation.

Among the good works proposed by the federation were scholarships for poor girls to attend the College of St. Catherine, an initiative that over the preceding four years had raised $48,000.[34]

Archbishop Brady was anxious to give public recognition to lay people who performed services beyond the ordinary. To do so he instituted a Service Medal and urged pastors to nominate worthy persons in their parishes, whom he would then honor at a conferral ceremony. For special individuals

---

34. Kueppers to "Madam President," December 30, 1957 (copy), AASPM, Brady Papers. I knew Mrs. Kueppers slightly; she was both charming and formidable.

he petitioned the Holy See for papal awards. The most special individual of all, however, I. A. O'Shaughnessy, presented a unique problem in this regard, as explained to Brady in the late winter of 1958 by Father Shannon, who had quickly become an intimate of St. Thomas's greatest benefactor. "In casual conversation I learned that Mr. O'Shaughnessy has thus far received three papal honors. He is a Knight of the Holy Sepulchre, a Knight of Malta, and a Papal Chamberlain. He is not a Knight of St. Gregory. However, his oldest son John is a Knight of St. Gregory."[35] The archbishop duly applied to the apostolic delegation, and the predictable result was that the philanthropist was enrolled as a Knight Commander of St. Gregory the Great with Star, while his wife received the Cross Pro Ecclesia et Pontifice.[36]

When Brady presented his case to the delegate for honoring the couple— aside from their many benefactions, their exemplary family life, and their advanced age—he also mentioned that in October they would celebrate their golden wedding anniversary. This happy occasion presented another problem, because not all the ecclesiastics interested in the O'Shaughnessys' well-being lived in St. Paul. Once again James Shannon provided the archbishop with the required information and also suggested a possible solution to the difficulty. The exact date, he wrote, was October 7, and the pastor of St. Mark's church in St. Paul, where they were married, had invited them to renew their vows there on that day.

> However, I also know that Father [Theodore] Hesburgh is putting pressure on them to observe the day with some solemnity on the Notre Dame campus. He offered to reserve the entire Morris Inn for them, their children, and their grandchildren.[37] Needless to say, this is a very attractive invitation for them, since it never has been possible for them in the past to have all the members of their large family together at one time. . . . With a little diplomatic pressure from you, I think we could persuade them to renew their marriage vows at St. Mark's in a private ceremony, and then go to Notre Dame for the family reunion.[38]

35. Shannon to Brady, March 3, 1958, AASPM, Brady Papers.

36. Brady to Cicognani, May 7, 1958 (copy), and Cicognani to Brady, July 8, 1958, AASPM, Brady Papers.

37. The Morris Inn is the hotel on the Notre Dame campus. O'Shaughnessy had given Notre Dame $2,180,000 for the classroom building named for him, the cornerstone of which was laid in November, 1951.

38. Shannon to Brady, March 3, 1958, AASPM, Brady Papers.

It would be easy to mock all this fussy attention, were it not for the fact that no one deserved it more than the great-hearted I. A. O'Shaughnessy.

As he rewarded publicly distinguished laity, even with papal honors on occasion, Archbishop Brady determined to do the same for his diocesan clergy. In the summer of 1957 no fewer than twenty-eight priests were named domestic prelates and so entitled to be addressed as "Monsignor." This large number of honorees was entirely unprecedented, and for good measure three years later five more received a touch of the purple.[39] Murray's board of priest-consultors, six strong, was disbanded and replaced by a board of nine. With the departure of Hilary Hacker as bishop of Bismarck, Brady appointed John Cullinan vicar general. Monsignor Cullinan was a much-loved and admired priest who had held a variety of weighty positions in the archdiocese, but now, at seventy-three, he was pastor of a large parish—St. Luke's in St. Paul—and not a full-time bureaucrat as the forty-four-year-old Hacker had been.[40] Clearly policy was to be set by the archbishop with a minimum of advice.

EARLY IN 1957 PETER BARTHOLOME, THE BISHOP OF ST. CLOUD, contacted Brady and urged him to take a more active role in promoting the Catholic Rural Life Movement, specifically by participating in the regional conventions then being planned. "The prime purpose of these conventions, of course, is to get the Rural Life Movement into the consciousness of the rural pastor and the rural family." More than 10,000 Catholic families live on the land, he pointed out, nearly fifty percent in most dioceses in the province and "very high even in St. Paul."[41] But the archbishop's mind was moving in a different direction; that "high" rural proportion in his own jurisdiction he was determined to reduce. It proved significant later in the year that of the nine new consultors Brady chose, only one, Cyril Popelka of New Prague, was pastor of a parish outside the Twin Cities metropolitan area. Another sign of things to come was a series of meetings the archbishop held between July 15 and 19 with clergy and laity in the towns of Benson, Delano, Granite Falls, New Ulm, and New Prague, at which were discussed, as the press put it vaguely, "distinctly rural problems that affect Catholics."[42] The purpose of this activity became clearer in December 1957, when it was announced that the

---

39. *CB,* July 23, 1957 and January 29, 1960.
40. *CB,* February 9 and February 16, 1957.
41. Bartholome to Brady, February 8, 1957, AASPM, Brady Papers.
42. *CB,* June 29, 1957.

Holy See had detached St. Paul's fifteen westernmost counties to create a new diocese of New Ulm, the character of which was almost exclusively rural.

At least twice during Archbishop Murray's time, adjustments of the boundaries within the huge St. Paul province and even the erection of a new diocese had been bruited about between Washington and St. Paul. In 1942 the apostolic delegate asked Murray about the feasibility of creating another diocese in Minnesota and a new province. The archbishop replied in exhaustive detail, several pages of demographic data and information about transport, the economy, and rural life in general. His conclusion went further than Cicognani's original tentative suggestion. Since the trains only run east and west, he said, and since the central Dakotas are virtually void of people, detach the western part of the archdiocese of St. Paul into a new diocese, and attach it to Sioux Falls. Take the present diocese of Crookston in northwestern Minnesota and associate it with Fargo. Hence, one new diocese and two new provinces.[43] Eleven years later the matter came up again, but this time more narrowly focused. Bishop Aloysius Muench of Fargo had suggested to the delegate that a new ecclesiastical province embracing the two Dakotas be set up. Observing state lines, Cicocgnani wrote, seems appropriate (a factor Murray had ignored in 1942); if so, would Sioux Falls or Fargo be an appropriate seat for an archbishop? "I most cordially endorse the undertaking," Murray replied. He judged that Fargo was "the most [sic] accessible by train" and therefore should receive preference. He explained, not much to the point, that the Catholic population of North Dakota was slightly larger, while the total population of South Dakota was slightly larger. And, clinching his argument, he concluded: "The discovery of oil in the Williston Basin in North Dakota has brought thousands of prospectors working out of Bismarck since the 1950 census was taken."[44]

There is no question of course that the final decision to divide the archdiocese of St. Paul was arrived at in Rome. But it is implausible in the extreme to suppose that the curial officials would have acted as they did without the agreement of Archbishop Brady or, indeed, without his active lobbying efforts. And, to be sure, there were good logistical reasons for him doing so. The eleven counties left to his jurisdiction were physically compact, and, though they still included some rural elements, the cultural emphasis was

---

43. Cicognani to Murray, February 2, 1942, and Murray to Cicognani, February 20, 1942 (copy), AASPM, Murray Papers.

44. Cicognani to Murray, October 12, 1953, and Murray to Cicognani, October 15, 1953, AASPM, Murray Papers.

clearly urban; Catholics in Faribault or even farmers around New Prague felt more akin to the rhythms of the nearby Twin Cities than did, say, their co-religionists in far-off Marshall or Graceville. "Distinctly rural problems" on the other hand, so the argument went, were best handled within a distinctly rural milieu. In previous years Archbishop Murray had toyed with one idea or another about jurisdictional realignment; William Brady, that whirlwind of initiative, took only a few months to arrive at what appeared to him a practical solution to a long-lingering anomaly. And fifty years after the fact, it remains hard to maintain that he was wrong.

Even so, the separation was not without its strains and complications. The raw statistics, however, are transparent enough and indeed precise. At the beginning of 1957 there dwelt in Minnesota 790,400 Catholics of whom 463,098 lived in the archdiocese of St. Paul. The fifteen counties comprising the new diocese counted 87,311 Catholics, which left St. Paul with, at least nominally, 375,787 communicants.[45] The ecclesiastical structure in New Ulm could claim in place ninety-three priests, 283 nuns, seven high schools, thirty-seven grammar schools, two hospitals, eighty-four parishes, and ten missions.[46] The future of regular sacramental administration appeared secure; enrolled in the St. Paul Seminary were twenty-nine students from parishes in the new diocese, eighteen in the theological department and eleven in the philosophical.[47]

But how the financial resources were to be divided was not so readily discerned. In this regard Brady had insisted in his first formal communication to his clergy that the central administration of the archdiocese stood on firm ground.

Rumors (which the archbishop has heard[48]) to the effect that the financial condition of the archdiocese is bad should be spiked at once. True, our parishes carry a heavy burden of debt, but the archdiocesan corporation is in good condition. Later, when it will be possible to do so, the Archbishop will give the clergy accurate information, for it is information that we should have in common, since so much depends on our common and

---

45. The comparative figures are a startling reminder of demographic shifts over the past half century. In 2007 there are roughly 750,000 Catholics in the archdiocese of St. Paul/Minneapolis and 69,000 in the diocese of New Ulm.

46. *CB*, May 23 and December 7, 1957.

47. Undated typed memorandum, AASPM, Brady Papers.

48. Brady habitually wrote his public documents in the third person.

united action. For the moment, be satisfied that the Archdiocese has no debts to be liquidated, but a good foundation for future positive and progressive planning.[49]

So it turned out that John Gregory Murray, in his simple lifestyle and with his obsession that debt was the ultimate evil, served his successor even beyond the grave.

With his usual sharp eye for detail, Archbishop Brady worked out the financial arrangements, "what we should be prepared to turn over to the Diocese of New Ulm." Three matters were simple and straightforward: "[Return] whatever funds we have received from the parishes [in New Ulm] for [the] 1958 cathedraticum, . . . diocesan needs, . . . and clergy assessment of $150 per priest." Dividing the assets of the archdiocese was more complicated and required a numerical formula. Those assets were divided into three main categories. The Diocesan Needs Fund was the largest, with its combination of bonds, saving certificates, and cash amounting to $576,000.37. Of this figure Brady determined—the records reveal no hint of negotiation—that New Ulm should receive seven and a half percent, or $43,200. The Clergy Fund (what Murray had called the Infirm Priests Fund[50]) held $375,563.07, of which twenty percent, $75,000, was to be allotted to the new diocese. Finally, the Charities Fund of $165,031.20 would contribute $16,500. Moreover the archdiocese had loaned money—in two instances a considerable amount—at three and a half to four and a half percent interest to nine parishes now subject to New Ulm. Brady directed that the seven lesser notes, totaling $63,000 in value, should be turned over to the new diocese as the lion's share of the contribution from Diocesan Needs, "and the rest in cash."[51]

The next area to be addressed had to do with clerical personnel. Technically the priests stationed in the two jurisdictions were frozen in place. But there were difficulties. At that time an archdiocesan priest could expect to serve as an assistant for perhaps fifteen years after ordination and then be assigned his first pastorate, usually in one of the smaller parishes across the countryside. After this period of seasoning he might be promoted to a larger parochial responsibility in the Twin Cities or their suburbs. Some priests, particularly those raised and nurtured amidst the rich cornfields in the west-

---

49. Brady to "Reverend Father," October 26, 1956 (copy), AASPM, Brady Papers.

50. See chapter 20, above.

51. Undated four-page memorandum, typed with handwritten addenda (often illegible), AASPM, Brady Papers.

ern part of the state, preferred to remain there, but many did not. "So that your information and mine will coincide," Brady wrote the new bishop of New Ulm in the spring of 1958, "I send you the following items concerning priests of our jurisdictions who (in varying degrees) may be interested in a change of diocese." He then listed six names of men now stationed in New Ulm who were either "anxious" or rumored to be strongly inclined to return to the archdiocese, and then two priests, at present in St. Paul, who had petitioned to be relocated in New Ulm along with two others who might be interested in doing so. "Obviously," he went on, "we cannot make wholesale changes, and there ought to be some equity." He cited one man's attitude that may have been fairly typical: "Father Donald Eichinger said he would never ask for a change but is not too happy in the countryside."[52] A few priests did manage to relocate, but there were no "wholesale changes."

The new bishop of the new diocese was fifty-five-year-old Alphonse Schladweiler, at the time of his appointment pastor of St. Agnes German parish in St. Paul. Born in Milwaukee, he was in grammar school by the time his family settled in Madison, Minnesota. He was ordained priest in 1929, and after a brief stint at Nativity in St. Paul he served as assistant at Holy Trinity Church in New Ulm, now his cathedral. His pastorates, before his transfer to St. Agnes in 1955, included those at Morgan, North Mankato, and Montevideo, all located, as was his home parish in Madison, within the precincts of what was now his diocese. This experience, along with his Germanic roots, seemed to make him an ideal choice to administer an area of farms and small towns heavily populated by the descendants of German immigrants. And so indeed Bishop Schladweiler, though he did not take on the task with any enthusiasm at first,[53] proved to be until he retired in 1975.

Alphonse Schladweiler was consecrated bishop in the usual solemn ceremony at the St. Paul Cathedral on January 29, 1958.[54] But he was not alone. Also being anointed with the sacred oils on that day was Leonard Philip Cowley, the new auxiliary bishop of St. Paul. Cowley had made his name as director of the Newman Center[55] at the University of Minnesota and as pastor of St. Olaf's Church in downtown Minneapolis; indeed, the two institutions

---

52. Brady to Schladweiler. April 26, 1958 (copy), AASPM, Brady Papers.

53. Interview with Msgr. John C. Ward. Schladweiler died in 1996, aged ninety-four.

54. *CB*, January 25, 1958.

55. For his episcopal motto Bishop Cowley chose St. Francis de Sales's definition of prayer—*cor ad cor loquitur*—just as Newman had done for his cardinal's coat of arms.

were linked financially, guaranteeing that the center and its ever-expanding services would not be starved of funding. Cowley, now forty-five, was a man of immense charm, witty and urbane, whose honeyed voice and wide culture made him a star performer from pulpit and platform. After fire destroyed the church and the adjoining rectory on Ash Wednesday night, 1953, Father Cowley wrote a brief and poignant account of the disaster, even as he laid plans for the magnificent new St. Olaf's on the same site, 2nd Avenue at 8th Street South.[56]

The elevation of Alphonse Schladweiler had another important consequence much to the liking of the authoritarian side of William O. Brady. Ten days after the bishops' consecration it was announced that Monsignor Rudolf Bandas had been appointed pastor of St. Agnes Parish. More remarkable still was the news that Archbishop Brady "reserves to himself the rectorship of the St. Paul Seminary," a post Bandas had held since 1945. Father David Dillon, a professor of theology, was named "administrative assistant to the rector."[57] At once ruthless and adroit, Brady accomplished this coup while Bandas was in Rome attending a meeting of the Congregation of Seminaries and Universities, of which he was a consultor. Since they were colleagues on the seminary faculty years before, Brady and Bandas had been a study in incompatibility. The archbishop had been rector before his appointment to Sioux Falls, and there can be little doubt that he intended to rule there again, whether directly or by proxy. Bandas, with his Vatican connections, was the obstacle. But St. Agnes was one of the great parishes in the archdiocese and assignment there could in no sense be considered a demotion. And to prevent any awkward questions being raised in Rome, the archbishop simply named himself rector, which canonically he was perfectly free to do, rather than put another priest in the office.

Brady as archbishop-rector appeared frequently though irregularly on the seminary campus. His interventions often reflected his own Sulpician training:[58] students were not to play games on Sundays; students were always to wear a hat in public, a straw in the summer and a black one after Labor Day. In a much more important matter he saw to it that promising young priests were sent to universities in this country and abroad for advanced degrees in hopes that the intellectual quality of the seminary faculty could be enhanced. Finally, the archbishop enjoyed the company of some of the older members of the faculty whom he had known for thirty years. Now and then

---

56. Leonard P. Cowley, *We Had a Fire* (Minneapolis, 1953).

57. *CB*, February 8, 1958.

58. See chapter 18, above.

he spent the night at the seminary. On one such occasion in August 1958, at breakfast the next morning, "between mouthfuls of cereal," he turned to David Dillon and said: "Father Dillon, I think you should know that I have appointed Msgr. [Louis] McCarthy rector of the seminary." Dillon, who for all practical day-to-day purposes had been acting rector over the past seven months, was stunned, and his silence testified to the bitterness and disappointment he felt. McCarthy had served on the seminary staff during the 1930s—at this moment he was rector of Nazareth Hall—and so he represented the old guard with whom Brady identified. The unfeeling, even coarse manner in which this change of assignment was communicated put a dark cloud—as happened all too often—over the archbishop's vaunted decisiveness.[59]

WILLIAM OTTERWELL BRADY WAS A GREAT COMMUNICATOR in both the spoken and the written word. And no doubt the way in which most of the people of the archdiocese of St. Paul came to know him was through the pages of the *Catholic Bulletin*. Even before Archbishop Murray died the coadjutor had begun to revamp the newspaper. The appearance of its front page was dramatically changed, its arrangement of material more attractively distributed. Brady's editor, Bernard Casserly, was a professional and highly regarded journalist, who had honed his skills at the *Minneapolis Star-Tribune*. Most of the trivial stories, stemming from the Catholic inferiority complex, disappeared. The paper was much less strident and pessimistic than before in its accounts of the fortunes of the Church overseas; indeed, with the obvious exception of news about the Vatican, reports from troublespots abroad—Juan Peron's Argentina, for instance—received comparatively little space. And the truly absurd—like the headline, "Reds in Italy Accused of Plot to Seize the Pope"[60]—would not have been tolerated on Casserly's watch.

In his first communication to his clergy as archbishop Brady marked out the emphasis he planned to place on the *Bulletin*.

The compliments of the clergy on the changes in the Catholic Bulletin are gratifying and encouraging. The Archbishop asks, however, that the clergy will understand how much time it will take to make the diocesan newspaper an effective instrument in parish and diocesan life. This cannot be done in a day. It may take a year or more. Already various

---

59. Athans, *To Work for the Whole People*, 208–220. I have personal knowledge of David Dillon's disappointment in 1958.

60. *CB*, February 3, 1951.

suggestions have been made on how we may obtain new subscribers and new readers. But the initial interest must be stirred up by the parish priests. What they can do now will be of help to us in the future when we will have come to the point of progress where we can present the paper as something necessary for every parish and every family.[61]

But without doubt the foremost contribution to the effort to improve the *Catholic Bulletin* was Brady's own weekly column. "The Coadjutor's Comments" appeared a few days before Murray's death,[62] after which it became "The Archbishop's Observations." He was not a stranger to this kind of journalism. During the 1930s, when he was on the faculty of the St. Paul Seminary, he wrote a column for the *Bulletin* called "Faith and Practice." In Sioux Falls he founded a monthly, *The Bishop's Bulletin,* for which he contributed "The Bishop's Monthly Letter." Written in the third person and located every issue on the left hand side of the front page, "The Archbishop's Observations" testified to this prior experience. The essays were pithy, smoothly written, colloquial without being in the least sentimental. They dealt with a dizzying number of issues, but always from an explicitly pastoral perspective. And they were didactic: no one who read them could doubt that he was being instructed by a writer serenely confident in his own authority. There was a kind of sprightliness in them as well, which suggests their author enjoyed the exercise and wanted his readers to enjoy it too. On the question of teenage dating, "Teenagers Can't Play at Being Adults," the column began:

Al Capp's annual Sadie Hawkins Day race in the newspaper comic pages has nothing comic in it. It reflects the matrimonial madness of more than Dogpatch. A sane appraisal is Mr. Phogbound's selfish, but shrewd, criticism (which we hope is Capp's real philosophy), that Sadie Hawkins Day is "unhoomin, unhealthy, un-American, and it's gotta be abolished." We do not take our morals from the funny pages nor our philosophy from Phogbound characters. But no words of the Archbishop could more forcefully decry the silly customs of boys who chase girls, or the "unhoomin, unhealthy and unchristian" teenage associations of steady company-keeping, which so often end in disillusionment or matrimonial misfits.[63]

---

61. Brady to "Reverend Father," October 29, 1956 (copy), AASPM, Brady Papers.

62. *CB,* October 6, 1956.

63. *CB,* November 9, 1957.

At times, especially on more somber subjects, the archbishop's prose could rise almost to the lyrical.

The old-fashioned wake was good for the neighbors, even if it has been ridiculed for its clay pipes and gossip which punctuated the prayers when the clocks struck the hours.

When the hearse moved away from the family door, it took with it people in black whose understanding of the funeral rites was deep because of anticipation as well as participation. The white gloves of the pallbearers and the naked brown earth that rimmed the opening of the grave spoke lessons of reverence and fact-facing which today are disguised by the mechanical lowering devices and mounds covered with artificial grass. Death can hardly be made cheerful for those who mourn, but it can be made meaningful for those who remain and whose weeping is more for themselves than for the dead they inter.[64]

One column stirred up something of a fuss. When Sister Duns Scotus, an instructor at Pacelli High School in Austin, performed with her students an experiment using a mouse that attempted to demonstrate how the impact of space-travel could have a negative affect on a living organism—the Soviet Union had launched its first "Sputnik" satellite in 1957—Humane Society enthusiasts were publicly outraged. In his "Observations" Archbishop Brady opined that such people would probably prefer to stuff Sister Duns Scotus into the nose-cone of a satellite. The brouhaha that followed drew reaction from many quarters, including the governor's office.

I have been very amused, and not a little entertained [wrote Governor Orville Freeman], by the comments in the daily papers reporting your remarks in connection with the very prominent "mousenik" affair down in Austin. I think they were extremely well chosen and an outstanding example of how humor, properly used, can make a point much better than either indignation or impassioned pleas. In this instance you have invoked many a chuckle around the state and surely got across the point which needed to be made with devastating clarity. I've enjoyed reading some of your other comments, and want to say that we surely value your opinion and your leadership as an outstanding Minnesotan.[65]

---

64. *CB*, October 31, 1958.
65. Freeman to Brady, January 14, 1958, AASPM, Brady Papers.

The archbishop was conscientious almost to a fault in grinding out the weekly essay, so important did he consider it as a pastoral tool. When he died suddenly and unexpectedly in 1961, Editor Casserly already had four "Observations" in hand.

ANOTHER INNOVATION IN THE *CATHOLIC BULLETIN* AT THIS TIME was the publication of the archbishop's schedule for the upcoming week. From the beginning of the episcopate efficiency and forethought were to be the watchwords. Brady insisted that pastors carry on all official business by mail. If a matter needed the archbishop's attention, and his alone, then he could be addressed directly; otherwise all communications should be sent simply to the chancery. "Let the principle be: if in doubt, write a letter. Thus we shall all save time." He strongly discouraged drop-in visits, as he did any changes or additions to a scheduled event that required his presence. Nor would he deal with any archdiocesan problems at home, his "two borrowed rooms" at the College of St. Catherine.

That domestic arrangement could not be permanent. "To mention such a matter is a bit disconcerting in view of the praise heaped on Archbishop Murray for having lived so simply. But his first charge to the new Archbishop was to provide a home where he and I could live together.[66] God disposed otherwise." Moreover, the apostolic delegate had given Brady "practically a command to provide a proper home for the Archbishop and for the guests of the archdiocese." This problem meshed with another just as sensitive. "Inquiries have been made at the Chancery whether the Archbishop will accept any offerings on the occasion of various functions or at other times when offerings are commonly made in other dioceses. Again, this matter is a delicate one for the new Archbishop since Archbishop Murray refused all such and the present Archbishop has no personal interest in the matter." He went on to pledge that he would accept no offerings "for himself personally." But when an auxiliary is appointed ("on this do not begin to speculate"), some provision will have to be made for him. Meanwhile, "since we must provide for an Archbishop's House, if any offerings are made, they will be placed in a special fund to provide such a residence or the furnishings thereto." In such an instance checks "should be made payable to the Chancery—this for tax purposes."[67]

---

66. The surviving record does not sustain this assertion.

67. Brady to "Reverend Father," October 29, 1956 (copy), AASPM, Brady Papers.

Thus were the initial steps taken toward the splendid edifice, at once arch-bishop's house and chancery, that now stands across Summit Avenue from the cathedral.

Along with the usual administrative and liturgical obligations—mitigated somewhat from 1957 by the aid of Bishop Cowley and more so from the summer of 1961 by the addition of a second auxiliary, the chancellor Gerald O'Keefe[68]—Archbishop Brady initiated a carefully defined set of policies. Reminiscent of the aspirations of Austin Dowling, he was particularly determined to expand Catholic secondary education in the metropolitan area. He noted with satisfaction that Our Lady of Peace High School for girls, recently located in St. Paul's midway district and conducted by the Sisters of Charity of the Blessed Virgin Mary, graduated its first class in 1957, and that the same year St. Bernard's parish in St. Paul, staffed by Benedictines from St. John's, announced its intention to open the second parochial high school in the city (the other was St. Agnes), which it did in 1959.[69] Meanwhile, St. Thomas Academy was finalizing plans to depart the campus it had long shared with the college and move to a new and spacious site in Mendota Heights.[70] Also in 1959 St. Margaret's Academy left its venerable but antiquated building in downtown Minneapolis for a twenty-eight acre campus on Upton Avenue North, where a facility accommodating 1,000 girls went up.[71] And as the Sisters of St. Joseph were relocating St. Margaret's, the Christian Brothers were building a new boys' high school in St. Louis Park, named for one of their own, St. Benilde.[72] On the other side of the metropolitan area, in Maplewood, the Benedictine Sisters welcomed students to the new Archbishop Murray Memorial High School in 1958, and a year later the Christian Brothers similarly greeted their male siblings to a school named for Mary Hill, wife of the celebrated Empire Builder.[73]

All this admirable expansion required a great deal of money—the relocation of St. Margaret's cost $2,500,000, for instance, and construction of Hill High School $1,350,000.[74] At the same time the demands for funds to support other Catholic institutions did not recede. In January 1959, St. Mary's Hospital

68. *CB*, July 7, 1961.

69. *CB*, July 19, 1957.

70. *CB*, January 29, 1960.

71. Mother Antonine to Brady, October 17, 1959, AASPM, Brady Papers.

72. The Christian Brother Benilde Romancon (1805–1862) was canonized in 1967.

73. *CB*, June 29, 1957 and May 15, 1958.

74. Mother Antonine to Brady, October 17, 1959, and *CB*, May 15, 1958.

in Minneapolis laid out plans for a \$6,800,000 addition, and six months later the College of St. Catherine announced an imminent \$10,000,000 fund drive.[75] The economic times were relatively good, but such sums remained formidable, even so. Such a circumstance did not deter the archbishop. To pay for the high schools, he proposed a five-year plan to raise \$10,000,000 by assessing the 116 parishes in the metropolitan area, the total to be reached by monthly installments.[76] The reaction at first was positive. Three Minneapolis parishes of various sizes and economic status provide examples: the Basilica of St. Mary pledged \$250,000 at \$4,000 per month; St. Joan of Arc \$40,000 and \$400; and tiny, impoverished St. Leonard of Port Maurice \$7,500 and \$75.[77] In the meantime, each of the new schools had to assume a prudent amount of debt, a course Brady readily agreed to.[78]

A parallel problem in the archbishop's judgment was the support of the diocesan seminaries, and this too had necessarily a financial component. A solution of sorts was suggested from a curious and edifying source. In the autumn of 1958, the bishops of the province invited Father Patrick Peyton to bring his Family Rosary Crusade to St. Paul. Peyton, a priest of the Congregation of Holy Cross, was famous for his promotion of family prayer over many years at vast outdoor rallies, on television and radio programs, and, not least, because of his familiarity with Hollywood celebrities. He was a good and simple man with a simple message: "The family that prays together stays together." On a crisp October Sunday no fewer that 225,000 people assembled on the grounds of the Minnesota state capitol to listen to Father Peyton and to pray the rosary together.[79]

Six months later, on April 16, 1959, Brady addressed a gathering of 600 priests and laymen at the College of St. Thomas. He told them that he had been deeply inspired by the Rosary Crusade for the right spiritual reasons, to be sure, but also because it demonstrated the latent power of the organized Catholic community. There is nothing we cannot accomplish, he said, if we

---

75. *CB*, January 30 and July 24, 1959.

76. Forty-three parishes in St. Paul, forty in Minneapolis, and thirty-three in the suburbs.

77. A folder of forms, n.d. [1958], AASPM, Brady Papers.

78. See, e.g., O'Keefe to Mother Antonine, October 19, 1958 (copy), AASPM, Brady Papers. How this arrangement ultimately worked out remains unclear. Many distracting events occurred in the interval, including the death of the archbishop.

79. For the arrangements of the rally see Quinn to O'Keefe, October 17, 1958. Joseph Quinn, C.S.C., was Peyton's assistant. The total expense was \$28,777.10, of which the archdiocese's share was \$16,634.55.

work together. Consider the difficulty the archdiocese faces in administering its seminaries. We never have enough priests—why else, he asked, did I find it imperative to adopt the policy of ordaining fourth-year theologians in February rather than in the customary June?[80]—and so we must never cease promoting vocations. But our two seminaries are bursting at the seams. At Nazareth Hall it has been necessary to restrict boarding students to those whose homes were too far away to commute—quite the opposite of Archbishop Dowling's intent in founding that institution. The major seminary is so crowded that there is scarcely enough room for all the students in the chapel. This flood of candidates is welcome in one important sense, but it has nonetheless driven expenses at the seminaries through the roof. What he proposed, therefore, was a program he called Opus Sancti Petri, the Work of St. Peter. Its object was to encourage vocations to the priesthood by all means—including a wholesome home life: "The family that prays together stays together"—and to furnish the required material support. He did not emphasize the monetary aspect of the Opus, but he did not neglect it either. After all, he pointed out, those buses rolling to and from Nazareth Hall had to be paid for.

An elaborate and permanent organization, reminiscent of Dowling's campaign for the Ireland Educational Fund,[81] was set up to forward the Opus, with a central office in downtown Minneapolis and designated representatives in every parish. Teams of volunteers were over several months to canvass each neighborhood door-to-door distributing relevant reading material and soliciting pledges of prayer and cash. The result of the first campaign, reported in the summer of 1959, was heartening: 102,000 people promised their prayers, and 52,000 donated $200,000.[82] The next year the returns were roughly the same, spiritually and materially, in response to Archbishop Brady's plea: "Give us your children, your prayers, your donations!"[83]

POPE PIUS XII DIED ON OCTOBER 9, 1958. THREE WEEKS LATER the seventy-seven year-old Angelo Roncalli, Patriarch of Venice, was, unexpectedly, elected his successor. The new pope, who took the name John XXIII, on the following January 25, surprised the Catholic world by announcing his intention to convene an ecumenical council, the second to be held at the

80. *CB*, February 9, 1957.
81. See chapter 16, above.
82. *CB*, April 24 and August 14, 1959.
83. "Observations," in *CB*, May 20, 1960.

Vatican and the twenty-first in the history of the Roman Church. The long and contentious preparations for this momentous meeting were handled by eleven commissions, each dedicated to a specific area of inquiry. Among them was the Pontifical Commission of Bishops and Diocesan Government, of which William O. Brady was one of three American members. Unlike his predecessor, the archbishop had always maintained his Roman connections, albeit in a casual way. But as the date of the opening session of the council approached—October 11, 1962—he went off to the eternal city much more frequently. In the winter of 1961 and again in the spring, commission business required his presence for a week or ten days each time.[84] He was scheduled to go again in September.

On September 22 "The Archbishop's Observations" appeared in the *Catholic Bulletin* as usual. But the day before that, in an airplane flying in the skies over Paris, Brady suffered his first coronary thrombosis. On landing at Leonardo da Vinci airport outside Rome, he was taken by ambulance to Salvator Mundi hospital; characteristically "he insisted on riding up front with the driver!" The next day, Sunday the twenty-third, he rested comfortably. "Monday he had another attack when he tried to get [to] a urinal at his bedside." Tuesday he did fairly well. On Wednesday came another and severe thrombosis, "and for a few minutes it looked like it would be fatal. After medication he rallied."[85] This report back to St. Paul was written by Dr. Charles Rea, the archbishop's friend and personal physician. His presence in the sick man's hospital room was due to the intervention of Senator Eugene McCarthy, who had "assisted Dr. Rea's clearance and I want you to know that I have," because he realized it would be a comfort to the archbishop and his sister. By a happy coincidence Sister Mary William Brady, having finished her term as president of St. Catherine's, was resident in Rome on a sabbatical studying art history. The senator cabled again the same day: "Asked our ambassador [to Italy] to give the Archbishop any assistance that might be needed. So please feel free to call the embassy if the staff can be of service. We assure you of our prayers for your brother's recovery."[86] McCarthy had apparently also expedited any passport awkwardness for Monsignor Francis Gilligan, Brady's close friend since Fall River days, who arrived in Rome at the middle of the week.

Archbishop Brady was restless and fretted about the future commitments he had made, since he had been told by Dr. Rea and the three Italian physi-

---

84. *CB*, September 29, 1961.

85. Rea to O'Keefe, September 28, 1961, AASPM, Brady Papers.

86. McCarthy to Sister Mary William, September 26, 1961 (two cables), AASPM, Brady Papers.

cians also in attendance—of whom Rea spoke highly—that he would need at least two months of complete rest. And, a practical man, he worried about insurance. "He is anxious that I tell you (I'm the temporary secretary!)," his sister wrote the chancellor, "to go to the upper left hand drawer of his desk at home and find the black record book which lists all the health and insurance policies that he holds."[87] Even so, Brady proved a cooperative patient, and his condition appeared to improve. "In fact," Rea reported, "we hope he is over the hump and will show improvement from now on."[88] "Today [Saturday, September 30] has been the best day Archbishop Brady has had to date. His blood pressure has been stabilized so that he needs no more stimulant. His pulse is slower. . . . Barring any more attacks he is on the way to recovery. I told him today that his critical week was over, and there was to be no more of those bad days."[89]

But "at 11:15 a.m. on Sunday, October 1, he suddenly gasped for breath," and three minutes later he was dead due to a massive coronary thrombosis. "The hospital chaplain and Sister Mary William were with him at the end. . . . It was providential that Sister Mary William was here, and Monsignor Gilligan as usual was a good tonic for him. . . . I consider it a privilege to have [been] able to do what I could medically, as I owe a great debt spiritually to His Excellency."[90] The next day Sister Mary William, Gilligan, and Rea met with John XXIII in the pope's private library. "The poor man, the poor man," they remembered the pontiff saying. On Wednesday, October 4, Monsignor Gilligan offered requiem Mass at Santa Susanna, the American church on the Via Venti Settembre; many Vatican grandees were in attendance, including Amleto Cicognani, so long apostolic delegate to the United States and now cardinal–secretary of state. On Thursday the Pan American plane carrying the body of the deceased and the mourners landed in New York after an eleven-hour flight. There a hearse took the archbishop's remains to a chapel on the grounds, where the bishop of Brooklyn presided at a Vespers service; among those present were Cardinal Spellman and Bishop Connolly of Fall River, the third of the "three wise men from the East."[91] The sad journey ended when the Northwest Orient plane set down in St. Paul at 9:15 p.m.[92]

87. Sister Mary William to O'Keefe, September 26, 1961, AASPM, Brady Papers.

88. Rea to O'Keefe, September 28, 1961, AASPM, Brady Papers.

89. Rea to O'Keefe, September 30, 1961, AASPM, Brady Papers.

90. Rea to O'Keefe, October 2, 1961, AASPM, Brady Papers.

91. See chapter 18, above.

92. *CB*, October 6, 1961.

Thousands passed the bier upon which rested Archbishop Brady's coffin during the two-day vigil that preceded the funeral on Monday, October 9. A flood of condolences poured into the chancery. One message, from Governor Elmer Andersen, seems in retrospect especially apt and just.

> I was greatly saddened to hear of the passing of Archbishop Brady. He was a distinguished spiritual leader whose ability to express his ideas in words readily familiar to all won him acclaim and a following that extended through the nation. To the 450,000 Catholics in the Archdiocese of St. Paul, as well as to those in the Province of St. Paul, . . . I extend my sincere condolences on this great loss.[93]

IN ONE SENSE WILLIAM OTTERWELL BRADY WAS FORTUNATE IN the timing of his premature death. He was only sixty-two years old and was a man of such vigor that he might well have expected at least another decade of intense activity. Had that indeed been the case, he might have witnessed the "resignation" of an auxiliary bishop who then contracted a civil marriage; the "resignations" of hundreds of his priests and religious; the abrupt collapse of his heretofore flourishing minor seminary; the gradual disintegration of discipline within his major; the plummeting Mass attendance and sacramental usage among the lay faithful; the bitter and corrosive controversy over artificial contraception. How would an Archbishop Brady—talented, principled and dedicated, but also self-confident, imperious, an alpha male if ever there was one—have coped with such turmoil?

The archbishop concluded one of his columns in the *Catholic Bulletin* ("A Code for Parents" who "frankly have been pampering their children much too much") with the rhetorical question, "Is the Archbishop just too old-fashioned?"[94] Perhaps not in 1959, but by then, though nobody knew it, the Church and indeed America stood on the cusp of drastic change. In the secular arena loomed Vietnam, Selma and Birmingham, the assassinations of the Kennedys and Martin Luther King, Woodstock, the Democratic National Convention in Chicago in 1968. As for the Catholic Church, the Second Vatican Council along with all the developments good and bad that followed in its wake—along with all the deep disagreements about its meaning and application—meant the end of more than an era. The Counter-Reformation

---

93. Andersen to O'Keefe, October 4, 1961 (telegram), AASPM, Brady Papers.
94. *CB*, September 11, 1959.

and the ecclesiastical culture it engendered were over, gone forever. William Brady was in many respects a Renaissance man; and, more to the point, he was the beau ideal of a Counter-Reformation bishop.

Perhaps nothing so clearly signals, in hindsight at least, the coming cultural shift than a sermon Brady delivered to a less than enthusiastic congregation at a national Liturgical Conference at St. John's Abbey in 1957.

> In your enthusiasm for liturgical prayer [he said in part] do not take the rosary away from us. . . . We all, I am sure, want our liturgical movement to foster liturgical song. The attempt, however, to adapt Gregorian notation to English phrases seems, to me at least, an uncomfortable Procrustean couch. And more than a few whose ears are untuned but whose hearts are pure, have drawn a possibly illogical but a very emotional conclusion in saying, "Please do not take away from us the hymns we knew in childhood."
>
> I do not wish to enter here into the sometimes noisy, intemperate and even disrespectful agitation for the vernacular. That is a special problem on which the Church has less than gently said, "Please do not take our Latin from us."[95]

As things turned out, the future lay with his somber listeners, not with him.

FINALLY, THE MOMENT HAS COME TO INVOKE THAT OVERUSED epigram: whatever goes around comes around. Just before Christmas 1961 the announcement arrived from Washington that the archbishop of Dubuque had been appointed archbishop of St. Paul. And so, as had happened 120 years before in the persons first of Lucien Galtier and Augustin Ravoux and then of Bishop Mathias Loras himself, up the Mississippi traveled the assurance that whatever vicissitudes the people of God in east-central Minnesota confronted along their pilgrim way, the gospel and the sacraments would dwell amongst them.

FINIS

---

95. Typed text in a folder of sermons, AASPM, Brady Papers.

MARVIN R. O'CONNELL

is professor emeritus of history at the University of Notre Dame
and author of numerous books, including *Edward Sorin*
(University of Notre Dame Press, 2001).